LAND DEED GENEALOGY

of

BEDFORD COUNTY TENNESSEE

1807 — 1852

Compiled by
Helen C. Marsh
&
Timothy R. Marsh

SOUTHERN HISTORICAL PRESS, INC.
c/o The Rev. Silas Emmett Lucas, Jr.
P.O. Box 738
Easley, South Carolina 29641-0738

ISBN 0-89308-610-X

INTRODUCTION

Land has been a prized possession of the human race from the beginning of civilization. The importance of recording the buying, selling and bequeathing of land or property by deed has for centuries been a very important stabilizing factor in the civilized world. A society without a policed system for regulating and recording the ownership of land and property would be a society in utter chaos. Throughout our history an extra effort has been exercised to protect the deeds and land records from destruction. Courthouse fires and the Civil War has been the major cause of destruction of deeds in the south. Historians and Genealogist often fail to recognize the importance of deeds in the research of local and family history. Land deeds may often contain "that missing link" or valuable information not recorded elsewhere. The land deeds in Bedford County are complete from formation in 1807 until 1852. Nine Deed Books, "UU" through "CCC" were destroyed in the Courthouse fire in 1863, however, many deeds that were destroyed in that fire were re-recorded immediately after the Civil War by the Grantees and Grantors, an additional help is an index called The Burned Index covering the period 1852-1861 and including names of Grantee and Grantor, dates and type of instrument. This Index Book is located in the Office of the Register of Deeds in Shelbyville, Tennessee. All deeds after the Civil War are intact. Early Tennessee Land Grants and Entries were recorded in separate Entry Books kept by the early Entry Takers of the County and were lost or destoyed many years ago. These Grants generally contained no genealogical information, however, copies of these grants may be found in the Tennessee State Archives in Nashville, Tennessee. The deed books of Bedford County contain North Carolina Military and General Grants, Occupant Grants, Small Tennessee Grants, often called waste land, one penny, nine penny, or School Land Grants. The material published in this book is presented in abstract form in order to conserve space. The primary purpose was to glean genealogical and historical material from the deeds, each and every deed in the Registers Office recorded from 1807 through 1852 was read and reread to make a determination as to the genealogical content. It is our sincere hope that the material contained herein will be helpful to the reader.

Helen C. Marsh
Timothy R. Marsh
1986

THE LANDS OF BEDFORD

Vast areas of the land lying within the present constituted boundaries of Bedford County, Tennessee were granted to early land speculators who were then living east of the Allegheny Mountains, at the close of the Revolution. Those presenting warrants were allowed to enter, locate, survey and file for grants to be issued out of John Armstrong's Land Office at Hillsborough, North Carolina, for ten pounds per hundred acres. There were over one hundred and thirty thousand acres granted to numerous grantees in various sizes up to five thousand acres each, in Bedford County.

The Blount brothers held grants for eighty five thousand acres of which about fifty thousand were located in the present bounds of Bedford County. Patton and Erwin, Alexander Outlaw and others later owned these grants that were all located on the Wartrace, Garrison and South or Barren Forks of Duck River, the major forks of said river. These grants were not issued for military service as many have assumed, the southern boundary line of the Military Reservation set aside for such purposes lay several miles to the north of Bedford County. Most of the land lying in between the large grants in addition to unappropriated lands were later issued as Tennessee Grants to holders of warrants that they had purchased from Soldiers of the North Carolina Line, these grantees were assignees of the soldiers. Other Tennessee Grants, generally for small acreages, called Waste Land, penny, twelve and one half cent, or School Grants, were issued for unappropriated lands in the county.

In 1807, at the direction of the Legislature, the county was surveyed and sectioned off into townships divided by range and section lines, crossing at six mile intervals. In early deeds, the section and range lines were often given, as was the surveyor's district, which was District Two (2) for Bedford County, not to be confused with Civil District Number Two. Within each section of six miles square, a tract of six hundred and forty acres was surveyed and set aside for benefit of the public schools, they were referred to as School Land tracts, so when deeds make reference to school land, it may mean one of the School Land Tracts, of which there were fifteen, not necessarily land upon which a schoolhouse was located. After 1846, these school tracts were auctioned off with approval of the Legislature and the local citizenry and grants issued to the purchasers by the State of Tennessee.

Editors

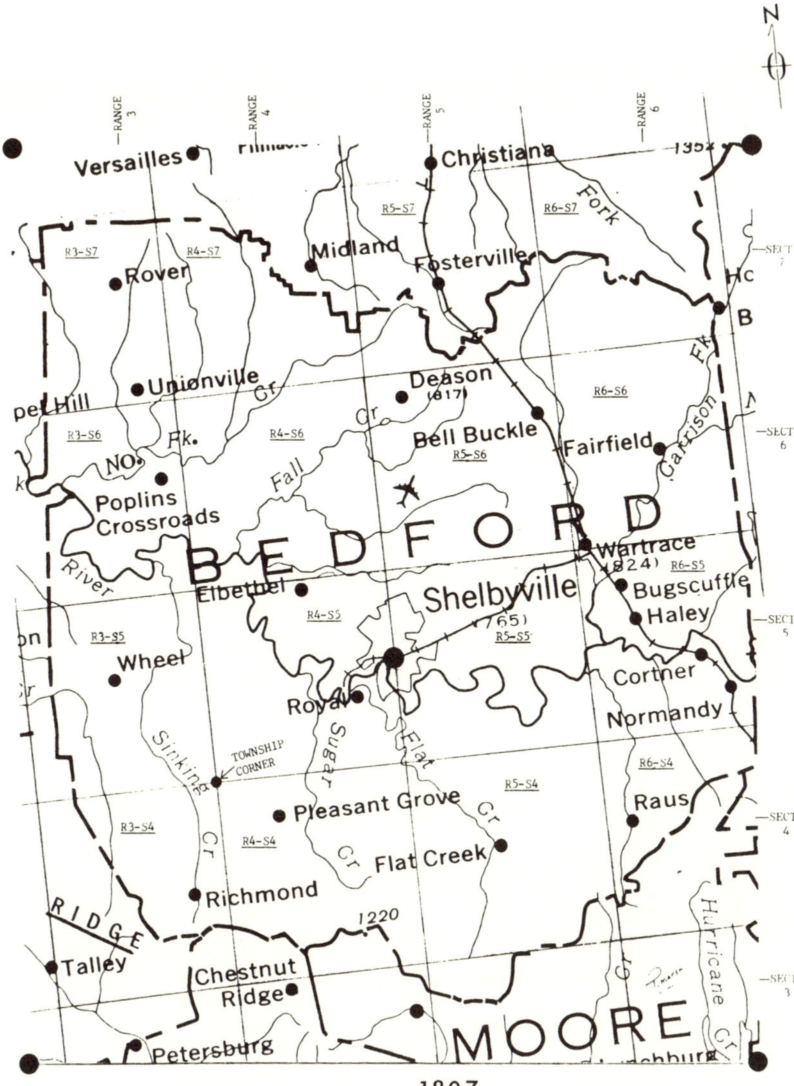

··1807··

COMPILED BY TIMOTHY R MARSH

RANGE & SECTION LINES

DEED BOOK "A"

Page 343 - Andrew Jackson to Enoch Enochs. 14 May 1809. Land situated lying and being in Bedford County, TN on Mulberry Creek, a branch of Elk River and about one mile above where Bedford County Court is now held. (Mrs. Payne's house). Ed Note: Most of Deed Book "A" is duplicated in Deed Book "B".

DEED BOOK "B"

Page 13 - J. Christopher of Washington Co., TN sold on 16th Aug 1807, a negro girl Milly to Polly Macklin, daughter of John Macklin. Wit: Henry Taylor and Stephen C. Taylor. Registered: June Term 1809.

Page 22 - John Southgate and Frances B. Southgate his wife of Norfolk, VA sold to William Newsom and William Newsom, Jr. of the same place. 18 Aug 1807, land in Williamson Co., TN on the south side of Duck River and on both sides of Rich Creek.

Page 154 - John Stone to John Glonenger. Power of Attorney. 23 Dec 1809. John Stone of Bedford County and his wife Magdaline one of the daughters of Leonard Sebold, late of Lebannon Township, County of Dauplin, PA, Yeoman, deceased, appointed as PA John Glonenger of Lebannon, Dauplin Co., PA. Wit: Thomas Greer and Alexander Greer. Registered: 24 Dec 1809.

Page 191 - Michael Campbell to John Philips. 18 Nov 1809. Michael Campbell, Executor of the Last Will and Testament of Philip Philips, deceased, of Davidson Co., TN, and John Philips of Smith Co., a Bond given by said Philip Philips given in his lifetime to Margaret Philips of the State of PA. Bond being transferred by Margaret Philips to John Philips and for consideration of one dollar paid by John Philips, one half of 640 acre tract granted to Philip Philips and Michael Campbell bearing date 21 Jun 1809. Land on Sinking Creek, waters of Duck River, adjoining school land and George Doherty Entry No. 40. Ed Note: Small portion of Village of Richmond was located on west end of this tract. Wit: Eli Talbot and Alexander Greer.

Page 202 - William Galbreath to Mathew Cunningham, PA 15 Nov 1809. William Galbreath of Adam Co., PA (later to Bedford Co, TN), Walter Galbreath, Robert Dixon and Mary his wife and William Dixon, an infant by his natural guardian and the said Robert of Orange Co., NC, Francis McKamie and Catharine his wife, William McKamie and Anne Galbreath of Guilford Co., NC of one part. Mathew Cunningham of Guilford Co., NC of the other part. William Galbreath, late of Orange Co., NC departed this life the year 1800 (appointed his father now deceased and Mathew Cunningham as his Executors). He died seized of tracts of land in Tennessee and leaving children, him surviving the aforesaid William Galbreath, Walter Galbreath, and John Galbreath (who died without issue), Catharine who intermarried with Francis McKamie, Mary who intermarried with Robert Dixon, Elizabeth who intermarried with Mathew Cunningham, and Jane(Ann) Galbreath who are his heirs. Land on south side of Duck River, adjoining lands of Samuel Patton, Jr., Thomas Nucholds, George Martin and Amos Balch. Francis and Catharine McKamie had a son William McKamie. Robert Dixon and wife Mary had a son William Dixon. (Land located west and south of Shelbyville. 30 acres reserved and offered as Seat of Justice if Commissioners desire. Offer not accepted.)
Wit: James Webb. Registered 27 Mar 1810.

DEED BOOK "B"

Page 240 - Zacheus Wilson to Benjah Gray. 350 acres 9 May 1808. Zacheus Wilson of Sumner Co., TN to Benjah Gray of Davidson Co., TN, land in Bedford Co. on north side of Duck River on waters of Caney Spring Creek, adjoining a 4000 acre tract of his father David Wilson and also Jonathan Wilson. Wit: George Realy and Charles Hays. Mero Dist. May Term 1808. Registered: April 1810.

Page 244 - Andrew Jackson to Rachel and Patsy Hays for 1500 acres. 13 July 1802. Andrew Jackson of Davidson Co., TN and Rachel Hays and Patsy Thompson Hays, daughters of Robert Hays of Davidson Co., TN, land being part of a 5000 acres lying on both sides of Duck River and granted to John Gray Blount and Thomas Blount by Patent No. 234. Wit: R. McGavock, R. Searcy and John Dickerson. Registered 28 Oct 1802 Williamson Co., TN, Book 1, page 166.

Page 246 - Robert Butler and Rachel Butler his wife to Patsy Thompson Hays. 15 Nov 1809. Robert Butler and his wife Rachel of Davidson Co., TN to Patsy Thompson Hays of Davidson Co., TN. (Same and part of above instrument.) Robert Butler hath intermarried with the said Rachel Hays. Land adjoins Charles Harryman. Registered: 10 Apr 1810.

Page 253 - Michael Robertson to John and Joseph Robertson for 1500 acres. 9 Oct 1804. Michael Robertson of Orange Co., NC to David Robertson, John Robertson and Joseph Robertson, sons of Michael Robertson and citizens of Williamson Co., TN. Land on north side of Duck River, about three miles above the mouth of Falling Creek, Martin Phifer's corner. This tract was granted by State of North Carolina to Michael Robertson by Grant No. 37, dated 10 July 1788. Recorded in Williamson Co., TN in Book 1, page 328. Wit: Thomas Rountree and Daniel McMahan. Registered 15 Apr 1810.

Page 313 - Samuel Maxwell's heirs to Newton Cannon for 355 acres 2 Aug 1810. Robert Maxwell, James Maxwell, Alexander Maxwell, Samuel Maxwell, William Lockhart, Thomas McNeely, William Phebb and Catherine Maxwell, all heirs of Samuel Maxwell, deceased, of Guilford Co., NC, sold to Newton Cannon of Williamson Co., TN, land in Bedford Co., TN on the south side of Duck River. Which tract was granted by State of Tennessee to Samuel Maxwell by Grant No. 280 for 355 acres. Land borders school land and Robert Smith. Wit: Howell Parkes and Willy Snell. Registered: 12 May 1810.

Page 316 - Robert Chapman to Patrick Gibson for 105 acres. 26 March 1810. Robert Chapman of Lincoln Co., TN. Land on Weakley Creek, waters of North Fork of Duck River, it being part of a Grant by State of North Carolina to Ebenezer Alexander. Land adjoins John Harris, Sr. Registered: 12 May 1810.

Page 321 - Martin Phifer to James Erwin. Power of Attorney. 27 Apr 1810. Martin Phifer of Cabarrus Co., NC appointed James Erwin, his son-in-law of Burk Co., NC, his Attorney. Land on waters of Duck River, Rutherford Co., TN, 5000 acres on Falling Creek. The Grant to him, No. 104, dated 10 July 1788 and one tract of land on Duck River of 2373 granted by State of North Carolina to his father, Martin Phifer, No. 38. Registered: 25 May 1810.

DEED BOOK "C" 1813 - 1815

Ed Note: Earliest sale of Town Lots of Shelbyville is in Deed Book "C".

Page 11 - Tennessee Grant to Nathaniel Taylor for 640 acres. No. 1639, for Military Service by Benjamin Skipper to State of North Carolina, Warrant No. 4778, Sealed 22 Aug 1807 by No. 61. Being in Williamson Co., TN, 2nd District, 3rd Range, 7th Section. Surveyed 18 Apr 1808. Reg: 27 Jun 1810.

Page 12 - Tennessee Grant to Newton Cannon for 150 acres. No. 1029. Certificate No. 318, dated 28 Aug 1807. Entered 12 Sep 1807 by No. 547. Granted to Newton Cannon, assignee of John Sloss in Rutherford Co., TN, 2nd District, 5 Range, 4th Section, on waters of Flat Creek, a south branch of Duck River. Sealed at Knoxville 8 Apr 1809. Reg: 28 --- 1810.

Page 13 - Tennessee Grant to Newton Cannon for 100 acres. No. 1030. Certificate No. 318, dated 28 Aug 1807. Entered 12 Sep 1807 by No. 546. In Rutherford Co., TN, 2nd District, 5th Range, 4th Section, on waters of Flat Creek, a south branch of Duck River. Surveyed 15 Oct 1807. Sealed at Knoxville 8 Apr 1809. Reg: 23 Jun 1810.

Page 14 - Tennessee Grant to Clement and Newton Cannon for 250 acres. No. 1035. Certificate No. 91, dated 25 Jul 1807. Entered -- of --, ---- by No. 221. Granted to Clement and Newton Cannon 250 acres in Williamson Co., TN, 2nd District, 3rd Range, 7th Section, on north side of Duck River on Wilsons Creek. Surveyed 19 Apr 1808. Sealed at Knoxville 10 Apr 1809. Reg: 28 Jun 1810.

Page 16 - Tennessee Grant to Newton Cannon for 50 acres. No. 770. Military Service by Joseph Richards to State of North Carolina, Warrant No. 4029, dated 3 Feb 1806. Entered 18 Mar 1808 by No. 251. Granted to Newton Cannon assignee of heirs of Joseph Richards. Land being in Bedford Co., TN on south side of Duck River, on the head waters of the Middle or Boiling Fork of Rock Creek of Duck River. Surveyed 19 Jul 1808. Sealed at Knoxville 7 Jan 1808. Reg: 28 Jun 1810.

Page 17 - Tennessee Grant to Newton Cannon for 700 acres. No. 1026. Certificate No. 318, dated 22 Aug 1807, by John Sloss. Entered 31 Aug 1807 by No. 442. Granted to Newton Cannon assignee of John Sloss. Land in Bedford Co., TN, 4th Range, 4th Section, on south waters of Duck River. Surveyed 30 May 1808. Seal at Knoxville 8 Apr 1809. Reg: 28 Jun 1810.

Page 18 - Tennessee Grant to Newton Cannon for 75 acres. No. 771. For Military Service by Joseph Richards to North Carolina, Warrant No. 4029, dated 3 Feb 1806. Entered 18 Mar 1808 by No. 247. Granted to Newton Cannon, assignee of the heirs of Joseph Richards. Land in Bedford Co., TN, south side of Duck River on waters of Middle or Boiling Fork of Rock Creek of Duck River. Surveyed 19 Jul 1808. Seal at Knoxville 7 Jan 1809. Reg: 8 Jul 1810.

Page 20 - Tennessee Grant to Newton Cannon for 65 acres, No. 774. For Military Service by William Rowland to North Carolina, Warrant No. 31, dated 20 Dec 1800. Entered 8 Feb 1808 by No. 145. Granted to N. Cannon, Assignee of John Rowland. Land in Bedford Co., TN, on south side of Duck River, Middle Fork

Of Rock Creek in the north boundary of a survey of Minos Cannon, Sr. Surveyed 20 Jul 1808. Seal at Knoxville, 7 Jan 1809. Reg: 9 Jul 1810.

Page 22 - Tennessee Grant to N. & C. Cannon for 428 acres. No. 567. For Military Service by Amos Paramore to North Carolina, Warrant No. 64, dated 6 Dec 1802. Entered 29 Aug 1807 by No. 393. Granted to N. & C. Cannon, assignees of Amos Paramore. Land in Rutherford Co., TN, 5th Range and 4th Section, on East Fork of Flat Creek of Duck River. Borders school land. Surveyed 14 Oct 1808. Seal at Knoxville on 5 Oct 1808. Reg: 9 Jul 1810.

Page 23 - Tennessee Grant to Newton Cannon for 150 acres. No. 1025. Certificate No. 318, dated 22 Aug 1807 obtained by John Sloss and entered 12 Sep 1807 by No. 545. Granted to Newton Cannon, assignee of John Sloss in 5th Range, 4th Section on East Fork of Flat Creek, a south branch of Duck River. Borders Matthew Cunningham survey. Surveyed 15 Oct 1807. Seal at Knoxville 8 Apr 1809. Reg: 9 Jul 1810.

Page 25 - Tennessee Grant to Newton Cannon for 125 acres. No. 773. For Military Service by William Rowland to North Carolina, Warrant No. 31, dated 20 Dec 1800 and entered 22 Sep 1807 by No. 593. Granted to Newton Cannon, assignee of John Rowlandto whom the Warrant issued for service of said William Rowland. Land being in Bedford Co., TN, 2nd Range and 4th Section, on Rock Creek of Duck River. Surveyed 19 Nov 1807. Seal at Knoxville 7 Jan 1809. Reg: 9 Jul 1810.

Page 28 - Edward Wade, son of William and Sarah Wade, born May 27, 1776.
Elizabeth Fisher, daughter of Michael and Christina Fisher, born September 29th 1789.
Edward Wade married to Elizabeth Fisher, daughter of Michael Fisher, 26 of February 1807.
William Stokes Wade, son of Edward and Elizabeth Wade, born March 27th 1808.
Martin Fisher Wade, son of Edward and Elizabeth Wade, born May 27th, 1809.
Patsey Wall Wade, daughter of Edw'd and Elizabeth Wade, born 25th of December 1810.

Page 32 - Tennessee Grant to Amos McLemore for 85 acres. No. 1638. Part of Warrant No. 626 for 640 acres issued to John Kennedy and founded on an Entry in office of Samuel Barton on 23 Mar 1802 by No. 265. Granted to Amos McLemore, assignee of John Kennedy. Land in Bedford Co., TN, on waters of Weakleys Creek. Borders an Entry of George Doherty. Surveyed 14 Feb 1809. Seal at Knoxville 17 Sep 1809. Reg: 24 Sep 1810.

Page 39 - Commissioners, Daniel McKissick, Benjamin Bradford, Berkley Martin, John Atkinson, Howel Dawdy, John Lane and William Woods. Commissioners for fixing the Seal of Justice in Bedford County now selling the Town Lots of the County Town of Bedford County and State of Tennessee.

Page 64 - Tennessee Grant to Jason Thompson for 240 acres. No. 1882. For Military Service by William Rowland to North Carolina, Warrant No. 31, dated 20 Dec 1800, entered 22 Sep 1807 by No. 589. Grant to Jason Thompson, assignee of William

Rowland. Land in Bedford Co., TN, on waters of Duck River, a small creek known as Rock Creek. Surveyed 5 Jan 1808 by George Mitchel, D.S. Seal at Knoxville 22 Jan 1810. Reg: 30 Nov 1810.

Page 76 - Tennessee Grant to Edward Bryeans for 100 acres. No. 1359. For Military Service by John Roundtree to North Carolina, Warrant No. 5137, dated 9 Dec 1797 and entered 11 Aug 1808 by No. 712. Granted to Edward Bryeans, assignee of the heirs of John Roundtree. Part of warrant in Bedford Co., on East Fork of Rock Creek of Duck River, bordered Entry No. 387 for 640 acres to John Baker. Surveyed 28 Sep 1808. Seal at Knoxville on 18 Jul 1809. Reg: 7 Dec 1810.

Page 78 - Tennessee Grant to Edward Bryeans for 90 acres. No. 1361. For Military Service by John Roundtree to North Carolina, Warrant No. 5137, dated 9 Dec 1797 and entered 19 Sep 1808 by No. 826. Granted to Edward Bryeans, assignee of John Roundtree, land in Bedford Co., on east waters of East Fork Creek, a south branch of Duck River. Borders Entry No. 387 in the name of John Baker. Surveyed 28 Sep 1808. Seal at Knoxville 18 Jul 1809. Reg: 8 Dec 1810.

Page 80 - Tennessee Grant to Edward Bryans for 200 acres. No. 1360. For Military Service by John Roundtree to North Carolina, Warrant No. 5137, dated 9 Dec 1797 and entered 11 Aug 1808. Granted to Edward Bryeans, assignee of the heirs of John Roundtree, part of warrant lying in Bedford County, on headwaters of East Fork of Rock Creek of Duck River. Bordered Captain John Medearis' west corner No. 43. Surveyed 23 Nov 1808. Seal at Knoxville 18 Jul 1809. Reg: 8 Dec 1810.

Page 82 - Tennessee Grant to Malcom Gilchrist for 200 acres. No. 1366. Certificate No. 269, dated 18 Aug 1807 obtained by Benjamin McCullock. Entered 8 Dec 1808 by No. 1032. Granted to Malcom Gilchrist, assignee of Benjamin McCullock. Land in Bedford Co., TN, on east waters of Big Flat Creek of Duck River. Borders an Entry No. 63 to David Ross. Surveyed 2 Jan 1809. Seal at Knoxville 18 Jul 1809. Reg: 8 Dec 1810.

Page 84 - Tennessee Grant to Malcom Gilchrist for 100 acres. No. 1367. Certificate No. 269, dated 18 Aug 1807, obtained by Benjamin McCullock and entered 8 Dec 1808 by No. 1033. Granted to Malcom Gilchrist, assignee of Benjamin McCullock. Land in Bedford County, on headwaters of East Fork of Rock Creek, a south branch of Duck River. Surveyed 1 Dec 1808. Reg: 4 Dec 1810.

Page 86 - Tennessee Grant to Joseph Coleman for 243 acres. No. 1780. Certificate No. 213, dated 1 Aug 1807, obtained by John Gray Blount and Thomas Blount and entered 27 Aug 1807 by No. 348. Granted to Joseph Coleman, assignee of John Gray Blount and Thomas Blount. Land in Bedford County. Adjoins 5000 acre grant by North Carolina to John Gray and Thomas Blount, on east, No. of Grant 219, No. of Warrant 1665, on waters of Wartrace Fork of Duck River. Surveyed 5 May 1809. Reg: 14 Dec 1810.

Page 88 - Tennessee Grant to Alexander Torrentine for 175 acres. No. 1524. Warrant No. 41, dated 1 Aug 1807, issued to William P. Anderson, Surveyor, and entered 4 Aug 1807 by No. 37.

Granted to Alexander Torrentine, assignee of William P. Anderson. Land in Bedford Co., TN, on north side of Duck River, bordering Anthony Newman Grant. Seal at Knoxville 24 Aug 1809. Reg: 18 Dec 1810.

Page 92 - Tennessee Grant to Alexander Torrentine for 100 acres. No. 1525. For Military Service by Malachi Russell to North Carolina, Warrant No. 637, dated 23 Apr 1784 and entered 5 Dec 1807 by No. 790. Granted to Alexander Torrentine, assignee of Malachi Russell, land in Bedford County, on Duck River. Seal at Knoxville 24 Aug 1809. Reg: 20 Dec 1810.

Page 115 - Mary Parker to Joshua Holt. 2000 acres. 19 Jul 1809. Mary Parker, late of Petersburg, VA and now of Nevenham, Shire of Glonester, Great Britain, England, sold to Joshua Holt of Orange Co., NC, land in Bedford Co., TN, on south side of Duck River and on east side of Sugar Creek, borders James Bradshaw, Charles McCommons, Amos Balch, George Martin, Richard Martin. Original granted to Robert McKemie on 16 Dec 1795. McKemie to Hugh Hunter and Hunter to Elias Parker and by Elias Parker by his Last Will to his widow Mary Parker.

Page 159 - Tennessee Grant to John Patrick, 100 acres. No. 1423. For Military Service by Jeremiah Litteral to North Carolina, Warrant No. 3175, dated 19 Dec 1785 and entered 3 Jul 1809 by No. 191. Granted to John Patrick, assignee of the heirs of Jeremiah Litteral. Land in Bedford Co., TN, on waters of Noah's Fork, a branch of Duck River. Surveyed 1 Jun 1808. Reg: 16 Mar 1811.

Page 161 - Tennessee Grant to James McCuistion, 274 acres. No. 619. Certificate No. 171, dated 30 Jul 1807 obtained by Alexander McCall and entered 6 Aug 1807 by No. 17. Granted to James McCuistion, assignee of Alexander McCall, being in Rutherford Co., TN, on north side of Duck River, on Hurricane Creek. Surveyed 25 Mar 1808. Reg: 18 Mar 1811.

Page 162 - Tennessee Grant to James McCuistion, 221 acres. No. 616. Warrant No. 258, dated 16 May 1803, issued to Robert McCuistion and entered 29 Aug 1807 by No. 377. James McCuistion assignee of Robert McCuistion. Land in Bedford County, on west waters of Big Flat Creek, a south branch of Duck River. Borders McCameys' Warrant No. 2267 and Edward Giles Entry No. 106. Surveyed 29 Apr 1808. Seal at Knoxville 1 Oct 1808. Reg: 18 Mar 1811.

Page 182 - Tennessee Grant to Newton Cannon, 317 acres. No. 1034. Certificate No. 177, dated 31 Jul 1807. Obtained by William Polk and entered 8 Aug 1807 by No. 55. Granted to Newton Cannon, assignee of William Polk. Land being in Rutherford Co., TN, on Thompson's Creek of Duck River, Surveyed 10 Sep 1807. Reg: 20 Apr 1811.

Page 189 - Tennessee Grant to Elijah Rutledge, 80 acres. No. 2244. For Military Service by Andrew Phillips to North Carolina, Warrant No. 4502, dated 22 Dec 1796 and entered 6 Dec 1808 by No. 1023. Granted to Elijah Rutledge, assignee of Andrew Phillips, part of warrant being in Bedford Co., TN, on waters of Weakleys Creek. Surveyed 15 Feb 1809 by George Tillman, D.S., Seal at Knoxville 8 May 1810. Reg: 11 May 1811.

Page 191 - Tennessee Grant to John Bryant, 60 acres. No. 2540. For Military Service by Benjamin Davidson to North Carolina, Warrant No. 3000, dated 30 Sep 1785 and entered 25 Feb 1809 by No. 1201. Granted to John Bryeans, assignee of Benjamin Davidson, land in Bedford Co., TN, on Sinking Creek of Duck River. Borders large lands of James Johnston. Surveyed 3 Jun 1809. Reg: 11 May 1811. (Recorded in Book C, page 202)

Page 194 - Tennessee Grant to Newton Cannon, 200 acres. No. 1947. Certificate No. 318, dated 22 Aug 1807, obtained by John Sloss and entered 31 Aug 1807 by No. 441. Granted to Newton Cannon, assignee of John Sloss. Land in Bedford Co., TN, on Dry Fork of Sugar Creek, a south branch of Duck River. Borders lands of John Thompson and Sharps and Sugans. Surveyed 1 Jun 1808. Reg: 24 May 1811.

Page 196 - Tennessee Grant to Thompson Wright, 160 acres. No. 965. For Military Service by John Jordon to North Carolina, Warrant No. 78, dated 1 Dec 1802 and entered 23 Jun 1808 by No. 550. Granted to Thompson Wright, assignee of the heirs of John Jordon. Land in Bedford Co., TN, on waters of Wartrace Fork of Duck River. Borders about 50 yards west of Timothy Sugg's house. Surveyed 27 Aug 1808. Reg: 24 May 1811.

Page 198 - Tennessee Grant to Thompson Wright, 55 acres. No. 966. For Military Service of John Jordon to North Carolina, entered 23 Jun 1808 by No. 551. Granted to Thompson Wright, assignee of the heirs of John Jordon. Land in Bedford Co., TN, on waters of Wartrace Fork of Duck River. Surveyed 27 Aug 1808. Reg: 1 Jun 1811.

Page 200 - Tennessee Grant to Thompson Wright, 425 acres. No. 964. For Military Service by John Jordon to North Carolina, Warrant No. 78, dated 18 Dec 1802, entered 18 Aug 1807 by No. 208. Granted to Thompson Wright, assignee of heirs of John Jordon. Land in Bedford Co., TN, on waters of Wartrace Fork of Duck River. Bordered Tilman Dickson. Surveyed 17 Aug 1808. Reg: 5 Jun 1811.

Page 202 - Tennessee Grant to Malcom Gilchrist, 75 acres. No. 2229. Certificate No. 274, dated 18 Jul 1809, obtained by Benjamin Williams and entered 7 Sep 1809 by No. 176. Granted to Malcom Gilchrist, assignee of Benjamin Williams. Land in Bedford Co., TN, on Sinking Creek, a south branch of Duck River. Borders on east of 650 acres for schools. Surveyed 27 Oct 1809. Reg: 1 Jun 1811.

Page 204 - Tennessee Grant to William Foster, 80 acres. No. 1652. For Military Service by James Sullivant to North Carolina, Warrant No. 3680, dated 10 Dec 1788 and entered 14 Nov 1808 by No. 754. Granted to William Foster, assignee of heirs of James Sullivant. Land in Bedford Co., TN, on headwaters of Alexanders Creek, a branch of North Fork of Duck River. Borders Richard Wright. Surveyed 20 Mar 1809. Reg: 2 Jun 1811.

Page 275 - Deed from Clement Cannon to the Commissioners, 100 acres, 2 May 1810. 100 acres for the site of the Town of Shelbyville &c., for $1.00. Land on north side of Duck River, beginning at a stake in River, 2 poles south of the mouth of Samuel Musgroves Spring Branch, running thence south 55° east

85½ poles to a small ash log and 2 cedars, thence east 48 poles to white oak and dogwood, thence north 146 poles and ½ pole to a stake, thence west 120 poles to a stake, thence south to beginning. Including Samuel Musgroves' improvements and spring. Part of a land granted to Robert Smith, late of Cabarrus Co., NC by Grant No. 15 from North Carolina and by Robert Washington Smith of the County of Cravens, NC. Reg: 22 Jun 1811.

Page 279 - James Torrentine to Church of Christ, 2½ acres. 21 Dec 1810. Land in Bedford Co., TN on the north side of Duck River near Thompson's Ford. Wit: Jno. Thompson. Reg: 22 Jun 1811.

Page 281 - John Newman to William Krowel (Crowell), 200 acres. 2 Nov 1810. John Newman of Davidson Co., TN as guardian of Jane and Anne Newman, daughters of Anthony Newman, deceased. William Krowel of Bedford Co., TN. Land in Bedford Co., part of 5000 acre Grant to Anthony Newman, on north side of Duck River. Wit: Michael Fisher. Reg: 22 Jun 1811.

Page 285 - Thompson Thompson to Anny Thompson, Deed of Gift. Thompson Thompson of Bedford Co., to his niece Anny Thompson, 1 negro woman. 25 Jul 1810. Wit: Jno. Thompson and Joseph Thompson. Reg: 22 Jun 1811.

Page 291 - Tennessee Grant to George Doherty, 3000 acres. No. 603. Warrant No. 1503, dated 5 Nov 1784 issued to George Doherty by John Armstrong, Entry Office for North Carolina. Entered 14 Aug 1807 by No. 152. Land in Williamson Co., TN, on a small creek that runs into North Fork of Duck River below the mouth of Weakleys Creek. Borders school land and Nathaniel Taylor and Thomas Thompson. Surveyed 8 May 1808. Reg: 10 Jul 1811.

Page 293 - Tennessee Grant to William Polk, 206¼ acres. No. 1107. For Military Service by David Rison to North Carolina, Warrant No. 1727, dated 24 Apr 1785 and entered 27 Aug 1807 by No. 345. Granted to William Polk, assignee of the heirs of David Rison, land in Bedford Co., TN, on Big Flat Creek, a branch of Duck River. Borders George Doherty. Surveyed 12 Jan 1809. Reg: 10 Jul 1811.

Page 295 - Tennessee Grant to Solomon Plumlee, 100 acres. No. 2486. Warrant No. 501, dated 4 Jan 1796, issued to Philip Newton by John Carter, Entry Taker for Washington County and entered 27 Dec 1808 by No. 1073. Granted to Solomon Plumlee, assignee of Philip Newton, land in Bedford Co., TN, on Wilsons Creek. Borders Abraham Byler and Robert Smith. Surveyed 26 Jul 1809 by George Tilman, D.S. Seal at Knoxville. Reg: 19 Jul 1811.

Page 296 - Elizabeth Giles to Newton Cannon, 472 acres. 13 Mar 1811. Elizabeth Giles of Sumner Co., TN sold to Newton Cannon of Williamson Co., TN, land in Bedford Co., TN, on waters of Duck River, of Flat Creek. Grant No. 1688 and Certificate No. 98, dated 25 Jul 1807 to Edward Giles and entered 12 Jul 1807 by No. 106. Elizabeth Giles for herself and the heirs of Edward Giles. Reg: 27 Jul 1811.

Page 299 - Tennessee Grant to John Blackwell, 480 acres. No. 2228. For Military Service by John Flinthon to North

Carolina, Warrant No. 5186, dated 9 Dec 1797 and entered 13 Jul 1808 by No. 612. Granted to John Blackwell, assignee of John Flinthon's heirs. Land in Bedford Co., TN, on headwaters of East Fork of Rock Creek, a south branch of Duck River. Surveyed 30 Nov 1808 by William Gilchrist, D.S. Reg: 4 Aug 1811.

Page 305 - Tennessee Grant to John Thompson, 300 acres. No. 1370. For Military Service by Edmund Dodd to North Carolina, Warrant No. 5309, dated 9 Dec 1797 and entered -- Jan 1809 by No. 171 as an Occupant Claim. Granted to John Thompson, assignee of Edmund Dodd, land, part in Bedford Co., TN, on north side of Duck River, near Anthony Newman's lands. Surveyed 9 Jun 1805(?). Reg: 9 Aug 1811.

Page 307 - Tennessee Grant to Thomas Thompson, 67 acres. No. 1512. Certificate No. 104, dated 25 Jul 1807, obtained by Thomas Taylor and entered 25 Mar 1808 by No. 261. Granted to Thomas Thompson, assignee of Thomas Taylor, land in Bedford Co., TN, on north side of Duck River. Borders school land. Surveyed 11 Nov 1808. Reg: 18 Aug 1811. (Recorded in Book C, page 115)

Page 313 - Benjamin McCuistion to Jno. and Elisha Marshal, 50 acres. 21 Jan 1811. Benjamin McCuistion of Bedford Co., TN, sold to John and Elisha Marshal, sons of Laven Marshall of Bedford Co., TN, land in Bedford Co., on north side of Duck River. Borders Entry of George Doherty. Reg: 3 Aug 1811.

Page 369 - Tennessee Grant to George Alexander, 1650 acres. No. 1689. Certificate No. 43, dated 14 Jul 1808, obtained by George Alexander and entered 12 Sep 1808 by No. 800. Granted to George Alexander and his heirs, land in Williamson Co., TN, on Weakleys Creek. Borders Grant to Ebenezer Alexander. Surveyed 20 Apr 1809. Reg: 21 Sep 1811.

Page 371 - Tennessee Grant to John Byler, 200 acres. No. 2459. Warrant No. 1522, dated 16 May 1797, issued to John Plumer by John Carter, Entry Taker for Washington County and entered 20 Aug 1810 by No. 229 as Occupant Claim. Granted to John Byler, assignee of John Plumer, land in Bedford Co., TN, on waters of Weakleys Creek. Borders John Harris and Charles Brandon. Surveyed 16 Mar 1810 by George Tilman, D.S. Reg: 25 Sep 1811.

Page 373 - Tennessee Grant to Benjamin McCuistion, 61 acres. No. 2280. For Military Service by Abel Litton to North Carolina, Warrant No. 92, dated 30 May 1804 and entered 20 Mar 1809 by No. 1296. Granted to Benjamin McCuistion, assignee of Abel Litton, land, part of a warrant in Bedford Co., TN, on waters of Wilsons Creek. Borders entry by Abraham Byler. Surveyed 3 Apr 1809 by George Tilman, D.S. Reg: 21 Sep 1811.

Page 374 - Tennessee Grant to Benjamin McCuistion, 120 acres. No. 2279. Warrant No. 1709, dated 19 Feb 1787, issued to David Ross and entered 1 Sep 1807 by No. 793. Granted to Benjamin McCuistion, assignee of David Ross, land in Bedford Co., TN, on a north branch of Duck River. Borders George Doherty. Surveyed 14 Jan 1809 by George Mitchell, D.S. Reg: 25 Sep 1811.

Page 378 - Tennessee Grant to Benjamin McCuistion, 110 acres. No. 1023. Certificate No. 331, dated 27 Aug 1807, obtained

By James McCuistion and entered 25 Sep 1807 by No. 607. Granted to Benjamin McCuistion, assignee of James McCuistion, land in Bedford Co., TN, on north side of Duck River, on Hurricane Creek. Surveyed 12 Apr 1808. Reg: 25 Sep 1811.

Page 377 - Tennessee Grant to Benjamin McCuistion, 129 acres. No. 747. For Military Service by Abel Litton for North Carolina, Warrant No. 92, dated 30 May 180_ and entered 25 Mar 1808 by No. 268. Granted to Benjamin McCuistion, assignee of Abel Litton, land in Bedford Co., TN, on waters of Duck River. Borders Howel Tatum. Surveyed 27 Mar 1808. Reg: 25 Sep 1811.

Page 379 - Tennessee Grant to Benjamin McCuistion, 62 acres. No. 2591. Certificate No. 331(?), dated 27 Aug 1807, obtained by James McCuistion and entered 15 Sep 1808 by No. 821. Granted to Benjamin McCuistion, assignee of James McCuistion, land in Bedford Co., TN, on a north branch of Duck River. Borders R. W. Smith and Amos Balch. Surveyed 15 Jan 1809. Reg: 22 Sep 1811.

Page 381 - Tennessee Grant to Benjamin McCuistion, 50 acres. No 2592. For Military Service by Litton (Abel) to North Carolina, Warrant No. 92, dated 30 May 1804 and entered 27 Nov 1808 by No. 960. Granted to Benjamin McCuistion, assignee of Abel Litton, land in Bedford Co., TN, on the north side of Duck River. Borders George Doherty and Robert W. Smith. Surveyed 3 Mar 1809. Reg: 28 Sep 1811.

Page 385 - Tennessee Grant to William Foster, 55 acres. No. 2845. Certificate No. 29, dated 7 Aug 1809, obtained by Thomas Dillon and entered 3 Jan 1810 by No. 2067. Granted to William Foster, assignee of Thomas Dillon, land in Bedford Co., TN, on Alexanders Creek, waters of Duck River. Surveyed 27 Feb 1810 by Cabell Vaughan, D.S. Reg: 1 Jun 1811.

Page 391 - Tennessee Grant to James Clinton, 300 acres. No. 2734(?). Certificate No. 209, dated 30 Jul 1810, issued to Sampson Sayers, Jr. and entered 12 Dec 1810 by No. 240 as Occupant Claim. Granted to James Clinton, assignee of Sampson Sayers, Jr., land in Bedford Co., TN, on both sides of Wilsons Creek of Duck River. Adjoins Robert Smith. Surveyed 18 Mar 180- by Alexander Torrentine, D.S. Reg: 8 Nov 1811.

Page 393 - Tennessee Grant to William Foster, 55 acres. No. 2845. Certificate No. 296, dated 17 Aug 1809, obtained by Thomas Dillon and entered 3 Jan 1810 by No. 2067. Granted to William Foster, assignee of Thomas Dillon, land in Bedford Co., TN, on Alexanders Creek, waters of Duck River. Surveyed 27 Feb 1810. Reg: 11 Dec 1811.

Page 395 - Tennessee Grant to Archibald Davis, 100 acres. No. 1955. Warrant No. 91, dated 12 Jan 1803, issued to Samuel Shannon and entered 2 Feb 1808 by No. 175. Granted to Archibald Davis, assignee of Samuel Shannon, land in Bedford Co., TN, on West Fork of Big Flat Creek, a south branch of Duck River. Surveyed 17 Nov 1808. Reg: 11 Dec 1811.

Page 403 - Tennessee Grant to Alexander Rutledge, 40 acres. No. 2457. Part of a Warrant No. 626 from Tennessee to John Kennedy and entered 16 Aug 1808 by No. 731. Granted to Alexander Rutledge, assignee of John Kennedy, land in Bedford Co.,

TN, on waters of Weakleys Creek. Surveyed 26 Nov 1808. Reg: 13 Dec 1811.

Page 405 - Tennessee Grant to Charles Brandon, 60 acres. No. 2458. For Military Service of William Reams to North Carolina, Warrant No. 4721, dated 15 Feb 1797 and entered 12 Sep 1809 by No. 1792. Granted to Charles Brandon, assignee of William Reams, land in Bedford Co., TN, on Clems Creek, north of Duck River. Borders William Clark and school land. Surveyed 14 Feb 1810. Reg: 13 Dec 1811.

Page 421 - Samuel Patterson to Andrew Patterson, 225 acres. 19 Sep 1811. Samuel Patterson of Wilson Co., TN sold to Andrew Patterson of Bedford Co., TN, land in Bedford Co., on north side of Duck River, adjoining entry of Ezekiel Alexander. Wit: William Patterson, Chas. Haskins and Thomas Gates. Reg: 16 Dec 1811.

Page 423 - Samuel Patterson to Thomas Patterson, 225 acres. 20 Sep 1811. Samuel Patterson of Wilson Co., TN, sold to Thomas Patterson of Smith Co., TN, land in Bedford Co., TN, on north side of Duck River, on waters of Spring Creek, adjoins Alexander Patterson. Wit: Alexander Patterson, Chas. Haskins, and Thomas Gates. Reg: 17 Dec 1811.

Page 425 - Samuel Patterson to William Patterson, 225 acres. 20 Sep 1811. Samuel Patterson of Wilson Co., TN, sold to William Patterson of Wilson Co., TN, land in Bedford Co., TN, on north side of Duck River, of Spring Creek. Adjoins Thomas Patterson and Andrew Patterson. Wit: Alexander Patterson, Charles Haskins and Thomas Gates. Reg: 17 Dec 1811.

Page 427 - Samuel Patterson to Alexander Patterson, 225 acres. 19 Sep 1811. Samuel Patterson of Wilson Co., TN, sold to Alexander Patterson of Wilson Co., TN, land in Bedford Co., TN, on waters of Spring Creek. Adjoins Ezekiel Alexander, Andrew Patterson and Aron Wilson. Wit: Charles Haskins, Thomas Gates and William Patterson. Reg: 18 Dec 1811.

Page 429 - North Carolina Grant to James Hunter, 1500 acres. No. 299. Being on north side of Duck River, on Alexanders Creek. Warrant from John Armstrong, Entry Taker, No. 1949. Reg: 17 Dec 1811.

Page 431 - Patton & Erwin to Matt Martin, 100 acres. 2 Apr 1811. James Patton and Andrew Erwin of Buncomb Co., NC sold to Matt Martin of Bedford Co., TN, land in Bedford Co., on waters of the Middle or Garrison Fork of Duck River. Reg: 18 Dec 1811.

Page 438 - McReynolds & Dunns to George W. Cahoon. 13 Jun 1811 for 163 acres. Lucy McReynolds and James McReynolds and John C. Dunn and Mary B. Dunn, all of Bedford Co., TN sold to George W. Cahoon of Bedford Co., TN, land in Bedford Co., TN, a part of a 1000 acre tract deeded to Benjamin Williams of North Carolina to Lucy McReynolds. The land where Joseph Trimble now living, on Spring Creek. Wit: John Atkinson and Joseph Trimble. Reg: 19 Dec 1811.

Page 453 - Tennessee Grant to Samuel McCuistion, 171 acres. No. 2270. 27 Aug 1807, entered 31 Aug 1807 by No. 413. Granted

TO Samuel McCuistion, assignee of James McCuistion. Land in Bedford Co., TN. Borders James McCuistion's land. Surveyed 24 Apr 1807 by Alexander Torrentine, D.S. Reg: 15 Jan 1812.

Page 454 - Tennessee Grant to James Smith, 15 acres. No. 2132. For Military Service of Burrell Smith to North Carolina, Warrant No. 1013, dated 26 May 1784 and entered 19 Apr 1809 by No. 1393, land in Bedford Co., TN, on waters of Alexanders Creek. James Smith, assignee of Burrell Smith. Land borders John Kockrell's land. Surveyed 21 Apr 1809 by James Smith, D.S. Reg: -- Jan 1812.

Page 456 - Tennessee Grant to James Smith, 50 acres. No. 2133. Warrant No. 741, dated 1 May 1805, issued to George D. Blackamore and entered 19 Apr 1809 by No. 1394. Granted to James Smith, assignee of George D. Blackamore, land in Bedford Co., TN, on south side of Duck River, on the headwaters of Rock Creek. Borders lands of William Donelson, William Nash, Michael Gleaves, John Overton and M. Gleaves. Surveyed 25 Apr 1809 by James Smith, D.S. Reg: 30 Jan 1811.
Also,
Tennessee Grant, No. 2134 for 54 acres. For Military Service of Burrell Smith to North Carolina, Warrant No. 1013, dated 26 May 1784 and entered 19 Apr 1809 by No. 392. Granted to James Smith, assignee of Burrell Smith, land in Bedford Co., TN, on the east drain of West Fork of Rock Creek. Borders Francis Nash. Surveyed 30 May 1809 by James Smith, D.S. Reg: 18 Jan 1812.

Page 459 - Tennessee Grant to James Smith, 50 acres. No. 2135. Certificate No. 181, dated 18 Feb 1809, obtained by Daniel Smith and entered 30 Aug 1809 by No. 1725. Granted to James Smith, assignee of Daniel Smith, land in Bedford Co., TN, on waters of Rock Creek, a branch of Duck River. Borders William Black, Fishing Ford, Rogers on north side of the Elk Ridge. Surveyed 15 Sep 1809 by James Smith, D.S. Reg: 18 Jan 1812.

Page 460 - Tennessee Grant to Elisha Hunter, 16 acres. No. 2144. Certificate No. 18-, dated 18 Feb 1809, obtained by Daniel Smith and entered 30 Aug 1809 by No. 572. Granted to Elisha Hunter, assignee of Daniel Smith, land in Maury Co., TN, on waters of Globe Creek. Borders George Mitchell, William Loftin, and William Nash. Surveyed 15 Sep 1809 by James Smith, D.S. Reg: 18 Jan 1812.

Page 462 - Tennessee Grant to John Wilkins, 120 acres. No. 2140. Certificate No. 18-, dated 18 Feb 1809, obtained by Daniel Smith and entered 30 Aug 1809 by No. 1728. Granted to John Wilkins, assignee of Daniel Smith, land in Maury Co., TN, on the head-drain of Globe Creek. Borders William Nash, William T. Lewis, and George Mitchell. Surveyed 15 Sep 1809 by James Smith, D.S. Reg: 26 Jan 1812.

Page 463 - Tennessee Grant to Robert Allison, 30 acres. No. 2454. Certificate No. 306, dated 21 Aug 1809, obtained by Benjamin McCullock and entered 29 Aug 1809 by No. 1719. Granted to Robert Allison, assignee of Benjamin McCullock, land in Bedford Co., TN, on waters of Clems Creek. Surveyed 28 Sep 1809 by George Tilman, D.S. Reg: 20 Jan 1812.

Page 465 - North Carolina Grant to Martin Phifer, 2373 acres. No. 38. In Bedford Co., TN, on north side of Duck River, including the mouth of Hurricane Creek. Surveyed 25 Jun 1810. Reg: 20 Jan 1812.

Page 466 - North Carolina Grant to Martin Phifer, 5000 acres. No. 2391. Also No. 104. Land in Bedford Co., TN, north side of Duck River, on waters of Falling Creek. Borders Caleb Phifer. Surveyed 27 Jun 1810. Reg: 26 Jan 1812.

Page 481 - Moses Yell to Joseph Kenady, 75 acres. 1 Jan 1811. Moses Yell of Bedford Co., TN sold Joseph Kennady of Bedford Co., TN, land in Bedford Co., TN, it being a part of a 750 acre of a 5000 acre of Andrew Jackson and now conveyed to him by Robert _utton and Rachel his wife. Borders lands of Rachel and Patsy Thompson Hays. Wit: James Jenkins, Samuel Phillips and James Yell. Reg: 11 M-- 1812.

Page 502 - Tennessee Grant to James Gage, 300 acres. No. 2437. Certificate No. 438, dated 2 Aug 1810, obtained by John McIver and William P. Anderson and entered 3 Aug 1810 by No. 221, as an Occupant Claim. Granted to James Gage, assignee of John McIver and William P. Anderson, land in Bedford Co., TN, on east waters of Big Flat Creek, a south branch of Duck River. Surveyed -- May 1808 by Daniel Gilchrist, D.S. Reg: 18 Mar 1812.

Page 504 - Tennessee Grant to William Shook, 50 acres. No. 2579. For Military Service by William Brown for North Carolina, Warrant No. 938, dated 19 Dec 1803 and entered 11 Jul 1809 by No. 1585. Granted to William Shook, assignee of William Brown, land, part of warrant lying in Bedford Co., TN, on east waters of Big Flat Creek. Surveyed 20 Oct 1809 by Malcom Gilchrist, D.S. Reg: 18 Mar 1812.

Page 516 - Andrew Erwin and James Patton of Buncomb Co., NC. 2 Apr 1811.

Page 639 - Tennessee Grant to Edward Wade, 50 acres. No. 338-. Certificate No. 63, dated 18 Aug 1808, obtained by Tilman Dixon and entered 4 Oct 1808 by No. 858. Granted to Edward Wade, assignee of Tilman Dixon, land in Bedford Co., TN, on south side of Duck River. Borders bank of Duck River, Hurricane Creek. Surveyed 21 Nov 1809 by William Gilchrist, D.S. Reg: 4 Feb 1812.

Page 548 - John Stone to Jacob Willhite (Wilhoite), 605 acres. 22 Mar 1812. Land located on both sides of Duck River. Borders Dempsey Powel's tract, Thomas Talbot's tract, Michael Robertson's tract. Wit: Joshua Holt and William Ray. Reg: 30 May 1812.

Page 606 - Tennessee Grant to John Atkinson, 100 acres. No. 3355. For Military Service of Roger Hilton for North Carolina, Warrant No. 3173, dated 19 Dec 1785 and entered 26 Aug 1809 by No. 1705. Granted to John Atkinson, assignee of the heirs of Roger Hilton, land in Bedford Co., TN, on north side of Duck River, on Wilsons Creek. Borders David Flemming. Surveyed 4 Sep 1809. Reg: (no date given)

Page 614 - Tennessee Grant to Martha Baker, 115 acres. No.1138. Warrant No. 1609, dated 30 Nov 1784, issued to Abraham Kuykendall

DEED BOOK "C"

by John Armstrong, Entry Taker of Claims for North Carolina, entered 8 Sep 1808 by No. 156. Granted to Martha Baker, assignee of Abraham Kuykendall, land in Bedford Co., TN, on Nall Creek, a fork of the Garrison Fork of Duck River. Borders John Nall.

DEED BOOK "D" 1812 - 1814

Page 27 - Burton Jordan to Hance and Jane Cunningham, 116¼ acres. 12 Jan 1812. All of Bedford Co., TN. Land in Bedford Co., TN.

Page 33 - Joel Dyer and others to Jesse Chafin, 274 acres. 6 Oct 1811. Joel Dyer, William Mitchell and Robert H. Dyer, all of Rutherford Co., TN, sold to Jesse Chafin of Rutherford Co., TN, land in Bedford Co., TN and entered in the name of Thomas Johnston. No. Entry 88, dated 11 Aug 1807. Surveyed 29 Aug 1808. Land on the Wartrace Fork of Duck River. Borders school land and Blount Grants. Wit: David Moore, David T. Man---g and Edward H. Chafin and Nathan Chafin.

Page 41 - James Patton and Andrew Erwin of Ashville, NC. 30 Mar 1812.

Page 47 - James Gilbert, Sr. to John Gilbert, of Bedford Co., TN. James Gilbert, Sr. to his son John Gilbert, land in Bedford Co., TN. Land on Thompsons Creek, 100 acers. 22 Jun 1812. Reg: 19 Sep 1812.

Page 48 - James Gilbert, Sr. to James Gilbert, Jr., 100 acres. James Gilbert, Sr. to his son James Gilbert, Jr., land on Thompsons Creek. 22 Jun 1812. Reg: 19 Sep 1812.

Page 59 - Tennessee Grant to William Shook, 24¼ acres. No. 3383. Certificate No. 232, dated 13 Aug 1810, issued to John Owens and entered 4 Oct 1810 by No. 2745. Granted to William Shook, assignee of John Owen, land in Bedford Co., TN, on east waters of Big Flat Creek. Borders Occupant Claim Survey of James Gage, Sampson Sawers. Surveyed 28 Feb 1811. Reg: 24 Oct 1812.

Page 61 - Tennessee Grant to Henry Miller, 200 acres. No. 3199. Part Warrant No. 626, dated 24 Jun 1807, issued to John Kennaday and entered 23 Mar 1808 by No. 263. Granted to Henry Miller, assignee of John Kennaday, land in Bedford Co., TN, on waters of Clems Creek. Surveyed 28 Dec 1808. Reg: 24 Oct 1812.

Page 64 - Tennessee Grant to Ruben McClerin, 100 acres. No. 3969. Warrant No. 501, dated 11 Jan 1796, issued to Philip Nalen and entered 12 Sep 1809 by No. 1791. Granted to Ruben McClerin, assignee of Philip Nalen, land in Bedford Co., TN, on waters of Wilsons Creek, north side of Duck River. Borders Robert Smith, Solomon Plumlee. Surveyed 25 Oct 1810. Reg: 24 Oct 1812.

Page 66 - Tennessee Grant to John Thompson, 528 acres. No. 2200. For Military Service of Moses Powell to North Carolina, Warrant No. 1783, dated 23 Apr 1785 and entered 7 Aug 1807 by No. 25. Granted to John Thompson, assignee of heirs of Moses Powell, land in Bedford Co., TN. Borders Samuel Patton, Amos Balch and Howel Talons and Story's line. Surveyed 24 Jul 1809 by

George Mitchell, D.S. Reg: 12 Nov 1812.

Page 69 - Joseph Allison & James Canon to Thomas Campbell, PA State of North Carolina, Iredell County. Joseph Allison of Iredell Co., and James Canon of Cabarrus Co., NC, appointed their friend Thomas Campbell of Murray (Maury) Co., TN, as their Attorney to recover and receive from William Woods of Giles Co., TN and John Homes, now of Bedford Co., TN, joint Bond, Warrant No. 61 in the name of William Black. William Woods and John Homes is believed to have violated every article of the agreement between them. Wit: Joseph Grey, J.P. and Samuel Long, J.P. 7 Sep 1812.

Page 72 - Tennessee Grant to Robert Allison, 240 acres. No.368. For Military Service by William Chaves for North Carolina, Warrant No. 5058, dated 6 Dec 1797 and entered 21 Jul 1809 by No. 1625. Granted to Robert Allison, assignee of the heirs of William Chaves, land in Bedford Co., TN, on north side of Duck River and on Clems Creek. Borders lands of John Wilson. Surveyed 28 Sep 1809 by George Tilman, D.S. Reg: 18 Nov 1812.

Page 74 - Tennessee Grant to David Floyd, Jr., 40 acres. No. 2511. Warrant No. 1644, dated 30 Nov 1784 issued to James Bosley and entered 6 Mar 1810 by No. 2221. Granted to David Floyd, Jr., assignee of James Bosley, land in Bedford Co., TN, on headwaters of Big Flat Creek. Surveyed 17 Apr 1810 by Daniel Gilchrist, D.S. Reg: 25 Nov 1812.

Page 130 - James Shriver to Jacob Harrington, 213 acres. 7 Jan 1812. James Shriver of Robertson Co., TN sold to Jacob Harrington and William Harrington of Bedford Co., TN, land in Bedford Co., TN, on waters of Duck River, it being a tract granted to the heirs of John Shriver. Land on east side of Thompsons Creek. Borders survey of Robert McCuistion, survey made for Alexander Cherry. Surveyed 18 Sep 1807. Wit: Charles Harrington and David Morgan. Reg: 22 Dec 1812.

Page 136 - John Gage to Heirs of Joseph Ake, 100 acres. 26 Sep 1812. John Ake of Bedford Co., TN sold to William Ake, Mitcham Lun Ake, Mary Ake, Callelow Brooks, Harper Ake, Joseph Henderson Ake, Nancy Sevier Ake, Jefferson Kelly Ake, and Russel Grundy Ake, heirs and heirs at law of Joseph Ake, deceased, of Bedford Co., TN, land in Bedford Co., TN, on Mill Creek, the waters of the Barren Fork of Duck River and on which is two grist mills and a saw mill. Wit: Samuel Brown, John Russeval, and William Boyd. Signed: John Gage. Reg: 22 Dec 1812.

Page 143 - J. A. Wilson and Steele to Nath'l Gilmore. James A.(C) Wilson and Joseph Steele to Nathaniel Gilmore. (Unionville).

Page 148 - The Division of A.(N). Gilmore to Eli Giles,350 acres. 4 Dec 1812. Between Archibald Johnston and his wife Elizabeth Johnston, Polly Gilmore and Jane H. Gilmore sold to Eli Giles of Sumner Co., TN, land in Bedford Co., TN, on waters of Duck River. Borders land of the heirs of John Locke survey and John Wilson. Wit: Edwin Alexander and A. Gilmore. Reg: 29 Dec 1812.

Page 151 - Tennessee Grant to James Neill, 50 acres. No. 3343. Certificate No. 142, dated 26 Jul 1809, obtained by Elisha

Walling and entered 4 Apr 1810 by No. 2295. Granted to John Neill, assignee of Elisha Walling, land in Bedford Co., TN, south side of Duck River, on waters of West Fork of Rock Creek. Borders Gordon's Trace, Laye's survey in name of David Ross. Surveyed 20 Jul 1810 by George Mitchell, D.S. Reg: 25 Jan 1813.

Page 153 - Tennessee Grant to John L. Jetton, 80 acres. No. 3857. Warrant No. 1386, dated 23 Jun 1784, issued to David Williams by Entry Taker John Armstrong, for North Carolina, lands and entered 2 Apr 1811 by No. 3088. Granted to John L. Jetton, assignee of David Williams, land in Bedford Co., TN, on head of Alexanders Creek, waters of Duck River. Borders survey of Samuel Nelson. Surveyed 20 May 1811 by Will McClain, D.S. Reg: 27 Jan 1813.

Page 155 - Tennessee Grant to John L. Jetton, 100 acres. No. 3856. For Military Service of Jonas Colgrove to North Carolina, Warrant No. 5192, dated 9 Dec 1797 and entered 8 May 1810 by No. 2368. Granted to John L. Jetton, assignee of Jonas Colgrove, land in Bedford Co., TN, near head of Alexanders Creek, waters of Duck River. Borders land on which James Wright now lives. Surveyed 20 May 1811 by Will McClain, D.S. Reg: 10 Feb 1813.

Page 157 - Tennessee Grant to Jason Thompson, 100 acres. No. 1883. Warrant No. 111, dated 31 Jan 1803, issued by Tennessee to Howel Tatum and entered 29 Aug 1809 by No. 350. Granted to Jason Thompson, assignee of Howel Tatum, land in Bedford Co., TN, on Dry Fork of Sugar Creek, a south branch of Duck River. Borders land granted to Anthony Sharpe and Thomas Dugan, land in name of Robert White. Surveyed 31 Mar 1808 by M. Gilchrist, D.S. Reg: 10 Feb 1813.

Page 159 - Tennessee Grant to Jason Thompson, 222 acres. No. 2113. Certificate No. 63, dated 10 Mar 1810, issued to Abraham Right and Jason Thompson and entered on 3 Apr 1810 by No. 208 as an Occupant Claim, assignee of Isaac Eaton. Granted to Jason Thompson and his heirs, land in Bedford Co., TN. Borders lands of Levi Campbell. Surveyed 19 Aug 1808 by John Drake, D.S. Reg: 10 Feb 1813.

Page 175 - James Patton and Andrew Erwin in Ashville, NC. Oct 1812.

Page 196 - John Huff to William Hopkins, PA.
John Huff appointed William Hopkins as Power of Attorney, to recover from Mathew Cunningham, his part of estate of William Galbreath, deceased, and also his part of estate of John Galbreath, deceased, as his rightful property as the true legitimate heir of the deceased. Reg: 13 Mar 1813.

Page 199 - Tennessee Grant to Charles Brandon, 90 acres. No. 3200. For Military Service by William Reams to North Carolina, Warrant No. 4726, dated 15 Feb 1797 and entered 13 Oct 1809 by No. 1882. Granted to Charles Brandon, assignee of William Reams, land, part of Warrant in Bedford Co., TN, on waters of Weakley Creek. Borders Alexander Rutledge and Elijah Rutledge and Wilson Clark. Surveyed 15 Mar 1810. Reg: 11 Mar 1813.

Page 201 - Tennessee Grant to Amos McLemore, 15 acres. No. 3198. Warrant No. 626, dated 24 Jun 1807 to John Kennedy, Pre-emption Claim of office of Samuel Barton, Entry Taker and entered 23 Mar 1808 by No. 266. Granted to Amos McLemore, assignee of John Kennedy, land in Bedford Co., TN, on waters of Weakleys Creek. Surveyed 27 Dec 1808 by George Tilman, D.S. Reg: 11 Mar 1813.

Page 207 - State of Georgia, Morgan County. 23 Mar 1813. Andrew Tannihill, formerly of State of Georgia and County of Franklin but now of Tennessee, County of Bedford, to Armsted Russel of Morgan Co., Georgia, land in Morgan Co., Georgia, 202½ acres, No. 179 (District plan). Reg: 23 Mar 1813.

Page 209 - John Warren to N. Branch, 105 acres. 2 Aug 1812. John Warren of Bedford Co., TN, for natural love for Nicholas Branch, Deed of Gift, land. Borders lands of Mathias Hoover. Wit: Martin Dyer and Martin Hoover. Reg: 24 Mar 1813.

Page 214 - David Low's lye Bill. David Low of Bedford Co., TN, intoxocated, did speak and say things about Joshua Holt, late of Orange Co., NC, now a citizen of Bedford Co., TN, also against Elenor Holt, wife of Joshua Holt, acknowledged 21 Sep 1812. Wit: Jos. B. Howell, William Hicks, Samuel Fleming and William Stuart and Nathaniel Hubart. Reg: 20 May 1813.

Page 223 - William and Walter Gilbreath to Robert Dixon, 126 acres. 16 Nov 1811. Walter Gilbreath of Orange Co., NC and William Gilbreath of Adams Co., PA sold to Robert Dixon of Orange Co., NC, land in Bedford Co., TN, 2nd District. Borders land of Roger Snell. Reg: 28 May 1813.

Page 253 - North Carolina Grant to William Branche, 5000 acres. No. 855. Land in Green Co., on waters of Duck River. Ten lbs per 100 acres. State Tax in Rutherford Co., TN. Plat on page 254. Green Co., NC. 1790. Reg: 7 Jun 1813.

Page 257 - Tennessee Grant to Walter Bernard, 330 acres. No. 3063. Certificate No. 246, dated 14 Aug 1807, obtained by Walter Bernard, heir of John Bernard and entered 11 Jan 1808 by No. 112. Granted to Walter Bernard and heirs, land in Bedford Co., TN, on Sinking Creek. Surveyed 27 Oct 1809 by William Gilchrist, D.S. Reg: 8 Jun 1813.

Page 280 - Tennessee Grant to Jeremiah Cherry, 500 acres. No. 469. For Military Service by Benjamin Kenneday for North Carolina, Warrant No. 3774, dated 24 Dec 1792 and entered 24 Aug 1807 by No. 297. Granted to Jeremiah Cherry, assignee of Benjamin Kenneday, land in Rutherford Co., TN, on Little Flat Creek of Duck River. Surveyed 9 Sep 1807. Reg: 28 Jun 1813.

Page 282 - Tennessee Grant to Alexander Torrentine, 100 acres. No. 3224. For Military Service by Malachi Russell for North Carolina, Warrant No. 637, dated 23 Apr 1784 and entered 27 Jul 1808 by No. 644. Granted to Alexander Torrentine, assignee of Malachi Russell, land in Bedford Co., TN, on Falling Creek, on north side of Duck River. Borders lands of Ephraim Payton. Surveyed 3 Mar 1809 by George Mitchell, D.S. Reg: 28 Jun 1813.

Page 284 - Tennessee Grant to William Caswell, 320 acres. No. 1523. For Military Service by William Caswell for North

Carolina, Warrant No. 158, dated 22 Oct 1783 and entered 24 Sep 1807 by No. 606. Granted to William Caswell and his heirs, land, a part of Warrant in Bedford Co., TN, on Alexanders Creek. Surveyed 4 Mar 1809. Reg: 28 Jun 1813.

Page 286 - Tennessee Grant to William Clark, 110 acres. No. 3239. For Military Service of Moses Leathers for North Carolina, Warrant No. 1207, dated 20 Sep 1784 and entered 23 Dec 1807 by No. 42. Granted to William Clark, assignee of Moses Leathers, land in Bedford CO., TN, on waters of Clems Creek, on north side of Duck River. Borders school land, Amos McLemore, Elijah Rutledge. Surveyed 30 Aug 1813 by George Tillman, D.S. Reg: 10 Aug 1813.

Page 288 - Stokly Donalson to William Henry, 500 acres. 10 Mar 1795. Stokly Donalson of Knox and Territory South of the River Ohio sold to William Henry of same afore Territory, land being in Middle District, about two miles above the Old Indian War Road and about one mile east of the War Trace Fork of Duck River. Borders Blount Grants. Reg: 29 Jun 1813.

Page 296 - Tennessee Grant to William Clark, 247 acres. No. 3238. For Military Service by Moses Leathers to North Carolina, Warrant No. 1207, dated 20 Sep 1784 and entered 23 Dec 1807 by No. 43. Granted to William Clark, assignee of Moses Leathers, land in Bedford Co., TN, on waters of Clems Creek, on north side of Duck River. Borders school land. Surveyed 30 Aug 1809 by George Tilman, D.S. Reg: 10 Aug 1813.

Page 298 - Tennessee Grant to John Allison and Thomas Cox, 100 acres. No. 2576. For Military Service by William Brown to North Carolina, Warrant No. 938, dated 19 Dec 1803 and entered 20 Oct 1808 by No. 901. Granted to John Allison and Thomas Cox, assignees of William Brown, land in Bedford Co., TN, on headwaters of Big Flat Creek of Duck River. Borders John Sloss. Surveyed 19 Nov 1808 by Daniel Gilchrist, D.S. (John Ellison). Reg: 11 Aug 1813.

Page 300 - Tennessee Grant to John Allison and Thomas Cox, 100 acres. No. 4129. For Military Service of William Brown for North Carolina, Warrant No. 938, dated 19 Dec 1803 and entered 4 Jul 1808 by No. 581. Granted to John Allison and Thomas Cox, assignees of William Brown, land in Bedford Co., TN, on waters of Big Flat Creek. Borders land of John Sloss. Surveyed 1 Oct 1810 by Daniel Gilchrist, D.S. Reg: 11 Aug 1813. (Ellison)

Page 302 - Tennessee Grant to John Allison and Thomas Cox, 50 acres. No. 2577. For Military Service by William Brown for North Carolina, Warrant No. 938 and entered 20 Oct 1808 by No. 902. Granted to John Allison and Thomas Cox, assignees of William Brown, land in Bedford Co., TN, on headwaters of Big Flat Creek. Surveyed 19 Nov 1808 by Daniel Gilchrist, D.S. Reg: 11 Aug 1813 (Ellison)

Page 304 - Tennessee Grant to Jonathan Ridgway, 90 acres. No. 793. Certificate No. 56, dated 20 Jul 1807, obtained by Martin Armstrong and entered 13 Aug 1807 by No. 133. Granted to Jonathan Ridgway, assignee of Martin Armstrong, land in Rutherford Co., TN, on one of the head branches of Alexanders Creek, a branch of the North Fork of Duck River. Borders Grant of Joseph Dixon. Surveyed 24 May 1808. Reg: 24 Aug 1812.

DEED BOOK "D"

Page 306 - Tennessee Grant to John Allison and Thomas Cox, 20 acres. No. 2572. For Military Service of William Brown for North Carolina, Warrant No. 938, dated 19 Dec 1803 and entered 19 Feb 1810 by No. 2160(0). Granted to John Allison and Thomas Cox, assignees of William Brown, land in Bedford Co., TN, on headwaters of Big Flat Creek. Surveyed 18 Apr 1810 by Daniel Gilchrist, D.S. Reg: 24 Aug 1812.

Page 314 - James M. Smith to William Harrison, 15 acres. 25 May 1812. James Smith of Buncomb, North Carolina sold to William Harrison of Bedford Co., TN, land in Bedford Co., waters of Alexanders Creek.

Page 316 - William Graham to Allen Leeper, 1 Oct 1812. William Graham of Mecklenburg Co., NC sold to Allen Leeper of Bedford Co., TN, land in Bedford Co., on west side of Rock Creek. James Graham, Attorney at Law for William Graham.

Page 318 - Tennessee Grant to John Harrison and Levin McNatt, 39 acres. No. 4060. Warrant No. 42, dated 24 Feb 1778, issued to Robert Kirkpatrick by John Carter, Entry Taker and entered 26 Oct 1809 by No. 5924. Granted to John Harrison and Levin McNatt, assignees of Robert Kirkpatrick, land in Bedford Co., TN, on West Fork of Big Flat Creek. Borders Mathew Dockrey. Surveyed 5 Jun 1810 by Daniel Gilchrist, D.S. Reg: 25 Aug 1813.

Page 324 - David Kerr to James Kerr, Bill of Sale. 9 Nov 1804. David Kerr of Rowan Co., NC, for love and affection for his son James Kerr of Rowan Co., NC, a negro girl named Dinah and two of her children, and others. Also other property. Wit: A. J. Brevard, Jos. Braly of NC. Reg: 30 Aug 1813.

Page 328 - Tennessee Grant to Abraham Byler, 100 acres. No. 319. Certificate No. 246, dated 14 Aug 1807 by Walter Brevard, heir of John Brevard and entered 7 Feb 1809 by No. 1176. Granted to Abraham Byler, assignee of Walter Brevard, land in Bedford Co., TN and Williamson Co., TN, on waters of Weakleys Creek. BordersGeorge Doherty's tract. Surveyed 19 Apr 1809 by George Tilman, D.S. Reg: 30 Aug 1813.

Page 330 - James Lock to Wade & Lock, PA 1182 acres. James Lock of Rowan Co., NC appointed Edward Wade and William Lock, both of Bedford County, his Attorney at Law, to receive possession of a tract of land in Bedford Co., TN. The land divided and allotted to him by his brothers. 1 Sep 1812. Wit: L. T. Baird.

Page 332 - Tennessee Grant to Abraham Byler, 100 acres. No. 4822. Warrant No. 626, issued to John Kennedy and entered 20 Mar 1808 by No. 255. Granted to Abraham Byler, assignee of John Kennedy, land in Bedford Co., TN, on Wilsons Creek. Borders Entry No. 249 of Newton Cannon, William White, Wilsons Creek. Surveyed 29 Dec 1808 by George Tilman, D.S. Reg: 23 Jun 1813.

Page 338 - John Smith, Sr. to Jno. Smith, Jr. 100 acres 30 Sep 1812. John Smith, Sr. of Pendleton, SC and John Smith, Jr. of Bedford Co., TN. Land on Falling Creek. Reg: 12 Sep 1813.

DEED BOOK "D"

Page 341 - John Parke to William S. Wilson, 500 acres. 20 Jun 1813. John Parke of Sumner Co., TN and William S. Wilson of Bedford Co., TN, land on north bank of Duck River. Reg: 12 Sep 1813.

Page 347 - Adley Alexander to George Ewing, 190 acres. 21 Jun 1813. Adley Alexander of Maury Co., TN sold to George Ewing of Maury Co., TN, land in Bedford Co., TN, on south side of Duck River, on Sinking Creek of the west fork of Duck River. Borders John Leeper. Reg: 13 Sep 1813.

Page 349 - Mary Doherty to James Ray, 636 acres. 22 Aug 1812. Mary Doherty of Williamson Co., TN sold to James Ray of Williamson Co., TN, land in Bedford Co., TN. Wit: George W. Parsons, John Moore and Michael Moore. Reg: 14 Sep 1813.

Page 361 - Tennessee Grant to Abraham Byler, 50 acres. No. 4823. Warrant No. 626. Part of a grant to John Kennedy for 640 acres. Pre-emption Claim and entered 23 Mar 1802 by No. 264. Granted to Abraham Byler, assignee of John Kennedy, land on waters of Wilson Creek. Borders line of Newton Cannon. Surveyed 28 Dec 1808 by George Tillman, D.S. Reg: 23 Jun 1813.

Page 363 - Tennessee Grant to John Atkinson, 50 acres. No. 4337. Certificate No. 322, dated 7 Sep 1809 to William Cochran and entered 31 Jan 1810 by No. 2117. Granted to John Atkinson, assignee of William Cochran, land in Bedford Co., TN, on waters of Wilson Creek. Surveyed 9 Feb 1810 by George Tillman, D.S. Reg: 17 Sep 1813.

Page 365 - Tennessee Grant to Jason Shuffield, 60 acres. No.4367. For Military Service by Roger Helton for North Carolina, Warrant No. 3173, dated 19 Dec 1785 and entered 13 Feb 1810 by No. 2151. Granted to Jason Shuffield, assignee of heirs of Roger Helton, land in Bedford Co., TN, on north side of Duck River, on waters of Wilson Creek. Borders lands of John Atkinson. Surveyed 17 May 1810 by George Tillman, D.S. Reg: 27 Sep 1813.

Page 367 - Tennessee Grant to William Lytle, 15 acres. No.3237. Certificate No. 310, dated 21 Aug 1807 and entered 24 Oct 1807 by No. 740. Land in Bedford Co., TN on waters of North Fork of Duck River. Borders Joseph Dixon. Surveyed 4 Mar 1809 by George Mitchell, D.S. Reg: 18 Sep 1813.

Page 369 - Tennessee Grant to William Caswell, 640 acres. No. 1522. For Military Service by William Caswell to North Carolina, Warrant No. 158, dated 23 Oct 1783 and entered 2 Sep 1807 by No. 466. Land in Bedford Co., TN. Borders Joseph Dixon. Surveyed 4 Mar 1809. Reg: 17 Sep 1813.

Page 371 - Tennessee Grant to Joseph Thompson, 112 acres. No. 3235. For Military Service by Moses Powell to North Carolina, Warrant No. 1783, dated 23 Apr 1783 and entered 2 Oct 1809 by No. 1843. Granted to Joseph Thompson, assignee of the heirs of Moses Powell, land in Bedford Co., TN, on Duck River. BordersJames Torrentine. Surveyed 11 May 1810 by W. P. Anderson, Reg. Surveyor. Reg: 19 Sep 1813.

Page 373 - Tennessee Grant to James Julen, 35 acres. No. 3369. For Military Service by Jeremiah Litteral to North Carolina, Warrant No. 3175, dated 19 Dec 1785 and entered 20 Mar 1809

BY No. 1297. Granted to James Julen, assignee of the heirs of Jeremiah Litteral, land in Williamson Co., TN, on the waters of Clems Creek. Borders Robert McCuistion and George Doherty and Abraham Byler. Surveyed 4 Apr 1809 by George Tillman, D.S. Reg: 20 Sep 1813.

Page 377 - Percy Yell to Moses Yell. Bond. 9 Dec 1802. Percy Yell of Jefferson Co., TN is bound unto Moses Yell, his father of the same County, for $10,000.00. Wit: John Underhill and Daniel Underhill. Reg: -- Jan 1803.

Page 379 - Benajah White to Nancy White. 1 Nov 1811. Wake Co., NC.Nancy Goodman, Regdon White of Lenoir County, Benajah White of Craven County, and Elizabeth Aldridge and husband of Green County, all of the State of North Carolina of the one part and Nancy White, wife of William White and daughters, viz, Nancy Barringer, Susan White, Elizabeth White, all of Wake Co., NC. That the said Nancy Goodman, Regdon White, Benajah White and Elizabeth Aldridge Goodman, Regdon White, Benajah White and Elizabeth Aldridge and husband, for $120.00. Regdon White, Nancy Goodman, Benajah White and Elizabeth Aldridge and husband grant unto Nancy White as aforesaid Nancy Barringer, Susan White, Elizabeth, Elnor White, Emma White, Gatrey White and Sophrona White, to them and their heirs &c, 1000 acres, land in Bedford County, TN, on waters of Sugar Creek. Borders property of their father Robert White. Wit: Henry Goodwell and R. W. Goodwell. Signed: Benajah White, Regdon White, Nancy Goodman, Drury Aldridge and Elizabeth Aldridge. Reg: 19 Oct 1812. (Land near Richmond area of Bedford Co., TN)

Page 383 - Tennessee Grant to Edward Bryant, 100 acres. No.3382. Certificate No. 274, dated 18 Jul 1809, entered 7 Sep 1809 by No. 1757. Granted to Edward Bryans, assignee of Benjamin Williams, land in Bedford Co., TN, on Bryans Creek, a south branch of Duck River, the first creek below Sinking Creek. Surveyed 28 Oct 1809 by William Gilchrist, D.S. Reg: 6 Dec 1813.

Page 385 - Tennessee Grant to John Coats, 65 acres. No. 4128. For Military Service by Edward Dodd to North Carolina, Warrant No. 5309, dated 9 Dec 1797 and entered 29 Mar 1809 by No. 1319. Granted to John Coats, assignee of Edward Dodd, land in Bedford Co., TN, north branch of Duck River. Borders George Doherty's land. Surveyed 2 Sep 1809 by George Mitchell, D.S. Reg: 9 Dec 1813.

Page 404 - Tennessee Grant to Robert Majors, 200 acres. No. 398. Certificate No. 166, dated 7 Jul 1810, issued to James Patton and Andrew Erwin and entered 14 May 1811 by No. 3152. Granted to Robert Majors, assignee of James Patton and Andrew Erwin, land in Bedford Co., TN, on Wartrace Fork of Duck River. Borders Alexander Outlaw. Surveyed 1 Nov 1814 by John Doak, D.S. Reg: 12 Dec 1813.

Page 410 - Tennessee Grant to Robert McCuistion, 300 acres. No. 3368. For Military Service by Jeremiah Litteral to North Carolina, Warrant No. 3175, dated 19 Dec 1785 and entered 20 Mar 1809 by No. 180, as Occupant Claim. Granted to Robert McCuistion, assignee of the heirs of Jeremiah Litteral, land in Williamson Co., TN, on the headwaters of Wilson Creek. Borders Newton and Clement Cannon. Surveyed 20 Mar 1808 by

DEED BOOK "D"

Alexander Torrentine, D.S. Reg: 20 Dec 1813.

Page 424 - Tennessee Grant to Joseph Dobbs, 75 acres. No. 3132. Certificate No. 179, dated 17 Feb 1809, issued to Sampson Williams and entered 12 Oct 1809 by No. 1877. Granted to Joseph Dobbs, assignee of Sampson Williams, land in Bedford Co., TN, on north side of Duck River. Borders John Sloss, David Ross and Newton Cannon. Surveyed 3 Sep 1810 by Daniel Gilchrist, D.S. Reg: 25 Dec 1813.

Page 426 - Tennessee Grant to William Little, 325 acres. No. 3236. Certificate No. 310, dated 21 Aug 1807, issued to William Little and entered 27 Jul 1808 by No. 643. Granted to William Little, land in Bedford Co., TN, on north side of Duck River. Surveyed 26 Jul 1809 by George Mitchell, D.S. Reg: 25 Dec 1813.

Page 428 - Tennessee Grant to William Caswell, 278 acres. No. 3333. For Military Service of Joseph Herndles to North Carolina, Warrant No. 432, dated 9 Mar 1784 and entered 27 Jul 1808. Granted to William Caswell, assignee of Joseph Herndles, land in Bedford Co., TN, on Fall Creek, a north branch of Duck River. Borders Mathew Lock and Phifer's land. Surveyed -- Feb 1811 by M. Gilchrist, D.S. Reg: 12 Jan 1814.

Page 430 - Tennessee Grant to William Caswell, 320 acres. No. 4590. For Military Service of William Caswell to North Carolina, Warrant No. 158, dated 22 Oct 1783 and entered 24 Feb 1812 by No. 741. Granted to William Caswell, land in Bedford Co., TN, on waters of Alexander Creek, a branch of North Fork of Duck River. Surveyed 13 Oct 1812 by Sam Bell. Reg: 6 Jan 1814.

Page 432 - Tennessee Grant to William Lytle, 150 acres. No. 1521. Certificate No. 310, dated 25 Aug 1807 by William Lytle and entered 24 Oct 1807 by No. 739. Granted to William Lytle, land in Bedford Co., TN, on North Fork of Duck River. Surveyed 2 Mar 1809. Reg: 11 Jan 1814.

Page 434 - North Carolina Grant to Robert McComick, 2000 acres. No. 21. Land on south side of Duck River and on east side of Sugar Creek. Borders point of a ridge, James Bradshaw, Charles McCommon, Amos Balch, and George Martin, and Richard Martin. Dated 10 Jul 1788. Reg: 11 Jan 1814.

Page 440 - Tennessee Grant to John Neill, 40 acres. No. 4421. Certificate No. 142, dated 26 Jul 1809, obtained by Elisha Waling(Walling) and entered 10 Jun 1810 by No. 2429. Granted to John Neill, assignee of Elisha Waling, land in Bedford County, TN, on waters of East Fork of Rock Creek. Borders Jason Thompson and Newton Cannon. Surveyed 26 May 1812. Reg: 11 Jan 1814.

Page 442 - Martha Thompson to Elizabeth and Zelphia Thompson, Deed of Gift. Martha Thompson of Sampson Co., NC, for love and affection for her daughters Elizabeth and Zelphia Thompson, two negro boys. Elizabeth and Zelphia Thompson under 21 years of age at this time. Dated 20 Jan 1787. Wit: Percy Johnston, Williamson Williams and Roger Snell. Reg: 12 Jan 1814.

Page 444 - David Justice to Heirs of James Clark, deceased. 800 acres. 20 Sep 1808. David Justice of Chatham Co., NC sold to James Clark, Thomas Clark, William Clark, Jesse Clark, Jos. Clark, Sarah Ray wife of Jno. Ray, Jenny Anderson wife of John Anderson, Hannah Clark, Elizabeth Clark, sons and daughters of William Clark, late of Orange Co., NC, deceased, who was brother and one of the heirs at law of James Clark, late of Orange Co., NC, deceased. Samuel Clark, Thomas Clark, Janne Gardner wife of Hezekiah Gardner of Randolph Co., NC, Catherine Webster wife of William Webster, Sarah Pratton wife of Paul Pratton, residence of the Western County, sons and daughters of Sarah Clark, sister and one of the heirs at law of James Clark, deceased. Jesse Clark of Tennessee, Sarah Clark, William Clark, Joseph Clark, Thomas Clark, Hyhram Clark and Catherine Clark of Kentucky, sons and daughters of Catherine Clark also sister and one of the heirs at law of James Clark, deceased. And Elizabeth Clark of Kentucky, also sister and one of the heirs at law of James Clark, deceased. Land in Bedford Co., TN, on both sides of Duck River. Wit: Jno. Linsey and Archabald Clark. Reg: 12 Jan 1813.

Page 453 - Tennessee Grant to Robert McCuistion, 301 acres. No. 3364. For Military Service of Alexander Gammill to North Carolina, Warrant No. 5150, dated 9 Dec 1797 and entered 14 Apr 1808 by No. 347. Granted to Robert McCuistion, assignee of the heirs of Alexander Gammill, land in Williamson Co., TN, on waters of Wilson Creek. Borders Newton Cannon. Surveyed 17 Nov 1808 by George Tillman, D.S. Reg: 19 Jan 1814.

Page 462 - Tennessee Grant to John Woods, 125 acres. No. 4333. For Military Service of John P-nany to North Carolina, Warrant No. 3370, dated 7 Jan 1786 and entered 11 Aug 1809 by No. 1651. Granted to John Woods, assignee of John P-nany, land in Bedford Co., TN, on west waters of Rock Creek. Borders William Black. Surveyed 25 May 1812 by Daniel Gilchrist, D.S. Reg: 24 Jan 1814.

Page 464 - Tennessee Grant to John Woods, 200 acres. No. 1553. Part of Warrant No. 1609, dated 30 Nov 1784, issued to Abraham Kuykendall, entered 9 Oct 1807 by No. 724. Granted to John Woods, assignee of Abraham Kuykendall, land in Bedford Co., TN, on East Fork of Rock Creek. Surveyed 29 Sep 1808. Reg: 13 Feb 1810.

Page 474 - Tennessee Grant to James Givins and John C. McLemore, 172½ acres. No. 3836. Certificate No. 1, dated 8 Jan 1810, issued to James Givins and John C. McLemore and entered 5 Feb 1810 by No. 2124, land in Bedford Co., TN, on Alexanders Creek, waters of Duck River. Surveyed 10 Mar 1810 by Thomas Coble Vaughan, D.S. Reg: 12 Mar 1814.

Page 480 - David Robertson to Michael and Joseph Robertson. 29 Jul 1813. Michael and Joseph Robertson, sons of David Robertson of Williamson Co., TN, bought land in Bedford Co., TN, on north side of Duck River. Wit: John Robertson, William Robertson and Jos. Robertson and John ------. Reg: 15 Mar 1814.

Page 482 - Tennessee Grant to Benjamin Carr, 228 acres. No.4263. For Military Service of James West for North Carolina, Warrant No. 4719, dated 15 Feb 1797 and entered 9 Jan 1810 by No. 2073. Granted to Benjamin Carr, assignee of James West, land in

Bedford Co., TN, on both sides of the North Fork of Duck River. Borders at mouth of Alexanders Creek, George Alexander's corner. Surveyed 15 Aug 1811 by M. Gilchrist, D.S. Reg: 22 Mar 1814.

Page 524 - John Medearis to Washington Davis Medearis, 622 acres. 2 Sep 1812. Washington Davis Medearis, son of John Medearis, bought land on East Fork of Rock Creek. Reg: 14 Apr 1814.

Page 541 - Tennessee Grant to John Woods, 200 acres. No. 1553. Part of Warrant No. 1609, dated 30 Nov 1784, issued to Abraham Kuykendall for North Carolina lands and entered 9 Oct 1807 by No. 1724. Granted to John Woods, assignee of Abraham Kuykendall, land in Bedford Co., TN, on East Fork of Rock Creek. Borders George Cathey's land. Surveyed 29 Sep 1808. Recorded before on page 464.

Page 545 - Tennessee Grant to Benjamin Carr, 112 acres. No.4264. Part of certificate No. 208, dated 28 Jul 1810, issued to William T. Lewis and entered 6 Aug 1810 by No. 2558. Granted to Benjamin Carr, assignee of William T. Lewis, land in Bedford Co., TN, on south side of Duck River. Reg: 10 Apr 1814.

Page 549 - Tennessee Grant to Archibald Adams, 122 acres. No. 3533. Part of certificate No. 363, dated 25 Nov 1809 and entered 22 Mar 1810 by No. 2252. Granted to Archibald Adams, assignee of Archibald Clinton, land in Bedford Co., TN, on south side of Duck River and on East Fork of Rock Creek, near Drydens Creek. Surveyed 12 Apr 1810 by George Mitchell, D.S. Reg: 10 Apr 1814.

Page 551 - Tennessee Grant to James Adams, 100 acres. No. 4306. Part of certificate No. 363, dated 21 Nov 1809 and entered 22 Mar 1810 by No. 2254. Granted to James Adams, land in Bedford Co., TN, south side of Duck River. Borders William Black. Surveyed 21 Jul 1810. Reg: 18 Apr 1814.

Page 560 - North Carolina Grant to Robert McComick, 2000 acres. No. 21. 10 lbs per 100 acres. Land in Bedford Co., TN, east side of Sugar Creek, south side of Duck River. Surveyed 5 Sep 1785 by R. Weakley, D.S. Reg: 19 Apr 1814.

Page 563 - Tennessee Grant to John Scott, 106¼ acres. No. 4903. Part of Warrant No. 565, dated 4 Jul 1812, issued to Robert Reed, a Soldier in the guard allotted the Commissioners for laying off the Military Boundary Line of West Tennessee, entered 16 Mar 1813 by No. 5090. Granted to John Scott, assignee of Robert Reed, land in Bedford Co., TN, on the East Fork of Rock Creek of Duck River. Borders home of James Walls and William Mitchell and John Dysart. Surveyed 23 Apr 1813 by Daniel Gilchrist, D.S. Reg: 25 Apr 1814.

Page 590 - Alexander Craig & wife to John Crage(Craig), PA Alexander Craig and Sarah his wife, appointed his father John Craig of Bedford Co., TN, his Attorney. He to convey to Nicholas Woodfin, Samuel McFerrin, James McMain, Moses Ashbrook, by a good and sufficient deed of land to them. Seal at Congdon, Harrison Co., Indiana Territory, 11 Nov 1813. Wit: David Floyd. Reg: 12 Jul 1814.

DEED BOOK "E" 1814 - 1815

Page 3 - Tennessee Grant to Robert Allison, 50 acres. No. 3937. Part of a Certificate No. 58, dated 27 Feb 1810, issued to William P. Anderson and entered 17 Feb 1812 by No. 3725. Granted to Robert Allison, assignee of William P. Anderson, land in Bedford Co., TN, on waters of Wilson Creek and Clems Creek, on north side of Duck River. Borders James Muse, William Patterson and James Mayfield, William Clark, William Hill and James McReynolds. Surveyed 19 Feb 1812 by George Tillman, D.S. Reg: 12 Jul 1814.

Page 5 - Tennessee Grant to Robert Allison, 10 acres. No. 4010. Part of Certificate No. 305, dated 21 Aug 1809 to Benjamin McCulloch, and entered 11 Jul 1810 by No. 2461. Granted to Robert Allison, assignee of Benjamin McCulloch, land in Bedford Co., TN, on north side of Duck River and on waters of Clems Creek. Surveyed 7 Sep 1810 by George Tillman, D.S. Reg: 12 Jul 1814.

Page 7 - Tennessee Grant to Robert Allison, 220 acres. No.4009. Part of Certificate No. 305, dated 21 Aug 1809 to Benjamin McCulloch and entered 13 Mar 1810 by No. 2234. Granted to Robert Allison, assignee of Benjamin McCulloch, land in Bedford Co., TN, on waters of Rock Creek. Borders William Wilbourn, Hays Blair and Felix Robertson. Surveyed 13 Feb 1812 by M. Gilchrist, D.S. Reg: 13 Jul 1814.

Page 11 - Tennessee Grant to Robert Allison, 140 acres. No.4011. Part of Certificate No. 58, dated 27 Feb 1810 issued to William P. Anderson and entered 6 Jul 1811 by No. 3243. Granted to Robert Allison, assignee of William P. Anderson, land in Bedford Co., TN, on waters of East Fork of Rock Creek. Borders William Wilbourn, Hays Blair and James Coffey. Surveyed 13 Feb 1812 by M. Gilchrist, D.S. Reg: 13 Jul 1814.

Page 13 - Tennessee Grant to Francis Patton, 49 acres. No. 5007. Part of Certificate No. 359, dated 23 Oct 1810 issued to John Brahan and entered 11 Jun 1811 by No. 3190. Granted to Francis Patton, assignee of John Brahan, land in Bedford Co., TN, on waters of Rock Creek. Borders William Wilbourn. Surveyed 14 Oct 1812. Reg: 14 Jul 1814.

Page 15 - Richard Brown to Terry Williams, 200 acres. 14 Sep 1814. Richard Brown sold to Terry Williams and his wife Sarah Williams, of Bedford Co., TN, land on waters of Rock Creek. Borders Shelbyville Road and Wooten's land. Reg: 13 Jul 1814.

Page 17 - Tennessee Grant to Francis Patton, 25 acres. No. 5008. Part of Certificate No. 142, dated 26 Jul 1809 issued to Elisha Walling and entered 4 Apr 1810 by No. 2294. Granted to Francis Patton, assignee of Elisha Walling, land in Bedford Co., TN, on waters of East Fork of Rock Creek. Borders James Smith and William Black. Surveyed 11 Apr 1810 by George Mitchell, D.S. Reg: 14 Jul 1814.

Page 45 - Dempsey Powell & others to Andrew Hartsfield, 265¼ acres. 29 Sep 1813. Dempsey Powell, Benton Powell, Caswell Powell and Jesse Powell of Wake Co., NC sold to Andrew Hartsfield, Sr. of Wake Co., NC, land in Bedford Co., TN. Borders James Fort. Wit: Henry Moringe, John Jelks and Dempsey Temple. Reg: 20 Jul 1814.

DEED BOOK "E"

Page 49 - Joseph Steele & others to Hugh McBride, 14 Feb 1814. Joseph Steele, John B. Gibson, James C. Wilson, James S. Wilson and John Wilson of Sumner, Williamson and Wilson Counties, TN sold to Hugh McBride of Bedford Co., TN, land in Bedford Co., on north side of Duck River (part of a 3000 acre tract granted to John Wilson). Wit: James S. Torrentine and Henry Pickle. Reg: 23 Jul 1814.

Page 63 - North Carolina Grant to John Newman, 1000 acres. No. 286. 10 lbs per 100 acres. Land on headwaters of Harpeth. Borders Robert Washington Smith. Mecklenburg Co., NC recorded in Book 12, page 66, Reg: 20 Jan 1796.

Page 65 - Thomas Stone and Caty Newman to Samuel Hart. 3 Jun 1814. Samuel Hart of Sumner Co., TN bought from Thomas Stone and Caty Newman of Hopkins Co., KY, administrators of estate of John Newman, deceased, formerly of Smith Co., TN, 1000 acres in Tennessee, on waters of Harpeth or Duck River. Wit: John Stone and Jos. Hart. Signed: Katy Newman. Reg: 25 Jul 1814.

Page 86 - John Haga to Mary Haga, 941 acres.
John Haga of Bedford Co., TN, for love and affection for his daughter Mary Haga of Bedford Co., TN. Dated 27 Jul 1814. Wit: Edward Wade and Jordan Holt.

Page 90 - Robert W. Smith to Ezra Allemong, PA
Robert W. Smith of Cabarrus Co., NC appointed Ezra Allemong of Rowan Co., NC, his Attorney, to receive for him, money from the State of Tennessee, also to sell his Tennessee lands. Signed: 13 Apr 1814. Reg: 4 Aug 1814.

Page 101 - Tennessee Grant to John Drake, 140 acres. No. 3906. Part of Certificate No. 205, dated 27 Mar 1809, obtained by Henry M. Rutledge and entered 25 Jun 1809 by No. 1535. Granted to John Drake, assignee of Henry M. Rutledge, land in Bedford Co., TN, on waters of Middle Fork of Duck River, adjoining lands of Joseph Coleman. Surveyed 7 Jul 1809 by John Drake, D.S. Reg: 14 Jul 1814.

Page 103 - Tennessee Grant to Alexander Outlaw, 312 acres. No. 717. Certificate No. 6, dated 16 Jul 1807 by Alexander Outlaw and entered 8 Aug 1807 by No. 50. Granted to Alexander Outlaw, land in Bedford Co., TN, on waters of War Trace Fork of Duck River. Surveyed 13 Jan 1808. Reg: 5 Sep 1814.

Page 114 - Andrew Erwin and James Patton to James Patton, 584 acres. 4 Oct 1812. Andrew Erwin and James Patton of Buncomb Co., NC sold to James Patton, Esq. of Bedford Co., TN, land on Strait Creek and the Garrison Fork of Duck River. Reg: 11 Sep 1814.

Page 121 - James Patton and Andrew Erwin to Thomas Patton. 19 Aug 1813. James Patton and Andrew Erwin of Ashville, NC sold to Thomas Patton of Bedford Co., TN, 1020 acres on Noahs Fork of Duck River. Reg: 11 Sep 1814.

Page 138 - Power of Attorney to Jno. D. Terrel. Bedford Co., TN. Our father Thomas McReynolds, deceased, formerly of Bedford Co., VA, died in the Revolutionary War, rendered service as an officer, Lieutenant and Captain in the Virginia Continental Line, we as his lawful heirs are entitled to lands in the

Virginia, We, John D. McReynolds, John C. Dunn who intermarried with Mary B. McReynolds, James McReynolds, Edward Whitworth who intermarried with Anna McReynolds, Thomas B. McReynolds and Elizabeth D. McReynolds, appoint John D. Tences of Georgia, Franklin Co., our Attorney. Signed 20 Sep 1814. Wit: James Ferguson, Jos. Crunk and Jas. McReynolds.

Page 185 - Richard Churchwell, Sr. to Richard Churchwell, Jr. Bill of Sale. Richard Churchwell, Sr. and wife of Maury Co., TN conveyed to Richard Churchwell, Jr. of Bedford Co., TN, all property. Signed 30 Apr 1812. Wit: Harrison Blagame, William Pool and William McBride. Reg: 6 Oct 1814.

Page 188 - James Patton to John Patton, 50 acres. 20 Jul 1813. James Patton conveyed to his son John Patton, both of Bedford Co., TN, land in Bedford Co., TN. Wit: James A. Wilson and James Andrews. Reg: 7 Oct 1814.

Page 208 - Alexander McCullock to John McClure, 166 acres. 27 Feb 1813. Alexander McCullock, one of the heirs of Benjamin McCullock, deceased, of Rutherford Co., TN sold to John McClure of Rutherford Co., TN, land in Bedford Co., TN, on or near the dividing ridge, dividing waters of Stones River from the waters of War Trace Fork of Duck River, part of a Tennessee Grant to Benjamin McCullock by Patent No. 2128, dated 11 Apr 1810. Reg: 11 Oct 1814.

Page 264 - Benjamin Bradford and others to Robert Hughes. Slaves. Benjamin Bradford, Hamilton Bradford and Mary Weatherford sold to Robert Hughes, slaves. Wit: Rees Hughes and Samuel Hughes. Reg: 21 Oct 1814.

Page 265 - Tennessee Grant to Archabald Adams, 44½ acres. No. 5253. Part of Certificate No. 645, dated 26 Jul 1811, issued to Joseph Philips and entered 25 Jan 1812 by No. 3673. Granted to Archabald Adams, assignee of Joseph Philips, land in Bedford Co., TN, on waters of East Fork of Rock Creek. Borders James Adams. Surveyed 15 Oct 1812. Reg: 21 Oct 1814.

Page 267 - Tennessee Grant to Archabald Adams, 22 acres. No. 3534. Part of Certificate No. 363, dated 21 Nov 1809, issued to James Adams and Archabald Clinton and entered 21 Apr 1810 by No. 2327. Granted to Archabald Adams, assignee of Archabald Clinton, land in Bedford Co., TN, south side of Duck River and on an east branch of the West Fork of Rock Creek. Surveyed 20 May 1810 by George Mitchell, D.S. Reg: 21 Oct 1814.

Page 269 - Tennessee Grant to Archabald Adams, 50 acres. No. 3537. Part of Certificate No. 363, dated 21 Nov 1809, obtained by James Adams and Archibald Clinton and entered 22 Mar 1810 by No. 2253. Granted to Archabald Adams, assignee of Archabald Clinton, land in Bedford Co., TN, east branch of West Fork of Rock Creek. Surveyed 10 Apr 1810 by George Mitchell, D.S. Reg: 22 Oct 1814.

Page 271 - Tennessee Grant to Archabald Adams, 50 acres. No. 3535. Part of Certificate No. 363, dated 21 Nov 1809, obtained by James Adams and Archabald Clinton and entered 22 Mar 1810 by No. 2257. Granted to Archabald Adams, assignee of Archabald Clinton, land in bedford Co., TN, on headwaters of Sinking Creek, of Rock Creek. Borders John Rogers, James

Leeper and David Ross. Surveyed 11 Apr 1810 by George Mitchell, D.S. Reg: 22 Oct 1814.

Page 273 - Tennessee Grant to Archabald Adams, 76 acres. No. 3536. Part of Certificate No. 363, dated 21 Nov 1809, obtained by James Adams and Archabald Clinton and entered 31 Jul 1810 by No. 2519. Granted to Archabald Adams, assignee of Archabald Clinton, land in Bedford Co., TN, on Rich Creek called Michael's Creek. Borders Thomas Sorrels. Surveyed 28 Aug 1810 by George Mitchell, D.S. Reg: 22 Oct 1814.

Page 275 - Tennessee Grant to Charles Brandon, 18 acres. No. 5592. Part of Certificate No. 558, dated 25 Jun 1812, obtained by Benjamin McCullock and entered 27 Jun 1812 by No. 4073. Granted to Charles Brandon, assignee of Benjamin McCullock, land in Bedford Co., TN, on waters of Clem Creek. Borders William Clark. Surveyed 9 Dec 1812 by Samuel Bell, D.S. Reg: 22 Oct 1814.

Page 277 - Tennessee Grant to Charles Brandon, 20 acres. No. 4047. Part of Certificate No. 609, dated 27 Jun 1811, issued to John Drake and entered 10 Jul 1811 by No. 3253. Granted to Charles Brandon, assignee of John Drake, land in Bedford Co., TN, on waters of Weakleys Creek. Borders John Byler. Surveyed 14 Dec 1811 by George Tillman, D.S. Reg: 22 Oct 1814.

Page 279 - Tennessee Grant to Charles Brandon, 40 acres. No. 4624. Part of Certificate No. 608, dated 27 Jun 1811, issued to John Drake and entered 18 Jul 1811 by No. 3268. Granted to Charles Brandon, assignee of John Drake, land in Bedford Co., TN, on waters of Weakleys Creek. Borders John Byler and Amos McLemore. Surveyed 14 Mar 1814 by George Tillman, D.S. Reg: 22 Oct 1814.

Page 281 - Tennessee Grant to Charles Brandon, 50 acres. No. 4623. Part of Certificate No. 578, dated 27 Feb 1810, issued to William P. Anderson and entered 14 Oct 1811 by No. 3476. Granted to Charles Brandon, assignee of William P. Anderson, land in Bedford Co., TN, on waters of Clems Creek. Borders William Hill. Surveyed 14 Dec 1811 by George Tillman, D.S. Reg: 22 Oct 1814.

Page 283 - Tennessee Grant to William Reed, 54 acres. No. 5895. Part of Certificate No. 644, dated 20 Jul 1811, issued to Joseph Philips, entered 30 Jan 1812 by No. 3678. Granted to William Reed, assignee of Joseph Philips, land in Bedford Co., TN, on Big Flat Creek. Borders lands granted to William Gilbreath, James Patton and Andrew Erwin. Surveyed 20 May 1813 by Daniel Gilchrist, D.S. Reg: 22 Oct 1814.

Page 285 - Tennessee Grant to John Dryden, 50 acres. No. 5141. Part of Certificate No. 481, dated 1 Mar 1811, issued to William Christmas and entered 13 Feb 1812 by No. 3708. Granted to John Dryden, assignee of William Christmas, land in Bedford Co., TN, on Rock Creek. Borders James Coffey and Robert Allison. Surveyed 22 Sep 1812 by Daniel Gilchrist, D.S. Reg: 22 Oct 1814.

Page 287 - Tennessee Grant to Daniel Shipman, 200 acres. No. 1217. For Military Service by Stokes Rochel to North

Carolina, Warrant No. 138, dated 19 Dec 1806 and entered 5 Aug 1807 by No. 54, as an Occupant Claim. Granted to Daniel Shipman, assignee of the heirs of Stokes Rochel, land in Rutherford Co., TN, on waters of Duck River. Surveyed 26 Aug 1807. Reg: 22 Oct 1814.

Page 289 - I, Titus Fox, Soldier in the 44th J-, do appoint my brother-in-law James Wood and Sarah Fox my wife, my lawfully Attorney, to receive money &c from the United States, should I not return home. Signed: 19 Sep 1814. Test: Sarah Lee. Signed: Titus (X) Fox. Oct Term 1814, proven. Reg: 26 Oct 1814.

Page 293 - Tennessee Grant to Kebble Terry, 200 acres. No. 6063. Warrant No. 2428, dated 25 Feb 1783, issued to Jeremiah Terry by Landon Carter, Entry Taker, and entered 4 Dec 1813 by No. 5860. Granted to Kebble Terry, assignee of Jeremiah Terry, land in bedford Co., TN, on waters of Clems Creek, waters of the North Fork of Duck River. Surveyed 31 Mar 1814 by Daniel Gilchrist, D.S. Reg: 15 Nov 1814.

Page 295 - Tennessee Grant to Samuel Wilson, 3000 acres. Grant No. 380, dated 17 Dec 1794 at request of John Wilson. Land in Bedford Co., TN, on north side of Duck River, on both sides of Spring Creek. Granted to Samuel Wilson by North Carolina by Grant No. 380. Borders Samuel Patterson. Surveyed 25 Aug 1814. Reg: 12 Dec 1814. Plat on same page.

Page 296 - North Carolina Grant to John Graham, 2000 acres. 15 Sep 1814. Reg: 19 Dec 1814. Plat on page 297-299.

Page 300 - Tennessee Grant to Hardy Murphy, 700 acres. No. 723. For Military Service of William Boswell to North Carolina, Warrant No. 3594, dated 29 Jun 1788 and entered 28 Aug 1808 by No. 363. Granted to Hardy Murphy, assignee of William Boswell, land in Bedford Co., TN, on the west waters of East Fork of Rock Creek. Borders John Medearis. Surveyed 16 Jun 1808. Reg: 28 Dec 1814.

Page 302 - Tennessee Grant to William Patterson, 83 acres. No. 3705. Warrant No. 1313, dated 10 Jul 1784, issued to William Patterson and entered 14 Oct 1807 by No. 735. Granted to William Patterson, land in Bedford Co., TN, on north waters of Duck River. Borders land of the heirs of Daniel Vaughan and James Grant. Surveyed 20 Aug 1810 by Malcolm Gilchrist, D.S. Reg: 28 Dec 1814.

Page 304 - Tennessee Grant to John Medearis, 3596 acres. No. 3179. Certificate No. 144, dated 27 Jul 1807, issued to Captain John Medearis and entered 8 Aug 1807 by No. 43. Granted to John Medearis, land in Bedford Co., TN, on east waters of Rock Creek. Borders school land. Sueveyed 17 Jan 1809 by M. Gilchrist, D.S. Reg: (no date).

Page 306 - Tennessee Grant to William P. Anderson, 640 acres. No. 1036. For Military Service by Lazarus McClurdy to North Carolina, Warrant No. 4649, dated 9 Feb 1797 and entered 1 Apr 1808 by No. 310. Granted to William P. Anderson, assignee of the heirs of Lazarus McClurdy, land in Bedford Co., TN, on both sides of Duck River. Borders Blount Grants. Surveyed 24 Sep 1808. Reg: (no date).

DEED BOOK "E"

Page 308 - John Warner, Sr. to John Warner, Jr. Sale of a negro girl. 21 Oct 1814. Wit: Abraham Fry and Nancy Wadsworth. Reg: 3 Jan 1815.

Page 310 - We, Jacob Fonts and Lewis Fonts, both of Clark Co., Indiana Territory, heirs of the Last Will and Testament of Col. Thomas Dougan, late of Randolph Co., NC, appointed their friend Capt. Michael Fisher of Bedford Co., TN, their Attorney, to collect monies from Thomas Dougan, deceased, sale of three tracts of land on waters of Sugar Creek. This 5 Sep 1812. Wit: Henry Culp and Edward Wade. Reg: 11 Jan 1815.

Page 364 - Tennessee Grant to Elisha Parker, 120 acres. No.3827. For Military Service of William Grimes to North Carolina, Warrant No. 1370, dated 10 Nov 1784 and entered 25 Aug 1807 by No. 325. Granted to Elisha Parker, assignee of the heirs of William Grimes, land partly in Rutherford Co., TN (and Bedford Co., TN), on Thompsons Creek of Duck River. Borders school land. Surveyed 12 Sep 1807 by Malcolm Gilchrist, D.S. Reg: 23 Jan 1815.

Page 366 - Tennessee Grant to Elisha Parker, 100 acres. No. 3828. For Military Service of William Grimes to North Carolina, Warrant No. 1370, dated 10 Nov 1784 and entered 31 Aug 1807 by No. 440. Granted to Elisha Parker, assignee of the heirs of William Grimes, land partly in Rutherford Co., TN, on west side of Thompsons Creek. Borders Robert McCuistion. Surveyed 19 Sep 1809 by Malcolm Gilchrist, D.S. Reg: 23 Jan 1815.

Page 368 - Tennessee Grant to Elisha Parker, 100 acres. No.3829. For Military Service by William Grimes to North Carolina, Warrant No. 1370, dated 10 Nov 1784 and entered 31 Aug 1807 by No. 132, as an Occupant Claim. Granted to Elisha Parker, assignee of the heirs of William Grimes, land partly in Rutherford Co., TN, on Thompsons Creek. Surveyed 5 Oct 1809 by Malcolm Gilchrist, D.S. Reg: 23 Jan 1815.

Page 370 - Tennessee Grant to Job Cooper, 50 acres. No. 5503. Part of Warrant No. 2502, dated 30 Nov 1784, issued to Elijah West and entered 2 Mar 1812 by No. 3770. Granted to Job Cooper, assignee of Elijah West, land in bedford Co., TN, on Weakley Creek. Borders Amos McLemore. Surveyed 25 Jun 1812 by Samuel Bell, D.S. Reg: 23 Jan 1815.

Page 372 - Tennessee Grant to Robert Adams, 55 acres. No. 5252. Certificate No. 645, dated 26 Jul 1811, issued to Joseph Philips and entered 25 Jan 1812 by No. 3674. Granted to Robert Adams, assignee of Joseph Philips, land in Bedford Co., TN, on waters of East Fork of Rock Creek. Borders James Adams. Surveyed 13 Oct 1812 by Daniel Gilchrist, D.S. Reg: 23 Jan 1815.

Page 374 - Jeremiah Chamberlain to Heirs of John Cunningham. 19 Aug 1814. Jeremiah Chamberlain of Granger Co., TN sold to Walter Galbreath, Francis McCamey and Catharine his wife, and Mathew Cunningham and Elizabeth his wife, and John Huff and Anna his wife, all of Bedford Co., TN, and William Galbreath of Adams Co., PA, and Mary Dixon widow of Robert Dixon of Orange Co., NC, all the heirs of John Galbreath, deceased, land granted to Jeremiah Chamberlain and William Galbreath, late of Orange Co., NC by State of North Carolina, 1000 acres in

Bedford Co., TN, on Big Flat Creek. Borders William Galbreath and Samuel Patton, Sr. Wit: Ja. Polk, C. McCanless. Reg: 31 Jan 1815.

Page 376 - Tennessee Grant to James Torrentine, 100 acres. No. 5235. Certificate No. 471, dated 19 Feb 1811, issued to Sampson Sawyers and entered -- Mar 1811 by No. 3063. Granted to James S. Torrentine, assignee of Sampson Sawyers, land in Bedford Co., TN, on Bryans Creek, a south branch of Duck River. Surveyed 11 Jul 1812. Reg: 24 Jan 1815.

Page 378 - Isaac S. Henderson to James Craser McRee & David Wilson McRee, 5000 acres. Isaac S. Henderson and Lucinda Henderson his wife of Mecklenburg Co., NC sold to James Craser McRee and David Wilson McRee of Iredell Co., NC, a certain tract of land being all the estate which came from David McRee, deceased, descended to Lucinda, ¼ part, lands in Giles, Lincoln, Bedford and Maury Counties, TN, which was conveyed by John Nelson to David, deed bearing date 11 Nov 1796 and registered in Davidson Co., TN on 16 Nov 1796 in Book "D", page 84 and also in Maury Co., TN. Wit: John Carson, John Reav(e)s and H. T. McRee. Reg: 11 Jan 1813. (Registered in Bedford Co., TN in Book "E", page 63.)

Page 383 - William E. Butler to King & Ditto. 30 Dec 1812. William B. Butler and Patsy T. Butler his wife of Davidson Co., TN sold to Benjamin King and William Ditto of Bedford Co., TN, land in Bedford Co., on waters of Little War Trace Fork of Duck River. Borders Moses Yell and Charles Harriman and Blount Grants. 750 acres. Reg: 31 Jan 1815.

Page 386 - Tennessee Grant to Aron Wilson, 400 acres. No. 6327 Part of Certificate No. 209, dated 30 Jul 1810, issued to Sampson Sawyers and entered 23 Oct 1812 by No. 3499 & 3500. Granted to Ann Wilson, assignee of Sampson Sawyers, Jr., land in Bedford Co., TN, on headwaters of Rock Creek. Borders Alexander Robertson. Surveyed 4 Aug 1812 by Daniel Gilchrist, D.S. Reg: 14 Dec 1814.

Page 418 - In tender affection of my brother William Speakman, I give all my property of every description. Signed 23 Apr 1814. Wit: Thomas Crutcher. Signed by Christian Williams. Reg: 31 Mar 1815.

Page 432 - Tennessee Grant to John Fisher, 10 acres. No. 4457. Part of Warrant No. 2212, dated 30 Jul 1784, issued to Alexander Johnston and entered 16 Aug 1810 by No. 2603. Granted to John Fisher, assignee of Alexander Johnston, land in Bedford Co., TN, on west waters of Rock Creek. Reg: 12 Apr 1815.

Page 434 - Tennessee Grant to John Fisher, 50 acres. No. 5548. Part of Warrant No. 2212, dated 30 Nov 1784, issued to Alexander Johnston and entered 1 Dec 1809 by No. 1992. Granted to John Fisher, assignee of Alexander Johnston, land in Bedford Co., TN, on Sinking Creek. Surveyed 2 Feb 1810 by George Mitchell, D.S. Reg: 12 Apr 1815.

Page 436 - Tennessee Grant to John Fisher, 50 acres. No. 5547. Warrant No. 2212, dated 30 Nov 1784, issued to Alexander Johnston and entered 7 Apr 1810 by No. 2308. Granted to John Fisher, assignee of Alexander Johnston, land in Bedford Co., TN, south side of Duck River and on Sinking Creek of Duck River. Borders John Paxton. Surveyed Apr 13, ----, by George Mitchell, D.S. Reg: 12 Apr 1815.

Page 438 - Tennessee Grant to John Fisher, 135 acres. No. 5545. Part of a Warrant No. 2212, dated 30 Nov 1784, issued to Alexander Johnston and entered 21 June 1809 by No. 1522. Granted to John Fisher, assignee of Alexander Johnston, land in Bedford Co., TN, on south side of Duck River, on west side of the West Fork of Rock Creek. Surveyed 30 ---, 1809 by George Mitchell, D.S. Reg: 12 Apr 1815.

Page 440 - Tennessee Grant to John Holmes, 17 acres. No. 5871. Part of Certificate No. 181, dated 18 Feb 1807, issued to Daniel Smith and entered 8 June 1810 by No. 2416. Granted to John Holmes, assignee of Daniel Smith, land in Bedford Co., TN, on east waters of East Fork of Rock Creek. Borders George Cathey. Including Holmes house and spring. Surveyed 24 Apr 1813 by Daniel Gilchrist, D.S. Reg: 12 Apr 1815.

Page 442 - Tennessee Grant to John Holmes, 6 acres. No. 5872. Part of a Warrant No. 1607, dated 30 Nov 1784, issued to James Kuykendall and Mathew Kuykendall and entered 25 July 1809 by No. 1617. Granted to John Holmes, assignee of John Kuykendall and Mathew Kuykendall, land in Bedford Co., TN, on east waters of Rock Creek. Borders a place known as "The Big Glade". Including a large sink-hole spring. Surveyed 24 May 1812 by Daniel Gilchrist, D.S. Reg: 12 Apr 1815.

Page 444 - Tennessee Grant to John Fisher, 150 acres. No. 5544. Part of Warrant No. 2212, dated 30 Nov 1784, issued to Alexander Johnston and entered 19 Dec 1808. Granted to John Fisher, assignee of Alexander Johnston, land in Bedford Co., TN, on west side of the West Fork of Rock Creek. Surveyed 27 Jan 1809 by George Mitchell, D.S. Reg: 13 Apr 1815.

Page 446 - Tennessee Grant to John Fisher, 55 acres. No. 5546. Part of a Warrant No. 2212, dated 30 Nov 1784, issued to Alexander Johnston and entered by No. 2602. Granted to John Fisher, assignee of Alexander Johnston, land in Bedford Co., TN, on Sinking Branch of Rock Creek. Borders Allen Leeper and Adley Alexander. Surveyed 17 Oct 1812 by Daniel Gilchrist, D.S. Reg: 13 Apr 1815.

Page 448 - Tennessee Grant to Job Cooper, 100 acres. No. 5501. Part of a Certificate No. 200, dated 23 July 1810, issued to William T. Lewis and entered 5 Apr 1811 by No. 3096. Granted to Job Cooper, assignee of William T. Lewis, land in Bedford Co., TN, on waters of Weakleys Creek, on north side of Duck River. Borders Elijah Rutledge and Charles Brandon and John Byler's Occupant Survey, and Amos McLemore. Surveyed 5 July 1811 by George Tillman, D.S. Reg: 13 Apr 1815.

Page 450 - Tennessee Grant to John Cooper, 50 acres. No. 5502. Part of a Certificate No. 627, dated 18 July 1811, issued to John Gray Blount and entered 6 Apr 1812 by No. 3883. Granted to John Cooper, assignee of John Gray Blount, land in Bedford Co., TN, on Weakleys Creek, a branch of the North Fork of Duck River. Borders John Byler and Nathaniel Walker. Surveyed 24 June 1812. Reg: 13 Apr 1815.

DEED BOOK "E"

Page 452 - Tennessee Grant to Daniel Parker, 68 acres. No. 6084. Part of Certificate No. 403, dated 6 Mar 1810, issued to Howel Tatum and entered 14 May 1810 by No. 2380. Granted to Daniel Parker, assignee of Howel Tatum, land in Bedford Co., TN, on north side of Duck River. Borders William Lytle and John Williams. Surveyed 20 Dec 1811 by Daniel Gilchrist, D.S. Reg: 13 Apr 1815.

Page 454 - Tennessee Grant to Thomas Parsons, 32 acres. No. 5969. Part of Certificate No. 309, dated 25 Aug 1809, issued to John Henderson and entered 27 June 1810 by No. 2444. Granted to Thomas Parsons, assignee of John Henderson, land in Bedford Co., TN, on north waters of Duck River. Borders John Thompson, John Payton and William Wilhight. Surveyed 30 Apr 1814 by Daniel Gilchrist, D.S. Reg: 13 Apr 1815.

Page 456 - Tennessee Grant to Daniel Parker, 136 acres. No. 6083. Part of Certificate No. 403, dated 6 Mar 1810, issued to Howel Tatum and entered 19 Apr 1810 by No. 2323. Granted to Daniel Parker, assignee of Howel Tatum, land in Bedford Co., TN, south side of Duck River opposite the mouth of Faling (Falling) Creek. Surveyed 23 Feb 1814 by Samuel Bell, D.S. Reg: 13 Apr 1815.

Page 458 - Tennessee Grant to Daniel Parker, 100 acres. No. 6082. For Military Service by Elisha Williams to North Carolina, Warrant No. 292, dated 9 Nov 1783 and entered 14 May 1810 by No. 2379. Granted to Daniel Parker, assignee of Elisha Williams, land in Bedford Co., TN, on north side of Duck River. Borders John Thompson and school land. Surveyed 18 Feb 1811 by Daniel Gilchrist, D.S. Reg: 13 Apr 1815.

Page 460 - Tennessee Grant to Malcolm Gilchrist, 14 acres. No. 5830. Part of Certificate No. 644, dated 26 July 1811, issued to Joseph Phillips and entered 25 Oct 1811 by No. 3508. Granted to Malcolm Gilchrist, assignee of Joseph Phillips, land in Bedford Co., TN, on the north waters of Duck River. Borders Amos Balch and Howel Tatum and Robert W. Smith and Benjamin McCuistion. Surveyed 5 Apr 1814. Reg: 13 Apr 1815.

Page 462 - Tennessee Grant to John Holmes, 150 acres. No. 4368. For Military Service of Norris Bowman to North Carolina, Warrant No. 5237, dated 9 Dec 1791 and entered 30 Mar 1808 by No. 292. Granted to John Holmes, assignee of Norris Bowman, land in Bedford Co., TN, on east waters of Rock Creek. Borders George Cathey. Surveyed 24 Mar 1812 by Daniel Gilchrist, D.S. Reg: 13 Apr 1815.

Page 469 - Abraham Howel to Andros Howel. Deed of Gift. Abraham Howell for love and affection for his son Andros Howel, all goods and chattels. Wit: Joseph Neil. Dated 20 Feb 1815. Reg: 14 Apr 1815.

Page 502 - Thomas Greer to the Baptist Church, 21 Jan 1815. Thomas Greerconveyed to the Baptist Church, so long as it continues to be a church, and for $5.00 to Thomas Greer, a tract of land, 1 acre, lying on the south side of Sugar Creek in Bedford Co., TN. Wit: Stephen Rogers. Reg: 18 Apr 1815.

Page 531 - Power of Attorney, Cabarrus Co., North Carolina. I, James Walker of said County and State, appoint Robert

Morrison of Bedford Co., TN, Power of Attorney, to receive any monies received from sale &c of his lands, situated on both sides of Sugar Creek. 21 Feb 1815. Reg: 27 Apr 1815.

Page 533 - Letter. Testamentary of James Johnston. Lincoln Co., NC. By the Justices of Lincoln County, it being certified to us that James Johnston is dead and made a Will and approved and constituted Robert Johnston and James Johnston, Jr., Executors. 1st Monday Oct 1805. Reg: 2 May 1815.
Page - Will. In the name of God, Amen. I, James Johnston of the County of Lincoln and State of North Carolina, being of sound mind and memory, do this first day of May one thousand eight hundred and five, make and publish this my Last Will and Testament in the manner and form following. Page 537 - A Copy of Last Will and Testament of James Johnston: In the name of God, Amen. I, James Johnston of the County of Lincoln County and State of North Carolina, being of sound mind and memory do this first day of May one thousand eight hundred and five, made and published this my Last Will and Testament in the manner and form following... First - I Will that all my just debts be paid and my body be buried in a decent and Christian like manner. Secondly - I Will and bequeath unto my son Robert Johnston all the plantation on which I now live with an exception of a small part taken off in this manner, Beginning at the beginning corner of the said tract, thence down the river to the mouth of the first branch, thence up said branch to a white oak marked this day and agreed upon by the said Robert Johnston and his brother James, thence to two white oaks on the mouth of a little ditch, thence up a dry hollow to a maple and an allum, thence to two small white oaks to other branch, thence down the last mentioned branch to within three or four poles of the meadow ground on said branch, thence down the east side of said branch to the pasture fence, thence across said branch with the ----- about three or four poles out of the meadow ground, thence up west side of said branch to the original line of Samuel Coburns(?)'s Old Tract, thence with said line to beginning corner of said Old Tract on the bank of the river also to my son, Robert, I bequeath two negroes, Joe and Jane. Thirdly - I Will and bequeath unto my son, James Johnston, all that tract of land purchased from Maj. John Nelson, lying immediately to Tools Ford on the Calaba River together with the past exempted from the Old Tract bequeathed to my son, Robert, as above specified, also, two negroes, Dick and Doll and hundred and fifty dollars in cash together with an entry of fifty acres of land at Tools Ford. Fourthly - I Will and bequeath to my son William Johnston, all that tract of land purchased of Ephraim and Isaac Henderson, lying on the east side of the river in Mecklenburg County. Containing by estimation two hundred acres also two negroes, Anthony and Aby, and one hundred and fifty dollars in casg which property both real and personal with the interest occurring thereupon shall be delivered to him when of age or sooner if thought proper by the Executors. Fifthly - I Will and bequeath to my son Henry Johnston the sum of fifteen hundred dollars to be put out at interest and thereof annually to be appropriated to his use as his circumstances may require. Sixthly - I Will and bequeath to my son-in-law John Hays, three negroes, sue and her children Clarissa and Jesse and five hundred dollars in cash, together with a bay mare, a bed and furniture which three negroes, mare, bed and furniture the said John Hays has already received. Seventhly - I Will and bequeath to my daughter

Margaret Johnston, a negro woman named Milly and her two children Charlotte and Kip and five hundred dollars in cash also a bed and furniture. Eightly - I Will and bequeath to my daughter Polly Johnston, three negroes, Hannah, Patience and Ben and five hundred dollars in cash with a bed and furniture. Ninthly - I Will and bequeath to my daughter Jane Johnston, three negroes, Franky, Ted and Nelly and five hundred dollars in cash with a bed and furniture. Tenthly - I Will and bequeath to my son Robert, the proper use and behoof of two negroes named Jesse and Dina for the span of four years for the support of the three youngest girls, my daughters. Its also my Will that my son James Johnston take to his proper use and behoof two negroes for the term of four years named Adam and Shield for the sum of eighty dollars yearly, to be paid annually to my three youngest daughters purpose of clothing them but if either of them should marry or die before the expiration of this term the money arising from hire of said negroes is to be equally divided between the several sisters. 11 - If any one of my legatees should die unmarried, that particular portion, mentioned as Willed, to be equally divided among the rest of the legatees. 12th - It is my Will that my three youngest children, viz, Patsy, William and Jane be schooled. To receive schooling out of the crops now upon the ground on both plantation this side the river in Lincoln County, &c. 13th - It is my Will that my son James Johnston be assisted in putting up and raising a house &c. 14th - I appoint John Hays, Robert Johnston and James Johnston, Executors. Wit: J. Abernathy and Wm. R. Sadler and H. Hunter. Reg: 10 May 1815.

Page 542 - Tennessee Grant to James Johnston, 2200 acres. No. 615. Certificate No. 139, dated 27 July 1807, issued to James Johnston and entered 21 Aug 1807 by No. 273. Granted to James Johnston and heirs, land in Bedford Co., TN, on Sinking Creek. Borders William Johnston, Nathaniel _______, and Thomas Dillahunty and Sinking Creek. Surveyed 20 Mar 1808. Reg: 10 May 1815.

Page 553 - George Mansker to Henry Miller. Bill of Sale. I, George Mansker of Williamson County, TN, do give forever to my daughter Mary Miller wife of Henry Miller of Bedford Co., TN and Town of Shelbyville, a negro girl name Patt now in her and said Henry's possession. 19 Jan 1815. Wit: George B. Balch and H. Dawdy. Reg: 11 May 1815.

Page 580 - Joseph Steele to James Williams. 10 Feb 1814. Joseph Steele for himself and John B. Gibson, James C. Wilson, James S. Wilson and John Wilson of Sumner, Wilson, Williamson and Bedford Counties, TN sold to James Williams of Bedford Co., TN, land in Bedford Co., on north side of Duck River, being a part of a 3000 acre tract originally granted to John Wilson. Borders Hugh McBride, Lock's land, and Burton Jordan. Wit: James Torrentine and Henry Pickle. Reg: 14 July 1815.

DEED BOOK "F" 1815 - 1817

Page 15 - William Lytle to James Torrentine. 3 Dec 1812. James Torrentine, administrator of estate of Alexander Torrentine of Bedford Co., TN one part and William Lytle of Rutherford Co., TN, land in Bedford Co., on headwaters of Alexanders Creek. Wit: John Thompson and Abram Thompson. Reg: 11 July 1815.

DEED BOOK "F"

Page 42 - Tennessee Grant to Mark R. Cockrell, 450 acres. No. 6014. Certificate No. 49, dated 27 Feb 1810, issued to William P. Anderson and entered 4 June 1811 by No. 3175. Granted to Mark R. Cockrell, assignee of William P. Anderson, land in Bedford Co., TN, on north bank of Duck River. Borders James A. Wilson, David Wilson and Justice's line. Surveyed 31 May 1813 by Samuel Bell, D.S. Reg: 28 July 1815.

Page 44 - Tennessee Grant to Amos McAdams, 15 acres. No. 6536. Part of a Certificate No. 338, dated 2 Nov 1809, issued to James Hill and entered 10 Dec 1813 by No. 5874. Granted to Amos McAdams, assignee of James Hill, land in Bedford Co., TN, on waters of Hurricane Creek of Duck River. Surveyed 1 June 1814 by Daniel Gilchrist, D.S. Reg: 12 Aug 1815.

Page 48 - James G. Jones and wife to Andrew Morrison, 133 acres. 22 Oct 1814. James G. Jones and Elizabeth his wife sold to Andrew Morrison, all of Bedford Co., TN, land in Bedford Co., TN. Borders Sharps upper tract on Duck River and including the Lot # 9 in the division among his heirs. Wit: Moses M. Robertson, John Kenny and John Robertson. Reg: (no date).

Page 50 - Peggy Clark to James Clark, 27 acres. 29 July 1814. Peggy Clark sold to James Clark, both of Bedford Co., TN, land in Bedford Co., TN, on waters of Big Flat Creek. Borders lands of William Higginbottom. Which said entry was made in the name of John Clark, Certificate No. 1564 for 200 acres, issued to John Strother, Entry No. 5929. Wit: John Woodrone, Benjamin Brittain and William Hall. Reg: 3 Sept 1815.

Page 64 - Tennessee Grant to William Dillard, 228 acres. No. 1054. For Military Service by William Dillard to North Carolina, Warrant No. 797, dated 5 May 1784 and entered 18 Aug 1807 by No. 207. Granted to William Dillard, land in Bedford Co., TN. Surveyed 20 May 1808. Reg: 19 Sept 1815.

Page 76 - Tennessee Grant to James Baird, 50 acres. No. 7315. Part of a Certificate No. 56, dated 27 Feb 1810, issued to William P. Anderson and entered 2 Feb 1811 by No. 2998. Granted to James Baird, assignee of William P. Anderson, land in Bedford Co., TN, south of Duck River. Borders Charles Fisher, the Duck River and Edward Wade. Reg: (no date).

Page 82 - Richard Hooper to Henry Rutherford, 213 acres. 26 Sept 1815. Richard Hooper, Attorney for William Martin of Moore Co., NC. Henry Rutherford of Williamson Co., TN. bought of Richard Hooper of Bedford Co., TN, part of 640 acres granted to William Martin, land in Bedford Co., TN, on west fork of East Fork of Rock Creek by Grant No. 679, dated 8 Dec 1800. Borders Thomas Garner. Reg: 9 Oct 1815.

Page 86 - Joseph Dobbs to William M. Crisp. 4 Feb 1815. Joseph Dobbs and Ann Dobbs his wife sold to William M. Crisp, all of Bedford Co., TN, land in Bedford Co. Wit: Jos. Neel and James Wilson. Reg: 9 Oct 1815.

Page 88 - Tennessee Grant to Charles Smith, 20 acres. No. 6475. Part of Certificate No. 75, dated 22 Aug 1811, issued to Alexander Hunter, entered 19 Aug 1811 by No. 3327. Granted to Charles Smith, assignee of Alexander Hunter, land in Bedford Co., TN, on east waters of Little Flat Creek. Borders Hord

Jones. Surveyed 27 Aug 1814 by Daniel Gilchrist, D.S. Reg: 9 Oct 1815.

Page 90 - Tennessee Grant to John Scott, 15 acres. No. 5409. For Military Service of David Hall to North Carolina, Warrant No. 4129, dated 6 Dec 1786 and entered 12 April 1810 by No. 2313. Granted to John Scott, assignee of David Hall, land in Bedford Co., TN, on East Fork of Rock Creek. Borders David Ross' 2005 acres. Surveyed 20 Apr 1815 by George Mitchell, D.S. Reg: 9 Oct 1815.

Page 92 - Tennessee Grant to John Scott, 36 acres. No. 5410. Certificate No. 28, dated Feb 5, 1810, issued to Elisha S. Hall, entered 12 Apr 1810 by No. 2311. Granted to John Scott, assignee of Elisha Hall, land in Bedford Co., TN, on East Fork of Rock Creek. Borders David Ross' Entry. Surveyed 20 Apr 1810 by George Mitchell, D.S. Reg: 9 Oct 1815.

Page 94 - Tennessee Grant to John Scott, 30 acres. No. 5408. For Military Service by David Hall to North Carolina, Warrant No. 4129, dated 6 Dec 1786 and entered 12 Apr 1810 by No. 234. Granted to John Scott, assignee of David Hall, land in Bedford Co., TN, on east waters of East Fork of Rock Creek. Borders lands in name of Trotter. Surveyed 7 Apr 1813 by D. Gilchrist, D.S. Reg: 9 Oct 1815.

Page 96 - Tennessee Grant to John Clark, 27 acres. No. 6561. Part of Certificate No. 1564, dated 13 Aug 1813, issued to John Strother and entered 8 Jan 1814 by No. 5929. Granted to John Clark, assignee of John Strother, land in Bedford Co., TN, on west waters of Flat Creek. Borders William Higginbottom. Surveyed 7 July 1814 by M. Gilchrist, D.S. Reg: 9 Oct 1815.

Page 105 - James Norvell to Marthy Johnston, Deed of Gift. James Norvell deeded a gift of a negro girl Nancy to his beloved granddaughter Marthy Johnston. 18 Feb 1815. Wit: William Norvell, John Norvell and Richard F. Jarratt. Reg: 1 Aug 1815.

Page 117 - Nathan G. Pinson and Oliver Williams to Heirs of Jacob Houber, deceased. 20 Jul 1814. Nathan G. Pinson of Lincoln Co., TN and Oliver Williams of Williamson Co., TN sold to Christian (Christopher) Houber, Mary Houber, Catharine Collins and her husband George Collins, Adam Houber, and Elizabeth Hay and her husband Jeremiah Hay, Sophia Houber, Jacob Houber, Henry Houber, Eve Houber, and Nancy Houber, heirs at law of Jacob Houber, deceased, all of Bedford Co., TN, except George Collins and Catharine his wife and Mary Houber of the District of Barnwell, South Carolina, land in Bedford Co., TN, on both sides of Rich Creek of Duck River. Borders Joel Laine and John Lewis. Wit: Jesse Brown, Jno. Hay, Jr., William M. Crisp and Martin Sims. Reg: 11 Oct 1815.

Page 121 - William Hartfield to Bidok Browning, 50 acres. 24 Apr 1815. William Hartfield sold to Bidok Browning, both of Bedford Co., TN, land in Bedford Co., on both sides of Powels Creek, adjoining lands of James Fort and Elizabeth Temple. Wit: Nathan Hartfield and Isiaah King. Reg: 11 Oct 1815.

Page 136 - James Lock to John Sanders, 104 acres. 17 Sept 1814. James Lock of Rowan Co., NC sold to John Sanders of Bedford Co., TN, land on north side of the North Fork of Duck River, it being part of 2000 acre granted to John Lock and his heirs by State of Tennessee by Grant No. 1063, dated 3 May 1809. Beginning at center of a spring in the north branch of North Fork, known as John Sanders Spring, it being also Nathan Wheeler's beginning corner. Wit: Samuel Bell and Nathan Wheeler. Signed by James Lock and William Lock as security. Reg: 12 Oct 1815.

Page 146 - Alexander McCullock to Benjamin McCullock. 10 July 1815. Alexander McCullock of Rutherford Co., TN, one of the heirs of Benjamin McCullock, deceased, and sole heir to the within claim by Deed of Release and partition from the other heirs, sold to Jonathan Wilborn, land which borders Hoover's land, McClure's line, on waters of Wartrace Fork of Duck River, land in Rutherford and Bedford Co., TN. Wit: Barkley Martin and Joel D. Harris. Reg: 17 Oct 1815.

Page 152 - Samuel Fleming to William Logan. 1 acre. 19 Jun 1815. Samuel Fleming sold to James Dixon, John McLeary, both of Bedford Co., TN and William Logan of Williamson Co., TN, Trustees of the Rock Spring Presbyterian Church, one acre of land on Samuel Fleming's south boundary line, east of the Fishing Ford Road and near south of the Rock Spring. Borders a cave and two sinks, being part of a tract granted to James Brandon by State of North Carolina, dated 10 July 1788 and conveyed by Brandon to Robert Weakley by Deed 18 Apr 1804 and registered in Davidson Co., TN. Wit: Jno. Atkinson and John B. Dixon. Reg: 17 Oct 1815.

Page 182 - Thomas Roberts and Mathew Lacy, Deed of Gift. Thomas Roberts and Mathew Lacy of Bedford Co., TN, jointly give to the three children of the said Roberts, to wit, Susannah, Ann and Thomas Roberts, they being the three only grandchildren of the said Lact, do give and bequeath to the said Susannah, Ann and Thomas Robert, Jr., negroes, nine in number. Wit: Elijah Parker and Enos Morgan. 12 June 1815. Reg: 27 Nov 1815.

Page 183 - Tennessee Grant to Amos McAdams, 40 acres. No. 7741. 14 Sept 1815. For Military Service of Craven Philips to North Carolina, Warrant No. 5195, dated 9 Dec 1797 and entered 5 July 1810 by No. 2456. Granted to Amos McAdams, assignee of the heirs of Craven Philips, land, part of a survey dated 1 June 1814, in Bedford Co., TN, on Hurricane Creek of Duck River. Borders Caleb Phifer, now in the name of James McAdams. Reg: 27 Nov 1815.

Page 185 - Samuel Breeden to Mason Breeden. Deed of Gift. Samuel Breeden of Bedford Co., TN, for love and affection for his beloved son Mason Breeden of Bedford Co., all his goods and chattels and other property. Wit: Rice Coffey and George B. Lowry. Reg: 27 Nov 1815.

Page 201 - Division of land between the heirs of John Sibley. 19 Oct 1813. Lot No. 1, borders Widow's Lot, 71 acres goes to Gabriel Sibley. Lot No. 2, borders Widow's Lot, 71 acres goes to Leonard Sibley. Lot No. 3, 71 acres goes to John Sibley. Lot No. 4, 51+ acres goes to Robert Sibley. Lot No. 5, 79 acres goes to Charles Sibley. Lot No. 6, 77 acres goes to Stephen Cook. Wisow not named. Signed by: John Radford, Samuel Radford, Hugh Houston, Alexander Osburn and Henry Fonderburg. Plat on page 204. Land on West Fork of Rock Creek. Reg: 30 Nov 1815.

Page 207 - Tennessee Grant to Joseph Neill, 31 acres. No. 7847. Part of a Certificate No. 1295, dated 31 Oct 1812, issued to Moses Humphreys and entered 4 Feb 1813 by No. 4849. Granted to Joseph Neill, assignee of Moses Humphreys, land in Bedford Co., TN. Surveyed 18 Feb 1813. Land on east waters of Bryeans Creek, a south branch of Duck River. Reg: 3 Jan 1816.

Page 209 - Tennessee Grant to Joseph Neill, 53 acres. No. 7846. Part of Certificate No. 1295, dated 31 Oct 1812, issued to Moses Humphreys and entered 4 Feb 1813 by No. 4847. Granted to Joseph Neill, assignee of Moses Humphreys, land on east waters of Bryeans Creek of Duck River. Borders Edward Bryeans. Surveyed 18 Feb 1813. Reg: 3 Jan 1816.

Page 211 - Tennessee Grant to Joseph Neill, 70 acres. No. 7845. Part of Certificate No. 426, dated 16 Jan 1811, issued to George W. Campbell and entered 9 Mar 1811 by No. 3048. Granted to Joseph Neill, assignee of George W. Campbell, land in Bedford Co., TN, on Bryeans Creek of Duck River. Borders Edward Bryeans. Surveyed 10 July 1812. Reg: 3 Jan 1816.

Page 213 - Tennessee Grant to Joseph Neill, 15 acres. No. 7848. Part of Certificate No. 1295, dated 31 Oct 1812, issued to Moses Humphreys and entered 4 Feb 1813 by No. 4848. Granted to Joseph Neill, assignee of Moses Humphreys, land in Bedford Co., TN, on east waters of Bryeans Creek. Borders Edward Bryeans. Surveyed 18 Feb 1813. Reg: 3 Jan 1816.

Page 215 - Tennessee Grant to Elijah Parker, 70 acres. No. 7849. For Military Service of Craven Philips to North Carolina, Warrant No. 5195, dated 9 Dec 1797 and entered 8 June 1808 by No. 482. Granted to Elijah Parker, assignee of the heirs of Craven Philips, land in Bedford Co., TN, on Thompsons Creek. Borders school land. Surveyed 9 Nov 1814. Reg: 3 Jan 1816.

Page 217 - Tennessee Grant to Elijah Parker, 40 acres. No.7874. Part of Warrant No. 1690, dated 19 Feb 1797, issued to David Ross by North Carolina and entered 3 Jan 1809 by No. 1081. Granted to Elijah Parker, assignee of David Ross, land in Bedford Co., TN, on Thompsons Creek. Surveyed 28 Nov 1809. Reg: 3 Jan 1816.

Page 219 - Tennessee to Elijah Parker, 30 acres. No. 7850. For Military Service of Craven Philips to North Carolina, Warrant No. 5195, dated 9 Dec 1797 and entered 8 Jan 1808 by No. 483. Granted to Elijah Parker, assignee of Craven Philips, land in Bedford Co., TN, on west waters of Thompsons Creek. Borders James Chambers, Thomas George and Elijah Parker. Surveyed 9 Nov 1815. Reg: 3 Jan 1816.

Page 277 - Michael Campbell to Catharine Boyet. 28 July 1814. Michael Campbell in his own right and as Executor of Philip Philips, deceased, of Davidson Co., TN conveyed to Catherine Boyet Hanegan, admrx. of John Boyet, deceased of Bedford Co., TN. Michael Campbell sold to Catherine Boyet and James Henagan, administrators, land in Bedford Co., TN, on waters of Rock Creek. Borders John Akin, Michael Campbell's old line. Reg: 3 Jan 1816.

Page 249 - Patsy Parker to John Wilson, deceased, heirs. 136 acres. 23 Oct 1815. Mrs. Patsy Parker, admrx. of Daniel

Parker, deceased, of Rutherford Co., TN, sold to James, Lemuel, Henry J. Davis, Margaret and Ellender Wilson, the heirs of John Wilson, deceased, land in Bedford Co., TN, on the north side of Duck River, opposite the mouth of Falling Creek. Borders school land. Wit: Ellender Wilson, Joseph Thompson and John Thompson. Reg: 21 Dec 1815.

Page 252 - Andrew Erwin to Heirs of Jacob Cross, 174 acres. 9 Oct 1815. Andrew Erwin of Augusta, Georgia, sold to the heirs of Jacob Cross of Bedford Co., TN, land in Bedford Co., on the waters of the Middle Fork of Duck River, a part of a 1364 acre tract granted by Tennessee to Norton Pryor by Patent No. 765. Borders Matt Martin. Reg: 19 Jan 1816.

Page 264 - Tennessee Grant to Andrew Erwin, 309½ acres, No. 6865. Part of Certificate No. 133, dated 14 June 1810, issued to John Scott and entered 22 July 1814 by No. 6565. Granted to Andrew Erwin, assignee of John Scott, land in Bedford Co., TN, on the waters of the Garrison Fork of Duck River. Borders Barkley Martin and Blount Grant. Surveyed 9 Sept 1814 by H. Grove, D.S. Reg: 1 Feb 1816.

Page 266 - Tennessee Grant to Andrew Erwin, 274 acres. No. 7308. Part of Certificate No. 430, dated 15 Apr 1813, issued to John C. McLemore and entered 17 Apr 1813 by No. 5209. Granted to Andrew Erwin, assignee of John C. McLemore, land in Bedford Co., TN, on Thompsons Creek. Borders Blount Grant and school land. Surveyed 25 Aug 1814. Reg: 1 Feb 1816.

Page 268 - Tennessee Grant to Andrew Erwin, 192½ acres. No. 6284. Part of Certificate No. 848, dated 17 Jan 1812, issued to John Brahan and entered 1 Feb 1813 by No. 4137. Granted to Andrew Erwin, assignee of John Brahan, land in Bedford Co., TN, on east waters of Shipmans Creek. Borders Moses Bridges and Blount Grant. Reg: 1 Feb 1816.

Page 270 - Tennessee Grant to Andrew Erwin, 384 acres. No. 6560. Part of Certificate No. 134, dated 14 June 1810, issued to John Scott and entered 22 July 1814 by No. 6577. Granted to Andrew Erwin, assignee of John Scott, land in Bedford Co., TN, on the Garrison Fork. Borders Matt Martin and Joseph Irvins. Surveyed 9 Sept 1814 by H. Grove. Reg: 1 Feb 1816.

Page 272 - Tennessee Grant to Andrew Erwin, 346 acres. No. 6864. Part of Certificate No. 133 and 136, dated 14 June 1810, issued to John Scott and entered 10 Sept 1814 by No. 6826. Granted to Andrew Erwin, assignee of John Scott, land in Bedford Co., TN, on the Garrison Fork of Duck River. Borders John Sutton. Surveyed 24 Sept 1814 by H. Grove, D.S. Reg: 1 Feb 1816.

Page 274 - Tennessee Grant to Andrew Erwin, 20 acres. No. 6283. For Military Service of Thomas Whitehead to North Carolina, Warrant No. 3199, dated 19 Dec 1785 and entered 3 Mar 1810 by No. 2216. Granted to Andrew Erwin, assignee of the heirs of Thomas Whitehead, land in Bedford Co., TN, on waters of Shipman Creek. Borders Thomas Logan of an Occupant Claim by Stephen Montgomery. Surveyed 12 Mar 1811 by Daniel Gilchrist, D.S. Reg: 1 Feb 1816.

Page 276 - Tennessee Grant to Archabald Adams, 57 acres. No. 7387. For Military Service by Johnston Parish to North

Carolina, Warrant No. 5295, dated 16 Dec 1797 and entered 21 Nov 1810 by No. 2839. Granted to Archabald Adams, assignee of the heirs of Johnston Parrish, land in Bedford Co., TN, on the East Fork of Rock Creek. Borders Cove Spring below where an Old Trace crosses fork of Rock Creek and known as Garden's Trace. Surveyed 21 Oct 1812. Reg: 1 Feb 1816.

Page 278 - Tennessee Grant to Archabald Adams, 25 acres. No. 7389. Part of Certificate No. 454, dated 5 Oct 1810, issued to William T. Lewis and entered 2 Oct 1811 by No. 3452. Granted to Archabald Adams, assignee of William T. Lewis, land in Bedford Co., TN, on west waters of East Fork of Rock Creek. Surveyed 10 Aug 1814. Reg: 1 Feb 1816.

Page 280 - Tennessee Grant to Archabald Adams, 32¼ acres. No. 7388. Part of Certificate No. 454, dated 5 Oct 1810, issued to William T. Lewis and entered 8 Aug 1814 by No. 6662. Granted to Archabald Adams, assignee of William T. Lewis, land in Bedford Co., TN, on waters of East Fork of Rock Creek. Borders survey of Robert Allison. Surveyed 28 Aug 1814. Reg: 1 Feb 1816.

Page 284 - Tennessee Grant to Joseph Thompson, 40 acres. No. 6914. Part of Certificate No. 1163, dated 5 Aug 1812, issued to Newton Cannon and entered 25 Feb 1814 by No. 6070. Granted to Joseph Thompson, assignee of Newton Cannon, land in Bedford Co., TN, on north side of Duck River. Borders Alexander Torrentine and John Thompson. Surveyed 26 Feb 1814. Reg: 1 Feb 1816.

Page 292 - Samuel White & others, Power of Attorney to Archabald White and others. We, Archabald White, Sr., Joseph White, Sr., John White, Jr., and Samuel White, Sr. of Cabarrus Co., NC, for considerations and good, we ordained &c, appoint friend Archabald White and Robert Morrison of Bedford Co., TN, their Attorney to transact any business pertaining to a tract of land in Bedford Co., on Sugar Creek, lying north of James Watkins and borders land of Amos Balch. 27 Dec 1815.

Page 293 - Cabarrus County, North Carolina. I, George Phifer, Clerk of Cabarrus Co., NC, do certify that David Houston and John B. Martin before whom the aboce, Power of Attorney, acknowledged at the time and are acting Justices of the Peace for said county, qualify. This 25 Dec 1815. Signed 28 Dec 1815 by Jno. B. Martin, J.P.

Page 294 - Cabarrus County, North Carolina. Joseph McCommons appoints his friend Archabald White of Bedford Co., TN, to convey the land which I, Joseph McCommons owns on Duck River. He is to return land and pay taxes and rent and receive rent. This 11 Dec 1815.

Page 295 - Cabarrus County, North Carolina. I, George Phifer, Clerk of Cabarrus Co., NC, certify that David Houston before whom the within Power of Attorney was acknowledged and now an acting J.P. of said county, qualified. Seal on 12 Aug 1815. Reg: 11 Mar 1816.

Page 296 - Tennessee Grant to Caleb Cox, 125 acres. No. 5890. By Certificate No. 125, dated 9 June 1810, issued to Caleb Cox and entered 16 Oct 1810 by No. 2773. Granted to Caleb Cox and his heirs, land in Bedford Co., TN, on waters of Weakleys Creek. Borders Benjamin Lemons and George Doherty. Surveyed 13 Feb 1812 by George Tillman, D.S. Reg: 11 Mar 1816.

Page 303 - Dyer & Green to William Hill, 200 acres. 13 Sept 1814. Joel Dyer and Sherwood Green, Executors of the Last Will and Testament of William Christmas, deceased, sold to William Hill of Bedford Co., TN, land in Bedford Co., TN, it being a Military Claim intered in the name of William Christmas, assignee of Sam. Pike, Grant No. 2643, about 200 acres. Borders Beverly Harris and James Wright. Wit: James L. Armstrong and Samuel Philips. Reg: 13 Mar 1816.

Page 307 - Samuel Patton to James W. Patton, 175 acres. 21 Dec 1814. Samuel Patton for love and affection for James W. Patton, a tract of land in Bedford Co., TN, on east side of Sugar Creek. Borders John Patton. Wit: William Patton and John Patton. Reg: 14 Mar 1816.

Page 309 - Samuel Patton to John Patton, 175 acres. 21 Dec 1814. Samuel Patton for love and affection for John Patton, land in Bedford Co., TN, on east side of Sugar Creek. Borders James W. Patton and Jonathan Barret. Wit: William Patton and James W. Patton. Reg: 14 Mar 1816.

Page 314 - William Hamilton to Francis Hamilton, 150 acres. William Hamilton sold to Francis Hamilton and his heirs, and for $1.00, land on north side of Duck River. Borders Joseph Hamilton. Reg: 15 Mar 1816.

Page 361 - The Heirs of McCarty to Richard Martin. 16 Jan 1797 by Deed convey to Jacob McCarty then of Robertson Co., TN, 400 acres on south side of Duck River, on Sugar Creek, it being part of Martin's part of a 534 acre tract granted by North Carolina to George Martin and Richard Martin, and Amos Balch. Grant date 10 July 1788, No. 16 of which said 400 acres, there is 325 acres taken by interference of an older claim having 75 acres taken now where as the said Richard Martin has conveyed to the heirs of Jacob McCarty, deceased, 75 acres, adjoins the 75 acres not taken up by older claims. We, James Tagert and Joseph McCarty, Executors of the Last Will and testament of Jacob McCarty, deceased. Wit: John R. Ross, Jacob W. Ross and William T. Ross. Reg: 18 Mar 1816.

Page 370 - Allen Leeper to James L. Ewing, 100 acres. 31 Dec 1815. Allen Leeper for love and affection he has for A. Leeper, his son-in-law and to his daughter Mary Ewing the said James L. Ewing's wife, given them land on West Fork of Rock Creek. Borders David Ross' survey. Reg: 18 Apr 1816.

Page 378 - James Fort and wife to John Stephens, 260 acres. 3 Oct 1815. James Fort and Chloe his wife of Worke Co., NC to John Stephens of Bedford Co., TN, land in Bedford Co., TN. Borders Charlotte Simms. Reg: (no date)

Page 386 - Tennessee Grant to Burton Jordan, 22 acres. No. 8312. Part of Certificate No. 1203, dated 17 Sept 1812, issued to the heirs of Thomas Wade and entered 28 Feb 1815 by No. 7587. Granted to Thomas Wade, land in Bedford Co., TN, on Weakleys Creek. Borders Where Jordan now lives and Robert Allison's land. Surveyed 17 Mar 1815. Reg. 21 May 1816.

Page 390 - Tennessee Grant to Ralph Williams, 100 acres. No. 5237. For Military Service of Joseph Perry to North Carolina, Warrant No. 3188, dated 19 Dec 1785 and entered 17 Aug 1809 by No. 1676. Granted to Ralph Williams, assignee of Joseph Perry, land in Bedford Co., TN, on waters of the North Fork of Duck River. Borders William Lytle. Surveyed 5 Oct 1812 by Samuel Bell, D.S. Reg: 31 May 1816.

Page 398 - Tennessee Grant to Manuel Cross, 50 acres. No. 6297. Part of Certificate No. 624, dated 15 July 1811, issued to Roderick Rawlins and entered 26 Sept 1812 by No. 4492. Granted to Manuel Cross, assignee of Roderick Rawlins, land in Bedford Co., TN, on waters of Bryans Creek. Borders a 50 acre survey of Edward Bryans. Surveyed 16 Feb 1813 by Daniel Gilchrist, D.S. Reg: 5 June 1816.

Page 400 - Tennessee Grant to Nathaniel Walker, 100 qcres. No. 5705. Part of Warrant No. 626, dated 24 June 1807, issued to John Kennedy and entered 23 Mar 1808 by No. 267. Granted to Nathaniel Walker, assignee of John Kennedy, land in Bedford Co., TN, on waters of Weakley Creek. Borders Charles Brandon and John Byler's Occupant Claim. Surveyed 16 Mar 1810 by George Tillman, D.S. Reg: 5 June 1816.

Page 402 - Tennessee Grant to James McReynolds, 100 acres. No. 4327. For Military Service of Roger Helton to North Carolina, Warrant No. 3173, dated the 19 Dec 1785 and entered 13 Feb 1810 by No. 2152. Granted to James McReynolds, assignee of the heirs of Roger Helton, land in Bedford Co., TN, on north side of Duck River and on the waters of Wilsons Creek. Borders John Atkinson and the Occupant Claim of David Fleming. Surveyed 17 May 1810 by George Tillman, D.S. Reg: 6 June 1816.

Page 404 - Tennessee Grant to Michael Fisher, 46½ acres. No. 6697. Part of Certificate No. 1090, dated 11 July 1812, issued to Henry Montford and entered 17 Sept 1812 by No. 4442. Granted to Michael Fisher, assignee of Henry Montford, land in Bedford Co., TN, on Falling Creek. Borders George Mitchell, Samuel Barton and now the property of Fisher's and Weatherrow, and Fall Creek. Surveyed 7 June 1814 by Daniel Gilchrist, D.S. Reg: 6 Mar 1816.

Page 406 - William Cross to John H. Anderson. 18 Sept 1815. William Cross and Hannah Cross his wife sold to John H. Anderson, land in Bedford Co., TN, Borders survey of Alexander Robertson. Wit: Duke Williams and William Barton. Reg: 25 June 1816.

Page 417 - Joseph Britton, Esq. of Bedford Co., TN, for consideration of the love and affection for his beloved daughter Elizabeth and now the wife of James C. Fulton of Bedford Co., TN, for $1.00, has conveyed unto James C. Fulton, his heirs &c., one negro woman Cealy with her three children, Bob, Dave, and Daniel. 6 Apr 1816. Wit: Jno. Wortham. Reg: 18 July 1816.

Page 423 - Jeremiah Dial to Henry Dial, 60 acres. 2 July 1814. Jeremiah Dyal of Bedford Co., TN sold to Henry Dial of same County, land in Bedford Co., on the headwaters of Falling Creek. Borders Martin Fifer (Phifer), and part of a tract granted to William P. Anderson and conveyed by Anderson and Coffee to Jeremiah Dial. Wit: Horatio Coop and John Coop. Reg: 18 July 1816.

Page 452 - Terry Williams to John Cockrell, Jr., 200 acres. 17 Mar 1816. Terry Williams and his wife (Sarah) Williams sold to John Cockrell, Jr. of Bedford Co., TN, land in Bedford Co. on West Fork of Rock Creek. Borders Richard Brown and Thomas Parker and the Shelbyville Road, and Wootons Old Trace. Wit: William Brown, Green Williams and William Alexander. Reg: 14 July 1816.

Page 502 - Nancy Spragins to China Spragins. 22 July 1816. Nancy Spragins for love and affection for China Spragins, convey to her and her heirs, property. Wit: Jesse Hall and James Hall. July Term 1816.

Page 504 - Tennessee Grant to Jeremiah West, 72 acres. No. 3290. Part of Certificate No. 434, dated 2 Aug 1810, issued to John McIvers and William P. Anderson and entered 7 Sept 1810 by No. 2663. Granted to Jeremiah West, assignee of John Ivers and William P. Anderson, land in Bedford Co., TN, on Rylies Creek, which includes the plantation where West now lives. Borders Isaac Hodge's Occupant Claim. Surveyed 31 Oct 1814. Reg: 24 July 1816.

Page 510 - Tennessee Grant to William Hill, 320 acres. No. 6422. For Military Service of John Dean to North Carolina, Warrant No. 167, dated 30 Nov 1808 and entered 21 Oct 1809 by No. 1988. Granted to William Hill, asignee of William Dean, heir at law of said John Dean, land in Bedford Co., TN, on Clems Creek. Borders Charles Brandon and Robert Allison's land where he now lives, and William Clark. Surveyed 15 Feb 1810 by George Tillman, D.S. Reg: 27 Jul 1816.

Page 515 - James Johnston to Logan Henderson, 1466 acres. 1 Dec 1815. Robert Johnston Surveying Executor of the Last Will and Testament of James Johnston, Sr., deceased, of Lincoln Co., NC, sold to Logan Henderson of Lincoln Co., NC, land in Bedford Co., TN, on both sides of Big and Little Sinking Creek. Borders tract conveyed to Newton Cannon by Robert Johnston as Executor of James Johnston, Sr., deceased. Reg: 30 Aug 1816.

Page 519 - William Petty to Joseph B. Porter. 18 Mar 1814. William Petty and Levina Petty formerly Levina Dilliard of Smith Co., TN sold to Joseph B. Porter of Maury Co., TN for locating a tract of land, 1298 acres by Entry No. 207 and $300.00, the land in the name of William Dilliard, gives Porter a tract of land in Bedford Co., TN, south of Duck River. The land was granted by Tennessee to William Dilliard by No. 1054. Levina Dilliard Petty, only heir of William Dilliard, deceased. Aug Term 1815 (Smith Co., TN)

Page 526 - Josiah Philips and wife Sarah Philips to John Philips. Gave all rights, titles &c to their son John Philips and his heirs. 26 Sept 1814. Wit: Henry Keely, John Rolston, Chester County, PA. Recorded in Book B, page 254 and 255.

Page 528 - Heirs of John Long to Rustly Anders. 20 July 1816. Sarah Long, widow of John Long, deceased, late of Sullivan Co., TN, Zacheus Wilson and Nancy his wife formerly Nancy Long, daughter and heir of John Long, Deceased, and Charles Long, William Long, John Long, Simon C. Long, Richard Long and Hugh Long, sons and heirs of John Long, deceased, and Hugh Wall and his wife Jane Wall formerly Jane Long, daughter of John Long, deceased, OF Bedford Co., TN, sold to Rustly Anders of Sullivan Co., TN, land of 560 acres in Hawkins Co., TN, on Panther Creek formerly known as Buffalo Creek, and on north side of Clinch River. This land was conveyed to John Long, deceased, by William Burk of Mason Co., Kentucky by deed dated 23 Dec 1794. Reg: 25 July 1816.

Page 542 - Andrew Erwin on 9 Oct 1815, in Augusta, Georgia.

Page 552 - Lewis Medlin to Resin Smith, 9 Feb 1816, on waters of Sinking Creek.

Page 567 - Andrew Erwin on 17 Mar 1817, in Augusta, Georgia.

Page 569 - Tennessee Grant to James Williams, 50 acres. No. 8311. Part of Certificate No. 305, dated 21 Aug 1809, issued to Benjamin McCullock and entered 11 July 1810 by No. 2469. Granted to James Williams, assignee of Benjamin McCullock, land in Bedford Co., TN, on north side of Duck River. Borders Robert Allison. Surveyed 5 June 1811. Reg: 27 Jan 1816.

Page 571 - Tennessee Grant to Larkin Edwards, 100 acres. No. 7467. Part of Certificate No. 306, dated 21 Aug 1809, issued to Benjamin McCullock and entered 20 Jan 1810 by No. 2102. Granted to Larkin Edwards, assignee of Benjamin McCullock, land in Bedford Co., TN, on north side of Duck River. Borders Anthony Newman. Surveyed 15 Oct 1814. Reg: 12 July 1815.

Page 573 - Tennessee Grant to Ann Wilson, Abram Gordon, 92 acres. No. 9193. 11 Apr 1792. Ephraim Gordon, a Private in the Battalion of Troops, raised per<u>suiant</u> to an Act of the General Assembly of the State of North Carolina, for the protection of the inhabitants of Davidson County and entered on the 17th and 24th day of March 1813 by No. 5104 and 5129. Granted to Ann Wilson, assignee of Ephraim Gordon, land in Bedford Co., TN, on waters of Rich Creek and Bryeans Creek of Duck River. Borders Rackoon (Raccoon) Spring. Surveyed 18 Feb 1814. Reg: 5 July 1817.

Page 591 - Michael Campbell to Bryan W. Nowlin. 9 Nov 1816. Michael Campbell for himself and as Executor of Philip Phillips, deceased of Davidson Co., TN, sold to Bryan W. Nowlin of Bedford Co., TN, land in Bedford Co., on Rock Creek. Wit: E. Chaffin and John H. Bills. Reg: 18 July 1817.

DEED BOOK "G" 1815 - 1817

Page 31 - Joseph Newman to Jeremiah Burns, Power of Attorney. Joseph Newman of Rutherford Co., TN appointed Jeremiah Burns of Bedford Co., TN, his Attorney, to apply at Col Anderson's office in Kentucky or at any other office in State of Ohio and procure a Military Land Warrant No. 2747 for 200 acres, issued to Joseph Newman for his service for the war as a Private of the Virginia Continental Line. Dated 16 Mar 1784 and issued by State of Virginia. Filed 12 Sept 1815 in Rutherford Co., TN.

Page 33 - Horne and others to Lane, Bill of Sale.
I, Anne Albertson, Levy Horne and Obediance of Bedford Co., TN, for $300.00 paid by John Lane of Bedford Co., 2 negroes, Sue and Terry. 1 June 1810. Wit: George Bussey, Joel H. Lane

and _____ Bussey. Reg: 25 July 1815.

Page 34 - Charles Snell and wife to Roger Snell, Bill of Sale. I, Charles Snell, Deborough his wife of Bedford Co., TN, conveyed to Roger Snell of Bedford Co., negro woman Peggy and a negro child Nelson. 4 Jan 1816. Wit: John Hale and John Deun(?). Signed by Charles Snell, Deborough Snell and Willie B. Snell. Reg: 25 July 1816.

Page 36 - James Gilbert, Sr. to William Gilbert, Deed of Gift. I, James Gilbert, Sr. of Bedford Co., TN, for love and affection for my son William Gilbert and for $1.00, conveyed 200 acres of land where James Gilbert now lives, also all goods and chattels of James Gilbert. 11 May 1816. Wit: Robert Wallace and William Wallace. Reg: 25 July 1816.

Page 45 - James Word to Heirs of John McLintick, 135 acres. 22 July 1816. James Word sold to John McLintick, Samuel McLintick, Robert McLintick, James McLintick, and George McLintick, heirs of John McLintick, deceased, land in Bedford Co., TN. Reg: 25 July 1816.

Page 47 - Edward Wade &c to James Word. 22 July 1816. Edward Wade, one of the acting Executors of John McLintick, deceased, of Bedford Co., TN sold to James Word, for $400.00 to George C. Gordon is paid and is acknowledged and by the Last Will and Testament of John McLintick, deceased, land in Bedford Co., TN. Borders John McCuistion's spring branch and Duck River for 67 acres. Reg: 25 July 1816.

Page 49 - Eben Wilson to Heirs of Daniel Williams, deceased, 69½ acres. 22 July 1816. Eben Wilson sold to the heirs of Daniel Williams, deceased, of Bedford Co., TN, land in Bedford Co., TN, on Falling Creek. Borders Richard Trotter's tract. Wit: Joseph Steele and Wilson Steele. Reg: 25 July 1816.

Page 69 - Felix Robertson to Elisha Hunter & wife and others. 226 acres. 1 Feb 1816. Felix Robertson, administrator of the estate of James Robertson, deceased, and William Shepperd, Sr. by his agent William Shepperd, Jr. sold to Elisha Hunter and Elizabeth his wife and John Sion Sherwood, James William Crawford, George and Mary Record, the heirs of John Record, deceased, of the County _____, TN. Dated 5 Feb 1811, land in Bedford Co., TN, on west side of Rock Creek. Surveyed 16 Feb 1809 by George Mitchell. Reg: 18 Oct 1816.

Page 96 - Mancil Crisp & wife to John H. Anderson, 50 acres. 19 Mar 1816. Mancil Crisp and Margaret his wife of Maury Co., TN sold to John H. Anderson of Bedford Co., TN, land in Bedford Co., TN, on Bryeans Creek. Borders Edward Bryan. Wit: Thomas Casey, David Grayham and Duke Williams. Reg: 25 Apr 1816.

Page 125 - I, Joseph Brittain, Esq., of Bedford Co., TN, and in consideration of the love and affection for my beloved daughter Jemima and now the wife of John Wortham of Bedford Co., TN, and for $1.00, conveyed one negro woman Winny and her three children Sam, Huldah and Nancy. 6 Apr 1816. Wit: James C. Fulton. Reg: 26 Apr 1816.

Page 148 - I, William Coble of Bedford Co., TN, for my good respect and esteem to my son Littleton Coble, do give a tract of land on the waters of West Rock Creek. Borders my land deeded by me to Robert Johnston, Willis Hopwood. 71½ acres. 16 Mar 1816. Wit: Thomas P. Gun and Hugh Smiley. Reg: 25 Apr 1816.

Page 156 - Tennessee Grant to James Wall, 2560 acres, No. 4310. For Military Service by James Wall to North Carolina, Warrant No. 630, dated 24 Apr 1784 and entered 8 Sept 1807 by No. 508. Granted to James Wall and his heirs, land in Bedford Co., TN, on waters of Rock Creek. Adjoins Jason Thompson and Newton Cannon's Entry, Philips and Campbell's Entry and William Black. Reg: 30 Oct 1816.

Page 162 - Cabarrus Co., North Carolina. 10 Oct 1809. We the under-subscribers being interested in a tract of land upon Duck River on waters of Sugar Creek, being part of a 5000 acre deed granted to Amos Balch and Company by North Carolina and whereas we the under-subscribers have a right and title to 1967 acres made over to Archabald White due by Amos Balch of Bedford Co., TN and made unto us now on record by Archabald White and John White, divers. We being a distance from said land, agree that our division shall be laid off in the following manner... John White division 200 acres is to join to William Balch on the north side of Balch's division. James Walls' division is 680 acres is to join the north side of John White division. Archabald White's division is 500 acres and to join James Walker's division on north. Hugh Edgars is to join Archabald White on the north, each division is to run east and west crossing said 5000 Grant. 10 Oct 1809. Wit: John Bradshaw and Nicholas White. Signed by James Walker, James White, Archabald White, Thomas White, John White, Arch. S. White, Jno. White, Wm. S. White, Jos. White, and Thomas White. Cabarrus Co., NC. July Term 1812. Proven in Court by John Bradshaw and Archabald White. Wit: G. Philips of Cabarrus Co., NC.

Page 164 - 16 Jan 1816. (C. Colwater) Thomas White of Cabarrus Co., NC sold to Archabald White of Bedford Co., TN, land mentioned in my father's Jno. White's Will, deceased, to me by virtue of said Will being in Bedford Co., TN on Sugar Creek (Colwater). Thomas White, one of the legatees of said John White. Jno. White, Testator. Wit: Josiah Bradshaw. Recorded in Cabarrus Co., NC in Book 8, page 459, 28 Mar 1816. Reg: 30 Oct 1816. NOTE: At one place in this instrument it states "Thomas White of Colwater".

Page 172 - 23 Oct 1816. Between Eliza Morgan, daughter of Simon Morgan, deceased, of Bedford Co., TN from Abner Chappel of Bedford Co., TN, land on Thompsons Creek, including the improvements where Charles Dunaway and his mother now lives and adjoining Benjamin King's land. 2 Surveys. Signed by Abner Chappel. Reg: 23 Oct 1816.

Page 197 - 14 Oct 1816. Benjamin Gates and Lucy Gates of Bedford Co., TN to Richard Long of Bedford Co., TN, land in Bedford Co. on waters of East Fork of Rock Creek, about 74 acres. Reg: 28 Oct 1816.

Page 210 - 3 Oct 1816. James Kerr and Selly Kerr to Benjamin Long, all of Bedford Co., TN, land in Bedford Co. on waters of the West Fork of Rock Creek, being part of a tract granted to David Kerr by Grant No. 3177. Reg: 28 Oct 1816.

DEED BOOK "G"

Page 229 - 19 Aug 1816. William Persons of Bedford Co., TN to Charles Persons of Bedford Co., son of William Person, for love and affection, conveys land in Bedford Co., TN, on waters of Big Flat Creek. The land conveyed to him by William Pearsons. 63 acres. Wit: David Floyd and Abraham Shook. Reg: -- Oct 1816.

Page 231 - 4 Jan 1816. John Jones to William Warner. Between Ephraim Davidson of Iredell Co., NC sold to William M. Warner of Bedford Co., TN, land on north side of Duck River, being part of a 1500 acres granted by North Carolina to George Davidson, dated 10 July 1788, Warrant No. 7028 and conveyed to Ephraim Davidson on 22 June 1797, 5 acres. Borders John Warner. John Jones, Agent. Reg: 16 Dec 1816.

Page 233 - Mississippi Territory of the United States, Jefferson County. We, Francis Baldridge and Elizabeth Baldridge his wife of Jefferson Co., Miss. Territory, appointed John Baldridge of the same county, their Attorney to take care of their interest in Tennessee. Elizabeth Baldridge to receive from the estate of her brother Alexander Turrentine, late of Nashville, Davidson Co., TN, deceased. This 14 Nov 1816. Reg: 9 Jan 1816.

Page 248 - We, Alexander Guy, John Guy, Samuel Guy, Sally Guy and Joseph Lawrence and his wife Margaret, and Ann Guy, all of Iredell Co., NC, appointed their brother William Guy of Bedford Co., TN, to receive any monies devised to them by the late Col. Alexander Work of Iredell Co., NC, to divide and survey all lands in Tennessee belonging to the estate of Alexander Worke, deceased, which belongs to them. Revoking the Power of Attorney to Gen. M. Stokes of Wilkes Co., NC so far as related to State of Tennessee. This 25 Feb 1816.

Page 255 - Zacheus Wilson to Daniel McGooding. 7 Dec 1815. Zacheus Wilson of Sumner Co., TN sold to Daniel McGooding of Logan Co., KY, land originally granted to David Wilson by Patent No. 3 and on Duck River. Borders survey of John Cathey. 375 acres. Reg: 14 Jan 1817. (Wilson is spelled in this instrument as Willson).

Page 257 - Benton Powell to John Sims, 194 acres. 28 Dec 1815. Benton Powell of Wake Co., NC sold to John Sims of Warren Co., NC, land in Bedford Co., TN. Borders Robert Temple, deceased, and Caswell Powell, deceased. Wit: D. Powel, William P. Turner, Samuel Marriott, Leonard P. Sims, Jno. S. Sims and Nancy Sims. Reg: 16 Jan 1817.

Page 261 - 2 Feb 1813. James Norvell to John Norvell. 150 acres. John Norvell, son of James Norvell, for love and affection he has for his son John Norvell, conveys land where James Norvell now lives, on War Trace Fork of Duck River. Borders John Whitehead and Bell Buckle Creek. Wit: David Knott, William Norvell and William Knott. Signed by James N. Norvell. Reg: 14 Jan 1817.

Page 264 - James Walker to John B. Walker, 227 acres. 26 Jun 1815. James Walker, Attorney for William Henry of Rhea Co., TN sold to John B. Walker of Bedford Co., TN, land in Bedford Co., TN, on waters of Garrison and Wartrace Forks of Duck River. Borders land conveyed by Henry to Joseph Walker. Wit: James Haggard, James Shinault and S. B. Patton. Reg: 14 Jan 1817.

Page 268 - Tennessee Grant to William O. Mahundro, 55 acres. No. 7469. Part of Certificate No. 52, dated 18 Jan 1814, issued to Christian Weaver and entered 3 Jan 1815 by No. 7362. Granted to William O. Mahundro, assignee of Christian Weaver, land in Bedford Co., TN, on the waters of the North Fork of Duck River. Borders William Litle. Surveyed 13 Feb 1815. Reg: 14 Jan 1817.

Page 269 - Tennessee Grant to Benjamin H. Lewis, 320 acres. No. 5763. Part of Warrant No. 625, dated 10 July 1784, issued to James Martin Lewis and entered 17 Sept 1812 by No. 4440. Granted to Banjamin H. Lewis, assignee of James Martin Lewis, land in Bedford Co., TN, on the north bank of Duck River. Borders David Justice. Reg: 15 Jan 1817.

Page 270 - Tennessee Grant to William Wyat, 16 acres. No. 3831. For Military Service of James Sullivan to North Carolina, Warrant No. 3680, dated 10 Dec 1788 and entered 4 May 1808 by No. 409. Granted to William Wyat, assignee of the heirs of James Sullivan, land in Bedford Co., TN, on the main fork of Big Flat Creek. Borders Giles Burditt. Surveyed 9 July 1808 by Daniel Gilchrist, D.S. Reg: 15 Jan 1817.

Page 271 - Tennessee Grant to Hezekiah Brown, 50 acres. No. 3832. For Military Service by Jesse Sharp to North Carolina, Warrant No. 5292, dated 15 Dec 1797 and entered 7 May 1808 by No. 417. Granted to Hezekiah Brown, assignee of Jesse Sharp, land in Bedford Co., TN, on main fork of Big Flat Creek. Reg: 16 Jan 1817.

Page 272 - Tennessee Grant to Hezekiah Brown, 50 acres. No. 3833. For Military Service of Jesse Sharp to North Carolina, Warrant No. 5292, dated 15 Dec 1797 and entered 7 May 1808 by No. 418. Granted to Hezekiah Brown, assignee of Jesse Sharp, land in Bedford Co., TN, on main fork of Flat Creek. Reg: 16 Jan 1817.

Page 275 - Tennessee Grant to Benjamin Carr, 41 acres. No. 6090. Certificate No. 1258, dated 1 Oct 1812, issued to Benjamin Carr and entered 8 Oct 1812 by No. 4570. Granted to Benjamin Carr, land in Bedford Co., TN, on north side of Duck River. Borders survey of Anthony Newman, Entry of Alexander Torrentine, John Thompson's grant, and school land. Surveyed 24 Feb 1814 by Samuel Bell, D.S. Reg: 16 Jan 1817.

Page 276 - Tennessee Grant to Barkley Martin, 30 acres. No. 6866. Part of Certificate No. 133, dated 14 June 1810, issued to John Scott and entered 17 Sept 1814 by No. 6869. Granted to Barkley Martin, assignee of John Scott, land in Bedford Co., TN, on waters of Garrison Fork of Duck River. Borders John Tilmond's land, Thomas B. Mosely, John Drake, Matt Martin and A. Erwin. Surveyed 29 Sept 1814 by H. Grove, D.S. Reg: 16 Jan 1817.

Page 273 - Tennessee Grant to Thomas Smith, 50 acres. No. 7160. Part of Certificate No. 434, dated 2 Aug 1810, issued to John McIvers and William P. Anderson and entered 3 Aug 1810 by No. 2551. Granted to Thomas Smith, assignee of John McIvers and William P. Anderson, land in Bedford Co., TN, on Rileys Creek. Surveyed 31 Oct 1814. Borders James Blyth's Occupant Claim. Reg: 16 Jan 1817.

DEED BOOK "G"

Page 274 - Tennessee Grant to James C. O'Riley, 400 acres. No. 5764. Certificate No. 1134, dated 15 July 1812, issued to James Patton and Andrew Erwin and entered 28 Sept 1812 by No. 4501. Granted to James C. O'Riley, assignee of James Patton and Andrew Erwin, land in Bedford Co., TN, on waters of Caney Spring Creek. Borders David Wilson, John Cockrell and David Justice. Surveyed 21 July 1813 by Andrew White, D.S. Reg: 16 Jan 1817.

Page 275 - Tennessee Grant to Benjamin Carr, 41 acres. No. 6090. Certificate No. 125, dated 1 Oct 1812, issued to Benjamin Carr and entered 8 Oct 1812 by No. 4570. Granted to Benjamin Carr and his heirs, land in Bedford Co., TN, on north side of Duck River. Borders Anthony Newman's Survey, Alexander Torrentine, John Thompson and school land. Reg: 16 Jan 1817.

Page 276 - Tennessee Grant to Barkley Martin, 30 acres. No.6866. Part of Certificate No. 133, dated 14 June 1810, issued to John Scott and entered 17 Sept 1814 by No. 6869. Granted to Barkley Martin, assignee of John Scott, land in Bedford Co., TN, on waters of the Garrison Fork of Duck River. Borders John Tilmond's field, Thomas B. Mosely, John Drake, Matt Martin, and A. Erwin. Surveyed 29 Sept 1814 by H. Grove, D.S. Reg: 16 Jan 1817.

Page 277 - 22 Jan 1816. William Hartsfield to Nathan Hartsfield, both of Bedford Co., TN, conveyed negroes (2). Wit: Isaiah King and Bedah Browning. Reg: 16 Jan 1817.

Page 285 - Tennessee Grant to James Randolph, 100 acres. No. 5967. Certificate No. 305, dated 21 Aug 1809, issued to Benjamin McCulock (McCullock) and entered 19 Mar 1810 by No. ---. Granted to James Randolph, assignee of Benjamin McCulock, land in Bedford Co., TN, on Wilson Creek of north side of Duck River. Borders John Atkinson. Surveyed 16 May 1810 by George Tilman, D.S. Reg: 19 Mar 1817.

Page 287 - I, Stokley Donelson of Hawkins County, Territory south of the Ohio River, have business to transact &c. I have engaged James Grant of Orange Co., NC, to go to any northward States and to transact and manage my affairs &c. 22 Sept 1792. Recorded in Orange Co., NC 23 Oct 1792 in Book E, page 565.

Page 291 - Oct Term 1816. Upon the Petition of Richard Locke, Robert Locke and his own right and also in his right as Executor of James Locke, deceased, by their Attorney Robert Weakley, setting forth that the State of North Carolina on 10 July 1788 granted to Mathew Locke by Grant No. 34, 5000 acres on both sides of North Fork of Duck River in Bedford Co., TN. Mathew Locke made a Will stating the tracts to his sons. Gen. Joseph Dickson is entitled to one half of said tract. The Will of Mathew Locke named his legitimate sons, Francis Locke, Richard Locke, Mathew Locke, James Locke, and Robert Locke and was published in the Clarion at Nashville. Recorded 29 Jan 1817 in North Carolina. Plat division on page 295. Reg: 22 Mar 1817.

Page 312 - George B. and Hezekiah J. Balch to Alfred Balch. 2 Nov 1816. George B. and Hezekiah J. Balch sold to Alfred Balch, all of Bedford Co., TN, Town Lot No. 39 in Shelbyville. Borders northwest corner of the brick house of Samuel and John N. Porter. Reg: 17 Apr 1817.

Page 314 - Andrew Erwin to the New Hope Meeting House. 24 Mar 1815. Andrew Erwin of North Carolina by his Attorney Henson Grove conveyed for $2.00, to Matt Martin, John B. Walker, Christopher Shaw, Vincent Smith, Jonathan Webster, James Slaton, and Barkley Martin, Commissioners for the New Hope Meeting House, citizens of Bedford Co., TN. Andrew Erwin sold a certain tract of land in Bedford Co., TN, on the Garrison Fork of Duck River, it being a part of a 5000 acre tract originally granted by State of North Carolina to John Gray and Thomas Blount by Grant No. 220. Borders on the Garrison Fork and John Scott. Deeded 4½ acres. Wit: John Atkinson and Thomas Patton. Reg: 27 Apr 1817.

Page 317 - Orange Co., NC. I, Daniel Torrentine, 12 Oct 1811, sold to Samuel Torrentine for $300.00, all my right &c to an undivided claim of the real estate of Alexander Torrentine, deceased. Wit: John Allison and James Torrentine. Orange Co., NC, Aug 1812. Recorded in Orange Co., NC in Book K, page 322. 7 Mar 1814. Reg: 17 Apr 1817.

Page 323 - Benjamin Hooper to James Hooper, 320 acres. 14 Oct 1816. Benjamin Hooper of Buckingham Co., VA sold to James Hooper of Bedford Co., TN, land in Bedford Co., TN, on the Middle Fork of Duck River. Reg: 15 Oct 1816.

Page 325 - We, Alexander McCorkle, Matthew McCorkle, Gilbert Milligan and Rebecca his wife, Charles Beatty of Lincoln Co., NC, James Conner guardian of Sally Lavania and Betsey Salina Beatty of Mecklenburg Co., NC, appointed William Guy of Bedford Co., TN, their Attorney, to pay and receive any monies due which is divided to us by the late Col. Alexander Worke of Iredell Co., NC, in the State of Tennessee also to divide and sell &c for us. 19 Oct 1816. Wit: John Allen, J. P. and Henry Conner, J.P. James Conner guardian for Sally L. Beatty and Betsey J. Beatty.

Page 329 - Tennessee Grant to Asa Fonville, 20 acres. No. 8582. Part of Certificate No. 1809, dated 7 July 1814, issued to Amos Balch and entered 15 Aug 1814 by No. 6689. Granted to Asa Fonville, assignee of Amos Balch, land in Bedford Co., TN, on waters of Caney Spring Creek. Surveyed 1 Feb 1813. Borders William Woods, David Williams and James Bruce. Reg: (no date).

Page 331 - Tennessee Grant to Jason Thompson, 300 acres. No. 7819. Part of Certificate No. 154, dated 9 Jan 1809, issued to Robert Espey and entered 12 Jan 1810 by No. 2083. Granted to Jason Thompson, assignee of Robert Espey, land in Bedford Co., TN, on the Garrison Fork of Duck River, including the place where Levi Campbell formerly lived. Surveyed 15 June 1815. Reg: (no date).

Page 333 - Tennessee Grant to James S. Turrentine, 50 acres. No. 8583. Part of Certificate No. 823, dated 30 Dec 1814, issued to William P. Anderson and entered 24 Feb 1815 by No. 7575 & 6. Granted to James S. Turrentine, assignee of William P. Anderson, land in Bedford Co., TN. Borders Richard Martin's Survey, Henry Pickle and James Neil. Surveyed 25 Feb 1815. Reg: (no date).

Page 335 - Tennessee Grant to John Harris, 30 acres. No. 8115. Part of Certificate No. 624, dated 15 July 1811, issued to

Rodrick Rawlings and entered 16 Oct 1812 by No. 4573. Granted to John Harris, assignee of Rodrick Rawlings, land in Bedford Co., TN, on waters of Weakleys Creek. Borders Ebenezer Alexander's grant, Abram Byler and Doherty's corner. Surveyed 15 Feb 1813. Reg: 27 Nov 1815.

Page 337 - Tennessee Grant to John Harris, 50 acres. No. 7615. Part of Certificate No. 645, dated 9 April 1813, issued to John Willson and entered 22 Sept 1813 by No. 5701. Granted to John Harris, assignee of the heirs of John Willson, land in Bedford Co., TN, on Weakleys Creek. Borders John Collins, Caleb Cox and Alexander's land. Surveyed 23 Sept 1813. Reg: 13 Sept 1815.

Page 377 - John Roberts and Sarah his wife, Lewis Medlin and Rachel his wife, Robert Medlin and Mary his wife, Elizabeth Brown and William Brown and Ruthy his wife, heirs and legatees of John Smith, deceased, all of Bedford Co., TN, sold to Reason Smith of Bedford Co., land in Bedford Co., TN, on waters of Sinking Creek. Land of 200 acres. Borders school land, George Doherty, Philip Phillips and Michael Campbell. Wit: William Medlin, Joseph Dunham and John England. Reg: 25 June 1817.

Page 418 - I, Michael Fisher of Bedford Co., TN, on 27 Jan 1817, granted and bequeathed to my son Martin Fisher, land on which I now live on, on the south side of Falling Creek. Borders James Harris and Henry Culp. 84 acres. Wit: Michael Fisher and John Maxwell. Reg: 25 Jan 1817.

Page 430 - North Carolina Grant No. 124, for 10 lbs per every 100 acres, granted to and paid by James Templeton, land of 120 acres on waters of Rutherfords Fork of Obion River. Borders James Davis and George Cathey. Plat on page 432. Reg: 10 Jul 1788.

Page 433 - 9 May 1815. David Yarborough and Helen M. Yarborough late Helen M. Doherty his wife of Orange Co., NC, William Bond and Frances W. Bond, late Frances W. Doherty his wife, and Mary Doherty of Williamson Co., TN, all heirs and devises of the late George W. Doherty of Orange Co., NC, deceased, sold to George W. Campbell of Nashville, TN, 1168 acres of land in Bedford Co., TN, on waters of Sugar Creek and Sinking Creek. Also, another tract of 300 acres in Lincoln Co., TN, on waters of Mulberry Creek of Elk River. Land whereon Byers Logan lived. Wit: James Giddins, William Wells, Henry Y. Houge and Francis Child.

Page 444 - Tennessee Grant to Robert Allison, 50 acres. No. 8846. Part of Certificate No. 1085, dated 11 July 1812, issued to Henry Montford and entered 13 Aug 1812 by No. 4251. Granted to Robert Allison, assignee of Henry Montford, land in Bedford Co., TN, on waters of Clems Creek, a branch of the North Fork of Duck River. Surveyed 21 Aug 1812. Reg: 10 Jun 1817.

Page 446 - Tennessee Grant to Robert Allison, 50 acres. No. 8845. Part of Warrant No. 2508, dated 30 Nov 1784, issued to Elijah West and entered 10 Feb 1813 by No. 4974. Granted to Robert Allison, assignee of Elijah West, land in Bedford Co., TN, on waters of Clems Creek. Borders James McReynolds. Surveyed 1 Feb 1814. Reg: 10 June 1817.

Page 448 - Tennessee Grant to Edward Wade, 80 acres. No. 8748. Part of Certificate No. 769, dated 15 Dec 1814, issued to James Bradshaw, Charles McCommons and Amos Balch and entered 21 Mar 1815 by No. 7666. Granted to Edward Wade, assignee of James Bradshaw, Charles McCommons and Amos Balch, land in Bedford Co., TN, on Bell Buckle the waters of the Wartrace Fork of Duck River. Borders James Coldwell and Alexander Outlaw's land. Surveyed 20 July 1815. Reg: 10 June 1817.

Page 450 - Tennessee Grant to Larkin Edwards, 10+ acres. No. 7468. Part of Certificate No. 869, dated 1 Feb 1812, issued to John McIvers and entered 6 July 1814 by No. 6509. Granted to Larkin Edwards, assignee of John McIvers, land in Bedford Co., TN, on North Fork of Duck River. Borders John Jackson and Felix Robertson. Surveyed 15 Oct 1814. Reg: 10 June 1817.

Page 452 - 23 July 1816. Matthew Cunningham and Betsey his wife, Francis McAmy (McCamey) and Catsey his wife, and Anne Huff, all of Bedford Co., TN, and Mary Dickson of Orange Co., NC sold to John B. Cummins of Bedford Co. land in Bedford Co., TN, on Big Flat Creek. Borders William Gilbreath and Jeremiah Chamberlain. (Catsey signed her name as Catherine McAmy). Wit: Joshua Holt and Elenor Holt. Reg: 10 June 1817.

Page 459 - 4 Jan 1817. James Ewing sold to Allen Leeper, John Reed, and John Woods, Commissioners for the Bethberi Church, in the Forks of Rock Creek, land for purpose of building a church upon and to bury the dead, on East and West Fork of Rock Creek. Reg: 11 June 1817.

Page 473 - Tennessee Grant to Littleberry Green and John Payton, 279 acres. No. 8555. For Military Service of Thomas Pearcy for North Carolina, Warrant No. 5154, dated 8 Dec 1797 and entered 12 Sept 1807 by No. 541. Granted to Littleberry Green and John Payton, assignees of Thomas Pearcy, land, bordering Michael Robertson and Howel Tatum's survey. Surveyed 31 July 1812. Land in Bedford Co., TN. Reg: 14 June 1817.

Page 480 - Tennessee Grant to Ann Wilson, 50 acres. No. 9194. Part of Warrant dated 14 Apr 1792, issued to Ephram Gordon, a Private in the Battalion of Troops raised pursuant to an Act of General Assembly of North Carolina for protection of inhabitants of Davidson Co., TN and entered 23 Oct 1811 by No. 3501. Granted to Ann Wilson, assignee of Ephram Gordon, land in Bedford Co., TN, on west waters of Rock Creek. Surveyed 7 Aug 1812. Reg: 6 Jan 1817.

Page 484 - I, Elizabeth Williams of Caswell Co., North Carolina, for natural love and affection which I have and bear towards my daughter in law Edy Williams the wife of Duke Williams and also towards her children by said Duke Williams, loan two (2) negroes which is now in her possession in Tennessee by the name of Philis and Simon and "afterward my decease" a negro girl Barbary now in my possession. 20 Oct 1816. Reg: 12 July 1817.

Page 496 - 27 July 1816 - Abraham Helton, Sr. of Bedford Co., TN sold to Abraham Helton, Jr., land in Bedford Co., on waters of Sinking Creek. Borders John Medearis and Daniel Davis. Land of 50 acres. Wit: B. W. H. Medearis and John Cook. Reg: 13 July 1817.

DEED BOOK "G"

Page 504 - Tennessee Grant to John White, 427 acres. No. 4383. For Military Service of Jonathan Jones to North Carolina, Warrant No. 111, dated 17 Dec 1804 and entered 26 Aug 1807 by No. 332. Granted to John White, assignee of Jonathan Jones, land in Williamson Co., TN, on headwaters of Cold Water Creek, a branch of Elk River. Surveyed 26 Oct 1807 by James Bright, D.S. Reg: 14 July 1817.

Page 522 - 28 April 1817. Michael Fisher, administrator of the estate of John Fisher, deceased, sold to Henry Verner, all of Bedford Co., TN, land on west waters of Rock Creek. Wit: John L. Neill and Edward Wade. Reg: 25 July 1817.

Page 544 - Tennessee Grant to William Hall, 320 acres. No. 6421. For Military Service of John Dean to North Carolina, Warrant No. 167, dated 30 Nov 1808 and entered 21 Oct 1809 by No. 1917. Granted to William Hall, assignee of William Dean, heir at law of John Dean, land in Bedford Co., TN, on the waters of Wilsons Creek. Borders grant of Samuel Wilson. Surveyed 15 Feb 1816 by George Tillman, D.S. Reg: 28 July 1817.

Page 546 - 31 Oct 1815. Margaret Alexander & Others to Josiah N. Alexander. Margaret Alexander and Nathaniel Alexander, Executors and heirs at law to Col. George Alexander, Jr., both of Cabarrus Co., NC sold to Josiah N. Alexander of Cabarrus Co., NC, land in Bedford Co., TN, between Alexanders and Weakley Creeks. Borders Daniel Davidson, Newton Cannon, Samuel Bell and Caswell and Dwiggins and Ebenezer Alexander. Land of 788 acres. Reg: 5 Aug 1817.

Page 558 - North Carolina Grant No. 106 (or 186). For ten pounds per 100 acres. To Edward Armstrong, land of 500 acres, on north side of Duck River, between the mouth of Caney Spring Creek and Spring Creek. Borders Duck River and David Justice. Plat on page 560.

Page 562 - 20 Sept 1817. James Anderton of Bedford Co., TN sold to William Thomas of Halifax Co., VA, land in Halifax Co., VA, where John Critington formerly resided, about 100 acres.

Page 569 - 20 Sept 1817. John Stone to William West. John Stone of Bedford Co., TN, Merchant, sold to William West of Lexington, Kentucky, land in Bedford Co., TN. Lot # 55 in Shelbyville.

Page 582 - Tennessee Grant to Robert McCuistion, 189 acres. No. 3365. For Military Service of Alexander Gammill to North Carolina, Warrant No. 5150, dated 9 Dec 1797 and entered 14 Apr 1808 by No. 350. Granted to Robert McCuistion, assignee of the heirs of Alexander Gammill, land in Williamson Co., TN, on waters of Wilsons Creek. Borders Entry of George Doherty. Surveyed 17 Nov 1808 by George Tillman, D.S. Reg: 30 Sept 1817.

Page 587 - 23 July 1816. Henry McCoy and James W. Stewart to Pinkston. Henry McCoy and J. W. Stewart, administrators of estate of William M. Hall, deceased, with the Will annexed, both of Rutherford Co., TN sold to William Pinkston of Williamson Co., TN, land in Bedford Co., TN, on North Fork of Duck River, including part of Weakleys Creek. Borders Hugh McBride. Wit: William Locke and James Williams. Reg: 24 Jan 1817.

DEED BOOK "G"

Page 589 - Tennessee Grant to James Adams, 50 acres. No. 5900. For Military Service by Reed Smith to North Carolina, Warrant No. 4363, dated 17 Dec 1796 and entered 20 Feb 1812 by No. 3732. Granted to James Adams, assignee of Reed Smith, land in Bedford Co., TN, on waters of East Fork of Duck River. Surveyed 3 Mar 1814 by Daniel Gilchrist. Recorded Sept 1814 (Nashville). Reg: (no date).

Page 591 - Tennessee Grant to James Adams, 63 acres. No. 7619. Part of Certificate No. 1863, dated 24 Aug 1814, issued to John C. McClamore (McLemore) and James Vacel, land in Bedford Co., TN, on waters of East Fork of Rock Creek. Borders George Horn, Polly Adams and Archabald Adams. Surveyed 8 Mar 1815. Reg: (no date).

Page 593 - Tennessee Grant to James Adams, 25 acres. No. 6276. For Military Service of Reed Smith to North Carolina, Warrant No. 4363, dated 17 Dec 1796 and entered 17 June 1814 by No. 6463. Granted to James Adams, assignee of Reed Smith, land in Bedford Co., TN, on waters of East Fork of Rock Creek. Borders Patton's survey. Surveyed 1 July 1814 by Daniel Gilchrist, D.S. Reg: 17 Nov 1814.

Page 595 - Tennessee Grant to James Adams, 7 acres. No. 5901. Part of Certificate No. 363, dated 21 Nov 1809, issued to Archabald Clinton and entered 30 Mar 1811 by No. 3035. Granted to James Adams, land in Bedford Co., TN, on waters of Rock Creek. Borders school land. Surveyed 2 July 1813 by Daniel Gilchrist, D.S. Reg: 2 Oct 1817.

Page 597 - Tennessee Grant to James Adams, 47 acres. No. 7383. Part of Certificate No. 135, dated 24 Aug 1814, issued to John C. McLemore and James Vacel and entered 26 Aug 1814 by No. 6754. Granted to James Adams, assignee of John C. McLemore and James Vacel, land in Bedford Co., TN, on headwaters of Mud Creek of Rock Creek. Borders Frqncis Patton and Henry Bishop. Reg: 2 Oct 1817.

Page 599 - Tennessee Grant to James Adams, 50 acres. No. 5899. Part of Certificate No. 363, dated 21 Nov 1809, issued to James Adams and Archabald Clinton and entered 13 June 1810 by No. 2425. Granted to James Adams, land in Bedford Co., TN, on waters of East Fork of Rock Creek. Borders William Black and Wall's Survey. Surveyed 28 Aug 1810 by George Mitchell, D.S. Reg: 3 Oct 1817.

Page 601 - Tennessee Grant to James Adams, 82 acres. No. 6423. Part of Certificate No. 363, dated 21 Nov 1809, issued to James Adams and Archabald Clinton and entered 13 Feb 1812 by No. 3709. Granted to James Adams, land in Bedford Co., TN, on waters of East Fork of Rock Creek. Borders James Hart and William Black. Surveyed 21 Jan 1814 by Daniel Gilchrist, D.S. Reg: 3 Oct 1817.

Page 603 - 25 Aug 1789. Between James Bradshaw, Charles McCommons, Andrew Campbell and William Balch of Mecklenburg Co., NC sold to Amos Balch of Green Co., NC, 500 acres of land on both sides of Sugar Creek, a branch of Duck River, Hawkins Co., TN. Borders George Martin, Amos Balch and Richard Martin. Cabarrus Co., NC, by Paul Barringer, Magistrate, signed 22 July 1817. Reg: 21 Mar 1817.

DEED BOOK "H" 1817 - 1818

Page 8 - 18 Mar 1817. Andrew Erwin to Jacob Coble, 64 acres. Andrew Erwin of Augusta, Georgia sold to Jacob Coble of Bedford Co., TN, land in Bedford Co., TN, on the north west side of the junction of the Garrison, a south fork of Duck River. Borders Matt Mullin's improvement. Wit: Henry Grove and John Ewell. Reg: 18 Mar 1817.

Page 10 - 27 Jan 1817. I, Michael Fisher of Bedford Co., TN for certain good reasons, I hereunto moving hath this day conveyed unto my son Jacob Fisher, land in Bedford Co., TN, on both sides of Falling Creek and it being part of the tract of land I now live on. Borders James Harris, Martin Fisher, and the Survey of William Lenore. About 95 acres. Wit: John Maxwell and Michael Fisher, Jr. Reg: 24 Jan 1817.

Page 16 - 19 Nov 1816. William Patterson and William Patterson, Jr. to Malcolm Gilchrist. William Patterson of Mecklenburg, NC and William Patterson, Jr. of Bedford Co., TN sold to Malcolm Gilchrist of Bedford Co., TN, land in Bedford Co., on headwaters of Butler's Creek. Borders land of the heirs of Daniel Vaughan, north Shelbyville Road and others. Including Nicholas Nall's house and where two of the Mr. Snelling now lives also one other tract in Bedford Co., on north side of Duck River bordering Walter Sims. 123 acres. Wit: George Graham and James Clark. Reg: 31 Jan 1817.

2 July 1817. Joseph and Ann Dobbs to Jabus Nowland (Nowlin). Joseph and Ann Dobbs sold to Jabus Nowlin, all of Bedford Co., TN, land in Bedford Co., on the waters of Rich and Bryants Creek, south of Duck River. Borders Racoon Spring and west of a Bubles Road leading from the Fishing Ford on Duck River, James S. Turrentine, and Edward Bryans. Wit: Joseph Neil and Jacob Webb. Reg: 27 Sept 1817.

Page 26 - 29 Apr 1817. John McClintock and wife to Daniel Treadwell. John McClintock and Frances McClintock his wife sold to Daniel Treadwell, all of Bedford Co., TN, Quit Claim, land of 120 acres which they claim as heirs of George Blessing, deceased. Borders E. McClain, branch of Duck River, and Duck River. The same being once conveyed by Charles Fisher and Edward Wade to Thomas Ross. Wit: Michael Earnhart and Elizabeth McClintock. Reg: 2 May 1817.

Page 29 - 29 July 1817. Clement Cannon to Andrew Cannon. Clement Cannon sold to Andrew Cannon, land in Bedford Co., TN. Adjoining town of Shelbyville and on part of 5000 Grant to Robert Smith. Borders Town of Shelbyville on southeast corner of Lot No. 4 whereon John B. Brown now lives, and Givins' corner. About 1+ acres. Wit: Eli Collins and William Wilson. Reg: 25 Sept 1817.

Page 43 - 8 Oct 1816. Joseph Dobbs to William Lemmons, 100 acres. Joseph Dobbs and Ann Dobbs his wife sold to William Lemmons, all of Bedford Co., land near head of Rock Creek, being a part of a 400 acre survey granted to Ann Wilson. Borders lands of John Wilson. Wit: Joseph Neil and Jabus Nowlin. Reg: 26 Sept 1817.

Page 61 - 8 July 1817. Joseph and Ann Dobbs to heirs of William Lemmon. Joseph and Ann Dobbs sold to the heirs of William Lemmon, deceased, of Bedford Co., TN, land of 50 acres, on west waters of Rich Creek. Borders survey of Newman, Nathan G. Pinson. Ann Dobbs formerly Ann Wilson. Wit: Joseph Neil and John Buchanan. Reg: 25 Sept 1817.

Page 63 - William Sanders to Frances Sanders, his wife. Bill of Sale. Whereas William Sanders, Sr., late of Bedford Co., TN, hath departed this life, having first made and published his Last Will and Testament, dated 7 Feb 1813. In Will, Sanders devised to Frances Sanders, his wife, a negro boy named Nelson and a negro girl Jenny left to "Fanny" Sanders, daughter of William Sanders, deceased. At the death of Frances Sanders, the widow of William Sanders, and whereas since the making and executing of the said Will, Claibourn Ragsdale intermarried with "Fanny" Sanders, daughter of William Sanders, deceased, goes to heirs of Claibourn Ragsdale and Fanny. Signed: 15 Jan 1815. Wit: John T. Ragsdale, Jesse Davis and John Resson. Reg: 26 Jan 1816.

Page 79 - 21 Dec 1816. B. M. Burrow to Ephraim Burrow, 125 acres. Banks M. Burrow of Bedford Co., TN conveyed to Ephraim Burrow of Guilford Co., NC, land in Bedford Co., TN, on west waters of Big Flat Creek. Borders William Burrow and Philip Burrow. Surveyed 20 Dec 1810. Wit: J. Burrow and Philip Burrow. Reg: 29 Sept 1817.

Page 81 - 5 June 1817. Michael Fisher to Martin Fisher, 51 acres. Michael Fisher, administrator of John Fisher, deceased, of Bedford Co., TN sold to Martin Fisher, land in Bedford Co., on Sinking branch of Rock Creek. Wit: Michael Fisher and John Fisher. Reg: 25 Sept 1817.

Page 95 - Jonathan Greaves (Graves) to Joseph D. Greaves (Graves) Jonathan sold to Joseph D. Greaves, a negro man William. Reg: 26 Sept 1812.

Page 101 - 30 Apr 1815. Alexander McCullock to Joel D. Harris, 104+ acres. Alexander McCullock of Rutherford Co., TN sold to the heirs of Benjamin McCullock, deceased, and sole heir to certain claim by Deed of Release and partition from the other heirs, sold to Joel D. Harris of Bedford Co., TN, all that land described, land in Bedford Co., on the waters of the Wartrace Fork of Duck River. Borders lands of Erwin(now Coffey's) and McClures land and Haywood's line. Wit: John G. Sims and P. B. Hays. Reg: 19 Mar 1816.

Page 108 - Dennis Grady to Margaret R. Medearis.
I, Dennis Grady give and deliver unto my granddaughter Margaret Rachel Medearis, daughter of Betty Medearis, my daughter, one negro girl Lively and her increase. Negro to work for the rise of Ghaikey Grady, my wife, during her life. Note: Ghaikey is also spelled Ghaked in same instrument). 31 Dec 1816. Wit: Dawson Grady and Harbert Smith. Reg: 27 Apr 1816.

Page 111 - Andrew Erwin on 18 Mar 1817 in Augusta, Georgia.

Page 117 - 5 Mar 1816. J. Patton and Erwin to Trustees of Fork Meeting House. James Patton and Andrew Erwin, late of Ashville, NC conveyed to Samuel King, William McGee and Samuel Tilford, Trustees of the congregation known by the name of the Fork Congregation, and their successors, for $25.00, conveyed 7 acres of land. Borders Charles Timmons and Samuel King. Wit: John B.

Pendegrest and W. Latimore. Reg: 25 May 1817.

Page 199 - Tennessee Grant to John C. Dunn, 300 acres. No. 4326. For Military Service by Roger Hilton to North Carolina, Warrant No. 3173, dated 19 Dec 1785 and entered 11 July 1809 by No. 1586. Granted to John C. Dunn, assignee of the heirs of Roger Hilton, land in Bedford Co., TN, on waters of Wilsons Creek. Borders Samuel Patterson, Jonathan Graves and Samuel Willson. Surveyed 10 Feb 1810 by George Tillman, D.S. Reg: 6 Nov 1817.

Page 121 - 16 Jan 1816. Robert W. Smith to Walter Sims. Robert W. Smith of Cabarrus Co., NC sold to Walter Sims of Philadelphia Co., PA, land in Bedford Co., TN, on both sides of Duck River, it being part of a survey for David Smith and granted to Robert Smith the father of said Robert Smith, by NC Grant. Borders Clement Cannon and Blount Survey. Reg: 15 Sept 1817.

Page 129 - 23 Oct 1817. Daniel King to Margaret E. King. Daniel King sold to Margaret E. King, a negro woman Charlite and child Mary Ann. Wit: J. D. Farley. Reg: 25 Oct 1817.

Page 130 - Daniel King to M. E. King, Bill of Sale. Daniel King sold to Margaret E. King, a negro boy Randol. 23 Oct 1817. Wit: J. D. Farley. Reg: 25 Oct 1817.

Page 131 - 23 Oct 1817. Daniel King to Margaret E. King, Bill of Sale. Daniel King sold to Margaret E. King, a negro boy Washington. Wit: J. D. Farley. Reg: 28 Oct 1817.

Page 132 - 23 Oct 1817. Daniel King to Margaret E. King, Bill of Sale. Daniel King sold to Margaret E. King, a negro girl Elizabeth. Wit: John D. Farley. Reg: 28 Oct 1817.

Page 133 - 23 Oct 1817. Daniel King to Margaret E. King, Bill of Sale. Daniel King sold to Margaret E. King, a negro boy Kelly. Wit: John D. Farley. Reg: -- Oct 1817.

Page 145 - North Carolina Grant to Caleb Phifer, No. 102, for 10 lbs per 100 acres, land of 5000 acres on Falling Creek. Borders Richard Trotter and Martin Phifer. 10 July 1788. Plat on page 147 & 149. Surveyed 27 July 1785. Reg: 30 Oct 1817.

Page 151 - North Carolina Grant to Richard Trotter, 4100 acres. No. 103. 10 lbs per 100 acres. Land in bedford Co., TN, on Falling Creek. Borders Caleb Phifer and John Wilson. Recorded in Rowan Co., NC in Book 12, page ---, 14 Apr 1790. Registered in Rutherford Co., TN in Book E, page 6 & 7, 29 May 1807. Plat on page 153 & 154. Surveyed 27 Oct 1817 by Samuel McLean.

Page 165 - James Grooms to his children, Deed of Gift. I, James Grooms of Bedford Co., TN, for love and affection which I have for my children Susana Guess wife of Joshua Guess, John Jones Grooms, Thomas Crooms, Elizabeth Grooms, Rebecah Grooms, Isaac Grooms, Sally Grooms and Henry Grooms, for $10.00 paid by my children, 6 head of horses and other stock of cattle &c, crops and house furniture, one note on Isham Hughs for $27.00, $25.00 on John Hathcock, Sr., $4.00 on John Mullins, $2.00 on Francis Arnold, $3½.00 on Joseph Dobbs and $4.00 on James Reeves and one rifle gun. My wife Polly Grooms to have use of property during our lives. Youngest child is Henry, under age 21 years. Joshua Guess to take the property until guardian is appointed. If there is a child born after this, it is to receive equal part. 26 Oct 1817. Wit: S. Casey. Reg: 20 Oct 1817.

Page 171 - 9 July 1817. John Rayburn to Joseph Alison (Elison). John Rayburn of Franklin Co., TN sold to Joseph Elison and Patsey Stone, administrators of the estate of James Stone, land in Bedford Co., TN, on waters of Duck River. Borders Garrison Fork of said River. Wit: Peter Lee and W. S. Watterson. Reg: 28 Oct 1817.

Page 250 - 29 Jan 1817. John Milton to Stephen Booth, 40 acres. John Milton sold to Stephen Booth, Executor of the estate of John Booth, deceased, and Tonzey Booth, Executrix, all of Bedford Co., TN, land in Bedford Co., TN, on waters of Alexander Creek, it being a part of a 3000 acre tract granted to Ebenezer Alexander by State of North Carolina. Wit: Caleb Cox and Evan Harris. Reg: 14 Mar 1818.

Page 262 - Matt Martin to Barkly and wife. Deed of Gift. I, Matt Martin of Bedford Co., TN, for love and affection I bear unto my brother Barkly Martin and his wife Rachael of Bedford Co., TN, land on which they reside. Borders John Donaldson's grant. When they die, to return to Matt Martin. 24 Apr 1815. Wit: Charles E. Watkins and Jno. Scott. Reg: 19 Mar 1818.

Page 297 - Tennessee Grant to Balch & Alexander, 22 acres. No. 10402. Part of Certificate No. 2184 & 2308, dated 25 Sept 1815 & 19 Feb 1816, issued to William P. Anderson and James Vasel and entered 20 Dec 1815 & 1 June 1816 by No. 8699 & 9289. Granted to Theron E. Balch and Joseph Alexander, assignees of William P. Anderson and James Vasel, land in Bedford Co., TN, on Duck River. Borders Amos Balch now lives, and Talbot's Survey and land of Thompson. Surveyed 2 June 1816. Reg: 26 Mar 1818.

Page 304 - I, Robert Allison of Bedford Co., TN, for love and affection and good will I bear toward my son James Allison of Bedford Co., TN, convey unto him land in Bedford Co., on waters of Rock Creek. Borders William Wilbourne and Hays Blair, Felix Robertson's Grant, and Hardy Murphy's Survey. Reg: 25 Mar 1818.

Page 312 - Tennessee Grant to Samuel Bell, 90 acres. No. 6911. Part of Certificate No. 306, dated 21 Aug 1809, issued to benjamin McCullock and entered 18 June 1811 by No. 3207. Granted to Samuel Bell, assignee of Benjamin McCullock, land in Bedford Co., TN, on waters of Alexanders Creek. Borders Ebenezer Alexander and Joseph Denson. Surveyed 3 Mar 1814. Reg: (no date).

Page 322 - W. Martin to Jacob Morton, Bill of Sale. William Martin conveyed to Jacob Morton, both of Bedford Co., TN, all his interest, claim to the estate of his father John Morton who died in Chatham Co., North Carolina in the year of 1783. Dated 1 April 1818. Wit: R. C. Thompson. Reg: 13 Apr 1818.

Page 324 - John Morton to William McDade, Bill of Sale. I, John Morton of Guilford Co., North Carolina sold to William McDade of Bedford Co., TN, one equal fourth part of the negroes and their offsprings bequeathed by John Morton, deceased, to his children at the death of his widow Ruth Morton, except Fortner and Bob which I have conveyed to Elijah Sparks of Richmond Co., Georgia, Mema a negro girl to George A. Gordon of Jackson Co., Georgia, Jacob to Peter Stroud of Berk Co., NC, also, Phebe and four children I have conveyed my part to Petway and Ferrington of Williamson Co., TN. I do nominate and appoint William McDade of Bedford Co., TN, my true and lawful Attorney to represent me in these sales &c. 11 April 1818. Wit: Edward Wade. Reg: 11 APril 1818.

Page 358 - 26 Dec 1816. Philip Burrow to Ephraim Burrow, 83 acres. Philip Burrow of Bedford Co., TN conveyed to Ephraim Burrow of Guilford Co., NC, land in Bedford Co., TN, on waters of Big Flat Creek. Borders John Boyd's old corner. Wit: Banks M. Burrow, Solomon Burrow and Jesse Mize. Reg: 21 May 1818.

Page 368 - Demsey Temple and Leonard C. Temple to John Sims. Demsey Temple and Leonard C. Temple, both of Bedford Co., TN, sold to John Sims of Bedford Co., land in Bedford Co., 200+ acres. Borders John Foster. Date 6 April 1818. Wit: Joshua Holt and A. Cannon. Reg: 23 May 1818.

Page 380 - 13 May 1817. Daniel Shipman to Elijah Parker, 10 acres. Daniel Shipman sold to Elijah Parker, both of Bedford Co., TN, land in Bedford Co., near head of Shipmans Creek. Borders land of Peter Daniel. Wit: Salley Shipman and Amelia Shipman. Reg: 26 May 1818.

Page 384 - 4 Sept 1815. Dougans devises to Daniel Gilchrist, 3100 acres. Jacob Fouts and his wife Mary Fouts, Lewis Fouts and his wife Sarah Fouts, William Montgomery and his wife Jane Montgomery, and Thomas Dougan of Clark County, Indiana Territory and Jacob Fouts and his wife Elenor Fouts of Wayne Co., Indiana Territory conveyed to Daniel Gilchrist of Bedford Co., TN, land in Rutherford Co., TN and Bedford Co., TN and on headwaters of the West Fork of Stones River and on the North Fork of Duck River. Borders Mathey Lock's tract. Reg: 27 May 1818.

Page 448 - 7 Feb 1818. Mary Ann Watkins to Elizabeth & Willis B. Watkins, all of Bedford Co., TN. Elizabeth and Willis B. Watkins, daughter and son of Mary Ann Watkins. For love and affection, granted unto Elizabeth and Willis B. Watkins, land in the Town of Shelbyville, Lot # 91. Wit: John H. Anderson and David McKissick. Reg: 1 July 1818.

Page 479 - William Dixon to John Dixon.
I, William Dixon of Bedford Co., TN, being at this time of sound mind and sober and of good memory, do for the good will, love and affection that I have, I do bear for my son John Dixon of Bedford Co., do give my tract of land whereon I now live in Bedford Co., on waters of Spring Creek. Borders W. Smith and Lacy McReynolds. Also give my negro man Frank and all my stock &c, tools and property and remains for the benefit of myself and my wife as long as we live. Wit: J. Atkinson and Jason Shuffield. Reg: 13 April 1818.

Page 486 (second page by this number) - Tennessee Grant to Abraham Byler, 35 acres. No. 10553. Part of Certificate No. 1637, dated 15 Nov 1813, issued to John C. McLemore and James Va<u>ulse</u>(Vasel) and entered 7 Aug 1815 by No. 8151. Granted to

DEED BOOK "H"

Abraham Byler, assignee of John C. McLemore and James Vaulse, land in Bedford Co., TN and Williamson Co., TN, on waters of Clements Creek. Borders Isaac Powell and George Doherty's land. Surveyed 19 Dec 1815. Reg: 6 Nov 1817.

Page 488 - John Williamson to Prisy Schooler.
I, John Williamson of Hawkins Co., TN, for love and affection for my daughter Pricilla Schooler wife of Samuel Schooler of Bedford Co., TN, and for $1.00, give a negro girl Amanda, in possession of L. Dotson. 24 Feb 1818. Wit: Robert J. McLemore and Lazarus Dotson. Reg: (no date).

Page 489 - Andrew Erwin to Potts & McKinne.
Andrew Erwin of Augusta Co., GA and his wife Jane Erwin sold to Potts & McKinne of City of New York, for money, 26 Mar 1818. Andrew Erwin and John McKinne, George Hargreaves, William Sims and Baird McKinne as witnesses, several tracts, all the following tracts of land and Town Lots in Franklin Co., TN, near head of South Fork of Duck River, 8500 acres, along with 2 grist mills, sawmill, one Stone Fort, one Public House, one Stone House, and one Stone Fort standing on said land. Also, tract of land in Bedford Co., TN, known by the Pleasant Retreat and Carter Nob<u>ol</u> Tract on which includes Three Forks of Duck River, to wit, the Middle Fork, the South Fork and the Western Fork together with a Brick Building House (Pleasant Retreat is what he called his house) and distillery situated thereon. Also, other land in Bedford Co., TN, 21500 acres over and above the foregoing, at this time cannot describe. Andrew Erwin and Jane Erwin his wife and Gideon, Joel and Joseph P. McKinne, 13 Sept 1817, endorsement bearing date 23 Mar 1818. Also, another tract of land, 200 acres in Lincoln Co., TN, which A. Erwin purchased of Samuel Buchanan, and also 620 acres on Elk River at the mouth of Swan Creek in Lincoln Co., TN, which Erwin purchased of Samuel Vance. Also, 500 acres on south side of Elk River originally granted to Andrew and James Patton. Also, The Bell Tavern Lot in Town of Fayetteville, on the northwest side of the Public Square. Also, one house and lot in Town of Fayetteville, TN, which cannot describe. Also, all that lot ot parcel of land in the City of Augusta, being the south east corner of the last known in plan of said City by No. 20. Also, other lands elsewhere. Wit: P. A. Willie, William H. Torrance and Benjamin H. Meigs (of Richmond Co., GA). Reg: 10 July 1818.

DEED BOOK "J" 1818 - 1819

Page 16 - Tennessee Grant to the heirs of Thomas Sorrels, 640 acres. No. 7636. For Military Service by Thomas Sorrels to North Carolina, Warrant No. 2961, dated 20 Sept 1785 and entered 19 Aug 1807 by No. 229. Granted to the heirs of Thomas Sorrels, land in Bedford Co., TN, on waters of Rock Creek. Surveyed 6 Jan 1807. Reg: 18 Aug 1818.

Page 18 - 1 May 1817. Clement Cannon to the Trustees of the <u>Dixon</u> (Dickson) Academy. Clement Cannon of Bedford Co., TN conveyed to the Chairman and Board of Trustees of the <u>Dickson</u> Academy and their successors in office. Clement Cannon donates to the Trustees for the use of the <u>Dixon</u> Academy, a certain tract or parcel of land situated and being in Bedford Co. Beginning on a stake four poles due north of the center of the north end of Martin Street in Shelbyville, running thence north 16 poles to a stake in Lencil Bobo's south boundary line, thence east with said Bobo's line 50 poles to a stake, thence south 16 poles to a stake on John Stone's line, thence west with said line 50 poles to the beginning. Containing 5 acres. Wit: George B. Balch and Littleberry Green. Reg: 18 Aug 1818.

Page 20 - Mary Ann Watkins to Elizabeth and W. Watkins, Bill of Sale. I, Mary Ann Watkins of Bedford Co., TN, for love and affection which I have for my daughter and son, Elizabeth and Willie B. Watkins and for $1.00, property, cow and calf, feather bed and furniture &c. 9 Feb 1818. Wit: Jno. H. Anderson and David McKissick. Reg: 18 Aug 1818.

Page 22 - William Dobbs to Elizabeth Copeland and heirs, Deed of Gift. I, William Dobbs of Bedford Co., TN, for love and affection for my daughter Elizabeth Copeland wife of Willis Copeland and the heirs of her body, I give unto Elizabeth Copeland, cattle. 1 Apr 1818. Reg: 18 Aug 1818.

Page 24 - Daniel Kinney to Mary E. Kinney, Deed of Gift. I, Daniel Kinney of Bedford Co., TN, give and bequeath unto my daughter Margaret E. Kinney, a negro girl Rachel. 23 Aug 1817. Reg: 18 Aug 1818.

Page 48 - 7 July 1818. Aaron Gamble to heirs of Enoch Doty, 100 acres. Aaron Gamble of Bedford Co., TN, conveyed to Melinda H. Doty and Preston L. Doty, heirs of Enoch Doty of Bedford Co., TN, land in Bedford Co., on headwaters of Powels Creek. Reg: 12 Sept 1818.

Page 54 - Andrew Erwin in Augusta, GA on 13 June 1818.

Page 56 - 3 July 1818. The heirs of Jacob Nichols, deceased, to Mede (Mead) Hale, 10 acres. The heirs of Jacob Nichols, deceased, namely Peggy Nichols wife and relict of said Jacob Nichols, deceased, Sally Nichols, Peggy Nichols, Caty Nichols, Nancy Nichols or Wiley Nichols, son of said Nancy, deceased, Betsy Nichols, Jacob Nichols and Suckey Nichols sold to Mead Hale, all of Bedford Co., TN, land in Bedford Co., on the waters of Noahs Fork. Wit: E. Watkins, Thomas Hale, ____ Starrett and John Brille. Reg: 22 Sept 1818.

Page 68 - Snelling & King to Frances King, 255 acres. 28 April 1818. Lemuel Snelling and John King, Executors of John King, deceased, of Bedford Co., TN sold to Frances King and her heirs, land on west side of the Hurricane Fork. Wit: John Payne and R. C. Thompson. Reg: 28 Sept 1818.

Page 122 - Anny Tharp to Thomzy Boothe. I, Anne Tharp, widow and relict of William Tharp of Bedford Co., TN, for $30.00 paid by Thomzy Boothe, all of dower land in Bedford Co., TN. 29 Sept 1818. Wit: Vincent Hearrlson and Edward Bruce. Reg: 5 Oct 1818.

Page 127 - James Erwin to A. Erwin, Bill of Sale. I, James Erwin sold to Andrew Erwin, Sr. of Richmond Co., GA, land on south fork of Duck River. Adjoins Wren Carter and Elias Yates and Riggs old place. Another tract on north side of Duck River and known as David Adams old place. Also, land bordering Hugh Davidson, one tract called Boyds old place. Also, land called George Whitson and Dady old place and land called Riley's old place including the mouth of Rileys Creek, also, tract called Byrons & Pickens old place, and others: Wall's place, Paynes old place, Hugh Brown's old place, King & McGee's tract, Murphee's & Harmons old place, Cyrus Sharpe old place, widow Pannels old place, and others. Wit: William Hodge and William Stevens. Signed 11 Sept 1818. Reg: 8 Oct 1818.

Page 147 - Jeremiah Whitworth to John S. Cook.
Jeremiah Whitworth of Buckingham Co., VA sold to John S. Cook and Abraham B. Routon, land in Buckingham Co., VA. Jeremiah Whitworth to Abraham B. Routon. Plat on page 149.

Page 152 - William Bond to William Knight. 25 June 1818.
William Bond and Frances Bond his wife of Williamson Co., TN sold to William Knight of Bedford Co., TN, land in Bedford Co. Borders Thomas and Alexander Greer's grant and Elisha Hall. Wit: J. Dougal and Melik. Brame. Reg: (no date)

Page 157 - William Oliver to William Knight.
William Oliver sold to William Knight, as guardian for me to my father's estate, property, negroes. 20 June 1817. Reg: 16 Nov 1818.

Page 158 - Devises of Ezekiel Alexander to Sarah Robison. 19 Jan 1813(8). Whereas we, Ezekiel Alexander and wife Agnes Alexander, Deborah Robison, Wallace Alexander, James Taylor Alexander, Ezekiel Roberson and my wife Elinor Roberson, all of Mecklenburg Co., NC, all legal heirs at law of Ezekiel Alexander, Sr., deceased, had bequeathed unto us together with us, ourselves, Sarah Robison of Bedford Co., TN by Ezekiel Alexander, deceased, land on Duck River of 1000 acres. Wit: William A. Robison and John C. Garrison. Reg: 16 Nov 1818.

Page 163 - Tennessee Grant to Nancy Gatewood, 13 acres. No.9527. Part of Certificate No. 627 & 1548, dated 18 July 1811 and 22 July 1812, issued to John G. Blount and Thomas Hubbard and entered 15 Apr 1814 by No. 6234. Granted to Nancy Gatewood, assignee of John G. Blount and Thomas Hubbard, land in Bedford Co., TN, on head waters of Rylie's Creek or Barren Fork of Duck River. Surveyed 5 April 1814. Reg: 23 Nov 1818.

Page 194 - Rachel Martin to Abraham Martin.
I, Rachel Martin of Bedford Co., TN, for the good will &c that I bear unto my nephew Abram Martin, Sr. of Bedford Co., TN, given a negro boy Jesse. 3 Oct 1818. Wit: Archibald Yell and Samuel Mitchell. Reg: 12 Dec 1818.

Page 202 - William Patterson to John H. Patterson.
I, William Patterson of Mecklenburg Co., NC, appointed John H. Patterson my grandson of Bedford Co., TN, as my Attorney. Reg: 23 Dec 1818.

Page 208 - Forrest & Others to Lucy Hurst. Power of Attorney.
We, Jonathan Forrest, James Mansfield, Aaron Collier, all of Lincoln Co., KY, appoint Lucy Hurst of Bedford Co., TN our Attorney and made acknowledged to William Hurst of Bedford Co., TN, to receive any monies of an undivided tract of land of William Hurst, Jr., deceased. 80 acres in Bedford Co., on east waters of Big Flat Creek. Borders William Haislett. Wit: Reuben Menafee and William Hutcherson. Reg: in Lincoln Co., KY

on 20 Oct 1818. Reg: (no date).

Page 210 - We, John Hurst, John Coffey* Elizabeth Hurst, James Hurst and Sary Hurst, all of Bedford Co., TN, appointed Lucy Hurst of Bedford Co., our Attorney. 80 acres belonging to the estate of William Hurst, Sr., of Bedford Co. Reg: 19 Sept 1818.

Page 214 - Devises of Hurst to William Hurst. 19 Dec 1818. John Hurst, Jonathan Hurst, James Hurst, John Coffey* Aaron Collier, James Mannafee (Menafee), Elizabeth Hurst and Sarah Hurst, heirs of William Hurst, Sr., deceased, late of Bedford Co., TN by their Attorney Lucy Hurst of Bedford Co. sold to William Hurst, Jr. of Bedford Co., land in Bedford Co., on east waters of Big Flat Creek. Borders school land. About 80 acres. Reg: 5 Jan 1819. * Spelled in instrument as Calffy.

Page 216 - Francis McCamey and wife to Robert and John McCamey. I, Francis McCamey and Catharine my wife formerly Catharine Galbreath, both of Bedford Co., TN, conveyed unto our two sons John McCamey and John McCamey, both of Bedford Co., land in Bedford Co., on waters of Big Flat Creek, land being Willed and Bequeathed by William Galbreath, deceased, to his daughter Catharine Galbreath now Catharine McKamey, about 220 acres. 11 Mar 1818. Wit: Joshua Holt, John Sutton and Joseph Steele, Justices of the Court. Reg: 6 Jan 1819.

Page 231 - 20 Oct 1817. William Doherty to H. Bradford, Deed of Gift. William Doherty sold to the heirs of Hamilton Bradford and Jane Bradford, all of Bedford Co., TN, for love and affection that William Doherty has for the heirs of Hamilton and Jane Bradford, a negro girl Rachel. Wit: Edmund Gray and John Bradford. Reg: 7 Oct 1818.

Page 233 - 7 Aug 1818. James H. McReynolds to James Joices, 99 acres. James H. McReynolds, Attorney for Eliza D. McReynolds and James H. McReynolds, himself, both of Alabama Territory, Tuscaloosa County, sold to James Joice of Bedford Co., TN, land in Bedford Co., on both sides of Spring Creek, land being part of 1000 acres entered in the name of Samuel Kerr and transferred to Benjamin Williams of State of North Carolina and by him Benjamin Williams, deceased, to Lucy McReynolds, in trust for her children, the heirs of Thomas McReynolds, deceased, the land being a part fell to Eliza D. McReynolds as her legacy of the 1000 acres. Reg: 7 Oct 1818.

Page 235 - 15 Aug 1818. McReynolds to Richard Graham, 74 acres. Eliza D. McReynolds by her Attorney James H. McReynolds and James H. McReynolds, himself, both of Tuscaloosa Co., Alabama Territory sold to Richard Graham of Bedford Co., TN, land in Bedford Co., TN, on waters of Spring Creek, it being part of 1000 acres of land entered in the name of Samuel Kerr and transferred to Benjamin Williams of North Carolina, Moore County, and by deed to Lucy McReynolds in trust for her children and heirs of Thomas McReynolds, deceased. Borders Edward Whitworth. Reg: 7 Oct 1818.

Page 241 - 8 Nov 1818. Jonathan Wilson to William Meek, 100 acres. Jonathan Wilson and Isreal Wilson Moore, Executors of the Last Will and Testament of Samuel Wilson, deceased, of Sumner Co., TN sold to William Meek of Bedford Co., TN, land in Bedford Co., TN, on Spring Creek. Borders James Wilson,

Samuel Wilson and Spring Creek. Wit: John Meek and James Wilson. Reg: 7 Jan 1819.

Page 243 - 28 Sept 1795. William Galbreath to William Galbreath, Jr. William Galbreath of Orange Co., NC sold to William Galbreath, Jr. of Mount Pleasant Township, York Co., PA, land, plantation or tract of land on south side of Duck River and on east side of Sugar Creek. Borders William Galbreath and Wllliam Chamberlain, and other buildings. Reg: 13 Jan 1819.

Page 265 - 15 Sept 1818. Fouts to Thomas Dougan. Jacob Fouts and his wife Mary (Polly) Fouts, Lewis Fouts and his wife Sarah Fouts, William Montgomery and his wife Jane Montgomery of Clark Co., Indiana, and Jacob Fouts and his wife Elenor Fouts of Wayne Co., Indiana sold to Thomas Dougan of Clark Co., Indiana, land in Bedford Co., TN, on headwaters of Sugar Creek and Powels Creek, it being part of a North Carolina Grant to Anthony Sharp and Thomas Dougan. Reg: 26 Feb 1819.

Page 276 - 23 Aug 1817. Daniel Kinney to William Kinney, 100 acres. William Kinney, son of Daniel Kinney and Elizabeth Kinney his wife. Daniel Kinney bequeathed land to William Kinney. Land in Bedford Co., TN, on waters of Sinking Creek. Borders Daniel Kinney. Wit: Benjamin W. H. Medearis and Jos. Harrison. Reg: 9 Dec 1819.

Page 277 - By Virtue of a Writ by Supreme Court of Errors and Appeals of 4th Circuit.(Land south of Farmington) 768 acres. We command you that of the Real Estate of 768 acres which was of Thomas Dillon and which at the time of his death descended to Charles R. Dillon, Mary Ann Dillon, Elizabeth Dillon, and Edward Dillon, heirs of the said Thomas Dillon, deceased, late in your County (Bedford Co., TN), you cause to be sold 768 acres of 2560 acres granted to James Wall, to satisfy debts. Heirs and additional heirs: Charles R. Dillon, Mary Ann Dillon, Elizabeth Sarah Dillon, George K. Dillon, Thomas David Dillon, and Edward Dillon. Land purchased by George Bernard. 23 July 1816. Reg: 9 Mar 1819.

Page 297 - Jonathan Ward to Stephen Boothe, 70 acres. 24 Oct 1816. Jonathan Ward of Bedford Co., TN sold to Stephen Boothe, Executor and Tounsey Boothe, Executor of the estate of John Boothe, deceased, both of Bedford Co., TN, land in Bedford Co., TN, on waters of Alexander Creek, it being part of a 3000 grant to Ebenezer Alexander by North Carolina. Borders Joseph Wallace. Wit: John Davis, Peter E. Ragsdale, and William Knott. Reg: 15 Mar 1819.

Page 321 - 6 Sept 1817. Walter Sims to John G. Sims, 2448 acres. Walter Sims of Philadelphia, PA sold to John G. Sims of Davidson Co., TN, land in Bedford Co., TN, on both sides of Duck river, being part of a 5000 acre surveyed for David Smith and granted to Robert Smith the father of Robert W. Smith. Wit: Walter W. Sims and David Sims. Reg: 25 Nov 1819.

Page 325 - 7 July 1818. John Roberson to Moses M. Roberson, 100 acres. John Roberson conveyed to his son Moses M. Roberson, all of Bedford Co., TN, land in Bedford Co., on waters of Sugar Creek. Borders John Roberson's tract whereon he now lives and Thomas Gray. Reg: 26 Mar 1819.

DEED BOOK "J"

Page 339 - Tennessee Grant to Samuel Bell, 115 acres. No. 11719. Part of Certificate No. 2282, dated 4 Jan 1816, issued to James Witherow and entered 16 Sept 1817 by No. 9562. Granted to Samuel Bell, assignee of James Witherow, land in Bedford Co., TN, on west side of Weakleys Creek. Borders John Lock, Ebenezer Alexander, Robert Allison, Nathaniel Walker and John Byler. Surveyed 30 Jan 1817. Reg: 6 Apr 1819.

Page 343 - Tennessee Grant to John Byler and Samuel Bell, 62+ acres. No. 11863. Part of Certificate No. 2285 & 2460, dated 4 Jan 1816 & 29 Aug 1816, issued to James Witherow and the heirs of David Carson and entered 19 Sept 1816 by No. 9599. Granted to John Byler and Samuel Bell, assignees of James Witherow, land in Bedford Co., TN, on west side of Weakleys Creek. Borders Ebenezer Alexander. Surveyed 5 Jan 1817. Reg: 6 Apr 1819.

Page 345 - Tennessee Grant to Samuel Bell, 50 acres. No. 11720. Part of Certificate No. 2282, dated 4 Jan 1816, issued to James Witherow and entered 10 Sept 1816 by No. 9552. Granted to Samuel Bell, assignee of James Witherow, land in Bedford Co., TN, on Alexanders Creek. Borders Ebenezer Alexander and Joseph Dixon. Surveyed 20 Dec 1816. Reg: 7 Apr 1819.

Page 348 - Na. Hendrix of Carter Co., TN appointed Abraham Byler, Esq. of Bedford Co., TN, his Attorney, to make an Warrant and make valid as I could do with my own assessment, the Warrant issued to Joseph and George Greenway and heirs of John Webb, deceased. 27 Dec 1817. Wit: Andrew Taylor, John Love, Thomas Maxwell and John Maxwell. Reg: 15 Apr 1819.

Page 356 - Articles between the Devises of David Wilson, dec'd. Articles of agreement intered into between the legatees of David Wilson, Deceased, about the division of land in Bedford Co., TN, on the north side of Duck River and a Caney Spring Creek, about 1096 acres granted to David Wilson, deceased, by North Carolina of 1788. Borders lands of the heirs of Zachariah Wilson, deceased, for Lot # 1; Lot # 2, James A. Wilson Lot conveyed to Zachariah Wilson; Lot # 3, William Wilson's Lot # 4; Mark Dodd's Lot # 5; Jonathan Wilson's Lot # 6; William Steels' Lot # 7; Z(achariah) Wilson, Jr.'s Lot # 8; David Wilson's Lot # 9. Will of David Wilson's Will made and division made 19 Sept 1803. Signed by: Elizabeth Wilson, William Wilson administrator of estate of Zachariah Wilson, James Wilson, William Wilson, Mark Dodd, Jonathan Wilson, William Steele, Zacheus Wilson and David Wilson. Signed 11 Auf 1817. Wit: Ezekiel Cherry and John Wallace. Reg: 7 Oct 1818.

Page 358 - Tennessee Grant to Amos McGuire, 7 acres. No. 1191-. Part of Certificate No. 2181, dated 25 Sept 1815, issued to William P. Anderson and entered 11 Jan 1816 by No. 876-. Granted to Amos McGuire, assignee of William P. Anderson, land in Bedford Co., TN, on waters of Falling Creek of Hurricane Creek. Borders land where said McGuire now lives, school land and George Doherty. Surveyed 9 Oct 1816. Reg: 4 May 1819.

DEED BOOK "K" 1819 - 1819

Page 3 - 23 Oct 1818. J. Tagert and Jos. McCarty to J. Robertson, 150 acres. James Tagert and Joseph McCarty of Alabama

Territory and Washington County, Executors of the Last Will and Testament of Jacob McCarty, deceased, sold to John Robertson of Bedford Co., TN, land in Bedford Co., south side of Duck River on Sugar Creek, it being part of a tract granted to George Martin, Richard Martin, Amos Balch by No. 16. Borders Holt's line, James Ross, Thomas and Alexander Greer. Wit: Thomas Greer and Joseph Greer. Reg: 14 May 1819.

Page 6 - John Cathey to Trustees of Union Meetinghouse, 1 acre. 13 June 1818. John Cathey conveyed to Joel Casy, Mark Dodd, George Allen, Ezekiel Cherry and Joseph Wallace, Trustees of the Union Meeting House and their successors in office, for $2.00, 1 acre of land. Also privilege of the spring near the said stage &c. Signed 13 July 1818. Wit: Samuel McCall and Hugh McClellan. Reg: 4 May 1819.

Page 12 - Joshua E. White &c to Richard Richardson, John Bolton, Carter Bolton and Darham T. Hall, all of Savanah, GA, Bill of Sale. 12 Mar 1819. Merchants in Trading, tracts of land of 309 acres in Bedford Co., TN. Borders the Barren Fork, Wren Carter, Elias Tate and Fergus Hall, Payne and Roberts. (Mortgage). Reg: 1 May 1819.

Page 68 - 11 Jan 1819. Between Jacob Waggoner sold to Peggy Nichols wife and relict of Jacob Nichols, deceased, Sally Nichols, Peggy Nichols, Caty Nichols, Nancy Nichols or Wiley, son of said heir Nancy Betsy Nichols, Jacob Nichols and Suckey Nichols, all of Bedford Co., TN, 10 acres, conveyed to the heirs of Jacob Nichols, deceased, land in Bedford Co., TN, on eastern waters of Noah's Fork of the Garrison Fork of Duck River, being a part of a tract entered by Joseph Waggoner. Reg: 24 May 1819.

Page 78 - Samuel Davidson to Catharine Davidson, Bond.
I, John Davidson of Rutherford Co., TN firmly bound unto Catharine Davidson of Bedford Co., TN for $3000.00. 31 Dec 1818. The condition of the above obligation is such that whereas my son Samuel Davidson on or about 8th of Sept last did depart this life and left no heir of his body to represent him. He died in possession of sundry pieces of property of both real and personal in the Town of Shelbyville. Settlement of estate should be made without delay. Catherine Davidson will release all her right title &c in the Tan Yard Lots in Shelbyville owned in co-partnership of Samuel W. Givins and Samuel Davidson to my son James Davidson, all her rights to a negro girl Dinah. Signed by John Davidson. Wit: Marget ______ and Samuel W. Givins. Reg: 25 May 1819.

Page 98 - 14 Nov 1814. John Peacock to Adam Peacock.
John Peacock, Jr. conveyed to Adam Alexander Peacock, son of Thomas Alexander Peacock. John Peacock for love and affection he has for Adam, land in Bedford Co., TN, on waters of the Wartrace Fork. Wit: William Murphy and W. Loyd. Reg: 27 May 1819.

Page 112 - 28 Nov 1818. John Wilson to James Wilson, 420 acres. John Wilson of Sumner Co., TN conveyed to James Wilson of Bedford Co., TN, for love and affection for his son, land in Bedford Co., TN, on Spring Creek. Wit: John Little and John Wilson. Reg: 28 May 1819.

Page 186 - Catherine Davidson to John Davidson.
John Davidson of Rutherford Co., TN has release and set over

to her and her heirs and assignees forever, one half of the house and lot which her husband Samuel Davidson lived and died in Shelbyville, all the property of her husband, personal property &c, tan yard lot in Shelbyville he owned with Samuel W. Givins, to James Davidson and her husband. Wit: Polly Kirk and Sally Haistell. Reg: 4 June 1819.

Page 188 - North Carolina Grant to Michael Robertson, 1500 acres. No. 37. Land on north side of Duck River. Beginning under clift of Duck River about 3 miles above the mouth of Falling Creek, Martin Phifer's corner. Surveyed 26 July 1795. Reg: in Davidson Co., TN in Book B, folio 250. Reg: 23 Nov 1790.

Page 194 - 3 Apr 1819. John Robertson to Robert A. Robertson, 150 acres. John Robertson of Bedford Co., TN for love and affection for Robert A. Robertson, granted and given land in Bedford Co., TN, on south side of Duck River on waters of Sugar Creek. Land being part of a grant to George Martin and Richard Martin and Amos Balch by No. 16. Borders Holt's land, James Ross' land, Thomas and Alexander Greer. Reg: 23 June 1819.

Page 202 - 22 Dec 1818. A. Shook to Moses Garrett, 46+ acres. Abraham Shook sold to the heirs of Moses Garrett, deceased, of Bedford Co., TN, land in Bedford Co. on headwaters of Big Flat Creek. For $400.00 paid by Cully Word, administrator of Moses Garrett, deceased. Borders Michael Prewett. Wit: William Hix and Cully Word. Reg: 23 June 1819.

Page 215 - 24 Feb 1819. Joseph Hastings & others to Stephen Hastings &c, 50 acres. Joseph Hastings, Robert Hastings, Thomas Cates and Martha Cates his wife, Samuel Pollock and Susanna Pollock his wife, all of Bedford Co., TN sold to Stephen Hastings and Henry Hastings, land in Bedford CO., TN, on waters of Big Flat Creek. Borders Ridge dividing Little Flat Creek from Big Flat Creek. Wit: Nathaniel Hubard, William H. Cates and Thomas Sanders. Reg: 24 June 1819.

Page 278 - 2 Feb 1819. Sarah Long to Charles Long. Sarah Long formerly Sarah Elliott, sister of Simon Elliott, deceased, of Bedford Co., TN sold to Charles and Isaac Elliott. Charles Elliott of Bedford Co., TN and Isaac Elliott of Sumner Co., TN, land and interests in real estate of Simon Elliott had at his death and which said Sarah had any title or claim by descent. Wit: S. E. Long and Hugh Long. Reg: 30 June 1819.

Page 286 - 17 Nov 1818. James Lock to Jesse Lay, 231 acres. James Lock of Rowan Co., NC sold to Jesse Lay of Bedford Co., TN, land in Bedford CO., on waters of North Fork of Duck River, it being a part of a 2000 acre tract granted to the heirs of John Lock, deceased, by State of Tennessee, also, a part of a division of George Lock. Wit: William Lock and Charles Wade. Reg: 1 July 1819.

Page 312 - 2 Feb 1819. Hugh Wall to Charles Long and Isaac Elliott. (Same as instrument on page 278).

Page 314 - 20 Jan 1816. William Hopwood to Willis Hopwood, Bill of Sale. I, William Hopwood of Bedford Co., TN, for $1.00 conveyed to Willis Hopwood of Bedford Co., one negro man slave Joshua, to be delivered to Willis Hopwood upon the death of myself and Nancy Hopwood. Wit: Hugh Smiley and John Bingham.

Page 316 - 7 Jan 1812. Redding Jones to Fanning Jones, 2100 acres. Fanning Jones sold to Redding Jones, both of Wake Co., NC, for $1000.00, land on south side of Duck River and on both sides of Rock Creek. It being the same tract of land conveyed to Fanning JOnes as surveying executors of Tengnal Jones, Sr., deceased, by deed surveyed 15 Dec 1810. Wit: William Daniel and Wiley Moss. Reg: 7 July 1819.

Page 318 - 26 May 1818. George W. Campbell to John McIver, PA I, George W. Campbell of Nashville, Davidson Co., TN, appoint John McIver of Fairfax Co., VA as my Attorney, to sell and dispose of the following land. One tract of 200 acres in Knox Co., TN, on south side of Holston River. One tract of 1280 acres in Maury Co., TN, adjoining Gordon's Ferry tract. One tract 424½ acres located partly in Bedford and Rutherford Co., TN, on waters of West Fork of Stones River. One tract of 800 acres in Bedford Co., TN, devised to me of the late George Doherty, it being same tract sold to Alfred Balch. Land in Lincoln Co., TN, Giles Co., TN, and Maury Co., TN, lands purchased by me in partnership with John Childress, Jenking Whiteside, William P. Anderson from said John McIver, assignee of Josiah Wilson and lands in name of Martin Armstrong and my portion. Wit: Robert A. Adams and Thomas Crutcher. Recorded in Nashville 18 Jan 1819. Reg: (no date).

Page 328 - Ephraim Burrow to Philip Burrow & Others, Trustees for Meeting House. 24 Oct 1818. I, Ephraim Burrow of Bedford Co., TN for $2.00 paid by Philip Burrow, Joshua Holt, John McNatt, Thomas Jones, Solomon Burrow, Trustees in Trust for the Methodist Episcopal Church and their successors in office, land beginning at north east of Pleasant Garden Meeting House and borders Philip Burrow. 1 acre and 20 poles. Wit: Banks M. Burrow and Ishmael Burrow. Reg: 20 July 1819.

Page 330 - 29 July 1815. William Long to Sarah Long, 50 acres. William Long of Lincoln Co., TN sold to Sarah Long of Bedford Co., TN, land in Bedford Co., on Caney Spring Creek. Borders Dry Creek. Wit: C. Long, Simon E. Long and Hugh Long. Reg: 20 July 1819.

Page 337 - 28 Dec 1818. Nancy Butler to Hugh Baird, 5 acres. Nancy Butler and James Butler her son sold to Hugh Baird, land in Bedford Co., TN, on waters of Big Flat Creek. Wit: William Ray and John Boswell. Reg: 20 July 1819.

Page 356 - 28 Dec 1818. Daniel Philips to William Fisher. Bill of Sale. We, Daniel Philips and Lucinda Philips of Maury Co., TN sold to William Fisher of Bedford Co., TN, negro boy. Wit: Henry Rone and Silvanus Fisher. Reg: 26 July 1819.

Page 357 - 11 Feb 1819. David Bell to Isaac H. Bell. I, David Bell of Bedford Co., TN, for $300.00, sold to Isaac H. Bell, all perishable property that I now claim and possess, together with plantation, & other articles and stock &c. Wit: William Allison and John Byler. Reg: 26 July 1819.

Page 358 - Tennessee Grant to Henry Pickle, 30 acres. No. 8584. Part of Certificate No. 823, dated 30 Dec 1814, issued to William P. Anderson and entered 24 Feb 1815 by No. 7577. Granted to Henry Pickle, assignee of William P. Anderson, land in Bedford Co., TN, on waters of Bryants Creek. Borders Joseph

DEED BOOK "K"

Neill, James S. Turrentine. Reg: 26 July 1819.

Page 362 - 28 Sept 1817. Ebenezer Alexander to James Morrison, 1000 acres. Ebenezer Alexander of Logan Co., KY sold to James Morrison of Mecklenburg Co., NC, land on North Fork of Duck River. Borders Joseph Wallens(?). Land being tract granted to Ebenezer Alexander, dated 10 July 1788. Reg: 26 July 1819.

Page 369 - 7 July 1818. Jonathan and Joseph D. Graves to Walter Sims, 391 acres. Jonathan Graves and Joseph D. Graves of Bedford Co., TN sold to Walter Sims of Philadelphia, PA, land in Bedford Co., TN, on both sides of Duck River, being part of a tract granted to Jonathan Graves by North Carolina by Patent and date 25 Nov 1797 and on which Jonathan Graves now lives. Borders Duck River, James Dixon and Robert Walker. Wit: John A. Hightower and John J. Green. Reg: 26 July 1819.

DEED BOOK "L" 1819 - 1820

Page 11 - S. and J. N. Porter to J. C. and N. E. Coldwell. 27 Feb 1817. S(amuel) and J. N.(John N.) Porter sold to J. C. and N. E. Coldwell, land in Bedford Co., TN, it being in Town of Shelbyville, on east side of the Public Square and being part of Lot No. 39, where Levi C. Roberts and ourselves have commenced building a brick house. Lot is 18 feet in front and length of said lot in back. Wit: William R. Hess and S. Henton. Reg: 28 July 1819.

Page 39 - Henry Miller to Sally, Nancy and Polly Walker. I, Henry Miller of Bedford Co., TN, on 2 Dec 1812, executor to John Walker estate of Bedford Co., deceased, to convey land in Bedford Co., on waters of Clems Creek, land which was granted to me by Tennessee Grant No. 3139, dated 11 July 1811. Borders George Doherty, Robert McCuistion's Occupant Claim. John Walker has departed this life since the contract, intestate, leaving three heirs, to wit, Polly Walker, Nancy Walker, and Sally Walker, lawful children of John Walker, deceased. This indenture made 30 Jan 1817. Wit: J. Haskell and Alfred M. Harris. Reg: 3 Aug 1819.

Page 43 - 22 May 1819. John Smith & Others to F. Haggard, PA We, John Smith in right of his wife Patsy Haggard now Patsy Smith and James Haggard being the legal heirs of Samuel Haggard, Sr., deceased, all of Bedford Co., TN, appoint Francis Haggard of Rone Co., TN, our Attorney, to act in their name to receive and recover, sell &c, land in Georgia, in County of Jackson, on waters of Turkey Creek, being the tract that Samuel Haggard, Sr., deceased, formerly lived on and died in possession of same. To attend to all the estate of our father, Samuel Haggard, Sr., deceased. Signed by John Smith, Jas. Haggard, Samuel Haggard and Alfred L. Haggard. Wit: John Meadows and Jesse Hall. Reg: 14 Aug 1819.

Page 45 - Tennessee Grant to Robert Allison, 40 acres. No.12493. Part of Certificate No. 2180, dated 25 Sept 1818, issued to William P. Anderson and entered 29 Dec 1818 by No. 8721. Granted to Robert Allison, assignee of William P. Anderson, land on waters of Clems Creek. Borders Jason Sheffield, John Atkinson and James McReynolds. Surveyed 4 Mar 1816. Reg: 17 Sept 1819.

Page 47 - Tennessee Grant to John Jones, 10 acres. No. 12491. Part of Certificate No. 66(?), dated 27 Feb 1810, issued to William P. Anderson and entered 20 Mar 1815 by No. 7655. Granted to John Jones, assignee of William P. Anderson, land in Bedford Co., TN, between Clems Creek and Wilson Creek. Borders Grant to Jonathan Graves. Surveyed 11 July 1815. Reg: 17 Sept 1819.

Page 49 - Tennessee Grant to John Jones, 10 acres. No. 12498. Certificate No. 2739, dated 22 July 1815, issued to Larken Edwards and entered 14 Sept 1815 by No. 8312. Granted to John Jones, assignee of Larken Edwards, land in Bedford Co., TN, on the Dividing Ridge between Wilsons and Clems Creek. Borders Graves survey. Surveyed 28 Mar 1816. Reg: 17 Sept 1819.

Page 51 - Tennessee Grant to Kimbrough Allison, 25 acres. No. 12499. Part of Certificate No. 1812, dated 7 July 1814, issued to Thomas Shute and entered 10 Oct 1815 by No. 8430. Granted to Kimbrough Allison, assignee of Thomas Shute, land in Bedford Co., TN, on waters of Clems Creek and Wilsons Creek. Surveyed 10 Mar 1816. Reg: 17 Sept 1819.

Page 71 - Andrew Erwin of Augusta, Richmond Co., GA, 9 Nov 1818 to Peter Hufman of Orange Co., NC.

Page 73 - 22 July 1818. Minos Cannon, Sr. to Minos Cannon, Jr., Robert Cannon and A. B. Morton. Minos Cannon, Sr. of Williamson Co., TN sold to Minos Cannon, Jr., Robert Cannon and Abraham B. Morton of Bedford Co., TN, land in Bedford Co., in the Town of Shelbyville, a part of Lot No. 54, fronting on the Public Square, including the house where Maj. Thomas Moore now lives. Reg: 21 Sept 1819.

Page 77 - 1 Oct 1818. Andrew Erwin to Jane Patton, 17+ acres. I, Andrew Erwin of Augusta, Georgia sold to Jane Patton of Bedford Co., TN, widow of Thomas Patton, late of Bedford Co., land in Bedford Co., on Noah's Fork of the Garrison Fork of Duck River, a part of a grant from North Carolina to John Gray Blount and Thomas Blount, No. 217. Wit: Neely S. Patton and Daniel Patton. Reg: 21 Sept 1819.

Page 96 - 15 Jan 1817. James & Clinton Norvell to John Norvell, 42+ acres. James Norvell and Clinton Norvell sold to John Norvell, all of Bedford Co., TN, land in Bedford Co., on the Wartrace Fork of Duck River, the west side of the said Fork. Borders John Norvell, Burrell Featherston, and Wartrace Fork of Duck River. Wit: William Murphry and John Davis. Reg: 23 Sept 1819.

Page 104 - James Morrison to Robert Morrison, 1000 acres. I, James Morrison of Mecklenburg Co., NC, having conveyed land to me by Ebenezer Alexander of Logan Co., KY, which ought to have been conveyed to my father for payment of said tract but through a mistake the deed has been conveyed to me the said James Morrison. I, therefore do for myself and my heirs &c do convey to Robert Morrison my father, the aforesaid tract of land on the North Fork of Duck River. Borders Joseph Wallace. This 27 Mar 1808. Reg: 24 Sept 1819.

Page 118 - 6 Apr 1819. James Norsworthy to Thomas Norsworthy, 164 acres. James Norsworthy for love and affection for his son Thomas Norsworthy, conveyed to him, land in Bedford Co., TN, on the waters of Sugar Creek. Land being one half of a tract granted to James Norsworthy for his Military Service to North Carolina, Warrant No. 144, dated 22 Dce 1806 and entered 21 Aug 1807 by No. 276. Wit: Neal Norsworthy and William F. Doty. Reg: 28 Sept 1819.

Page 130 - 7 July 1819. John Barrett to Jemima Barrett, 50 acres. John Barrett conveyed to Jemima Barrett, both of Bedford Co., TN, land in Bedford Co., on the waters of Powels Creek, adjoining land of Enoch Doty and Aaron Gambill, during her natural life and I for myself and my heirs, Executors &c do convey to Jemima Barrett all said land. Wit: Daniel Williams and David Rozar. Reg: 1 Oct 1819.

Page 142 - 9 Nov 1818. Jesse Burnam to Hickerson Burnam, PA I, Jesse Burnam appointed Hickerson Burnam, his Attorney, to attend to Thomas Bell of Bedford Co., TN, a General Warrant Right & Title to 50 acres in Bedford Co., on Bryans and Sinking Creek, a bond given by me to Thomas Bell. Wit: James Nall and William Burnham. Reg: 13 July 1819.

Page 143 - 9 Nov 1818. George Lock to Mary Smith, 250 acres. Plat of land on page 143. I have conveyed to Mary Smith of Rowan Co., NC, agreeable to the Last Will and Testament of George Lock, deceased, land in Bedford Co., TN, between the North Fork and Weakleys Creek. Borders lands of William Short. Wit: William and James Lock. Reg: 2 Oct 1819.

Page 153 - 8 Nov 1816. Ann White to John Lane, PA
I, Anna White of Raleigh, NC appoint friend John Lane of Bedford Co., TN, my Attorney, for me and in my name as Executrix of the Last Will and Testament of my husband William White, to divide or cause to be divided, 3 tracts of land in Tennessee between Newton Cannon, Esq. and the Devises of William White, deceased. 9 July 1807. Wit: William Hill. Reg: 13 Oct 1819.

Page 162 - 4 Mar 1819. William Patterson, Sr. to John H. Patterson. I, William Patterson, Sr. of Mecklenburg Co., NC, appointed my grandson John H. Patterson of Bedford Co., TN, my Attorney, to sell or receive any grant locations or warrants for my lands. Reg: 28 Oct 1819.

Page 169 - 13 Apr 1819. Thomas G. Polk and Mary E. Polk to Joseph Sloss, 493½ acres. Thomas G. Polk and Mary E. Polk his wife, both of Mecklenburg Co., NC sold to Joseph SLoss of Bedford Co., land in Bedford Co., on south side of Duck River, it being granted to Richard Trotter by Tennessee No. 2499. Borders Jones' line and John Lewis' tract. Recorded in Franklin, TN. Reg: 2 June 1819.

Page 171 - 24 Aug 1818. George Hargrove, John McKenne, William Sims and Barna McKinne, assignees of A. Erwin, A. Erwin Groc. & Co., Erwin & Co. sold to James Erwin, 17205 acres. George Hargrove and others by their Attorney Andrew Erwin of Augusta, GA sold to James Erwin of Bedford Co., TN, he being the highest bidder at Public Sale. I, J. McKinne, at the brick house near the Three Forks of Duck River, conveyed to James Erwin. Borders one tract called "Walls Old PLace" on south fork of Duck River. Adjoining Walls Old Place, Riggs Old Place, and other tracts. Reg: 2 Dec 1819.

DEED BOOK "L"

Page 181 - 15 Sept 1819. James Neill, Sr. to James & John L. Neill, 120 acres. James Neill, Sr. conveyed to James Neill, Jr. and John Neill, land in Bedford Co., TN, on waters of Sinking Creek, it being part of land conveyed to James Neill, Sr. on 29 July 1817 by Newton Cannon. Wit: Alexander L. Neill and Andrew Neill. Reg: 15 Oct 1819.

Page 189 - 5 July 1819. Susanna Pennington to Isaac Whitworth, 100 acres. Susanna Pennington and Levi Pennington, administrators of Elijah Pennington, Sr., deceased, sold to Isaac Whitworth land in Bedford Co., TN, near head of a hollow, the waters of Noahs Fork of the Garrison Fork. Wit: John King and John Pennington. Reg: 15 Oct 1819.

Page 213 - 22 Oct 1819. George Haywood to John J. Daniel, 50 acres. George Haywood of Lauderdale Co., Alabama Territory sold to John J. Daniel, Executor of William Daniel of North Carolina, land in Bedford Co., TN, on West Fork of Rock Creek. Wit: David Craghead and James B. Craghead. Reg: 29 Nov 1819.

Page 223 - Plat of David Adams tract. Reg: 8 Dec 1819.

Page 235 - 15 Dec 1819. Jonathan Graves to Zadock Daniel, 160 acres. Jonathan Graves of Lauderdale Co., Alabama sold to Zadock Daniel of Wake Co., NC, land in Bedford Co., TN, on waters of Wilson Creek. Wit: Theo. F. Bradford and John Sims. Reg: 26 Dec 1819.

Page 237 - 2 Jan 1809. Jonathan Graves to Zadock Daniel, 600 acres. Jonathan Graves of Rutherford Co., TN sold to Zadock Daniel of Granville Co., NC, land in Bedford Co., TN, on North Fork. Wit: Lenord H. Sims and J. S. D. Graves. Reg: 26 Dec 1819.

Page 239 - 27 Nov 1817. Wilson Coats to William Coats, 75 acres. Wilson Coats conveyed for love and affection he bears for his son William Coats, land in Bedford Co., TN, it being part of Smith's 2000 acre tract. Wit: J. L. Neill, W. P. Whitny, and John Williams. Reg: 9 Dec 1818.

Page 245 - 6 Sept 1819. Abraham Wood to Arthur Campbell, 747 acres. Abraham Wood, Attorney in fact for Abraham Wood, Jr. sold to Arthur Campbell, land in bedford Co., TN, on waters of Flat Creek. Wit: William Ray, Solomon Campbell and Benjamin Campbell. Reg: 15 Oct 1819.

Page 247 - 25 Sept 1819. John Allison, Sr. to John Allison, Jr., 153 acres. John Ellison conveyed to his son John Ellison, Jr., land in Bedford Co., TN, on waters of Rich Creek. Borders Thomas Sorrels. Wit: Thomas Dryden and Joseph S. Ellison. Reg: 27 Dec 1819.

Page 250 - 21 Sept 1819. John Ellison to Thomas Ellison, 140 acres. John Ellison conveyed to Thomas Ellison his son, land in Bedford Co., TN, on waters of Rich Creek. Borders Jason Thompson and John Null. Wit: Thomas Dryden and Joseph S. Ellison. Reg: 27 Dec 1819.

Page 319 - Tennessee Grant to John Thompson, 25 acres. No. 5332. An Entry made in Surveyor's office by No. 60721, dated 25 Feb 1814. Founded on a Certificate for 101 acres of land, dated

17 Jan 1814. Granted to John Thompson and his heirs, land in Bedford Co., TN, on Duck river. Borders Anthony Newman's tract and Benjamin Carr, and school land. Surveyed 14 Oct 1814. Reg: 31 Dec 1819.

Page 321 - Tennessee Grant to John Thompson, 25 acres. No. 5329. An Entry No. 7546, dated 10 Feb 1815, Certificate No. 1896, issued to John Thompson, land in Bedford Co., TN, on south side of Duck River. Borders Thompson's land and school land. Surveyed 10 July 1815. Reg: 31 Dec 1819.

Page 323 - Tennessee Grant to John Thompson, 101+ acres. No. 5331. Certificate No. 649, dated 29 Mar 1814, issued to John Thompson, land dated 17 Jan 1814. Granted to John Thompson, land of 76+ acres in Bedford Co., TN, on south side of North Fork of Duck River. Beginning at the mouth of a branch running into North Fork. Borders school land. Surveyed 14 Oct 1814. Reg: 31 Dec 1819.

Page 325 - Joseph G. Conway to H. Conway, Bill of Sale. I, Joseph Conway sold to Henry Conway, both of Bedford Co., TN, a negro man Warner, he being Willed to Joseph by Thomas Conway his father, after the death of his mother Lydia Conway. The said Thomas Conway's then wife which negro man Warner has been sent for by a certain Robert Boyes of KY, in the Federal Court of United States in Nashville. 21 Dec 1819. Wit: Spencer Henton and John G. Carothers. Reg: 15 Oct 1819.

Page 327 - William Dickson (Dixon) to Keziah Smith, Deed of Gift. I, William Dixon of Bedford Co., TN, being of sound mind and good memory, for love and affection that I have for my daughter Keziah Smith wife of Benjamin Smith, give a negro girl Syntha. 1 Mar 1818. Wit: John Atkinson. Reg: 13 July 1818.

Page 329 - John and Tabitha Warner to John Warner, Bill of Sale. We, John Warner, Sr. and Tabitha Warner his wife sold to John Warner, Jr. a negro woman Dinah. 8 Apr 1817. Wit: William Stagg and Nancy Buchanan. Reg: 23 Apr 1817.

Page 331 - William Dixon to Jedidiah Dixon, Bill of Sale. I, William Dixon of Bedford Co., TN, being of sound mind and good memory, for good will and affection that I have for my son Jedidiah Dixon, give my negro boy Michael. Michael is to remain the only use and benefit of myself and my wife Mary Dixon during both our lives and after that period of time the property of Jedidiah Dixon and his heirs. 14 Mar 1818. Wit: John Atkinson. Reg: 18 July 1818.

Page 332 - William Dixon to John Warner & Others, Deed of Gift. I, William Dixon of Bedford Co., TN, being of sound mind and good memory, do for the love and good will and affection, do give to my three daughters, to wit, Kezia Smith, Ann Perry and Unie Warner and their heirs, all my household and kitchen furniture also one negro woman Margaret and her increase from this time, however said property to remain the property of me and my wife Mary Dixon, during our natural lives and after our death, said property to be equally divided among the three daughters. This 16 May 1818. Wit: John Atkinson. Reg: 18 Jul 1818.

Page 336 - 8 Sept 1819. William Stamper to John T. Forrest, 300 acres. William Stamper of Granville Co., NC sold to John T.

Forrest of Orange Co., NC, land in Bedford Co., TN, on the North Fork of Duck River. Borders Daniel's line. Recorded in Granville Co., NC, 9 Sept 1819.

Page 338 - Devises of James Clark to Samuel Torrentine. The heirs of James Clark, deceased, of Orange Co., NC, for $50. paid by Samuel Torrentine of Bedford Co., TN, undivided tract of land of 800 acres deeded to the heirs of James Clark by David Justice, all our eighth parts of the fourth part of said 800 acres on Duck River, adjoining Samuel McDaniel. Land begins about two miles above the mouth of Rock Creek. Signed by: James Clark, Thomas Clark, Jesse Clark, Joseph Clark, John Clark, Sarah Rone, Joseph Smith, Hanah Smith, John Anderson, and Ginny Anderson. 9 Oct 1818. Wit: Andw. W. Broom and Thomas Taylor (of Orange Co., NC). Recorded in Orange Co., NC 31 Mar 1819.

Page 343 - Elenor Clark to William Clark, PA. I, Elenor Clark of Warren Co., TN, appointed my son William Clark, Power of Attorney, to sell and convey all my right claim and interest in 800 acres, granted to James Clark, deceased, and in Bedford Co., TN, on Duck River, of which I hold one fourth. 24 June 1818. Recorded in Warren Co., TN. 10 Aug 1818.

Page 344 - William Clark to Samuel Torrentine, 200 acres. I, William Clark of Davidson Co., TN, as Power of Attorney for my mother Elenor Clark who is one of the heirs of the said James Clark, deceased. One fourth part is her part sold to Samuel Torrentine, adjoining lands of Samuel McDaniel. Wit: J. W. Hall, James Torrentine and Orville Thompson. Reg: 20 Mar 1820.

Page 346 - 28 Sept 1818. Clark's Devises to Samuel Torrentine, 247 acres. James Clark, Thomas Clark, Jesse Clark, and Joseph Clark, heirs of William Clark, deceased, all of Orange Co., NC sold to Samuel Torrentine of Bedford Co., TN, land being undivided one fifth part, about 247 acres in Bedford Co., TN, on waters of Clems Creek, on the north side of Duck River. Borders school land. Wit: Thomas Taylor and John Anderson (of NC). Reg: 20 Mar 1820.

Page 349 - 9 Oct 1818. James Clark heirs to Alexander Torrentine, 110 acres. James Clark, heir of William Clark, deceased, of Orange Co., NC, acting by an agreement with Thomas Clark, William Clark, Jesse Clark, and Joseph Clark, under a Power of Attorney sold to the heirs and legatees of Alexander Torrentine, deceased, land in Bedford Co., TN, on waters of Clems Creek. Borders school land, Amos McLemore and Elijah Rutledge and Alexander Rutledge. Reg: 22 Mar 1820.

Page 352 - Clark's heirs to Samuel Torrentine, Power of Attorney, of NC. James Clark, Thomas Clark, Jesse Clark, and Joseph Clark, heirs at law of William Clark, deceased, of Orange Co., NC, to sell, transfer &c, all title and interest we have in a certain Military Land Warrant issued by the State of Tennessee to William Clark for 640 acres, No. 994 and dated 2 May 1817. Reg: 22 Mar 1820.

Page 373 - 13 Dec 1819. Fanny W. Bond to John Dougal, 80 acres. Fanny W. Bond now widow of William Bond of Williamson Co., TN sold to John Dougal of Bedford Co., TN, land in Bedford Co., on waters of Powels Creek on south side of Duck River. Borders school land. Wit: John Robeson and Aaron A. Gamble. Recorded

23 Mar 1820.

Page 414 - 31 July 1818. John Bradford to Knight Dalby, 100 acres. John Bradford sold to Knight Dalby, both of Bedford Co., TN, land in Bedford Co., on south side of Bradfords Creek, it being the place whereon Bradford now lives. Borders land of Benjamin Bradford, Spradlin's line. Wit: William Doherty, John Meadows and Edward B. Dalby. Reg: 27 Mar 1820.

Page 442 - 12 Dec 1819. William Caple to Branson D. Caple, 71 acres. William Capleconveyed to Branson D. Caple, son of William Caple, land in Bedford Co., TN, on West Fork of Rock Creek. Borders Littleton Caple and Thompson's line. Reg: 28 Mar 1820.

Page 448 - Richard W. Caswell agreement to Alexander Torrentine. Alexander Torrentineagrees to locate a certain Military Land Warrant for 1280 acres, No. 158, issued to William Caswell, also another Military Land Warrant for 278 acres, No. 482, issued to Joseph Hudlen and assigned to William Caswell, land, 11 Aug 1817 (Orange Co., NC). Reg: 29 Mar 1820.

Page 454 - 9 Apr 1818. Barkley Martin to George W. Hively, Lot No. 127. Commissioners of Bedford Co., TN, being satisfied that George W. Hively did in the lifetime of my deceased brother Barkley Martin, purchased of him a certain Lot in Shelbyville, known as Lot No. 127, and George W. Hively paid full amount. Now, I, Matt Martin, Executor of the Last Will and Testament of my brother Barkley Martin, deceased, to fulfill requests, to deed to George W. Hively said Lot No. 127. Wit: Joseph Steele and Joshua Holt. Reg: 30 Mar 1820.

Page 458 - 13 Dec 1819. Fanny W. Bond to Aaron Gambill, 200 acres. Fanny W. Bond, now widow of William Bond of Williamson Co., TN, sold to Aaron Gambill of Bedford Co., TN, land in Bedford CO., on waters of Powels Creek. Borders John Sloss and school land. Wit: John Robeson and J. Dougal. Reg: 30 Mar 1820.

Page 462 - Elliott Bussey to George Smith, Bill of Sale. I, Elliott Bussey sold to George Smith, both of Bedford Co., TN, ine fifth part of the negroes now in the possession of my mother Lucy Bussey and I, as an heir of my father George Bussey, deceased, delivered to George Smith, Jr., to take possession of the negroes, Bill, Charley, and Jack. 13 Dec 1819. Wit: John McClintock and James Torrentine. Reg: 12 Jan 1820.

Page 464 - Joseph Kennady to James Gibson, Bill of Sale. I, Joseph Kennady give unto James Gibson, son of Thomas N. Gibson, a bay mare, for good will I have for James Gibson. 1 Sept 1818. Wit: And. Cannon and James Young. Reg: 1 Apr 1820.

Page 465 - John D. Farley to Sanders & Muse, Bill of Sale. I, John D. Farley, for $1400.00 for which Richard Sanders and Isaac Muse, a security for me as administrator of the estate of Elizabeth Farley, deceased, I have sold unto Sanders & Muse, nine negroes, to wit, Mingo, Hannah, Hiram, Paton, Cealy, Rebecca, Elenor, Vince, and Julia and other property. 12 July 1819. Reg: 12 July 1820.

DEED BOOK "L"

Page 493 - Edward Wade, son of William and Sarah Wade, born 17th Day May 1777.
Elizabeth Fisher, daughter of Michael & Christina, born 29th Day Sept 1789.
Edward Wade married Elizabeth Fisher, daughter of Michael & Christina, 26th day Feb 1807.
William Stokes Wade, son of Edward & Elizabeth Wade, born the 27th day March 1808.
Martin Fisher Wade, son of Edward & Elizabeth Wade, born 17th day July 1809.
Ann Wade, daughter of Edward & Elizabeth Wade, born the Nov the 30th 1812.
Patsy Wade, daughter of Edward & Elizabeth Wade, born 25th Nov 1810.
Edward Wade, son of Edward & Elizabeth Wade, born 23rd Sept 1814.
Elizabeth Wade, daughter of Edwd. & Elizabeth Wade, born 10th Dec 1817.
Margaret Jane Wade, daughter of Edward & Elizabeth Wade, born 9th day July 1819.
Mary Thompson Wade, daughter of Edward and Elizabeth Wade, born July 26th 1821.
Michael Fisher Wade, son of Edward & Elizabeth Wade, born June 3rd 1824.
Marma Duke Mitchell Wade, son of Edward & Elizabeth Wade, born 27th March 1826.
Nancy M. Wade, daughter of Elizabeth & E. Wade, born 18th day July 1828 and of the Independence of the United States, the fifty second.

Page 495 - North Carolina Grant to John Wilson, 3000. No. 315. For ten pounds for every 100 acres. Granted to John Wilson, land on Weakleys Creek, a branch of North Fork of Duck River. Plat on page 496. 9 April 1813. Reg: (no date).

Page 506 - Hugh Edgar to Samuel Edgar, Power of Attorney. I, Hugh Edgar of Wayne Co., Ohio, appointed Samuel Edgar of Washington Co., PA, my Attorney, to receive from Archibald White, John White, James Walker and James Bradshaw, their heirs, Executors or Administrators, a deed of a tract of land which was conveyed to them 26 Aug 1789 by Amos Balch of North Carolina, dated 12 Aug 1788. This 1 April 1819. Reg: (no date).

Page 526 - George Adams to David Riggs, 110 acres. I, George Adams sold to Charles Long and David Riggs, all of Bedford Co., TN, land in Bedford Co., TN, on waters of Wilsons Creek, the land being land where I now live on. Borders William White, James White and Philip Walker. Wit: Anson Furguson and William McDaniel. Reg: 8 Apr 1820.

DEED BOOK "M" 1820 - 1821

Page 3 - Tennessee Grant to Joseph Nance, 38 acres. No. 13758. Part of Certificate No. 1434, dated 5 Mar 1813, issued to Daniel Ship for 100 acres and entered 25 Oct 1814 by No. 7002. Granted to Joseph Nance, assignee of Daniel Ship, land in Bedford Co., TN, on waters of Falling Creek. Surveyed 25 Nov 1814. Borders James McAdams, Phifer's corner, John Burrow, and Alexander Torrentine. Reg: 20 Jan 1820.

DEED BOOK "M"

Page 31 - 11 Feb 1820. Rezin Smith to Sarency Brown, 85 acres. Rezin Smith sold to Sarancy Brown, Sabring Brown, and Smith Brown, Rosylind Brown and James Williss and John Williss, all of Bedford Co., TN, land in Bedford Co., TN, on headwaters of Sinking Creek. Borders a point on a ridge south of where Joseph Williss now lives, John Smith, Jr., Philip Phillips and Michael Campbell's corner. Wit: Benjamin Taliferro and Nancy Meeks. Reg: 8 April 1820.

Page 39 - Robert Morrison to William Morrison & Others, 1000 acres. I, Robert Morrison, Sr. of Mecklenburg Co., NC, give and grant unto my (5) sons, William, John, James, Robert and Thomas Morrison, land on North Fork of Duck River. Borders Joseph Wallace' corner. Land being part of a 3000 acre granted to Ebenezer Alexander of Logan Co., KY and of which I purchased by Patent, dated 10 July 1788. My son William is to have 250 acres. John shall have 200 acres. Remainder to be equally divided among my three other sons, James, Robert and Thomas Morrison. 1 April 1808. Reg: 6 June 1820.

Page 61 - North Carolina Grant to Adam Meek, 1000 acres. No. 287. Ten lbs per 100 acres. Granted to Adam Meek, land on south side of Duck River. Borders Duck River. Plat on page 62.

Page 63 - Adam Meek to Joseph Wallace, Power of Attorney. Adam Meek of Mecklenburg Co., NC appointed Joseph Wallace, James Meek and John Wilson of Tennessee, my Attorney in my name and to my son. I desire recovery of my tract of land on Duck River. 14 July 1808. Wit: D. Cowan, J.P. and George Maxwell, J.P. Reg: (no date).

Page 105 - Tennessee Grant to Nicholas Anthony, 15 acres. No. 9587. Part of Certificate No. 631, dated 23 Feb 1813, issued to Benjamin McCullock and entered 3 April 1813 by No. 5164. Granted to Nicholas Anthony, assignee of Benjamin McCullock, land in Bedford Co., TN, on waters of Thompsons Creek.Surveyed 1 Oct 1814. Borders Peter Shofner. Reg: 28 June 1820.

Page 107 - Tennessee Grant to Nicholas Anthony, 15 acres. No. 9588. Part of Certificate No. 631, dated 23 Feb 1813, issued to Benjamin McCullock and entered 3 April 1813 by No. 5165. Granted to Nicholas Anthony, assignee of Benjamin McCullock, land in Bedford Co., TN, on waters of Thompsons Creek. Borders Peter Shofner. Surveyed 1 Oct 1814. Reg: 28 June 1820.

Page 109 - John Morrison & Others to Samuel Garrison, Bill of Sale. We give to Samuel Garrison, the negro boy Caleb, formerly the property of brother Thomas Morrison, deceased. 24 Oct 1815. Wit: Jany Bradshaw, E. D. Morrison and Mathy Russell. Signed by William Morrison, John Morrison, Elizabeth Anderson, Robert Calne, Jas. W. Bradshaw, Thomas Parks, Jas. Morrison, and Robert Morrison. Reg: 8 April 1820.

Page 111 - Archabald Cathey to Rebecka Cathey, Deed of Gift. I, Archabald Cathey for love and affection I have for my daughter Rebeckah Cathey, 6 negro slaves, Easter, Jude, Candes, Ned, Frank and Rachell and their increases, also a mare and colt and other property. also 75 acres of land on which I now live. Borders William Knott. 20 April 1819. Reg: 29 June 1820.

DEED BOOK "M"

Page 113 - Joseph Wallace to Thomas Gibson, Bill of Sale. We, Joseph Wallace and Elizabeth Wallace of Bedford Co., TN sold to Thomas Gibson of Lincoln Co., TN, a negro woman Jenny and her child Nelson. 13 Feb 1819. Wit: Rezin Smith and Ruth Brown. Reg: 8 April 1820.

Page 114 - Patience Jones to Louisia and Parthenia Clemmons, Deed of Gift. I, Patience Jones of Bedford Co., TN, for good will and affection which I have for Louisia and Parthenia Clemmons of Bedford Co., minor heirs of Joseph B. Clemmons, have together with the sum of $1.00, property (personal). 15 Feb 1820. Wit: Jos. McGuffin and Jos. B. Clemmons. Reg: 8 April 1820.

Page 117 - Jas. McAdams to John and Jas. McAdams, Bill of Sale. I, James McAdams, Sr. sold to my sons John N. McAdams and James McAdams, all of Bedford Co., TN, personal property. 31 Jan 1820. Wit: John Trollinger. Reg: 29 June 1820.

Page 119 - John Cates to Peter Saling, Power of Attorney. I, John Cates of Howard Co., Mississippi, appoint Peter Saling my Attorney to settle all my business in Tennessee. 22 Feb 1819 at Franklin, Mississippi. Reg: (no date).

Page 120 - John and Frances McLintock to John Warner, Bill of Sale. We, John McLintock and Frances McLintock formerly Frances Bussey of Bedford Co., TN sold to John Warner, Jr. property of George Bussey, deceased, father of Frances McLintock, also three negroes, Betsy, Charity, and Jack, which formerly belonged to George Bussey, deceased, but now in possession of Lucy Brown widow of George Bussey, deceased. 4 April 1820. Wit: John Robinson and John Stephens. Reg: 8 April 1820.

Page 125 - -- April 1820. Samuel Briggs to Charles Briggs & others, Bill of Sale. I, Samuel Briggs of Wake Co., NC for natural love and paternal affection I bear for by beloved children, Charles Briggs, Samuel G. Briggs, Duncan D. Briggs, Anne Eliza Briggs and Patsy (Betsy) D. Briggs, granted to them slaves (8). 4 April 1820. Wit: G. M. Morton and John Bruce. Reg: 8 April 1820.

Page 129 - John Sims to Nancy Davis, Deed of Gift. For affection I have for my daughter Nancy Davis formerly Nancy Sims, I give two negroes Nulley and Peter. She shall keep until I shall want the two negroes by name of Molly and John, for services she is to tender unto me. 13 April 1818. Wit: Theo. F. Bradford and Jas. McKissick. Reg: 13 April 1818.

Page 159 - 2 April 1819. Joshua E. White and S. White to Benjamin and John Gott. Joshua E. White and Steel White of Savannah, GA sold to Benjamin and John Gott and sons of Seed, England, land of 642 acres in Bedford Co., TN, on Barren Fork of Duck River. Borders Pickens old place, Adams tract and others. Reg: 12 July 1820.

Page 165 - 3 Aug 1812. Heirs of David Allison to A. Jackson. Alexander Allison, John Allison, William Allison for himself as administrator of Peggy Allison, deceased, of the State of Georgia, brothers and sisters of David Allison formerly of the City of Philadelphia, deceased, sold to Andrew Jackson of Davidson Co., TN. He is indebted to A. Jackson, transferred land in Bedford Co., TN. (Wilkes Co., Georgia). Reg: 12 July 1820.

Page 182 - Tennessee Grant to Alexander Torrentine, 49 acres. No. 14285. For Military Serivce by Malchi Russell to North Carolina, Warrant No. 637 for 640 acres, dated 23 April 1784 and entered 5 Dec 1807 by No. 796. Granted to Alexander Torrentine, assignee of Malchi Russell, land of 49 acres in Bedford Co., TN, on north side of Duck River. Borders Anthony Newman, Duck River, James Torrentine and John Thompson. Surveyed 24 Feb 1814. Reg: 28 Aug 1820.

Page 234 - Alexander Findley to Margaret Findley, Bill of Sale. For $200.00 paid by Margaret Findley and for supporting my mother Nancy Findley during her natural life, I sell and deliver property after the death of my mother Nancy Findley, cattle &c. 17 June 1820. Signed by Alexander Findley. Wit: Philip T. Burford. Reg: 4 Sept 1820.

Page 295 - Tennessee Grant to Andrew Erwin, 100 acres. No. 13757. Part of Certificate No. 1805, dated 7 July 1814, issued to George Martin for 858 acres and entered 5 Dec 1815 by No. 8645. Granted to Andrew Erwin, assignee of George Martin, land in Bedford Co., TN, on Straight Creek, waters of Garrison Fork of Duck River. Surveyed 22 Dec 1815. Reg: 4 Oct 1820.

Page 316 - Martin and Anna Perry to John Warner, Bill of Sale. I, Martin Perry and Anna Perry his wife sold to John Warner, Jr., all of Bedford Co., TN, a negro boy Archabald and called "Asa". 29 May 1817. Wit: Mary Dixon and Edward Whitworth. Reg: 13 Jan 1820.

Page 329 - Plat of Michael Robison.

Page 331 - Tennessee Grant to Benejah Gray, 300 acres. No. 6477. Part of Certificate No. 340, dated 2 Nov 1809, issued to William Hill and entered 30 Mar 1810 by No. 2274. Granted to Benejah Gray, land in Bedford Co., TN, between Wilson and Spring Creek. Borders Samuel Wilson and Charles Brandon. Surveyed 6 Mar 1811 by George Tillman, D.S. Reg: 23 Nov 1820.

Page 339 - 27 Jan 1817. John Baldridge to Samuel & James Torrentine. John Baldridge, Agent and Attorney for Francis Baldridge and Elizabeth Baldridge his wife, heirs and legatees of Alexander Torrentine, deceased, the said John Baldridge being of Jefferson Co., Mississippi Territory as also the said Francis and Elizabeth sold to Samuel Torrentine and James Torrentine, both of Bedford Co., TN, land belonging to the estate of Alexander Torrentine, deceased. Wit: D. Torrentine and Nancy Torrentine. Reg: 26 Sept 1817.

Page 343 - 29 Mar 1820. Levi C. Roberts to Female Academy, one half acre. Levi C. Roberts conveyed to James L. Armstrong, Jesse Evans, M. D. Mitchell, Clement Cannon and James A. McLore, Commissioners of the Shelbyville Female Academy, for $25.00, land in Bedford Co., TN, and east of the Town of Shelbyville and near the same. Wit: John C. Coldwell and Michael Green. Reg: 16 Oct 1820.

Page 345 - 18 Feb 1820. Theo. F. Bradford to Female Academy, 10 and three fourth acres. Theoderick F. Bradford sold to James L. Armstrong, Clement Cannon, M. D. Mitchell, Jesse Evans, and Jas. A. McClorie, Trustees of a Female Academy for $900.00 by Commissioners or Trustees, conveyed land lying east of Town of Shelbyville. Borders M. D. Mitchell, Wilson Coats, Levi C. Roberts, and Haskell's line. Wit: William H. Iredell and ----- Young. Reg: 24 Nov 1820.

Page 385 - Theophilus Thompson to Newcombe Thompson, North Carolina. I, Theophilus Thompson, Sr. for $450.00 paid by Newcombe Thompson, one negro man Harvy. I reserve to myself the possession and service of said Harvy during my natural life for my own use. 3 Sept 1819. Wit: William Hill and Kenneth Anderson. Reg: 4 Dec 1820.

Page 396 - North Carolina Grant to Thomas Talbot, 2000 acres. No. 13. Granted to Thomas Talbot, land on Duck River. Borders Alexander Greer and crossing Lick Creek. 10 July 1788. Warrant No. 1434. Surveyed by William Martin, Daniel White and Alexander McLure, C.C.

Page 420 - 17 July 1818. Anna White to Newton Cannon, 3000 acres. Anna White, Executrix of estate of William White, late of North Carolina of Wake County by John Lane, Esq., of Bedford Co., TN, her Attorney sold to Newton Cannon of Williamson Co., TN, for consideration of services rendered in locating, surveying &c tracts of land, granted to Newton Cannon, land in Bedford Co., TN, on Wilsons Creek, it being part of a 1000 acres granted by State of Tennessee to William White, deceased, by No. 617. Wit: Isaac Phillips, Larken Edwards and J. Buckhannon. Reg: 3 Oct 1820.

Page 424 - 17 July 1818. Anna White to Newton Cannon, 300 acres. (same as above instrument) land in Bedford Co., TN, on waters of Sugar Creek and Sinking Creek. Borders Robert White. Wit: Larken Edwards, James Buckhannon, Nicholas Gentry and James K. McDaniel. Reg: 3 Oct 1820.

Page 448 - 19 Feb 1812. Daniel McClaren, 3rd to Daniel McClaren, Sr. Daniel McClaren, Sr. of Bedford Co., TN and Daniel McClaren, 3rd of Bedford Co., TN, land in Bedford Co., TN, on waters of Caney Spring Creek. Borders Samuel Fleming, Richmond's corner and Daniel McClaren, Sr., where he now lives. 270 acres. Wit: John Rickman and Daniel Rickman. Reg: 3 Oct 1820.

Page 450 - 27 Dec 1815. Daniel McClaren, Sr. to Daniel McClaren, Jr., 194 acres. Daniel McClaren, Sr. sold to Daniel McClaren, Jr., both of Bedford Co., TN, land for good will and love for Daniel McClaren, Jr. Conveyed land on Caney Spring Creek. Borders Hugh H. Loverns' corner. Wit: John C. Dunn, John Rickman, and Elisha Falwell. Reg: 2 Oct 1820.

Page 472 - Joseph Lytle to William Lytle, Deed of Gift. I, Joseph Lytle for good will and affection which I have for my son William Lytle, both of Bedford Co., TN, my goods and chattels now being in my present dwelling house in Bedford Co., personal property, also a note on hand and also 133 acres of land being in Virginia, Henry Co., on waters of Turkey Cock Creek. 7 Oct 1820. Reg: 10 Oct 1820.

Page 474 - 11 Jan 1820. William Armstrong to William Gibson, Deed of Gift. I, William Armstrong for in consideration of the parental affection and my support for upwards of 20 months past and so long as I live with, my son-in-law William Gibson and his wife Margaret Gibson, my daughter, conveyed all my property of which I possess. Wit: Owen Medlin and Lewis Medlin. Reg: 2 Oct 1820.

Page 490 - Tennessee Grant to Samuel Patton, 20 acres. No. 13521. Part of Certificate No. 1385, dated 30 Jan 1813, issued to Benjamin McCullock for 500 acres, dated 25 Sept 1813 by No. 8369. Granted to Samuel Patton, assignee of Benjamin McCullock, land in Bedford Co., TN, on waters of Sugar Creek. Surveyed 26 Sept 1815. Reg: (no date).

Page 496 - Tennessee Grant to Thomas B. Mosley, 75 acres. No. 14707. Part of Certificate No. 140 and 1812, dated 16 June 1810 & 7 July 1814, issued to John Scott for 100 acres, the latter to Thomas Shute for 1106 acres and entered 26 Oct 1815 by No. 8496. Granted to Thomas B. Mosley, assignee of John Scott and Thomas Shute, land in Bedford Co., TN, on waters of the Garrison Fork. Borders Mosley's corner called "The Tomahawk Corner", and Samuel U. Gillespie. Surveyed 1 Nov 1815. Reg: 12 July 1820.

Page 500 - Tennessee Grant to Joseph Haynes, 50 acres. No. 13839. Part of Certificate No. 1805, dated 7 July 1814, issued to George Martin for 858 acres, granted 5 Aug 1815 by No. 8146. Granted to Joseph Haynes, assignee of George Martin, land on waters of Noahs Fork. Borders Hail's land, Andrew Erwin's claim. Surveyed 22 Dec 1815. Reg: 15 Aug 1820.

Page 502 - Daniel Bussey to John Warner, Bill of Sale. I, Daniel Bussey sold to John Warner, Jr., property that I as heir or legatee of my father George Bussey, deceased, negroes. A slave now in the possession of my mother Lucy Bussey. 6 April 1820. Wit: John Bryant, Hamilton Bradford and Edward Wade. Reg: 1 Jan 1821.

Page 504 - Joseph Brittain to James Brittain, Bill of Sale. I, Joseph Brittain for love and affection for my son James Brittain, given to his three negroes. 8 Sept 1820. Wit: Thomas C. Fulton and Aaron Boyd. Reg: 1 Jan 1821.

Page 506 - David Luster, Sr. & Others to Thomas H. Luster, PA South Carolina. We, David Luster, James Luster, John Luster and Simon Luster of Greenville District, SC, appointed Thomas H. Luster of Bedford Co., TN, our Attorney, to sell and receive of Executors or Administrators of William Luster, deceased of Mississippi near Washington or Natches, all estate, real and personal William Luster died possessed of, for us the heirs. 13 Sept 1820. Reg: 21 Feb 1821.

Page 516 - Chatham Co., North Carolina. I, Daniel Carrell of NC, Chatham County, appoint Edward Carrell of same County, my Attorney, to recover from Edward Warren and Robert Waite, Executors, late of Bedford Co., TN, all portion of estate of Edward Warren, deceased, of which I may be entitled in right of my wife Polly, under the Last Will and Testament of Edward Warren, deceased. 16 Aug 1824. Reg: (no date).

DEED BOOK "N" 1821 - 1821

Page 4 - 28 Apr 1819. Jesse Davis to John Davis, 39+ acres. Jesse Davis conveyed to John Davis, both of Bedford Co., TN, for consideration of the service &c and for Davis' other good and value, given to John Davis, land in Bedford Co., TN, the same whereon John Davis now lives. Borders William Norvell and Jesse Davis. Wit: C. J. Ragsdale and Benjamin Booth. Reg: 2 Mar 1821.

Page 18 - 8 Oct 1816. Joseph & Ann Dobbs to John Wilson, 100 acres. Joseph Dobbs and Ann Dobbs his wife sold to John Wilson, land in Bedford Co., TN, it being part of a 400 acre survey granted to Ann Wilson. Borders Alexander Robertson and crosses Rich Creek. Wit: Joseph Neill and Josiah Davis. Reg: 3 Jan 1821.

Page 40 - 1 Dec 1819. George W. Cahoon to the heirs of Forsythe, 109 acres. George W. Cahoon of Blount Co., Alabama Territory sold to the following children of Benjamin Forsythe, deceased, to wit, Elizabeth B. Smalling, Sally A. Perry, Effey J. Forsythe, Bethunia H. Forsythe, James N. Forsythe, and Mary L. Forsythe, all of Bedford Co., TN, and Elizabeth B. Cowan is to live on the said place where she now lives, sold land in Bedford Co., TN, it being part of a 1000 acre tract devised from Benjamin Williams of North Carolina to Lucy McReynolds. Borders Spring Creek. Wit: John Long and Ansel H. Ferguson. Reg: 4 Jan 1821.

Page 43 - 26 Feb 1820. Abraham Helton to Peter Helton. Abraham Helton, Sr. conveyed to Peter Helton, both of Bedford Co., TN, on headwaters of Sinking Creek, on the west branches. Wit: Joseph A. Brantly and Samuel S. Austin. Reg: 24 Mar 1821.

Page 45 - 27 July 1819. James P. Balch to Theron E. Balch, 120 acres. James P. Balch sold to Theron E. Balch, both of Bedford Co., TN, land on both sides of Duck River in Bedford Co., TN, the right whereof he devises from his grandfather Samuel Patton, lying on the north end of the survey on which Amos Balch now lives on the west by Talbots' land. Wit: Lewis Campbell and Joseph Alexander. Reg: 3 Jan 1821.

Page 63 - 16 Aug 1820. James Norvell to Norvell McGee, 26 acres. James Norvell, Sr.sold to Norvell McGee land in Bedford Co., TN, beginning at corner of a tract conveyed by James Norvell, Sr. to John Norvell, Sr. by Deed of Gift. Borders Featherston's land, and the Bell Buckle Creek. Wit: John Norvell, Sr. and David Norvell. Reg: 4 Jan 1821.

Page 79 - Sheriff Bill of Sale to John Hooper. Sheriff to sell property of Richard Hooper, desk &c, 2 large Bibles, books and other personal property in Bedford Co., TN. John Hooper being highest bidder. 4 Oct 1820. Reg: 3 Jan 1821.

Page 82 - 26 July 1820. Richard Hooper to John Hooper, Mortgage. For $225.18. Personal property. Wit: J. W. McBride and Thomas Powdrall. Reg: 30 Mar 1821.

Page 98 - Catherine Clark to Jesse Clark, Power of Attorney. I, Catherine Clark of Garrard Co., KY, appointed Jesse Clark of Rutherford Co., TN, my Attorney, to sell land in Bedford Co., TN, it being one fourth part of an undivided tract deeded by David Justice to James Clark's heirs. Borders Duck River about one mile above the mouth of Rock Creek. 22 Oct 1820.

DEED BOOK "N"

Page 103 - Samuel Smalling to Forsythe Devises, Relinguishment. I, Samuel Smalling of Bedford Co., TN, do relinguish all my claims to a negro girl Franky, now in possession of E. B. Cowan. One sixth part of said negro girl the other five parts to belong to the other heirs of Benjamin Forsythe, deceased, to wit, Sally A. Perry, Effey J. Forsythe, Catharine H. Forsythe, James N. Forsythe, and Mary P. Forsythe. 2 Dec 1819. Wit: Edward Whitworth and A. Perry. Reg: 14 Dec 1820.

Page 106 - Tennessee Grant to Andrew Erwin, 40 acres. No. 1475. Part of Certificate No. 1613, dated 14 Oct 1813, issued to John C. McLemore for 620 acres and entered 17 June 1815 by No. 7966. Granted to Andrew Erwin, assignee of John C. McLemore, land in Bedford Co., TN, on the Barren Fork of Duck River. Borders Blount grant No. 233. Surveyed 10 Oct 1815. Reg: 11 Apr 1821.

Page 108 - Tennessee Grant to Andrew Erwin, 150 acres. No. 14758. Certificate No. 1119, 1120 and 1121, dated 15 July 1812, issued to James Patton and Andrew Erwin, 50 acres each, and entered 16 Oct 1815 by No. 8455. Granted to Andrew Erwin, assignee of James Patton, land in Bedford Co., TN, on said Erwins Stone Fort Mill Creek. Borders James Nelson's cabin. Surveyed 16 Nov 1816. Reg: 11 Apr 1821.

Page 110 - Tennessee Grant to James Patton and Andrew Erwin, 14¼ acres. No. 14756. For Military Service by Zachariah Davis to North Carolina, Warrant No. 3167, dated 19 Dec 1785, for 640 acres and entered 25 June 1812 by No. 4070. Granted to James Patton and Andrew Erwin, assignees of the heirs of Zachariah Davis, land in Bedford Co., TN, on headwaters of Wartrace Fork of Duck River. Borders Benjamin McCullock's corner and Brother's line. Surveyed 21 Mar 1816. Reg: 15 Aug 1820.

Page 112 - Hugh Edgar to Samuel Edgar, Power of Attorney. I, Hugh Edgar of Wayne Co., Ohio, appointed Samuel Edgar of Washington Co., PA, my Attorney, to receive from Archabald White, John White, Joseph White, James Walker, and James Bradshaw, to assign a deed for 285 acres, agreeable to an Article of Agreement executed by Amos Balch of North Carolina, now in Tennessee, to Hugh Edgar, dated 12 Aug 1788. Said deed was conveyed by Amos Balch to Archabald White, deceased, by and bearing date -- Aug 1789. Recorded in Stark Co., Ohio. Reg: 26 Mar 1821.

Page 123 - Tennessee Grant to Daniel Berrycroft, 105 acres. No. 14813. Part of Certificate No. 1369, dated 16 Jan 1813, issued to William T. Lewis for 600 acres and entered 9 Feb 1813 by No. 4964. Granted to Daniel Berrycroft, assignee of William T. Lewis, land in Bedford Co., TN, on Sinking Creek. Borders Walter Bernard and Sinking Creek. Surveyed 30 June 1815. Reg: 17 May 1821.

Page 142 - North Carolina Grant to Anthony Newman, 5000 acres. No. 127. 10 lbs per 100 acres. Granted to Anthony Newman, land on north side of Duck River, above Felix Robertson and John Jackson's surveys. Recorded in North Carolina 10 July 1788. Plat on page 144 and 145. Reg: 12 May 1821.

Page 158 - 28 Oct 1820. Humphy M. & Jane Cunningham to William Pickens, 100 acres. Hance M. Cunningham of Lawrence Co., Alabama and Jane Cunningham of Bedford Co., TN, sold to William

Pickens, land in Bedford Co., TN. Wit: Andrew Hammel and James N. Cunningham. Reg: 11 Apr 1821.

Page 160 - 10 Apr 1820. Robert Adams to James Adams, 110 acres. Robert Adams conveyed to James Adams, son of said Robert Adams, land on south side of Duck River and on Dryden's Fork of Rock Creek. Borders survey of John Holmes, and school land. Reg: 11 Apr 1812.

Page 199 - North Carolina Grant to Stockley Donalson, 5000 acres. No. 297. Ten lbs. per 100 acres. Located about two miles above the Old Indian War Trace Road and about one mile east of the Wartrace Fork of Duck River. Recorded Patent date at Newburn. 22 Feb 1795, No. 297.

Page 212 - 13 Nov 1812. William Patterson, Jr. to Archabald Cathey, 100 acres. William Patterson, Jr. of Mecklenburg Co., NC sold to Archabald Cathey of Williamson Co., TN, land in Bedford Co., TN, on north waters of Duck River. Borders Blount grant and Daniel Vaughan. Wit: John Stone and Daniel Gilchrist. Reg: -- May 1817.

Page 242 - Tennessee Grant to Joseph Brittain, 60 acres. No. 14720. Part of Certificate No. 1369, dated 16 Jan 1813, issued to William T. Lewis for 600 acres and entered 25 Jan 1813 by No. 4915. Granted to Joseph Brittain, assignee of William T. Lewis, land in Bedford Co., TN, on waters of Caney Spring Creek. Borders Robert Weakley's survey, William Marshall and John Atkinson. Surveyed 12 July 1819. Reg: (no date).

Page 244 - Tennessee Grant to James McCuistion, 100 acres. No. 14808. Certificate No. 18, dated 4 May 1808, issued to Daniel McKissick for 181+ acres and entered 10 Aug 1808 by No. 703. Granted to James McCuistion, assignee of Daniel McKissick, land in bedford Co., TN, on north side of Duck River. Surveyed 1 Mar 1809. Borders Benjamin McCuistion. Reg: 5 Aug 1820.

Page 256 - Tennessee Grant to Isaiah Alexander, 50 acres. No. 13234. Part of Certificate No. 1316, dated 2 July 1817, issued to John Humphrey for 500 acres and entered 23 Feb 1818 by No. 10705. Granted to Josiah N. Alexander, assignee of John Humphrey, land in Bedford Co., TN, on waters of Weakleys Creek and Alexanders Creek. Borders Thomas Callon. Surveyed 25 Feb 1818. Issued by Murfreesborough, 13 Mar 1819. Reg: (no date).

Page 268 - Tennessee Grant to Thomas Callon, 200 acres. No.13422. Certificate No. 267, dated 13 Sept 1810, issued to Newton Cannon for 200 acres and entered 26 Jan ---- by No. 2956. Granted to Thomas Callon, assignee of Newton Cannon, land on headwaters of Weakleys Creek. Surveyed 2 Aug 1814. Reg: 27 June 1821.

Page 272 - 13 Sept 1819. Peter Saling and John Cates to Nicholas Anthony, 50 acres. Peter Saling, agent for John Cates of Howard Co., Mississippi Territory sold to Nicholas Anthony of Bedford Co., TN, land on waters of Thompsons Creek. Borders Samuel Brown and Robert's land. Wit: John Cates, John Tillman and Henry Snow. Reg: 8 Apr 1821.

Page 280 - John Peacock, Sr. to James & Catherine Peacock. I, John Peacock, Sr. for love and affection for my grandchildren,

DEED BOOK "N"

Thomas James Peacock and Catherine Jane Peacock, the children of my daughter Mary Peacock the wife of Thomas H. Peacock, a negro boy child Ned, to Thomas James Peacock and Catherine Jane Peacock, a negro girl Hannah. 7 Dec 1812. Wit: Jeremiah Dial and Stephen Murphy. Reg: 23 Mar 1813.

Page 289 - Daniel Low to William Low, Deed of Gift.
I, Daniel Low, for love and affection for my son William Low, both of Bedford Co., TN, a negro girl Mimey. --- --, 1812. April Term 1821. Reg: 8 Apr 1821.

Page 293 - John Warner, Sr. to John Warner, Jr., Bill of Sale.
I, John Warner, Sr. to John Warner, Jr., negro boy Squire. The negro boy is to remain with John Warner, Sr. until his death. 19 Jan 1819. Reg: 13 Jan 1821.

Page 294 - Irvin Hide, Attorney for Samuel Thompson and William H. Oliver. I, Irvin Hide of Bedford Co., TN, as agent for William H. Oliver of Madison Co., Alabama sold to Samuel Thompson of Bedford Co., TN, a negro man Wyatt. 15 June 1820. Signed 2 Apr 1821. Reg: 8 Apr 1821.

Page 296 - 6 Sept 1817. William Hartsfield to Nathan Hartsfield, for negro. Both of Bedford Co., TN, for 4 negroes. Wit: Bedy Browning and Isaiah King. Reg: 8 Apr 1821.

Page 297 - 30 Mar 1820. Howel Dawdy to Thomas Blythe, Jr.
Howel Dawdy of Bedford Co., TN sold for $500.00 to Thomas Blythe, Jr. of Lincoln Co., TN, also for caring for myself and wife Feby during our natural lives, I grant and deliver to him, 6 tracts of land in Bedford Co., TN. One tract of 15 acres, adjoining Town of Shelbyville, on the west and borders Jesse Evins line. One tract of 75 acres which Howel Dawdy purchased of William Coats, adjoining the Academy on east. Another tract or Lot in Shelbyville No. 86 where Dawdy now lives. Another tract or Lot in Shelbyville, No. 98. Also, tract ot Lot in Shelbyville, No. 105, and also Lot No. 133. Reg: 28 June 1821.

Page 300 - Howel Dawdy to Thomas Blythe, Bill of Sale.
Howel Dawdy of Bedford Co., TN sold to Thomas Blythe of Lincoln Co., TN, negro man Tom and other personal property. 30 Dec 1820. Wit: Ed. Wade. Reg: 8 Apr 1821.

Page 302 - E. Henderson to James D. Henderson.
I, Elam Henderson for love and affection for my son James D. Henderson, both of Bedford Co., TN, land in Bedford Co., in the Town of Farmington, Lot No. 2. 3 Apr 1820. Reg: 8 Apr 1821.

Page 308 - 15 Nov 1819. Thomas C. Polk & Mary E. Polk to Jos. Steele, 2336 acres. Thomas G. Polk and his wife Mary E. Polk of Mecklenburg Co., NC sold to Joseph Steele of Bedford Co., TN, land in Bedford Co., on Falling Creek. It being part of a North Carolina Grant to Richard Trotter. Reg: 11 July 1821.

Page 319 - 16 June 1821. Willis Hopwood to Meeting House, 2½ acres. Willis Hopwood of Bedford Co., TN conveyed to the members of the Baptist Church, who do may or shall assembly together as a church to worship God and carry on and keep up Gospel Decipline on the premises hereafter to be named. I, Willis Hopwood for and in consideration of the good will I have for the above named church and people, I have granted unto them a certain piece or parcel of land in Bedford Co., TN, on waters of the West Fork of Rock Creek. Borders survey of Abner Pillow. Wit: Burgess Harden and John L. Harden. Reg: 13 July 1821.

Page 365 - Philip Burrow to Mary Burrow, 19+ acres. I, Philip Burrow of Bedford Co., TN give to Mary Burrow, my daughter, land in bedford Co. Borders Pleasant Garden Meeting House. 9 Mar 1821. Signed by Philip Burrow, Jr. Wit: Charles Jones and Alfred Burrow. Reg: 14 July 1821.

Page 383 - 15 May 1820. James Purryear to Sary Purryear, 15 acres. James Purryear sold to Sary Purryear, both of Bedford Co., TN, land in Bedford Co., on waters of Barren Fork, Riley's Creek and adjoins Blythe's tract whereon Sary Purryear now lives. Wit: Samuel Purryear and Robert Purryear. Reg: 14 Jul 1821.

Page 395 - 3 July 1821. James B. Porter to Nathan Adams & others, 1088 acres. James Porter & Frances M. Porter formerly Frances M. Bond of Williamson Co., TN, sold to Nathan Adams and his wife Sarah Adams formerly Sarah Porter, Polly Porter and John Porter of Williamson Co., TN and devises of Nathaniel Porter, deceased, Frances W. Porter formerly wife of William Bond. Sold land in bedford Co., TN, survey date 27 Apr 1821, on waters of Sinking Creek. Land sold to Samuel Porter, Nathan Adams, Sarah Adams, Neely Porter and John Porter. Wit: James P. Porter and A. W. -----. Reg: 13 July 1821.

Page 400 - 19 Jan 1821. John F. Forrest to Robert Cannon, 300 acres. John Forrest of Orange Co., NC sold to Robert Cannon of Raleigh, NC and Alexander Mason, John Taylor of Orange Co., NC, Fannin M. Jones of Wake Co., NC, and William Scott of Madison Co., Alabama. John F. Forrest on 29 Sept 1820 executed a promissory note to Alexander Mason for $800.00 due in 88 days, Thomas W. Scott, Attorney. Land in Bedford Co., TN (to sell) on north side of Duck River. Borders Graves' old corner and Daniel's corner. Reg: 13 Sept 1821.

Page 404 - 3 July 1821. Mary Doherty to Samuel Porter & Others, 942 acres. Mary Doherty, femme sole, of Williamson Co., TN sold to Samuel Porter, Nathan Adams and his wife Sarah Adams formerly Sarah Porter, Polly Porter and John Porter, heirs and decises of Nathaniel Porter, deceased, formerly of Bedford Co., TN. Mary Doherty, by bond dated 11 Sept 1812 executed by her to Nathaniel Porter in his life time for $2626.95 pd to her, land in Bedford Co., TN. Wit: James P. Porter and James B. Porter. Reg: 13 Sept 1821.

Page 426 - The Heirs of John Galbreath to Walter Galbreath, 183 acres. We, all of Bedford Co., TN, being a part of the heirs, devises and legatees of John Galbreath, deceased, of Orange Co., NC sold to Walter Galbreath of Orange Co., NC, land in Bedford Co., TN, on Big Flat Creek. The same as John Galbreath, deceased, in his lifetime purchased of Jeremiah Chamberlain and being his part of a 5000 acre tract entered in name of William Galbreath and Jeremiah Chamberlain. Signed by Legatees: William Galbreath, Mat. Cunningham, Elizabeth Cunningham, Ann Huff, Catherine McKamey and Francis McKamey. Wit: Joshua Holt and William Ray. Reg: 11 Oct 1821.

Page 428 - The Heirs of John Galbreath to William Galbreath,

DEED BOOK "N"

We, all of Bedford Co., TN, being of the heirs of John Galbreath, deceased, of Orange Co., NC conveyed to William Galbreath of Adams Co., PA, land in Bedford Co., TN, on Big Flat Creek. 15 Jan 1819. Reg: 4 July 1821.

Page 431 - Edward R. Anderson to Wardlaw & Thompson, Bill of Sale. I, Edward R. Anderson, for $90.00 from Joseph Wardlaw and John Thompson, sold to them one set of surgical instruments and my supply of medicine and shop furniture, and other items. 4 Sept 1821. Reg: (no date).

DEED BOOK "O" 1821 - 1822

Page 31 - 23 Dec 1821. Jacob Whitworth to Abram Finly, 150 acres. Jacob Whitworth, George Hill, John Hill and Samuel Whitworth, all of Bedford Co., TN sold to Abram Finly land in Bedford Co., TN, on waters of Wartrace Fork of Duck River, it being a part of a 5000 acre grant to the Blounts by North Carolina, by No. 219. Borders M. Gilchrist. Wit: Arch Chaffin and Erasmus Hill and Ballard Coldwell. Reg: -- Oct 1821.

Page 35 - 6 June 1821. Lockhart, Executor to Abraham Byler, 100 acres. James Lockhart, surviving Executor of John Strother, deceased, of Botetourt Co., VA sold to Abraham Byler of Bedford Co., TN, land in Bedford Co. Borders Nathaniel Taylor and Jonathan Plumly. Reg: 15 July 1821.

Page 37 - 29 Aug 1821. Lewis Medlin & Others to Resen Smith, 100 acres. Lewis Medlin and Rachel Medlin his wife formerly Rachel Smith, Robert Medlin and Mary Medlin his wife formerly Mary Smith, John Roberts and Sarah Roberts his wife formerly Sarah Smith, and Ruthy Brown formerly Ruthy Smith sold to Resen Smith, all of Bedford Co., TN, land in Bedford. Whereas John Smith, Jr. brother of Resen, Rachel, Mary, Sarah, and Ruthy, died seized in fee of a tract of land of 100 acres, being on the headwaters of Sinking Creek, without issue to his body, leaving the said parties to this deed and Joseph Waller(Wallen) and Elizabeth Waller(Wallen) formerly Elizabeth Smith, brothers and sisters as heirs of his body, which said tract of 100 acres was conveyed to John Smith, Jr. by John Smith, Sr. by deed dated 30 Sept 1812. Borders Philip Phillips and Michael Campbell. Signed by Lewis Medlin, Rachel Medlin, Robert Medlin, Mary Medlin, John Roberts, and Ruthy Brown. Wit: William Medlin and John England. Reg: 1 Oct 1821.

Page 55 - 10 Sept 1821. Jacob Wilhoit to John Wilhoit, 200 acres. Jacob Wilhoit, Sr. conveyed to John Wilhoit, for love and affection for his son John Wilhoit, land in Bedford Co., TN, on both sides of Duck River. Wit: A. B. Morton and William Ray and John Hall. Reg: 10 Oct 1821.

Page 57 - 10 Sept 1821. Jacob Wilhoit to William Wilhoit, 200 acres. Jacob Wilhoit, Sr. conveyed to William Wilhoit, for love and affection for his son, land in Bedford CO., TN, land in Bedford Co., TN, on both sides of Duck River. Borders Michael Robertson. It includes a mill. Wit: A. B. Morton, William Ray and John Hall. Reg: 10 Oct 1821.

Page 69 - John Graham & others to Richard Graham, 168½ acres. We, John Graham and James Graham of Bedford Co., TN, also

Joseph Graham, William Graham, Samuel Graham, Ezekiel Graham, and Griffith R. Graham of North Carolina, by our Attorney Alexander Graham and Alexander Graham of GA for himself, being all heirs at law of William Graham, late of the State of North Carolina and County of Mecklenburg, devises do for consideration of Richard Graham who is also an heir at law of William Graham, deceased, land in Bedford Co., TN, on waters of Spring Creek. Borders Haile's line, John Graham, and James Graham. 11 Oct 1820. Wit: Edw. Whitworth and Samuel Garrison. Signed by John Graham, Robert Graham, Joseph Graham, William Graham, Samuel Graham, Ezekiel Graham, Griffith Graham by Alexander Graham, Attorney in part, A. Graham. Reg: 6 Oct 1821.

Page 83 - Graham's devises to John Graham, 168½ acres. We, James Graham and Richard Graham of Bedford Co., TN also Joseph Graham, William Graham, Samuel Graham, Ezekiel Graham, and Griffith R. Graham of North Carolina by their Attorney in fact Alexander Graham and Alexander Graham of Georgia for himself, all heirs at law of William Graham, late of Mecklenburg Co., NC, do for and in consideration of John Graham who is also an heir at law of William Graham, deceased, relinguishes all rights &c to deceased estate, to land on waters of Spring Creek. Borders Haile's line, James Graham, and James Sheppherd. 11 Oct 1820. Reg: 6 Oct 1821.

Page 101 - 3 Jan 1822. Jesse Parker to Susannah Parker, 100 acres. Jesse Parker conveyed to Susannah Parker, mother of said Jesse Parker of Bedford Co., TN, for love and affection for his mother Susannah Parker, land which he inherited from his father, it being where Susannah Parker now lives. Also another tract of 30 acres which fell to James Paskell by his intermarriage with Elizabeth Parker, daughter of Susannah and sold by him to James to John McClintock. Wit: S. Torrentine and Sarah Torrentine. Reg: 9 Jan 1822.

Page 129 - 19 Dec 1821. Philip T. Burford to Abram Shook, 250 acres. Philip T. Burford of Bedford Co., TN of one part and Elizabeth C. Morris, Rebecca Shook, William Shook, Lurane Shook, and Lucinda Shook of other part, all of Bedford Co., TN, heirs and legatees of Abraham Shook, deceased. Philip T. Burford guardian of Rebecca, William, Lurena and Lucinda Shook, minors and heirs of Abraham Shook, deceased, and Elizabeth C. Morris being their mother and Relict of Abraham Shook, deceased, is indebted to one third part of the under described land and the guardian, sold said land to John Davidson in order to pay Andrew Erwin. Land sold is same purchased of Alexander Smith and Gideon Pillow, in Bedford Co., TN, on waters of West Fork of Rock Creek. Borders Alfred Blair and Burford's Spring. Wit: Michael Green and Samuel Thompson. Reg: 9 Jan 1822.

Page 131 - Sally Brewer to William Brewer, Deed of Gift. I, Sally Brewer of Bedford Co., TN, for $1.00, paid by William Brewer, given to my son William Brewer, one sorrel mare, 4 head of cattle being all my stock, meat cattle, 8 head hogs being all my stock of hogs, 2 featherbeds and furniture. 18 Jan 1822. Reg: 19 Jan 1822.

Page 135 - 30 June 1821. Stephen Murphrey to John W. and Thomas Peacock. Stephen Murphrey conveyed to Thomas A. Peacock and John W. Peacock, Executors of estate of John L. Peacock for heirs and creditors of estate, all of Bedford Co., TN, land in Bedford Co., TN, on the Wartrace Fork of Duck River, bordering the north east corner of 170 acre tract of land to Jno. L. Peacock. Wit: S. E. McGrew and Thomas Coldwell. Reg: 6 Jan 1822.

Page 137 - 4 Aug 1821. James Baker to William Baker, Bill of Sale. I, James Baker sold to William Baker, both of Bedford Co., TN, his crop of corn he is now growing and other personal property. Wit: David Gordon and T. Ann Dunaway. Reg: 9 Jan 1822.

Page 138 - 30 Nov 1821. Thomas McMullen to John Green McBride, Deed of Gift. I, Thomas McMullen of Williamson Co., TN, give and bequeath unto my nephew John Green McBride, one bay mare, saddle and bridle, one red cow and yearling, two featherbeds and furniture. And I do further appoint my brother in law Hugh McBride to take care of the property until John Green McBride shall be 21 years of age. Wit: G. Davis. Reg: 9 Jan 1822.

Page 141 - 10 Dec 1821. Robert Harrison to William Harrison, 30 acres. Robert Harrison sold to William Harrison, both of Bedford Co., TN, land in Bedford Co., on waters of Alexanders Creek. Borders William Nash, Jr. and Caswell's line. The same being granted by Tennessee to Robert Harrison by No. 1369, dated 16 Jan 1813. Wit: William Damron and Moses Guest. Reg: 9 Jan 1822.

Page 159 - 18 Sept 1821. Andrew Hartsfield to Nathan Hartsfield, 50 acres. Andrew Hartsfield, Sr. of Wake Co., NC conveyed to Nathan Hartsfield of Bedford Co., TN, land in Bedford Co., on waters of Powel Creek. Borders Demsey Powel's land. Reg: 15 Jan 1822.

Page 162 - 2 Jan 1822. James Norvell, Sr., James Norvell, Jr. to Norvell McGee, 43 acres. James Norvell, Sr. and James Norvell, Jr. conveyed to Norvell McGee, all of Bedford Co., TN, land in Bedford Co., on Wartrace Fork of Duck River. Borders Bell Buckle Creek and Burrell Featherston. Wit: Thomas M. Bagly, John Norvell, Sr. and David Norvell. Reg: 9 Jan 1822.

Page 178 - 9 Dec 1819. Andrew and Martha McBroom to Josiah Baldridge. Andrew McBroom and Martha his wife, which Martha is one of the sisters and legatees of Alexander Torrentine, late of Bedford Co., TN, now deceased, conveyed to Josiah Baldridge, late of North Carolina, Orange Co., land of estate of Alexander Torrentine, deceased, in Bedford Co., TN, of which Alexander Torrentine died seized and possessed of at the time of his death. Wit: Richard B----- and Samuel McBroom. Reg: (no date).

Page 182 - North Carolina Grant to Andrew Neal, 2000 acres. No. 391. 10 lbs per 100 acres. Land on waters of Caney Spring, north side of Duck River. Borders Robert Weakley and Samuel Graham. Plat on page 183. Reg: 2 Apr 1822.

Page 204 - 6 Feb 1819. Isaac Wood from John Newman, 100 acres. JOhn Newman, Executor of Anthony Newman, deceased, of Nashville conveyed to Isaac Wood of Bedford Co., TN, land. Part of Anthony Newman's 5000 acre grant (NC). Wit: John G. G---, P. J. Scudder and Charles Wortham. Reg: 4 Apr 1822.

Page 218 - 13 Sept 1820. Nathan Adams to Elender Trice, 80 acres. Nathan and Sarah (Sally) Adams of Williamson Co., TN, conveyed to Elender Trice of Bedford Co., TN, land in Bedford Co., on Little Sinking Creek. Borders Benjamin Gambill (Gamble). Wit: W. D. Medearis, Thomas Smith and John Trice and George Crump. Reg: 2 Apr 1822.

Page 222 - 27 Mar 1822. James Ray to John Ray, 115 acres. James Ray for love and affection and for $1.00, conveyed land in Bedford Co., TN, on waters of Sinking Creek. Wit: James D. Anderson and B. W. H. Medearis. Reg: 2 Apr 1822.

Page 272 - 25 Jan 1822. William Crowel to Peter Crowel, 48 acres. William Crowelconveyed to Peter Crowel his son, land in Bedford Co., TN, on south side of Duck River and adjoining the land now in possession of Samuel Crowel and others. Wit: Jno. McMullen and Jacob Crowel. Reg: 4 Apr 1822.

Page 297 - 12 Dec 1821. William Crowel to Samuel Crowel, 113 acres. William Crowel conveyed to Samuel Crowel his son, land in Bedford Co., TN. Borders William Crowel, John Newman and Duck River. Wit: John McMullen and George Smith. Reg: 25 June 1822.

Page 304 - 27 Mar 1822. James Ray to Alexander Ray, 82 acres. James Ray sold to Alexander Ray, both of Bedford Co., TN, for $1.00, land in Bedford CO. Borders James Ray. Wit: James D. Anderson and B. W. H. Medearis. Reg: 27 June 1822.

Page 308 - Benjamin W. H. Medearis to William Brady, Power of Attorney. I, B. W. H. Medearis appoint William Brady of Murfreesborough, Rutherford Co., TN, Attorney for me while I reside in North Carolina. Reg: 10 Apr 1822.

Page 309 - William Waite and George Waite to Jos. Gray, Bill of Sale. William Waite and George Waite sold to Joseph Gray, all of Bedford Co., TN, negro girl. Wit: Hamilton Bradford and R. Waite. Reg: 3 Apr 1822.

Page 310 - 8 Sept 1821. Nathan and Sally P. Adams to Benjamin Gamble, 50 acres. Nathan Adams and Sally his wife of Williamson Co., TN sold to Benjamin Gamble of Bedford Co., TN, land on Little Sinking Creek. Nathan Adams and Sally P. Adams, being heirs of Nathan Porter, deceased. Wit: W. D. Medearis, Thomas Smith, John Trice, and George Crump. Reg: 2 Apr 1822.

Page 312 - 1 Apr 1822. Sally P. Adams, wife of Nathan Adams, examined by Justices of Bedford Co., TN, relative to her deed to Benjamin Gamble. Wit: John Thompson, A. Byler and Allen Perry, all J.P.'s.

Page 313 - 6 July 1821. Articles between Jane Thompson & Others. Articles between Jane Thompson, widow of the late Samuel Thompson, deceased, and Thomas Thompson, Thomas Durham in right of Ellenore Durham formerly Ellenor Thompson, and Samuel Thompson, Jr., all of which except the widow, are lawful heirs and children of Samuel, deceased, all of Bedford Co., TN. Samuel Thompson, deceased, at his death who died testate, seized of two tracts of land in bedford Co., and on waters of West Rock Creek, of 254 acres, the same being conveyed by Thomas Joyce to Samuel Thompson. Bearing date Sept 1818 and one tract bearing date

15 Aug 1818 from John Cockrell to Samuel Thompson for 223 acres in same neighborhood and adjoining above tract. Widow desires her dower and to divide among heirs. Widow to get 100 acres. Borders Thomas Thompson and Thomas Durham. Plat on page 317. Wit: Philip T. Burford and Thomas Ross. Reg: 10 Apr 1822.

Page 318 - 27 Nov 1821. Samuel King & Others to T. H. Barnard, 80 acres. Samuel King, John McGee and Ann McGee, administrators of William McGee, deceased, sold to T. H. Bernard, all of Bedford Co., TN, land in Bedford Co., on Barren Fork of Duck River, part of a 5000 acre grant No. 223. Borders Mill Dam in T. H. Bernard's line, Timmons' line and Barren Fork of Duck River. Wit: Lemuel Sneling (Snelling) and James S. Cathey. Reg: 29 June 1822.

Page 320 - 27 Nov 1821. Samuel King & Others to Daniel Johnston &c, 57 acres. Samuel King, John B. Pendergast for themselves, John McGee and Ann McGee, administrators of William McGee conveyed to Daniel Johnston and Thomas H. Bernard, all of Bedford Co., TN, land at the Three Forks of Duck River. Beginning at junction of the South Barren and Garrison Fork. Wit: Lemuel Sneling (Snelling), James S. Cathey, William Bernard, and John A. Arnold. Reg: 15 Jan 1822.

Page 332 - 4 Oct 1819. Fanning Jones, Jr. to Fanning Jones, Sr.,1050 acres. Fanning Jones, Jr. of Wake Co., NC conveyed to Fanning Jones, Sr. of Wake Co., NC, land in Bedford Co., TN, it being one half or one undivided tract of land of 2100 acres which was divided by the Last Will and testament of his father Redding Jones, to be equally divided between John R. Jones and myself, land on Duck River, all the woods, water &c. Wit: William Durenes and Richard Smith. Reg: 2 July 1822.

Page 343 - 3 May 1822. Valentine Thomas to Laughlin, Power of Attorney. I, Valentine Thomas of Frederick Co., MD, appointed Samuel H. Laughlin, Attorney of Rutherford Co., TN, to recover in the name of John N. Porter against Samuel Porter and assignee by John N. Porter to me. Also, to take care of Order of Sale levied on a tract of land in Bedford Co., TN, lately descended to the heirs of Nathaniel Porter, deceased. Wit: L. Rucker and Samuel Anderson. Reg: 3 July 1822.

Page 349 - 27 Nov 1821. John and Ann McGee to Johnston & Bernard, 14 acres. John McGee and Ann McGee, administrators of William McGee, deceased, conveyed to Daniel Johnston and T. H. Bernard, land in Bedford Co., TN, on south side of Barren Fork of Duck River. Adjoining Johnston and Bernard Mill Tract above the river and the Race that afford the water to the Mills. Wit: Lemuel Sneling (Snelling) and James S. Cathey. Reg: 11 July 1822.

Page 376 - Tennessee Grant to Henry Davis and John Dickson, 33½ acres. No. 15524. Certificate No. 1046, dated 30 Sept 1817, issued to James Randolph and entered 3 Aug 1818 by No. 10962. Granted to Henry Davis and John Dickson, assignees of James Randolph, land in Giles Co., TN, on south side of Duck River. Surveyed 3 Apr 1819. Reg: 28 July 1821.

Page 378 - 25 Oct 1821. Peter Singleton to William Stone, 311 acres. Peter Singleton sold to William Stone of Pittsylvania Co., VA, land in Bedford Co., TN, near Terry's Ford on Duck

River. Wit: Wiley Daniel and Moses H. Prewett. Reg: 15 Aug 1822.

DEED BOOK "P" 1822 - 1822

Page 9 - 1 July 1822. Porter & Thomas to Daniel Davis, 50 acres. John N. Porter of Rutherford Co., TN and Valentine Thomas of Frederick Co., MD by Samuel H. Laughlin, his Attorney conveyed to Daniel Davis of Bedford Co., TN, land in Bedford Co., on waters of Sinking Creek, it being same, a part of a tract formerly owned by Nathaniel Porter, deceased. Borders Sinking Creek, William M. Russell, and Taliaferro's line. Wit: A. B. Morton and Thomas H. Fletcher. Reg: 26 Sept 1822.

Page 16 - 1 July 1822. John N. Porter and V. Thomas to William M. Russell, 100 acres. John N. Porter of Rutherford Co., TN and Valentine Thomas of Frederick Co., MD by Samuel H. Laughlin, Attorney, conveyed to William M. Russell of Lincoln Co., TN, land in Bedford Co., TN, on waters of Sinking Creek, the same being a part of a tract formerly owned by Nathaniel Porter, deceased. Reg: 2 July 1822.

Page 18 - 4 June 1821. John Strother by James Lockhart to John Hartsfield, 248 acres. James Lockhart surviving executor of John Strother, deceased, of Botetourt Co., VA, sold to John Hartsfield, assignee of John Hartsfield, assignee of Andrew Hartsfield, assignee of Frances May, deceased, late of Nashville, TN, land in Bedford Co., TN, on Martin's Creek. Borders land granted to Anthony Sharp and Thomas Dougan, and land granted to Demsey Powell. Reg: 27 Sept 1822.

Page 20 - 15 Sept 1821. William McGuire, Sr. to William McGuire, Jr., 86 acres. William McGuire, Sr. conveyed to William McGuire, Jr., both of Bedford Co., TN, it being a part of a tract conveyed by Benjamin King and William Ditto to William McGuire, Sr., for 300 acres, where William McGuire now lives. Borders land where Neely McGuire first settled. Land included the plantation where on William McGuire, Jr. now lives. Wit: Samuel Philips and John W. Gollonthan. Reg: 12 Dec 1821.

Page 61 - Daniel Meaders to Elizabeth Meaders, Bill of Sale. I, Daniel Meaders of Warren Co., TN but at present in Bedford Co., TN, for love and affection I bear for my daughter Elizabeth Meaders and for $.25, conveyed a negro girl Vilet. I do not agree to relinguish the possession of during my life but after my death, negro girl is to be the property of my daughter Elizabeth and her heirs. 10 Dec 1821. Wit: Jno. Pott and Samuel Haggard. Reg: 12 July 1822.

Page 83 - North Carolina Grant to Tignall Jones, 2100 acres. No. 131. 10 lbs per 100 acres. To Tignall Jones, land on both sides of Rock Creek. Borders Duck River on the upper side of Rock Creek. Plat on page 85 and 86. Surveyed 24, 25 & 26 June 1822 by Joseph Neill, D.S.

Page 88 - Fanning Jones and John Jones, Article Agreement. We have agreed to the division of our tract of 2350½ acres, agreeable to the lines run by John Lane, Esq. (See Plat on pages 85 & 86). 28 June 1822. Wit: John M. Lane.

DEED BOOK "P"

Page 91 - 1807. Walter and William Galbreath to Roger Snell. There was conveyed to Roger Snell by John Galbreath, 284 acres of land whereas the same is lawful to the undersigned by the Last Will and Testament of William Galbreath, Sr., relinguish to Roger Snell, all lands. 19 June 1819. Wit: Theo. F. Bradford and Newcom Thompson. Reg: 4 Oct 1822.

Page 92 - 6 July 1821. Samuel Thompson's devises, Articles of Agreement &c. Between Jane Thompson, widow of the late Samuel Thompson, deceased, and Thomas Durham and Ellena his wife formerly Ellena Thompson, Thomas Thompson and Samuel Thompson, Jr., all heirs of late Samuel Thompson, deceased, and all of Bedford Co., TN. Samuel Thompson died intestate. They have agreed to the division of estate. Wit: Philip T. Burford and Thomas Ross. Reg in Book P, page 95. Reg: (no date).

Page 98 - 11 Apr 1822. Alexander W. Brandon to Richard Brandon, Power of Attorney. We, Alexander W. Brandon and Abel Cowan of Rowan Co., NC and Frederick Dinkins and Sarah his wife of Mecklenburg Co., NC, appointed our well beloved friend Richard Brandon of Giles Co., TN, our Attorney, to oversee for us in the lands we hold in Bedford Co., TN, on both sides of Alexander Creek, on land we hold by virtue of the Last Will and Testament of Alexander Work, deceased. Reg: 7 Oct 1822.

Page 100 - 18 Mar 1822. John S. Brandon to Richard Brandon, Power of Attorney. We, John S. Brandon and Ann Lock of Giles Co., TN and James P. Percell and Margaret Percell his wife of Wilson Co., TN, appointed Richard Brandon of Giles Co., TN, our Attorney, to oversee for us our lands in Bedford Co., TN, on both sides of Alexander Creek or any other lands we hold by virtue of the Last Will and Testament of Alexander Work, deceased. Wit: George Lock and B. B. Watson. Reg: 9 Oct 1822.

Page 112 - 18 Sept 1821. Andrew Hartsfield to Nathan Hartsfield, 50 acres. Andrew Hartsfield, Sr. of Wake Co., NC conveyed to Nathan Hartsfield of Bedford Co., TN, for love and affection for his son Nathan Hartsfield and for $50.00, land in Bedford Co., TN, on waters of Powels Creek. Borders Demsey Powell, deceased, land of his heirs. Wit: H. J. Hayes, T. Pullen and Micajah Hill. Reg: 15 Oct 1822.

Page 127 - Henry Saling to James Hall, Power of Attorney. We, Hickerson Burnum and Henry Saling, late of Bedford Co., TN but now resident of Howard Co., Mississippi, appoint our friend James Hall formerly of Bedford Co., TN but now resident of Clay Co., MO, our Attorney to oversee our business or land we sold in August or September 1820 to Thomas Greer, on waters of East Fork of Rock Creek, to convey a good deed to said land. 24 Sept 1822. Reg: 28 Oct 1822.

Page 133 - 10 Oct 1822. Robert Reed to William Reed, 104 acres. Robert Reed conveyed to William Reed, both of Bedford Co., TN, 2 tracts of land in Bedford Co., on Big Flat Creek. 1st tract borders Andrew Erwin Entry, Andrew Reed, and William Reed's grant. 2nd tract granted to William Reed by Tennessee by No. 5895, dated 20 July 1811 and surveyed 20 May 1813, borders land granted to William Galbreath, James Patton, and Andrew Erwin, and Sim's survey. Wit: William Gore and Robert McKamey. Reg: 18 Nov 1822.

DEED BOOK "P"

Page 135 - 25 June 1822. Fanning Jones to Ezekiel Briant, 160 acres. Fanning Jones sold to Ezekiel Bryant, both of Bedford Co., TN, for $100.00, one certain quarter section of land, to wit, the north east quarter of Section 18 of Township 15 north, in Range 3 east, which land was granted by United States to Ira Williams for his Military Service in the Military Tract in the State of Illinois. Wit: John M. Lane and Joseph Neill. Reg: 17 Oct 1822.

Page 142 - 9 Oct 1822. Robert Reed to Andrew Reed, 70 acres. Robert Reed sold to Andrew Reed, both of Bedford Co., TN, land in Bedford Co., on Big Flat Creek. Borders Minos Cannon survey, Big Flat Creek, William Galbreath and Jeremiah Chamberlain's line. Wit: Jno. Reed, Robert McKamey and William Gore. Reg: 12 Oct 1822.

Page 172 - 20 Sept 1822. Peter and Samuel Crowell to John Capley, 387 acres. Peter Crowell and Samuel Crowell, acting administrators of estate of William Crowell, deceased, all of Bedford Co., TN sold to John Capley, of Bedford Co., land in Bedford Co., on north side of Duck River, it being part of 200 acre tract purchased by William Crowell from John Newman. Borders lands of Samuel Crowell, Peter Crowell and Thomas Shearin, Duck River, and John Thompson, Esq. Peter and Samuel Crowell are sons of William Crowell, deceased. Wit: Jno. McMullen and Samuel Earls. Reg: 10 Oct 1822.

Page 176 - 28 May 1822. Richard Brandon & Others to William Wallace (Walker), 189 acres. Richard Brandon of Giles Co., TN, for himself as Executor of Alexander Lock, deceased, and agent for Ann Lock, John J. Brandon, James Peral and his wife Margaret Peral, Alexander W. Brandon, Abel Cowan, Frederick Dinkins and Sarah Dinkins his wife conveyed to William Walker, of Rutherford Co., TN, land in Bedford Co., TN, on waters of North Fork of Duck River, it being a part of the Devise land of to the heirs of John Brandon as legatees or devises of Alexander Work, deceased. Borders Brandon tract. Signed by Richard Brandon, John S. Brandon, Ann Lock, James Peral, Margaret Peral, Alexander Brandon, Abel Cowan, Frederick Dinkins, Sarah Dinkins by their agent Richard Brandon. Wit: Charles Wade, Absolem Peardy and George Sanders. Reg: 10 Oct 1822.

Page 195 - 5 Sept 1822. James & Robert Fullerton to George Ewing, 10 acres. James and Robert Fullerton, administrators for estate of Adam Fullerton, deceased, of Bedford Co., TN, sold to George Ewing of Bedford Co., land in Bedford Co., on Sinking Creek, a branch of Rock Creek. Wit: Jacob Fisher and Samuel McCrory. Reg: 12 Oct 1822.

Page 209 - 12 Oct 1822. Wren Carter to John B. Bates, 100 acres. Wren Carter of Madison Co., Alabama sold to John B. Bates of Bedford Co., TN, land on the north side of the South Fork of Duck River, a part of a grant for 5000 acres granted to Blount brothers. Wit: William Cribbs and Moses Payne. Reg: 29 Nov 1822.

Page 217 - 28 May 1822. Richard Brandon & Others to Charles Wade. (Same as page 176) Richard Brandon & Others sold to Charles Wade, on Alexanders Creek. Reg: 12 Oct 1822.

DEED BOOK "P"

Page 238 - 28 May 1822. Richard Brandon to William Dameron, 189 acres. (Same as on page 176), land on Alexanders Creek. Reg: 12 Oct 1822.

Page 241 - 17 Oct 1818. John Cates to Nicholas Anthony, Power of Attorney. I, John Cates of Howard Co., MO, appointed Nicholas Anthony of Bedford Co., TN, Attorney, for myself. Wit: William Carothers and William Logan. Reg: 16 Oct 1822.

Page 248 - 10 Aug 1818. Thomas Callon to Robert Cannon. Thomas Callon of Cabarrus Co., NC sold to Robert Cannon of Williamson Co., TN, land in Bedford Co., TN, in Town of Shelbyville and known by No. 16 & 33. Reg: 2 Jan 1823.

Page 256 - 12 Dec 1815. William Norvell to Church, 1 acre. William Norvell conveyed to Daniel Owen, David Norvell, John Ragsdale, Burrell Featherston, William Ashbrooks, and Jeremiah Dial, Trustees in Trust for use and purpose herein after mentioned, all of Bedford Co., TN. William Norvell for and in consideration of the love of God and for the encouragement of his Holy Worship, hath given, granted, conveyed and confirmed by these presents doth give unto the Trustees and their successors, land in Bedford Co., TN. Beginning on east of William Norvell's dwelling house and north of the New Meeting House, about one acre for the purpose to build thereon a House of Worship for the use of the members of the Methodist Episcopal Church in the U.S.A. Reg: 26 July 1817.

Page 260 - 12 Apr 1822. Abel and James W. Parsons to Thomas Gregory. Abel Parsons of Bedford Co., TN and James W. Parsons of Giles Co., TN, set over to Thomas Gregory of Bedford Co., claims to land as remainder of estate of our deceased father Thomas Parsons. We also release claim on Elizabeth Parsons, Administrix, with Will annexed of Thomas Parsons. Reg: 12 Apr 1823.

Page 270 - 2 June 1821. John W. Peacock & Thomas to Stephen Murphree. John W. Peacock and Thomas A. Peacock, acting Executors of Last Will and Testament of John Peacock, deceased, conveyed to Stephen Murph<u>rey</u>, all of Bedford Co., TN, land in Bedford Co., TN, on waters of Wartrace Fork of Duck River. Signed: John William Peacock and Thomas A. Peacock. Reg: 3 Jan 1823.

Page 279 - 12 Nov 1821. William B. McGee & Sally to William King, 27 acres. William McGee and Sally McGee his wife of Bedford Co., TN, conveyed to William King of Morgan Co., Alabama, one ninth part of a tract descended to the heirs of Francis King, deceased, who was father of Sally McGee, land in Bedford Co., TN, on west side of the Garrison Fork of Duck River. Begins at center of the Garrison, a few yards above where the road crosses Fork. Borders McGee & Tilford survey which includes the Mills on the Fork, Francis King's field, and near the mouth of Wartrace Creek. Wit: Edward Easly and Arthur Hamlin. Reg: 13 July 1822.

Page 282 - 12 June 1821. Edward Easly and Frances to William King, 27 acres. Edward Easly and Frances Easly his wife of Bedford Co., TN, conveyed to William King of C----- Co., Alabama, one ninth part of a tract descended to the heirs of Francis King, deceased, who is the father of Frances Easly, land in Bedford Co., TN, on west side of the Garrison Fork. Begins at center of the Garrison Fork, a few yards above where the road crosses the Ford which includes their Mill. Reg: 15 June 1821.

Page 284 - 19 Jan 1819. John B. Cummings to William Galbreath, 1 acre. John B. Cummings of Bedford Co., TN conveyed to William Galbreath of Adams Co., PA, land on west of his west boundary line as called in a deed executed to him by William and Walter Galbert by deed and bearing this date. Wit: Jos. Brittain and Theo. F. Bradford. Reg: 17 Apr 1819.

Page 288 - 19 Feb 1821. James Walker to John McGee, 60 acres. James Walker sold to John McGee, both of Bedford Co., TN, land in Bedford Co., on Shipmans Creek, being the place whereon James Walker now lives. Wit: Charles Timmins and William P. Chamberlain. Reg: 11 July 1821.

Page 292 - 28 May 1822. Richard Brandon & Others to William Lock, 189 acres. Richard Brandon of Giles Co., TN, for himself and Executors of Alexander Lock, deceased, and agent for Ann Lock widow of Alexander Lock, deceased, and agent for James Peral and Margaret Peral his wife, John S. Brandon, Alexander W. Brandon, Abel Cowan, Frederick Dinkins and Sarah Dinkins his wife conveyed to William Lock of Bedford Co., TN, land in Bedford Co., TN, on waters of the North Fork of Duck River, it being part of the division laid off to the heirs of John Brandon as legatees of Alexander Lock, deceased. Borders John Thompson. Wit: John Thompson and Pinston. Reg: 13 Aug 1823.

Page 295 - 6 June 1821. James Lockhart to Moses H. Prewitt, 314 acres. James Lockhart surviving Executor of John Strother, deceased, of R----- Co., VA and Paterick Prewitt, Moses H. Prewitt, Hiram Edde, Moses Edde, Malvina Edde, Patience Edde, Elizabeth Womack and Michael Womack, heirs of Michael Prewitt, deceased, by his Last Will, land in Bedford Co., TN. Borders Michael Prewitt, school land and Flat Creek. Reg: 9 July 1823.

Page 302 - 18 Jan 1823. John Limmons to Isaac Shinault. We, Washington Lumby and Elizabeth Lumby his wife formerly Elizabeth Shinault, John Limmons and Anna Lemons his wife formerly Anna Shinault, in full faith and confidence in our friend James Shinault who is also co-heir within the estate of Isaac Shinault, appointed James Shinault, our Attorney to oversee of the estate of Isaac Shinault which was decreed to us at Jan Term 1822, against Howel Dawdy, Administrator against John Jackson of Missouri or any other persons in Missouri or elsewhere. Reg: 23 Jan 1823.

Page 305 - 4 June 1822. Thomas Talbot to Lavina Beck & Others. Thomas Talbot of Davidson Co., TN conveyed to Lavina Beck, Susanne C. Beck and Georgiana Beck of Davidson Co., TN, land in Bedford Co., TN. Beginning at north boundary line of North Carolina Grant to Thomas Talbot, crosses Duck River. Wit: Jo. H. Talbot and E. Talbot. Reg: 22 Feb 1823.

Page 309 - 3 Jan 1823. Clinton Norvell to William Norvell, Bill of Sale. I, Clinton Norvell of Lawrence Co., Alabama, appointed my friend William Norvell of Bedford Co., TN, my Attorney, to sell and receive of moneys on sale of negroes. Reg: 3 Jan 1823.

Page 326 - 2 July 1821. John Balch to Alfred and Samuel Balch. John Balch conveyed to Alfred M. Balch and Samuel P. Balch, all of Bedford Co., TN, undivided land situated in Bedford Co., TN and which was devised to Ann Balch, mother of John Balch by the Last Will and Testament of Samuel Patton, Sr. Devised to her and her male heirs. Reg: 15 Mar 1823.

Page 330 - 26 Feb 1823. Articles of Agreement between the heirs of A. Torrentine. We, the heirs and legatees of Alexander Torrentine, deceased, viz, Samuel Torrentine, who claiming in his own right as also by purchase from Daniel Torrentine and from John Baldridge, agent of Francis Baldridge and Elizabeth Baldridge his wife formerly Elizabeth Torrentine, James Torrentine in his own right as also tenants in common with Samuel Torrentine in the purchase from John Baldridge, agent, as aforesaid John Watson and Jane his wife formerly Jane Torrentine, and Thomas Wood who claims by purchase from Josiah Baldridge who purchased from Andrew McBroom and Martha his wife formerly Martha Torrentine, being all of lawful age and heirs and leggatees of Alexander Torrentine, deceased, land of 278 acres in Bedford Co., TN, on Fall Creek. Borders Mathew Lock's tract, and Phifer's survey. Wit: Isaiah Lemmond and James Torrentine. Reg: 15 Jan 1823.

Page 333 - 8 Feb 1822. Richard W. Caswell to Jas. Turrentine, 598 acres. Benjamin McCullock in right of his wife as administrator of Richard W. Caswell, deceased, of Rutherford Co., TN conveyed to James Turrentine in his own right as one of the legal heirs of Alexander Turrentine, deceased, and as agent of Samuel Turrentine and other heirs and legatees of Alexander Turrentine, deceased, of Bedford Co., TN, land in Bedford Co., on Fall Creek. Wit: Thomas Williams and John Williams. Reg: 18 Mar 1823.

Page 337 - 4 June 1821. John W. McGimsey to Moses Payne, 122 acres. John W. McGimsey and Mary McGimsey his wife of Town of Shelbyville, Bedford Co., TN, sold to Moses Payne of Bedford Co., TN, land in Bedford Co., on the south or Barren Fork of Duck River. Borders Wren Carter, J. Ewell, S. Payne(Shrewsberry Payne). The same land as being the tract of which Shrewsberry Payne lived upon which said interest and claim of the said John W. and Mary his wife to said tract of 122 acres is their undivided one sixth part of tract which they are entitled as one of the heirs of Shrewsberry Payne, deceased. Signed by J. W. McGimsey and Polly McGimsey. Wit: Minos Cannon and Thomas C. Moore. Reg: 17 Feb 1822.

Page 356 - Dec Term 1819. John Wortham, Sheriff to Joseph and Cathartine Drake. Thomas Drake lately in said Court had recovered against Joseph Drake and Catharine Drake. Sheriff was commanded to levy on the goods and chattels and tenements of Joseph and Catharine Drake to be found in bedford Co., TN, 13 Oct 1819, William Norvell, High Sheriff, found 495 acres in 3 tracts as property of said Joseph and Catharine Drake. Also, John Tuck lately recovered against Joseph and Catharine Drake and Randolph Bates and Sheriff was to levy on goods and chattels of Said Drake's and Bates in bedford Co., on 495 acres.

Page 365 - 7 Nov 1822. Thomas Sanders to Thomas B. Moseley, Bill of Sale. I, Thomas Sanders, administrators of estate of Edward Ragsdale, deceased, sold to Thomas B. Moseley, a negro girl Jenny, one of the negroes of the estate of Edward Ragsdale. Wit: Frances Ragsdale, M. W. _. Haile. Reg: 8 Apr 1823.

Page 366 - 18 Mar 1823. John Adkinton and John Wortham to James C. O'Reilly. We, John Adkinson and John Wortham, administrators with Will annexed of Samuel Fleming, deceased, as administrator against Henry Crabb(?) and other creditors and against John Furguson and others, assignees and legatees under Will of Samuel Fleming, deceased, sold to James C. O'Reilly, a negro girl Mary. Reg: 8 Apr 1823.

Page 368 - 1 Nov 1822. John Jakes to Rachael Martin, Bill of Sale. Mrs. Rachael Martin paid $200.00 for negro boy Gilbert. Wit: John Scott, J. J. Mitchell, Samuel Mitchell and John T. Ragsdale. Reg: 8 Apr 1823.

Page 388 - Tennessee Grant to Joseph Long, 17 acres. No. 17971. Part of Certificate No. 1369, dated 16 Jan 1813, issued to William T. Lewis for 600 acres and entered 26 Feb 1813 by No. 5036. Granted to Joseph Long, assignee of William T. Lewis, land in Bedford Co., TN, on headwaters of Thompsons Creek. Beginning at a beech marked J.L. the north west corner of a 50 acre survey in name of said Long on which he now lives. Surveyed 17 Sept 1814. Reg: 16 June 1823.

Page 390 - Tennessee Grant to Joseph Long, 50 acres. No. 17973. For Military Service of Garrot Whitlock to North Carolina, Warrant No. 3192, dated 19 Dec 1795 for 640 acres and entered 7 July 1809 by No. 1570. Granted to Joseph Long, assignee of Garrot Whitlock, land in Bedford Co., TN, on west side of Thompsons Creek, west of a spring out of which Samuel Cross uses water. Surveyed 28 Nov 1819. Seal date at Murfreesboro on 4 Sept 1822. Reg: (no date).

DEED BOOK "Q" 1823 - 1823

Page 3 - 23 Nov 1822. Jacob Fuller to Joseph Green, Deed of Gift. I, Jacob Fuller of Bedford Co., TN, for love and affection for my daughter and son-in-law Joseph Green and Anny Green of Bedford Co., give negro woman Fillis, a negro child Caroline, cattle and furniture, and other property. Wit: L. B. Green and Hugh Morgan. Reg: 15 Jan 1823.

Page 28 - 24 Aug 1819. Thomas Cummings to Sarah Endsley, 150 acres. Thomas Cummings of Bedford Co., TN, conveyed to Sarah Endsley widow of Andrew Endsley, deceased, for the lawful heirs of said Andrew Endsley, deceased, of Bedford Co., TN, agreeable to the Lasy Will and Testament of Andrew Endsley, deceased, authorizing Sarah Endsley to purchase land &c, the land in Bedford Co., TN, on west waters of East Fork of Rock Creek. Borders Felix Robertson, Blackwell's corner and Smiley's line. Reg: 15 Oct 1819.

Page 30 - John Reed to the Church of Christ.
I, John Reed of Bedford Co., TN, for benefit of the community, given a parcel of land adjoining the Village of Farmington upon which a cabin now stands which was and is intended for a House of Instruction. Be it understood that I do voluntary give unto Horatio Mullins, George Neill and D. Dryden of Bedford Co., one quarter of an acre to be laid off from my body of land and

that the said quarter of an acre is to include the School House or cabin aforesaid, the shape and form of which quarter of an acre may be a square, oblong or otherwise. Wit: McClure & Robert Dysert. Reg: 15 Jan 1823.

Page 32 - 25 Oct 1822. Gabriel Jones to Robert Allison & Others. I, Gabriel Jones of North Carolina for love and affection I bear for Robert Allison and the children of Jane Allison, deceased, all of Tennessee except Jane Williams daughter of James Allison who lives in Mississippi, the said Robert and James being brothers of my late wife Mary formerly Mary Allison, given negro slaves which came to my wife, to wit, Solomon and his wife Richard and their children, Jenny, Franky, Tabby, Solomon, Tempy, Jimmy, Mary and John. Wit: Thomas Littlejohn and William Allison. Reg: 14 Jan 1823.

Page 34 - 16 July 1821. John G. Brown to Mary Friddle, Bill of Sale. I, John G. Brown of Bedford Co., TN sold to Mary Friddle of Bedford Co., 120 acres of land adjoining Mary Friddle and widow Reynolds, on Big Flat Creek, and other personal property. Wit: Henry Jones and Hugh Baird. Reg: 9 Oct 1821.

Page 35 - 14 Jan 1823. James Norsworthy to Thomas Norsworthy, Power of Attorney. I, James Norsworthy of Perry Co., TN, appointed my beloved son Thomas Norsworthy of Bedford Co., TN, my Attorney, to transact by business everwhere. Wit: Edward Wade and John Barrett. Reg: 27 Mar 1823.

Page 36 - 8 Dec 182_. Andrew Kerr, Devises to Archabald Walker, Obligation. We, Catherine Kerr, David Kerr, Joseph Gass and his wife Jane Gass, Margaret Kerr, John Kerr and Catherine Kerr, all of Jefferson Co., TN, are bound unto Archabald S. Walker of Bedford Co., TN, land for $500.00. Land on both sides of Sugar Creek. Borders lands of Charles McCommons and John Bradshaw. Wit: Richard Bradshaw and William Rankins. Reg: 28 Mar 1823.

Page 66 - 29 Aug 1820. John White and Archabald White, Agreement. I, John White of Cabarrus Co., NC and Archabald S. White of Madison Co., Alabama, agreement to pay money of Archabald S. White to pay $600.00 by 25 Dec 1824. I, John White in my own name and in the name of Samuel, Archabald and Joseph White, as by a Power of Attorney to me, claim to land on Sugar Creek deeded to Archabald White, Sr. by Amos Balch. Wit: Ozne W. Bradshaw and Eva S. Bradshaw. Reg: 17 Oct 1822.

Page 80 - 9 Oct 1822. Joseph Brittain to James Brittain, 194 acres. Joseph Brittain sold land to James Brittain, my son, land in Bedford Co., TN, on north side of Duck River, a part of a 1000 acre grant to Amos Balch by North Carolina. Wit: Thomas Dover and John Wortham. Reg: 3 April 1823.

Page 82 - 9 Oct 1822. Joseph Brittain to James Brittain, 7 acres. Same as above, land in Bedford Co., TN, on north side of Duck River. Wit: Thomas Dover and John Wortham. Reg: 12 Oct 1822.

Page 90 - 7 Apr 1823. John Scott to Mary Scott Yell, Deed of Gift. I, John Scott of Bedford Co., TN, for love and affection for my granddaughter Mary Scott Yell, conveys a negro boy John and negro girl Penelope. Reg: 9 Apr 1823.

Page 91 - 29 Dec 1821. Archer Cathey to James Cathey, Deed of Gift. For love and affection for his son James Cathey, conveys a negro boy Moses who is now in possession of said James Cathey. Wit: William Ditto and John Lain. Reg: 9 Apr 1823.

Page 118 - Edward and Anne Whitworth to Samuel Whitworth, PA I, Edward Whitworth and Anna Whitworth of Bedford Co., TN, appointed Samuel Whitworth of Bedford Co., our Attorney, to recover or receive from Oliver McReynolds of "Cammel" Co., VA, administrator of estate of James McReynolds, late of "Cammel" Co., VA, one sixth part of said estate that comes to the heirs of Thomas McReynolds, deceased. Thomas McReynolds, deceased, who lived in Moore Co., NC. Reg: March Term 1810 Term.

Page 122 - 15 June 1822. Solomon Dews to George A. G. B. Dews. We, Solomon Dews and Nancy R. Dews of Bedford Co., TN, for love and affection we have for our son George Alexander Galvestor Bannester Dews of Bedford Co., give for $1.00, negro man Moses who is now in the possession of Archibald Atkinson of Isle of Wight, VA. The said negro Moses was bequeathed unto Nancy R. Dews by the Last Will and Testament of Thomas Carroll, deceased, her former husband, during her natural life. Wit: James L. Armstrong and Jesse Taylor. Reg: 22 May 1823.

Page 124 - 12 Apr 1822. George W. Haywood to John Haywood, Deed of Mortgage. I, George Haywood convey to my father John Haywood, all my estate both real and personal. Wit: Turbeville and Margaret Duffey on 2 Jan 1823. Wit: John D. Lane and E. Haywood. Reg: (no date).

Page 125 - Tennessee Grant to Joseph Long, 5 acres. No. 17972. Part of Certificate No. 701, dated 7 May 1814, issued to Ephraim Payton for 640 acres and entered 24 Feb 1816 by No. 8971. Granted to Joseph Long, assignee of Ephraim Peyton, land in Bedford Co., TN, on waters of Thompsons Creek. Surveyed 15 Mar 1816. Reg: at Murfreesboro, TN Oct 1822.

Page 126 - Tennessee Grant to Joseph Long, 20 acres. No. 17970. Part of Certificate No. 51, dated 10 Sept 1807, issued to Samuel Smith for 275 acres and entered 20 Feb 1810 by No. 2194. Granted to Joseph Long, assignee of Samuel Smith, land in Bedford Co., TN, on headwaters of Thompsons Creek. Surveyed 5 Apr 1810. Borders Keeble Terry. Reg: 12 Oct 1822.

Page 172 - 5 Apr 1823. James McCuistion, Sr. to Anthony McCuistion, 110 acres. James McCuistion conveyed to Anthony McCuistion, both of Bedford Co., TN, land in Bedford Co., on waters of Hurricane Creek. Borders James McCuistion, Thomas McCuistion and Benjamin McCuistion. Wit: Benjamin McCuistion and Thomas McCuistion and James McCuistion. Reg: 17 Apr 1823.

Page 176 - 17 Mar 1823. George Crump to Elizabeth Crump, 50 acres. George Crump conveyed to Elizabeth Crump, both of Bedford Co., TN, land in Bedford Co., on waters of Sinking Creek. Borders John Medearis and Peter Garrins. Wit: Peter Helton, Thomas Brown and James Helton. Reg: 17 Apr 1823.

Page 178 - 15 Dec 1821. Samuel Reed to Elijah Parker, 60 acres. Samuel Reed of Limestone Co., Alabama conveyed to Elijah Parker of Bedford Co., TN, land in Bedford Co., on headwaters of Little Flat Creek. Borders Abner Chappel and Keeble Terry. Wit:

Elijah Parker, Jr. and Landrum Spann. Reg: 17 Apr 1823.

Page 194 - 14 Oct 1822. Abraham B. Routon & Others to George Hooper, 130 acres. Abraham B. Routon and Ann his wife, and John Cooke and Charlott his wife sold to George Hooper, land in Bedford Co., TN. Wit: Francis Mosley, S. S. Mosley and Richard Gilliam. At a court for Buckingham Co., VA, 14 Oct 1822, this indenture was acknowledged by Abraham B. Routon and John S. Cooke. Reg: 4 July 1823.

Page 196 - Archabald Cathey to James Cathey, Deed of Gift. For love and affection for his son James Cathey, he gives to him a negro boy Moses who is in the possession of James Cathey. 29 Dec 1821. Wit: William Ditto and John Lain. Reg: 8 Apr 1823.

Page 199 - 1820. James Norsworthy to Neal Norsworthy, 106 acres. James Norsworthy conveyed to Neal Norsworthy, both of Bedford Co., TN, for love and affection for his son Neal Norsworthy, land in bedford Co., TN, on waters of Sugar Creek. Borders Thomas Greer and Alexander Greer, Dougans and Sharp's line and Carlisle' survey. Said land is a Land Grant to James Norsworthy for his Military Service to North Carolina, Warrant No. 144, dated 22 Dec 1806 and entered 21 Aug 1807 by No. 276. Also, deed reserve that the James Norsworthy and Barbary his wife during their natural lives shall have and be in full possession of all the land and tenements on the east side of Thompsons Ford Road except one acre of ground which contains the dwelling house wherein the said Neal Norsworthy now lives and outbuildings extending to the spring and after death of James and Barbary Norsworthy, shall be in possession of Neal Norsworthy. Wit: Jas. McKissick and Thomas Norsworthy. Reg: 5 July 1823.

Page 209 - 6 Apr 1813. Peter Chilcut to Perlina Chilcut, Deed of Gift. I, Peter Chilcut of Bedford Co., TN, for love and affection for my daughter Perlina Waddle Chilcut, personal property. Wit: Thomas Cary and Isham Harris. Reg: 23 July 1823.

Page 222 - David Ross' Last Will and Testament.
I, David Ross of Richmond do make this my Last Will and Testament. To my son Frederick Augustus Ross, land which I have put into the possession of my son David Ross, Jr. and also 36 slaves. To my son David Ross, Jr., land in his possession, called "Mount Ida & Red House Plantation", about 1400 acres and also 36 slaves. I give to my four children and heirs to be equally divided among them namely Eliza Myers wife of Jacob Myers, Amanda A. Duffield wife of John Duffield, and Frederick A. Ross, and David Ross, Jr. Nominated Frederick A. Ross, my son in law Jacob Myers and friend Thomas T. Bauldin, Executors of this Last Will and Testament. This 24 April 1817. Wit: John Jameson, Sewell Osgood, and M. H. Rice. Court at Henrico Co., VA, 6 May 1817 David Ross, deceased, proven. Recorded in Overton Co., TN 26 Feb 1821 in Register's office in Book E, from page 126 to 129. Reg: in White Co., TN, 4 July 1821 in Register's office in Book G and pages 79 & 80. Reg: in Warren Co., TN in Register's office in Book D, pages 151, 152, 153, 27 Aug 1821. Reg: in Franklin Co., TN in Register's office in Book H, pages 53, 54, 55, & 56. Reg: in Bedford Co., TN, 2 Aug 1823.

Page 225 - 10 Apr 1820. David Ross devises to Frederick A. Ross.
Jacob Myers and Eliza Myers his wife, John Duffield and Amanda his wife, and Benjamin Lewis, all at present of Sullivan Co., TN conveyes to Frederick A. Ross at present of Sullivan Co., TN, land in Sullivan and Hawkins Counties, TN, David Ross the elder on 4 April 1817 made and published his Last Will and Testament and on the 4 May 1817 departed this life. See Will on page 222. Executors to sell land in Kentucky. Wit: Perly Fairbanks and David W. R. Myers. Reg: 2 Aug 1823.

Page 232 - 21 Mar 1818. David Ross devises to F. A. Ross. Jacob Myers and Eliza his wife, John Duffield and Amanda his wife, and David Ross conveyed to Frederick A. Ross (see page 222 & 225). David Ross departed this life on 4 May 1817. Reg: (no date).

Page 247 - 18 Feb 1823. Solomon Dews to Starling Newsom, Mortgage. George Alexander Galveston Banester Dews by his father and guardian Solomon Dews of Bedford Co., TN sold to Starling Newsom of Bedford Co., a negro woman Nelly. Wit: Benj. Strother and James Deery. Reg: 9 July 1823.

Page 256 - 28 May 1822. Brandon devises to John Thompson, 190 acres. Richard Brandon of Giles Co., TN for himself and Executor of Alexander Lock, deceased, and agent for Ann Lock, James Pernal and Margaret his wife, John S. Brandon, Alexander W. Brandon, Abel Cowan, Frederick Dinkins and Sarah Dinkins his wife conveyed to John Thompson of Bedford Co., TN, land in Bedford Co., on waters of Alexanders Creek, waters of North Fork of Duck River. Borders William Dameron. Wit: Richard Brandon and John S. Brandon. Reg: 9 July 1823.

Page 279 - 2 July 1823. Jordan C. Holt to John Whitsel, 60 acres. Jordan C. Holt and Peggy his wife sold to John Whitsel, all of Bedford Co., TN, land in bedford Co., on waters of Sinking Creek, known as Lot No. 5. The land being the jointly by Jacob Wilhoit. Reg: 9 July 1823.

Page 283 - 2 July 1823. John Barrett to John Whitsell, 51¼ acres. John Barrett and Fanny his wife sold to John Whitsell, all of Bedford Co., TN, land in Bedford Co., on waters of Big Sinking Creek, known as Lot No. 2. Reg: 9 July 1823.

Page 297 - 1 Apr 1822. Benjamin Huddleston to Stephen Huddleston, Bill of Sale. I, Benjamin Huddleston conveyed to Stephen Huddleston, both of Bedford Co., TN, personal property. Wit: John Huddleston and David Huddleston. Reg: 16 July 1823.

Page 298 - Thomas A. Peacock to Amos McAdams, 40 acres. Whereas Wilson Loyd, late of Bedford Co., TN, now deceased, did on 29 Oct 1815 made and execute his certain bond to Amos McAdams on land of 40 acres in Bedford Co., on waters of Hurricane Creek. Reg: 7 July 1823.

Page 315 - 7 June 1823. James Lockhart to Aaron Gamble, 207 acres. James Lockhart, surviving Executor of the Last Will and Testament of John Strother, deceased, of Botetourt Co., VA conveyed to Aaron Gamble of Bedford Co., TN, land in Bedford Co., on waters of Powels Creek, it being the land that William Bond, deceased, of Williamson Co., TN, deeded to Aaron Gamble, dated 14 Apr 1812. Wit: S. Anderson, William F. Rawling and William Rawlins and Lewis Rawlins. Reg: 1 Oct 1823.

Page 317 - 1 Jan 1822. McGee devises to Daniel Johnston, 11½ acres. William McGee, deceased, heirs and John McGee conveyed to Daniel Johnston, land in Bedford Co., TN, on the Garrison Fork of Duck River. Borders Garrison Fork, Mill formerly conveyed by King to McGee & Tilford. John McGee and Ann McGee, heirs of William McGee, deceased, James Burrow, John Thompson, W. B. McGee and Samuel K. McGee for themselves heirs and Administrators or Executors, sold to Daniel Johnston. Wit: T. H. Bernard, William Hooser and Hugh Davidson. Reg: 9 July 1823.

Page 334 - 26 Dec 1822. John Denny to Elizabeth and Archabald Cook, 25 acres. John Denny sold to Elizabeth and Archabald Cook, all of Bedford Co., TN, land in Bedford Co., on East Fork of Rock Creek. Wit: D. Appleby, James Rogers and D. Jose. Reg: 5 July 1823.

Page 340 - 16 Jan 1823. Michael Fisher to George W. Parsons, Bill of Sale. I, Michael Fisher for love and affection for his daughter Peggy and her husband George W. Parsons and for $30.00, a negro girl Amy. Reg: 9 July 1823.

Page 356 - 16 Oct 1823. Benjamin Coats to James Coats, Power of Attorney. I, Benjamin Coats of Wilson Co., TN, appointed James Coats, my Attorney, to oversee my property, management of two lots. No. 1, borders the land which Wilson Coats my father held in his life time and on which he died, on the north bank of Duck River. Also, lot in Town and known as Lot No. 129, in Shelbyville. I have a brother James Coats of Bedford Co., TN, which I appoint as my Attorney. Wit: Laven S. Martial and Percy Yell. Reg: 18 Dec 1823.

Page 366 - 4 Aug 1823. John McCorkle to William Lemmons, 100 acres. Jane McCorkle and John McCorkle, both of Bedford Co., TN conveyed to William Lemmons of Bedford Co., land in Bedford Co., on north side of Duck River just below the mouth of the North Fork and being a part of a 2000 acre tract originally granted to John Graham, dated 10 July 1788. Borders Felix Roberson and John Jackson. Wit: Charles Wortham and John S. Gibson. Reg: 16 Oct 1823.

DEED BOOK "R" 1823 - 1824

Page 1 - 15 Apr 1823. James L. Armstrong and John J. Sims to Smith Arnold. John G. Sims and James L. Armstrong, surviving Trustees of John G. Sims conveyed to Smith Arnold, land being a part of land conveyed by Sims to Armstrong and Minos Cannon, deceased, by Deed of Trust, dated 5 Oct 1822. 100 acres. Wit: Thomas Davis and Edward Wade. Reg: 13 Aug 1823. (Page 3 - sells to Thomas Holland) and (Page 5 - sells to John Moore).

Page 7 - 14 Apr 1823. Michael Holt to John Comb, 266 acres. Michael Holt, Jane Holt his wife sold to John Comb, land in Bedford Co., TN, on waters of Sugar Creek and Sinking Creek. Wit: John A. Maars (Marrs), and William Combs. Reg: 18 Apr 1823.

DEED BOOK "R"

Page 15 - 18 Mar 1823. Atkinson & Wortham to William Guy. We, John Atkinson and John Wortham, administrators with Will annexed of Samuel Fleming, deceased, of Bedford Co., TN, as administrators complainants against Henry Crabb and other creditors and against John F. Ferguson and other devises and legatees under the Will of Samuel Fleming, deceased, has sold unto William Guy, negro boy Stephen. Wit: John M. Lane and Abram Martin, Jr. Reg: 19 Aug 1823.

Page 17 - 1 June 1823. Andrew Erwin to George Newton. Erwin for $1.00, land in Bedford Co., TN, on Knob Creek. Beginning on the line of George Newton where the wagon road crosses Knob Creek between the Academy, thence south to line of the brick house tract. For the use only of the Academy whereon is established and use as a Church. Wit: Jno. _. Erwin, A. Martin and Jno. B. Dickson. Reg: 26 Aug 1823.

Page 33 - We, Daniel Dryden, guardian for Nancy Gates, William A. Gates, Benjamin D. Gates and Alexander Gates, minor children of Allen Gates and his wife Elizabeth, and Thomas Powelwell and his wife Eliza, Abram Lorance and his wife Susan Lorance, the said Eliza and Susan being also children of said Allen Gates and his wife Elizabeth have this day received from Elias Billington $455.00 for negro boy George. The negro was left to Elizabeth Gates during her life by the Will and Testament of William H. Allen and after her death to go to her children. -- day of ---, 1823. Reg: 30 Aug 1823.

Page 57 - David Yarborough and Helen M. Yarborough, late Helen M. Doherty his wife of Orange Co., NC, and Frances W. Bond, late Frances W. Doherty, and Mary Doherty of Williamson Co., TN, heirs and devises of the late George Doherty of Orange Co., NC sold to William P. Anderson of Franklin Co., TN and James Lockhart of Botetourt Co., VA, surviving executors and devises of John Strother, deceased, late of Davidson Co., TN and executor of George Strother, deceased, a devise likewise of John Strother, deceased, land on a small creek that runs into the North Fork of Duck River below the mouth of Weakleys Creek, about 3000 acres. Borders school land. Also, land on both sides of the Middle Fork of Normans Creek of Elk River in Lincoln Co., TN, bordering school land. Also, a tract on both sides of the main East Fork of Flint River in Lincoln Co., TN, and other tracts elsewhere. Reg: 9 Oct 1822.

Page 66 - 10 July 1822. James B. Porter and Frances W. Porter, late Frances W. Doherty and Frances W. Bound (Bond) now Frances W. Porter of Williamson Co., TN, heirs and devises of the late George Doherty of Orange Co., NC sold to William P. Anderson of Franklin Co., TN and James Lockhart of Botetourt Co., VA, surviving executors of John Strother, deceased, late of Davidson Co., TN, and executor of George Strother, deceased &c, sold to David Yarborough and Helen M. his wife late Helen M. Doherty, Mary Doherty and Frances W. Porter, did on 1 Sept 1821 executed a deed for land &c. Reg: 15 Oct 1823.

Page 97 - 22 Sept 1822. Thomas Miles to David Logan, Devises, 161 acres. Thomas Miles of Wilson Co., TN conveyed to the heirs of David Logan, deceased, of Bedford Co., TN, viz, Martha Floyd the daughter of David Logan, Polly Breecheen, Sarah Breecheen, both daughters of David Logan, Benjamin Logan, Talton Logan, Lucinda Logan, Mary Logan, John Logan, and Agness Logan, all heirs of David Logan, land in Bedford Co., TN, on East Fork of Rock Creek. Borders James Walls, William Mitchell, John Dysert. Wit: John Bruce and S. Anderson. Reg: 16 Oct 1823.

Page 138 - Margaret Nichols to William B. Nichols, Mortgage. I, Margaret Nichols of Bedford Co., TN, for love and affection for William B. Nichols of Jackson Co., Alabama, and for $1.00, for a negro boy Anderson. Wit: A. W. Haton, Catherine Nichols, and Margaret Nichols. Reg: 16 Oct 1823.

Page 161 - 4 Nov 1824. Sims & Green to John G. Sims, Mortgage. Walter B. Sims and John S. Green sold to John G. Sims, administrator with Will annexed of Walter Sims, deceased, of Davidson Co., TN, land in Giles Co., TN, also land in Bedford Co., TN. Also, another tract in Bedford Co., of 150 acres on north side of Duck River, being opposite Sims' Mill on Duck River and other tracts of land elsewhere. Wit: O. B. Hays and Jno. Bell. Reg: Nov Term 1823.

Page 167 - 1 Aug 1823. James & Samuel Torrentine, Agreement. Maj. Samuel Torrentine and his brother James Torrentine, both of Bedford Co., TN, agree to start business together. Wit: James Torrentine and Charles Torrentine. Reg: 5 Jan 1824.

Page 171 - 15 Nov 1821. Bates Smithwick to William King, 254 acres. Bates Smithwick and Polly Smithwick his wife of Bedford Co., TN sold to William King of Morgan Co., Alabama, for $50.00, part of a tract of land divided to the heirs of Francis King, deceased, who was father of Polly Smithwick and to whom Polly together with her husband Bates Smithwick or heirs, land in Bedford Co., TN, on west side of the Garrison Fork of Duck River. Wit: Edward Easly. Reg: 17 Oct 1823.

Page 180 - 20 Nov 1823. William Norvell to Edward Cage, 267½ acres. William Norvell, Sr., John Norvell, Jr., James Norvell, Jr., and Nathan Norvell of Bedford Co., TN conveyed to Edward Cage of Bedford Co., land in Bedford Co., on waters of the Wartrace Fork. Borders William Norvell, Jesse Davidson's field, and Bell Buckle Creek. Wit: Francis Yancy, Thomas Norvell, and Wilson J. Cage. Reg: 29 Jan 1824.

Page 192 - 17 Nov 1823. Mark Harden to Robert Allison, 320 acres. Mark Harden of Rockingham Co., NC sold to Robert Allison of Bedford Co., TN, land in Bedford Co., on Clems Creek. Borders Charles Brandon's survey, John Wilson's tract, Robert Allison's corner of which he now lives, and William Clark's line. Wit: William Ogilvie, Kimbrough Allison, James Ray and Richard Wright. Reg: 29 Jan 1824.

Page 209 - 29 Nov 1823. Thomas Blythe to Levi C. Roberts, 75 acres. Thomas Blythe, Jr. of Lincoln Co., TN sold to Levi C. Roberts of Bedford Co., TN, land in Bedford Co., northeast of the Town of Shelbyville, being part of a tract purchased by Wilson Coats, deceased, from Clement Cannon. Wit: Jonathan Floyd and Thomas Washbourn. Reg: 30 Jan 1824.

Page 211 - 17 June 1813. Samuel Wilson to James Bruce, 450 acres. Samuel Wilson of Sumner Co., TN sold to James Bruce of Sumner Co., TN, land in Bedford Co., TN, on Spring Creek. Borders James Wilson where he now lives, and Aaron Wilson, and Patterson's land. Wit: George Crocket. Reg: 29 Mar 1824.

Page 213 - 25 Mar 1823. John Porter & Others to William M. Russell, 4 acres. John N. Porter and Catharine his wife of Rutherford Co., TN, and Samuel Laughlin, agent to Valentine Thomas of Rutherford Co., TN, and Nathan Adams and Sally his wife of Williamson Co., TN, and Stephen Porter and Mary his wife of Lincoln Co., TN conveyed to William M. Russell of Lincoln Co., TN, land in Bedford Co., TN, on Sinking Creek, including Porter's Old Mill, land formerly belonging to Nathaniel Porter, deceased. Wit: Benjamin W. H. Medearis, Thomas Smith, James Barben and Charles Russell. Reg: 16 Jan 1824.

Page 215 - 10 Jan 1824. James Coldwell to Edward Cage, 100 acres. James Coldwell of Madison Co., TN sold to Edward Cage of Bedford Co., TN land in Bedford Co., on waters of Wartrace Fork of Duck River. Wit: John Davis, Lemuel Sutton and William Norvell. Reg: 29 Jan 1824.

Page 235 - 24 Dec 1821. Amos West & Others to James Alexander, 100 acres. Amos West, Elijah West, Sally W. Lee of Nicholas Co., KY, and Eli West of Fayette Co., Ohio conveyed to James Alexander, Jr. of Rutherford Co., TN land in Bedford Co., on waters of Alexanders Creek, being land granted to Elijah West, deceased. Borders James Alexander and lands on which Moses Gess lives on. Wit: Nathan Adams, William Vinson, Field Coleman and William Trotter. Reg: 27 May 1824.

Page 237 - 13 Dec 1823. John Hooper to George W. Hooper, Bill of Sale. I, John Hooper of Tuscaloosa, Alabama, for the good will and affection for my nephew George W. Hooper, son of Richard Hooper of Tuscaloosa, Alabama, give to him articles of personal property among of which is a large Bible, and furniture. Wit: Moses Chastenbery, M.C. Jose, William A. Gates and David Dryden. Reg: 12 Apr 1824.

Page 277 - 6 Apr 1824. John Eakin to Sarah Pearson, 108½ acres. John Eakin of Shelbyville, Bedford Co., TN, conveyed to Sarah Pearson, Washington Bobo, Samuel Bobo, Elizabeth Bobo, Hettie Bobo, Burrel Bobo, Lucretia Bobo, children of Elijah and Sally Bobo of Bedford Co., land in Bedford Co., on the headwaters of Big Flat Creek, for Sarah Pearson for her natural life and at her death goes to the heirs of Elijah and Sally Bobo. Wit: Alexander Eakin and Kindred Pearson. Reg: 8 Apr 1824.

Page 305 - 3 Feb 1824. James L. Armstrong to William B. Sutton, Bill of Sale. I, James L. Armstrong for love and affection for my daughter Marianne, I give to her husband William B. Sutton, a negro girl Daphne. Reg: 4 June 1824.

Page 306 - 27 Jan 1824. Catherine Drake and David Marshall to Rachael Martin, Bill of Sale. Mrs. Rachael Martin was sold a negro boy Joseph. Wit: William S. Waterson, John T. Ragsdale and Jas. McMahon. Reg: 10 Apr 1824.

Page 327 - 25 Apr 1823. O. B. Hays to Andrew Greer & Others, 175 acres. Oliver B. Hays of Davidson Co., TN sold to Andrew Greer, Louisa B. Evins and Alexander Greer of Bedford Co., TN, children of Alexander Greer, deceased, land in Bedford CO., TN, on the south west corner of Grant No. 40 for 5000 acres to A. & T. Greer. Borders Sugar Creek. Reg: (no date).

DEED BOOK "R"

Page 329 - 18 Nov 1823. D. & Polly Blessing to Giles Burdett, 84¼ acres. David Blessing and Polly Blessing his wife sold to Giles Burdett, all of Bedford Co., TN land in Bedford Co. Borders Wilson Coats, deceased. Wit: Jas. Brittain and W. R. Burdett. Reg: 29 Jan 1824.

Page 342 - 14 Jan 1824. Thomas and Neal Norsworthy to James Lockhart, 41 acres. Thomas Norsworth, Attorney in fact for James Norsworthy and Neal Norsworthy to both whom James Norsworthy executed Deed of Conveyance to land by Grant to James Norsworthy for 312 acres on waters of Sugar Creek in Bedford Co., TN, sold to James Lockhart surviving executor heir &c of John Strother, deceased, land being part of the above mentioned tract. Borders John Strother's survey. Wit: Robert Cannon and _____ Conway. Reg: 29 Jan 1824.

Page 360 - 3 Apr 1824. John King to Nancy King, -- acres. John King conveyed to Nancy King, both of Bedford Co., TN, bequeathed to Nancy King the land, the plantation whereon John King now lives. Borders Dickinson's land, Frances King, and land John King ourchased of Peter Lee. Nancy King to have during her natural life, the same land left to John King by John's father at his death. Wit: _. Starrett and Charles B. King. Reg: 8 Apr 1824.

Page 362 - 5 Feb 1824. James Mason to Elizabeth Jane & R. Whitehead, Bill of Sale. I, James Mason sold to Elizabeth Jane and Redden Whitehead, all of Bedford Co., TN, property. Wit: Sary Whitehead. Reg: 8 Apr 1824.

Page 365 - John Whitehead to Ja. Whitehead. 27 Oct 1823. Both of Bedford Co., TN, property. Wit: Samuel More and _____ Burwell. Reg: 8 Apr 1824.

Page 378 - 18 Dec 1822. Thomas & Samuel Bell to Isaac Bell. Thomas Bell of Bedford Co., TN and Samuel Bell of Franklin Co., Alabama, conveyed to Isaac Bell of Franklin Co., Alabama, land in Bedford Co., on waters of Noah's Fork of the Garrison Fork. Borders Samuel & Robert Hughes, Thomas Boman, Nancy Wetherford's peach orchard, where Jonathan Webster lives, and John Welch lived in 1816. Several tracts. Reg: 12 July 1824.

Page 409 - 9 June 1824. David Green to the Devises of William Treace, 140 acres. David Green and John Payton, Sr., on 27 Sept 1819 conveyed unto William Treace, land in Bedford Co., TN, it being a part of a 640 acre tract granted to John and William Payton by Tennessee No. 323. Borders Nathan H. Schooler and George Tilman. William Treace is now dead, leaving a widow and three children, Nancy now married to John Hickerson and Samuel Treace all of whom are minors and Christina, all heirs of William Treace, deceased. Wit: John H. Anderson and Edward Wade. Reg: 9 Sept 1824.

Page 430 - 7 July 1824. Joseph Robinson to John Robinson, 100 acres. Joseph Robinson of Williamson Co., TN conveyed to John Robinson, his son, of Williamson Co., TN, for love and affection for his son, land in Bedford Co., TN, on north side of Duck River, it being a part of a 1500 acre tract granted to Michael Robinson, Sr. by North Carolina and the same being a part of my division. Borders John Robinson, Sr. and Asa Fonville. Wit: John Robinson, Sr. and Benjamin McCuistion. Reg: 13 July 1824.

Page 430 - 2 Apr 1824. John N. Hart to Jacob Lowrance, 100 acres. John N. Hart, agent for the heirs of James Hart of Iredell Co., NC sold to Jacob Lowrance of Maury Co., TN, for consideration of the claims of Jacob Lowrance for the heirs of John Baird, deceased, originally of Buncomb Co., NC, to a part of a warrant in the name of James Hart, deceased, for 2214 acres. James Hart, deceased, being bound by Bond to Collen Campbell, Esq. Wit: Thomas A. Harris and Elijah Harris. Reg: 18 Sept 1824.

Page 450 - 29 Oct 1821. Daniel McLaren to John Richman, Deed of Gift, 150 acres. I, Daniel McLaren, Sr. for love and affection for John Richman and Susannah Richman his wife, she being my daughter, they living in Bedford Co., TN, given land in Bedford Co., TN, on waters of Caney Spring Creek. Wit: J. Atkinson and Ruben McLaren (McClaren). Reg: 15 July 1824.

Page 452 - 29 Oct 1821. Daniel McLaren to John C. Lewis, 213 acres. I, Daniel McLaren, Sr. for love and affection for John C. Lewis and Elizabeth Lewis his wife, she being my daughter of Bedford Co., TN, given land in Bedford CO., TN, on waters of Caney Spring Creek. Wit: J. Atkinson and Ruben McLaren (McClaren). Reg: 15 July 1824.

Page 458 - 29 Mar 1823. Daniel McLaren to J. & Nancy Atkinson, Deed of Gift, 200 acres. I, Daniel McLaren, Sr. of Hickman Co., TN, for love and affection for John Atkinson and Nancy Atkinson his wife, she being my daughter, given land whereon I, Daniel McLaren, Sr. formerly lived, on waters of Caney Spring Creek. Wit: John Richman and William Wheeler. Reg: 13 July 1824.

Page 489 - Sally & Moses Payne to Zebediah Payne, Bill of Sale. Sally Payne and Moses Payne, administrators of Shrewsberry Payne, deceased, of Bedford CO., TN, sold to Zebediah Payne, a negro boy William. Wit: A. B. Ross and Walton Payne. Reg: 13 July 1824.

Page 493 - 15 Mar 1824. Moses Payne to Zebediah Payne, Bill of Sale. I, Moses Payne, Jr. relinguish to Zebediah Payne, all of Bedford CO., TN, all my personal property. Wit: William Cribbs and Walton H. Payne. Reg: 13 July 1824.

Page 496 - 16 Dec 1823. Sally, Moses and Micager Payne to Zebediah Payne, Bill of Sale. I, Sally, Moses and Micager Payne all of Bedford CO., TN, relinguish unto Zebediah Payne of Bedford Co., all rights &c to negro girl Selah and 40 acres of land the same being on which Sally now lives and part of 131 acres belonging to Shrewsberry Payne and it being the dower, also other property. Wit: W. McConel and Walton Payne. Reg: 13 July 1824.

Page 498 - 9 Nov 1810. Thomas Beaty to Graham Devises. I, Thomas Beaty of Iredell Co., NC, for love and affection for my beloved grandchildren, David B. Graham, William Graham, Peggy Graham, Nancy H. Graham, and Jenny L. Graham and Elenor C. Graham, give a negro woman China. Wit: William Graham. Reg: (no date).

Page 504 - I, Elisha Gunn, one of the heirs and legatees of Elisha Gunn, Sr., deceased, sold to William M. Dorman, negro girl Phily. Elisha Gunn, Sr., deceased, was father of Elisha Gunn. Wit: Giles Burdett and W. B. Burdett. This 6 May 1824. Reg: 5 Dec 1824.

DEED BOOK "S" 1825 - 1825

Page 3 - Tennessee Grant to Samuel Lockhart, 100 acres. No.1539. Part of Certificate No. 146, dated 28 July 1807, obtained by Samuel Lockhart and entered 13 Aug 1808 by No. 717. Granted to Samuel Lockhart, land in Bedford Co., TN, on east waters of Big Flat Creek. Sueveyed 17 Nov 1808. Reg: (no date).

Page 63 - 18 July 1822. Archabald Yell to Samuel Phillips, 75 acres. Archabald Yell of Shelbyville, Bedford Co., TN sold to Samuel Phillips of Bedford Co., land in Bedford Co., being part of Robert Butler and Patsy his wife to Moses Yell and a part of that tract as Willed Moses Yell to his son Archabald Yell. Borders James Yell, plantation where Jane Yell now lives, and Phillips' line. Wit: A. Martin, Jesse Taylor and John G. Sims. Reg: 13 Jan 1825.

Page 67 - 19 June 1824. John Harris to Susanna Harris, 43 acres. John Harris conveyed to Susanna Harris, both of Bedford Co., TN, land in Bedford Co., on waters of Alexanders Creek of North Fork. Borders Joseph P. Morrison. Wit: Eva Harris and John Harris. Reg: 12 Oct 1824.

Page 81 - 26 July 1822. Abraham Wood to Thomas Dean, 10 acres. Abraham Wood of Independence Co., Arkansas conveyed to Thomas Dean of Bedford CO., TN, land in Bedford Co., on waters of Big Flat Creek. Borders cabin of Abraham Wood. The land being the land on which Davis Womack formerly lived. Wit: John H. Anderson and George Floyd. Reg: 14 Jan 1825.

Page 85 - 10 Apr 1824. Robert P. Harrison to Alexander Newton, 5 acres. Robert P. Harrison sold to Alexander Newton, land in Bedford CO., TN. Borders south east corner of the Dixon Academy land, James Deery, and George Davidson formerly Bobo. Wit: Thomas Davis and George Davidson. Reg: 18 Jan 1825.

Page 118 - 5 July 1824. William Omehundro Devises to William Gullett, 55 acres. James Y. Omehundro, William Omehundro, Richard Omehundro, and Elizabeth McGuire, legatees, sold to William Gullett, all of Bedford Co., TN, land in Bedford Co., TN, sold to Waitman Gullett, land granted to William Omehundro, deceased, land on waters of North Fork. Borders William Lytle. Elizabeth McGuire wife of Francis McGuire. Wit: John Shaw and Silas Simmon(?). Reg: 14 Oct 1825.

Page 122 - 1 Apr 1824. James Hart to Collen Campbell, -- acres. John N. Hart of Iredell Co., NC, agent for the heirs of James Hart, deceased, sold to Collen Campbell of Maury Co., TN, for services performed by Campbell by locating, surveying and obtaining a grant, deeded him land. Borders Thomas Davidson. Land in Bedford CO., TN, on west waters of East Fork of Rock Creek. Wit: Joel Darnell and Thomas Davidson. Reg: 14 Oct 1824.

Page 148 - 4 Nov 1823. Joseph Wallace to John England, 18 acres. Joseph and his wife Elizabeth Wallis sold to John England, all of Bedford Co., TN, land in Bedford Co., on headwaters of

Sinking Creek. Borders John Roberts. Land being the seventh part of a 100 acre survey deeded to John Smith, to John Smith and others, John Smith being deceased and died without issue and Elizabeth Wallace wife of Joseph Wallace being a sister of John Smith, deceased. Reg: Oct Term 1824.

Page 156 - 11 Jun 1821. Daniel Kenny & Devises to Thomas P. Kenny, 200 acres. William Kenny and Alexander Davidson, Margaret E. Davidson wife of Alexander Davidson, Elizabeth Kenny the widow of Daniel Kenny, deceased, and Jane Kenny of Bedford Co., TN conveyed to Thomas P. Kenny, land in Bedford Co., TN, on waters of Big Sinking Creek. Borders Humphry Cunningham, William Kenny. Wit: William Cunningham and Richard Talifero. Reg: 12 Oct 1825.

Page 161 - 29 July 1824. Alexander Davidson & Others to H. Cunningham, 105 acres. Alexander Davidson and Margaret his wife, William Potter and Jane his wife, and Elizabeth Kenny, all of Bedford Co., TN, sold to Humphry Cunningham of Bedford Co., land on waters of Sinking Creek, it being part ot a Tennessee Grant to Amos Johnson. Signed by Alexander Davidson, Margaret Davidson, William Potter, Jane Potter, and Elizabeth Kenny. Wit: George M. Cunningham and Isaac Doty. Reg: 14 Oct 1824.

Page 163 - 7 Feb 1820. Robert Adams to Alexander Adams, 100 acres. Robert Adams sold to Alexander Adams, both of Bedford Co., TN, land in Bedford Co., on Drydens Fork of Duck River. Borders William Shockley, William Williams, and James Miller. Reg: 14 Feb 1825.

Page 167 - 20 Feb 1824. Anna White to Richard Wright, 200 acres. Daniel L. Barringer, Attorney for Anna White, Executrix of the Last Will and Testament of William White, deceased, of Raleigh, NC sold to Richard Wright of Bedford Co., TN, land in Bedford Co., on waters of Wilson Creek, being part of a 1000 acre tract granted to William White, late of Raleigh. Borders James Stem and Nathan Shuffield. Wit: Isham Sims, Arthur Shuffield and William Collins. Reg: 7 Apr 1825.

Page 171 - 23 July 1823. George Waite to Morgan & Others, Quit Claim. Received of Robert Morgan as Agent and Attorney for David Sims, Willis Cannon and John Miller, $6.16 in full for land sold at Sheriff's Sale of Bedford Co., TN on 5 April 1823. Wit: P. J. Scudder. Reg: 14 Feb 1825.

Page 172 - 30 July 1823. Frederick Denkins & Others to Thomas Swann, 189 acres. Richard Brandon of Giles Co., TN, for himself and as Executor of Alexander Lock, deceased, and Agent for Ann Lock widow of Alexander Lock, deceased, and Agent for James Peral and Margaret Peral his wife, John S. Brandon, Alexander W. Brandon, Abel Cowan, Frederick Denkins and Sarah Denkins his wife conveyed to Thomas Swann of Bedford Co., TN, land in Bedford Co., on waters of the North Fork of Duck River, it being a part of the division of land of the heirs of John Brandon as devises of Alexander Lock, deceased. Borders William Lock. Reg: 14 Feb 1825.

Page 231 - 17 Feb 1824. Joseph Steele to Price C. Steele, 123 acres. Joseph Steele of Bedford Co., TN, for love and affection for his son Price C. Steele, part of his legacy of his father's estate in Bedford Co., TN, on Falling Creek. Borders William Rowland. Wit: V. H. Steele and Wilson Steele. Reg: 29 Apr 1825.

Page 235 - 5 Feb 1825. John Stokes, Sr. to William Stokes, Thomas Stokes and John H. Stokes. John Stokes, Sr. conveyed to William Stokes, David Stokes, Thomas Stokes and John H. Stokes, all of Bedford Co., TN, and for $40.00, land in Bedford Co., the same being the place where said Stokes now lives. Borders Tignal Jones and Rock Creek. Wit: John Stokes. Reg: 29 Apr 1825.

Page 250 - 24 July 1824. I, Abram Hill sold to Rebecca Hill, a negro man Lewis. Wit: Hillard Dixon and Thomas Dixon. Reg: 13 May 1825.

Page 260 - 5 Jan 1824. Joseph Steele to Wilson Steele, 168 acres. Joseph Steele for love and affection for his son Wilson Steele, part of a legacy of his father's estate, land on west side of the North Fork of Falling Creek. Wit: P. C. Steele and V. H. Steele. Reg: 12 Feb 1825.

Page 324 - 2 Dec 1823. Elizabeth Mayfield to Abraham Mayfield. I, Elizabeth Mayfield for love and affection for Abraham Mayfield and his family, conveys negroes, at my death. Wit: Elizabeth J. Tucker and William Mayfield, Robert Ray and Joseph Neill. Reg: 26 July 1825.

Page 333 - 28 Mar 1825. Joseph and Little Hickerson to Thomas and Henry Powers, 25 acres. Joseph and Little Hickerson sold to Thomas and Henry Powers, land in Bedford Co., TN, on west side of Brewers Branch, waters of Barren Fork. Reg: 19 Sept 1825.

Page 379 - Dec Term 1824. Circuit Court of Bedford County, TN William Hartsfield, complainant against John _. Stephens and Louisa D. Stephens, minor heirs of Allen Stephens, deceased, by their guardian John Stephens and Nathan Hartsfield, Defendants. A deed conveyed of 300 acres for 50 lbs of North Carolina currancy in year 1811. A contract with John Fort who had married one of the daughters and heirs of Dempsey Powel, dec'd, for land of 300 acres in Bedford Co., which he claimed in right of his wife as one of the heirs of Dempsey Powel, deceased. William Hartsfield moved to Bedford Co., TN from North Carolina with his family in 1811 and settled upon that division of Dempsey Powell land which had been assigned to John Fort and his wife. William Hartsfield was read a letter which Solomon Hartsfield proved he wrote by the direction of his father to William in 1811. The father was Andrew Hartsfield. There was a Andrew Hartsfield, Jr. mentioned in instrument. Reg: 12 Sept 1825.

Page 389 - John Reagor & Others to James Reagor & Others. John Reagor, Isaac Reagors, David Floyd and Catharine Reagor sold to James Reagor, Abraham Reagor, William Reagor and A. W. Reagor, all of Bedford Co., TN, the landed estate of Anthony Reagor, deceased of Bedford Co., -- day of Sept 1824. Wit: George Floyd, Thomas Dean and Jonathan Hurt. Reg: 12 May 1825.

Page 390 - 11 May 1825. Jefferson Scott to Sarah Trotter. Jefferson Scott conveyed to Sarah Trotter wife of George Trotter,

Sr., for $1.00, confirmed unto Sarah Trotter, all of Jefferson Scott's right, title, interest &c held by him under the Will of his father William Scott, deceased, three tracts of land in Bedford Co., TN, one tract on waters of Obed River, other on waters of Forked Deer River which tract was part of Alexander ______ estate who by his Last Will and Testament, devised to William Scott, deceased. Bourbon Co., KY, 26 May 1825. Reg: (no date).

Page 396 - 2 May 1825. John W. Peacock to Thomas A. Peacock. John W. Peacock conveyed to Thomas A. Peacock, both of Bedford Co., TN, land in Bedford Co., on waters of Wartrace Fork and known as estate of John Peacock, deceased, by No. 14. Wit: Thomas Coldwell and Stephen Murphree. Reg: 13 Aug 1825.

Page 404 - 24 Feb 1821. I, Joseph Brittain for love and affection for my beloved daughter Mary and now the wife of Aaron Boyd, all of Bedford Co., TN. Mary Boyd is my 3rd daughter. For $1.00, conveyed unto Mary Boyd a negro woman Fan and her children. Wit: John Wortham and John F. Ferguson. Reg: 14 Nov 1825.

Page 408 - 7 Nov 1825. James Shepherd to Elizabeth Marbury, Bill of Sale. I, James Shepperd of Williamson Co., TN, for love and affection which I have for my grandchild Elizabeth Marbury, negro slaves, which are now in the possession of Leonard W. Marbury. Elizabeth Marbury is under age of eighteen, if she should die before age of eighteen, the gift is void and the slaves are to go to my children. Wit: M. Gilchrist and H. Suggs. Reg: 14 Nov 1825.

Page 410 - 1 July 1822. H. McCoy and James Stuart to Hugh McBride, 126 acres. Henry McCoy and James H. Stuart of Rutherford Co., TN, administrators of the estate of William Mull, deceased, sold to Hugh McBride of Bedford Co., TN, land in Bedford Co. Borders heirs of John Lock, deceased, William Lock Survey, banks of the North Fork. Wit: S. Anderson and A. Byler. Reg: 23 Nov 1825.

Page 417 - 11 Nov 1818. James Lock to William Lock, 424 acres. I, James Lock of Rowan Co., NC, sold to William Lock of Bedford Co., TN, land in Bedford Co., on waters of the North Fork, it being a part of a 2000 acre tract granted to the heirs of John Lock by State of Tennessee, also a part of the estate of George Lock, deceased. Borders William Short, James Lock's division, William Lock, George Lock, deceased, and Mary Smith. Wit: Edward Cooper and John Thompson. Reg: 12 May 1825.

DEED BOOK "T" 1825 - 1826

Page 11 - 24 Feb 1821. Joseph Brittain to Aaron Boyd, 200 acres. Joseph Brittain for love and affection for his beloved daughter Mary and now the wife of Aaron Boyd, conveyed land in Bedford Co., TN, on waters of Caney Spring Creek. Wit: John Wortham and John F. Ferguson. Reg: (no date).

Page 43 - 1 Aug 1825. Jeremiah Dial to Ragsdale & Sample. Jeremiah Dyal of one part and Dronysues M. Ragsdale and William Sample, all of Bedford Co., TN, other part, Jeremiah Dyal, Jesse Scott, Alexander Freeman and William Knott, being equally interested in boring for salt water upon a tract of land belonging to Dyal and were each to bear a portion of the expense and each bear the benefits, on one acre of ground around the well. Jesse Scott sold one half of his interest to Robert Cooper. Wit: William Gilchrist and William Knott. Reg: 13 Aug 1825.

Page 57 - 9 Mar 1825. Mathew Cunningham to Robert Reed, 100 acres. Mathew Cunningham and Elizabeth Cunningham his wife, Jeremiah Cunningham, and Catherine Cunningham daughter of Mathew Cunningham, all of Bedford Co., TN, William Word and wife Mary, sold to Robert Reed of Wayne Co., TN, land in Bedford Co., TN, on Flat Creek. Borders Mathew Cunningham, William Reed and William Galbreath. Wit: Robert McFarling and Robert Baker. Reg: Aug Term 1825.

Page 61 - 15 Apr 1825. Sally Payne to Elizabeth Payne, 40 acres. Sally Payne widow of S. B. Payne, deceased, of Bedford Co., TN, conveyed to Elizabeth Payne daughter of Sally Payne of Bedford Co., for $100.00, sold land to my daughter Elizabeth Payne during my natural life or until my death, land in Bedford Co., on the Barren Fork. Borders Zebediah Payne, Argus Payne, Elizabeth Payne's line, and the land laid off to her out of her father's tract. The land being the Dower land that belonged to S. B. Payne at the time of his death. Wit: George Cotner and Walter H. Payne. Reg: May Term 1825.

Page 63 - 15 Apr 1825. Sally Payne to Elizabeth Payne. (Same as above instrument). Wit: Zebediah Payne, George Cortner and Walter H. Payne. Reg: 10 June 1826.

Page 64 - 30 Apr 1825. Sally Payne to Elizabeth Payne. Sally Payne conveys to Elizabeth Payne, personal property. Wit: Z. Payne and Anthony Troxler. Reg: 11 Jan 1826.

Page 68 - 9 Mar 1825. Mathew Cunningham & Others to William Reed, 100 acres. Mathew Cunningham and Elizabeth Cunningham his wife, William Word and his wife Mary, Elizabeth Cunningham and Catherine Cunningham, daughters of Mathew Cunningham of Bedford Co., TN, sold to Robert Reed land in Bedford Co.,on waters of Flat Creek. Wit: Robert McFarland and Robert Baker. Reg: 12 Jan 1826.

Page 93 - 6 Aug 1825. Andrew Reed to Thomas Holland, Jr., 24 acres. Andrew Reed and Malinda Reed his wife sold to Thomas Holland, Jr., all of Bedford Co., TN, land in Bedford Co., on north side of Duck River, a tract formerly owned by William Coats, deceased. Borders Widow Coats Dower. Reg: 15 Aug 1825.

Page 136 - 30 Jan 1824. Edward Cage to John Sutton & Others, 1 acre. Edward Cage conveyed to John Sutton, Thomas A. Peacock, Stephen Murphy and William Knott, Commissioners, appointed to superintend the establishing and erecting a school house on the premises or land in Bedford Co., on waters of Wartrace Fork. Borders Cage. They are to use the spring called Winston(?) Spring. Wit: John Bradford, William Norvell and John Norvell. Reg: 19 Feb 1826.

Page 138 - Tennessee Grant to Robert Allison, 13+ acres. No. 1310. 12½¢ per acre. Entered 19 Oct 1824, in Bedford Co., TN, 15 Jan 1825, on west side of Clems Creek. Borders James Williams, Robert Allison and Kimbrough Allison. Reg: 10 Feb 1826.

Page 140 - Tennessee Grant to Robert & Kimbrough Allison, 310 acres. No. 139. 12½¢ per acre. Entered 14 Apr 1824, land in Bedford Co., TN, on waters of Clems and Wilson Creek. Survey date 3 June 1824. Borders Robert Allison, Sr.'s land where he now lives, James Williams, Jonathan Graves and land where Kimbro Allison now lives, and William Hill. Reg: 23 May 1825.

Page 165 - Tennessee Grant to Henry Haynes, 45 acres. No. 14532. Certificate No. 624, dated 15 Jul 1811, issued to Roderick Rawlins for 273 acres and entered 13 Nov 1812 by No. 4726. Granted to Henry Haynes, assignee of Roderick Rawlins, land in Bedford Co., TN, on waters of John Byler's branch of Weakleys Creek. Surveyed 21 Feb 1814. Borders John Byler, Cooper's line, Abraham Byler, and Alexanders land. Reg: 20 Mar 1826.

Page 167 - Tennessee Grant to Henry Haynes, 7 acres. No. 14533. Certificate No. 624, dated 15 July 1811, issued to Roderick Rawlins for 273 acres and entered 9 Mar 1819 by No. 11218. Granted to Henry Haynes, assignee of Roderick Rawlins, land in Bedford Co., TN, on Weakleys Creek. Borders land where Henry Haynes lives, Abraham Byler, and Job Cooper. Reg: 20 Mar 1826.

Page 176 - 16 May 1825. William McGuire, Sr. to William McGuire, Jr., 81 acres. William McGuire, Sr. conveyed to William McGuire, Jr, both of Bedford Co., TN, land in Bedford Co., on waters of Wartrace Fork. Borders Malcolm Gilchrist's land, Samuel Philips, William Dillon and the Little Wartrace Fork of Duck River. Wit: Samuel Philips and W. F. Richerson. Reg: 19 Nov 1825.

Page 202 - -- Sept 1825. John King and Agnes King to Bates Smithwick, 82 acres. John King and Agnes King sold to Bates Southwick, all of Bedford Co., TN, land on west side of the Garrison Fork. Borders Dickens Jones and Francis King. Wit: William Hooser and B. Starrett. Reg: 18 Feb 1826.

Page 223 - 8 Feb 1826. William Critington to Mary Thogmorton, Deed of Gift. I, William Critington, for love and affection for my daughter Mary Thogmorton and for $1.00, for her during her natural life, a negro girl Sealah, but to none others, at her death to the issues of her body. Reg: 18 Apr 1826.

Page 224 - I, being called by Mrs. Jane Frazier to survey 107 acres in Bedford Co., TN, on west side of Wartrace Fork and on both sides of Bradfords Creek, it being where Mrs. Jans Frazier now lives. Borders Harrison land and John Taylor. Plat on page 224. Reg: 17 Apr 1826.

Page 263 - 14 Jan 1826. Jacob Lense to John Lense, 48 acres. Jacob Lentz for love and affection for John Lentz, $200.00 as a legacy of the last of Jacob Lentz, given to John Lentz, land in Bedford Co., TN, on south side of Duck River. Borders George Bussey, Nancy Bussey. Wit: John Thompson and John Warner. Reg: 27 Apr 1826.

Page 266 - 6 Jan 1826. Ben. Lentz and his wife Penelopy to Jacob Lentz, 76 acres. Benjamin Lentz sold to Jacob Lentz, all of Bedford Co., TN, land in Bedford Co., on south side of Duck River, it being part of a tract divided between the heirs of George Bussey, deceased, and known by No. 2 Penelopy Bussey now the wife of Benjamin Lentz. Wit: John Warner and Nancy

Lentz. Reg: 27 Apr 1826.

Page 312 - 20 Sept 1825. A. S. White to Robert Allison, 143 acres. Ziza Morrison, Archabald Walker and Archabald S. White sold to Robert Allison, all of Bedford Co., TN land in Bedford Co., on waters of Weakley Creek, it being part of 3000 acre tract granted by North Carolina to Ebenezer Alexander. Borders William Allison, Benjamin Strickler, Knight Dalby and William Allison. Reg: 18 May 1826.

Page 322 - 8 Jan 1825. John Baker to Eliza Ann Baker Dabny 550+ acres. John Baker, Sr. of Montgomery Co., TN conveyed to Eliza Ann Baker Dabny of Montgomery Co., TN, for love and affection for his granddaughter and for $1.00, land in Bedford Co., TN. Wit: Cordall Norfleet and The. F. Norfleet. Reg: (no date).

Page 330 - 12 Aug 1825. For love and affection which I have for my son Samuel Barber Kennedy and for $5.00, personal property. Signed John Kennedy. Wit: Richard Warner. Reg: 8 Jun 1826.

Page 333 - 7 Feb 1826. Miller & Green.
John Miller conveyed to Edmund Green, both of Bedford Co., TN, land in Bedford Co., they bought jointly of Elizabeth Sims guardian of the minor heirs of David Sims, deceased. John Miller is to have 97 acres of the east end and Edmund Green is to have 61 acres of west end. Wit: James Younger and Percy Yell. Reg: 9 June 1826.

Page 335 - 28 Sept 1825. Elizabeth Sims guardian to Walter, David and Rebecca Sims of Sumner Co., TN, conveyed to Edmund Green and John Miller of Bedford Co., TN, land in Bedford Co., it being the estate belonging to David Sims, deceased, to satisfy a debt. 157 acres. Reg: (no date).

Page 345 - 16 May 1825. Jesse Powell to Elizabeth Temple, 349 acres. Jesse Powell of Wake Co., NC conveyed to Elizabeth Temple of Bedford Co., TN land in Bedford Co., on north side of Duck River, opposite the mouth of Sugar Creek. Borders Michael Robison. Wit: Allen Rogers, ---- -----, and Robert Fleming. Reg: 17 Aug 1826.

Page 350 - 16 Feb 1825. Anna Brown to Minerva Brown & Others. I, Anna Brown for good will and affection I have for my two children, daughter Minerva Ann Brown and Hubbard William Brown, given property. Wit: William Burnett, H. S. Wilson and Isaac Hornsby. Reg: 24 Aug 1826.

Page 351 - 12 July 1821. Bates Smithwick to Alfred Smithwick, Bill of Sale. I, Bates Smithwick am bound to my son Alfred Smithwick, in a negro woman. Reg: 12 May 1826.

Page 355 - 7 Mar 1825. Joseph White & Others to Archabald S. White, 500 acres. We, Joseph White, John White, Esther White, David White, Samuel D. White, James White, Isabel White, and Zinas White, all of Cabarrus Co., NC sold to Archabald S. White of Bedford Co., TN, land in Bedford Co., on waters of Sugar Creek and adjoining James Walker on the north. Wit: Stephen B. Black and Johnson V. Biggs. Reg: 3 Sept 1826.

DEED BOOK "T"

Page 367 - 23 Sept 1825. Drake, Marshall & Anderson to Anthony Thomas. Joseph Drake, Daniel Marshall and Catharine Drake of Bedford Co., TN and William B. Anderson of Franklin Co., TN sold to Anthony Thomas of Bedford Co., land in Bedford Co., on waters of Wartrace Fork, where A. Thomas now lives. Wit: Gray Linch, David Thomas, Thomas Davis, and George Davidson. Reg: 18 Nov 1826.

Page 359 - 15 Nov 1825. Jacob Landers to Abel Landers, 14 acres. Jacob Landers conveyed to Abel Landers, both of Bedford Co., TN, land in Bedford Co.,on waters of Thompson Creek, being a part of 200 acres granted by Tennessee No. 15877, to Phebe, Henry, Abell, Jacob, Sary, Robert and Elizabeth Landers. Borders land of Abel Landers and heirs of James Walker, deceased. Wit: David Chamberlan and Henry Landers. Reg: 29 Sept 1826.

Page 361 - 15 Nov 1825. Abel Landers to Henry Landers, 13 acres. Abel Landers conveys to Henry Landers, both of Bedford Co., TN, land in Bedford Co., on waters of Thompson Creek, being part of 200 acres granted to Phebe, Henry, John, Abel, Jacob, Saray, Robert, and Elizabeth Landers by Tennessee No. 15877. Borders Abel Landers and heirs of James Walker. Wit: David Chamberlan and Jacob Land<u>is</u>. Reg: 29 Sept 1826.

Page 366 - 14 Nov 1825. John Ray to Thomas Williams, Power of Attorney. I, John Ray of Bedford Co., TN, and now about to remove from Bedford Co. sold 50 acres in Bedford Co., on headwaters of Thompson Creek to Thomas Simmons of Lincoln Co., TN, and I have appointed Thomas Williams of Bedford Co., my Attorney. Reg: 19 Nov 1825.

Page 367 - 22 June 1820. Frankey Sibley & Others to Strangeman Hutchings, 50 acres. Frankey Sibley, Robert Sibley, Charles Sibley, John Sibley, Stephen Cook, Leonard Sibley and Gabriel Sibley, land in Bedford Co., TN, on West Fork of Rock Creek, which was Willed to Frankey Sibley by John Sibley, deceased, Borders John Record's heirs. Wit: John Bills, John H. Bills and William Hutchins. Reg: 12 Aug 1825.

DEED BOOK "U" 1826 - 1827

Page 11 - 6 July 1826. Job Cooper, Sr. to Job Cooper, Jr., 42 acres. Both of Bedford Co., TN, land in bedford Co., on waters of Weakleys Creek. Borders Amos McLemore. Wit: George C. Cooper and Joel Kimmons. Reg: 18 Feb 1826.

Page 19 - 26 June 1826. Willis Cannon to Jno. McNary Thompson. Willis Cannon of Bedford Co., TN conveyed to John McNary Thompson of Maury Co., TN. Whereas Leticia Cannon wife of Willis Cannon did on 8 Nov last(1825) with Willis Cannon, executed and delivered to James Porter a general warrantee deed for land in Rutherford Co., TN, of about 270 acres of which Willis Cannon held in right of his wife Leticia Cannon and which was devised from Jason THompson, the father of Leticia, by Deed of Gift and for $1.00, sold to John McNary Thompson. Also land in Bedford Co., TN, it being a part of 5000 acres formerly belonging to the estate of Walter Sims, deceased. Wit: A. Yell, A. Martin and Robert McCrary. Reg: 27 Apr 1826.

Page 22 - 8 Feb 1826. William Crittendon to Elizabeth Smith. I, William Crittendon of Bedford Co., TN, for love and affection I have for my daughter Elizabeth Smith and $1.00, a negro girl Eleanor. Reg: 27 Apr 1826.

Page 28 - 17 Dec 1825. James McCuistion, Sr. to Benjamin F. McCuistion, 136 acres. James McCuistion, Sr. conveyed to Benjamin F. McCuistion of Bedford Co., son of James McCuistion, Sr., for love and affection, land in Bedford Co., TN, on waters of Hurricane Creek. Borders James McCuistion, Sr., Thomas McCuistion, Anthony McCuistion, James McCuistion, Jr. He is to receive this land until after Jean McCuistion's death, his mother. Wit: Samuel McCuistion and A. McCuistion. Reg: 18 Feb 1826.

Page 50 - Tennessee Grant to James Williams, 24 acres. No. 9491. Part of Certificate No. 58, dated 27 Feb 1810, issued to William P. Anderson and entered 14 Oct 1811 by No. 3477. Granted to James Williams, assignee of William R. Anderson, land in Bedford Co., TN, on waters of Clems Creek. Borders Robert Allison and James Williams. Surveyed 3 Apr 1812. Reg: 12 June 1826.

Page 52 - 9 Sept 1825. Edward Chaffin to Abner Houston, 215 acres. Edward Chaffin of Bedford Co., TN conveyed to Abner Houston of Mecklenburg Co., NC, land in Bedford Co., TN, on West Rock Creek. Wit: John H. Bills and Strangeman Hutchins. Reg: 18 Feb 1826.

Page 69 - Tennessee Grant to William Hartsfield, 49 acres. No. 13446. For Military Service by John Ralph to North Carolina, Warrant No. 3103 for 64 acres, dated 8 Dec 1785 and dated 22 Jan 1818 by No. 1060. Granted to William Hartsfield, assignee of John Ralph, land in Bedford Co., TN, between Powell's and Sugar Creek. Borders Strother's survey, Powels' line and Dougan corner. Reg: 20 June 1826.

Page 71 - Tennessee Grant to William Hartsfield, 53¼ acres. No. 9589. Part of Certificate No. 645, dated 9 Apr 1813, issued to the heirs of John Wilson and entered 26 Apr 1815 by No. 7828. Granted to William Hartsfield, assignee of the heirs of John Wilson, land in Bedford Co., TN, on east waters of Sinking Creek. Borders Tabby Boyd. Surveyed 6 June 1815. Reg: 20 June 1826.

Page 73 - Tennessee Grant to William Hartsfield, 80 acres. No. 7212. Part of Certificate No. 645, dated 9 Apr 1813, issued to the heirs of John Wilson and entered 25 June 1814 by No. 6495. Granted to William Hartsfield, assignee of the heirs of John Wilson, land in Bedford Co., TN, on waters of Sinking Creek. Surveyed 7 Oct 1814. Reg: 20 June 1826.

Page 83 - 3 Jan 1826. James Patton to Elisha A. Patton, 100 acres. James Patton of Bedford Co., TN, for love and affection for his son Elisha A. Patton, given and granted unto him, land on waters of Caney Spring Creek of Bedford Co., TN. Borders Hugh McClelans' corner. Wit: G. H. Allen, _olly Patton and Robert M. Walton. Reg: 22 June 1826.

Page 93 - 28 Mar 1825. Frederick A. Ross to William Neese, 332 acres. I, Frederick A. Ross of Hawkins Co., TN sold to William Neese, land in Bedford Co., TN, on waters of Duck River, formerly the name of Mount Misory. Wit: Jos. Francis, Jacob Bunes and P. Carter. Reg: 4 July 1826.

Page 108 - 20 May 1824. Thomas Wright to Richard Wright and Robert Wright, 106 acres. Thomas Wright of Bedford Co., TN, for love and affection for his two sons Richard & Robert Wright, granted unto them land in Bedford Co., on waters of the Garrison Fork. Adjoining James M. Yell, Andrew Erwin, the same tract which Thomas Wright now lives. It is to be equally divided. Wit: Jonathan Smith and James M. Yell. Reg: 12 May 1826.

Page 121 - 9 Nov 1810. Thomas Beasley to David B. Graham. I, Thomas Beasley of Iredell Co., NC, for love and affection for my grandchildren, David B. Graham and Ellen C. Graham, given unto them one negro woman China. Wit: H. W. M. Graham and Jos. Graham. Reg: 8 Aug 1826.

Page 141 - 4 Oct 1824. John Bonner to John, Troy and Russell Nall, 90 acres. John Bonner of Warren Co., TN sold to John Nall, Troy Nall and Russell Nall, minor sons of James Nall of Bedford Co., TN land in Bedford Co., on Noahs Fork and Nalls Creek. Wit: Neiley S. Patton and A. D. Foster. Reg: 15 Feb 1826.

Page 144 - 26 April 1825. William McGuire, Sr. to William McGuire, Jr. I, William McGuire of Bedford Co., TN, for love and affection for my son William McGuire, Jr., personal property and balance of the estate, negroes excepted. He is to maintain William McGuire, Sr. and Mary his wife, during their natural lifes. Wit: Samuel Phillips and J. W. Gollithan. Reg: 19 Nov 1825.

Page 148 - 14 Apr 1825. Rachael Martin to Samuel Mitchell. I, Rachel Martin, of Bedford Co., TN, for respect and friendship for Samuel Mitchell of Bedford Co.,, boy slave Lewis. Wit: William Gilchrist and S. C. Edgar. Reg: 19 Aug 1825.

Page 152 - 18 July 1825. Margarett Nichols to Jacob Nichols. I, Margarett Nichols for love and affection for my son Jacob Nichols and also to my great grand daughter, to wit, Nancy Nichols, had given 3 negroes, Joseph and Daniel, to Jacob Nichols and Franky to Nancy Nichols. The negroes were left to me by my husband's Last Will. Wit: John Vannoy. Reg: 12 Aug 1825.

Page 158 - 27 May 1825. Mary Davidson to Miles Davidson. I, Mary Davidson for love and affection for my grandson Miles Davidson, given a sorrel filly now in the possession of my son John Davidson. Reg: 19 Aug 1826.

Page 162 - 14 Aug 1826. Moses M. Robinson to Henry Verner. Moses Moore Robinson sold to Henry Verner, both of Bedford Co., TN, land in Bedford Co., TN, on waters of Sugar Creek. Wit: James Younger, Melch Brame and Aaron Gambill. Reg: 19 Aug 1826.

Page 184 - 19 Oct 1825. Charles Shipman and Jacob Shipman. Charles Shipman and Jacob Shipman conveyed to Daniel Shipman. Daniel Shipman, Sr. conveyed to us land of 50 acres each as being part of 200 acres granted to Daniel Shipman, Sr. by Tennessee and conveyed to us including the house and orchard. They are to convey unto Daniel Shipman, Sr. everything necessary to keep him from suffering and to take care of him as long as he shall live a natural life. Wit: Abel Landis and Reuben Shipman. Reg: 19 Aug 1826.

Page 197 - 8 Nov 1824. Wiley Vincent & Others to Andrew Wilson, 60 acres. Wiley Vincent, William J. Bennett and Richard Bennett of Sumner Co., TN sold to Andrew Wilson of Sumner Co., TN, land in Bedford Co., TN. Borders James Gourly and Dodd's line. Wit: William Glover and David Wilson. Reg: 10 Nov 1826.

Page 199 - 10 Nov 1826. Miles Wilson to Elizabeth Cherry & Others, Deed of Gift. I, Miles Wilson of Bedford Co., TN, for natural love and affection for my niece Elizabeth W. Cherry, give her personal property, including one large Family Bible. I give unto niece Sarah L. Cherry, personal property. I give unto my nephew William L. Cherry, personal property. I also give unto my nephew John K. Cherry, personal property. I give unto my nephew Samuel W. Cherry, personal property. Also, give unto my niece Martha K. Cherry, personal property. Wit: Joseph Ross and Ezkl. Cherry. Reg: 13 Nov 1826.

Page 201 - 7 Dec 1825. Joseph and Jane B. McKissick to David Dryden, 30 acres. Joseph McKissick and his wife Jane B., both of Bedford Co., TN, sold to David Dryden of Bedford Co., land in Bedford Co., on Sugar Creek, being a part of an original survey granted by North Carolina to Alexander Greer and Thomas Greer and a part of a 295 acre tract belonging to Joseph and Jane B. McKissick. Borders Joseph A. Greer, Joseph and Jane B. McKissick, Sugar Creek. Wit: A. Greer, Richard Williamson and John Bennett. Reg: 16 Nov 1826.

Page 203 - 25 Aug 1825. Frances Holt & Others to Henry Holt. Frances Holt wife of John Holt, Sr., deceased, James Holt, Koonrad Kimbro and Rachael Kimbro his wife, John Holt, Jr., Michael Holt, William Holt, Joseph Holt, and James Franklin and Elizabeth Franklin his wife, and John Smith and Barbry Smith his wife conveyed to Henry Holt, all heirs of John Holt, Sr., deceased, of Bedford Co., TN, land being near the Wartrace Fork and being the same place where John Holt, deceased, formerly lived. Borders Francis Cox. Wit: Michael Holt and Charles McGuire. Reg: 17 Nov 1826.

Page 208 - 22 Apr 1824. John Kuton to George Stephens, 200 acres. John Kuton of Franklin Co., TN conveyed to George Stephens, William Stephens, Wiley Stephens, James Stephens, Anna Stephens, Eliza Stephens and Orra Stephens, for love and affection, land in Bedford Co., TN, on Cards Creek, a branch of Garrison Fork of Duck River. Borders Cards Creek and James Mitchell. Elizabeth Card, their mother, is to have and enjoy the tract during her natural life and after her death, the land is to be equally divided between George, William, Wiley, Anna, Eliza, and Orra Stephens. Reg: Nov Term 1825.

Page 222 - 28 Aug 1826. John T. Dabny to John Larue, 515+ acres. John T. Dabny and Eliza Ann Baker Dabny his wife, of Montgomery Co., TN sold to John Larue of Bedford Co., TN, land in Bedford Co., on East Fork of Rock Creek. Land granted to John Baker. Reg: (no date).

Page 226 - 14 Aug 1826. John B. Jackson to David Chadwell, Power of Attorney. I, John B. Jackson of Lawrence Co., Alabama, appointed David Chadwell of Maury Co., TN, Attorney to recover from George Cahoon and James Reed, Executors of the Last Will and testament of Zacheus Wilson, late of Bedford Co., TN,dec'd, all land, chattels, money and other estate that I am entitled to from George Cahoon and James Reed, in right of my wife Louisa Jackson formerly Louisa Wilson, a daughter and one of the legatees of Zacheus Wilson, deceased. Recorded in Lawrence Co., Alabama. Reg: (no date).

Page 231 - 29 Dec 1825. Mathew Cunningham and Elizabeth Cunningham & Others to Robert Reed, 5 acres. Mathew Cunningham and Elizabeth Cunningham his wife, Jeremiah Cunningham, William Word and his wife Mary Elizabeth, and Catharine Cunningham daughter of Mathew Cunningham, all of Bedford Co., TN conveyed to Robert Reed of Bedford Co., for $31.00, land in Bedford Co., on waters of Flat Creek. Borders land of Mathew Cunningham, William Galbreath survey, and Kennedy land. Wit: John Kims and William Reed. Reg: 8 Dec 1826.

Page 249 - 9 Jan 1826. Benjamin Lentz and Penelope Lentz to John Warner, Bill of Sale. We, Benjamin Lentz and Penelope Lentz formerly Penelope Bussey, both of Bedford Co., TN, sold to John Warner, Jr. negroes. Penelope being heir and legatee of George Bussey, deceased, father of Penelope Lentz. The negroes now in possession of John Warner. Wit: Jacob Lentz and Nancy Lentz. Reg: 18 Feb 1826.

Page 250 - 5 Dec 1825. George Smith to John Warner, Bill of Sale. I, George Smith, Jr. sold to John Warner my interest in negroes belonging to estate of George and Lucy Bussey, deceased, which was conveyed to me by Elliott Bussey one of the heirs of George and Lucy Bussey. Wit: John S. Frazier and James B. Armstrong. Reg: 17 Jan 1827.

Page 251 - 15 Feb 1826. Nancy Bussey to John Warner, Bill of Sale. We, Nancy Bussey and John McClintock, guardian of Nancy Bussey, daughter of George Bussey and Lucy Bussey, deceased, all of Bedford Co., TN, sold slaves to John Warner, Jr. Wit: Jacob Lentz and Shadrack Brown. Reg: 18 Feb 1826.

Page 253 - 5 Mar 1825. Edmund Kimmons to John Barrett, 43 acres. Edmund Kimmons and Nelly his wife sold to John Barrett, all of Bedford Co., TN, land on waters of Sinking Creek. Borders Porter's land. Wit: John H. Anderson and Edward Wade. Reg: 18 Jan 1827.

Page 260 - 5 Aug 1822. William Burdett, Sr. to William Burdett, Jr., 70 acres. William Burdett, Sr. conveyed to William Burdett, Jr., both of Bedford Co., TN, for love and affection for my son, land on Big Flat Creek. Borders Giles Burdett's survey. The land includes the improvement whereon William Burdett, Sr. now lives. Wit: Giles Burdett and Samuel Stewart. Reg: 18 Feb 1826.

Page 265 - Tennessee Grant to John Sutton, 20+ acres. No. 23483. Part of Certificate No. 1805, dated 7 July 1814, issued to George Martin for 858 acres and entered 25 Feb 1820 by No. 11545. Granted to John Sutton, assignee of George Martin, land in Bedford Co., TN, on waters of Hurricane Creek. Borders John Peacock survey. Surveyed 31 May 1821. Reg: 1 June 1825.

DEED BOOK "U"

Page 269 - 31 Oct 1826. Lewis Gant to Lewis and John Gant, 100 acres. Lewis Gant, Sr. for love and affection for Lewis and Jonathan Gant, conveyed unto them, land in Bedford Co., on Big Sinking Creek. Wit: Michael Fisher, James Cheaves and Henry Gilmore. Reg: 24 Jan 1827.

Page 287 - 5 Sept 1826. George Tilman to Silas Tilman, 250 acres. George Tilman for love and affection for Silas Tilman, his son, given him land in Bedford Co., TN, on north side of Duck River, it being part of a tract granted to John and William Payton. Wit: Asa Fonville and Isreal Fonville. Reg: 25 Jan 1827.

Page 298 - 7 Nov 1826. James Brittain, admr. of Joseph Brittain to Thomas Powel, 200 acres. James Brittain, Executor of Joseph Brittain, deceased, conveyed to Thomas Powel, all of Bedford Co., TN, land in Bedford Co. Borders corner of Joseph Brittain, deceased, survey, Murdock's corner and James Nowlin. Reg: 25 Jan 1827.

Page 338 - 3 Oct 1826. Lewis Gant to William A. Gant, 4 negroes. I, Lewis Gant, Sr., for love and affection for my beloved son William A. Gant, conveyed 4 negroes. Wit: Michael Fisher, James Cheaves and Henry Gilmore. Reg: 15 Nov 1826.

Page 344 - 10 Nov 1826. John McCuistion & Others - John Ingram, Agreement. We, the heirs of John Ingram, deceased, relinguish all claims, to wit, John McCuistion and Peggy his wife, Samuel Ingram and the heirs of Thomas Ingram, deceased, Ruben Nance and Frances his wife, Thomas S. Parsons and Susanna his wife, Thomas G. Watkins and Elizabeth his wife, we have this day received satisfaction in full of all the estate of John Ingram, deceased. Wit: Thomas Hamilton, A. McCuistion, Nathan H. Schooler and James Knott. Reg: 3 Feb 1827.

Page 358 - 11 Sept 1826. Daniel Patton to William Patton, Bill of Sale. I, Daniel Patton of Bedford Co., TN sold to William Patton of Charlestown, SC, a negro girl Susan, now in possession of our mother Jane Patton with whom she is to remain until called for by my brother William Patton. Wit: A. Martin and William McMichael. Reg: 15 Mar 1827.

Page 359 - 13 Apr 1817. John Scott to the Trustees of New Hope Meeting House, 113 poles. John Scott conveyed to Jonathan Webster, Christopher Shaw, John B. Walker, James Slaton, Matt Martin, and Vincent Smith, Trustees of the New Hope Baptist Meeting House of Bedford Co., TN, for $1.00, land in Bedford Co., on the Garrison Fork. Borders lands of John Scott near the Meeting House. Wit: John Ewell and W. S. Waterson. Reg: 5 Apr 1827.

Page 361 - 10 Feb 1827. John D. Stovall to A. Martin and Joseph R. Drake. I, John D. Stovall of Rutherford Co., TN sold to Abram Martin and Joseph R. Drake, both of Bedford Co., TN, 2 negroes, which I am entitled in right of my wife Mary H., formerly Mary H. Drake and one of the children of Kitty Drake and which 2 negroes were conveyed by deed to the present and future children of said Kitty Drake by Thomas Thogmorton of Nicholas Co., KY, bearing date 27 Oct 1823. Reg: 17 Feb 1827.

DEED BOOK "U"

Page 367 - 13 Mar 1823. Amos, Alfred and James Balch to Newcum Thompson, 4 acres. Amos Balch, Alfred and James C. Balch conveyed to Newcum Thompson, land in Bedford Co., TN, part whereon Amos Balch and Alfred Balch now lives, on road leading from Shelbyville to Columbia near Amos Balch's Spring Branch. Borders Samuel and Newcum Thompson's corner of their Tanyard tract. Wit: Joseph Alexander and Samuel Thompson. Reg: -- Apr 1827.

Page 369 - 18 Aug 1826. Elizabeth Temple to Dempsey P. Temple and D. C. Temple, 349 acres. Elizabeth Temple for love and affection for her sons Dempsey P. Temple and D. C. Temple, conveyed land in Bedford Co., TN, on north side of Duck River and being the tract whereon Elizabeth Temple now lives. Borders Duck River and Michael Robinson's survey. Wit: John Robinson, John Wilhoite and Robertson Horton. Reg: 9 Apr 1827.

Page 371 - 4 Nov 1822. Amos Balch, Alfred, Samuel and James Balch to S. & N. Thompson, 1 acre. Amos Balch, Alfred, Samuel and James Balch conveyed to Samuel and Newcum THompson, land in Bedford Co., TN, adjoining lands of Newcum Thompson near Duck River and on Amos Balch Spring Branch. Located on the Big Road. Wit: Edward Wade and Joseph Anderson. Reg: 9 Apr 1827.

Page 375 - 13 Feb 1827. James Coats, Attorney in fact for Benjamin Coats to Wyeth Hunter. James Coats of Bedford Co., TN, Attorney for Benjamin Coats of Wilson Co., TN, by letters, dated 16 Oct 1823 conveyed to Wyeth Hunter of Bedford Co., land in Bedford Co., in Town of Shelbyville, Lot No. 129. Wit: John H. Anderson and James Deery. Reg: 9 Apr 1827.

DEED BOOK "W" 1827 - 1828

Page 28 - 1 Aug 1825. Henson Brown & wife to R<u>eizon</u> Smith, 7 acres. Henson S. Brown and Elizabeth Brown <u>formerly</u> Elizabeth Ingle conveyed to R<u>eazin</u> Smith, all of Bedford Co., TN, that whereas John Smith, Jr. brother of Nancy Ingle who was mother of Elizabeth Brown formerly Ingle, deceased, seized of land of 100 acres, without issue of his body and whereas Nancy Ingle mother of Elizabeth became entitled to one-seventh part of the land which is bordered by Philip Phillips and Michael Campbell on Sinking Creek, and whereas Nancy leaving seven children, to wit, Rezin, Sally, Lucinda, William, James, Nancy Ingle and Elizabeth Brown formerly Elizabeth Ingle who are entitled to the interest of their mother Nancy Ingle. Rezin Smith has purchased from Henson S. Brown and Elizabeth his wife, all their interest in 100 acres divided into seven parts. Reg: 10 Feb 1826.

Page 30 - 28 Apr 1826. William Kell<u>ey</u> to Francis Kell<u>ey</u>(Keller), 50 acres. William Kell<u>ey</u> conveyed to Francis H. Kell<u>er</u> and Joseph Kell<u>er</u>, all of Bedford Co., TN, the undivided part of land in Bedford Co., the same being William Kell<u>ey</u>'s undivided part as a legatee of Ruben Kell<u>er</u>, deceased, of land conveyed to Ruben Kell<u>ey</u> by Patton & Erwin of NC (Ashville), dated 11 Mar 1811. Registered in Deed Book C, page 400. <u>Note</u>: All Kell<u>ey</u> should be Kell<u>er</u>. Wit: William Jones and Ruben Kell<u>ey</u>. Reg: 17 Apr 1827.

Page 32 - 23 July 1824. Samuel Plumlee to Joseph Rushing, 20 acres. Samuel Plumlee, administrator of estate of Thomas Plumlee, deceased, of Bedford Co., TN, sold to Joseph Rushing, land in Bedford Co., on waters of Weakleys Creek. Borders Benjamin Lemons. Wit: Evan Rushing and Solomon Maxwell. Reg: 17 Feb 1827.

Page 34 - 14 Oct 1826. Nathan Forrest to William Forrest, 50 acres. Nathan Forrest sold to William Forrest, for $1.00, land in Bedford Co., TN, on waters of Caney Spring Creek, being a part of a 3000 acre survey of Samuel Wilson. Borders Zachariah Minton where he now lives and formerly Nathan Forrest. Wit: Robert Church and Huston Patterson. Reg: 6 Apr 1827.

Page 40 - 19 May 1825. Henry Killingsworth to James McDaniel's heirs, 75 acres. Land in Bedford Co., TN, on waters of West Rock Creek. Wit: Edward Chaffin and Eli Cheek. Reg: 7 Feb 1827.

Page 53 - 15 Apr 1826. William Jones to Francis and Joseph Keller for -- acres. William Jones sold to Francis H. Keller and Joseph Keller, all of Bedford Co., TN, land in Bedford Co., the same being William Jones' part which he lately purchased of Polly Keller, one of the legatees of Ruben Keller, deceased, conveyed to Ruben Keller by Patton & Erwin of Ashville, NC. Wit: William Kelly and Ruben Kelly. Reg: 7 Feb 1827.

Page 57 - 5 Feb 1827. Peter R. Proby to Washington Walch for -- acres. Peter R. Proby sold to Washington Walch, both of Bedford Co., TN, land in Bedford Co., on waters of Little Flat Creek and Thompsons Creek. Borders the south west corner of a tract whereon James M. Proby now lives on and deeded to him by Taylor Lane, tract whereon Washington Walch now live and tract whereon Peter R. Proby now lives. Wit: James M. Proby and John Dean. Reg: 17 Feb 1827.

Page 73 - 4 Oct 1826. John Burns to William Burns, 65 acres. John Burns, for love and affection for his son William Burns, both of Bedford Co., TN, granted unto him land in Bedford Co., on waters of Falling Creek. Borders lands of Joseph Glover, Trotter's land, James Clardy, and Phifer's tract. Reg: 13 Apr 1827.

Page 79 - 13 Nov 1821. Richard and Jonathan Parker to Ezekiel Brown, 161 acres. Richard and Jonathan Parker, both of Green Co., Alabama, conveyed to Ezekiel W. Brown of Bedford Co., TN, land in Bedford Co., on waters of Thompsons Creek, entered in three entrys, two of which is granted to John Epps and other to John Epps' heirs, to wit, Priscilla and Francis Epps which was in possession of John Epps at the time of his death. Borders school land. Wit: James McGill, Samuel Parker and Charles Parks (Parker ?). Reg: 14 Apr 1827.

Page 89 - 23 Jan 1827. James Patton and James E. Patton to Trustees of Union Meeting House. James Patton and James E. Pattonconveyed to Thomas Church and John Scott, Trustees of the Union School, land of one acre and 36 poles, in Bedford Co., TN, on waters of the Garrison Fork, it being part of the land bought by James Patton of James Patton and Andrew Erwin and is included in the Blount's Grant No. 220. Beginning at a small tree about one pole southwest of a small spring, the first in the hollow above what is known by the name of the Big Spring of the branch that empties into the Garrison Fork below the mouth of Straight Creek and on same side of fork that Straight Creek is located. Including said School House and Spring. Wit: Jno. S. Wood and P. M. Walker. Reg: 17 Feb 1827.

Page 91 - 15 Apr 1826. William Jones to Francis & Joseph Keller, -- acres. William Jones sold to Francis and Joseph Keller, all of Bedford Co., TN, land in bedford Co., the same being the one eighth part of a tract inherited by his wife Nancy Jones formerly Nancy Kelley one of the legatees of Ruben Kelley, deceased, conveyed to Ruben Kelley by Patton & Erwin of Ashville, NC, deed dated 11 Mar 1811 and recorded in Deed Book C, page 400 Bedford Co., TN. Wit: William Kelly and Ruben Kelley. Reg: 17 Feb 1827.

Page 117 - 11 Jan 1827. Isaac Holmes to Joseph Keller, 100 acres. Isaac Holmes at present of Warren Co., but formerly of Bedford Co., TNsold to Joseph Keller of Bedford Co., land in Bedford Co., it being part of a 200 acre tractoriginally bought of Col. A. Erwin. Beginning on top of a ridge whereon Isaac Holmes formerly lived, borders Thomas Drake, Dennis Holmes, Ephraim B. Gallyer, Henson Grove and Ruben Kelly. Wit: William Kelley and Francis H. Keller. Reg: 17 Feb 1827.

Page 137 - 20 July 1826. Alexander and Ann Null to Samuel Winsted, 17 acres. Alexander Null and Ann Null his wife sold to Samuel Winsted, all of Bedford Co., TN land in Bedford Co., on east side of the East Fork of Rock Creek, it being a part of a tract granted by North Carolina to George Cathey. Borders East Fork of Rock Creek. Reg: 17 Nov 1826.

Page 143 - 24 Oct 1825. Daniel Marshall to Portland J. Curle, 125 acres. Daniel Marshall for himself and in right of his wife Nancy, late Nancy Drake and his said wife Nancy and Joseph Drake, all of Bedford Co., TN conveyed to Portland J. Curle of Rutherford Co., TN, land in Bedford Co., on waters of War-trace Fork. Reg: 27 Apr 1827.

Page 158 - 9 Nov 1825. Agreement with the heirs of Peter Bos-well, deceased. Walter S. Sorrel, William Marlow, Robert Ray-bourn, George Boswell and William S. Boswell, all of this time of Bedford Co., TN and heirs of the estate of Peter Boswell, deceased, formerly of State of Virginia and County of Fairfax and as there never has been any administration on the estate of Peter Boswell, deceased, and the heirs now being of full age have come together and made a final settlement of the estate of the legatees, to wit, Walter B. Sons who became one of the heirs by marriage with Martha Boswell a daughter of Peter Bos-well, William Marlow who became heir by marriage with Elizabeth Boswell a daughter of Peter Boswell, and Robert Raybourn who became heir by marriage with Mary Boswell a daughter of Peter Boswell, also George Boswell a son of Peter Boswell, deceased, William F. S. Boswell a son of Peter Boswell, deceased. Wit: William Beanes Sutton and Charles F. Sutton. Reg: 19 Nov 1825.

Page 162 - 6 May 1824. Allman Jarner's Certificate. Granville Co., NC. William Callen, Jr. and Isreal Hargrove came before me one of the Justices of the Peace for Granville Co., NC and made oath that they believe Allman Jarner to be a free man for the following reasons, to wit, that Allman Jarner was raised in Granville Co., NC and was always reputed to be the son of Phill and Betty Jarner who embarked from Virginia to Granville Co., NC and passed for free persons, moreover Allen Jarner was bound to Ruben Smith of Granville Co., NC and stayed until he attained the age of twenty one. The following description of his person and age: height five feet and seven inches and a half, of light complexion, a scare about an inch long on left cheek, a flesh mark on his under lip rather on the left side and is between twenty seven and twenty eight years of age. Signed by William R. Hargrove, J.P. Reg: 24 May 1827.

Page 167 - 5 Nov 1825. Jacob Troxler to Eve Linn, Agreement. Before the Holy Estate of Matrimony is performed between Jacob Troxler, Sr. and Eve Linn, both of Bedford Co., TN, upon the following conditions, to wit, That I, Jacob Troxler, Jr. relinguishes all claim &c to any property of real, personal &c to Eve Linn's property. Signed Jacob (X) Troxler and Eve Linn. Wit: William Heaslett and Jacob Kizer. Reg: 19 Nov 1825. NOTE: Eve, 2nd wife.

Page 175 - 6 Nov 1826. John Moore, Sr. to John Moore, Jr., Bill of Sale. I, John Moore, Sr., of Bedford Co., TN, sold to John Moore, Jr, a negro woman Hannah, a negro boy Washington, and a son of Hannah. Reg: 15 Nov 1826.

Page 178 - Dempsey Powell procession for 132 acres. Plat on page 178. Dempsey P. Temple, Attorney for Dempsey Powell and by virtue of a survey and division made for the heirs of Dempsey Powell, deceased, agreeable to his Last Will and Testament, of a tract of land granted to Dempsey Powell, deceased, by Grant No. 12, dated 10 July 1788 for 1977 acres and the part being allotted to Dempsey Powell, Jr., surveyed 132 acres for Dempsey Powell, Jr. in Bedford Co., TN, on south side of Duck River a short distance above John Sims Mill. Borders John Stephens and Sims Mill Tract. Wit: Granville H. Frazier and Thomas Pettus. Reg: 18 July 1827.

Page 180 - 15 May 1827. Dempsey P. and Leonard Temple, 363 acres. Plat on page 180. At request of Dempsey P. Temple and by virtue of a deed from Elizabeth Temple to Dempsey P. Temple and Leonard C. Temple, dated 18 Aug 1826. Part of land was transferred to Jesse Powell and by him to Elizabeth Temple on 6 May 1825. Land in Bedford Co., TN, on north side of Duck River opposite the mouth of Sugar Creek. Borders John Robinson, Duck River, stake opposite mouth of Temple Mill Race, and Michael Robinson. Wit: Joseph B. Powell and THomas Pettus. Reg: (no date).

Page 184 - 21 Feb 1827. Ann Neill to Allen Leeper, 3 Lots. Ann Neill widow of Alexander Neill, deceased, and one of the heirs of George Cathey, deceased, sold for $2.00, to Allen Leeper, both of Bedford Co., TN, 3 Town Lots in Town of Farmington, Bedford Co., TN. Wit: W. J. Whitthorn and Spencer Eakin. Reg: 16 May 1827.

Page 186 - 6 Mar 1827. James Hobbs to A. D. Foster, 10 acres. James Hobbs of Morgan Co., Illinois sold to Anthony D. Foster of Bedford Co., TN, land in Bedford Co., on waters of Noahs Fork. House and Spring where A. D. Foster now lives. Wit: William Farrar and Thomas Bell. Reg: 19 July 1827.

DEED BOOK "W"

Page 188 - 22 Jan 1827. The Heirs of James Shinault to John Lemmons, 100 acres. Margaret Shinault, Walter Shinault, John Shinault, Stephen Shinault, William Shinault, John Yeary and Zach Davis, all of Fayette and Hardeman Counties, TN sold to John Lemons of Bedford Co., TN, land in Bedford Co., on Noahs Fork of the Garrison Fork, granted by Tennessee to Isaac Shinault, No. 21134 and being part of Warrant No. 1692. Borders James Hobbs, Noahs Fork, and Harrison's tract. Wit: Absalom Garland, Jos. Beasley and Asa Lemmons. Reg: 16 May 1827.

Page 192 - 3 Aug 1824. Elijah Parker, Sr. to Elijah Parker, Jr., 160 acres. Both of Bedford Co., TN, land in Bedford Co., on east waters of Thompsons Creek. Borders tracts survey of Elijah Parker, Sr. Wit: James Walker and Jeremiah Spann. Reg: 16 May 1827.

Page 194 - 15 May 1827. Robert Church to William M. Forrest & Others, Deed of Gift. I, Robert Church purchased at Constable Sale of Elias Pate vs Jonathan Forrest, personal property. Sale 9 Dec 1826. Also, I, Robert Church of Bedford Co., TN, for friendship and affection and for $1.00, sold to William Masson Forrest, Sarah Jane and Williamson Forrest, infant children of Jonathan Forrest the above personal property bought at Constable Sale. Reg: 19 July 1827.

Page 199 - 19 Jul 1826. John Robison, Jr. to John Robison, Sr., 100 acres. John Robison, Jr. conveyed to John Robison, Sr., both of Bedford Co., TN, land in Bedford Co., it being a part of a 1500 acre tract granted by North Carolina to Michael Robison and same being a part of Joseph Robinson and my division of tract of 500 acres. Borders John Robison, Sr., Duck River, and Asa Fonville. Wit: David Robinson and John Wilhoite. Reg: 16 May 1827.

Page 203 - 27 Feb 1827. Martin Fisher to Michael Fisher, 84 acres. Martin Fisher conveyed to Michael Fisher, both of Bedford Co., TN, land in Bedford Co., being on north side of Duck River and south side of Falling Creek, being part of tract on which Michael Fisher now lives. Borders James Harris, Henry Culp and Falling Creek. Wit: Jacob Fisher and William J. Eakin. Reg: 16 May 1827.

Page 205 - 28 Apr 1827. Neely S. Patton to Daniel Patton, Sr., 70 acres. Both of Bedford Co., TN, land in Bedford Co., on Nalls Creek. Borders Burnams Branch, Top of Ridge, James Keel's line and Patton's land. Wit: _. H. Searcy and William McMichael. Reg: 16 May 1827.

Page 254 - 8 Sept 1825. S. J. Whitworth to Effy Whitworth, Quit Claim. I hereby relinguish all my right title and interest to the land left me by my mother Elizabeth Whitworth to Effy Whitworth, for a negro boy Henry. Wit: Jos. D. Graves and Edward Whitworth. Reg: 16 May 1827.

Page 256 - Easter Clinton to Thomas Clinton. Both of Bedford Co., TN, conveyed a negro girl. Reg: 16 May 1827.

Page 277 - 14 Sept 1826. Stokley H. Enochs to Samuel Ingram, Power of Attorney. I, Stokley H. Enochs of Carroll Co., TN, appointed Samuel Ingram, my Attorney to oversee my part of the estate which is coming to me or my wife from the estate of James McCuistion, late of Bedford Co., TN. Wit: H. H. Brown. Reg: 3 Sept 1827.

Page 286 - 11 Mar 1816. Robert Allison to John Allison, 110 acres. I, Robert Allison has granted unto my son John Allison, both of Bedford Co., TN, land that I, Robert Allison, bought of Larkin Edwards and lying in Bedford Co., on the north bank of Duck River. Borders Anthony Newman's survey, Jackson and Robinson land. Wit: Kimbro Allison and Preston McClure. Reg: 18 Aug 1827.

Page 311 - 24 July 1827. Lewis Gant to Keziah Aldridge, Deed of Gift. Lewis Gant, Sr. of Bedford Co., TN, for love and affection for his daughter Keziah Aldridge of Lawrence Co., Alabama, gives unto her two negroes. Wit: M. Fisher and Charles Fisher. Reg: 18 Aug 1827.

Page 337 - 6 Aug 1827. Lewis Gant to Peggy Aldridge, Bill of Sale. Lewis Gant, Sr. of Bedford Co., TN, conveyed unto Peggy Aldridge his daughter of Lawrence Co., Alabama, two negroes, one girl Ann and one boy Tom. Wit: M. Fisher and Charles Fisher. Reg: 18 Aug 1827.

Page 345 - 24 Jan 1827. Ephraim D. Dickson & Others, Agreement. We, Ephraim D. Dickson, John B. Dixon, William W. Dickson and Bennett S. Dickson, all being legatees of James Dickson, after leaving his Last Will and Testament, all of the tract whereon he lived on at the time of his death, it being about 696 acres. The heirs has decided to divide the land. Ephraim D. Dickson gets 200+ acres. Bennett S. Dickson gets 96+ acres. William W. Dickson gets 200 acres, John B. Dickson gets 200 acres. Wit: J. Wortham, Archabald Clinton and A. J. Wilson. Reg: 17 Nov 1827.

Page 351 - Tennessee Grant to Thomas Washburn, 20 acres. No. 15819. Part of Certificate No. 2459, dated 29 Aug 1816, issued to the heirs of David Carson for 640 acres and entered 28 Apr 1817 by No. 10108. Granted to Thomas Washburn, assignee of the heirs of David Carson, land in Lincoln Co., TN, on West Fork of the East Fork of Mulberry Creek, waters of Elk River. Surveyed 16 May 181_9_(?). Reg: 20 Dec 1827.

Page 357 - 2 Oct 1824. I, Jane Galespie of Bedford Co., TN, for love and affection for my grandchildren, Elizabeth B. McNutt, Isabell W. McNutt, Jane A. McNutt, and Mary P. McNutt, the children of my daughter Margret V. McNutt now the wife of William B. McNutt, all of Bedford Co., TN, give a negro girl Zelpha. Wit: Thomas A. Peacock and John Tailor. Reg: 18 Aug 1825.

Page 359 - 8 Jan 1823. Joseph Davidson to Isaac Muse, Bill of Sale. Whereas William Davidson, Sr. conveyed unto Peggy, William, Betsey, Polly, Melinda, Jenny and Joseph Davidson, his children, on 20 July 1808, a negro woman Hannah and her only child, a certain Jesse Farly purchased without the consent of the heirs or children and Jesse Farly purchased from five of the children, their interest in the negro woman and her child. Jenny and Joseph Davidson still hold their interest in the negro woman. We, Jenny Russell formerly Jenny Davidson and Lewis Russell her husband, and Joseph Davidson sold slave to Isaac

Muse. Wit: Richard Muse and Andrew Davidson. Reg: 29 Dec 1827.

Page 388 - 5 Nov 1827. Nancy Kizer to Jacob Kizer, 186 acres. Nancy Kizer, Executrix of Valentine Kizer, deceased, of Bedford Co., TN conveyed to Jacob Kizer, land in Bedford Co. Jacob Kizer paid unto Valentine Kizer in his life time for land in Bedford Co., on Big Flat Creek. Borders Jacob Hunter and William Wallace. Wit: William F. Doherty and William Kizer. Reg: 29 Dec 1827.

Page 390 - 17 Nov 1827. Nancy Kizer to William Kizer, 200 acres. Nancy Kizer, Executrix of Valentine Kizer, deceased, of Bedford Co., TN, for $1.00, conveyed unto William Kizer land in Bedford Co., on Flat Creek. Borders Prewett survey. Wit: William Wallace and Jacob Kizer. Reg: 29 Dec 1827.

Page 413 - 27 Aug 1827. George A. Harbar to Peter Wood, 40 acres. Catharine Harbar and George A. Harbar sold to Peter Wood land in Bedford Co., TN, on waters of Rich Creek and being the 4th and 5th Lot of a tract of land in plat of division between the heirs of Jacob Barbar. Wit: Martin W. Oakly and Sarah White. Reg: 29 Dec 1827.

Page 415 - 28 Jan 1826. William S. Watterson to Philamon Keele, 300 acres. William S. Watterson sold to Philamon Keele, both of Bedford Co., TN, land whereon William S. Watterson now lives, at the head spring of Patrick's Branch. Borders John Keeton, top of ridge, Jonathan Webster and Thomas Patton. Wit: A. Erwin and Nathan Ellis. Reg: 26 Jan 1828.

Page 421 - 12 Jan 1826. William S. Mayfield to James Brittain, Bill of Sale. Whereas William S. Mayfield has intermarried with Sally Brittain of Bedford Co., TN and whereas by the Last Will and Testament of Joseph Brittain, deceased, Sally was entitled to one third of the negroes living on the land at Brittain's death. Amongst whom were five negroes. Sally was to have her one third at the time of her intermarring and whereas James Brittain has this day purchased from William S. Mayfield her interest in the five negroes and the interest of Sally his wife. Wit: William Gilchrist and John S. Frazer. Reg: 30 Jan 1828.

Page 423 - 7 June 1827. John F. Furgerson to James Brittain, Bill of Sale. I, John F. Furgerson of Bedford Co., received from Jas. Brittain, Executor of Jos. Brittain, deceased, $600., it being the amount of myself and wife Amelia Furgerson formerly Amelia Brittain, property of two mares. Wit: Samuel Escue. Reg: 29 Dec 1827.

Page 424 - 13 Jan 1826. Philip Marcus to Martin Adams. I, Philip Marcus of Bedford Co., in behalf of my wife Peggy, alias Margaret, who is one of the lawful heirs of Richard Thomason, relinguish to Martin Adams, all rights title &c, as heir of estate or Richard Thomason at his death. Wit: Adam Miller, B. N. Copeland and Nathan Ballard. Reg: 29 Dec 1827.

Page 426 - 20 Dec 1823. James Bradshaw and wife to Elliott Rucker, 20 acres. James W. Bradshaw and Sarah Bradshaw his wife of Bedford Co., conveyed to Elliott Rucker of Bedford Co., land in Bedford Co., on waters of Weakleys Creek. Borders Robert Coldwell and Robert Morrison's survey. Wit: William

Page 442 - 10 Aug 1827. James S. Walker to Nancy Kizer, 591¼ acres. James S. Walker and Maria A. Nicholson and Alfred O. Nicholson, the legal heirs and devises of Osburn Nicholson, deceased, all of Maury Co., TN one part and Nancy Kizer, Executrix of the Last Will and Testament of Valentine Kizer, deceased, of Bedford Co., TN, other part. James S. Walker and Maria A. his wife, Calvin H. Nicholson and Alfred O. Nicholson for $1800. paid by Valentine Kizer in his lifetime to Osburn P. Nicholson in his lifetime, and for another $1.00, conveyed to Nancy Kizer, land in Bedford Co., TN, on both sides of Big Flat Creek. Borders James Dickson, and crossing of Holts Creek. Wit: William Wallace and Jacob Kizer. Reg: 1 Feb 1828.

Page 445 - 18 Jan 1826. Michael Green to James Claxton, Bill of Sale. I, Michael Green sold unto James Claxton for $100.00, a negro woman and her three young children which belong to the male heirs of John McClintock, deceased, and willed to them by him, that is to say, Samuel McClintock's part which fell to him by his father's Will and he has transferred them to me, Michael Green. Wit: Jas. H. Mosly and Jos. Thompson. Reg: 29 Dec 1827.

Page 448 - 5 Nov 1827. Nancy Kizar to William Wallace, 395 acres. Nancy Kizar, Executrix of the Last Will and Testament of Valentine Kizar, deceased, of Bedford Co., sold to William Wallace land in Bedford Co., on Big Flat Creek. Borders James Dickson and crossing Holts Creek, Jacob Kizer. Wit: William F. Doughlin and Jacob Kizar. Reg: 29 Dec 1827.

Page 450 - Tennessee Grant to Thomas Washburn, 64+ acres. No. 3077. 12½¢ per acre and entered 5 July 1824, granted to Thomas Washburn, land in Bedford Co., TN(now Lincoln Co.) on West Fork of East Fork of Mulberry Creek of Elk River. Borders Aaron Cunningham's tract, Jonathan Floyd's lot, Washburn's peach orchard, and James Gowen's Spring Branch. Surveyed 28 Oct 1824. Reg: 2 Feb 1828.

Page 452 - Tennessee Grant to Thomas Washburn, 5 acres. No.16728. Part of Certificate No. 149, dated 17 Dec 1808, issued to Samuel Patton for 276 acres and entered 28 April 1817 by No. 10109. Granted to Thomas Washburn, assignee of Samuel Patton, land on West Fork of East Fork of Mulberry Creek of Elk River. Borders Washburn's survey of 65 acre survey whereon Washburn now lives. Surveyed 16 May 1817. Reg: 11 Apr 1822.

Page 458 - 12 Sept 1826. George Ewing to James Ewing, Power of Attorney. I, George Ewing of Wythe Co., VA, appointed my son James Ewing of Wythe Co., VA, my Attorney, to receive from the Executor of my deceased brother James Ewing, late of Bedford Co., TN, whatever I am entitled to under the Will of James Ewing, deceased. Reg: 5 Feb 1828.

Page 337 - (misnumbered, should be 537) 25 Oct 1824. John McBride to William McBride, 80 acres. John McBride conveys unto William McBride for Christian love and affection, land in Bedford Co., TN, being on McBride's Creek, a fork of the Garrison. Wit: Rice Hughes and Samuel Hanna. Reg: 12 May 1824.

Page 340 - (misnumbered, should be 540) 19 Mar 1825. James McCuistion, Sr. to Jas. McCuistion, Jr., 79 acres. For love and affection for James McCuistion, Jr., conveys land in Bedford

Co., TN, on waters of Hurricane Creek. Wit: Benjamin McCuistion, Anthony McCuistion and Samuel Ingram. Reg: (no date).

DEED BOOK "X" 1827 - 1827

Page 8 - 24 Nov 1826. John D. Stovall to Rachel Martin, Bill of Sale. I, John D. Stovall, as a legatee or one of the heirs of John Drake, deceased, sold negro boy Joseph to Rachel Martin, conveyed to Rachel Martin by Catherine Drake and Daniel Marshall for $250.00, said negro. Wit: Samuel Clay and Samuel Mitchell. Reg: 11 Apr 1827.

Page 56 - 13 Aug 1826. James McMahan, administrator of William McMahan to T. B. Mosely. James McMahan, administrator of the estate of William McMahan, deceased, of Bedford Co., TN sold to Thomas B. Mosely of Bedford Co., land in Bedford Co., on waters of Garrison Fork for a consideration made by my father William McMahan now deceased for $120.00 paid on 8 Mar 1825. Borders John Tillman's tract and land deeded to my father by Alexander Outlaw, Sr. of Dallas Co., Alabama, John Riggs, assignee of my father William McMahan. Wit: N. L. Majors, James Shinault and James Croft. Reg: 25 Apr 1827.

Page 64 - 24 Apr 1827. Jason Thompson to Robert C. Thompson. Jason Thompson of Davidson Co., TN, for love and affection for my daughter Letitia Cannon of Bedford Co., TN, and for $5.00 paid by Robert C. Thompson of Bedford Co., a negro slave. Reg: 13 May 1827.

Page 69 - 4 May 1825. Sarah House to D. P. T. House, Bill of Sale. I, Sarah House of Bedford Co., TN sold tc D. P. T. House a negro man Stephen. The slave was left to Sarah House by her deceased husband Dudly House. Wit: John W. Howe and Leonard Harmon. Reg: 15 May 1827.

Page 84 - 17 Feb 1825. Stephen Booth, Sr. to James Booth and Samuel Clay, 100 acres. I, Stephen Booth, Sr. relinguish my right and title &c to land in Bedford Co., TN, on waters of Wartrace Fork. Borders David Thomas' land, Linch's line. The land is the tract that I, Stephen Booth, Sr. has given to my son James Booth. In the year 1812 which tract James Booth has conveyed to Samuel Clay for $800.00. Wit: Peter Daniel and N. L. Majors. Reg: 18 May 1827.

Page 92 - 4 Mar 1827. Agness Hughs to James Deery, Mortgage. I, Agness Hughs have for $51.56¼, mortgage unto James Deery, property, my dower of 111 acres left to me by my husband Josiah Hughs, deceased, and other personal property. Wit: William F. Dougherty and Thomas McCuistion. Reg: 25 May 1827.

Page 116 - 29 Feb 1827. Larkin, Hance Davidson to Elish Holt, 120 acres. Hance Davidson, Executor of William Davidson, deceased, and John Larkin of Franklin Co., TN sold to Elish Holt of Bedford Co., TN, land in Bedford Co., on Dawdys Creek, a south branch of the Barren Fork. Borders William Green. Wit: A. Martin and John Davidson. Reg: 15 May 1827.

Page 161 - 16 Feb 1827. John and Esther Reed to Nathaniel Dryden, 1 acre. John Reed and Esther Reed his wife sold to Nathaniel Dryden, a lot in the Town of Farmington, Bedford Co.,

TN. Borders the Public Square on the Shelbyville Road. Wit: David Appleby and Christy McElhannon. Reg: 16 May 1827.

Page 174 - 15 July 1825. Edmund Austin to James Deery & Others. Edmund Austin of Williamson Co., TN conveyed to John Sims, James Deery, James McCorkle and Joseph Steele, Elders and Representatives of the Presbyterian Church in Town of Shelbyville, Bedford Co., TN, for $60.00, paid by the Elders, sold a certain Lot in Town of Shelbyville, known as Lot No. 24. Wit: A. B. Morton and Robert Cannon. Reg: 19 Aug 1826.

Page 179 - 20 Dec 1826. John Sutton to William Sutton, 100 acres. John Sutton sold to William Sutton, Jr., both of Bedford Co., TN, and for $1.00, two tracts in Bedford Co., on headwaters of the Garrison Fork, of 50 acres each. Borders John Sutton, & Thomas Blair. Wit: John Sutton and John Brants(?). Reg: 17 Feb 1827.

Page 223 - 10 Feb 1827. John Reed and wife to Michael C. Josse. John Reed and Esther Reed his wife, for $50.00, sold to Michael C. Josse, a Lot in Village of Farmington of one half acre and known as Lot No. 36. Borders Lot No. 25. Wit: David Appleby and Christy McElhanon. Reg: 1st Monday Feb 1827.

Page 256 - 18 Jan 1827. John B. Craighead and Others to Newcum Thompson, 162 acres. John B. Craighead, Lavina Craighead his wife, Robert Payne and Susanah C. Payne his wife, and John McNairy Robertson guardian for Georganne C. Beck of Davidson Co., TN sold to Newcum Thompson of Bedford Co., TN, land in Bedford Co., on north side of Duck River, being part of a 2000 acre tract granted to Thomas Talbot. Borders Duck River. Wit: Nathan Ewing, Jn. Robertson and H. Roland. Reg: (no date).

Page 266 - 2 Aug 1826. John Reed and Esther Reed to Thomas H. Shockley. John Reed and his wife Esther Reed formerly Esther Cathey sold to Thomas H. Shockley, all of Bedford Co., TN, 2 Town Lots in Town of Farmington, Lot No. 8 and Lot No. 21. Lot No. 8 borders southwest corner of the Public Aquare and west side of Huntsville Street and Lot No. 21 and Lot No. 7. About ¼ acre. Lot No. 21 borders Lot No. 8 in west margin Huntsville Street, Lot No. 2, Lot No. 22. About ½ acre. Wit: James Dryden and John D. Reed. Reg: 12 May 1827.

Page 273 - 10 Feb 1827. John Reed and Esther Reed to Joshua Graham. John Reed and his wife Esther sold to Joshua Graham, all of Bedford Co., TN, Lot of one acre in Town of Farmington, Bedford Co., TN. Borders Lot No. 21, Huntsville Street, Lot No. 27. Wit: D. Appleby and Christy McElhanon. Reg: 16 May 1827.

Page 277 - 10 Feb 1827. John Reed and Esther his wife to Thomas Powdrell, ½ acre Lot. John Reed and Esther Reed his wife formerly Esther Cathey sold to Thomas Powdrell, all of Bedford Co., TN, Lot in Town of Farmington. Borders Huntsville Street. Wit: Christy McElhanon and David Appleby. Reg: 22 Sept 1827.

Page 283 - 10 Feb 1827. John Reed and Esther his wife to Joshua Graham, ½ acre. John Reed and Esther his wife sold to Joshua Graham, a Lot in Town of Farmington, Bedford Co., TN, on east side of East Fork of Rock Creek, being part of Grant No. 107 granted by North Carolina to George Cathey, Lot known as Lot

DEED BOOK "X"

No. 7. Borders on Columbia Road and Lot No. 21. Wit: Christy McElhanon and D. Appleby. Reg: 16 May 1827.

Page 339 - 2 July 1827. William B. Benson to Jeremiah Cleveland. William B. Benson of Bedford Co., TN indebted to Jeremiah Cleveland of Granville District, SC. Wit: A. Martin and Rice Cleveland. Reg: 25 Nov 1827.

Page 368 - 13 Aug 1818. John Sanders to George Sanders, Quit Claim Deed. We, John Sanders and Henry Wormath sold to George Sanders, all of Bedford Co., TN, land on east side of the North Fork, it being two thirds of an undivided part of 324 acres willed by George Sanders, Sr. to Peter Sanders, deceased, containing 108 acres. Wit: John Thompson and John Rogers. Reg: 14 Jan 1828.

Page 370 - 13 Aug 1818. George Sanders and Henry Wormath, all of Bedford Co., TN sold to John Sanders, land on east side of North Fork. Wit: John Thompson and John Rogers. Reg: 29 Dec 1827.

DEED BOOK "Y" 1828 - 1828

Page 12 - 2 Feb 1828. William Waite to George Waite, Deed of Gift, 192 acres. William Waite, Sr. conveyed to his son George Waite, for love and affection, land in Bedford Co., TN, on waters of Wartrace Fork, being the place whereon George Waite now lives. Borders John Bowers. Wit: Jas. Haggard, Samuel Haggard and James Haggard, Jr. Reg: 15 Feb 1828.

Page 19 - 2 Feb 1828. William Waite, Sr. to Robert Waite, 48 acres. William Waite, Sr.conveyed to his son Robert Waite, for love and affection, land on waters of Wartrace Fork, being the place whereon Robert Waite now lives. Wit: Jas. Haggard, Samuel Haggard and Jas. Haggard, Jr. Reg: 16 Feb 1828.

Page 42 - 10 May 1824. James Torrentine to the Church of Christ, 2 acres. James Torrentine conveyed to Joseph Steel, James Torrentine, John Morrison, Michael Fisher, George Smith, Sr., George Smith, Jr., and Archabald Torrentine as Trustees of the Church of Christ at New Hope Meeting House near Thompsons Ford and their successors, land in Bedford Co., TN, on north side of Duck River at Thompsons Ford. Borders Duck River. Wit: Thomason Thompson and George W. Parsons. Reg: 15 Feb 1828.

Page 52 - Plat of Estate of William Newsom, deceased, by Last Will &c by request of the widow and executor. 100 acres of land into 4 Town Lots. Four Boys: James drew Lot No. 1, Jerry No. 2, Lewis No. 3, and Francis No. 4. On south bank of Duck River, Smith's grant, and now owned by Lyles & Bond. Surveyed 13 Dec 1827 by John Thompson, D.S. and William Thompson and Eben Lacy, chaincarriers. Reg: 22 Apr 1828.

Page 54 - James Newsom's tract of 20 acres. (Play) 101 acres. By Last Will and Testament of William Newsom, deceased, and whereon he lived. No. 1 fell to James Newsom. William Newsom, deceased, signed his Last Will and Testament on 24 Dec 1827. Signed by Starling Newsom. Reg: 22 Apr 1828.

Page 56 - Plat of Jerry Newsom's tract of 30¼ acres. (Same as instrument on page 54). Lot No. 2.

Page 58 - Plat of Lewis Newsom's tract of 30½ acres. (Same as instrument on page 54 & 56). Lot No. 3.

Page 60 - Plat of Francis Newsom's tract of 20 acres. (Same as instrument on page 54, 56, & 58).

Page 83 - 25 Jan 1828. James Neill to William Neill, 100 acres. James Neill conveyed to William Neill his son, for love and affection for his son William, his part of James Neill's estate, both real and personal, land in Bedford Co., TN, on waters of Sinking Creek. Borders north west corner of James Neill's land, Gant and Dryden's land. Dividing the spring formerly used by James Neill. Wit: Jas. Ewing, William D. Orr, and J. W. Walker. Reg: 15 Apr 1828.

Page 85 - 10 Aug 1803. Thomas McGuire to William McGuire, Bill of Sale. I, Thomas T. McGuire of Pulaski Co., KY sold to William McGuire of Madison Co., KT, negroes. Wit: Will Hess and Margaret D. Hess. Reg: 25 Apr 1828.

Page 90 - 29 Dec 1827. Mary Teter to William Vancleve, Deed Trust, 85 acres. Mary Teter conveyed to William Vancleve, both of Bedford Co., TN, for $1.00, land in Bedford Co., being the same which was last conveyed from William Weaver to Mary Teter. Borders Banjamin Ransom. Mary Teter is bound unto William Carter in two bonds. Reg: 15 Feb 1828.

Page 114 - 6 Aug 1827. Daniel Gilchrist to Commissioners of Poor House, 130 acres. Daniel Gilchrist conveyed to Joshua Holt, Joseph Steele, and Samuel Philips, commissioners of the Poor House of Bedford Co., TN, for $475.00 sold a tract of land in Bedford Co., on headwaters of Butlers Creek. Borders land of the heirs of Daniel Vaughan, land of George Doherty's heirs now claimed by William Polk, land of William Foster, Elijah Bomar, G. Galathans' corner and Butlers Creek. Wit: William Gilchrist and James Fulton. Reg: 30 Apr 1828.

Page 119 - 11 Feb 1828. James Erwin to Ruben Manly, 25 acres. James Erwin at present of New Orleans conveyed to Ruben Manly of Bedford Co., TN, land on Bedford Co., on waters of the Wartrace Fork. Signed by James Erwin's Attorney, A. Erwin, Jr. Wit: John C. Coldwell and Robert Logan. Reg: 15 Feb 1828.

Page 123 - 24 Aug 1815. (Plat on this page). William Guy and William Lock's plat and certificate of survey of 520 acres. Land where they now live. The 520 acres has been divided into 2 equal parts. Surveyed 23 Aug 1815 by William Gilchrist, D.S. Reg: 1 May 1828.

Page 134 - 5 Feb 1828. John T. Street to Alexander Street, Mortgage. John T. Street of one part and Alexander Street of other part. Whereas Anthony Street of Lunenburg Co., VA, now deceased, by his Last Will and Testament, loaned to his wife Polly during her life, negroes, and at her death the negroes are to go to his four children and whereas the said Polly intermarried with John T. Street after the death of her former husband Anthony Street. After the marriage of John T. Street and Polly Street removed to the State of Tennessee bringing with the the negroes. Reg: 14 Feb 1828.

Page 149 - Plat of Robert Hunters and certificate of possession for 1269 acres. Survey date 15 Dec 1820.

Page 152 - 18 Apr 1827. Albert G. Henderson to Burrell Fetherston (Featherston), Bill of Sale. I, Albert G. Henderson sold to Burrell Fetherston, land that I have in the estate inherited from my grandfather Robert Smith to my mother Elizabeth Henderson. The personal part now in the possession of Mary Smith of Rutherford Co., TN. Wit: William P. Temple and D. M. Davis. Reg: 3 Jun 1828.

Page 163 - 29 Sept 1827. Robert Berry and wife to Sarah Twitten. Robert Berry and Rebecka his wife, Joseph Sharp and Julia Ann his wife, John Scott, James Scott and Jane Scott of Augusta Co., VA conveyed to Sarah Twitten wife of George Twitten of Kentucky, land in Bedford Co., TN. Whereas Col. Alexander Worke, late of Iredell Co., NC and by his Last Will and Testament devises unto the children of his several sisters of whom Rebecah Scott was one. Rebecah Scott having departed this life leaving, Sarah Twitten, Rebecah Berry, Julia Ann Sharp, Jane Scott, John Scott, and James Scott, her children. Sarah Twitten purchased from the heirs of William Scott and half share of the heirs of Alexander Scott, part of heirs of Ebby Scott being the devises of John Scott, Jane Scott, Robert Berry and Rebecah his wife and Joseph Sharp and Julia Ann his wife. Reg: 30 Jun 1828.

Page 189 - 23 Oct 1826. Alexander Neill and wife to John Reed. We, Alexander Neill and Ann his wife, for love and affection for John Reed and his wife Esther, all of Bedford Co., TN, conveyed land in Bedford Co., on East Fork of Rock Creek. Wit: Hosea Mullins and Nathan Dryden. Reg: 3 May 1828.

Page 191 - 23 Oct 1826. Alexander Neill and wife to Vilett Cathey, 833+ acres. We, Alexander Neill and Ann his wife, for love and affection for Vilett Cathey, all of Bedford Co., TN, conveyed to her land in Bedford Co., on East Fork of Rock Creek. Wit: Hosea Mullins and Nathaniel Dryden. Reg: 11 July 1828.

Page 195 - 1 Apr 1828. Ann Neill to John Orr, 100 acres. Ann Neill for love and affection for John Orr, conveyed unto him land in Bedford Co., TN, on East Fork of Rock Creek. Wit: Nathaniel Dryden and Hosea Mullins. Reg: 6 May 1828.

Page 228 - 22 May 1828. James Brittain to Dorothy Brittain, Bill of Sale. I, James Brittain for love and affection for my mother Dorothy Brittain and $1.00, his part of 5 negroes. Reg: 10 May 1828.

Page 237 - 10 May 1828. James Cooper to Washington Cooper. I, James Cooper for natural love and affection for my daughter Mary Tune and her eight children: Frances, William, James, Bedford, John, Elizabeth, Charles, and Mary Louisa, and for $1.00 paid by Washington B. Cooper, all of Bedford Co., TN, sold personal property. Some of the property is at the house of John Tune husband of Mary Tune. Wit: Jonathan Cooper. Reg: 16 May 1828.

Page 243 - 24 Apr 1828. Eben (Ebenezer) Wilson to Fortus Wilson's heirs, 65 acres. Eben Wilson conveyed to the heirs of Fortus Wilson, land on Falling Creek. Borders John Claxton. Heirs of Fortus Wilson, to wit, Darcas Jean Wilson and Elender Wilson. Wit: William Burnett and James Harris. Reg: 16 May 1828.

Page 257 - 20 Feb 1828. Thomas P. Whitney to James G. Whitney, Lot and Store House. Whereas by the Last Will and Testament of William O. Whitney, deceased, bearing date 31 Jan 1825, there was bequeathed unto Thomas P. and James G. Whitney, sons of William O. Whitney, Lot and Store House in Shelbyville. Wit: William B. Sutton and James R. White. Reg: 16 May 1828.

Page 263 - 5 May 1828. James and William D. Ewing to James U. Ewing, 295 acres. James Ewing of Rutherford Co., TN and William D. Ewing of Maury Co., TN, Executors of the Last Will and Testament of James Ewing, deceased, conveyed to James U. Ewing, land in Bedford Co., TN, on west side of Rock Creek. Borders Joseph P. Ewing. Reg: 16 May 1828.

Page 275 - 1 Sept 1827. Hannah Spain to James A. Spain, Deed of Gift. I, Hannah Spain for love and affection for my son James A. Spain, give unto him a negro girl Milly. Wit: John Sims, L. P. Sims and John Streeter. Reg: 16 July 1828.

Page 276 - 1 Sept 1827. Hannah Spain to Abigal Spain, Deed of Gift. I, Hannah Spain for love and affection for my daughter Abigal Spain, give unto her a negro girl Matilda. Wit: John Sims, L. P. Sims, and John Streeter. Reg: 16 May 1828.

Page 277 - 27 Oct 1827. Hannah Spain to Ann Sally Blagg, Deed of Gift. I, Hannah Spain for love and affection for my daughter Ann Sally Blagg wife of John Blagg, give unto her a negro boy Richmond. Wit: Henry Spain and Charity Jordan. Reg: 16 May 1828.

Page 278 - 1 Sept 1827. Hannah Spain to Polly T. Morton, Deed of Gift. I, Hannah Spain for love and affection for my daughter Polly T. Morton wife of Isaac Morton, give unto her a negro girl Clary. Wit: John Sims, L. P. Sims and John Streeter. Reg: 30 July 1828.

Page 279 - 29 Aug 1827. Hannah Spain to Kitty Hartsfield, Deed of Gift. I, Hannah Spain for love and affection for my daughter Kitty Hartsfield wife of Jacob Hartsfield, giv unto her a negro girl Reves. Wit: John Sims, Andrew Browning and Bedey Browning. Reg: 16 May 1828.

Page 289 - 12 Feb 1828. Judith Ringstaff to John Ringstaff, Lot No. 107. Judith Ringstaff conveyed to John Ringstaff, both of Bedford Co., TN, all Judith Ringstaff's dower unto two tracts of land in Bedford Co., Lot No. 107 and also land on north side of an alley running east and west in town of Shelbyville. Judith Ringstaff widow and relict of Henry Ringstaff, deceased. Land borders John Ragsdale's grass lot north of Shelbyville, about three acres. Wit: Michael Green and Isham Sims. Reg: 16 May 1828.

Page 299 - 14 Oct 1816. Agreement between the Phifers, 2373 acres. Martin Phifer, John F. Phifer, John N. Phifer, George A.

Phifer, and Mary Simmons of Cabarrus Co., NC. They are entitled to a tract of land, on the north side of Duck River in Bedford Co., TN, being a grant by North Carolina to Martin Phifer, Sr., by Patent No. 38, dated 10 July 1788, land to be divided. Reg: 8 Aug 1828.

Page 305 - 24 Feb 1823. Samuel Balch to Alfred Balch, 120 acres. Samuel Balch conveyed to Alfred and James Balch, land where Alfred Balch now lives in Bedford Co., TN, which tract was divided to the male heirs of Amos Balch by our grandfather Samuel Patton, deceased. Borders Samuel Patton, Jr., Sugar Creek, and Thomas Talbot. Wit: Joseph Alexander and Edward Wade. Reg: 12 Aug 1828.

Page 329 - 21 June 1828. Joseph McKisick to John Robeson, 151 acres. Joseph McKisick and Jane B. McKisick his wife sold to John Robeson, all of Bedford Co., TN, land in Bedford Co., on waters of Sugar Creek, on south side of the McKisick Fork of Duck River. Borders Dryden's land. Wit: Amos Balch, Thomas Greer and Robert C. Thompson. Reg: 16 Aug 1828.

Page 331 - 5 May 1828. Eli Cleveland to Smith Crawford, 170 acres. Eli Cleveland, Administrator of Morton Jones, deceased, late of Bedford Co., TN, conveyed to Smith Crawford land in Bedford Co., on Dawdys Creek. Morton Jones in his lifetime entered into bond on 18 Sept 1825 with Smith Crawford. Borders Willis Green. Wit: A. Erwin, Jr. and G. W. Essleman. Reg: 16 Aug 1828.

Page 355 - 10 Mar 1827. Nathaniel Porter devises to Susannah Penington, 25 acres. The heirs of Nathaniel Porter, deceased, late of Bedford Co., TN, conveyed to Susannah Penington land in Bedford Co., on Big Flat Creek. Borders where Penington now lives. SIgned by Nathan Adams, Sally P. Adams, Stephen Porter, Mary Porter and J. N. Porter. Wit: Joseph Porter, George Crump, Rachel Penington and James Russell. Reg: 16 Aug 1828.

Page 377 - 21 June 1827. Samuel Roseborough to James Lockhart. Samuel Roseborough, Attorney for heirs of William Roseborough, deceased, of Lincoln Co., TN, sold to James Lockhart surviving Executor of John Strother, deceased, of Davidson Co., TN, land in Bedford Co., TN, on West Fork of Rock Creek. Borders Francis Nash. Wit: Porterfield, Bright and Samuel Mitchell and John C. Coldwell. Reg: 16 Aug 1828.

Page 387 - 18 Jun 1828. J. C., N. E. and Thomas Coldwell to James Brittain, Bill of Sale. We, John C. Coldwell, Nathaniel E. Coldwell of Bedford Co., TN and Thomas Coldwell of Warren Co., TN sold to James Brittain of Bedford Co., 4 negroes. Wit: John Eakin, THomas M. Coldwell and M. D. Mitchell. Reg: 16 Aug 1828.

Page 389 - 1 July 1828. Kenneth L. Anderson to Daniel Johnston, 70 acres. It was commanded by Sheriff of Bedford Co., TN that the lands and tenaments of Walter Burnard, V. A. Burnard and R. H. Burnard, minor heirs of Thomas H. Burnard, deceased, in Bedford Co., should make the sum of $1678.61¼ and cost of suit which in the same Court, Anny McGee, Allen Knight and Catherine Timmons hath removed against them and he should make return thereof of Court. Three writs came unto Kenneth P. Anderson and issued on land. One tract of 102 acres, one of 70 acres, one of 50 acres, and one of 5 acres, in Bedford Co., on waters of Duck River, for sale. Land borders junction of Barren and Garrison Fork, Charles Lucas and a Mill. Wit: Edward Wade and J. H. Burnett. Reg: 27 Sept 1828.

Page 393 - 7 Feb 1828. Alexander J. Worke to Theophilus Falls, 2473+ acres. Both of Iredell Co., NC. Land in Bedford Co., TN, on both sides of Duck River. Borders Joseph Dickson's survey. Reg: 30 May 1828.

Page 421 - Moses Thompson to Joseph Cloud, 46 acres. Whereas Aaron Thompson, now deceased of Bedford Co., TN, Executed to Joseph Cloud, his bond for $425.00, dated 15 Nov 1821, land in Bedford Co., and in the neighborhood of West Fork of Rock Creek. Borders Nowlin's, Paxton's, and Polk's lands. Wit: James Reed, William D. Orr and Alexander Orr. Reg: 16 Aug 1828.

Page 424 - 30 May 1828. John Davis to Willie Ledbetter, Bill of Sale, to R. Warner. We, John Davis and Willie Ledbetter, acting administrators of estate of William Knott, deceased, of Bedford Co., TN, negro slaves. Wit: Rezen Thompson and William Williams. Reg: 16 Aug 1828.

Page 432 - 26 June 1828. Minor Wilks to Eliza Wilks and Others. I, Minor Wilks of Bedford Co., TN, for the regard I have for my four children, to wit, Eliza Wilks, Elizabeth Wilks, Mary Ann Wilks and Franklin Wilks, grant unto them personal property. Wit: William Justice and M. D. Yell. Reg: 16 Aug 1828.

Page 455 - 24 Sept 1820. Richard Brown to Frances Turner. Richard Brown of Wilson Co., TN conveys to Frances Man (Mann), late Frances Turner, Executors of the Last Will and Testament of Isham Turner, deceased. Isham Turner, in his lifetime, paid unto Richard Brown $300.00, sold to Frances Mann, late Frances Turner, a tract of land in Bedford Co., TN, on Rock Creek. Wit: William Allen, Joel Eckles and William Walker. Reg: 24 Dec 1828.

Page 457 - 16 Mar 1824. William Hamilton to Theophilus Hamilton, Bill of Sale. I, Will Hamilton for love and affection for my son Theophilus Hamilton, both of Bedford Co., TN, give personal estate. William Hamilton and Marian his wife. Reg: 2 Nov 1828.

Page 459 - 3 Dec 1814. William Hamilton to Theophilus Hamilton, 150 acres. William Hamilton conveyed to Theophilus Hamilton, both of Bedford Co., TN, for $1.00, land on north side of Duck River. Borders Billington's line, John Hamilton's corner and the Columbia Road. Wit: David Artes(?), Sorrel White and John S----. Reg: 2 Nov 1828.

Page 465 - 3 Mar 1828. Nancy Dalby(Dolby) to William Fleming, Bill of Sale. I, Nancy Dalby, one of the heirs of Micajah Bullock, deceased, late of Granville Co., NC, for myself and my heirs, relinguish a negro woman Poly, which was the property of Micajah Bullock, deceased, to William Fleming of Granville Co., NC. Negro left in possession of his daughter Frances in his lifetime and in which Frances Bullock is since married to William Fleming. Nancy Dalby of Bedford Co., TN. Wit: Theo. F. Bradford and John Dalby. Reg: 3 Mar 1828.

DEED BOOK "Y"

Page 484 - 1 May 1828. Sarah Ray to Robert Ray.
I, Sary Ray widow and relict of William Ray, deceased, late of Bedford Co., TN, for $100.00 paid by Robert Ray, guardian of Charles Ray, Fout Ray, Polly and Hugh Ray, minor heirs of William Ray, deceased, land which belonged to William Ray, my late husband, on south side of Duck River. Borders Duck River, and Thompson's line. Wit: Hugh Ray and Thomas Ray. Reg: (no date).

Page 494 - 3 Oct 1826. Elizabeth Nall to Perlina Nall.
I, Elizabeth Nall for natural love and affection for my daughter Perlina Nall, both of Bedford Co., TN, granted unto her a mare and two colts which is now in my possession and on the plantation where I now live, also personal property. Wit: Andrew Vannoy and Jane Vannoy. Reg: 3 Nov 1828.

Page 496 - 20 Aug 1828. William Carothers to A. Crothers.
I, William Carothers for love and affection for my oldest son Archabald Carothers, both of Bedford Co., TN, two negro boys. Wit: Robert Kelle and William B. Herndon. Reg: 3 Nov 1828.

Page 503 - 21 Apr 1827. Zadoc Wood, Sr. to Zadoc Wood, Jr., 50 acres. Both of Bedford Co., TN, land in Bedford Co., on waters of the Wartrace Fork. Borders R. Cunningham. Wit: C. D. Wood and George Waite. Reg: 3 Nov 1828.

Page 505 - William Pillow and Abner Pillow of Maury Co., TN and Gideon Pillow of Giles Co., TN and Mordecai Pillow of Davidson Co., TN conveyed to Ebenezer Elliott of Maury Co., TN, land on Rock Creek. Borders John Redford, John Cockrell, & Meeting House. 371 acres. Wit: Y. W. Egnew and Rob. Mack. Reg: 3 Nov 1828.

Page 508 - Franklin, Williamson County, TN, 2 June 1825. Chancery Court. John Atkinson and John Wortham, administrators with Will annexed of Samuel Fleming, deceased, vs John Ferguson, Elizabeth Ferguson, Rebecca Tomlinson, Samuel Tomlinson, Wiley Tomlinson, Samuel Ferguson, Abraham D. Fleming, Elizabeth Fleming, David C. Summington, John Fleming, John W. Fleming, Henry Crabb, Archable and George M. Neill, Joel Riggs and Alexander McCorkle, minors of Hugh Tomlinson, deceased. Court surveyed a tract of 1050 acres, the real estate of Samuel Fleming, deceased, late of Bedford Co., land was laid off. Reg: (no date).

DEED BOOK "AA" 1829 - 1830

Page 2 - 14 Sept 1825. Heirs of Joseph Taylor to John Taylor. Whereas Joseph and John Taylor about 20 years ago entered into partnership and worked for many years, they purchased two tracts, one from Nathaniel Hays for 175 acres and one from Joseph Cook for 200 acres. Deed was made to Joseph Taylor and in February 1823 divided the two tracts but Joseph Taylor died without executing a deed to John Taylor for said land. Sarah Campbell, Alexander Stuart and Mary his wife, Samuel Thompson and Nelly his wife, Josiah Blair and Jemmy his wife, Mary Taylor and Elizabeth Taylor, heirs of Joseph Taylor, sold to John Taylor, land in Bedford Co., TN, on west side of Wartrace Fork. Wit: John Williams and James H. Vance. Reg: 6 Feb 1827.

Page 9 - 10 Nov 1826. S. E. Richardson and wife to James

Thompson, 98 acres. Samuel E. Richardson and Harriett Richardson sold to James Thompson, all of Bedford Co., TN, land in Bedford Co., on north side of Duck River, it being part of land belonging to the estate of Joseph Thompson, deceased, No. 8. Borders Torrentine's corner, James Thompson and Duck River. Wit: James Turrentine and George Fisher. Reg: 9 Feb 1829.

Page 16 - 13 Nov 1826. Thomas Whiteside - John B. Dickson, Sheriff. At Davidson Co., TN to Sheriff of Bedford Co., TN in favor of Washington Jackson and James Erwin, surviving partners of the late firm of Kirkman, Jackson & Erwin vs Thomas Whiteside, Richard C. Whiteside, David Whiteside, James Whiteside, William Whiteside, John Johnson and wife, Newton Parker and wife, James Lafferty, Jane Lafferty, John Lafferty, James McGolick and Isabella McGolick, as heirs of Jenkins Whiteside, deceased. The land in Bedford Co., TN, on Duck River. Wit: William Gilchrist and Benjamin G. Marshall. Reg: 10 Feb 1829.

Page 19 - Return of the division among the heirs of Caleb Phifer.
Lot No. 1, to John N. Phifer and Ann his wife.
Lot No. 2, to Elizabeth Moore.
Lot No. 3, to A. C. McCree(McRee) and Barbary his wife.
Lot No. 4, to William Houston and his wife Sarah.
Lot No. 5, to Robert McKinzie and Mary his wife.
Lot No. 6, to Nathaniel Alexander and Esther his wife.
Surveyed and Divided, 4 Feb 1829, land in Bedford Co., TN, on waters of Fall Creek, north of Shelbyville, 5000 acres, same being conveyed to Caleb Phifer by North Carolina. Plat on page 20. Reg: 10 Feb 1829.

Page 21 - 16 Apr 1828. Thomas Sanders - Fanny Sander's Deed of Relinguishment. Whereas the Last Will and Testament of William Sanders, deceased, late of Bedford Co., TN, I, Fanny Sanders widow of William Sanders, are entitled to a life estate or dower in land in Bedford Co., TN, which is in possession of Thomas Sanders son of William Sanders, being the same tract on which Thomas is now living on the south side of Duck River and east of Shelbyville, and whereas for love and affection I have for my son Thomas Sanders and for 10 shillings, relinguish all claims and titles to Thomas Sanders. Wit: A. Cathey, D. D. Sanders and David Owen. Reg: 10 Feb 1829.

Page 22 - Petition for the heirs of Caleb Phifer for a division of land. Petition of William Houston and his wife Sarah, Elizabeth Moore, Robert McKenzie and Mary his wife, John N. Phifer and Ann his wife, A. C. McRee in right of his deceased wife Barbara, Cornelius McRee, Caleb P. McRee by right of Mary Ann McRee and Margaret McRee who was an infant under age of twenty one years by their father and next friend A. C. McRee, Robert W. Smith and Margaret his wife, Caleb P. Alexander, Samuel S. Harris and Jane his wife, Eliza Mears, Francis Lock and his wife Sarah, Elam Harris and Mary his wife, Nancy Alexander an infant under the age of twenty one by her guardian and next friend Samuel S. Harris, Esther Alexander who is under twenty one years by her guardian and next friend Elam Harris, Charles and John Anderson who are also under twenty one years by their guardian and next friend Caleb P. Alexander, all of North Carolina, represented that Caleb Phifer of Cabarrus Co., NC, departed this life sometime in the year 1811. He died seized of a tract of land in Bedford Co., TN, containing about 5000 acres. Caleb Phifer made and published his Last Will and Testament and proven in County Court of Cabarrus Co., NC. He divided among six daughters, to wit, Esther Alexander, Elizabeth Moore, Sarah Houston, Barbara McRee, Mary and Ann Phifer. Esther Alexander has departed this life since the death of her father and leaving your petitioners, Margaret who has intermarried with Robert W. Smith, Jane who intermarried with Samuel S. Harris, Sarah who intermarried with Francis Lock, Mary who has intermarried with Elam Harris, Eliza Mears relict of J. A. Mears, deceased, Caleb P. Alexander, Nancy Alexander, Easter Alexander, Charles and John Alexander her heirs at law surviving her, Barbara one of the daughters has departed this life since the death of her father leaving A. C. McRee who claims to be a tenant by the courtesy and your petitions, Cornelius McRee, C. P. McRee, Mary Ann and Margaret McRee her heirs at law surviving her. Sarah who intermarried with William Houston, also a daughter, and Elizabeth Moore also one of the daughters and Mary who intermarried with Robert McKenzie also one of the daughters. Ann who intermarried with John N. Phifer is also a daughter. Sometime in the year 1817 a Power of Attorney signed by the devises, their husbands was delivered unto Joseph Steele, J. N. Alexander and Wilson Steele empowering them to divide land equally, to wit, Elam W. Harris, Mary Harris, Caleb P. Alexander, Eliza Mears, Sarah Lock, Francis Lock. Reg: 11 Feb 1829.

Page 28 - 1 Oct 1828. James Yell to Samuel Philips.
James Yell sold to Samuel Philips, both of Bedford Co., TN, land in Bedford Co., on headwaters of eastern branch of Butlers Creek, it being part of land that Moses Yell, deceased, bought of Robert Butler and Rachel Butler his wife. Borders Archabald Yell's land he sold to Philips last spring, T. F. Bradford's land, Thomas McGuyre, Sr.'s land he purchased of James Yell, East Fork of Butlers Creek, and James and Alexander C. Yell. Reg: 12 Feb 1829.

Page 29 - 19 Jul 1828. Sally Holt to Henry Holt.
Sally Holt of Grainger Co., TN, sold to Henry Holt of Bedford Co., TN, land in Bedford Co., on north side of Duck River, it being the twelfth part of an undivided land of 100 acres of which John Holt died seized and possessed and one twelfth part descended to Sally Holt, one of the legatees of Henry Holt. Wit: Joseph Rich, G. W. Rich and Isaiah Meakiff. Reg: 12 Feb 1829.

Page 30 - 30 Apr 1828. Peter Graves' lease to John Kimbro.
I, Peter Graves of Bedford Co., TN, leased unto John Kimbro of Bedford Co., 113¼ acres of land and a distillery in Bedford Co., the tract that I (Graves) and Kimbro now live on. Borders land of Clement Cannon and crossing Thompsons Creek. Lease is during the natural life of Peter Graves, Margaret Graves his wife, and John Kimbro and Elizabeth Kimbro his wife. Contract was made in the year 1818. Levy Kimbro rendered service for Peter Graves in 1825, gets the distillery. Both Kimbros to receive all property after death of Peter and Margaret Graves. Wit: Elijah Parker, Jr. and Jonathan Parker. Reg: 13 Feb 1829.

Page 43 - 31 Jan 1829. Lancaster Lovet to Enoch Lovet.
I, Lancaster Lovet of Bedford Co., TN, being of sound mind and it being my wish to possess my son Enoch Lovet land in Bedford Co. Borders my son Green Lovet's corner, Samuel Harper and Ruth Brown. Wit: Daniel Looney. Reg: 20 Feb 1829.

Page 44 - 31 Jan 1829. Lancaster Lovet to Green Lovet. Lancaster Lovet and Green Lovet, both of Bedford Co., TN. I, Lancaster Lovet, possess my son Green, the part of my farm whereon I now live and where on my dwelling house now stands. Borders William McKinney's corner. Green Lovet to take possession after my death and the death or marriage of ny beloved wife Kitty. Wit: Daniel Looney. Reg: 20 Feb 1829.

Page 52 - 25 Mar 1826. Samuel Patton to Joseph Patton, 81 acres. For love and affection for his son Joseph Patton, granted unto him land in Bedford Co., TN, on south side of Duck River. Borders Samuel Patton. Wit: James Gammill and Joseph Alexander. Reg: 24 Feb 1829.

Page 62 - 26 Nov 1828. Elizabeth Wallace, Admrx. to John Cartmill, 175 acres. Elizabeth Wallace, surviving administratrix of Robert Wallace, deceased, of Bedford Co., TN, sold to John Cartmill of Bedford Co., land in Bedford Co., on the Wartrace Fork. Borders T. F. Bradford, Wartrace Fork and William Peacock. Wit: John Slade, William Wallace and William M. Cartmill. Reg: 26 Feb 1829.

Page 75 - 8 Jan 1829. Allen Leeper to Lile A. Ewing and Rebekah his wife, 203½ acres. Allen Leeper conveyed to Lile A. Ewing and Rebekah his wife, for love and affection for his son-in-law and his daughter, Lile A. Ewing and Rebekah Ann his wife, land in Bedford Co., TN, on West Fork of Rock Creek. Borders David Ross' and, James Ewing, near Leeper's Mill. Wit: William L. McCleary and Calvin H. Ewing. Reg: 2 Mar 1829.

Page 80 - 31 Jan 1829. James E. Patton to Joseph Couch, 74 acres. James E. Patton conveyed to Joseph Couch, both of Bedford Co., TN, land conveyed by the Last Will and Testament of James Patton, deceased, to his son James E. Patton, on Middle Fork of Garrison Fork of Duck River. Borders James Patton's land, Garrison Fork, excluding within which is not sold but reserved expressively for the only use of a graveyard forever, it being set apart by James Patton in his lifetime, containing one half acre for graveyard. Wit: Michael Stevens and Jno. Stevens. Reg: 3 Mar 1829.

Page 83 - 12 Sept 1824. Thomas P. Kinney and Elizabeth Kinney to William Potter, 100 acres. Thomas P. Kinney, Alexander Davidson and Margaret Davidson his wife and Elizabeth Kinney, all of Bedford Co., TN sold for $1.00 to William Potter of Bedford Co., land in Bedford Co., on waters of Sinking Creek. Borders Humphrey Cunningham. Wit: Humphrey Cunningham and G. W. Cunningham. Reg: 3 Mar 1829.

Page 84 - Thomas Talbert to J. R. Talbert, Elizabeth Pepper, Patsy Myers and John H. Talbert. Whereas William Talbert, late of Bedford Co., TN, died possessed of property in Bedford Co., both real and personal, I, Thomas Talbert of Jackson Co., TN, relinguish and signe over to James R. Talbert, Patsy Myers, John H. Talbert and Elizabeth Pepper, all the estate William Talbert, deceased, as the next of kin and father of William Talbert, deceased, except one fifth part to be equally divided among James R., Patsy, John H., Elizabeth and myself. This 3 Feb 1829. Wit: O. H. Searcy and A. Martin. Reg: 3 Mar 1829.

DEED BOOK "AA"

Page 102 - 17 Nov 1827. Richard Ellkins and Maacha Ellkins to Mahala Ellkins. Sold a negro woman Blythe. Wit: Asa M. Ellkins. Reg: 10 Mar 1829.

Page 102 - 17 Nov 1827. Richard Ellkins and Maacha Ellkins to Matilda Ellkins. Sold a negro girl Susy. Wit: Asa M. Ellkins. Reg: 10 Mar 1829.

Page 103 - 26 Mar 1828. Richard Ellkins to Maacha Ellkins. Both of Bedford Co., TN, sold negroes. Wit: Asa M. Elkins. Reg: 10 Mar 1829.

Page 105 - 2 Feb 1829. Elijah Floyd to Hosea H. Floyd and Norman Finney, 154 acres. I, Elijah Floyd sold to Hosea H. Floyd a tract of land of David Floyd, deceased, of which Elijah Floyd is an assignee of David Floyd, deceased. Land includes the spring that David Floyd, deceased, formerly made use of. Borders Yates' Mill on Big Flat Creek, and Charles Jones. Wit: A. W. Puryear, Alex. Finney and Thomas Crawford. Reg: 13 Feb 1829.

Page 108 - 17 Oct 1828. Edmund Hodges, Sr. and Others to William S. Watterson, 400 acres. Edmund Hodges, Sr., Edmund Hodges, Jr. and Charles Hodges, Sr. sold to William S. Watterson, land in Bedford Co., TN, on Garrison Fork. Borders E. Hodges, Sr. and E. Hodges, Jr., Gideon Green and Peter Starns. Which land includes where Hodge now lives. Wit: James A. Brantley and Isaac Chrisman. Reg: 12 Mar 1829.

Page 111 - 26 June 1802. Joseph Dickson to Alexander Worke. Joseph Dickson of Lincoln Co., NC sold to Alexander Worke of Iredell Co., NC, land in Bedford Co., TN, on both sides of North Fork. Wit: R. Worke, Alexander Worke, Jr., and Hannah Worke. Reg: 23 Mar 1829.

Page 132 - 22 Feb 1828. Jariot Shearin's heirs to Thomas Shearin, 750 acres. Mary Shearin relict of Jariot Shearin, deceased, and William Shearin and Turner Shearin, all of Haywood Co., TN conveyed to Thomas Shearin of Bedford Co., TN, land in Bedford Co. Mary Shearin, William Shearin and Turner Shearin, all heirs and legatees of William Shearin, deceased, and is entitled to part of land which is undivided, as heirs of William Shearin, deceased, which land was granted by North Carolina to William Shearin by Grant No. 47, dated 10 July 1788. Borders Anthony Newman and Alexander Robertson. Wit: Charles Wortham. Reg: 18 May 1829.

Page 138 - 2 May 1825, Franklin, Williamson Co., TN. Atkinson & Wortham vs The Heirs of Samuel Flemming & Others. Chancery Court. John Atkinson and John Wortham, administrators with the Will annexed of Samuel Flemming, deceased, complainants vs John F. Furguson, Elizabeth Furguson, Rebecca Tomlinson, Samuel A. F. Tomlinson, Willie Tomlinson, Samuel Ferguson, Abraham D. Flemming, Elizabeth Flemming, David C. Summington, John Flemming, John W. Flemming, Henry Crabb, Archibald and George M. Neil, Joel Riggs and Alexander McCorkle, administrators of Hugh Tomlinson, deceased, Defts. Land of 1050 acres of estate of William Flemming, deceased, late of Bedford Co., TN, is to be laid off in lots. Plat on page 138. On west side and near Spring Creek, on the road on the north boundary line near the Baptist Meeting House. Reg: 20 May 1829.

DEED BOOK "AA"

Page 143 - 30 Oct 1828. Heirs and Devises of Moses Yell to Alexander Yell. John Brooks and Sally Brooks his wife of Maury Co., TN, John A. Moor and Nancy his wife, and Archibald Yell of Bedford Co., TN, heirs and devises of Moses Yell conveyed to Alexander C. Yell of Bedford Co.,in the division of property in the Last Will and Testament of Moses Yell, deceased, land in Shelbyville, Lot No. 57 and on the Public Square and bordered on east by Martin Street, south by Lane Street, west by Lot No. 65, and north by small alley. Reg: May 20, 1829.

Page 176 - 24 Feb 1829. A. Erwin, Jr. to Abraham Myers. Andrew Erwin, Jr. of Bedford Co., TN, as administrator of William Talbot, deceased, and as surviving partner of the firm of Talbot & Erwin conveyed to Abraham Myers of Jackson Co., TN. Wit: O. H. Searcy, James H. Shields and A. Erwin. Reg: 27 May 1829.

Page 178 - 2 Jan 1828. William Shearin's heirs to Thomas Shearin, 750 acres. Elizabeth Shearin, relict of John Shearin, deceased, and William Shearin, Polly Borough formerly Polly Shearin and now the wife of James Borough, and Rebecca Shearin, all of Bedford Co., TN conveyed to Thomas Shearin land, a part of undivided estate of William Shearin, deceased. Borders Anthony Newman, Alexander Robertson. Wit: William S. Mayfield and Richard H. Sims. Reg: 28 May 1829.

Page 186 - Tennessee Grant to Samuel Philips, 300 acres. No.8092. Paid 12½ cents per acre. 15 Dec 1826, granted to Samuel Philips land in Bedford Co., TN, on both sides of Duck River. Surveyed 21 Dec 1826. Borders David Ross, Blount brothers, crosses Duck River, where a road leading from Shelbyville to the Pond Spring and John Gilbert. Reg: 18 Jun 1828.

Page 187 - Tennessee Grant to Newton Cannon, 640. No. 8093. 12½ cents per acre. 15 Dec 1826, survey date 18 Mar 1827 by No. 1129. Land in Bedford Co., TN, dated 18 Mar 1827. Borders Samuel Philips and Duck River and the Blount brothers. Reg: 29 May 1829.

Page 188 - Tennessee Grant to Robert and Clement Cannon, 698 acres. No. 8096. 1cent per acre. Entered 9 Apr 1827 by No. 1192, survey date 9 July 1829, land in Bedford Co., TN, on both sides Duck River. Borders Newton Cannon and Freeman Burrow. Reg: 29 May 1829.

Page 206 - 19 Dec 1828. Edward Ragsdale to Thomas A. Peacock, 7 acres. Edward Ragsdale sold to Thomas A. Peacock, both of Bedford Co., TN, land in Bedford Co., on headwaters of Fall Creek. Borders Susan Peacock and known on the plan of the estate of John Peacock, by Lot No. 4. Wit: Andrew Bailey and Minor Wilkes. Reg: 6 Jun 1829.

Page 212 - 2 May 1829. Lewis Gant, Sr* to Lewis Gant, Jr., 640 acres. Lewis Gant, Sr. conveyed to Lewis Gant and Jonathan Gant, Jr., land in Bedford Co., TN, for love and affection for his beloved sons Lewis and Jonathan Gant, the land being on both sides of Big Sinking Creek. Borders School Land. Wit: Charles Fisher and James Cheves. Reg: 8 June 1829.

* Gant is spelled in this instrument as Gaunt.

Page 222 - 17 Jan 1828. William P. Samples to S. Murphree, Deed of Trust, 207 acres. William P. Samples one part and Stephen Murphree, John Hornsby, Thomas A. Peacock and Frederick Frazer, all of Bedford Co., TN, other part, land in Bedford Co., TN, on waters of Wartrace Fork of Duck River. Borders Bell Buckle Creek, Burrell Featherston and John Norvell. Wit: David Murphree and Jas. Kelly. Reg: 10 Jan 1829.

Page 228 - 10 Oct 1828. Ziza Morrison and Susannah Morrison to John Bradshaw, 57 acres. Ziza Morrison and Susannah Morrison of Bedford Co., TN, conveyed to John Bradshaw of Bedford Co., Deed of Trust. Land in Bedford Co., TN, on waters of Sugar Creek whereon she now lives, which was deeded by Archibald S. White to Susannah Morrison. Also, personal property. Wit: A. Yell and Samuel Escue. Reg: 15 Jun 1829.

Page 241 - 9 Jul 1828. John Atkinson to Joseph J. Marshall, 51 acres. John Atkinson for inconsideration for his son-in-law Joseph J. Marshall, both of Bedford Co., TN, by virtue of his marriage to Virginia Atkinson a daughter of John Atkinson, give unto him land in Bedford Co., TN, on waters of Spring Creek, on west side of said creek. Wit: George R. Scott and Owen Vincent. Reg: 26 Jun 1829.

Page 243 - 8 Oct 1828. George Higgs and Effie J. Higgs to James Joice, 25 acres. George Higgs and Effie J. Higgs conveyed to James Joice, all of Bedford Co., TN, part of estate left to said Effie J. Higgs as her legacy of Benjamin Forsythe, deceased, land in Bedford Co., on waters of Spring Creek, it being part of 1000 acre entered in the name of Samuel Kerr and transferred to Benjamin Williams of Moore Co., NC and by him Benjamin Williams, deceased, to Lucy McReynolds in trust for her children the heirs of Thomas McReynolds, deceased, and by recent transfer to Elizabeth B. H. Forsythe widow of Benjamin Forsythe, deceased. Wit: J. Atkinson and J. B. Sheffield. Reg: 26 Jun 1829.

Page 263 - Tennessee Grant to John G. Adams, 8 acres. No. 7576. 12½ cents per acre. Entered 14 May 1825. Survey date 18 July 1825, in Bedford Co., TN, on waters of Wilson Creek. Borders Batt Stovall whereon he now lives, land whereon Mathew Russell now lives, and William Clark's land. Reg: 4 Aug 1829.

Page 264 - Tennessee Grant to John G. Adams, 10 acres. No. 7204. 12½ cents per acre. Entered 6 May 1825 by No. 577. Survey date 16 May 1825. Land in Bedford Co., TN, on waters of Wilsons Creek. Borders William Clark, Robert Allison, and where B. Stovall now lives. Reg: 4 Aug 1829.

Page 271 - 10 Aug 1829. George Roberts and John Knott, Division of property. Whereas Elizabeth Roberts, late of Bedford Co., TN, entitled to property &c also several negroes, we, George Roberts and John Knott have and distributes of the said Elizabeth Roberts, deceased, in order to affect a division of the property among ourselves being the only distributees of Elizabeth Roberts, the said George Roberts in his own right and John Knott took first lot of negroes and George Roberts took the second lot of negroes. Wit: James Brittain and A. Martin. Reg: 18 Aug 1829.

Page 276 - Mary H. Bell to Mary Ann Patton, Deed of Gift. I, Mary H. Bell of Lexington District, SC, for love and affection for my niece Mary Ann Patton, daughter of John and Ann Patton, now residing in Tennessee, given a negro girl Betta. Wit: John C. Bell, Harriett Hart and Eliza Ann Heron. Signed at Pearl Springs, Lexington District, SC. Reg: 1 Sept 1829.

Page 283 - 3 Aug 1829. Nancy A. Marshall to Portland J. Curl, 125 acres. Nancy A. Marshall wife of Daniel Marshall and daughter of John Drake, deceased, of Bedford Co., TN sold to Portland J. Curl of Bedford Co., land in Bedford Co., on waters of Wartrace Fork. Borders land formerly of William Henry and Jackson land. The land being part of the tract whereon Portland J. Curl now lives. Nancy A. Marshall being now twenty years of age. Wit: S. C. Edgar. Reg: 1 Sept 1829.

Page 290 - 3 Aug 1829. Hugh Thomison and Jane Caroline his wife formerly Jane Caroline Endsley of Lincoln Co., TN sold to Hugh B. Smiley of Bedford Co., TN, land in Bedford Co., on headwaters of East Fork of Rock Creek. Borders lands surveyed for Felix Roberson, Smiley's land, and Julia F. Endsley's division. 40 acres. Wit: Hugh Smiley and Jane B. Lowry. Reg: 2 Sept 1829.

Page 292 - 9 Aug 1828. David Chamberland and Phebe Chamberland his wife to William Walker, 100 acres. All of Bedford Co., TN. David and Phebe Chamberland sold to William Walker land in Bedford Co., on waters of Thompsons Creek, it being a part of a undivided tract belonging to the heirs of James Walker, deceased. Borders land granted to Clement Cannon, school land, and William Wilborn and Hays Blair's grant. Wit: Daniel Shipman, Ezekiel Smith, Abel Landers and Reuben Shipman. Reg: 3 Sept 1829.

Page 298 - 28 Nov 1828. John Reed, Esther Reed his wife sold to Gabriel Silby, land in Bedford Co., TN, on East Fork of Rock Creek, 80 acres. Wit: John Ellison and H. W. Ligget. Reg: 3 Sept 1829.

Page 325 - 23 May 1829. Loudon Co., Virginia. This day, Isabella Credler formerly Isabella Kaighn but miscalled in the Will of John Kaighn, deceased, formerly of Chester Co., Burlington, New Jersey. <u>Arabella</u> made oath before me the undersigned Justice of the Peace for said county that she was married to Samuel Kaighn, deceased, mentioned in the Last Will and Testament who departed this life about the 3rd day of September year of 1808, that John B. Kaighn recently of Leesburg in Loudon but who wrote to William Chilton, Esq., Attorney at Law on 1st March last from Pleasant Retreat in the State of Tennessee, is the son of Samuel Kaighn, deceased, and herself, that Samuel having departed this life at his residence in Fairfax County near Alexandria. She about the year 1810 removed to Loudon County that she has often heard her deceased husband Samuel speak of his Uncle John Kaighn living in Philadelphia and knows that he received letter from him. She further states that John B. Kaighn is the only son of Samuel Kaighn, deceased. She further states that she knows that John B. Kaighn through his late guardian William Chilton, Esq., to have settled with the Executor of John Kaighn, deceased, for the personal property or Philadelphia property to which he was entitled. Signed by Sam Edwards.

At the same time and place, Mary Monroe widow of Andrew Monroe, deceased, made oath that she is the mother of Isabella Credler. She said Isabella, her daughter, had in her first husband

husband Samuel Kaighn, deceased, that during her life they lived in Fairfax County near Alexandria, that John B. Kaighn is the son of Samuel and Isabella, called in the Will of John Kaighn, deceased, Arabella, that affiant knows this fact and that she has often heard Samuel Kaighn, deceased, speak of his Uncle John Kaighn near Philadelphia and that John B. Kaighn his grandson is now in the State of Tennessee attending to lands devised him by his relation John Kaighn, deceased. Reg: 28 Sept 1829.

Page 327 - Last Will and Testament of John Kaighn of Chester County , of Burlington, New Jersey, being advanced age.
1st - Just debts be paid.
2 - To my relation Ann Edwards my large Bible and my dwelling house.
3 - To my relation Ann Edwards, Samuel Edwards, Elizabeth Edwards, Sarah the wife of Joseph Collins, and Charles Edwards, my dwelling house retreat in Morristown and all the remainder of my estate.
4 - To the above relations, all the household and kitchen furniture &c of Morristown, also all my books. And to my friend Samuel Jones, books and pamplets to the Library Company at Morristown.
5 - To Samuel Edwards all my interest of 3/8 of estate at Main Square in Wormouth Co., New Jersey.
6 - I give my four story house, No. 5 Lombard Street, unto Abigail Graves and Elizabeth Gardiner, John Graves, Sarah Graves, Abigail Graves, Jr., and Charles Graves, to share equally.
7 - To John Kaighn, Jr. my Lot and back Kitchen on the east of and adjoining the above four story house during his natural life and after his death, goes to heirs of John Kaighn, deceased.
8 - To Kaighn, son of Samuel Kaighn and Asabella his wife, late of Fairfax Co., VA, not far rom Alex ndria, and to William Kaighn all my estate in three tenements on Mead Alley in District of Southwork.
9 - To William Kaighn, my Lot in Middletown, Dalphin Co., PA.
10 - Kaighn, son of Samuel, my share of 5000 acres purchased in company with Levi Hollingsworth of Philadelphia, located on Duck River of Tennessee and other properties in Tennessee.
11 - A Lot at corner of Broad and Square Street, to be sold.
12 - My Executors pay unto the heirs of Joshua Gibbs, deceased, monies from estate of Joshua Gibbs, deceased.
13 - Appoint John Welch, Merchant and Benjamin R. Morgan, Esq. of Philadelphia.
Will signed 11 May 1812. Wit: James Matlock, David Vandeweer and William Roberts. Reg: 28 Sept 1829.

Page 330 - 22 Oct 1828. We, Johnathan Floyd, David Floyd, George Floyd, Enoch Floyd, John Davis and William Reaves for $100.00 to each of us, we assign to Elijah Floyd, Hosea K. Floyd, and Norman Finney, jointly, our interest in the land estate of David Floyd, deceased, of Bedford Co., TN. Wit: A. W. Ragor, A. Norman and John Newton. Reg: 6 Oct 1829.

Page 332 - 22 May 1829. Articles of Agreement.
Mary McGuyre, Thomas McGuyre and William McGuyre and Cornelius McGuyre, John McGuyre, Peter Lee in behalf of his wife, Henry Holt in behalf of his wife, and Solleman West in behalf of his wife but is not present, all the legatees of William McGuyre, Sr., deceased, sold to Thomas McGuyre, Sr. negroes. Date of Aug 1803, four negroes. Thomas McGuyre, Sr. delivers to Henry Holt, administrator of William McGuyre's, deceased, estate and

negroes. Wit: Samuel Philips. Reg: 6 Oct 1829.

Page 333 - 13 Jan 1829. John Turner to William Turner. John Turner conveyed to his son William Turner, both of Bedford Co., TN, all his lands and possession now under his control, after the decease of John Turner or otherwise be equally divided among his three brothers and three daughters. Wit: Jno. McMullen. Reg: 9 Aug 1829.

Page 335 - 12 Feb 1829. Thomas G. Polk amd Mary E. Polk his wife to Dennis Springer. Thomas G. Polk and Mary E. Polk his wife of Rowan Co., NC sold to Dennis Springer of Bedford Co., TN, land in bedford Co., 975 acres, being on Faling (Falling) Creek. Borders Joseph Steele, William Enochs. Wit: N. Chambers and W. White. Reg: 3 Nov 1829.

Page 338 - 28 Jan 1828. Anderson Ivy to James Ivie, 50 acres. Ancerson Ivie conveyed to James Ivie, both of Bedford Co., TN, for love and affection for my son James Ivie, land on West Fork of Rock Creek. Borders Wilsons Road, William Miller, Abednge Robertson, and Sink Hole Spring. Wit: John A. Ivie and Ezekiel Billington. Reg: 3 Nov 1829.

Page 341 - 28 Oct 1829. Nancy Spraggins to Nancy Casey, Deed of Gift. I, Nancy Spraggins of Bedford Co., TN, for love and affection for my beloved grand daughter Nancy Casey a daughter of Nathaniel Casey who intermarried with my daughter China Spraggins of Hardin Co., TN, given unto her property which is in my possession. Wit: P. L. Ragsdale and John W. Hamlin. Reg: 5 Nov 1829.

Page 342 - 8 Sept 1829. I, James Neill, Sr. of Bedford Co., TN for $450.00 paid by my son Andrew Neill, on a note of 25 Dec 1830, transferred unto him a negro boy Harry. Wit: William Gilchrist and George C. Neill. Reg: 12 Nov 1829

Page 342 - 9 Oct 1828. William Polk of Wake Co., NC to Thomas G. Polk of Rowan Co., NC, for love and affection, granted land in Bedford Co., TN. Reg: 13 Nov 1829.

Page 344 - 10 Feb 1825. James and Ann McKnight to John A. Hart and Adaline Hart. James McKnight and Ann his wife heirs of James Hart of Iredell Co., NC conveyed to John A. Hart and Adaline Hart of Iredell Co., NC, land in Bedford Co., TN, on East Fork of Rock Creek. Borders John Baker. Wit: Richard Allison, Joseph Hall and J. H. McLaughlin. Reg: 28 Nov 1829.

Page 351 - 29 Oct 1829. William Reagor and A. W. Reagor to James B. Reagor and Abraham Reagor. All of Bedford Co., TN. William and A. W. Reagor, heirs of Anthony Reagor, deceased, transferred tract of land on which he had died containing 220 acres except that part which had been transferred by the heirs to William and James B. Reagor and Abraham Reagor heirs... We, William and A. W. do hereby claim to the same. Also, we transfer to James B. and Abraham Reagor all our interest as heirs &c to above mentioned to Anthony Reagor, deceased. Wit: John Casteel and Henry Casteel. Reg: 3 Dec 1829.

Page 351 - 28 Sept 1829. Thomas Poteet of Western District to Elizabeth Blythe the wife of the deceased James Blythe and Jane Ruth Polly Ann nearly three of age, John Y. and Lotty under age of (blank) of Bedford Co., TN land on Rileys Creek. Borders Barren Fork, Jeremiah West. 135 acres. Wit: Hillis Green and Cathrine Green. Reg: 4 Dec 1829.

Page 365 - 5 Sept 1828. Reece Porter and Elizabeth Porter his wife of Haywood Co., TN sold to John and Spencer Eakin of Bedford Co., TN, land in Bedford Co., on headwaters of Sinking Creek. Borders lands of Col. Newton Cannon. 54+ acres. Wit: Alexander Eakin and William Eakin. Reg: 8 Dec 1829.

Page 369 - 11 Nov 1829. Michael Green, Edmund Green, William Galbreath and James R. White, Trustees of Littleberry Green, late of Bedford Co., Tn sold land to Reuben Reynolds of Williamson Co., TN, it being the land where Littleberry Green, lately lived and deeded by him on 21 Oct 1824 to Michael Green, Edmund Green, William Galbreath and James R. White. Beginning near Robert Walker's spring at the water edge of the north side of Duck River, near Wilsons Creek, 200 acres. Wit: John Thompson and J. S. White. Reg: 9 Dec 1829.

Page 383 - 9 Feb 1829. John N. Phifer and Ann his wife of Cabarrus Co., NC by Joseph Steele of Bedford Co., TN, their Attorney conveyed to James Cooper of Bedford Co., land in Bedford Co., on waters of Hurricane Creek, being part of land allotted to Ann Phifer as heir of Caleb Phifer, deceased. 214 acres. Wit: W. Carter and Richard Warner. Reg: 12 Dec 1829.

Page 389 - 12 Jun 1829. Matt Martin to Barkley Martin. For love and affection for his son Barclay Martin and for $1.00, land in Bedford Co., TN, on waters of Middle Fork of Duck River. Borders Matt Martin, Andrew Erwin, John Tillman, Peter Sailing. Rachel Martin survivor of her husband Barkley Martin. Wit: John S. Cooke and Tavner Haley. Reg: 15 Dec 1829.

Page 408 - 7 Nov 1827. Richard Brandon of Giles Co., TN for himself and as Executor of Alexander Locke, deceased, and agent for Ann Locke widow of Alexander Locke, deceased, and agent for James Peral and Margaret Peral his wife, John S. Brandon, Alexander D. Brandon, Abel Cowan, Lucretia Cowan his wife, Shederick Denton and Sarah Denton his wife, conveyed to Benjamin Barnhill of Rutherford Co., TN, land in Bedford Co., TN, on North Fork, it being a part of the division laid off to the heirs of John Brandon as legatees or devises of Alexander Worke, deceased. Borders William Walker, William Guy now lives. 174 acres. Wit: Hiram Myers, Robert Lee and Charles Myers. Reg: 26 Jan 1830.

Page 413 - 29 Oct 1829. William Reagor, James B. Reagor and Abraham Reagor conveyed to A. W. Reagor, transferred all their interest to tract of land on which A. W. Reagor now lives, about 98 acres. William Reagor, James B. Reagor and Abraham Reagor, heirs of Anthony Reagor, deceased. Wit: John Casteel and Henry Casteel. Reg: 27 Jan 1830.

Page 428 - 9 Feb 1830. I, John Gilpin of Bedford Co., TN, for $1.00, convey to my daughter Nancy C. Gilpin after the death of myself and wife Clary Gilpin, a negro girl Charlotte. Wit: Thomas L. Bond and James B. Gilpin. Reg: 10 Feb 1830.

Page 429 - (Plat of Robinson property). Survey requested by John Robinson and Joseph Robinson for the dividing line on 17

Feb 1830, as heirs of Michael Robinson, land in Bedford Co., TN, about three miles above the mouth of Falling Creek, north of Duck River. Borders Martin Phifer.17 Feb 1830. Reg: 1 Mar 1830.

Page 435 - 9 Nov 1829. Dennis Springer to Sarah Holden & Others. Dennis Springer of Bedford Co., conveyed to Sarah Holden, John B. Nash, William Nash, Mary Ann Stewart, George W. Nash, Thomas Nash, Nancy Nash, Franklin Nash, Paton S. Nash, and Amanda Nash, the heirs of Thomas Nash, deceased, of Rutherford Co., TN, land in Bedford Co., TN, on waters of Falling Creek. Thomas C. Nash and William Vinson, Esq., administrators of estate of Thomas Nash, deceased. Land begins above the mouth of Hurricane Creek. About 112 acres. Wit: George M. Nash, Guynn Foster and John N. Vinson. Reg: 4 Mar 1830.

Page 444 - 11 Feb 1830. John Sanders & Others to Lewis Newsom. John Sanders and his wife Elizabeth, late the wife of William Newsom, deceased, and Thomas Sanders of Bedford Co., TN sold to Lewis Newsom of Bedford Co., during the natural life time of Elizabeth Sanders, land in Bedford Co., on south side of Duck River, it being one third part of a tract of land whereon William Newsom lived, containing 101 acres by the Last Will and Testament of William Newsom, deceased, bequeathed to Elizabeth his wife the right of one third of 101 acres. Executor was Starling Newsom. Wit: John Thompson and John Gilbert. Reg: 5 Mar 1830.

Page 455 - 6 Jan 1830. Henry Cook to Martha L. Cook. Henry Cook and Martha L. Cook his wife of Bedford Co., TN conveyed to James Garrett of Williamson Co., TN, land in Bedford Co., on waters of Wilson Creek. Borders Robert McCuistion. 300 acres. Wit: Presley Jones, William Collins and Darrington Garrett. Reg: 8 Mar 1830.

Page 456 - 17 Apr 1829. Thomas McCall to William and Samuel McCall, 100 acres. Thomas McCall conveyed to his two sons William and Samuel McCall land in Bedford Co., TN, on north side of Duck River. Borders Mercelles Cook and William Neal. Wit: James McClelan and William McClelan. Reg: 8 Mar 1830.

Page 460 - 8 Apr 1829. Joseph Steele to Carlos D. Steele. Joseph Steele for love and affection for his son Carlos D. Steele, both of Bedford Co., TN, land in Bedford Co., on Falling Creek, being a part of the estate of his father. Borders Spring Branch. Wit: Lewis Tucker and John Steele. Reg: 10 Mar 1830.

Page 461 - 12 Dec 1829. William Gammil to William Gamble (Gammil). William Gammil conveyed to his son William Gammil, Jr., both of Bedford Co., TN, land in Bedford Co. Borders William Gammel, Jr., Alexander Greer, Joshua Holt. Wit: Amos Balch and Robert Parks. Reg: 10 Mar 1830.

Page 472 - 29 Sept 1829. Andrew Patterson from James N. Forrest, land, a residue of my father's estate of Nathan Forrest that is to come unto me. About 25 acres. Wit: J. Wortham and F. M. Jones. Reg: 12 Mar 1830.

Page 473 - 3 Nov 1829. Nicholas Anthony to John Shoffner, Deed of Trust, 200 acres and 50 acres. Nicholas Anthony of one part and Virginia Ann Ruthy Hill and Walter Burnard, minor heirs of Thomas H. Burnard and by their guardian John Shoffner of the second part. Nicholas Anthony for $1.00 transferred unto John Shoffner, land in bedford Co., TN, on Thompsons Creek. Borders James Gilbert. Also a tract on Thompsons Creek, borders Samuel Brown and Roberts tract. Also a note on Wilson Brown fir title to 40 acres, also personal property. Wit: William Gilchrist and Ezekiel W. Brown. Reg: 16 Mar 1830.

Page 495 - 20 Sept 1828. M. Sanders to his heirs, Deed of Gift. I, Marion Sanders of Bedford Co., TN, for love and affection for my beloved grand children, William J. Black, Robert R. Black, Henry B. Black, Susan Winters, Faney Black, Mary Black, Cassa Black, Martha A. Black, as soon as they become of age, personal property. The property is left in the possession of Mark and Fanna Black, their father and mother, for the use of the grand children. Wit: J. B. Shuffield and William Wright. Reg: 17 Mar 1830.

Page 503 - 30 Dec 1829. John H. Kaighn to Peggy Furguson, 50 acres. John H. Kaighn of Loudon Co., VA conveyed to Peggy Furguson widow of John Furguson, land on which Peggy Furguson resides, the same on which was conveyed to her husband in his lifetime by James Robertson, land in Bedford Co., TN, on waters of the Garrison Fork. Wit: A. Erwin and Richard Muse. Reg: 18 Mar 1830.

Page 504 - 15 Jan 1827. Joseph Steele to Volney H. Steele. Joseph Steele for love and affection for his son Volney H. Steele, both of Bedford Co., TN, conveyed unto him land in Bedford Co., TN, as part of the estate of his father, land in Falling Creek. Borders each side of the Spring Branch, Josiah Springer, James Cooper, Rowland's line and P. C. Steele. 138 acres. Wit: William Rowland and P. C. Steele. Reg: 18 Mar 1830.

Page 514 - 9 Feb 1829. Furgus Hall to Lewis W. Hall. Furgus Hall for $1.00 conveyed to Lewis W. Hall, both of Bedford Co., TN, land in Bedford Co., on waters of South Fork of Duck River, a part of a 405 acre tract, also houses and buildings &c. Wit: A. Martin and John B. Bates. Reg: 20 Mar 1830.

DEED BOOK "BB" 1830 - 1832

Page 9 - 9 Sept 1826. James Sheppard, Jr. to James Sheppard, Sr., 200 acres. James Sheppard, Jr., of Bedford Co., TN conveyed to James Sheppard, Sr., of Williamson Co., TN, land in Bedford Co., on waters of Wilsons Creek. Borders Tignal Martin, John Scott, Benjamin Smith and Benson Smith. Wit: Martha Lock. Reg: 26 Mar 1830.

Page 11 - 5 Dec 1829. We, John Shuffield and Mary Shuffield, administrators &c of Bright Roberts, deceased, sold by the highest bidder, a negro man Wiley and belonging to the estate of Bright Roberts, deceased, to Ephraim Hunter. Wit: John Laws and J. F. Furguson. Reg: 26 Mar 1830.

Page 13 - Nov Term 1827. We, Ephraim D. Dickson, John B. Dickson, William H. Dickson and Bennet S. Dickson, all being legatee and devises of James Dickson and in possession of the Last Will and Testament of the deceased. He left to legatees, land whereon he lived at the time of his death, 696 acres. To Ephraim Hunter, 200+ acres. To Bennet S. Dickson 96+ acres. To William W. Dickson 200 acres and borders Bennet S. Dickson. To John B. Dickson 200 acres and borders William W. Dickson and E. D. Dickson. Wit: John Wortham, Archibald Clinton, John Wortham and B. Faver. Reg: 30 Mar 1830.

Page 21 - 8 Feb 1830. I, Rachel Martin of Bedford Co., TN, for love and affection for Benjamin G. Marshall, gives a slave boy Joseph. Wit: Samuel Mitchell and Samuel Clay. Reg: 5 May 1830.

Page 24 - 2 Nov 1829. Joseph Wallace and Elizabeth his wife to Rezin Smith, all of Bedford Co., TN, conveyed to Rezin Smith 85 acres in Bedford Co., on headwaters of Sinking Creek. Borders John Smith, Jr., Philip Philips and Michael Campbell. Wit: Rezin Ingle and John England. Reg: 7 May 1830.

Page 26 - 10 Aug 1827. James S. Walker and Maria A. Walker his wife formerly Maria A. Nicholson, Calvin H. Nicholson and Alfred O. Nicholson, the legal heirs and devises of Osburn P. Nicholson, deceased, all of Maury Co., TN sold to Nancy Kiser, Executrix of the Last Will and Testament of Valentine Kiser, deceased of Bedford Co., TN, land in Bedford Co., on both sides of Big Flat Creek. Valentine Kiser in his lifetime ourchased of Osburn P. Nicholson said land. Borders James Dickson. 591 acres. Wit: William Wallace and Jacob Kiser. Reg: 17 Mar 1830.

Page 29 - 7 Dec 1827. Joseph R. Drake, Catharine Drake, Nancy A. Marshall, Mary H. Stovall, Daniel Marshall and John D. Stovall of Bedford Co., TN except John D. Stovall and Mary H. Stovall who are of Rutherford Co., TN and James J. Marshall of Rutherford Co., TN, land in Bedford Co., TN, on waters of Wartrace and Garrison Forks. Borders road that leads from Davis' Mill on the Garrison Fork to Murfreesboro in Rutherford Co., TN, Mosley's land, Thomas' land. 249 acres. Wit: Josiah Marshall, William Smith and Walter Marshall. Reg: 25 May 1830.

Page 31 - 2 Jan 1829. I, William Carithers of Bedford Co., TN, for love and affection for his son Robert Carithers, gives a negro woman Eve and her two children. Wit: R. _. Cunningham, Samuel Haqqard and Richard Davis. Req: 7 June 1830.

Page 50 - 3 May 1830. Archabald C. Adams to Robert Sims, 113 acres. Archabald C. Adams sold to Robert Sims, son-in-law of Archabald C. Adams, both of bedford Co., TN, for love and affection for Robert Sims, gives land in Bedford Co., on East Fork of Rock Creek. Wit: Thomas Ellison and John Ellison. Reg: 27 July 1830.

Page 53 - 18 Feb 1829. Moses M. Sanders to Hamilton V. Turner, both of Bedford Co., TN. Moses M. Sanders conveyed to Hamilton V. Turner all rights as a legatee of David Sanders, deceased, the one fifth part or share of 125 acres in three surveys, whereon Moses M. Sanders and William H. Sanders now lives, land in Bedford Co., between Rock Creek and Duck River. Borders David Appleby and Hamilton V. Turner and others. Wit: David Appleby and David C. Creswell. Reg: 27 July 1830.

Page 53 - 15 Feb 1829. William H. Sanders to Hamilton V. Turner. Both of Bedford Co., TN sold all rights as a legatee of David

Sanders, deceased, the one fifth part or share of 125 acres in three surveys, whereon William H. Sanders and Moses M. Sanders now lives, land in Bedford Co., TN, between Rock Creek and Duck River. Wit: Appleby, Archabald Cook and David C. Creswell. Reg: 28 Jul 1830.

Page 56 - 18 May 1829. Elizabeth and Archabald Cook to John Denny, all of Bedford Co., TN, land in Bedford Co., on waters of East Fork of Rock Creek. 25 acres. Wit: David Appleby and Alexander C. Denny. Reg: 13 May 1830.

Page 60 - 1 May 1817. I, Martin Shofner for good will and affection for my daughter Sally Dean and for $1.00, land of 40 acres in Bedford Co., TN, on Thompson Creek. Borders Elijah Parker's entry. Wit: John Shofner and William Holt. Reg: 31 July 1830.

Page 62 - 22 Mar 1830. I, Margaret Furgerson for love and affection for my beloved grand daughter Mary Cross daughter of James Cross and Peggy P. Cross his wife formerly Peggy P. Furgerson, all of Bedford Co., TN, conveys personal property. Wit: G. G. Osborne and William P. Finch. Conditions to above deed: Should Mary Cross die before she arrives of age of maturity the above property is to return to Margaret Furgerson. Reg: 3 Aug 1830.

Page 62 - 29 Jul 1829. William Hanby to Williamson Smith. William Hanby of Bedford Co., TN sold to Williamson Smith of Maury Co., TN and Gabriel Hanby guardian for Paulina Jane Moore of Patrick Co., VA, for $1.00, paid by Williamson Smith, negroe slaves. Wit: John Moore and Henry S. Wilson. Reg: 4 Aug 1830.

Page 66 - 22 Oct 1829. John Lane and John M. Lane. John Lane conveyed to John M. Lane, both of Bedford Co., TN, for love and affection for John M. Lane, conveyed for $500.00, land on south bank of Duck River. Borders Rich Creek. Wit: John Wortham and W. D. Orr and James Shaw. Reg: 7 Aug 1830.

Page 67 - 13 Feb 1830. Samuel Appleby, David Appleby, David Dryden and Richard Mitchell of Bedford Co., TN and Henry Morgan of Lincoln Co., TN sold to John Denny of Bedford Co., land in Bedford Co., on waters of East Fork of Rock Creek. Borders John Wood's survey. 25 acres. Wit: Mathias Brower and Alexander C. Denny. Reg: 10 Aug 1830.

Page 71 - 12 Feb 1827. Sarah A. Gibson, Elijah R. Parish and Catharine his wife and Elizabeth Sappington of Williamson Co., TN and Josiah E. Giles and Mary his wife of Davidson Co., TN conveyed to William Brown of Bedford Co., TN land in Bedford Co., on waters of Weakleys Creek. 34 acres. Wit: T. T. Pettus and R. C. Tisdale. Reg: Feb Term 1827.

Page 79 - 6 May 1830. Washington D. Medearis to David Yancy. Washington D. Medearis conveyed to his son-in-law David Yancy for love and affection for his daughter, all of Bedford Co., TN, land in bedford Co., on East Fork of Rock. Borders Thomas Smith, George Lowe's corner, and others. 100 acres. Reg: 28 Sept 1830.

Page 103 - 2 Nov 1829. Hiram Davison and Sally Davison of Hickman Co., TN and daughter of David Sanders, deceased, conveyed to Hamilton V. Turner of Bedford Co., TN, land or their claim to 125 acres of land in three surveys of where David Sanders, deceased, formerly lived and William H. Sanders now lives, on south side of Duck River between Rock Creek. Borders lands of David Appleby and Hamilton V. Turner and others. Wit: David Appleby and David V. Creswell. Reg: 9 Nov 1830.

Page 104 - 11 Aug 1830. Benjamin F. McCuistion of Ray Co., MO and his mother Jane McCuistion of Bedford Co., TN conveyed to William Moody of Bedford Co., land in Bedford Co., on waters of Hurricane Creek. Borders grant of James McCuistion, deceased, Thomas McCuistion, Willie B. Stone and Samuel McCuistion. 137 acres. Wit: Thomas McCuistion and David Burton. Reg: 9 Nov 1830.

Page 107 - 15 May 1830. James Cooper to Jonathan Cooper. James Cooper for love and affection for his daughter Mary Tune wife of John Tune of Bedford Co., TN, and for $1.00, sold land to Jonathan Cooper, on South Fork of Fall Creek. Borders James McAdams, Clardy's corner, Rowland's corner, Alexander's land, and that was laid off for Ann Phifer. 163 acres. Wit: D. S. Springer and William Cooper. Reg: 11 Nov 1830.

Page 109 - 10 Jul 1830. I, Nancy Reaves wife of Tobias Reaves of Bedford Co., TN, has entered and published disgraceful reports against the good name &c of Jane S. Arnold wife of Alsey Arnold of Bedford Co., to wit, that she, Jane S. Arnold, had been guilty of adultry with Lewis Newsom, Jr. of Bedford Co. This testimonial bears witness that Nancy Reaves had had no reason, truth or foundation for charging Jane S. Arnold with adultry or any obscene disgraceful conduct with Lewis Newsom or with any other person and that I, Nancy Reaves did knowingly and wickedly to gratify revenge &c toward Jane S. Arnold, utter and publish the allegation charged by me against Jane S. Arnold, knowing the same to be false. Wit: Thomas J. Purdie, Francis Arnold, Benjamin B. Morgan, and Darling D. Arnold. Reg: 11 Nov 1830.

Page 110 - 12 Aug 1830. Lewis Philips and his wife Peggy and William B. Philips and his wife Polly and William Meeks conveyed to Richard Warner, all of Bedford Co., TN, land in Bedford Co., on south side of Duck River. Borders James F. Meeks. 180 acres. Wit: William Burditt and D. D. Arnold. Reg: 11 Nov 1830.

Page 112 - 11 Apr 1829. I, James Hester of Bedford Co., TN sold to William Burnett my share of seven negroes willes to me by my grandmother Ann Hester formerly of Franklin Co., NC, now deceased. Wit: R. C. Thompson and K. L. Anderson. Reg: 11 Nov 1830.

Page 115 - 21 May 1830. William Bigham conveyed to Hugh B. Bigham, son of William Bigham, both of Bedford Co., TN, for love and affection, land in Bedford Co., on West Rock Creek. 80½ acres. Wit: S. Bigham and Richard Hill. Reg: 18 Nov 1830.

Page 137 - 17 Nov 1825. Marget Gibson and William Gibson, administrators of estate of William L. Gibson, deceased, of Marion Co., Alabama sold to Josiah Brecheen of Bedford Co., land in Bedford Co., on waters of Sinking Creek. Borders Newton Cannon's survey. 100 acres. Wit: William Rosson and Henry B. Rosson. Reg: 3 Dec 1830.

DEED BOOK "BB"

Page 138 - 30 Dec 1828. Lemuel Perry and Sally A. Perry his wife formerly Sally A. Forsythe sold to Allen Perry, all of Bedford Co., TN, land in Bedford Co., on waters of Spring Creek. 106 acres. Borders land belonging to the heirs of Benjamin Forsythe, deceased. Wit: J. Atkinson and James B. Shuffield. Reg: 3 Dec 1830

Page 140 - I, Catharine Drake of Bedford CO., TN conveyed to John D. Marshall and William A. Marshall my grandchildren who are children of Daniel Marshall and Nancy his wife, and my daughter. For love and affection for my daughter Nancy A. Marshall, John and William Marshall, my grandchildren, and also all the lateful begotten heirs of the body of Nancy A. Marshall hereafter, grant two negro boys Mark and Jack. Wit: John Gowen, James Jakes and S. E. Edgar. Reg: 4 Dec 1830.

Page 143 - 8 Sept 1828. Logan Co., KY - John Neill of Logan Co., KY and James Neill and Hannah Harris and also Robert Neill of Robertson Co., TN, also George Cathey and Peggy his wife of Bedford Co., TN and George Neill and his wife Elizabeth Neill and Robert M. Walter and his wife Ester E. Walter, Martha M. Shockly and John Orr and Ann Neill of Bedford Co., and the eldest brothers of William Neill, deceased, heirs at law of William Neill, a Lieutenant in the Continental of North Carolina Service and he, William Neill, being killed in battle in service and being in this State without any children and we the heirs and being the brothers and sisters of William Neill, appoint Samuel Ragsdale of Monroe Co., Mississippi their Attorney to oversee and sell and recover of the legatees of East Tennessee College 2560 acres of land, being on Big Hatchie River, the grant being founded in Hardeman Co., TN. Signed by: Cyntha Neill, John Neill and James Neill. Others signed: Sarah Neill, Hannah Harris, Robert Neill, George Neill, Elizabeth H. Neill, Robert M. Walter, Esther E. Walter, Angeline M. Shockly, John Orr, Ann Neill, George Cathey and James Neill. Reg: 13 Dec 1830.

Page 146 - 26 Apr 1830. Dorcas Garret of Bibb Co., Alabama widow and relict of James Garret, late of Bedford Co., TN. Dorcas Garret for $1.00 paid by her son Asa Garret of Bibb Co., Alabama, granted unto him all the dower and third of all other properties, land in Bedford Co., on waters of Duck River. 110 acres. It being same which was deeded by Jonathan Webster to the heirs &c of James Garret, deceased. Wit: J. B. Clark, J. Erwin and John G. Ackin. Reg: 24 May 1831.

Page 147 - 26 Apr 1830. John A. Goodson and Nancy his wife, late Nancy Garret and William Coffee and Elizabeth his wife late Elizabeth Garret, all of Bibb Co., Alabama, which Nancy and Elizabeth are daughters and heirs of James Garret late of Bedford Co., deceased, and Asa Garrett of Bibb Co., Alabama. JonathanWebster deeded on 19 Sept 1814 and recorded in Bedford Co., TN, land to heirs of James Garrett, deceased, in Bedford Co., on waters of Duck River, the place where the widow Garret then lived. 110 acres. Wit: J. Erwin, John G. Ackin and J. B. Clark. Reg: 21 Dec 1830.

Page 161 - 4 Sept 1830. Matthew Cunningham, Jr., the son of Matthew Cunningham, Sr. and Elizabeth Cunningham his wife in right of Thomas and Matthew Cunningham, Jr. was not of age where they gave title to two tracts of land to William Reed and Robert Reed which I was thought to be an heir from a clause of the

Last Will and Testament of William Galbreath, deceased, which was the prior owner of the two above mentioned tracts of land which he hereafter described. I, now Matthew Cunningham, Jr. of Bedford Co., being now of lawful age, do convey unto William Reed and Robert Reed, land in Bedford Co., on waters of Big Flat Creek. Wit: Alexander Smith and William Robinson. Reg: 3 Feb 1831.

Page 162 - 26 Aug 1830. John Ellison, Sr. for love and affection for the heirs of Joseph Ellison, son of John Ellison, conveys land in Bedford Co., TN, on waters of Rich Creek. Borders Robert Hunter, where Ephraim Hunter now lives and Thomas Jarrel. 140 acres, being the place where the plantation whereon the heirs now lives. Wit: John Harkness and Samuel Harkness. Reg: 3 Feb 1831.

Page 168 - 12 Dec 1829. Hugh T. Montgomery and wife Lucretia F. Montgomery of Rutherford Co., TN conveyed to Alexander P. Richmond, 34 acres. Lucretia H. Montgomery, late wife of John Gregory, deceased, of Bedford Co., TN. Wit: Nathan Chaffin and Daniel H. Johnson. Reg: 5 Feb 1831.

Page 177 - 7 Nov 1830. John Reed and Louisy Reed his wife sold to Robert Waite, all of Bedford Co., TN, land in Shelbyville, Bedford Co., TN, it being a part of a tract formerly belonging to Wilson Coats, deceased, and known as Lot No. 9. 26 acres. Reg: 15 Feb 1831.

Page 182 - 6 Nov 1830. Rezin Ingle, Sally Ingle and Lucretia Hatley formerly Lucretia Ingle and Mack Hatley sold to Rezin Smith, all of Bedford Co., TN, whereas John Smith, Jr., brother of Nancy Ingle who was mother of Rezin Ingle, Sally Ingle and Lucretia Hatley. John Smith, Jr. now deceased, died seized of 100 acres of land. Borders Philip Philips and Michael Campbell on Sinking Creek. The land being where Nancy died leaving seven children, to wit, Rezin, Salley, Lucretia, William, James and Nancy and Rezin Ingle, who are entitled to interest of said land. Reg: 19 Feb 1831.

Page 189 - 26 Aug 1830. John Ellison, Sr. to John Ellison, Jr. Both of Bedford Co., TN. For love and affection for his son John Ellison, Jr., gives land in Bedford Co., on waters of Rich Creek. Borders Thomas Sorrel's survey, Thomas Ellison and where John Williamson now lives. 220 acres. It being the plantation and where I, John Ellison, Sr., now live. Wit: Samuel Harkness and John Harkness. Reg: 22 Feb 1831.

Page 203 - 7 Feb 1830. (Plat on page 203) William Heaslett, Sarah Hubbard, John Norman, John Hubbard and Robert McElvaney and being the lawful heirs of Nathaniel Hubbard, all of Bedford Co., TN sold to James Brittain and Smauel Doak of Bedford Co., land in Bedford Co., on waters of Flat Creek near the head of a spring on north side of a branch including the spring. 19 acres. Reg: 4 Mar 1831.

Page 212 - 16 Aug 1830. Josiah Hooser and Atlantic his wife conveyed to John B. King, distributive share of land descending to Atlantic Hooser from her father Francis King, deceased. Borders the Garrison Fork, Mullins' land, Samuel Snelling, Hugh Snelling and others and being the tract of land on which Benjamin R. King and Mary King now reside. Wit: G. Starrett and B. R.

King. Reg: 10 Mar 1831.

Page 221 - 15 Mar 1829. Jesse McLean of Lincoln Co., TN to John McLean, son of John McLean. Jesse McLean for love and affection for his son John McLean, land in Bedford CO., TN, on the headwaters of Rock Creek, being a part of a 2500 acre survey to David Ross. Borders survey of David Ross and now of David Gossadge, Thompson's corner, land where Nowlin Wright now lives. 80 acres. Wit: G. Cummings and John Cummings. Reg: 14 Mar 1831.

Page 233 - 13 Jan 1831. Robert McElvany in behalf of his wife Nancy, John Hubbard in behalf of himself, William Heaslett in behalf of his wife Melvinia, John F. Norman in behalf of his wife Milly, Sarah Hubbard relict of Nathaniel Hubbard, deceased, in behalf of himself sold to Jonathan Norman, land in Bedford Co., TN, on waters of Big Flat Creek. Borders James Brittain's land, Edmund Wards' tract. The land includes where John Lawwell formerly lived, of 110 acres. Wit: James Wortham and Thomas Dean. Reg: 21 Mar 1831.

Page 235 - 4 Feb 1831. James Gilbert and Polly his wife to William James. James Gilbert and Polly his wife of Bedford Co., TN sold to William James of Chatham Co., NC, land in Chatham Co., NC. Borders Peter Smith's land. 150 acres. It being part of the distributive share coming to Polly Gilbert of the real estate of Richard James, her late father, deceased. Wit: A. Yell and John Warner. Reg: 22 Mar 1831.

Page 243 - 4 Feb 1831. James Gilbert and Polly his wife of Bedford Co., TN sold to John H. Hawkins of Chatham Co., NC, land in Chatham Co., NC, on Bear Creek and on a public road joining lands of Daniel Perry and lands laid off for the dower of widow James, it being part of a distributive share coming to Polly Gilbert of a undivided tract on which is a small mill that contains two acres which her late father Richard James died possessed. Wit: A. Yell and John Warner. Reg: 24 Mar 1831.

Page 250 - 5 Feb 1831. William Bingham to Timothy Parker. William Bingham for love and affection for Timothy Parker, both of Bedford Co., TN, land in Bedford Co. Borders Samuel Bingham. 7½ acres. Wit: William Bingham and Samuel Bingham. Reg: 25 Mar 1831.

Page 257 - 10 Jan 1831. Abel Landers to Pheby Landers. Both of Bedford Co., TN. Abel Landers conveyed to Pheby Landers land in Bedford Co., on waters of Shipmans Creek. Borders George Doherty's survey, Pheby Landers is trustee for Sarah Ann Nutt wife of Daniel Nutt. Sarah Ann Nutt is to use and occupy land for her natural life. Wit: John McMullen and William Shipman. Reg: 26 Mar 1831.

Page 259 - 8 Jan 1831. David Nutt and wife Sally A. to Abel Landers, all of Bedford Co., TN, land in Bedford Co., on waters of Thompsons Creek, being a part of a tract granted by State of Tennessee to Pheby Landers, widow. Wit: Jno. Harrison and Daniel Shipman, Sr. Reg: 29 Mar 1831.

Page 268 - 9 Aug 1828. Davis Chamberlain and Phebe Chamberlain his wife to Ezekiel Smith, all of Bedford Co., TN, land in

Bedford Co., TN, on Thompsons Creek, it being a part of a undivided tract of land belonging to the heirs of James Walker, deceased. Borders Clement Cannon's land, school tract, William Wilburn and Hays Blair grants. Wit: William Walker, Daniel Shipman and Abel Landers. Reg: 5 May 1831.

Page 272 - 5 Jan 1831. I, Catharine Nichols of Bedford Co., TN, for obligation of my brother Jacob Nichols to support me during my natural life &c, I have sold two negroes, a boy Abraham and a girl Harriet, my share of the estate of Jacob Nichols, deceased, and land on which Jacob Nichols now lives. Wit: W. Wallace and William Hall. Reg: 19 May 1831.

Page 275 - 6 Dec 1823. James Cooper sold to Dennis Springer in right of his wife Sarah, all of Bedford Co., TN, land in Bedford Co., on Weakleys Creek. 100 acres. Wit: Washington B. Cooper and James H. Lile. Reg: 20 May 1831.

Page 286 - 13 Feb 1830. William Gammill to Anthony Coble. William Gammill bound himself to his son Andrew Gammill to make a Deed of Gift for 50 acres, where Andrew Gammill settled but before the deed was made Andrew Gammill sold his right to Alfred M. Balch and Balch sold his right to Anthony Coble. All of Bedford Co., TN. The land in Bedford Co., on waters of Sugar Creek where Alfred M. Balch now lives. Borders Greer's line, Alexander Greer's line, and Joseph Patton. 50 acres. Wit: Jordan C. Holt and Margaret Holt. Reg: 23 June 1831.

Page 289 - 10 Oct 1830. I, Elizabeth B. Smalling of Bedford Co., TN, for love and affection for my three children, James M. Smalling, Susannah C. Smalling and Benjamin F. Smalling, give a negro woman Frankey and her increase. Wit: Nathaniel Peay and Solomon Jacobs. Reg: 12 July 1831.

Page 290 - 4 Apr 1825. We, Branch J. Copeland and Zulima his wife of Bedford Co., TN, sold a negro woman and child Peggy and John to Martin Adams. Wit: Adam Miller and Thomas C. A. Miller. Reg: 12 July 1831.

Page 324 - 21 Apr 1831. James McKisick and Polley V. McKisick his wife to Roger Snell, all of Bedford Co., TN, land in Bedford Co., on Sugar Creek. Borders Dryden's line and Joseph A. Greer. 110 acres. Reg: 20 July 1831.

Page 333 - 23 Sep 1830. Ann Neil to George Neil, son of Ann Neil. For Love and affection for her son George Neil, conveyed land in Bedford Co., TN, on East Fork of Rock Creek, being a part of a 2500 acre North Carolina Grant to George Cathey. Borders George Cathey's grant. Wit: Richard McRee and Robert M. Walter. Reg: 22 July 1831.

Page 334 - 12 Mar 1831. Robert Hunter to Edwin C. Hunter. Both of Bedford Co., TN. Robert Hunter for love and affection for his son Edwin C. Hunter, conveyed land in Bedford Co., on Sinking Fork of Rock Creek. Borders James Walls' line and George Cathey. Wit: David Appleby, Richard McRee and Samuel D. Dysart. Reg: 22 July 1831.

Page 335 - 11 Dec 1826. I, William Crittendon, Sr. of Bedford Co., TN, did in his lifetime give to his son Joel Crittendon a tract of land of 50 acres in Bedford Co. Signed by John

Crittendon, John Martin, Lorenzo C. Whitworth, Shelby B. Crittenton, Robert Thogmorton, John and Elizabeth Smith, and William Crittendon. Wit: John Tillman and Richard Cunningham. Reg: 8 Aug 1831.

Page 339 - 20 Jun 1827. Sheriff to the heirs of Fanning Jones, deceased. Sheriff to sell all claim and interest that Archibald Clinton and Matthew Clinton had in 150 acres of land in Bedford Co., TN, on Wilsons Creek, including the farm whereon Easter Clinton now lives and adjoins lands of John C. Wilson. Land sold to cover debt of Fanning Jones, deceased. Land sold to Mary Fanning, Martha A., Sarah S., Catharine and Addielade Jones, heirs of Fanning Jones, deceased. Wit: John B. Dickson. Reg: 26 Sept 1830.

Page 375 - 16 Sep 1829. Orville H. Searcy of Bedford Co., TN to Alexander McMichell, James McMichell and William McMichell of Bedford Co., land on Bedford Co., on Noah's Fork. Borders Noah's Fork and Mrs. Patton's corner, Jones' tract, and Mrs. McMichell. 115 acres. Wit: Andrew Vannoy and George T. Jetton. Reg: 3 Nov 1831.

Page 379 - 7 Feb 1830. Daniel McClarren of Hickman Co., TN to Sussanah C. Rickman of Bedford Co., TN, for love and affection for his daughter Sussanah Rickman, sold to her two negroe boys, Rickmon and Jacob. Also one fourth of all land granted to him. Wit: Edward Whitworth, J. R. Wilson, Zachary Wilson and J. B. Boyd. Reg: 7 Nov 1831.

Page 379 - 5 Oct 1829. Mathew McCorkle, Charles Beaty, Gilbert Milligan and Rebecca Milligan his wife, George Little and Elizabeth S. Little his wife, Alexander McCorkle, all of Lincoln Co., NC and Jane Alexander of Iredell Co., NC conveyed to William Guy of Bedford Co., TN, land in Bedford Co., on waters of North Fork of Duck River. Borders William Guy's land, and the family of Guy's and heirs of Col. Alexander Worke, late of Iredell Co., NC, David Sears, and Brandon & Locke families. 525 acres, it being part of a lot of land laid off to the McCorkle family heirs &c of late A. Worke. Wit: Francis McCorkle and Mordicia Howard. Signed by: Matt. McCorkle, Gilbert Milligan, Rebeccah Milligan, Charles Beaty, George Little, Betsey S. Little, Jane Alexander and Alex. McCorkle. Reg: 9 Nov 1831.

Page 382 - 13 Sep 1831. James Beard and Jane Beard his wife and formerly Jane Cross the legal heir of Jacob Cross, deceased, of Marion Co., Illinois conveyed to George W. Weaver of Maury Co., TN, land in Bedford Co., TN, on waters of the Garrison Fork. Borders Robert Magers (Majors), Dudly Hail's tract, and lands of the late Jacob Cross, deceased. 174 acres, by survey by the Last Will and Testament of Jacob Cross, deceased, was willed to his legal heirs and there being six shares. Signed 30 Sept 1831. Wit: B. M. Simpson and Jesse M. Wade. Reg: 10 Nov 1831.

Page 384 - 5 Nov 1831. David Doak to Samuel Doak, both of Bedford Co., TN, both formerly of Adair Co., KY. David Doak is indebted to Samuel Doak for $503.68+ which is due, convey unto Samuel Doak all mis legacy coming to him in right of his wife Jane Doak and the daughter of Hugh Beard, deceased, of Jackson Co., Alabama. Wit: James Brittain and Jno. M. Cannon. Reg: 10 Nov 1831.

Page 386 - 10 Aug 1831. Ezeccal (Ezekiel) Smith and wife Salley sold to Abel Landers, all of Bedford Co., TN, land in Bedford Co., on waters of Thompsons Creek, it being a part of a 100 acres belonging to the heirs of James Walker, deceased, and which tract is undivided and we, Ezecal Smith and wife Salley have sold to Abel Landers. Borders Clement Cannon tract and school land. Reg: 11 Nov 1831.

Page 392 - 16 Sep 1831. Mary Dixon alais Mary Freeland of Bedford Co., TN sold to Samuel Stewart of Carroll Co., TN. Land in Bedford Co., TN, on Big Flat Creek, it being the same that William Galbreath, her father, willed to her in his Last Will and Testament. Mary Dixon for and inconsideration that the said Samuel Stewart shall maintain, attend to and provide for said Mary in a decent manner during her natural life, relinguished all her right title claim and interest in the land, it being the tract whereon she now live. Borders Francis McCamy's heirs, Hundley Wiggins, William Dickson tract willed to him by William Galbreath, and the Phillips' land. 200 acres. Wit: Jordan C. Holt and Abraham Adell. Reg: 18 Nov 1831.

Page 397 - 1 Dec 1831. Abraham B. Morton of Shelbyville, Bedford Co., TN to John C. Hall, Archabald C. Hall, Samuel Hall, Lindsey Hall, William Russell and his wife Tabitha Russell formerly Tabitha Hall, and Rhody Hall now married to a gentleman whose name is not known, heirs and distributees of Doctor Elisha S. Hall. Elisha S. Hall in his ligetime and his administrators since his death paid A. B. Morton $700.00 for tract of land in St. Francis, Louisiana and known in the plan to town by Lot No. 1. Wit: William Gilchrist and Shad. S. Brown. Reg: 6 Dec 1831.

Page 410 - 14 Jun 1830. I, David Riggs of Bedford Co., TN, for love and affection for my son Andrew S. Riggs, give land in Bedford Co., on waters of Flat Creek. Adjoining Roger Snell and whereon I now live. Also all residue of my property. I give to my daughter Marian Kenady, a negro girl Chery. I also give unto my present wife Abigail Riggs, a horse, bridle and saddle. I will remain in control of above property for my natural life. Wit: Augustus H. White and James P. Anderson. Reg: 17 Jan 1832.

Page 414 - 20 Apr 1831. Edward Ragsdale to Thomas A. Peacock. Both of Bedford Co., TN. Conveyed two tracts of land, one known in the plan of the real estate of John Peacock, Sr., deceased, by No. 4 and 15½ acres, other tract not known on said plan which joins the same No. 4 and 49 acres, it being a deed made by T. R. Peacock and Susan B. Peacock on 20 Oct 1828. Land in Bedford Co., TN, on waters of Fall Creek. Also other personal property. Wit: Benjamin Ragsdale and Stephen Murphree. Reg: 23 Jan 1832.

Page 421 - 15 Sept 1830. James Cross and Lavina Cross to Robert Dennison, all of Bedford Co., TN., land in Bedford Co., on waters of Garrison Fork. 58 acres, it being 2/6th of a tract of land of which Jacob Cross, deceased, died possessed. Adjoining lands of John L. Neill, Dudly Hail, Robert Majors, Jr., James McMahan and William Cross. James and Lavina Cross are legal heirs of Jacob Cross, Deceased. Wit: Green B. Green and Jackson Buckly (?). Reg: 24 Jan 1832.

Page 424 - 18 Oct 1831. Benjamin McCuistion for love and affection for his son John C. McCuistion, both of Bedford Co., TN, gives land in Bedford Co., northwest of Shelbyville. Wit: Benjamin F. McCuistion and John T. Neil. Reg: 30 Jan 1832.

Page 425 - 18 Oct 1831. Benjamin McCuistion for love and affection for his son Samuel B. McCuistion, both of Bedford Co., TN, gives land in Bedford Co., northwest of Shelbyville. Wit: Benjamin F. McCuistion and John T. Neil. Reg: 31 Jan 1832.

Page 427 - 5 Nov 1831. Carter Crow and Caroline his wife to Samuel Mitchell, all of Bedford Co., TN. Carter Crow and his wife Caroline legal heirs of Charles Keezee(?), deceased, conveyed land on waters of Wartrace Fork, 75 acres. Borders Anthony Thomas, Elijah Dyer and the tract that David Thomas purchased of Gilchrist. Wit: Giles Burditt and John Sims. Reg: 31 Jan 1832.

Page 428 - 3 Sept 1831. Catherine Russell to Eve Troxler, both of Bedford Co., TN. Catherine Russell sold to Eve Troxler and after her death to William Troxler, heir of Eve Troxler, land in Bedford Co., TN, on east of Flat Creek. Borders lands of Lockhart. 76 acres. Wit: Henry Lynn and Jesse Koons. Reg: 31 Jan 1832.

Page 441 - 1 Nov 1831. Thomas Patterson for love and affection for his son Alexander D. Patterson, both of Bedford Co., TN, gives land in Bedford Co., on waters of West Fork of Rock Creek. Borders lands of Richard Brown and Thomas Parker and Andrew McCrory. 50 acres. Wit: S. Bigham and James Reed. Reg: 3 Feb 1832.

Page 443 - 10 Nov 1831. Thomas Powell and his wife Sally to John Whitesell, all of Bedford Co., TN. Thomas Powell and Sally his wife sold to John Whitesell land in Bedford Co., on waters of Sinking Creek. 50 acres. Reg: 3 Feb 1832.

Page 448 - 12 Mar 1822. William Dixon, one of the sons of Robert Dixon, late of North Carolina, deceased, to James Dixon, another son of Robert Dixon, deceased and Nancy Dixon a daughter of Robert Dixon, deceased, conveyed lands in Bedford Co., TN. Robert Dixon, deceased, died intestate. Land adjoins Roger Snell and the Patton land. 223 acres. Mary Freeland former widow of Robert Dixon, deceased, of North Carolina, requests, and William Dixon for himself and as purchaser of Margarett Stewart part in the above land and guardian for Nancy Dixon, idiot, and James Dixon, to be equally divided. Wit: Jacob Greer, Joseph Haistings and Robert Haistings. Reg: 4 Feb 1832.

Page 451 - 14 Feb 1829. I, John Spain of Lawrence Co., TN, bequeath unto my daughter Abigail R. Gamble, one negro girl Matilda. Wit: John Blagg and Jacob Hartsfield. Reg: 4 Feb 1832.

Page 452 - 14 Feb 1829. I, John Spain of Lawrence Co., TN, bequeath unto my daughter Kitty H. Hartsfield, a negro girl Milly. Wit: John Blagg and Thomas J. Gamble. Reg: 4 Feb 1832.

Page 453 - 1 Nov 1830. William S. Mayfield and Sally his wife to William Forrest, land in Bedford Co., TN, on waters of Caney Spring Creek. Borders Dodd's land, Richard Walker, John Polk, and Jonathan Wilson. 181 acres. Wit: A. Turrentine and David Bass at Abraham Mayfield's house. Reg: 7 Feb 1832.

Page 454 - 8 Feb 1831. William S. Mayfield and Sally his wife to Ephraim Harris, all of Bedford Co., TN, sold land in Bedford Co., on waters of Caney Spring Creek. and borders Frederick Taylor, Joshua Coleson, Aaron Boyd, Thomas Murdock and Philip Brittain. 270 acres. Wit: Archillus Turrentine and David Ray. Reg: 7 Feb 1832.

Page 458 - 19 Feb 1831. Alexander Webb and Mary E. Webb his wife to Stephen Nowlen, all of Bedford Co., TN, sold land in Bedford Co., on the fork of West Fork of Rock Creek. Wit: Light Nowlen and Benjamin Clark. Reg: 13 Feb 1832.

Page 459 - 15 Feb 1831. Fanney Sims and Robert Sims, Executrix and Executor of Brigg Sims, deceased, to Thomas Greer, all of Bedford Co., TN, by the Last Will and Testament of Brigg Sims, sold to Thomas Greer, land in Bedford Co., on Sugar Creek. 113 acres. Wit: Peter Chilcutt and Jno. L. Neill. Reg: 13 Feb 1832.

Page 460 - 7 Nov 1831. W. R. Nunn of Williamson Co., TN one part as administrator of estate of James Sheppard, deceased, with Will annexed and Benjamin Little of Bedford Co., other part, but Benjamin Little having departed this life leaving a Will and the said Will gave and bequeathed the tract of land to his wife Patsy Little during her lifetime or widowhood and then to his daughter Permelia Little. Left land in Bedford Co. Wit: Samuel Philips and Richard Wright. Reg: 13 Feb 1832.

Page 466 - 28 Sept 1831. Owen Medlin and Mary Harrison, Executor of Jonathan Harrison, all of Bedford Co., TN, for $50.00, sold land in Bedford Co., on waters of Sinking Creek. Borders Rezin Smith. 122 acres, one half which land was decreed to Robert Brooks of Lincoln Co., TN, a distributee of Matthew Brooks, deceased, and Robert Brooks' land being taken by Mary Harrison for 122½ acres divided in an undivided survey by Lewis Medlin to Jonathan Harrison. Wit: John Davis and Henry Moore. Reg: 14 Feb 1832.

Page 469 - 5 Nov 1831. Herman Reid and Martha his wife to Samuel Mitchell, all of Bedford Co., TN. Herman Reid and his wife Martha legal heir of Charles Keezee, deceased, sold to Samuel Mitchell, land in Bedford Co., on waters of the Wartrace Fork. Borders Archibald Caruthers. Wit: Samuel Clay and John Sims. Reg: 14 Feb 1832.

Page 473 - 14 Aug 1829. David Blessing and his wife Mary to Joseph Marlow, all of Bedford Co., TN, sold part of a Town Lot in Shelbyville, Bedford Co., known as Lot No. 65. It being the lot fell to David Blessing and his wife Mary as the heirs of Wilson Coats, deceased. Wit: Samuel Escue and S. N. McClain. Reg: 21 Feb 1832.

Page 484 - 6 Dec 1830. Charles Lavender, John Lavender and Bird Lavender to Howard Carlton, all of Bedford Co., TN, sold land in Bedford Co., on waters of Caney Spring Creek, being a part of a tract conveyed to them by Charles Long and Isaac Elliot. Borders John Lavender's corner. 78½ acres. Wit: James Billington and Miles Wilson. Reg: 13 Mar 1832.

Page 485 - 15 Mar 1831. We, William Wade and Martin Wade are bound unto William Murphree, his heirs and assigns for $500.00. Edward Wade, Michel Wade and Marmaduke M. Wade has claims on property relinguished their rights to William Murphree. Land on Fall Creek. Wit: William Gilchrist. Reg: 13 Mar 1832.

Page 506 - 16 Jul 1828. Willie Robertson and Mary Robertson his wife, both of Wake Co., NC to John Simms of Bedford Co., TN, sold land in Bedford Co., on waters of Duck River. Borders lands of John Simms and others. 50 acres. It being the land left by Caswell Powell to Mary Powell who is now Mary Robertson. Wit: John Ligon and William B. Dunn. Reg: (no date).

Page 507 - 11 Dec 1830. John Sutton to William B. Sutton and Charles F. Sutton, all of Bedford Co., TN, for love and affection for his son William B. Sutton for his natural life and remainder to Charles F. Sutton, interest to hold for the use and benefit of every son and daughter lawfully begotton by William B. Sutton, land in Bedford Co., on Duck River. Borders Samuel Patton, Amos Balch, Wilhoite's line, Duck River and Samuel Thompson. 350 acres. Wit: K. L. Anderson and Thomas R. Anderson . Reg: 21 Mar 1832.

Page 509 - 2 Aug 1825. We, Thomas T. Taylor and Rachel Taylor his wife, Seth T. Casly and Francis Casly his wife, sold to Amos McAdams, a negro girl Easter who was willed to Rachel and Francis and Lewis W. and John W. Walker by their brother Phillip Walker, deceased, to be sold when John W. the youngest comes to Lawful age. Wit: James Harmon and A. C. Yell. Reg: 21 Mar 1832.

Page 510 - 26 Jan 1824. We, John Lane and Peggy (Margaret) Lane his wife, James B. Armstrong and Rebecca Armstrong his wife, all of Bedford Co., TN, sold a negro woman Sharlott, to Amos McAdams. Wit: William Norvell and George C. Armstrong. Reg: 21 Mar 1832.

Page 521 - 20 Sept 1831. I, James McBride, for myself, my heirs and assigns, sold to Pleasant and Fieldin McBride, all my right title claim and interest in the estate of John McBride, deceased, both real and personal property. Wit: William S. Watterson and William McBird. Reg: 27 Mar 1832.

Page 522 - 7 Feb 1832. I, Aron Williams sold to Robert McCuistion, all my right, title and interest in and to the estate of my father Andrew Williams, deceased, the same being one eighth part of the estate. Wit: William Gilchrist. Reg: 27 Mar 1832.

Page 523 - 15 Sep 1831. I, Henry Bibbs of Madison Co., Alabama, for love and affection for my only daughter Mary Bibbs, a negro girl Mary. Wit: Aron Boyd and Joel Riggs. Reg: 27 Mar 1832.

Page 536 - 14 Feb 1831. Sterling Brown and his wife Mary Brown formerly Mary Lock sold to James Turrentine, all of Bedford Co., TN, land in Bedford Co., on waters of Weakleys Creek. Borders R. W. Lock and R. Allison. 78 acres. Wit: William B. Sutton and John W. Mayfield. Reg: 13 Apr 1832.

Page 537 - 20 Nov 1821. Lewis Turner and Tomsey Turner of Smith Co., TN sold to James Harris of Bedford Co., TN, 140 acres of land in Bedford Co., on Alexanders Creek. Borders the land whereon James Harris now lives, and Elet Buckers' land. Wit: Zenas C. Morrison, Mary Booth, George Landers and Joseph Morris. Reg: 13 Apr 1832.

Page 538 - 3 Jan 1832. William G. Wood and his wife Sarah Wood to David H. Williams, all of Bedford Co., TN, sold land in Bedford Co., on north side of the Barren Fork, it being a part of land conveyed from Theo. F. Bradford to Blan Maupin, drawn by Sarah Wood supposed to be Lot No. 3 and of 9 acres. Wit: Blan Maupin and Sarah Maupin. Reg: 15 Feb 1832.

Page 539 - David H. Williams bought from William G. Wood and Sally his wife, sold land in Bedford Co., TN. Sally Wood is aged and infirmed and cannot travel to the Court to be examined as to free will and consent to execute a deed. Reg: 13 Apr 1832.

Page 540 - 31 Dec 1831. William G. Wood and Sarah Wood his life sold to Charles Timmons, all of Bedford Co., TN, on south side of Barren Fork, Lot No. 2 and of 15 acres. Borders Charles Timmons and Payne's land. Wit: Blan Maupin and Sarah Maupin. Reg: 15 Feb 1832.

Page 542 - 3 Jan 1832. William G. Wood and Sarah Wood his wife, sold to Blan and Gabriel Maupin, all of Bedford Co., TN, land in Bedford Co., on south side of Barren Fork. It being the 7th part, 16+ acres. Wit: D. H. Williams and Sidney Williams. Reg: 15 Feb 1832.

Page 545 - 3 Feb 1832. William Heaslett, Robert McElvany, John Hubbard and John F. Norman, all of Bedford Co., TN sold to Sarah Hubbard widow and relict of Nathaniel Hubbard, deceased, of Bedford Co., for natural love and affection for their beloved mother and mother in law and widow and relict, conveyed a negro girl Alse, belonging to the estate of Nathaniel Hubbard, deceased. Wit: James C. Tribble and Robert Snody. Reg: 14 Feb 1832.

Page 548 - 20 Feb 1832. John McNairy of Davidson Co., TN one part and his brothers Nathaniel A. McNairy and Boyd McNairy of Davidson Co., TN other part, for love and affection for his brothers, conveyed unto them land in bedford Co., TN, on the east side and adjoining the Town of Shelbyville, Bedford Co., TN, at Cull Camp Ford. Wit: J. H. Hall and John McNairy. Reg: 14 Apr 1832.

Page 553 - 13 Sep 1819. Daniel T. Barnes of Rutherford Co., TN one part and Swepson Sims of Rutherford Co., TN other part, for $1.00, sold to Swepson Sims in trust for Susan S. Barnes wife of Daniel T. Barnes and her two children Swepson F. Barnes and Gabriel Barnes and the other children who maybe born, who are all infants under 21 years, negro slaves. Reg: 23 Apr 1832.

Page 555 - 31 Oct 1831. I, Leroy Taylor of Washington Co., TN, appoint my son Wilson Taylor of Washington Co., TN, my Attorney to try and collect of my son John Taylor of Bedford Co., TN, $200.00. John Taylor, administrator of my son Joseph Taylor, deceased, who died intestate in Bedford Co., TN. Wit: John Kennedy and William P. Chester. Reg: 27 Apr 1832.

Page 559 - 30 Sep 1829. Elizabeth Moore of Rowan Co., NC one part and Edward Cross and Margret his wife of Rowan Co., NC other part, land in Bedford Co., TN of 870 acres and the plantation whereon Edward Cross lives. Wit: James B. Hampton. Reg: 8 May 1832.

Page 560 - 4 May 1830. Elizabeth Moore of Cabarrus Co., NC one part and George A. Phifer of Cabarrus Co., NC other part, land in Bedford Co., TN, on waters of Duck River. Borders Trotter's line, Ann Phifer's Lot. 833 acres. Wit: Jno. Young and J. Phifer. Reg: 8 May 1832.

Page 561 - 18 Apr 1832. Thomas McCuistion and Ann McCuistion his wife sold to Robert McCuistion, all of Bedford Co., TN, all claims in estate of Andrew Williams, deceased. Ann McCuistion is one of the daughters of Andrew Williams, deceased. Wit: William H. Purvis and Joseph McCuistion. Reg: 8 May 1832.

Page 562 - 31 May 1830. Samuel Bell and Isaac Bell of Franklin Co., Alabama sold to Henry Bell of Bedford Co., TN, land in Bedford Co., on Weakleys Creek. 277 acres. Reg: 11 May 1832.

Page 566 - 26 Mar 1831. Hamilton White, Jr. of Pittsylvania Co., VA of one part and John Chandler and Samuel E. White of second part and William Chandler and Martha B. his wife of the third part, for love and affection he has for his sister Martha B. Chandler wife of William Chandler, slaves and other property. Halifax Co., VA, recorded 23 Jan 1832. Reg: 26 May 1832.

DEED BOOK "CC" 1832 - 1833

Page 2 - 19 Mar 1832. Robert Allison, Sr. to Kimbrough Allison, both of Bedford Co., TN, for good will and affection for Kimbrough Allison, conveyed two tracts of land in Bedford Co., on waters of Clems Creek and Wilsons Creek. No. 1 bounded by school land and land conveyed by Robert Allison, Sr. to Thomas Allison, 124 acres, same being the residue of a 178 acre tract conveyed to Robert Allison, Sr. by Solomon Christopher and Michel Wade. No. 2 bounded by James Muse, William Patterson and James Mayfield, William Clark, William Hill, James McReynolds, 50 acres. Wit: T. Allison, E. Buchanan and J. T. Neil. Reg: 1 Jun 1832.

Page 3 - 6 Mar 1832. Lenord C. Temple to Jordon C. Holt, both of Bedford Co., TN, sold land in Bedford Co., on waters of Sugar Creek, adjoining lands of William Gambel, Joseph A. Greer, Alfred Balch and others, same being the land laid off for Catherine M. Greer now Catherine M. White and wife of James R. White, land being same tract of land levied on by Sheriff of Bedford Co. by virtue of Execution which issued from the Circuit Court of Bedford County, dated 15 Aug 1829 and sold at public auction at Court House on 10 Nov, bought by John Streeter and later on 12 Feb 1830 transferred to Lenord C. Temple. Land of 200 acres. Wit: Jno. H. Anderson and Daniel McKisick. Reg: 1 Jun 1832.

Page 5 - 13 Apr 1832. David Jones, administrator with will annexed of Fanning Jones, deceased, and Thomas Powdrell, both of Bedford Co., TN, sold to Ephraim Hunter of Bedford Co., land in Bedford Co., in the Village of Farmington. Wit: Henry L. Davis and James Eakin. Reg: 1 Jun 1832.

Page 8 - 11 Feb 1831. Mathew P. Hannah, administrator of Samuel Hannah, deceased, of Lincoln Co., TN to William S. Watterson of Bedford Co., TN, land in Bedford Co., on McBrides Creek, a branch of Garrison Fork of Duck River. Same land that David Sorrel purchased of A. Erwin, J. Patton & Erwin and deeded by Sorrel to Waugh Finley and Johnson and by Waugh Finley and Johnson to Samuel Hannah, deceased. Bordered Watterson's line, Gregory's line, Jacob's line and McBrides line. Wit: James A. Brantley and William T. Harris. Reg: 1 Jun 1832.

Page 13 - 4 Jan 1832. George T. Harris to Elizabeth Parker, both of Bedford Co., TN, conveyed 190 acres on Alexanders Creek. Wit: Evan Harris, Esq. and Martha Harris. Reg: 1 Jun 1832.

Page 15 - 8 Feb 1832. Henry Shearin of Haywood Co., TN to Thomas Shearin of Bedford Co., TN. Henry Shearin who is heir and representative of Jacent Shearin, late of Bedford Co., deceased, became legally constituted to part of a tract of land which was granted by State of North Carolina to William Shearin, deceased, by Grant No. 47, dated 10 July 1788 and bounded by Anthony Newman, Alexander Roberts and Robertson's line. 750 acres. Wit: William Cook and George Capley. Reg: 1 Jun 1832.

Page 21 - 28 Mar 1832. Harriet Hunter of Johnston Co., NC to Thomas O. Hunter of Johnston Co., NC, land in Bedford Co., TN, which descended from Osburn Hunter, late of Johnston Co., NC, deceased, to Thomas O. Hunter, Emily Frilick and Harriet Hunter, children and heirs of Osburn Hunter, deceased. Wit: J. McLeod and Willis H. McLeod. Reg: 5 Jun 1832.

Page 22 - 28 Mar 1832. We, James Frilick and Emily Jane Frilick wife of James, appoint Thomas O. Hunter, our Attorney, to oversee to pay and receive any monies on land in Bedford Co., TN, on lands belonging to Osburn Hunter, deceased, of NC. Reg: 5 Jun 1832.

Page 71 - 4 Jan 1832. Nancy Butler, heir of Isaac Butler, heir and administratrix of James Butler, deceased, Thomas Dean, administrator of James Butler, deceased, sold to Hiram Holt and Thomas Newsom. Nancy, Esther and Thomas having first advertised the premises and was sold to Holt and Newsom, land in Bedford Co., TN on Big Flat Creek. Borders Butler's 100 acres and where he now lives. 18 acres. Wit: Henry Reynolds and David Beard. Reg: 22 Jun 1832.

Page 78 - 11 May 1832. For love and affection I have for my grandson Linseley Dobbs, part of estate of William Dobbs, deceased, both personal and mixed or real to which I may be entitled to as the widow and relict of William Dobbs, deceased, it being a childs part of the estate, as long as he supports and maintains me. Signed by Keziah Dobbs. Wit: George Bussey and John Dobbs. Reg: 23 Jun 1832.

Page 84 - 23 May 1831. Joseph Wardlaw of Aleganey Co., PA to John and Spencer Eakin of Shelbyville, Bedford Co., TN, land in Shelbyville and Lot No. 37. Wit: John W. Cowan and William Eakin. Reg: 26 Jun 1832.

Page 87 - We, Mary and Sarah Damron sold to James Hart, all of Bedford Co., TN, furniture and implements and being in the hands of William Damron, cattle and numerous items. Wit: D. V.

Page 88 - 8 Mar 1832. Articles of Agreement between Francis Jackson of Williamson Co., TN one part and Mary Allison of Bedford Co., TN other part, whereas there is an intended marriage between Francis Jackson and Mary Allison and it is anticipated that Mary will have given to her by her father Robert Allison, some negro slaves and whereas it is not expected that Mary will ever have any issue of her own body, now in case she never has, it is hereby agreed by Francis Jackson that if the intended marriage should take place and there should be no issue of Mary, then Mary shall have full power to do what she pleases with the slaves received from her father, or from his estate after his death, and it is further agreed that if Mary should die before Francis Jackson, then and in that case Francis Jackson binds himself, his heirs, executors, administrators &c to give and surrender up all the slaves to be equally divided by the brothers and sisters of Mary, viz, James Allison, William Allison, Jr., Elizabeth Williams, Thomas Allison, Sally Williams, John Allison and Kimbrough Allison. Wit: James Ogilvie, Elijah Buchannon and William Ogilvie. Reg: 27 Jun 1832.

Page 91 - 9 Jan 1832. Christopher Shaw to Robert C. C. P. Shaw, both of Bedford Co., TN, for love and affection for his son Robert C. C. P. Shaw, gives land in Bedford Co., on waters of Puncheon Camp Creek. Borders Joseph Eoff, William Eoff and James Robertson. 109 acres. Another tract on Puncheon Camp Creek, borders T. L* D. W. Shaw and William Sharp. 160 acres. Another tract of land on Puncheon Camp Creek, borders James Sutton and Christopher Shaw. 47½ acres. Wit: Jno. Scott and T. L* D. W. Shaw. Reg: 27 Jun 1832.
* could be S.

Page 93 - 9 Jan 1832. Christopher Shaw to Christopher G. W. B. Shaw, both of Bedford Co., TN, for love and affection for his son C. G. W. B. Shaw, gives several tracts of land in Bedford Co., TN. One tract borders the Garrison Fork, McBride's land and William Lee, of 107 acres. Another tract, land formerly property of Thomas Kindall and bordered by Garrison Fork and Kindall's land, of 48 acres. Also, another tract of land formerly Kindall's lying on south side of the Garrison Fork and a small distance above the above described tract, bordering the Garrison Fork, of 1 acre. Another tract lying on south side of the Garrison Fork and the above last described land, of 15 acres. Another tract formerly property of John Jackson, borders the Garrison Fork, of 10+ acres. Making in all 134½ acres. Wit: Jno. Scott and Joel H. Webster. Reg: 27 Jun 1832.

Page 95 - 28 Nov 1831. Christopher Shaw to T. L* D. W. Shaw, for love and affection for his son, gives 9 acres of land in Bedford Co., TN. Borders Christopher Shaw, James Morrison, William Eoff, line dividing Bedford and Rutherford Counties, and Sharp's land. In all 404 acres. Wit: Charles Moore, James A. Brantley and W. P. Harris. Reg: 28 Jun 1832.

Page 97 - 16 May 1828. John Eakin and Giles Burditt, both of Bedford Co., TN, witnessed that whereas by a Deed of Indenture, dated 11 Nov 1823 from John Blessing and Matilda Blessing his wife there was conveyed to John Eakin and Giles Burditt a tract of land in Bedford Co. Borders Lot No. 3 of Wilson Coat's, deceased, and the widow Coats corner. 53½ acres. The above land to be divided. Wit: Joseph Wardlaw and Garnet G. Cole. Plat on page 97. Reg: 28 Jun 1832.

Page 99 - 28 Dec 1831. Nancy Butler widow of Isaac Butler, deceased, Esther Butler widow of and administratrix of James Butler, deceased, and Thomas Dean administrator of the estate of James Butler, deceased, sold to Hiram Holt and Thomas Newsom, all of Bedford Co., TN, land as advertised, on which Isaac and James Butler formerly lived and of which they died in possession and sold to Hiram Holt and Thomas Newsom. The land in Bedford Co., on waters of Big Flat Creek. Borders Jonathan Norman's land purchased of Nathaniel Hubbard, deceased, heirs, Edmond Word's land, and Jacob Wilhoite's land. 114 acres, including the land where Esther now lives. Wit: Henry Reynolds and David Beard. Reg: 28 Jun 1832.

Page 101 - 5 May 1832. Robert Williams and Julia F., his wife, formerly Julia F. Endsley, and Hugh B. Smiley, all of Bedford Co., TN, on headwaters of East Fork of Rock Creek. Borders lands of Felix Robeson, Hugh B. Smiley purchase of Hugh Thomison and Jane Caroline his wife by deed, Blackwell's line, McAdams' corner. 60 acres. Reg: 28 Jun 1832.

Page 106 - 29 Jun 1832. I, James T. Byler sold to Nancy Byler, both of Bedford Co., TN, gives a negro boy Henry, one negro boy Peter and one negro girl Caroline. Wit: A. Oslin and John Byler. Reg: 9 Jul 1832.

Page 106 - 29 Jun 1832. I, James T. Byler sold to Nancy Byler, both of Bedford Co., TN, horses, furniture and other personal property. Wit: Alanson Oslin and John Byler. Reg: 9 Jul 1832.

Page 107 - 10 Feb 1832. John Reed and his wife Esther Reed conveyed to Alexander B. Reed, Hosea Mullins and his wife Peggy formerly Peggy Reed, and Isaac W. Walker and his wife Violet Walker formerly Violet Reed, for love and affection, they being the sons and daughters, land in Bedford Co., TN, on East Fork of Rock Creek. Borders Violet Cathey, John Orr, Orr's line. 100 acres. Another tract of land conveyed to Isaac W. Walker and his wife Violet, nee Reed, borders Almond B. Reed and Mullin's line. 80 acres. Wit: John T. Neal and John Harkness. Reg: 9 Jul 1832.

Page 129 - 12 Jul 1831. Between the heirs at law of Abraham Shook, deceased, to wit, William B. Shook, Wade Griffin and Lucinda his wife sold to Burgess Harden of Bedford Co., land in Bedford Co., sold land to Burgess Harden. Land on Rock Creek. Borders William Cawfield and Blair's corner. 200 acres. Reg: 7 Aug 1832.

Page 130 - Tennessee Grant to Thomas Allison, 33 acres. No. 7615. 9 Aug 1826. 1¢ per acre. Land in Bedford Co., TN, on waters of Rock Creek. Borders John Ellison, Sr. now lives and John Ellison, Jr. Reg: 7 Aug 1832.

Page 158 - 9 Apr 1832. Leonard C. Temple sold to Demsey P. Temple. both of Bedford Co., TN, land in Bedford Co., on north side of Duck River opposite and below the mouth of Sugar Creek, it being a part of a 1900 acre tract granted to Demsey Powel and deeded to Jesse Powell to Elizabeth Temple and by her to her two sons, Leonard C. and Demsey P. Temple and they agreed to likewise, land in Bedford Co., on south side of Duck River near John Sim's Mill, it being a part of the tract granted to Demsey Powel and bequeathed by Demsey Powel to Leonard C. Temple and Demsey P. Temple. Borders John Sims' Mill tract, John Stephens, Elizabeth Temple and the Duck River. 132 acres. Wit: John Sims and Richard H. Sims. Reg: 23 Aug 1832.

Page 159 - 10 Apr 1832. Leonard C. Temple to Demsey P. Temple, both of Bedford Co., TN, sold land in Bedford Co., on north side of Duck River opposite and below the mouth of Sugar Creek. Same as above instrument, and where Demsey P. Temple now lives. Borders at the mouth of the Mill Race, the original corner of the Powel tract, and Duck River. Wit: John Sims and Richard H. Sims. Reg: 23 Aug 1832.

Page 163 - 23 Oct 1830. Thomas Murdock and Mary his wife to James Williams, all of Bedford Co., TN, land in Bedford Co., on waters of Wilsons Creek. Borders Adam Allen's line and Adam Miller's line. 142 acres. Wit: Aaron Boyd and J. B. Shuffield. Reg: 23 Aug 1832.

Page 165 - 30 Sept 1831. John Stokes, David Stokes, Thomas Stokes, and John Stokes, Jr. of Bedford Co., TN sold to Robert Nix of Maury Co., TN, land in Bedford Co., on south side of Duck River. Borders Tignal Jones and Rock Creek. 240 acres. Wit: James Elliot and E. Hudson. Reg: 23 Aug 1832.

Page 174 - 8 Mar 1832. Pleasant Ewell to Alexander McMichael, James McMichael and William McMichael, all of Bedford Co., TN, land in Bedford Co., on Nall's Creek and Noah's Fork. 39 acres. Borders Nall's Creek at mouth of William Ross' Spring Branch, Solomon Hart's Spring Branch, and Noah's Fork. Wit: T. L. D. W. Shaw and John Patton. Reg: 28 Aug 1832.

Page 176 - 15 Aug 1832. John L. Neill to Washington Sims, Brigg Sims, Zachariah Sims, John Sims, Burrel Sims, Robert W. Sims, Sally Johnson wife of Benjamin Johnson, Polly L. Hedley wife of John Hedley, Elva D. Robertson wife of Bennett Robertson, Nancy C. Morrison wife of Henry C. Morrison, Franky Dryden wife of James Dryden, Hally(?) Sims, Sophinia Sims, children and heirs of Brigg Sims, deceased. On 5 Jan 1829, sold to Brigg Sims in his lifetime 196½ acres. Land in Bedford Co., on East Fork of Rock Creek. Wit: Jas. McKisick and W. D. Orr. Reg: 30 Aug 1832.

Page 180 - 16 Jun 1832. John Sanders, Jr. sold to George Sanders, both of Bedford Co., TN, land in Bedford Co., belonging to John Sanders, Sr., deceased. John Sanders, Jr. being an heir of John Sanders, Sr., deceased. Wit: Evan Harris and Hiram Mayfield. Reg: 30 Aug 1832.

Page 183 - 10 Jul 1832. David Jones, surviving administrator of Fanning Jones, deceased, sold to Fanning M. Jones , all of Bedford Co., TN, land in Bedford Co., on south side of Duck River and on Rock Creek and upper side of the mouth of Rock Creek, it being corner of original tract of 2100 acres granted by North Carolina to Tignal Jones in 1788. Wit: William Gilchrist, William H. Conway and W. S. Mayfield. Reg: 30 Aug 1832.

Page 211 - 8 Nov 1830. Morgan Murry of Bond Co., Illinois sold to Erwin McAdams of Lincoln Co., TN, land in Bedford Co., TN, on north side of the Elk Ridge on the headwaters of the Middle Fork of Rock Creek whereon Mary Murry formerly resided. Morgan Murry, acting as Power of Attorney from Mary Murry and Jordan

Jordan Murry, all of Bond Co., Illinois, sold land in Bedford Co., TN, on north side of the Elk Ridge, on the headwaters of the Middle Fork of Rock Creek, whereon Mary Murry formerly resided. Borders George Cummings, John Endsley, top of the ridge, it being the County Line, west side of Mary Murry, David Ross' line, and Jesse McClain. 119 acres. Wit: George Cummings and Milton Cummings. Reg: 7 Sep 1832.

Page 214 - 29 Apr 1829. George Clanton of Rutherford Co., TN to Dudley Clanton of Bedford Co., TN, for love and good will for Dudley Clanton, gives him land in Rutherford Co., TN and Bedford Co., TN, on the waters of Mill(?) Fork of Stones River. Borders George Clanton, William Williams, Guinn & McLemore's line, and William Foster. 50 acres. Reg: 11 Sep 1832.

Page 217 - 29 Jul 1828. William W. Bullock to Leonard Bullock, both of Bedford Co., TN, land bequeathed my wife Ann by her uncle Jeremiah Bullock, deceased. Also, one other legacy of land which I, W. W. Bullock, purchased of my brother-in-law Samuel Bullock which land is in Granville Co., NC. Wit: Adam Miller and James N. Grooves. Reg: 11 Sep 1832.

Page 219 - 30 Jun 1832. Theophilus Falls, Trustee of Alexander J. Worke of Iredell Co., NC to William Houston of Bedford Co., TN, land in Bedford Co., on south side of the North Fork of Duck River. Starting at middle of the road leading from Shelbyville to Murfreesboro, joins James Hart, Springer's line, Pinkerton's house, and A. J. Worke's heirs. 611 acres. Alexander J. Worke, one of the legatees of Col. Alexander Worke, deceased. Wit: Jonathan Cooper and Hugh Pinkerton. Reg: 13 Sep 1832.

Page 233 - Fire Company. We, the undersigned persons, resident within the Corporation of the Town of Shelbyville, do agree to form our selves into a company for the purpose of extinguishing fire, to be known by the name of Shelbyville Fire Company. John G. Smith, Wilkins Blanton, W. J. Riddle, N. Thompson, Jr., W. R. Burditt, Richard Crackel, W. E. Deery, John Marcum, Robert Mathews, William S. Jett, Robert T. Cannon, James Terry, Anderson Vannoy, Jordantia Waite, Joseph B. Mason, Joseph Dukes, William B. Smith, Willis W. Wilhoite, James C. Martin, Erwin J. Frierson, William Eakin, Thomas M. Coldwell, Thomas Eakin, James Davidson, Samuel Escue, T. H. Reeves, T. Rowland, Robert Moffatt, Miles W. Moody, N. E. Coldwell, Thomas Lipscomb, Joseph Vannoy, G. W. Fogleman, Josephus White, Richard D. Graham, John H. Hudson, James Story, Preston Frazer, Robert Stevenson, Thomas C. Whiteside, Abner Gaither, William T. Ross, William Gilchrist, W. M. Nelson, J. R. Pinson, W. B. M. Brame, J. R. Deery, Henry Douglass, R. C. Dobson, Jno. T. Shanks, Jos. Shanks, R. Welden, John Mitchell, Volney H. Steele, D. Galbreath, Charles Shanks, H. M. Watterson, Daniel McKisick, and Joel H. Burditt. (Sep 1832)

Page 235 - 3 Sep 1831. William and Bennett Robison, Executors of Will of Abednego Robison, deceased, of Bedford Co., TN sold to Hampton Liggett of Maury Co., TN, land in bedford Co. Borders Robert Clenden's line. 101 acres. 2nd tract, borders Allen Leeper. 26 acres. Reg: 17 Sep 1832.

Page 246 - 25 Jul 1832. William and Charles J. Russell to John Ray, all of Bedford Co., TN, land in Bedford Co., on Sinking Creek of 4 acres and known by the name of Porter's Old Mill. Borders the Old Mill and land being part formerly belonging to

Nathaniel Porter. deceased. Wit: James Ray and Joshua E. Percevell. Reg: 19 Sep 1832.

Page 247 - 30 May 1832. Linsey Dobbs & others to Jeremiah Dobbs. Linsey Dobbs and John White and Willis Coplin are firmly held and bound as joint heirs unto Jeremiah Dobbs, Edward Stevenson, John Bryeans, and Benjamin Penn for $5000.00 for division of personal property of William Dobbs, deceased, estate. Keziah Dobbs wife of William Dobbs, deceased, to receive a child's part of the estate. They decided to make Linsey Dobbs a legal and lawful heir by Deed of Gift, made in May Court in 1832. He gets 50 acres of land in bedford Co., TN, on Big Sinking Creek. Land joins Lewis Gant's land, he also gets a negro woman Queen, left with Keziah Dobbs and at her death goes to Linsey Dobbs. Wit: John Trolinger. Reg: 20 Sep 1832.

Page 252 - 13 Aug 1832. John and Rebecca Jameson to Robert B. Mopin (Maupin). John and Rebecca Jameson of Bedford Co., TN sold to R. B. Maupin of Bedford Co., TN, land in Bedford Co., on north side of the Barren Fork. Borders Teo. F. Bradford land conveyed to R. B. Maupin. Reg: 21 Sep 1832.

Page 253 - 10 Aug 1832. John and Rebecca Jameson to Charles Timmins. John and Rebecca Jameson his wife sold to Charles Timmons, all of Bedford Co., TN, land in Bedford Co., on waters of Shipmans Creek. Borders Payne's land. 150 acres. Reg: 21 Sep 1832.

Page 257 - 6 Feb 1832. Robert Waite to the Church of Christ. I, Robert Waite of Bedford Co., TN, granted unto the Baptist Church of Christ now constituted at Friendship Meeting House, the following parcel of land. Beginning in the center of the spring now made use of said Meeting House and running east 13 poles to a stake, thence south 13 poles to a stake, thence west 13 poles to a stake, thence north 13 poles to beginning. Containing 1 acre and 9 sq. poles. This indenture witnesseth whereas the said Meeting House was built for a Liberty Meeting House to be free for the Presbyterians, Methodists, and United Baptist to preach in and for a public school house and provided these conditions are complied with, I, Robert Waite, will and do &c hereby bind myself, my heirs, Executors or administrators will &c warrant and forever defend the aforesaid land including said Meeting House to the said Baptist Church forever. Reg: 21 Sep 1832.

Page 258 - 3 Sep 1831. Power of Attorney from Elizabeth Robeson to Executors of Abednego Robeson, deceased. Elizabeth Robeson widow of A. Robeson. Wit: Samuel McCurdy and John Vincent. Reg: 24 Sep 1832.

Page 258 - 4 Jun 1832. An Acquital from the heirs of Robert Allison, deceased. We, the heirs of Robert Allison, Sr., deceased, have rescinded a Bill of Sale from Francis Jackson and Mary Jackson his wife, conveying all their rights &c to all negroes of Robert Allison, Sr., deceased, for the delivering of which negroes Francis Jackson did execute a written agreement before his marriage to Mary his wife, to us the undersigned at the death of Mary his wife. Mary is legal heir of Robert Allison, deceased. Signed by the heirs, James Allison, William Allison, Robert Allison, Thomas Allison, John Allison, Kimbro Allison, Elizabeth Williams, Sally Williams, James Williams, and William Williams. Wit: Elijah Buckhanan, William Ogilvie and Jesse Covington. Reg: 21 Sep 1832.

Page 262 - Davidson & Vance to John Walker.
Agreeable to the Last Will and Testament of George Whitton, deceased, Samuel Vance and Hugh Davidson, Executors, on 6 Sep 1826, to sell at public auction all the tract of land on which deceased lived. Robert Ferguson was highest bidder. Ferguson unable to meet payments and was sold to John Walker. The land in Bedford Co., TN, on Noah's Fork. 62 acres. Beginning at a spring now used by John McMahan. Borders on road from Davis' Mill to McMinnville, Jacob Nichols, Hoopers & Whitworth, now Roulin & Robinett's line. Reg: 25 Sep 1832.

Page 266 - 3 Sep 1832. William and Bennett Robeson to Hampton Liggett. William and Bennett Robeson, Executors of the Will of Abednego Robeson, deceased, of Bedford Co., TN sold to Hampton Liggett of Maury Co., TN, land in Bedford Co. Borders James White and Anderson Ivies. Wit: Samuel McCurdy and Jno. Vincent. Reg: 28 Sep 1832.

Page 267 - 4 Jun 1832. Francis Jackson and Mary Jackson to heirs of Robert Allison. Francis Jackson and Mary Jackson his wife and formerly Mary Allison, sold to heirs, James Allison, William Allison, Robert Allison, Thomas Allison, John Allison, and Kimbro Allison and Elizabeth Allison Williams and Sally Williams, heirs of Robert Allison, Sr., deceased, sold negroes. Wit: William Ogilvie, Elijah Buckhanan and Jesse Covington. Reg: 27 Sep 1832.

Page 268 - 11 Aug 1832. Elizabeth H. Fulton to heirs of James C. Fulton. I, Elizabeth H. Fulton widow and relict of James C. Fulton, deceased, relinquish all rights &c to a negro girl Rachel, willed and devised by James C. Fulton to his daughter Dorothy H. Fulton who has since died. Wit: Joseph H. Brittain. Also devises the court to appoint John H. Hall to oversee her business. Reg: 28 Sep 1832.

Page 270 - 23 Jun 1832. John W. Walker to Samuel Philips. I, John W. Walker, one of the heirs of Philip Walker, Jr., deceased, sold to Samuel Philips, all my interest in estate of my brother Philip Walker, deceased, it being one fourth of a negro girl and child, Esther and Lewis, it being willed to me by my brother Philip Walker, deceased. Wit: B. L. Philips and Thomas M. Coldwell. Reg: 4 Oct 1832.

Page 271 - 4 Feb 1832. David H. and Sydney Williams to Blan and Gabriel Maupin. David H. Williams and his wife Sydney Williams sold to Blan Maupin and Gabriel Maupin, all of Bedford Co., TN, land in bedford Co., on south side of the Barren Fork and it being a part of the widow Sarah Maupin's dower of 114 acres. Reg: 4 Oct 1832.

Page 276 - 11 May 1831. From the heirs of Jane Greer, deceased to Harrel Wiggins. James McKisick and his wife Polly, James G. Whitney and his wife Manerva H., James R. White and his wife Catharine C., Nathan Evans in right of his deceased wife Louisa, Richard S. Williamson in right of his deceased wife Betsey, Joseph McKisick and his wife Jane B., Joseph Greer, Alexander Greer, and Andrew Greer, being heirs of Jane Greer, deceased, late of Bedford Co., sold to Harrel Wiggins of Franklin Co., TN land in Bedford Co., TN, on Sugar Creek. 304 acres. Signed by, J. G. Whitney, Manerva H. Whitney, Joseph McKisick, Jane B. McKisick, James McKisick, Polly V. McKisick, Jos. S. Greer, Andrew Greer, R. S. Williamson, James R. White, Catharine C. White, and Alexander Greer. Wit: John W. White and James A. Walker. Reg: 2 Nov 1832.

Page 287 - 13 Jan 1832. Robert Cook and Naomi L. his wife to William P. Finch. Robert G. Cook and Naomi L. his wife, late of Smith Co., TN sold to William P. Finch of Bedford Co., TN, land in Bedford Co., on waters of the Wartrace and Garrison Fork. Borders west side of road leading from Davis' Mill to Murfreesboro, TN. 249 acres. Wit: H. Rennals and George W. Foster. Reg: 15 Nov 1832.

Page 289 - 19 Mar 1832. Robert Allison to Thomas Allison. Robert Allison, Sr. conveyed to Thomas Allison, for love and good will, land in Bedford Co., TN, on both sides of Clems Creek. Borders Charles Roan, John Wilson, Robert Allison and William Clark. 266 acres. Wit: John T. Neil, Elijah Buckhanan and _. Allison. Reg: 15 Nov 1832.

Page 301 - 29 Oct 1832. Ezekiel Reynolds to Joseph Cleek & Others. Ezekiel Reynolds sold to William Cleek, Ezekiel Cleek, Joseph Cleek, James Cleek, Polly Ann Cleek, and Samuel Cleek, heirs of Michael Cleek, deceased, all of Bedford Co., land in Bedford Co., on south side of Duck River, being a part of a 2000 acre tract granted to Alexander Robertson by the State of North Carolina and part of a 400 acre tract which was conveyed to Reynolds by John Parker. Borders the farm on which Michael Cleek formerly live. 219 acres. Wit: Christian Harbar and John O'Neal. Reg: 24 Nov 1832.

Page 309 - 2 Jul 1832. Theophilus Falls to Hugh Pinkerton. Theophilus Falls, Trustee of Alexander J. Worke of Iredell Co., NC sold to Hugh Pinkerton of Bedford Co., TN, land in Bedford Co., on the south side of the North Fork. Borders original tract of William Houston and Pinkerton's house. 102 acres. Wit: William Cooper and Jeremiah B. Nichols. Reg: 25 Nov 1832.

Page 314 - 27 Sep 1832. Robert Hill to Lydda Hill. Robert Hill and Lydda Hill, both of Maury Co., TN, sold to Lydda Hill all the land in Bedford Co., TN, on Thomas Creek. Borders Hugh Bigham. 32½ acres. Wit: S. Bigham and William Bigham. Reg: 27 Nov 1832.

Page 323 - 5 Nov 1832. Nathaniel Johnson to James Johnson. Nathaniel Johnson conveyed to James Johnson, both of Bedford Co., TN, for love and affection for his son James M. Johnson, land in Bedford Co., being part of a tract conveyed from John G. Sims to Nathaniel Johnson by deed dated 19 Jan 1824. Borders Duck River about one mile and a half above Shelbyville near William Carter's corner, Willis Cannon and J. C. Hobb's Mill. 105 acres. Wit: Henry H. Anderson and James C. Morrison. Reg: 13 Nov 1832.

Page 325 - 22 Apr 1811. William Newsom & Others to Robert C. Jennings. William Newsom, Sr. and Mary his wife of Prince Ann Co., VA and his son William Newsom, Jr. and his wife Sarah of King & Queen Co., VA sold to Robert Cary Jennings of Norfolk, VA, land in Williamson Co., TN, on south side of Duck River and on both sides of Rich Creek. 1057 acres, being one half of tract John Sevier sold to John Southgate and Frances B. his wife, who conveyed same to William Newsom, Sr. and his son William Newsom, Jr. Deed dated 9 Apr 1803 and ordered to be registered in Davidson Co., TN and by Deed dated 18 Aug 1807 recorded in Court for Norfolk, VA on 25 May 1808. Borders Theiphilus Hunter and Joel Lane. Reg: 17 Dec 1832.

Page 328 - 24 Apr 1811. Robert C. Jennings to Morgan Tomkies (Temple). Robert Cary Jennings and Allice his wife sold to Morgan Tomkies (Temple), land in Williamson Co., TN, on Rock Creek, south side. 1057½ acres. Reg: 18 Dec 1832.

Page 330 - 22 Apr 1811. William Newsom & Others to Robert C. Jennings. William Newsom, Sr. and Mary his wife of Prince Ann Co., VA and his son William Newsom, Jr. and his wife Sarah of King & Queen Co., VA sold to Robert Cary Jennings of the Borough of Norfolk, VA, 1057½ acres in Williamson Co., TN, on south side of Duck River and on both sides of both forks of Rich Creek. Reg: 19 Dec 1832.

Page 334 - 18 Aug 1807. Southgate and wife to Newsom. John Southgate and Frances B. Southgate his wife of the Borough of Norfolk, VA sold to William Newsom, Sr. and William Newsom, Jr. of the same place, land of 2115 acres in Tennessee, on south side of Duck river and on both sides of both forks of Rich Creek. Borders Theophilus Hunter. Reg: 19 Dec 1832.

Page 352 - 10 Apr 1832. Dempsey P. Temple to L. C. Temple, 240 acres. Dempsey P. Temple conveyed to Leonard C. Temple, both of Bedford Co., TN, land in Bedford Co., on north side of Duck River, opposite and below the mouth of Sugar Creek, it being a part of a tract granted to Dempsey Powell and deeded by Jesse Powell to Elizabeth Temple and by her given to her two sons the said Dempsey and Leonard C. Temple. Wit: John Sims and Richard H. Sims. Reg: 1 Jan 1833.

Page 372 - 25 Aug 1832. John Scott to Mary Shaw. John Scott sold to Mary Shaw a yellow girl Cribby, belonging to the estate of the late C. Shaw, deceased, not disposed of by his will which was by the County Court of Bedford Co., last session, ordered to be sold. Wit: T. S. D. W. Shaw. Reg: 17 Jan 1833.

Page 378 - 2 Jun 1832. Willis and Elizabeth Cooplin* to Linsey Dobbs. Willis Cooplin and John White of Waine (Wayne) Co., TN and Elizabeth Cooplin and Nancy White sold to Linsey Dobbs of Waine (Wayne) Co., TN land in Bedford Co., TN, of 50 acres. Borders school land, Gant's line and Sinking Creek. Wit: William A. Gant and Jeremiah Dobbs. Reg: 18 Jan 1833.
*Cooplin could be Copeland.

Page 393 - 4 Mar 1832. William Perry and Bethenia Perry his wife, formerly Bethenia Forsythe conveyed to Allen Perry of Pickens Co., Alabama, land of 31 acres in Bedford Co., TN. Borders Sheffield's land and the lands belonging to the heirs of Benjamin Forsythe. Wit: A. J. Rose and B. F. Roper of Pickens Co., Alabama. Reg: 12 Feb 1833.

Page 398 - 29 Oct 1832. Hatton Hamilton to Lemuel Wheeler, both of Bedford Co., TN, sold land in Bedford Co. Borders Duck

River and Middleton Hamilton. 156 acres. Wit: Thomas Medlin, Archabald Donnell, J. T. Neil and John O'Neal. Reg: 15 Feb 1833.

Page 399 - 11 Dec 1832. David Green & Tabitha C. Burton & Kenneth L. Anderson. Whereas a marriage is shortly intended to be had and solemnized between David Green and Tabitha C. Burton, they desire on both parties that the property now owned by one should not become responsible for the debts or contracts of the other. Wit: William Gilchrist for Green & Burton, J. Cunningham and William M. Nelson. Reg: 21 Feb 1833.

Page 403 - I, Leonard W. Marbury for and in consideration of a bond which Blackman Dobson now holds on me, dated 7 Nov 1825 Conditioned to be void on the payment of $700.00 to my daughter Elizabeth Marbury now the wife of Blackman Dobson, with interest on said $700.00 from 10 Nov 1827 until Elizabeth should attain the age of eighteen or marry if she married before that and Blackman Dobson agrees to receive the negroes. 28 Jan 1833. Wit: William Gilchrist and N. Thompson. Reg: 27 Feb 1833.

Page 405 - Two parties, viz, Mordicai Kelly of Sumner Co., TN and Anny his wife originally Anny Ensley, spinster, of the first part and Enoch Ensley of Davidson Co., TN and Parker Alexander of Mississippi of other part. Mordicai Kelly is possessed of six negroes and now in possession of Mordicai Kelly. Now, Mordicai Kelly sold for $10.00 to Enoch Ensley and Parker Alexander, for love and affection which Mordicai Kelly bears for wife Anny, and Felix, Alfred, Lurany and Enoch, her children. Wit: William H. Hagard and George W. Spain. Reg: 27 Feb 1833.

Page 444 - 12 Feb 1833. I, Elizabeth Temple of Bedford Co., TN, for love and affection for James A. Dixon, Elizabeth Dixon, Mary T. Dixon, Nancy M. Dixon, Jane M. Dixon, Isabella M. Dixon, and Robert T. Dixon, children of John B. Dixon and my daughter Charlotte B. Dixon wife of John B. Dixon, gives them negroes, personal property also conveys to L. C. Temple property. Wit: L. P. Sims and B. S. Dickson. Reg: 13 Mar 1833.

Page 453 - 26 Jul 1832. Fanny Sims, widow and relict of Briggs Sims, deceased, Washington Sims, Briggs Sims, Zachariah Sims, John Sims, Burwell Sims, Holly Sims, Dolphia Sims, James Dryden and Frances his wife formerly Frances Sims, John Hadley and Polly his wife formerly Polly Sims, Benjamin Johnson and Sally Johnson his wife formerly Sally Sims, Bennet Robertson and Elva D. Robertson formerly Elva D. Sims, Clinton Morrison and Nancy Morrison his wife formerly Nancy Sims, all heirs and legatees of Briggs Sims, deceased sold to Robert W. Sims, all of Bedford Co., TN, land in Bedford Co., on Rock Creek. 196 acres. Wit: Briggs G. Sims, Zachariah Sims, Benjamin Johnson and Burwell Sims. Reg: 14 Mar 1833.

DEED BOOK "DD" 1833 - 1834

Page 4 - 4 May 1831. Joseph T. Elliott of Morgan Co., Illinois to the rest of the heirs of Ebenezer Elliott, deceased, late of Bedford Co., TN. Ebenezer Elliott paid $200.00 to Joseph T. Elliott, in his lifetime and Joseph T. Elliott acknowledged same. Joseph Elliott sold to the heirs of Ebenezer Elliott, deceased, all the undivided share or interest that Joseph T. Elliott has in the estate of Ebenezer Elliott, deceased, his father, land in Maury and Bedford Counties, TN (2 tracts). Reg: 16 Mar 1833.

Page 7 - 13 Feb 1833. Samuel Mc. Patton and Jane Patton his wife, Elender Patton his mother of one part, they being of Bedford Co., TN and Jonathan Mosley of Bedford Co., of other part, sold land in Bedford Co., to Jonathan Mosley, on waters of Sugar Creek. Borders corner of a small graveyard, and James Gammel's corner. 46 acres. Wit: Joseph Trice and William Mosley. Reg: 18 Mar 1833.

Page 18 - 9 Feb 1833. Mary Maxfield to Nancy Ann Maxfield the daughter of Mary Maxfield, for love and affection for her daughter Nancy Ann Maxfield and for the maintaining and support of Mary Maxfield, has given unto Nancy Ann Maxfield personal property. Wit: Evan Harris, Weathersbee Haynes, D. O. Hughes and Josiah Springer. Reg: 23 Mar 1833.

Page 20 - 24 Nov 1831. Miles Wilson to John Robinson, both of Bedford Co., TN, sold 150 acres of land in Bedford Co., TN and being a part of a 5000 acre tract granted to David Wilson by State of North Carolina. One hundred acres fell to Miles Wilson in a division of the heirs of Zacheus Wilson, the other 50 acres sold by William Wilson to David Casson, by David Casson to Richard Walker, by Richard Walker to Miles Wilson by deed and laid off. Borders Ezekiel Cherry's corner, John Walker, and near the Fork of Caney Spring Creek. Wit: William Neil, Jno. K. Cherry, J. H. L. Neil and James Cathey. Reg: 29 Mar 1833.

Page 24 - 1 Mar 1833. I, Samuel Thomas*to Joseph Thompson, Jr., both of Bedford Co., TN, sold for $1.00, a negro woman Rose and her infant child Creasy. Samuel Thompson for love and affection for his grandson Joseph Thompson, son of Samuel's son Joseph Thompson. Wit: George Davidson and John C. Coldwell. Reg: 4 Apr 1833.
* Should be Thompson.

Page 26 - 13 Feb 1833. Willis Cannon and Letsy Cannon to Catharine Cannon, Samuel T. Cannon, Martha Cannon, Jason H. Cannon and Letsy Cannon, children of Willis and Letsy Cannon, for love and affection for their children, and for $100.00 to them paid by Clement Cannon and James Brittain, the friends of the said children, also, land in Bedford Co., TN, on south side of Duck River, it being part of a tract belonging to the estate of Walter Sims. Borders Minos Cannon's purchase from David Sims, and Edmond Green's line. 200 acres. Another tract of land on waters of Duck River and Flat Creek. Borders Edmond Green and Jacob Whitten's corner. 70 acres. Another tract on south side of Duck River. Borders land whereon Northern Johnson now lives, Winchester Road, below Sims' Mill, and Robert More's line. 106 acres. Also, personal property, Reg: 7 Apr 1833.

Page 44 - 2 Jan 1832. William Polk of Wake Co., NC to Thomas G. Polk of Rowan Co., NC, for love and affection for his son Thomas G. Polk and for $5.00, sold land in Bedford Co., TN, adjoining Town of Shelbyville. Reg: 1 May 1833.

DEED BOOK "DD"

Page 50 - 15 Feb 1832. William Burditt, Sr. of Bedford Co., TN, has four children, to wit, Giles, Jesse, Polly who is married to Ambrose Crain, and William Burditt, leaves after his death to each one an equal portion of his estate, which is about $3000.00. Wit: William Gilchrist and William Norvell, Sr. Reg: 2 May 1833.

Page 54 - 15 Apr 1833. I, William Morrison and Elenener Morrison his wife of Montgomery Co., TN, appoint their son Robert W. Morrison of Williamson Co., TN, their Attorney to oversee their interests &c in the estate of Ann Wilson, deceased, in Bedford Co. Reg: 6 May 1833.

Page 56 - 17 Oct 1832. Robert S. Means, W. C. Means and John W. Means of Cabarrus Co., NC to Nathaniel T. Means of Bedford Co., TN, land in Bedford Co., on Duck River to which we are entitled under the will of Alexander Worke, deceased, of Iredell Co., NC, which land has been partitioned and 70 acres left to each of the said Robert, William, and John. Wit: D. W. Barringer. Reg: 8 May 1833.

Page 57 - 30 Sep 1831. John Stokes, Sr., David Stokes, Thomas Stokes and John Stokes, Jr. of Bedford Co., TN to Robert Nix of Maury Co., TN, land in Bedford Co., on south side of Duck River. Borders Tignal Jones and near the mouth of Rock Creek. 240 acres. Wit: James Elliott and E. H. McLean. Reg: 8 May 1833.

Page 65 - 5 Mar 1833. I, Jason Thompson of Davidson Co., TN, for natural love and affection for my grandson Jason T. Brittain, a son of my daughter Maria Brittain, and for the sake of the name, I give unto Jason Thompson Brittain, a negro girl Harriet. My grandson was named for me. Wit: Robert Mathews and Wilson J. Riddle. Reg: 13 May 1833.

Page 69 - 11 May 1831. James McKisick and his wife Polly V. McKisick to David Dryden, all of Bedford Co., TN, land on Sugar Creek of Bedford Co. Borders on west bank of Sugar Creek and Joseph A. Greer's line. 5 acres. Reg: 14 May 1833.

Page 70 - Received this date of Mrs. Mary Shaw, Executrix and John Scott, Executor of the Last Will and Testament of the late Christopher Shaw, deceased, personal property &c. Wit: Josh. P. Scott. Reg: 14 May 1833.

Page 72 - North Carolina Grant to William Lanear, 1500 acres. No. 126. 10 pounds per 100 acres. Located on north side of Duck River including the mouth of Falling Creek. 10 July 1780. Plat on page 72. Reg: 17 May 1833.

Page 73 - 24 Sep 1832. Abraham Alen (Allen) and Nancy C. Alen (Allen) his wife of Monrose Co., Illinois to Robert Dennison of Bedford Co., TN, sold land in Bedford Co., on waters of the Garrison Fork. Borders lands of John L. N---, Dudley Hall, Edward A. Mosely and Robert and William Eoff. 174 acres. Wit: Walter B. Seales and Rufus Riches. Reg: 17 May 1833.

Page 86 - 26 Oct 1831. I, William Low for love and affection for William W. Barksdale, all of Bedford Co., TN, grants to him one half interest in two horses in possession of William Low. Reg: 22 May 1833.

DEED BOOK "DD"

Page 86 - 13 Apr 1833. I, James Weaver of Bedford Co., TN. made Deed of Gift to Margaret Ann Docia Balch, daughter of James C. Balch of Rutherford Co., TN, on heifer. Wit: Martha Newton and Amos Balch. Reg: 22 May 1833.

Page 101 - 17 Dec 1832. James Allison, Robert Allison, Thomas Allison, John Allison, Kimbrough Allison, William Williams and Elizabeth Williams his wife, and James Williams and Sally Williams his wife conveyed to William Allison, land on Clems Creek whereon Robert Allison, deceased, last lived, of 760 acres. Borders John Wilson, Thomas Allison, Robert Allison's place where he lived, William Ogilvie, Alexander Moon's line, and Clems Creek. Reg: 7 Jun 1833.

Page 108 - 3 Nov 1832. I, Stephen White of Rutherford Co., TN, for love and affection for my grandson Julius Peacock, the son of my daughter Frances who married John W. Peacock, now living in Bedford Co., TN and about to remove to Perry Co., TN and remove his son Julius with him, do give a negro girl Louisa. Wit: Thomas A. Peacock and Burrell Featherston. Reg: 13 Jun 1833.

Page 112 - 18 Mar 1833. Nancy Tyson formerly Nancy Forrest, widow of Nathan Forrest, deceased, of Bedford Co., TN sold to Brittain H. Forrest son of Nathan Forrest, deceased, land or share of his father's estate. Nancy Tyson, Executrix of Nathan Forrest, deceased, of Last Will and Testament. Borders James N. Forrest. 20 acres. Wit: John Laws and A. B. Bowen. Reg: 14 Jun 1833.

Page 116 - -- --- 1833. Thomas Long to Mary Williamson, Executrix of the Last Will and Testament of her husband John Williamson, deceased, land in Bedford Co., TN, on Rich Creek. Borders James Elison, Thomas Allison and William Chapman. 86 acres. Wit: J. W. Riggs and Ephraim Hunter. Reg: 17 Jun 1833.

Page 116 - 2 Oct 1832. William P. Hix to James W. Patton, both of Bedford Co., TN. William P. Hix is one of the heirs of John Hix, entitled to one fifth. 50 acres. Wit: Jacob Greer and John Patton. Reg: 17 Jun 1833.

Page 122 - I, Wilie B. Watkins of Bedford Co., TN, intermarried Ann Eliza Kincaid and believing she was entitled to nine negroes. James Kincaid the father of my wife Eliza. Wit: L. B. Knott. Reg: 26 Jun 1833.

Page 123 - 14 May 1832. John L. Wood and Rebecca E. Wood his wife formerly Dickerson sold to Lemuel Snelling, all of Bedford Co., TN, land in Bedford Co., on the Garrison Fork, a tract formerly owned by William Dickerson, deceased, and by his Last Will and Testament conveyed to Rebecca E. Wood formerly Dickerson, his second daughter. Borders the Garrison Fork, Daniel Gilchrist, William Hooser, Esq., and widow Dickerson. 100 acres. Wit: K. L. Anderson and Giles Burdett. Reg: 28 Jun 1833.

Page 129 - 4 Jan 1833. Jane Cunningham daughter of Mathew Cunningham and Elizabeth Cunningham his wife, in right of them, as I, Jane Cunningham was not of lawful age when they perfected a title to two tracts of land to William Reed and Robert Reed who was thought to be an heir, forms a claim of the Last Will and Testament of William Galbreath, which was the prior owner of said tracts. I, Jane Cunningham of Bedford Co., TN, now of age, do convey to William and Robert Reed, land in Bedford Co., on waters of Big Flat Creek. 200 acres. Wit: James Orrick and Andrew Reed. Reg: 31 Jul 1833.

Page 130 - 11 Feb 1833. Elbert Clark and his wife Elizabeth Clark sold to Hiram Maxfield, all of Bedford Co., TN, land in Bedford Co., on waters of North Fork. Borders the mouth of Alexanders Creek and North Fork. 29 acres. Wit: Evan Harris. Reg: 31 Jul 1833.

Page 138 - 25 May 1832. John Reed and his wife Esther Reed conveyed for love and affection for Benjamin C. Brantly and his wife Elizabeth M. Brantly formerly Eliza M. Reed, they being the son-in-law and daughter of John and Esther Reed, and for $1.00, conveyed to them land in Bedford Co., on west side of East Fork of Rock Creek. Borders Isaac W. Walker and John Orr. 95 acres. Wit: Alexander B. Reed and John W. Walker. Reg: 16 Aug 1833.

Page 154 - 10 Feb 1831. Ruthy Shearin to John Capley, Sr., all of Bedford Co., TN. Ruthy Shearin of whom is heir and legatee of William Shearin, deceased, and became legally entitled to part of tract of land, undivided, as the heir. Land was granted by North Carolina to William Shearin by Grant No. 47, dated 10 July 1788. Borders Anthony Newman, Alexander Robertson, and Duck River. 750 acres. Wit: Peter Capley, Paul Capley and John Capley. Reg: 26 Aug 1833.

Page 159 - 5 Nov 1832. Nathaniel Johnson to John B. Johnson, both of Bedford Co., TN for love and affection for his son John B. Johnson and for $1.00, conveyed land in Bedford Co., being a part of a tract of land conveyed by John G. Sims to Nathaniel Johnson on 19 Jan 1824. Borders Willis Cannon, and near the Winchester Road, and William Carter. 105 acres. Wit: Henry H. Anderson and James W. Morrison. Reg: 29 Aug 1833.

Page 160 - 7 Aug 1832. Edward Whitworth of Bedford Co., TN to Mary L. Forsythe of Fayette Co., TN, land sold to Edward Whitworth as part of the Lot that has been held in common among the heirs of Benjamin Forsythe, deceased. Borders Edward Whitworth, Allen Perry, Oakly and James Joyce. 16 acres. Wit: Thomas Higgs and Louis Turner. Reg: 29 Aug 1833.

Page 163 - 31 Aug 1833. Daniel McKisick of one part and William Heaslett and David McKisick of second part and William Heaslett of third part, all of Bedford Co., TN. Daniel McKisick on 15 Feb 1825 became guardian of the heirs of Jno. W. McGimpsey, viz, Mary E. Pelina and John W. McGimpsey, and was bonded on 15 Feb 1825, property of land in Bedford Co., and east of Town of Shelbyville, including the dwelling house where I, D. McKisick now live. Wit: J. D. Henderson. Reg: 31 Aug 1833.

Page 170 - 5 Sep 1833. I, Henry Davis of Bedford Co., TN, having full faith in my brother Thomas Davis of the Town of Shelbyville, Bedford Co., do appoint him my Attorney. He is to purchase apartment of goods in Philadelphia. Reg: 6 Sep 1833.

Page 170 - 22 Feb 1832. Frederick Chandler sold to Mathew Chandler, Hartwell Chandler and Henry Chandler, negroes. Wit: Elias Palmer, James W. Leland, John Shofner and Loton Shofner.

DEED BOOK "DD"

Reg: 10 Sep 1833.

Page 174 - Ambrose Crain vs John B. Dickson, Absolom Lowe, Giles Burditt, Thomas Landers, William Burditt and William R. Burditt. In Equity. A judgement was at Feb Term 1826 of Bedford County Court, rendered against Walter Burnard, Virginia Ann Burnard and Robert H. Burnard, minor heirs of Thomas H. Burnard, deceased, in favor of Anna McKee on 18 Feb 1826. Tract of 5 acres with a Spinning Factory, Cotton Gin and Bailing Screws in Bedford Co., on Barren Fork. Absolom Low was highest bidder. Reg: 7 Oct 1833.

Page 178 - 5 Dec 1833. John Tillman & Others purchased slaves of Rachael Martin, belonging to her by the Last Will and Testament of her late husband Barkley Martin, deceased. They agreed to pay her $900.00 a year for the rest of her life. Wit: William P. Finch. Reg: 8 Oct 1833.

Page 182 - 18 Oct 1830. Mary Friddle and Martin Friddle, both of Bedford Co., TN. Mary Friddle sold to Martin Friddle land in Bedford Co., on waters of Big Flat Creek and being the land and plantation whereon Martin Friddle now lives. Borders Jane Reynolds' land, Murry's lane, John Reynolds and Martin Friddle's 6 acres purchased of Robert Prewitt. 138 acres. Wit: John G. Brown and John Reynolds. Reg: 15 Oct 1833.

Page 183 - 25 Aug 1832. My father, Bushrod Webb of Bedford Co., TN, has provided 250 acres of land which he has caused to be deeded to me and my heirs &c and executed this day by John W. Nelson of Shelby Co., TN. It being the tract of land whereon my father and mother now resides for and in consideration of which my father Bushrod Webb and mother Catharine Webb is to remain and hold possession of the said land during their natural lives. Signed by John A. Webb. Wit: James Alexander and Robert C. Batts. Reg: 15 Oct 1833.

Page 187 - -- Mar 1833. I, Jackson Lile of Bedford Co., TN, for love and affection for my daughter Clairy Lile, conveyed a negro girl Isabel. Reg: 15 Oct 1833.

Page 195 - 19 Jan 1833. Nancy Golanthan, Mar<u>ry</u> West formerly Marry Golanthan and Joshua F. West who married Mar<u>ry</u> Golanthan of Bedford Co., TN sold to William Young of Bedford Co., land in Bedford Co., on headwaters of Butlers Creek. Borders land of the heirs of Daniel Vaughan, Elijah Bomar and Butlers Creek. 20 acres. Wit: James Jones and William Bomar. Reg: 12 Feb 1833.

Page 204 - 19 Mar 1833. Nancy Tyson formerly Nancy Forrest, widow and Executrix of Nathan Forrest, deceased, conveyed to Brittain H. Forrest, son of Nathan Forrest, all of bedford Co., TN. Nancy Tyson in compliance with the Last Will and Testament of Nathan Forrest, deceased, land in Bedford Co., on waters of Spring Creek. Borders Thomas B. Forrest. 3 acres. Wit: John Laws and R. A. Bowen. Reg: 31 Oct 1833.

Page 214 - 15 Jan 1830. I, Robert Waite of Bedford Co., TN, am bound unto Cynthia Haggard formerly Cynthia Meadows, Mariah, Jane, Henderson Riley, Sarah Elizabeth and Julia Meadows, all children of William Meadows of Bedford Co., land in Bedford Co., on waters of Wartrace Fork, adjoining lands of Henry Holt,

Theoderick F. Bradford and Michael Holt for 107 acres. Wit: Pumphry Meadows and W. K. Daley. Reg: 8 Nov 1833.

Page 214 - 26 May 1829. Reubin Kelly to Joseph Keller, both of Bedford Co., TN. Reubin Kelly sold to Joseph Keller and Francis Keller all his undivided land which my father Reubin Kelly died and possessed of 400 acres in Bedford Co., on the waters of the Garrison Fork, his undivided part being 50 acres. Wit: Thomas Couch and James Armstrong, on 4 Nov 1833. Reg: 8 Nov 1833.

Page 217 - 3 Sep 1832. Richard Lock, late of Roan Co., NC, deceased, died possessed of land in Bedford Co., TN, he made a Last Will and Testament and appointed Joseph Byrd and George Lock, both of Roan Co., NC, as his Executors, impowered them to sell land in Bedford Co. and George Lock by his agent Mathew B. Lock vested unto him by law, Richard Lock sold to William Roane of Burke Co., NC, all the land in Bedford Co. Lot No. 4 as laid off to Richard Lock now deceased, of 6000 acres granted by North Carolina to Mathew Lock, Sr. the father of Richard Lock. Land on headwaters of Duck River. Reg: 9 Nov 1833.

Page 219 - 2 Nov 1833. Robert McFarland sold to Robert Baker and Mary Pratt and Henry Pratt, devises of William Pratt, land in Bedford Co., TN, on Duck River. 703 acres. Wit: Benjamin McFarland and James Haley. Reg: 11 Nov 1833.

Page 220 - 12 Oct 1833. Henderson Meadows sold to Samuel Haggard, both of Bedford Co., TN, all his interest in the estate of deceased father, the late Michael Meadows, according to his Last Will and Testament, all land and negroes. Wit: J. W. Norvell, E. G. Meadows and R. Haggard. Reg: 11 Nov 1833.

Page 221 - 12 Oct 1833. William Meadows to Samuel Haggard, both of Bedford Co., TN, land and negroes belonging to the estate of his deceased father, the late Michael Meadows, according to his Last Will and Testament. Wit: Hamilton Bedford and G. G. Osborne and R. Haggard. Reg: 11 Nov 1833.

Page 223 - 7 Sep 1830. Polly Kelly to Joseph Keller and Francis H. Keller, all of Bedford Co., TN, land in Bedford Co., of which her father Reubin Kelly died seized and possessed, 400 acres on waters of Garrison Fork, 50 acres being her part. Wit: Nathaniel T. Kelly and Lavica Kelly. Reg: 13 Nov 1833.

Page 224 - 10 Aug 1833. I, George Tilmon of Hinds Co., Mississippi, appointed Wade Nowlin of the same County and State, my Attorney, to sell lands in Bedford Co., TN. Reg: 14 Nov 1833.

Page 232 - We, Mathew B. Lock and Ann C. Byers, heirs of Richard Locke, deceased, of Iredell Co., NC, sold to William Roane of Burke Co., NC, land in Bedford Co., TN, known as Lot No. 4, is a 5000 acre grant by North Carolina to Mathew Locke and divided among the heirs of Mathew Locke, Richard being one of the heirs. Division made in January 1817. 344 acres. Wit: D. T. Coldwell and D. W. Barringer. Reg: 25 Nov 1833.

Page 233 - 13 Aug 1833. Bediah Browning and Elizabeth his wife of McCracken Co., KY sold to Wilie Stevens of Bedford Co., TN, land in Bedford Co. Borders James Fort, Browning's corner and William Hartsfield. 50 acres. Wit: B. Snell and John Stephens of McCracken Co., KY. Reg: 24 Nov 1833.

Page 234 - 1 Aug 1833. Bediah Browning of McCracken Co., KY to Wilie Fort of Bedford Co., TN, land in Bedford Co. Borders Stephen's fence, William Hartsfield land he gave to Browning's wife, and Stephen's plantation. 50 acres. Wit: James Stephens and Ransom Stephens. Reg: 26 Nov 1833.

Page 236 - 18 Nov 1828. James Crow to the Heirs of Polly S. Turnage, deceased, viz, Mar<u>ry</u> Jane Turnage, Narcissa C. Turnage and William Whitefield Turnage, all of Bedford Co., TN, land in Bedford Co., on south side of Duck River, being a part of a 2000 acre grant by North Carolina to Alexander Robertson. Borders Samuel C. Card of Madison Co., TN. 61 acres. Wit: Joseph Neil and Samuel H. Card. Reg: 27 Nov 1833.

Page 239 - 10 Jun 1833. I, Elizabeth Daniel to James Deery, both of Bedford Co., TN. Elizabeth Daniel sells her right title and claim of one third part of 50 acres of land that her husband Thomas Daniel purchased from Jeremiah Clanch. Reg: 30 Nov 1833.

Page 241 - We, Zacheus Wilson and Louisa Wilson his wife of Dyer Co., TN, has appointed William S. Mayfield of Bedford Co., TN, their Attorney, to oversee their interests &c coming to them from the estate of Aron Wilson, deceased. Wit: M. Mitchell and A. Pursell. Reg: 20 Jan 1833.

Page 243 - 7 Nov 1833. John N. Phifer and his wife Ann Phifer of Bedford Co., TN to Travis C. Nash of Rutherford Co., TN, land in Bedford Co., on waters of Fall Creek. Borders Edward Haley, George A. Phifer and Trotters old line. 219 acres. Wit: Wilson Steele and Nathan H. Schooler. Reg: 4 Dec 1833.

Page 245 - 4 Nov 1833. Edward Cress and Margaret his wife of Bedford Co., TN to Travis C. Nash of Rutherford Co., TN, land in Bedford Co., for 429 acres, be the one half a tract originally belonging to Mrs. Elizabeth Moore as former deed will show (above record). Borders Phifer's Lot and Trotter's old line. Wit: William Eakin and Spencer Eakin. Reg: 5 Dec 1833.

Page 247 - 3 Jul 1833. George Campbell to Richmond Campbell. George Campbell conveyed to his son Richmond Campbell land on Powel Creek of Bedford Co., and where George Campbell now resides. Borders George Campbell, William Campbell, Adam's line and James Campbell. 147 acres. The above land will not be in possession of Richmond Campbell until after the death of his father George Campbell and his wife Anny Campbell. Wit: Joseph Adams and J. Dougal. Reg: 12 Dec 1833.

Page 248 - 9 Dec 1833. I, George Sanders of Bedford Co., TN, for love and affection for my children, John Sanders, David Sanders, Mary Sanders and Elizabeth Sanders and also for $1.00, given unto them all the goods and chattels. Wit: James D. Clark and H. Maxfield. Reg: 12 Dec 1833.

Page 249 - 9 Dec 1833. George Sanders to John Sanders, David Sanders, Mary Sanders and Elizabeth Sanders, sons and daughters of George Sanders and his wife Elizabeth Sanders, all of Bedford Co., TN, for love and affection for their children, conveyed land in Bedford Co., on waters of North Fork. Borders Robert Cannon, Elizabeth Parker and George Harris and Nathan Wheeler.

40 acres. It being part of the estate of John Sanders, deceased. Wit: James D. Clark and Hiram Maxfield. Reg: 13 Dec 1833.

Page 250 - We, children and heirs of Thomas Lee, deceased, and Mary Lee widow of Thomas Lee, deceased, agree to live together as former to have done and whenever they may become seperated or Mary Lee does become unable to do for herself, then she is to live with which of the children of Thomas Lee, deceased, she may think proper and they are bound to pay Mary Lee or who ever she lives with for one year or the time she lived with them $45.00 per year for her lifetime or widowhood. Signed by Mary Lee, Mary Lee, Sarina(?) Lee, Margaret Lee, Sarah M. Lee, William Lee, S. T. Lee, John Lee, and Martin Hopkins. Wit: William H. Harrison and R. Puckett and George W. Smith. Reg: 18 Dec 1833.

Page 251 - 13 Feb 1833. I, John M. Puckett sold to P. Puckett, both of Bedford Co., TN, all claim and interest in the estate of Arthur Puckett, deceased, negroes, land and stock, this property now in the hands of Lucy Puckett and will remain there during her natural life which P. Puckett gives me (John M.) $225.00. Wit: John W. Harrison and William H. Harrison. Reg: 18 Dec 1833.

Page 254 - 24 Dec 1833. John Wortham, Commissioner &c to James Joyce, both of Bedford Co., TN. Whereas Lemuel Perry and Sarah his wife is in their petition against James Graham and Elizabeth his wife, George Higgs and Effy J. his wife, and Mary T. Forsythe by her guardian George Higgs at the June Term 1831 of Circuit Court of Bedford Co., TN, for to sell a tract of land in Bedford Co., on Spring Creek. 6 acres. It being all of Lot No. 1 of the original tract of Benjamin Forsythe, deceased. Wit: William Moody. Reg: 26 Dec 1833.

Page 255 - 7 Feb 1833. Nancy Dickson and Bennet S. Dickson to John B. Wortham, all of bedford Co., TN, land in Bedford Co., on Wilson Creek. 112+ acres. Borders John Wortham, James Dickson and Bennet S. Dickson's land which fell to him with his brothers, of his father's tract. Wit: J. Worthan as to Mrs. Dickson and William W. Dickson as to Mary Dickson. Reg: 26 Dec 1833.

Page 257 - 2 Oct 1833. Samuel M. Patton and Elenor Patton to James Dickson, all of Bedford Co., TN, land in Bedford Co. Borders Roger Snell and Jonathan Mosely. 59¼ acres. Wit: Jacob Greer and Randolph Newsom and William M. Wilson. Reg: 2 Jan 1834.

Page 259 - 2 Aug 1833. Jesse Rogers and Mary his wife to William H. Miles, all of Bedford Co., TN, land of 50 acres in Bedford Co., on waters of Little Flat Creek. Wit: John H. Miles and Willie B. Snell. Reg: 2 Jan 1834.

Page 259 - 12 Jun 1833. John Finley and Argen Finley his wife of Pickens Co., Alabama to Isaac Troxler of Bedford Co., TN, land and interest in same of 122 acres in Bedford Co., on Barren Fork. Borders Duck River, John Ewell, S. Payne and Wren Carter. The land being of which Shrewberry Payne lived upon at the time of his death and land laid off to Sally Payne wife of Shrewberry Payne, as we are heirs of S. Payne. Reg: 2 Jan 1834.

Page 263 - 3 Jul 1833. George Campbell to his son Charles Campbell, both of Bedford Co., TN, land in Bedford Co., and where Charles Campbell now resides. Borders James Campbell. 101 acres. Wit: James Philips and Jno. Dougal. Reg: 8 Jan 1834.

Page 266 - 14 Nov 1833. Clement Cannon to his son Henry Cannon, both of Bedford Co., TN, land in Bedford Co., and on south of Town of Shelbyville. Borders land that Clement Cannon sold to James L. Armstrong, and George Davidson. 14 acres. Wit: James McKisick and Alexander H. McKisick. Reg: 9 Jan 1834.

Page 267 - 7 Jan 1834. William Gilchrist of Shelbyville, Bedford Co., TN conveyed to Thomas Davis, John Eakin, Erwin J. Frierson, Robert P. Harrison, James Deery, and William Gilchrist, Trustees of the Shelbyville Female Academy, and for $50.00, to build a Female Academy in the Town of Shelbyville, land in Town Plan as Lot No. 50. Reg: 10 Jan 1834.

Page 269 - 5 Jan 1832. George T. Harris and Elizabeth Parker to Simeon Gilly, all of Bedford Co., TN, land in Bedford Co., on Alexanders Creek. Borders John Rawlings and Rushing's line. 300 acres. Wit: John Rushing and Evan Harris. Reg: 10 Jan 1834.

Page 273 - 7 May 1832. Mathew McCorkle, Alexander McCorkle, Gilbert Milligan and Rebecca Milligan his wife, Charles Beaty and George Little and Elizabeth L. Little his wife, all of Lincoln Co., NC and Jane Alexander of Iredell Co., NC sold to Abraham Landers of Bedford Co., TN, land in Bedford Co., on waters of Alexander Creek, joining lands of George Jones and others, being part of 945 acres belonging to the McCorkle family and heirs of the late Col. Alexander Worke of Iredell Co., NC. The land whereon said Landers now lives. Wit: Thomas Ward and M. Sigmas. Signed at Lincolnton, NC 18 July 1832. Reg: (no date).

Page 276 - 7 May 1832. Instrument same as above, one part and Thomas Alfred of Bedford Co., TN other part, land in Bedford Co., TN, on both sides of Alexander Creek. Joining lands of Abraham Landers and Guy and Others. Wit: Thomas Ward and M. Sigmas. Reg: 16 Jan 1834.

Page 298 - 12 May 1833. Robert Wilson, Sr. to Robert Wilson, Jr., his son, for love and affection for his son, land in Bedford Co., TN, on north branch of the Barren Fork, and where Robert Wilson, Sr. now lives. Borders James Puryear and land whereon Robert Wilson, Jr. now lives, and widow Blythe's land. 75 acres. Wit: William Hodge and Alexander Hodge. Reg: 5 Feb 1834.

Page 303 - -- Feb 1834. Joseph M. Harris and Mary Ann Harris his wife sold to Hugh Snelling, all of Bedford Co., TN, land in Bedford Co., near The Three Forks of Duck River, it being a part of land formerly belonging to William Dickinson, Lot No. 1. Borders land of Mrs. Dickinson widow of William Dickinson, deceased, now lives, the Garrison Fork, and William Hooser. 100 acres. Wit: D. P. T. House and Alex. H. McKissick. Reg: 11 Feb 1834.

Page 304 - 21 Dec 1833. John M. Endsley to Willis Burgess and

Cyntha Burgess his wife, all of Bedford Co., TN, land in Bedford Co., on headwaters of Rock Creek, it being a part of 1540 acres granted to Minos Cannon, Sr. 100 acres. Wit: James B. Lowry and John Cummings. Reg: 12 Feb 1834.

Page 313 - 30 Nov 1833. We, John McEwen and Ann McEwen, both of Bedford Co., TN, for $1.00, sold to Alexander Neal, property. Wit: William Neal and Allen Brown, Sr. Reg: 21 Feb 1834.

Page 315 - 22 Feb 1834. I, James H. Hadley of Williamson Co., TN, appointed James Holmes of Bedford Co., TN, my Attorney, to oversee of the heirs at law of Joshua Hadley, deceased, a deed to Jesse Arnold for 100 acres of land in Bedford Co., on Hurricane Creek. Borders school land and lands of Joshua Hadley. Wit: D. D. Arnold and Samuel B. McCuistion. Reg: 21 Feb 1834.

Page 334 - 1 Feb 1834. Archibald C. Adams of Bedford Co., TN to John Ellison, Alexander B. Reed and Henry Bishop, all of Bedford Co., for the interest I feel in the advancement of the spread and success of the Redeemer Kingdom and in particular in the bounds and vicinity of that branch of it denominated The Hopewell Congregation under the care of the Cumberland Presbytery, I have conveyed to the Trustees and Congregation, on the waters of the East Fork of Rock Creek, being a part of that tract on which I now live. Borders Robert W. Linn. 1 acre and use of the Adam's Spring, to be for a site for the Meetinghouse for a graveyard and to include the Camp Ground. Wit: Robert W. Sims and Thomas Ellison. Reg: 26 Feb 1834.

Page 335 - 24 Oct 1833. Lawrence Co., Alabama. It is ordered that James Aldridge be appointed guardian of Mary Ann C. Aldridge, Jesse G. Aldridge, Jane Louisa Aldridge, James R. Aldridge, Kezia M. Aldridge, and Andrew J. Aldridge, children of Kezia Aldridge, deceased, heirs in right of their mother, (daughter) of Lewis Gant, late of Bedford Co., TN, deceased, all children are infants under age of twenty one years. 18 Dec 1833. Reg: 26 Feb 1834.

Page 348 - 1 Jun 1832. James Wilson to Samuel Wilson, both of Bedford Co., TN, for love and affection for his son Samuel Wilson for a legacy and a portion of his estate valued at $1000.00, conveyed land in Bedford Co., on waters of Spring Creek, including the place whereon Samuel Wilson now lives. Borders Fleming's line and Samuel Wilson. 100 acres. Wit: John Thompson and Jason B. Shuffield. Reg: 28 Feb 1834.

Page 352 - 3 Jul 1833. George Campbell to James Campbell, both of Bedford Co., TN, James Campbell is son of George Campbell, and was conveyed land in Bedford Co., on Powell Creek. Borders Charles Campbell. 151 acres. Wit: James Philips and Jno. Dougal. Reg: 1 Mar 1834.

Page 355 - 19 Nov 1833. South Carolina. We, John Dean, Samuel Miller, Burnett H. Allgood, Elisha Bobo, Samuel Coldwell, Thomas Dean, Henry Dean, Joel Dean, Jr., Alfred Dean and Abram Dean are bound unto Joel Dean, Jr. in sum of $500.00. Joel Dean, Jr* has given up his note to the other named people, or they pay $25.00 yearly during his natural life. He will make his home with any of his children and they be allowed a charge.
* probably Joel Dean, Sr.

Signed by John Dean, Samuel Miller, Barnett H. Allgood, Henry Dean, Joel Dean, Jr., Alfred Dean, Abram Dean, Samuel Coldwell, Elisha Bobo, and Thomas Dean. Reg: 6 Mar 1834.

Page 356 - I, Mary Ann Watkins conveyed to Willie B. Watkins of Bedford Co., TN, Lot No. 91, which Winningham now lives. He is to rent the same and give the proceeds to Mary Ann Watkins. Borders Corporation, Benjamin Strickler and John B. Pinson. Willie B. is to get the property for building Mary Ann Watkins a house eighteen feet by twenty and chimney to it, one story high and at her death to go to Willie B. Watkins. Wit: J. Cunningham and M. Cunningham. Reg: 8 Mar 1834.

Page 357 - 28 Jan 1834. Robert McFarland, Mary Pratt and Tency Pratt devises of William Pratt, deceased, and Robert Baker sold to James Deery of Bedford Co., TN, land in Bedford Co. Borders Thomas McFarland and William Pratt. 71 acres. Wit: J. Cunningham and Jno. Hastings. Reg: 14 Mar 1834.

Page 360 - 1 Mar 1827. Plat on page 360. George Landers of Bedford Co., TN conveyed to Ridly Morgan and Nathan Frizzle, Deacons of the Baptist Church, Bedford Co., for love and desire he hath for the promotion of the Christian Religion of the North Fork Church at Mount Pisquay Meetinghouse for use of the Baptist Denomination, land in Bedford Co., on waters of the North Fork of Duck River, including Mount Pisquay Meetinghouse. Borders the road leading from Shelbyville to Nashville. 1 acre. Wit: John Larrimore and David Frizzle. Reg: 14 Mar 1834.

Page 361 - 3 Feb 1834. I, Hanson S. Brown, administrator of Thomas Brown, deceased, of Bedford Co., TN, sold to Mary Brown of Bedford Co., a negro boy London. Wit: William Eakin. Reg: 14 Mar 1834.

Page 362 - 22 Dec 1832. Joseph W. Camp and his wife Margaret N. Camp of Madison Co., Mississippi sold to Thomas Brown of Bedford Co., TN, land in Bedford Co. Wit: William H. Conway and Alexander Robinson. Reg: 14 Mar 1834.

Page 378 - 2 Jul 1832. William Bingham, Sr. to William Bingham, Jr., both of Bedford Co., TN, for love and goodwill for William Bingham, Jr., conveyed to him land in Bedford Co. Borders Samuel Bingham, Isaac J. Miller and the ridge between Rutherford and Bedford Counties. 92 acres. Wit: Isaac J. Miller and William W. Miller. Reg: 24 Mar 1834.

Page 381 - 14 Aug 1833. Joel Lawrance of Bedford Co., TN to Joseph Lawrance of Rutherford Co., TN. Joel Lawrance for love and affection which he has for his daughter Elizabeth Murphy wife of Cedar Murphy and the children of the said Elizabeth Murphy now born and which she may hereafter have, and for $1.00 by Joseph Lawrance, the son, sold personal property &c. Wit: Charles Lisenby and W. W. B. Morris. Reg: 25 Mar 1834.

Page 387 - 3 Oct 1833. John Hamilton and Polly his wife sold to Abel Landers, all of Bedford Co., TN, land in Bedford Co., on waters of Thompsons Creek. Borders lands of Clement Cannon and school land. Wit: E. W. Brown and David Nutt. Reg: 7 Apr 1834.

Page 390 - 31 Oct 1832. Solomon Maxwell, Daniel Maxwell, Johnathan King, Mashea Hail of Randolph Co., Illinois, and Keziah Rushing and Rushing & McGuffin of Bedford Co., TN, all lawful heirs of Thomas Maxwell, Sr., deceased, conveyed to Thomas Maxwell, Jr. of Bedford Co., land in Bedford Co., on Clems Creek. Borders Thomas Thompson and Richard Varable.* 82 acres. Wit: James T. Byler and Caleb Cox. Reg: 8 Apr 1834.
* could be Venable.

Page 394 - Greenville District, South Carolina. I, Jeremiah Cleveland, Sr. of Greenville District, South Carolina, for love and affection for my son Jeremiah Cleveland, Jr., land in Bedford Co., TN, on the Garrison and Wartrace Fork. 1431 acres. Borders mouth of Wartrace Fork, Kenchin Stokes, Rice Coffee and Robert Waite, and the Garrison Fork. Wit: William Robinson and George E. W. Nelson. Reg: 12 Apr 1834.

Page 400 - 24 Oct 1833. Robert McKenzie and wife Mary sold to William Houston and wife Sarah, all of Bedford Co., TN, land in Bedford Co., on both sides of Dry Fork of Fall Creek. Borders Houston's corner and Martin Phifer's line. 60 acres. Reg: 19 Apr 1834.

Page 401 - 24 Oct 1833. William Houston and wife Sarah sold to Robert McKenzie and his wife Mary, all of Bedford Co., TN, land in Bedford Co., on north side of Dry Fork of Fall Creek. Borders McKenzie's line, Edward Crisp and McKee's line. 60 acres. Reg: 19 Apr 1834.

Page 403 - 1 Dec 1833. Samuel Walker and Rachael Walker to William Yates, all of Bedford Co., TN, land in Bedford Co., on waters of Sugar Creek, adjoining lands of James McKisick, John Bradshaw, Nathan Evans, and others. 225 acres. Wit: Jas. Staggs and Robert Parks. Reg: 22 Apr 1834.

Page 405 - 23 Jan 1834. James Allison to Thomas H. Allison. For love and affection for his son Thomas H. Allison, all of Bedford Co., TN, conveyed land in Bedford Co., on East Fork of Rock Creek. Borders Isaac B. Larue, Richard Allen and Gabriel Blackwell. 107 acres. Wit: William Williams, Sr. and Wesley Williams. Reg: 24 Apr 1834.

Page 407 - 21 Dec 1833. Mary Endsley, Executrix of John Endsley, deceased, of Bedford Co., TN, Alfred C. Anderson and Damaris his wife formerly Damaris Endsley of Lincoln Co., TN, Willis Burges and Cynthia Burges his wife formerly Cynthia Endsley, Isaac N. Endsley and Bedford Endsley of Bedford Co., conveyed to John M. Endsleyof Bedford Co., land in Bedford Co., on waters of East Fork of Rock Creek, it being a part of Hardy Murphy land. Borders Murphy's spring and Felix Roberson. 150 acres. Wit: James B. Lowry and John Cummings. Reg: 29 Apr 1834.

Page 408 - 21 Dec 1833. Mary Endsley, Executrix of John Endsley, deceased, of Bedford Co., TN, alfred C. Anderson and Damaris his wife formerly Damaris Endsley of Lincoln Co., TN, Willis Burges and Cynthia Burges his wife formerly Cynthia Endsley, John M. Endsley and Bedford Endsley of Bedford Co. conveyed to Isaac N. Endsley of Bedford Co., land in Bedford Co., on waters of East Fork of Rock Creek, it being part of Hardy Murphy survey. Borders Murphy's spring and John M. Murphy. 150 acres. Wit: James B. Lowry and John Cummings. Reg:29 Apr 1834.

Page 416 - 2 May 1834. I, James Nichols sold to Blan Maupin, borh of Bedford Co., TN, all title and interest which is now in the hands of Sary Blanton, Executrix and Guardian of the minor heirs of William Blanton, deceased, from account sale that may fall to my wife Mary as one of the lawful heirs of William Blanton's estate of five negroes, also land where Sary Blanton now lives, all falling to me by Mary my wife, being an heir of the estate, also personal property. Wit: D. P. T. House and Ehody Anthony. Reg: 2 May 1834.

Page 427 - 11 Nov 1833. We, John L. Neill, Theodrick F. Bradford, John Tillman, Thomas B. Moseley, Edward A. Moseley, Henry C. Martin and Matt Martin, Jr., all of Bedford Co., TN, for love and affection they have for Elizabeth Martin widow of Abram Martin, deceased, and for $1.00. Wit: James Scruggs and David Thomas. Reg: 12 May 183_3_(4).

Page 429 - 3 Jan 1834. Ruth Harris to James Harris, Jr., both of Bedford Co., TN, for love and affection Ruth Harris has for James Harris, conveys a negro boy Stephen. Wit: James H. Neil and Mary Harris. Reg: 12 May 1834.

Page 430 - 17 Oct 1833. John Noblet, Jacob Noblet, Thomas Noblet, Isaac Conwell and his wife Rutha Conwell, William Philips and Catharine Philips his wife, Aron L. Hindman and Sarah Hindman his wife conveyed to William Noblet, all of Bedford Co., TN, land that Robert Noblet died in possession and fell to us as heirs of Robert Noblet, land in Bedford Co., TN, on waters of Flat Creek. Borders John Noblet. 100 acres. Wit: Jordan C. Holt and Jacob Albright. Reg: 14 May 1834.

Page 435 - 1 Mar 1834. Hilery Mosely, Sr. of Charlotte Co., VA conveyed to Edward A. Mosely of Bedford Co., TN, his son, for love and affection for his son Edward A. Mosely and for $1.00, land in Bedford Co., TN, on waters of the Wartrace Fork. Recorded in Charlotte Co., VA on 7 Mar 1834.

Page 447 - 17 May 1833. William D. Orr, Sheriff of Bedford Co., TN conveyed to Erwin J. Frierson of Bedford Co., for $160.04. for case against Robert C. Thompson, John Cockrill and Mary Bell Thompson, heirs of Robert C. Thompson, deceased, land of 17 or 18 acres in Town of Shelbyville, on the Skull Camp Road. Borders James Brittain and by heirs of James Brittain, by heirs of Peter Chilcut, and lands on which Robert C. Thompson formerly resided when a citizen of Shelbyville. Wit: William D. Means and A. H. McKisick. Reg: 25 May 1834.

Page 452 - -- Nov 1833. William Bowden to Travis Bowden, both of Bedford Co., TN, conveyed land and plantation in Bedford Co., on north bank of Barren Fork. Borders Joseph Jameson. 160 acres. Wit: Frederick W. Bowden and Elmer Bowden. Reg: 25 May 1834.

Page 457 - 3 Nov 1828. The heirs of Abraham Shook, deceased, viz, James Long and Rebecca his wife, James Harmon and Lurena (Lucinda) his wife, all of Bedford Co., TN conveyed to Burges Hardin of Bedford Co., land in Bedford Co., on waters of the West Fork of Rock Creek. Borders Rambo's corner, William Caufield and Blair's corner. 200 acres. Signed by Elizabeth Miner, James Long, Rebecca Long, James Harmon, Lucinda Harmon, William Shook, Wade Griffin, Lucinda Griffin. Wit: Jabus Nowlin,

Light Nowlin, George W. Nowlin and Jonathan Bradford. Reg: 7 Jun 1834.

Page 459 - 30 Apr 1832. Benjamin Kimbro and his wife Ann to Allen Knight, all of Bedford Co., TN, land in Bedford Co., on Barren Fork, being No. 4 as laid off of the estate of Frederick Payne, deceased. Borders land of Frederick Payne. 13 acres. Wit: Frederick Shofner. Reg: 7 Jun 1834.

Page 462 - We the undersigned Attorneys appointed by A. C. McKee of Cabarrus Co., NC, for the purpose of directing and allotting to his four children, namely, James C. McKee, Caleb P. McKee, Mary Ann McKee and Margaret E. McKee, land in Bedford Co., TN. Dated 183-(blank). Signed by John N. Phifer, Robert McKinsey and Moses W. Moore. Plat on page 463. Reg: 8 Apr 1834.

Page 467 - 1 Nov 1833. James Ewing of Bedford Co., TN and W. D. Ewing of Maury Co., TN, Executors of the Last Will and Testament of James Ewing, deceased, conveyed to James V. Ewing of Bedford Co., land in Bedford and Maury Counties, TN, on west side of Rock Creek, it being a part of 643 acre tract conveyed to James Ewing, deceased, by Hezekiah Davis. Borders William McClure. 250 acres. Signed by James Ewing and William D. Ewing. Wit: William McClure and John McClure. Reg: 9 Jun 1834.

Page 478 - 18 Dec 1832. John Thompson of Bedford Co., TN and Joseph P. Thompson in Trust for Ann Gates wife of Allen Gates her natural lifetime and then for her children forever, wit, Julian, Margarite, Woodson, Clay, Spencer, Carrol, Harriet, for love and affection John Thompson has for his sister Ann Gates and her children, names Joseph P. Thompson her Trustee of land in Bedford Co., on Rock Creek whereon Gates now lives. 40 acres. Wit: P. H. Thompson and Ann C. Thompson. Reg: 10 Jun 1834.

Page 484 - 13 Apr 1834. William Willis conveyed to William S. Willis, for love for his nephew William Willis, a mare colt now in possession of his father and mother. William S. Willis being an infant son of Philip Willis. Wit: Benjamin Kimbro and John Bennett. Reg: 23 Jun 1834.

Page 494 - 1 May 1834. Mathew Cunningham, Sr. and Elizabeth Cunningham his wife, Jeremiah Cunningham, William Word and his wife Mary, Samuel Neely and his wife Elizabeth, Katharine Cunningham, Mathew Cunningham, Jr. and Jane Cunningham, sons and daughters of Mathew Cunningham, Sr., all of Bedford Co., TN sold to John Reed of Bedford Co., land in Bedford Co., on waters of Big Flat Creek. Borders John Reed, William Galbreath, Huff's line and Andrew Reed. 28 acres. Wit: Wilson C. Reed and Enoch Trott. Reg: 14 Jul 1834.

Page 497 - 11 Jul 1834. James Deery conveyed to Gerdentia Waite, Julia P. Waite, Elisheba Waite, Artimetia Waite, Francis P. Waite, Sarah P. Waite, Magdalen R. Waite, and Amanda M. Bradford, heirs of Robert Waite, deceased, all of Bedford Co., TN, land in Shelbyville, Bedford Co., being one half of five sixth of a Lot No. 55 and Lot No. 55 being the lot on which the Shelbyville Inn now stands, on the north side of the Public Square. Wit: George M. Lindsay and John R. Deery. Reg: 15 Jul 1834.

DEED BOOK "DD"

Page 499 - 11 Jun 1834. Hugh Houston and Benjamin R. Cheek, of Bedford Co., TN, Executors of the Last Will and Testament of Jeremiah Cheek, deceased, conveyed to Thomas D. Cheek of Bedford Co., land in Bedford Co., on West Fork of Rock Creek. Borders Philip Campbell. 180 acres. Wit: Levi Cockran, Samuel Omund, Wesley A. Piles and John F. Boyete. Reg: 15 Jul 1834.

Page 506 - 17 Dec 1832. We, Robert Patterson and Elia Patterson his wife sold to Sherwood Dunegan a negro girl Emaline. Wit: Joseph H. Brittain and Jefferson Rhea. Reg: 22 July 1834.

Page 506 - 7 Oct 1833. John Capley to James Aron, both of Bedford Co., TN. John Capley, his heirs and assigns forever, my interest in my wife's part of her father's estate John Capley, deceased, which is the eighth part of her father's estate, as her dower, land in Bedford Co., on north side of Duck River, adjoining lands of Crowels and the tract old Peter Crowel, the Shearin tract, Smith's tract. 114 acres, and also her interest and portion of a part of her father's interest in the Shearin tract held under the interest of Rutha Shearin in the Shearin tract, be the same on which Shearin's survey lies adjoining the above tract of land and I, the said Aron and my wife Cena sell unto John Capley land. Wit: Moses Aron and William H. Aron. Reg: 22 Jul 1834.

Page 513 - 29 Jul 1834. Harrison Word to William Word, both of Bedford Co., TN. William Word sold to Harrison Word land belonging to the heirs of Thomas Word, deceased, adjoining Elijah Lacy, Joshua Holt and John Hix and others in Bedford Co., on waters of Big Flat Creek. Wit: Thomas Dean and Edmond Word. Reg: 30 Jul 1834.

Page 515 - 9 Nov 1833. James McKisick and Polly McKisick his wife sold to Roger Snell, all of Bedford Co., TN, land in Bedford Co., on Sugar Creek. Borders Herrel Wiggins, Sugar Creek and Roger Snell's line. 137 acres. Reg: 2 Aug 1834.

Page 521 - 31 Dec 1833. Thomas J. and Martin M. Lane, Executors of Thomas Lane, deceased, sold to Lanson Harris, all of Bedford Co., TN, land in Bedford Co., on waters of Rich Creek. Borders Christian Harbour. 125 acres. Wit: John M. Lane and Robert Lane. Reg: 9 Aug 1834.

Page 531 - 9 Aug 1834. John M. Presgrove and Rachael Presgrove to Andrew Presgrove, all of Bedford Co., TN, land in Bedford Co., on North Fork. Borders North Fork. 40 acres. Wit: W. M. Presgrove and H. S. Wilson. Reg: 15 Aug 1834.

Page 544 - 21 Aug 1834. Hosea Mullins and his wife Peggy Mullins sold to Benjamin C. Brantly, all of Bedford Co., TN, land in Bedford Co., on Rock Creek. Borders on East Fork of Rock Creek. 100 acres. Reg: 22 Aug 1834.

Page 554 - 2 Jun 1834. William Osburn and his wife Nancy of Tipton Co., TN sold to John Orr of Bedford Co., TN, land in Bedford Co., on West Fork of Rock Creek, being one fifth part of a tract of land formerly owned by David Sanders, deceased, of Bedford Co. Reg: 1 Sep 1834.

Page 573 - 30 Jul 1833. John Robinson, Sr. to John Robinson, Jr., both of Bedford Co., TN, for love and affection for his

John Robinson, Jr., his son, 151 acres of land in Bedford Co., TN, on waters of Sugar Creek. Borders McKisick Fork of Sugar Creek, Evan's line and Dryden's corner. Wit: Benjamin Strickler and Jos. Rowland. Reg: 15 Sep 1834.

DEED BOOK "EE" 1834 - 1835

Page 13 - 4 Aug 1834. Jacob Anthony and wife Phebe conveyed to Abel Landers, all of Bedford Co., TN, land in Bedford and that part of land which Henry Landers, deceased, in possession of his deceased land of 12½ acres of the whole tract of the deceased's 125 acres. Borders lands of Abel Landers, John Landers and others and being on waters of Thompsons Creek. Henry and Phebe Landers are legatees of Henry Landers, deceased. Wit: J. Kimbro and John Eakin. Reg: 9 Oct 1834.

Page 14 - 25 Jul 1833. William Prince and Presly Prince from Robert C. Daniel, all of Bedford Co., TN, sold land of 50 acres in Bedford Co., on Thompsons Creek. Borders John Dean, Nathan Prince's land where he now lives, Parker's survey and R. C. Daniel. Wit: Elijah Parker and John Dean. Reg: 11 Oct 1834.

Page 15 - Michael Moore, Henry Moore, Samuel Moore, Charles R. Moore, and Benjamin R. Delk and Martha his wife formerly Martha Moore, heirs and legatees of Henry Moore, deceased, of Bedford Co., TN. Commissioners to divide the estate of Henry Moore, deceased, consisting of land and negroes and other property. Divided into nine lots. Charles R. Moore drew a negro boy Joseph, Henry Moore and Samuel Moore of Lincoln Co., TN, and Michael Moore, David R. Moore, Margarite Moore, Mary Moore, Elizabeth Moore, Benjamin R. Delk and Martha his wife, for $1.00. Wit: J. S. Brown and Jas. M. Ray. Reg: 11 Oct 1834.

Page 32 - 6 May 1834. William Moody of Bedford Co., TN sold to John W. Peacock of Perry Co., TN, land in Bedford Co., on Hurricane Creek, it being the place where William Moody did live and now occupied by his widow Coldwell and it being the land that the said Moody purchased of Benjamin F. McCuistion and Jane McCuistion his mother. 165 acres. Borders Jacob Morton, Benjamin McCuistion. Wit: C. D. Cannon and Thomas Holland. Reg: 23 Oct 1834.

Page 43 - We, Samuel Phillips and Gerdentia Waite, administrators of Robert Waite, deceased, sold to James J. Fowler, a negro girl Caroline, on 25 Sept 1834. Reg: 30 Oct 1834.

Page 49 - 8 Jan 1834. Brumfield Long to Thomas Long, both of Bedford Co., TN, for love and affection for Thomas Long, conveyed land in Bedford Co., on East Fork of Rock Creek, being the tract on which Thomas Long now lives. Borders Allen Gates and William Newsom. 25 acres. Wit: G. H. Allen and D. B. Crawford. Reg: 30 Oct 1834.

Page 62 - 1 May 1834. I, Washington D. Medearis for $20.00 sold to Joel Yowel, Elisha Bagly, A. G. Jones, H. Hollingsworth, Thomas Smithe, David Yancy and Gabriel Blackwell, all of Bedford Co., TN, except Joel Yowel, A. G. Jones and Elisha Bagly of Lincoln Co., TN, Trustees appointed by the Deciples of Christ in the vicinity of East Fork of Rock Creek, a Lot of land on the head of East Fork of Rock Creek, adjoining Medearis and

Elizabeth Blackwell, Francis Jordan and road leading from Gibson's Gap to Meek's Mill on Duck River. 2 acres. To build them a Meeting House or for them to meet and worship in and intertain such congregation as attend their meetings. Wit: Hugh Smiley and Gabriel Blackwell. Reg: 14 Nov 1834.

Page 66 - 12 Sept 1834. Phillip Burrow of Carroll Co., TN, by his agent Nimrod Burrow sold to David Low of Bedford Co., TN, land in Bedford Co., on Thompsons Creek. Borders Adam Euless, David Low, David Gilbert, and Whitesides' line. 40 acres. Wit: William Jenkins and Iredell Low. Reg: 10 Nov 1834.

Page 72 - 24 Nov 1834. I, William Blakely, Sr. of Bedford Co., TN, for love and affection for his son William Blakely, Jr. and his wife Elizabeth Blakely and their children, to wit, James T. Blakely, Mary E. Blakely, Isaac D. Blakely, Nancy M. Blakely, Elizabeth M. Blakely, William C. Blakely, Minerva J. Blakely, John W. Blakely, Louisa C. Blakely, and Newton M. Blakely. Should my son William and Elizabeth his wife should have any more children, they are to have equal share, granted personal property. Wit: Robert Clark and Polly M. W. Clark. Reg: 22 Nov 1834.

Page 82 - 13 Jul 1834. I, John Wallis of Henry Co., VA, for love and affection for Sarah Hanly of Bedford Co., TN, lent unto her during her natural life, a negro woman Sucky and after the death of Sarah Hanly, I give the negro woman to surviving children of Sarah Hanly. Wit: James A. Wallis and Jos. Shelton. Reg: 14 July 1834 in VA.

Page 83 - 6 Dec 1834. Jemima H. Hight of Bedford Co., TN, appointed my friend James Bruce, Sr. of Halifax Co., VA, to rent lands, hire negroes, sue for recover and receive monies coming to me. Also, I have confidence of my brother Melchizedick Brame of Bedford Co., TN and appoint him my Attorney to receive of James Bruce, Sr., any monies due me. Wit: W. B. M. Brame and Isreal Fonville. Reg: 8 Dec 1834.

Page 85 - 13 Feb 1828. Humphrey C. Furgerson and Harriett C. his wife of Bedford Co., TN sold to David Vance Davidson of Bedford Co., land in Bedford Co., on Barren Fork, being the one third part devised to Harriett C. Furgerson, is entitled as the widow of James Davidson, deceased, and which was awarded her by Bedford County Court in 1827, being a part of the land that James Davidson resided on at his death. Borders Hugh Davidson, Jr., Heirs of White, deceased. 300 acres. Reg: 10 Dec 1834.

Page 100 - 2 Aug 1831. Thomas Dean, administrator of estate of James Butler, deceased, and Nancy Butler and Esther Butler of Bedford CO., TN. Large amount of claims against the estate of James Butler, deceased. Thomas Dean ordered to pay off debts. Wit: Abner Gaither and Riley Yates. Reg: 20 Dec 1834.

Page 118 - 18 Oct 1834. Robert C. Jennings and Chancy Jennings his wife and James Dillon and Kitty Dillon his wife conveyed to Harrison Word, all of Wilson Co., TN, their interest in a parcel of land belonging to the heirs of Thomas Word, deceased, and adjoining lands of Elijah Lacy, Joshua Holt, Sr. and John Hix and others, land in Bedford Co., on waters of Big Flat Creek. Wit: James C. Word, John Word, William A. Jennings and Jas.

Davidson. Reg: 29 Dec 1834.

Page 122 - 27 Dec 1834. William R. Martin and Eliza G. Martin his wife formerly Eliza G. Brown to Thomas B. Jeffreys and Alexander B. Moon, all of Bedford Co., TN. That whereas Ermina Brown widow of John Brown and mother of Eliza G., departed this life on the 23 day of August 1834 in Bedford County, passed a negro man Abram and a negro woman Phebe and other valuable property, also, Eliza G. and six other children, in all seven children, all heirs of Ermina Brown. William R. and Eliza G. sold to Thomas B. Jeffreys and Alexander B. Moon in the estate of Ermina Brown and also estate of Edmond Wilson her (Ermina) father. Reg: 30 Dec 1834.

Page 126 - 5 Jan 1835. James Morrison sold to James Deery, both of Bedford Co., TN. James Morrison is indebted to James Deery by note, one note given by James Morrison and his son James H. Morrison, due in 1834. Reg: 5 Jan 1835.

Page 128 - 3 Nov 1834. Robert Dysart one part and Dysart of the said Robert Dysart of other part, for love and affection for Robert Dysart, conveyed to him a tract of land in Bedford Co., TN, on East Fork of Rock Creek. Borders East Fork of Rock Creek, R. C. Dysart, Robert Dysart and Rock Creek. 205 acres. Wit: William Williams and Lile A. Ewing. Reg: 10 Jan 1835.

Page 143 - 28 Jan 1834. Robert McFarlin, Robert Baker and Mary Pratt and Henry Pratt, devises of William Pratt, deceased, of Bedford Co., TN, sold to John Hastings of Bedford Co., land in Bedford Co. 132 acres, being a part of a tract (703 acres) that Robert McFarlin, William Pratt and Robert Baker purchased of Frederick A. Ross, lying on the waters of Big Flat Creek. Wit: J. Cunningham and James Deery. Reg: 14 Jan 1835.

Page 145 - 14 Dec 1833. I, Joseph D. Dickson of Madison Co., TN, for love and affection for my nephew George T. M. Holt, granted personal property. The property is to remain in the hands of George T. M. Holt's father A. M. Holt until George arrives at the age of twenty one. Wit: Daniel C. Rodgers. Reg: 15 Jan 1835.

Page 146 - 3 Nov 1834. Robert Dysart to James P. Dysart, for natural love and affection for his son James P. Dysart, conveyed land in Bedford Co., TN, on Mud Creek. Borders Alexander Dysart and Phillips & Campbell's old line. 115 acres. Wit: William Williams, Jr. and Lile A. Ewing. Reg: 16 Jan 1835.

Page 148 - 17 June 1834. Unionville was then called Union Campground.

Page 149 - 3 Nov 1834. Robert Dysart to Robert C. Dysart his son, for love and affection for Robert C. Dysart, conveyed to him land in Bedford Co., TN, on East Fork of Rock Creek. Borders East Fork of Rock Creek. 113 acres. Wit: Lile A. Ewing and William Williams, Jr. Reg: 16 Jan 1835.

Page 150 - 3 Nov 1834. Robert Dysart to Alexander Dysart his son, for love and affection for his son Alexander Dysart, conveyed unto him land in Bedford Co., TN, on East Fork of Rock Creek. Borders Phillips & Campbell's land now the land of the heirs of Benjamin Logan. 118 acres. Wit: Lile A. Ewing and William

Williams, Jr. Reg: 16 Jan 1835.

Page 151 - 14 Jan 1835. Nicholas Newton and Sarah J. Newton his wife to James W. Patton, all of Bedford Co., TN, land in Bedford Co., on Big Flat Creek, it being that part of 50 acres that John Hix died and seized and possessed of which Nicholas Newton and his wife is heir of John Hix, is entitled, a fifth part. Borders Patton & Nichols. 50 acres. Wit: John Hale and W. Gay. Reg: 17 Jan 1835.

Page 153 - 18 Dec 1827. Elizabeth Cummins and Jane Cummins heirs of John Cummins, deceased, and Elanor Cummins widow of John Cummins, deceased, all of Bedford Co., TN, sold to Abner Houston of Bedford Co., land in Bedford Co., on waters of Rock Creek. 88½ acres. Wit: Hugh Houston and Henry Thompson. Reg: 17 Jan 1835.

Page 154 - 18 Dec 1827. Robert Hunter and Rebecca Hunter his wife to Abner Houston, all of Bedford Co., TN, land on West Fork of Rock Creek, it being the undivided share of Robert Hunter and Rebecca Hunter, as heirs of John Cummins, deceased. Borders Phillips & Campbell. 88½ acres. Wit: Hugh Houston and Henry Thompson. Reg: 19 Jan 1835.

Page 162 - 28 Oct 1834. Isaac and Maria Bullock to Leonard Bullock, all of Bedford Co., TN, land in Granville Co., NC, adjoining lands of Richard Bullock and James Downey and others, it being the same given them by Jeremiah Bullock, deceased, of Granville, Co., NC. Wit: Samuel Redford and S. Murdick. Reg: 21 Jan 1835.

Page 174 - 31 July 1834. Allen Leeper of Bedford Co., TN one part and Members of the United Baptist Church who as may or shall assemble together as a church in order to worship, for good will for the church and people, granted and conveyed to them land and being in Bedford Co., TN, on waters of West Rock Creek. 1 acre. Wit: James Reed and Catran S. Reed. Reg: 24 Jan 1835.

Page 185 - 2 Sep 1834. John Reed and his wife Esther Reed to Nathaniel Dryden, all of Bedford Co., TN, land on Rock Creek. Borders John Orr, East Fork of Rock Creek, John Russel and Eakins line and Columbia Road. 100 acres. Wit: R. M. Dryden and J. W. Walker. Reg: 28 Jan 1835.

Page 193 - 23 Jan 1835. Jane Wilson to Samuel Vest, both of Bedford Co., TN, land by Last Will and Testament of Jane Wilson's husband, James Wilson, deceased, bequeathed to her, his home and included 100 acres and other effects that she may desire to keep except that is given to his children by his Will and she to apply to herself and her nine children until they come of age. Jane Wilson appointed Samuel Vest her trustee. Wit: John Thompson and Samuel Wilson. Reg: 30 Jan 1835.

Page 194 - 14 Apr 1834. Acy Tilman of Bedford Co., TN one part and the members of the United Baptist Church, to assemble together as a church to worship God, for good will for said church and people, granted a parcel of land in Bedford Co., on waters of West Rock Creek. 1 acre. Wit: Benjamin Bingaman and H. J. Gilmore. Reg: 31 Jan 1835.

Page 196 - 20 Oct 1834. We, Samuel Stewart and Peggy (Margaret) Stewart sold all right in land in Orange Co., NC, on waters of Big (blank), being our interest in Mary Dixon dowry land in the tract whereon Robert Dixon, deceased, sold said land to James Dixon. Wit: William Dixon and James McKisick. Reg: 31 Jan 1835.

Page 198 - 20 Oct 1834. Samuel Stewart of Carroll Co., TN to Mary Dixon alias Mary Freeman of Bedford Co., TN, land in Bedford Co., on waters of Big Flat Creek. Borders Francis McKamey, Wiggins' line, William Dixon and Phillips' land. 200 acres. Wit: Jonathan Briant and Jacob Greer and James N. Patton. Reg: 31 Jan 1835.

Page 201 - 26 Jul 1824. John Lock of Cabarrus Co., NC to Mary Chunn wife of William Chunn, David C. Lock and Margarett Lock of Rowan Co., NC, granted unto them one fourth part of a tract of land in Bedford Co., TN, originally the property of Mathew Lock, deceased. Borders in the Gap of the Cedar Nobb and Joseph Dickenson. 408 acres. Wit: James McCullock and John McCullock. Reg: 3 Feb 1835.

Page 201 - 19 Feb 1834. Salisbury, Rowan Co., NC. We, William Chunn and Mary his wife and David C. Lock of Rowan Co., NC appointed William H. Trent of Rowan Co., NC, his Attorney, to make sell our interest in a tract of land in Bedford Co., TN, of 480 (acres). Reg: 3 Feb 1835.

Page 208 - 1 Apr 1834. Sarah Crews, late wife of George Crews, deceased, of Bedford Co., TN to Uriah Cross of Bedford Co., land in Bedford Co., on north side of Duck River on Hamilton Creek, the tract of land that George Crews, deceased, owned at his death and containing 28 acres. Now Sarah Crews sold all her right to the one third of the above described land. Borders William Horsley. Wit: K. L. Anderson and Jo. Thompson. Reg: 5 Feb 1835.

Page 209 - 26 Jun 1833. Isaac Rainey, Sr. and George R. Rainey, both of Bedford Co., TN conveyed to Barzellia T. Rainey of Bedford Co., land in Bedford CO., on north side of Duck River, it being a part of a tract conveyed to Isaac Rainey, Sr. by James C. O'Kelly and Samuel Craig. Borders Polly Mills and John Beck. 300 acres. Wit: J. N. Rainey and Abraham T. Lillard. Reg: 6 Feb 1835.

Page 213 - 24 Dec 1834. John T. Cooper, Executor of R. Cooper, deceased, of Rutherford Co., TN to Edward Whitman of Bedford Co., TN, land in Bedford Co., on Falling Creek, the land conveyed by R. Cooper, deceased, to Joshua Springer and by the said Springer to said Whitman. Borders Cooper's line, Martin Phifer's line, and bank of Falling Creek. 200 acres. Wit: Josiah Springer. Reg: 16 Feb 1835.

Page 214 - 14 Feb 1835. Stephen Keneday and his wife Polly Keneday to John Limmons, all of Bedford Co., TN, land in Bedford Co., 300 acres and it being the land on which Edward Teal, father of Polly, resided at the time of his death and purchased by E. Teal from James Hively and adjoins the lands of John Limmons, William Farrow and others. Wit: William S. Baskette and W. Guy. Reg: 18 Feb 1835.

DEED BOOK "EE"

Page 216 - 9 Aug 1834. Margarett Furgerson, H. W. Furgerson, John Furgerson and James C. Furgerson to William D. Finch, all of Bedford Co., TN, land in Bedford Co., on waters of Garrison Fork, it being the place on which Margarett Furgerson now lives. Containing 50 acres. Borders William D. Finch, Richard Muse, Isaac Muse, John Bradford and Mary Suggs. It being the land purchased by John Furgerson, deceased, of James Robertson. Margarett Furgerson wife of the said John Furgerson, deceased. John Furgerson, deceased, willed said land to Margarett by Deed of Gift and one from John H. Kaign. Wit: J. E. Scruggs and G. G. Osborne. Reg: 20 Feb 1835.

Page 219 - 24 May 1828. James MacMahon, administrator of his father William MacMahon, deceased, sold to John T. Cook, all of Bedford Co., TN, land of 6 acres, located on western branch of the Garrison Fork. Borders land whereon Cook now lives, and Matt Martin. Wit: W. Moseley, James Mason and Enoch T----(?) Reg: 23 Feb 1835.

Page 220 - 23 Feb 1835. Thomas C. Neely and Mary Neely his wife sold to Fanning Jones, all of Bedford Co., TN, land of 100 acres decreed by William Hamilton in his Last Will and Testament to Mary Neely formerly Mary Hamilton, Barbary Hamilton and Nancy Hamilton, daughters and children of Middleton who as heir, a son of William Hamilton, land on north side of Duck River in Bedford Co., TN. Borders Fanning Jones, Duck River, and George May. 100 acres. The above land conveyed to the children of Middleton Hamilton. Reg: 24 Feb 1835.

Page 221 - 15 Dec 1828. Thomas A. Peacock to Edward Ragsdale, both of Bedford Co., TN, land in Bedford Co., on waters of the Wartrace Fork and known in the plan of the real estate of John Peacock, Sr., deceased, by No. 14. Borders lands of John Peacock, Sr., deceased. 15½ acres. Reg: 24 Feb 1835.

Page 226 - 27 Jan 1835. Matt Martin, Sr. to Henry C. Martin, both of Bedford Co., TN, for love and affection for his son Henry C. Martin, conveyed land in Bedford Co., on waters of the Garrison Fork. Borders John S. Nall. 342 acres. Wit: Matt Martin, Jr., F. Hughey and S. Neill. Reg: 26 Feb 1835.

Page 233 - 5 Dec 1834. I, Barkley Martin of Muscogee Co., GA, for love and affection for Elizabeth Martin, widow of Ambroc Martin, deceased, and for $5.00, conveyed to Elizabeth Martin all my interest as one of the distributees in the personal estate of Abram Martin, deceased. Wit: Henry C. Martin and Matt Martin, Jr. Reg: 2 Mar 1835.

Page 243 - 12 Nov 1834. I, Rachael Martin, for regard I have for Martha Ann Thomas Ragsdale and Joshua Perry Ragsdale, children of John T. and Frances Ragsdale and for $1.00, give unto them a horse, mare and colts. Wit: A. Martin and J. L. Neill. Reg: 5 Mar 1835.

Page 247 - Bedford County Court issued a writ to the Sheriff of Bedford Co., TN to make known to the heirs of Joseph Hastings, deceased, to wit, Frances Marian Hastings, Sopha Caroline Hastings, John Hayman Hastings, Delphe Ann Hastings, William Smart Hastings, and Margarett Fanny Hastings, minor heirs of Joseph Hastings, deceased, to appear in next Court of Pleas and Quarter Sessions to show cause why the estate of Joseph Hastings, dec'd, has not been sold to satisfy debts. About 94 acres on head of Butlers Creek. Reg: 11 Mar 1835.

Page 248 - 5 Jan 1835. I, Jacob Nichols one part, for personal property of his deceased father, belonging to him, sold to me by Catharine Nichols of Bedford Co., TN, my sister, for the upkeep and support during her natural life. Wit: William Wallace and William Hall. Reg: 13 Mar 1835.

Page 265 - 3 Apr 1835. John Scott, by Deed of Gift, registered in Bedford Co., TN, give to Mary S. Yell, daughter of undersigned by first wife Mary Yell, daughter of John Scott, negroes. The undersigned being about to remove from State of Tennessee to the Territory of Arkansas with his family, except the said Mary S. Yell, his oldest daughter and being desirous of taking with them two of the negroes given to Mary S. Yell as aforesaid by her grandfather John Scott. The undersigned Archibald Yell. He will deliver said slave to Mary S. Yell when she reaches age of 21 years. Wit: James McKisick and E. J. Frierson. Reg: 3 Apr 1835.

Page 272 - 5 Jan 1833. We, Joseph Greer and Caroline Greer his wife of Bedford Co., TN, sold to Thomas Greer, Sr. of Bedford Co., negroes. Wit: George W. Greer and John A. King. Reg: 8 Apr 1835.

Page 273 - 8 Apr 1835. Negroes by the Last Will and Testament of Elizabeth Williams of Caswell Co., NC, bequeathed to the children of Duke Williams of whom my wife is one, which said legacy has not been received from the Executor of said Elizabeth and I for my wife to receive the property due her. For $1.00 to me paid by Christopher Williams sold to Christopher Williams all my right title in negroes. Signed by Robert P. Harrison on 8 Apr 1835. Reg: 10 Apr 1835.

Page 275 - 10 Nov 1834. Agreement between Peggy Stewart widow of William Stewart, deceased, one part and Samuel Stewart of second part and Jesse Guerly and his wife Jemima of the third part and Demarious D. Hicks and Malinda his wife of the fourth part, James C. Gambill and Martha his wife of the fifth part, William Stewart, Jr., of the sixth part, John Hicks and Nelly his wife of the seventh part, Jordan C. Holt who binds himself for John Stewart, a minor son of William Stewart, Sr., of the eighth part, Moses Smiley and Lucinda his wife of the nineth part, Joshua Holt who binds himself for Joshua Stewart and William H. Stewart, minor children of Joshua Stewart, deceased, who was a son of William Stewart, deceased, of tenth part, and John Barrett who binds himself for Benton Barrett and Lucinda Barrett, minor children of Rachael Barrett, deceased, who was a daughter of William Stewart, Sr. of the eleventh part, by the Last Will and Testament of William Stewart, deceased, equal share of his estate. Reg: 12 Nov 1835.

Page 282 - 27 Jan 1829. I, Richard Cunningham, for love and affection for my son James T. Cunningham, bequeath unto him all the land whereon I now live, about 200 acres in Bedford Co., TN. Borders mouth of Alexander Creek, William Waite, Road leading from Davis' Mill to Shelbyville, Norvells land and center of the Wartrace Fork. Wit: Jas. Arnold and R. Waite. Reg: 5 May 1835.

DEED BOOK "EE"

Page 290 - I, George E. Low of Tipton Co., TN, for love and affection for my brothers children, the heirs of my brother William Low, deceased, the third part of land where the widow Low, my mother Martha, now lives and being in Bedford Co., TN, on waters of Rock Creek, of 300 acres. Wit: Isaac B. Low, M. W. Oakley and William W. Barksdale. Reg: 19 May 1835.

Page 293 - 5 Feb 1835. William Chunn and Mary his wife and David C. Locke of Rowan Co., NC and William H. Trent and Margarett his wife of Bedford Co., TN sold to Samuel Anderson of Rutherford Co., TN, 480 acres in Bedford Co., TN. Borders William Guy's field, west of the Turnpike Road, Guy's Knobb, Joseph Dickerson and Lock's heirs land. The land being a part allotted to Matthew Locke. Wit: James C. McRee and H. Means. Reg: 2 Jun 1835.

Page 327 - 3 Aug 1835. John S. Booth, Abel W. Booth and Josiah Eley in right of his wife Martha, those of the heirs and legatees of William T. Booth, deceased, sole heir of John Booth, deceased, all of Bedford Co., TN, except Abel W. Booth of Wilson Co., TN conveyed to Jeremiah B. Booth of Wilson Co., TN, land in Bedford Co., on waters of Alexander Creek, a west branch of the North Fork, it being a part of a grant issued to Ebenezer Alexander. Borders Joseph Wallis. 70 acres, it being an undivided tract of land between the heirs of William T. Boothe, deceased, and sole heir of John Boothe, deceased, there being five in number of heirs. Wit: John F. Thompson and John Thompson. Reg: 4 Aug 1835.

Page 334 - 26 Mar 1835. William Damron, Polly Damron and Sally Damron sold to C. D. Steele as Trustee for Claiborne Logan, all of Bedford Co., TN. They are indebted to Logan, deliver personal property. Wit: Thomas G. Watkins and James R. Clark. Reg: 10 Aug 1835.

Page 337 - 11 Oct 1834. The heirs of Shadrick Forrest, deceased, sold to John H. Wilson, all of Bedford Co., TN, land that the said Shadrick Forrest willed to his wife Jane Forrest during her natural life. Borders Elisha Forrest, McLean's corner and Columbia Road leading from Columbia to Murfreesboro. 240 acres. Wit: Lawson H. Rickman and Elisha Forrest. Reg: 11 Aug 1835.

Page 339 - 27 Oct 1834. Martin Shofner to Eve Holt, his daughter, both of Bedford Co., TN, for love and affection for his daughter Eve Holt, gives land in Bedford Co., on waters of Thompson Creek. Borders school land. 70 acres. Wit: William Jenkins and Jno. Dean. Reg: 11 Aug 1835.

Page 340 - 1 Nov 1828. William Frizzell and Nathan Frizell to Hiram Harris, all of Bedford Co., TN, land in Bedford Co., adjoining the lands of Worke, Springer, Volney Steele and Peter Rushing. 104 acres. Wit: William Carter and P. C. Steele. Reg: 12 Aug 1835.

Page 345 - 13 Aug 1834. Gray J. Jones to Robert McCrory, both of Bedford Co., TN, sold all undivided interest as heir at law of Robert and Sarah B. Jones, land in Bedford Co., TN, on waters of West Rock Creek. Borders near bank of West Rock Creek. 50 acres. Gray J. Jones is heir of Robert and Sarah B. Jones. Wit: John W. Houston, Henry Thompson and Samuel Davis. Reg: 13 Aug 1835.

Page 359 - 28 Jan 1835. Robert Patterson and Celia Patterson sold to Jepthah Ezell, all of Bedford Co., TN, land on Caney Spring Creek, being a part of Shadrack Forrest, deceased, land. 131 acres. Wit: J. T. Furgerson and J. H. Holt. Reg: 18 Aug 1835.

Page 371 - 9 Jul 1835. Thomas O. Hunter of Bedford Co., TN, and as agent and Attorney for James Frelin and Emilt Jane Frelin his wife of North Carolina sold to Charles Hooper, land in Bedford Co., TN, on waters of Rich Creek and adjoins lands of Thomas O. Hunter and others. Borders Thomas O. Hunter, near bank of Rich Creek and Theophilus Hunter. 400 acres. Wit: John M. Lane and Matt Martin. Reg: 21 Aug 1835.

Page 373 - North Carolina Grant to David Vance, No. 88. 10 lbs per 100 acres. Land of 100 acres on south side of Duck River and on both sides of Rock Creek. Borders Tignall Jones. Plat on page 373. Surveyed 12 Mar 178<u>5</u>(?). Reg: 29 May 1807.

Page 374 - 22 Oct 1834. I, David Vance of Buncomb Co., NC appoint William Orr of Bedford Co., TN my Attorney, to oversee my property in Bedford Co. Reg: 21 Aug 1835.

Page 375 - 16 Oct 1834. William C. Shapherd of Williamson Co., TN sold to Darrington Garrett of Bedford Co., TN, land in Bedford Co. Borders Benjamin Smith whereon he now lives. 129 acres. Wit: W. Nunn and James Garrett. Reg: 22 Aug 1835.

Page 376 - 9 Oct 1834. Isham Oneal sold to Benjamin Logan, deceased, both of Bedford Co., TN. To wit, Daniel M. Logan and John <u>O</u>.(?) Logan and Tarleton J. Logan and Francis Marion Logan and Morgan Logan and Benjamin T. Logan, land in Bedford Co., on waters of Rock Creek. 46 acres. Wit: Andrew Dysart and Moses Oneal. Reg: 25 Aug 1835.

Page 378 - 5 Dec 1833. I, Edward Hord of Bedford Co., TN, for good will and affection for my daughter Permelia Slaten, a negro girl Nancy, or to my daughter Martha, a boy Leonard and a horse and saddle and other items and 44 acres on Noahs Fork formerly owned by her deceased husband Abel Slaten and sold for his debts and now owned by me. Wit: E. Hord, Jr. and A. Erwin, Sr. Reg: 28 Aug 1835.

Page 379 - 28 Mar 1835. I, Pleasant Puckett sold to William Harrison, both of Bedford Co., TN, all rights, claim &c to the estate of Arthur Puckett, deceased. Wit: H. G. Lane and John H. Harrison. Reg: 7 Sep 1835.

Page 379 - 31 Aug 1835. John Robinson, Sr. to Joseph Robinson his son, all of Bedford Co., TN, for love and affection for his son Joseph, conveyed unto him land in Bedford Co. Borders James Robinson, Martin <u>Fiffer</u>(Phifer) and J. C. Coldwell. 250 acres. Wit: James Gregory and Thomas S. Patton. Reg: 1 Sep 1835.

Page 396 - 6 Dec 1834. Thomas J. and Milton M. Lane, Executors of Thomas Lane, deceased, of Giles Co., TN sold to Joseph Click of Giles Co., land in Bedford Co., TN, on waters of Duck River. Borders Christian Harbin. 100 acres. Wit: John M. Lane and Robert Lane. Reg: 11 Sep 1835.

DEED BOOK "EE"

Page 406 - 30 Sep 1835. Daniel K. Hime to Mary Ann Hime, both of Bedford Co., TN, land in Bedford Co., on waters of Big Flat Creek. Borders the dower tract. Including the Rocky Spring. About 30 acres. Land of the widow and heirs of John Hime, deceased. Reg: 30 Sep 1835.

Page 409 - 1 Jul 1835. Henry Harber and of the heirs of Jacob Harber, late of Bedford Co., TN to George A. Harber of Bedford Co., land in Bedford Co., on Rich Creek and known as ,ot No. 1 and also his part of his mother's dowry known by Lot No. 1. Wit: Jeremiah Hay and John Penn. Reg: 3 Oct 1835.

Page 410 - 16 Feb 1835. Malcolm Gilchrist of Lawrance Co., Alabama sold to Bennett Word of Bedford Co., TN, land in Bedford Co. Borders land of Word, William T. Neil where he now lives. 100 acres. Wit: S. Word and C. Word. Reg: 6 Oct 1835.

Page 413 - 31 Jul 1835. I, Mary C. Marshall of Wilkerson Co., Mississippi, for natural love for Elizabeth Martin, widow of Abram Martin, deceased, and for $1.00, conveyed all interests &c in personal estate of Abram Martin, deceased. Wit: Henry C. Martin and William Galleghy. Reg: 6 Oct 1835.

Page 417 - 4 Nov 1834. Rebecca Sims to Mary E. Sims, for love and affection for Mary E. Sims, has given unto her land purchased by Rebecca Sims by a Court Order at Nashville on 27 Sept last, 400 acres about one mile above the Fishing Ford of Duck River in Bedford Co., TN, also a tract of 150 acres below the Fishing Ford of Bedford Co. of which is a grist mill and two tracts, one of about 250 acres and other about 213 acres. Also 160 acres and one of 150 acres and a grist mill above Shelbyville. Wit: Elizabeth Scudder and Ridgeway Davis. Reg: 10 Oct 1835.

Page 420 - 3 Feb 1835. James Erwin of Fayette Co., KY by his Attorney Andrew Erwin, Jr. of Nashville, TN sold to Thomas Drake of Bedford Co., land in Bedford Co. on headwaters of Knob and Straight Creek, branches of Garrison Fork. Borders John Strand and Jno. McDaniel. 96 acres. Reg: 12 Oct 1835.

Page 422 - 11 Oct 1835. Thomas Drake, Jr. to Elizabeth Thogmorton, both of Bedford Co., TN, for love and affection towards his sister Elizabeth Thogmorton, sold land in Bedford Co., on waters of Knob and Straight Creek, being the same land on which Thomas Drake, Sr. resided at the time of his death. Reg: 12 Oct 1835.

Page 429 - I, Elizabeth Jones of Bedford Co., TN, for love and affection for my granddaughter E. L. Robinett and because of my advanced age and helpless condition, conveyed all and singular my goods and chattels. Wit: James Walker and Patton M. Walker. Reg: 21 Oct 1835.

Page 430 - 20 Oct 1835. Joseph Robinson, as Executor of Robert J. Robinson sold to John C. Coldwell of Bedford Co., TN, notes and land in Bedford Co. Borders Michael Robinson, Joseph Green, Martin Phifer's corner, Columbia Road and Stevens corner. 150 acres. Wit: James H. Graham and William F. Long. Reg: 22 Oct 1835.

Page 431 - 16 Oct 1835. William Damron, Polly Damron, Sally Damron and Samuel Woodfin to James Hart as Trustee for Joseph Steele, all of Bedford Co., TN, indebted to Joseph Steele, personal property &c. Wit: Volney H. Steele and Stephen Hart. Reg: 23 Oct 1835.

Page 432 - 28 Apr 1835. Johnathan Webster, Sr. and Joel H. Webster, both of Bedford Co., TN to John G. Walker of Bedford Co. Jonathan Webster, Moses Hart and Joel H. Webster sold land including the place whereon Joel H. Webster now lives, to John G. Walker. Land in Bedford Co., on waters of Burnum branch of Nalls Creek. Borders lands of Patsy Baker, now Patsy Burnum. 8 acres. Wit: Moses M. Coss(?) and G. Green. Plat on page 433 & 434. Reg: 26 Oct 1835.

Page 441 - 13 Jul 1832. I, John Scott of Bedford Co., TN, for love and affection for my wife Sarah Scott and for her support, granted and conveyed a mullatto boy child Humphrey Clinker. Wit: Josh P. Scott and Robert J. Scott. Reg: 28 Oct 1835.

Page 441 - 16 Oct 1835. Sarah Polk, Executrix of the Last Will and Testament of William Polk of Wake Co., NC sold to William London of Bedford Co., TN, land in Bedford Co. Borders Record's corner, Andrew McCrory's line and Beavin's line. 640 acres. Reg: 29 Oct 1835.

Page 443 - 19 Oct 1835. Joseph McKisick and his wife Jane B. McKisick sold to Roger Snell, all of Bedford Co., TN, land in Bedford Co. Borders Robinson's line, Nathan Evans' line Richard Williamson's line and Roger Snell's line. 128 acres. Reg: 31 Oct 1835.

Page 445 - 15 Jan 1833. James Brittain now deceased and Samuel Doak executed to Hiram Holt and Thomas Newsom, a certain bond, land in Bedford Co., TN, on waters of Big Flat Creek, adjoining the lands of William Heaslet and others, the same being the lands purchased by James Brittain and Samuel Doak at the sale of Nathaniel Hubbard, deceased, known as the Tanyard tract. 20 acres. Reg: (no date).

Page 445 - 12 Aug 1835. William F. Long, Executor of the Last Will and Testament of James Brittain, deceased, and Samuel Doak sold to Hiram Holt, land in Bedford Co., TN, on waters of Flat Creek. Borders William Heaslet and Hubbard's line. 19 acres. Wit: James H. Graham and H. F. Holt. Reg: 5 Nov 1835.

Page 446 - 12 Feb 1835. William Allison to James P. Allison his son, for goodwill and affection for his son James P. Allison, conveyed land that William Allison purchased of the heirs of Robert Allison, deceased. 679 acres. Borders John Wilson, west bank of Clems Creek, Thomas Allison, land whereon Robert Allison, deceased, lived, Kimbrough Allison, William Ogilvie and William Shaw. Wit: Jos. H. Lile and W. Lile. Reg: 6 Nov 1835.

Page 448 - 16 Jan 1819. William Gregg of Colwell Co., KY to Hugh Caruthers of Giles Co., TN, 400 acres of land in Bedford Co., TN, on south side of Duck River and it being part of 2000 acre granted to Alexander Robinson. Borders Wilson's line, Runnel's line and Wilson Craig. Wit: Robert A. Caruthers and John Goodrum. Reg: 6 Nov 1835.

DEED BOOK "FF" 1835 - 1837

Page 3 - 26 Jul 1834. Jason Wilson and Lucinda Wilson his wife of Hardeman Co., TN to Fanning Jones of Bedford Co., TN, land in Bedford Co., on Duck River. 200 acres. Borders on Columbia Road, Billington's corner and Theophilus Hamilton. Wit: Jno. H. Bills. Reg: 12 Nov 1835.

Page 4 - 30 Apr 1835. James Morgan, Mary Morgan and Amanda Morgan to Alsey Arnold, all of Bedford Co., TN. Morgan is indebted to Darling D. Arnold for $34.50. Wit: J. D. Dial and Mary Arnold. Reg: 9 Nov 1835.

Page 5 - 3 Nov 1835. James Erwin of Fayette Co., KY by his Attorney Andrew Erwin, Jr. of Nashville sold to James Frizzle of Bedford Co., TN, land in Bedford Co., on waters of the Wartrace Fork. Borders lands of William Norvell, Abraham Finley, Absalom Manley and Baxter Ragsdale, where he and also William Norvell formerly lived. 95 acres. Reg: 12 Nov 1835.

Page 13 - 18 Sep 1835. George Arnhart to Benjamin Arnhart his son, both of Bedford Co., TN, for love and affection for his son, conveyed land in Bedford Co., on south west branch of Duck River. Borders Culp's line, bank of Duck River, Dyer's line, Daniel Arnhart's line, and Mr. Freeman's line. 226 acres. Wit: Hartwell Freeman and Jacob Lantz(Lentz). Reg: 20 Nov 1835.

Page 16 - 15 Nov 1835. Rebecca Sims vs Walter P. Sims & al Franklin, TN. To sell mortgaged property, (1) Land in Giles Co., TN, (2) Land in Bedford Co., TN of 200 acres, (3) 150 acres in Bedford Co., on north side of Duck River, and others. Thomas A. Gordon purchaser of Giles Co., TN, Walter B. Sims, John G. Sims, Ann Sims and Boyd McNairy Sims, children and heirs of John G. Sims, deceased. Reg: 25 Nov 1835.

Page 18 - 12 Mar 1819. John G. Sims to Walter Sims. John G. Sims of Bedford Co., TN and Walter Sims of Davidson Co., TN, sold land in Bedford Co., on south side of Duck River above the Town of Shelbyville. Borders Duck river. 5 acres. Wit: Jno. A. Marrs and E. S. Tunstall. Reg: 25 Nov 1835.

Page 19 - 6 Sep 1817. John G. Sims of Davidson Co., TN to Walter Sims of Philadelphia, PA, land on north side of Duck River in Bedford Co., TN, it being a tract of land of 2448 acres granted to John Sims by Walter and dated -- day Sept 1817. Beginning at a branch on the north side of Duck River, being the first branch that empties into Duck river below the Mill Dam belonging to Walter and John, above the Town of Shelbyville. 350 acres. Reg: 25 Nov 1835.

Page 22 - 2 Nov 1835. Nicholas Anthony of Bedford Co., TN to Edward Trabue and Charles Trabue of Davidson Co., TN, land in Bedford Co., one of the tracts described as being on Barren Fork of Duck River. Borders junction of Barren Fork and Garrison Fork, Charles Lucas, a mill, and south edge of the race to mouth of race. 70 acres. Another tract of 5 acres in Bedford Co., on Barren Fork. Beginning in middle of a spring on the west edge of the first branch emptying into the Barren Fork below Bernards Old Factory. Wit: Thomas C. Whiteside. Reg: 2 Dec 1835.

Page 23 - 28 Apr 1835. We, Elijah Rushing, Elizabeth Rushing, Jeremiah Rushing, and Elvira Deason, heirs of John Rushing, deceased, all of age, that our mother is a widow and that she has several small children to raise and support and that the estate is small, we jointly agree that she, our mother, have the remainder of the estate after paying our father's just debts. Wit: Jesse Deason, William Burrow and Elijah Rushing. Reg: 3 Dec 1835.

Page 30 - 23 Nov 1811. Sarah Clifft of Bedford Co., TN sold to John Hall of Bedford Co., land in Bedford Co., on waters of Sugar Creek. 110 acres, including the plantation whereon Sarah Clifft now resides. Wit: Thomas Morrison. Reg: 5 Dec 1835.

Page 34 - 2 Jan 1833. John Odom of Madison Co., MO sold to Elias Stilwell of Bedford Co., TN, land in Bedford Co., on east side of West Rock Creek. Borders east bank of Rock Creek and Peter Woods. 50 acres. Wit: John Osborn and John Devin. Reg: 11 Dec 1835.

Page 35 - 5 Dec 1835. George Clark of Williamson Co., TN sold to Allen Thornbrough of Bedford Co., TN, land in Bedford Co., on headwaters of Wilson Creek. Borders Widow Bailey, old road leading to Shelbyville, Elmore's land, and Kelly's land. 50 acres. Wit: James Carson and William J. Marshall. Reg: 12 Dec 1835.

Page 36 - 10 Mar 1835. William Chunn and Mary his wife of Rowan Co., NC sold to Samuel Anderson of Rutherford Co., TN, land in Bedford Co., TN. Borders Francis Locke one of the (5) sons of Matthew Locke, deceased, and Joseph Duke. Mary Chunn being entitled to one third of 480 (acres) as one of the children of Matthew Locke, deceased. Reg: 12 Dec 1835.

Page 37 - 12 Dce 1835. Theophilus Falls, Trustee of A. J. Worke of Iredell Co., NC to William T. Ball of Rutherford Co., TN, sold land in Bedford Co., TN, on North Fork of Duck River. Borders Ball's land and Jordan's land. 100 acres. Wit: Thomas C. Rankin and Robert Allison. Reg: 14 Dec 1835.

Page 39 - Whereas James Brittain, now deceased, executed to Leonard Marbury, his bond and bearing date of 24 Mar 1832, deed to land on west side of the Town of Shelbyville. Bond endorsed on 12 Feb 1833, L. M. Marbury made a deed to Peter Morgan, signed 25 Mar 1833 by Peter Morgan. Wit: Joseph Kingcaid(Kincaid) and W. J. Riddle.

Page 40 - 4 Jul 1835. William F. Long, Executor of the Last Will and Testament of James Brittain, deceased, to Susan Morgan, wife and relict of Peter Morgan, deceased, and Melinda Morgan only heir of Peter Morgan, deceased, sold land of 50 acres in Bedford Co., TN, on west boundary line of Town of Shelbyville. Borders the Tan Yard Lot of Eakins, John A. Marrs Brick Yard, John C. Coldwell, and Robert Cannon. Wit: C. W. Black and James H. Graham. Reg: 14 Dec 1835.

Page 41 - 12 Dec 1835. Theophilus Falls, Trustee of Alexander J. Worke of Iredell Co., NC to Thomas C. Rankin of Bedford Co., TN, sold land in Bedford Co., on North Fork of Duck River. Borders Pinkerton's corner and Houston's corner. 469 acres. Wit: Robert Allison and William B. Jordan. Reg: 14 Dec 1835.

Page 42 - 3 Nov 1835. William H. Miles to John H. Miles, James H. Miles, William Anderton and Judith H. Anderton his wife, all of Bedford Co., TN, sold land in Bedford Co., on waters of Big Flat Creek. Borders land of George Doherty. 150 acres. Wit: William F. Long. Reg: 18 Dec 1835.

Page 43 - 3 Nov 1835. William H. Miles to John H. Miles, James H. Miles, William Anderton and Judith H. Anderton his wife, all of Bedford Co., TN, sold land in Bedford Co., on waters of Big Flat Creek. Borders John H. Miles, John Hastings and H. F. Hastings. 13 acres. Wit: William F. Long. Reg: 18 Dec 1835.

Page 44 - 12 Dec 1835. William T. Ball of Rutherford Co., TN to William B. Jordan of Bedford Co., TN, land in Bedford Co., on waters of North Fork of Duck River. Wit: W. J. Long. Reg: 18 Dec 1835.

Page 46 - 24 May 1834. Alexander Neil of Lawrance Co., Alabama to Andrew Neil of Bedford Co., TN, land in Bedford Co., on waters of Little Sinking Creek, for 50 acres being part of willed land by James Neil to Alexander and Andrew Neil by his Last Will and Testament and contained in the eighth item of said will and allotted in said demise said "James Old Place" I formerly lived upon and described in will as lying between the land given to my son William Neil, deceased, and that given to my son Samuel Neil, the part now sold is the one half of tract mentioned in will and called the "Old Place" of 50 acres. Wit: Nathaniel King and John L. Neil. Reg: 21 Dec 1835.

Page 48 - I, William Austin, held and formerly bound, of Bedford Co., TN, unto John Polk of Lincoln Co., TN, for $75.00. Land in Bedford Co. and Lincoln Co., TN, on waters of Big Flat Creek and also on waters of West Mulberry Creek. Borders near County Line, William Noblett and Grammer's line. Also, includes land where John Polk now lives. Wit: Henry Morgan and Grason Auston. Reg: 22 Dec 1835.

Page 49 - 18 Sep 1835. George Arnhart, Sr. to Daniel Arnhart his son, both of Bedford Co., TN, for love and affection for his son Daniel. Daniel Arnhart agrees to maintain George Arnhart and his wife during their natural life, land in Bedford Co., on south bank of Duck River. Borders Duck River, Culp's line, Benjamin Arnhart, John Warren's corner, and Henry Arnhart's corner. 178 acres. Wit: Hartwell Freeman and Jacob Lentz. Reg: 22 Dec 1835.

Page 50 - 10 Dec 1835. Elizer Stilwell of Bedford Co., TN one part and William McGregor and Peter Phifer of Maury Co., TN and Benjamin Thompson, Hugh Houston, Elias Stilwell and John Osburn of Bedford Co., Trustees and their successors for Mount Carmel Meeting House of other part, for affection Eleazer Stilwell for the Methodist Episcopal Church worshipping at Mount Carmel Meeting House and for the neighborhood and all mankind, grant unto the above named Trustees, two tracts of land. One, Beginning at the south west corner of Mount Carmel Grave Yard, of one acre and 68 poles. Second, Another one acre of land, whereon a new meeting house is about to be built. Wit: Edward D--- and Thomas D. Cheek. Reg: 24 Dec 1835.

DEED BOOK "FF"

Page 57 - 1 Jul 1834. James Brown and Mary D. Brown his wife to William Knight, all of Bedford Co., TN, 108 acres in Bedford Co., on east side of Powels Creek. Borders Melchezedick Brame, Thomas Greer, and Powels Creek. Wit: O. W. Knight and G. B. Knight. Reg: 28 Dec 1835.

Page 60 - 24 Dec 1835. Burrell G. White of Rutherford Co., TN to Calvin Creecy of Bedford Co., TN, for $1.00, sold land to Burrel G. White, on waters of the Wartrace Fork in Bedford Co. Borders Drury Daniel and John Robertson. 122 acres. Wit: Stephen W. Jamison, Robert F. Elkins and A. H. White. Reg: 2 Jan 1836.

Page 73 - 5 Jan 1836. I, William H. Harrison sold to Mary Jane Puckett and William Rufus Puckett, all of Bedford Co., TN, all the right, title, claim and interest that was conveyed to my by Pleasant Puckett of the estate of Arthur Puckett, deceased, it being one seventh part of the estate, and paid for by Mary Jane Puckett and William Rufus Puckett. Reg: 5 Jan 1836.

Page 86 - 8 Jan 1836. I, David Norman of Bedford Co., TN, appointed my brother Jonathan Norman of Dickson Co., TN, my Attorney, to oversee my business in settling with the administrators of my mother Martha Norman, deceased, in Union Cistrict, South Carolina. Reg: 8 Jan 1836.

Page 87 - --Jan 1836. We, John S. Crawly and Sarah K. Crawly his wife, sold to Robert M. Whitman, a negro woman Prudence and her child Martha. Wit: John W. White and Richard Fowler. Reg: 8 Jan 1836.

Page 87 - 28 Fbe 1835. I, Sarah Ray, give two negroes, Jenny and Jesse, unto my son David Ray. Wit: Robert Ray, A. B. Hammett and Thomas Ray. Reg: 9 Jan 1836.

Page 89 - 25 Dec 1835. James T. McKelvey of Mecklenburg Co., NC to Alexander B. Moon of Bedford Co., TN, land in Bedford Co., on waters of North Fork of Duck River. Borders William Short's tract, on dividing line of William and George Locke, and Mary Campbell formerly Mary Smith. 250 acres. Reg: 11 Jan 1836.

Page 90 - 13 Nov 1835. John L. Neill, Jr. and James D. Neill, both of Bedford Co., TN, land in Bedford Co., on Little Sinking Creek, being part of a 392½ acres purchased by James Neill now deceased and part of a tract laid off by James Neill, deceased, to James and John L. Neill, Jr. by deed dated 15 Sep 1819. Borders Andrew Neill, Henderson's line, Neill's spring, and Old Pulaski and Shelbyville Road. 60 acres. Wit: William D. Orr and James Neill, Jr. Reg: 11 Jan 1836.

Page 92 - 14 Dec 1835. Dudley Clanton of Bedford Co., TN to Richard Smith of Rutherford Co., TN, two tracts of land, being a part in Rutherford Co. and a part in Bedford Co., on waters of Alexanders Creek. (1) of 50 acres, borders William Williams, McLemore's line and James Foster. (2) of 51 acres, borders Caswell's line. Reg: 11 Jan 1836.

Page 94 - 20 Dec 1832. Nancy Meeks of Lincoln Co., TN to Solomon Durrett of Bedford Co., TN, land in Bedford Co., on headwaters of Sinking Creek. Borders Philip Philips and Michael Campbell.

Exception of 17 acres which was laid off for Joseph Wallis and Elizabeth Wallis his wife formerly Elizabeth Smith. Another exception of 21 acres sold to John Ingland. Reg: 12 Jan 1836.

Page 95 - 5 Sep 1835. Simeon Marsh of Giles Co., TN to John B. Fowler of Bedford Co., TN, land in Bedford Co.,on waters of Rock Creek. 302½ acres. Wit: James C. Record and William London. Reg: 12 Jan 1836.

Page 98 - 20 Dec 1832. Nancy Meeks of Lincoln Co., TN to Solomon Durrett of Bedford Co., TN, land in Bedford Co., on headwaters of Sinking Creek. Borders John Strother and Malcolm Gilchrist. 25 acres. Wit: Thomas N. McLain and Rezin Smith. Reg: 12 Jan 1836.

Page 101 - 2 Feb 1835. Elias Yates sold to Samuel Yates his son, both of Bedford Co., TN, for love and affection for his son Samuel Yates, conveyed unto him land in Bedford Co., on waters of Barren Fork. Borders Allen Knight which he purchased of Nicholas Coble, Fergus Hall, and John B. Bates. 90 acres. Wit: Allen Knight and John Knight. Reg: 13 Jan 1836.

Page 111 - 9 Dec 1834. John Lee of Shelby Co., Illinois to Isham H. Lain(Lane) of Bedford Co., TN, land in Bedford Co., on waters of Alexanders Creek. Borders John A McLane. 20 acres. Wit: Drury D. Lain and Rutherford Lain. Reg: 15 Jan 1836.

Page 114 - 24 Aug 1835. I, Jeremiah Dobbs for love and affection for my grandson Joseph Dobbs, son of John Dobbs, all of Bedford Co., given one sorrel filly. Wit: John T. Neil and David Bledsoe. Reg: 15 Jan 1836.

Page 119 - 23 Dec 1835. Noble L. Majors of Bedford Co., TN to Burrell G. White of Rutherford Co., TN, land in Bedford Co., on Wartrace Fork. Borders Benjamin W. Smithson. 2 acres. Wit: Robert H. Majors and A. H. White. Reg: 18 Jan 1836.

Page 122 - 28 Dec 1832. James Erwin of Fayette Co., KY by his Attorney A. Erwin, Jr. to Elias Yates of Bedford Co., TN, land in Bedford Co., on Barren Fork or South Fork. Borders Elias Yates, Willis Green, and the mouth of Dawdy Creek, and John B. Bates. 69¼ acres. Reg: 19 Jan 1836.

Page 122 - 1 Oct 1834. Eppy Crews of Hardeman Co., TN and Thomas Holdon and Temperance Holdon his wife of Bedford Co., TN, to Uriah Cross of Bedford Co., for $25.00, land that George Crews owned at the time of his death. 28 acres. Land on north west side of Hamilton Creek. Borders William Horsby, John G. Sims' heirs and Uriah Cross. Wit: Alsey Arnold and A. Arnold. Reg: 19 Jan 1836.

Page 123 - 3 Jan 1835. John Philips to Jesse Philips, both of Bedford Co., TN, for love and affection for his son Jesse and for $1.00, land in Bedford Co., on west branch of Sugar Creek, it being a part of a 640 acres belonging to John Philips. Borders George Doherty, Gant's, and Miles Philips. 129½ acres. Wit: William H. Craig and Jarred Bishop. Reg: 19 Jan 1836.

Page 124 - 3 Jan 1835. John Philips to Miles Philips, both of Bedford Co., TN, for love and affection for his son Miles Philips, land in Bedford Co., on west branch of Sugar Creek, being a part of a 640 acres of John Philips. Borders George Doherty, and where Thomas Harper lately lived, and Jesse Philips. 136 acres. Wit: William H. Craig and Jarred Bishop. Reg: 19 Jan 1836.

Page 125 - 14 Aug 1834. William Sugg to Nehemiah Sugg, both of Bedford Co., TN, one half interest in two tracts whereon William Sugg now lives, the building excepted. Nehemiah is to have the use of the plantation as is contained by the following, viz, all the plantation lying north of the cross fence which runs from the barn westwardly to the creek, and west of the apple and peach orchard to the road and part of the field lying eastwardly of the orchard &c. He is to get said land &c at the death of William Sugg and Jemima Sugg, also, half of the spring and all the buildings &c. Wit: Harbert Sugg and Aquilla Sugg. Reg: 20 Jan 1836.

Page 127 - 16 Jan 1835. John S. Wood of Lewis Co., MO to William J. Finch of Bedford Co., TN, land in Bedford Co., on Straight Creek of the Garrison Fork. Borders William Galleghy, Enoch Haynes and Jacob Anderson. 127 acres. Wit: William Jones and E. D. Jones. Reg: 20 Jan 1836.

Page 129 - 30 Dec 1835. Dempsy J. Sutton to Sarah Sutton, both of Bedford Co., TN, land in Bedford Co., on waters of Alexander Creek. Borders Jordan Holden. 65 acres. Wit: Alexander Sutton and Henry Vincent. Reg: 20 Jan 1836.

Page 131 - 18 Nov 1833. Widow and Legatees, Polly Garrett, Sally Martin, Nancy Martin, Wilson Garrett and Moses Garrett, John Garrett, Samuel Garrett, Joseph Garrett one part and Samuel Coldwell other part, land in Bedford Co., TN, on waters of Big Flat Creek, adjoining lands of William Shook, James Trible and Samuel Coldwell. Borders William Shook near Levi Shook's house, Samuel Coldwell and James Trible. 6 acres. Wit: Charles E. Stewart, Welcome Covey and William W. Coldwell. Signed by Polly Garrett, Joseph Garrett, Asa Martin, Nancy Martin, Wilson Garrett, Joseph Garrett and Moses Garrett, Benjamin Martin, Sarah Martin, William Martin, Benjamin and Sarah Martin by their Attorney. I, James McKisick, Clerk of Court of Pleas and Quarter Sessions, certify that the execution of the within deed from Polly Garrett, Joseph Garrett, Asa Martin, Nancy Martin, Wilson Garrett, Moses Garrett, Benjamin Garrett and Sarah his wife, to Samuel Coldwell for 46 acres. William Martin, Attorney for Benjamin and Sarah Martin and the said Sarah Martin. Reg: 21 Jan 1836.

Page 136 - 30 Sep 1835. Jane Walker and Martha Walker, heirs of James Walker, deceased, to William Yates, all of Bedford Co., TN, land south west end of the field adjoining the place on which John Bradshaw lived at the time of his death which was bequeathed to Jane and Martha Walker during their lives by their ancestor James Walker, deceased, by his Last Will and Testament, which will bears date in Jan 1825. Wit: Samuel Walker and E. H. Moore. Reg: 23 Jan 1836.

Page 150 - 11 Nov 1835. I, James W. Lovins of Shelby Co., Illinois, having special trust and confidence in Andrew Flemming of Bedford Co., TN, appoint him my Attorney to oversee my interest in the estate of Jane Forrest widow of Shadrick Forrest, late of Bedford Co., TN. Reg: 31 Feb 1836.

DEED BOOK "FF"

Page 152 - 14 Nov 1835. Margaret Jones of Calaway Co., KY to John Biggers of Bedford Co., TN, land in Bedford Co., on McCurleys Fork, on east branch of West Fork of Rock Creek. Borders lands of Roseborough, McCurleys Creek, Smith's line, Anna McDaniel, Orr's line, and Nash's old west line. 186 acres. Margaret Jones reserves two poles square including graves where their daughter Polly is buried, for a burying ground. Wit: Elisha Garrett and Benjamin Bingaman. Reg: 7 Feb 1836.

Page 154 - 3 Feb 1836. George Newton to Ballard Coldwell, both of Bedford Co., TN. Whereas Alexander Newton of Madison Co., Mississippi, did on 7 May 1834, executed a Deed of Trust to George Newton for land in Bedford Co. Borders the Dixon Academy, James Deery and the heirs of Thomas Moore, deceased. 5 acres. Reg: 10 Feb 1836.

Page 156 - 13 Feb 1836. George Davidson of Bedford Co., TN to Herbert Owens of Williamson Co., TN. Whereas at a public sale on 4 Feb 1834 against Robert E. Thompson, John Coldwell Thompson and Mary Bell Thompson, only heirs at law of Robert C. Thompson, deceased, Erwin J. Frierson purchased all rights and of the heirs of interest in land of which Robert C. Thompson died seized and possessed, being in Bedford Co. Adjoining Town of Shelbyville on the Skull Camp Ford Road. Borders Daniel McKisick and the heirs of James Brittain, deceased, Peter Chilcutt and the street leading east from Shelbyville that goes from the north east corner of the public aquare. 17 acres. Wit: Thomas C. Whiteside and Robert Mathews. Reg: 13 Feb 1836.

Page 157 - 1 Nov 1834. Plummer Shofner and Elizabeth Shofner his wife to John Smith, all of Bedford Co., TN, land in Bedford Co., on waters of Thompson Creek, on the east side of said Creek. 20½ acres. Borders John Landis. Wit: F. Shofner and Austin Shofner. Reg: 16 Feb 1836.

Page 160 - 10 Feb 1836. John S. Hix to James W. Patton, both of Bedford Co., TN, land in Bedford Co., it being that part of fifty acres of land that John Hix died seized and possessed of, which John as one of the heirs of John Hix is entitled to a fifth part. 50 acres. Wit: W. B. M. Brame and J. A. Blakeman. Reg: 17 Feb 1836.

Page 161 - 18 Dec 1833. William R. Caswell, James E. Grundy and Benjamin McCullock of Rutherford Co., TN to Isham Lane of Bedford Co., TN, land in Bedford Co., on Alexanders Creek, being a part of a tract known by the name of Caswell's Tract. Borders Moses Guest's corner. Wit: Rutherford Lain and Drury H. Lain. Reg: 17 Feb 1836.

Page 164 - 5 Dec 1834. Jesse Alexander of Henry Co., TN to John C. Wilson of Bedford Co., TN, land in Bedford Co., on the North Fork. Borders Moor's land and Wortham's land. Wit: M. T. Span and W. Wilson. Reg: 17 Feb 1836.

Page 165 - -- Jan 1835. Henson S. Brown and Elizabeth Brown his wife, John S. Brown and his wife Sarah Brown, James Ingle and Nancy Ingle of Bedford Co., TN and Mark Hatley and Lucredia Hatley his wife of Cole Co., MO, by their Attorney John S. Brown of one part and John Patton of Bedford Co., other part, 150 acres of land in Bedford Co., on waters of Sugar Creek. Borders John Whitsell and A. Balch. Wit: Joseph Morton. Reg: 18 Feb

1836.

Page 166 - Whereas John A. Marrs, now deceased, by his Last Will and Testament, devised that all his real property should be sold to highest bidder. Robert P. Harrison and Joseph C. Strong, administrators of John A. Marr's will. About one half mile or one mile from Shelbyville. Borders the Columbia Road, Joseph Kincaid, Benjamin McCuistion, James G. Whitney, and others and Benjamin Strickler. 50 acres. Reg: -- Feb 1836.

Page 168 - 20 Mar 1835. James Erwin of New Orleans to Abraham Manly of Bedford Co., TN, land in Bedford Co., on headwaters of Wartrace Fork. Borders Whitworth's corner. 52 acres. Wit: Nathan Chaffin and Samuel Whitworth. Reg: 19 Feb 1836.

Page 170 - 1835. Thomas J. and Martin M. Lane, Executors of Thomas Lane, deceased, to Wily Oneal, land in Bedford Co., TN. Wit: John M. Lane and Samuel Winstead. Reg: 19 Feb 1836.

Page 176 - 1 Feb 1834. John F. Tomlins for himself and as agent for Robert Cary Jennings of the Borough of Norfolk, VA one part and Charles Hopper of Bedford Co., TN, other part. Land in Bedford Co., on Rich Creek, being the residue oa a tract of 2015 acres originally granted by North Carolina to John Lewis about 10 July 1788. Borders William Newsom, Charles Hopper and Thomas Hopper. Reg: 23 Feb 1836.

Page 177 - 15 Jul 1835. We, William L. McKinley and Nancy McKinley of Gibson Co., TN, sold to James B. Simmons of Gibson Co., all interest in estate of William Simmons, Sr., deceased, who was a resident of Bedford County, TN at the time of his death and of which Nancy McKinley is a daughter and heir at law. Wit: C. S. Simmons and David Huddleston. Reg: 23 Feb 1836.

Page 179 - 2 Nov 1835. Virginia Ann Norfleet, Ruthy H. Bernard and Walter Bernard, all heirs of Thomas H. Bernard, deceased, by their guardian James G. Barksdale of 1st part and Nicholas Anthony of 2nd part and James G. Barksdale 3rd part. N. Anthony sold to James G. Barksdale, land in Bedford Co., TN, on Thompson Creek. Borders Anthony's tract. 200 acres. Another 50 acre tract on Thompson Creek. Borders Samuel Brown and Robert's tract. Wit: Thomas C. Whiteside. Reg: 25 Feb 1836.

Page 182 - 31 Oct 1835. We, Robert McElvaney and Nancy his wife for $34.00 paid by John F. Norman, all of Bedford Co., TN, land in Bedford Co., whereon Sarah Hubbard now lives and in which she holds a life estate. Borders William Heaslett, John Evans, Samuel Coldwell and Hiram Holt's Tanyard. Wit: Zacharias Cheshire and William Heaslett. Reg: 26 Feb 1836.

Page 191 - 28 Jan 1834. James J. Brown and Nancy M. Brown to James Allison, all of Bedford Co., TN, land in Bedford Co., on East Fork of Rock Creek. Borders Cummings' corner, Davis' land, Wallis' land, and Thomas Cummings' corner. 50 acres. Wit: Albert Anderson and David Revis. Reg: 1 Mar 1836.

Page 192 - 19 Jan 1835. Joseph Hill of Henry Co., TN to William D. Hill of Bedford Co., TN, land in Bedford Co., on waters of Weakley's Creek and adjoins Doherty's and Gilchrist. 100 acres. Wit: Thomas Black and John Patterson. Reg: 1 Mar 1836.

Page 197 - 6 Feb 1836. Patrick H. Loving to Sherwood Dunegan, both of Bedford Co., TN, sold goods and chattels, a certain piece of leased land of Robert Patterson for a term of seven years, 1 Jan 1834 and adjoining John F. Ferguson and Joseph H. Brittain, on land formerly owned by Robert and Celah Patterson now owned by Jephtha Ezzell. Borders tract formerly owned by Elizabeth Lovins now belonging to John F. Ferguson. 25 acres on waters of Caney Apring Creek. Wit: Aaron Boyd. Reg: 3 Mar 1836.

Page 198 - 16 Apr 1835. Thomas Haddock and Nancy Haddock his wife, late of Bedford Co., TN to Samuel Morton of Williamson Co., TN, 100 acres in Bedford Co., being their part of a tract of 290 acres which Martha Kimbro, deceased, gave in her Last Will and Testament to John G. Haddock and wife, Thomas Haddock and wife, and James M. Taylor. Land borders Daisey's land, James M. Taylor's land, and William Kidd's land. Reg: 3 Mar 1836.

Page 199 - 11 Feb 1836. Thomas G. Polk of Rowan Co., NC to John Hutton of Bedford Co., TN, land in Bedford Co., on waters of Hurricane Creek. Borders Archibald Yell's land now owned by Coleman Jackson, and Amos McAdams. 166 acres. Also another tract bordering the above tract, and Amos McAdams. 50 acres. Reg: 8 Mar 1836.

Page 200 - 4 Oct 1835. James Sheppard of bedford Co., TN to Madison R. Hughs of Williamson Co., TN, land in Bedford and Williamson Counties, TN, on headwaters of Spring Creek and adjoining Samuel Davis, William C. Sheppard and James Graham, Austin Sheppard, and William H. Alford and John Hughes. Reg: 4 Mar 1836.

Page 203 - 13 Mar 1835. James Erwin of City of New Orleans to Wilson E. Rushing of Bedford Co., TN, land in Bedford Co., on headwaters of the Wartrace Fork. Borders Absalom Manley's corner, William Norvell, Thomas Rushing, and James Frizzle's corner. 39 acres. Wit: Nathan Chaffin and Samuel Whitworth. Reg: 8 Mar 1836.

Page 205 - 14 Jan 1836. Robert Snoddy and James C. Tribble, administrators of Peter Tribble, deceased, to Henry Lynn, all od Bedford Co., TN, land in Bedford Co., on waters of Big Flat Creek, it being the tract whereon Peter Tribble, deceased, formerly lived. Borders C. C. Hix's land on which he now lives, P. H. Prewitts' line, James Cheshire, and Daniel Kizzer's corner. 141½ acres, including the plantation where Lynn now lives. Wit: Hiram Holt and P. H. Prewitt. Reg: 9 Mar 1836.

Page 207 - 20 Oct 1828. Thomas A. Peacock and Susan B. Peacock to Edward Ragsdale, all of Bedford Co., TN, land in Bedford Co., on headwaters of Falling Creek. Tract 1, borders John Peacock, Jr., deceased, Stephen Murphree, H. Bailey, and John Sutton. Tract 2, borders John Sutton and John Peacock. Wit: John W. Peacock and Andrew Bailey. Reg: 9 Mar 1836.

Page 210 - 28 Jan 1836. Jane Reynolds and Willis Hastings, both of Bedford Co., TN. Jane Reynolds sold to Willis Hastings land in Bedford Co., on waters of Big Flat Creek, being part of a tract on which she now lives. Borders land purchased from Jane Reynolds by Robert Hastings, deceased, now owned by Josiah

Hastings, William Hurst, and lands where Willis Hastings now lives, and where Josiah Hastings now lives. 15 acres. Wit: Josiah Hastings and William N. Fuller. Reg: 9 Mar 1836.

Page 213 - -- Nov 1833. William Bowdon, Sr. to William Bowdon, Jr., both of Bedford Co., TN, land in Bedford Co., on north branch of Barren Fork. Borders bank of the Spring Branch and Samuel Johnson. 160 acres. Wit: Frederick W. Bowdon and Elmer Bowdon. Reg: 10 Mar 1836.

Page 213 - 19 Dec 1835. James Burrow and Margaret his wife to Thomas C. H. Miller, all of Bedford Co., TN, land in Bedford Co., on waters of Wilson Creek. Borders Adam Miller on land where he now lives and James Williams. 80 acres. Wit: Pearce Wilhoit and James Jones. Reg: 10 Mar 1836.

Page 216 - 1 Jan 1836. James Wilson of Rutherford Co., TN to Wilson Turrentine of Bedford Co., land in Bedford Co., on waters of North Fork. Borders Turrentine's tract whereon he now lives and John Wilson. 48+ acres. Reg: 11 Mar 1836.

Page 218 - 20 Jul 1835. Charles Hopper of Bedford Co., TN to Hollin Collins of Maury Co., TN, land in Bedford Co., on waters of Rich Creek, a part of the original tract which formerly belonged to Theophilus Hunter adjoining land of Thomas O. Hunter, and Peter Woods. 125 acres. Wit: John Oneal and W. S. Anderson. Reg: 12 Mar 1836.

Page 222 - 8 Apr 1832. Arch. Walker to Samuel Walker, both of Bedford Co., TN, relinguishes all rights and interest in land in Cabarrus Co., NC, on waters of Coddle Creek on the east side of same. Borders Andrew Walker, Thomas White and James Burnes. 50 acres. Wit: Thomas Dryden and Nathaniel White. Reg: 14 Mar 1836.

Page 223 - 18 Aug 1834. I, William Siler of Shelby Co., Illinois, son of Frederick Siler, deceased, of Bedford Co., TN, sold to William A. Fleming, negroes and stock, household and kitchen furniture. Mary Siler wife of Frederick Siler, deceased. Wit: B. H. Siler. Reg: 14 Mar 1836.

Page 225 - 15 May 1830. Robert Hastings to Josiah Hastings, his son, of Bedford Co., TN, land in Bedford Co., on a west branch of Big Flat Creek. Borders D. D. Hix, the Columbia-Winchester road, Robert's line, heirs of Valentine Kizer, dec'd. 49 acres. Wit: John H. Hubbard, George Hudlow and Willis Hastings. Reg: 15 Mar 1836.

Page 226 - 11 Aug 1835. Erwin McAdams of Lincoln Co., TN to Joseph McAdams of Bedford Co., TN, land in Bedford Co., on waters of East Fork of R.(Rock) Creek. Borders John McEndsley, Betsey Lowery, Cumming's line and T. C. K. W.'s line. 100 acres. Wit: John McAdams and Jesse McAdams. Reg: 15 Mar 1836.

Page 229 - 30 Oct 1835. William A. Lemmons of Bedford Co., TN, for himself and as agent and Attorney for Samuel Stratton and Fine Stratton of Henderson Co., TN sold to John Penn of Bedford Co., TN, land in Bedford Co., on Rich Creek adjoining lands of Charles Hopper and others. Borders Newsom's tract and Nathan G. Pinson. 47 acres. Wit: Hiram Harris and Jesse W. Burrow. Reg: 16 Mar 1836.

DEED BOOK "FF"

Page 229 - 8 Dec 1834. Archibald Carothers and his wife Juliet Carothers and Eliza Adams of Bedford Co., TN and William G. Woodson of Braken Co., KY sold to Samuel Clay of Bedford Co., TN, land in Bedford Co., on waters of the Wartrace Fork. Borders road leading from Davis' Mill to Murfreesboro by Liberty Meeting House in Samuel Clay's line near Clay's spring and where he now lives. This being the same tract surveyed by John B. Hamilton to John Adams in 1 Sept 1829. Wit: Francis Vannison(?), John Jakes and Vinson R. Allen. Reg: 16 Mar 1836.

Page 232 - (no date). We, Malcolm Gilchrist and Daniel Gilchrist now of Alabama, appoint our brother William Gilchrist of Bedford Co., TN, our Attorney to oversee of the sale of their interests in Tennessee. Wit: A. V. Brown and A. M. Ballantine. Reg: 17 Mar 1836.

Page 238 - 24 Mar 1836. George Neill to Robert M. Walter, both of Bedford Co., TN, for $5.00, land in Bedford Co., on waters of Rock Creek, adjoining a tract of George Cathey, 50 acres transferred to Alexander Neill, deceased, and was estate of the said deceased. Page 239 - 27 Nov 1835. I, Ann Neill of Bedford Co., TN, for love and affection for my daughter Esther E. Walter of Bedford Co., land in Bedford Co., on waters of Rock Creek. Borders Cathey, Kimbro Ogilvie, mouth of the spring branch, and George Neill's Mill Dam. 93 acres. Wit: George Neill and Jno. Crawford. Reg: 28 Mar 1836.

Page 239 - 24 Mar 1836. I, John Orr of Bedford Co., TN, in behalf of my daughter Margaret L. Orr and my son William L. Orr, are held and firmly bound unto Robert M. Walter of Bedford Co., for $300.00. Wit: John Ramsey and James Eakin. Reg: 28 Mar 1836.

Page 240 - 18 Mar 1835. David B. Crawford and Algeline Crawford sold to Robert M. Walters, all of Bedford Co., TN, land in Bedford Co., on waters of Rock Creek and joining land of George Cathey of North Carolina. Wit: John Ramsey and James Eakin. Reg: 28 Mar 1836.

Page 243 - -- Mar 1835. Samuel Wilson, Executor and Jane Patterson, Executrix of the Last Will and Testament of James Wilson, deceased, sold to Robert S. Patterson, all of Bedford Co., TN, by the Last Will and Testament whereon his mill stands should be sold. We, Samuel Wilson and Jane Patterson, Executor and Executrix of said Will sold unto Robert S. Patterosn, land in Bedford Co., on Spring Creek. Borders William Meek. 36 acres, including a Mill Dam. Wit: T. J. W. Miller and John Goad. Reg: 29 Mar 1836.

Page 246 - (no date). I, Robert Powell of Bedford Co., TN, for love and affection for my wife Mary L. and my sons Thomas P. and Lymon R. and my grandsons Robert James Powell and Richard Henry Powell, sons of my son Thomas P., for $1100.00 Reserving to myself property during my life time, granted to my wife the south division of my land to be divided into two parts. If my wife survivies me, she is to have the south division during her natural life and at her death to go to my son Thomas P. The negroes goes to my son Thomas P., $200.00 to my son Lymon R. also to my daughter Elizabeth H. Whitaker $1.00. Negroes to the two grandsons. Wit: Elem Pucket and Littleberry Turner and Monroe W. Turner. Reg: 30 Mar 1836.

Page 250 - 1 Jul 1835. William Pyland, one of the heirs of Jacob Harber, late of Bedford Co., TN, deceased, to George A. Harber of Bedford Co., land in Bedford Co., on Rich Creek, known as No. 7 and also his part of my mother's dowery known by Lot No. 1 in the plat of the division. 70 acres. Wit: Jeremiah Hay and John Penn. Reg: 31 Mar 1836.

Page 251 - 6 Dec 1834. Thomas J. and Milton M. Lane, Executors of Thomas Lane, deceased, both of Giles Co., TN sold to William Click of Bedford Co., TN, land in Bedford Co., on Duck River. Borders Lawson Harriss. 125 acres. Wit: John M. Lane and Robert Lane. Reg: 31 Mar 1836.

Page 251 - 2 Oct 1835, Lexington. Jesse Taylor and Christopher H. Williams, both of Henderson Co., TN. Christopher H. Williams in trust for Eliza W. Harrison of Bedford Co., TN, a negro woman Barbara. C. H. Williams is to hold slave. Reg: 31 Mar 1836.

Page 255 - 31 Jul 1830. Andrew Erwin to John Davidson, both of Bedford Co., TN, land in Bedford Co., on Barren Fork, the same being sold by A. Erwin to Abram Shook on 27 Dec 1813, previous to the payment of which said Shook departed this life leaving no will and on 5 Oct 1818 Philip Berford, administrator and guardian of legatees, was ordered to sell land debt to Erwin. John Davidson was purchaser. Land borders north bank of Barren Fork and Hugh Davidson. 100 acres. Wit: G. W. Erwin, Hugh Davidson and A. Erwin, Jr. Reg: 2 Apr 1836.

Page 257 - 5 Aug 1835. Alexander Robinson to William H. Craig, both of Bedford Co., TN, land in Bedford Co., on waters of Sugar Creek. Borders Michael Marsh. 91 acres. Wit: A. M. Loyd and William H. Hicks. Reg: 3 Apr 1836.

Page 258 - 10 Jul 1832. Thomas G. Polk of Rowan Co., NC to Daniel Gilchrist of Bedford Co., TN, land in Bedford Co. Borders John Eakin, north side of McMinnville Road, Nelson's corner, and McFarland's line. 294 acres. Wit: Robert P. Harrison, John R. Coffey and Jno. A. Marrs. Reg: 4 Apr 1836.

Page 259 - (no date). I, Spencer Haynie of Bedford Co., TN, sold to James Mullins as Trustee for the benedit of James W. Dickerson, a bay mare and a crop made this year on Lettitia Dickerson's farm. Wit: A. P. Haynie and J. Holt. Reg: 5 Apr 1836.

Page 263 - 26 Mar 1836. Preston Frazier of Green Co., Alabama to Granville H. Frazier of Washington Co., Mississippi, and Mary Temple of Bedford Co., TN, land in Bedford Co., near the Town of Shelbyville. Borders lands of James Brittain, deceased, lands that formerly owned by the heirs of B. S. Thompson, deceased, and now the property of Mr. Owen, their step father, which property I, Preston Frazier, purchased of Martha A. R. Thompson on 10 Mar 1834. Wit: Henry B. Files(Fields) and James Yeats. Reg: 5 Apr 1836.

Page 264 - 26 Mar 1836. Preston Frazier of Green Co., Alabama to Granville H. Frazier of Washington Co., Mississippi and Mary Temple of Bedford Co., TN, Town Lot in Shelbyville. Borders William Gilchrist, Clement Cannon, and Square. Lot is known in plan as Town Lot No. 78. Also conveyed a negro boy Tom.

Wit: John Pemberton and James Eastham. Reg: 15 Apr 1836.

Page 265 - (no date). We, James Allison, William Allison, Robert Allison, Thomas Allison, John Allison, and Sally and James Williams, and Elizabeth and William Williams, heirs of Robert Allison, deceased, conveyed land unto Kimbrough Allison, it being the land that our father bought of Barnabas McCallister. 100 acres on waters of Wilson Creek in Bedford Co., TN. Borders John Adkinson, David Fleming and Kimbrough Allison. Wit: Thompson Faulk and John W. Wheeler. Reg: 6 Apr 1836/

Page 266 - 13 Aug 1830. Samuel Wilson of Carrol Co., TN to Hezekiah Briant of Bedford Co., TN, land in Bedford Co., on waters of Spring Creek, it being a part of a 3000 acre tract granted to Samuel Wilson. 50 acres. Wit: E. Cherry, John W. Lavender, John P. Briant. Reg: 6 Apr 1836.

Page 268 - 14 Oct 1835. I, Jesse Burr and Mary Burr my wife, to W. A. Simmons, all of Bedford Co., TN, land in Bedford Co., on waters of Rich Creek, which formerly belonged to William Simmons, deceased. Wit: Hiram Harris and Abram Batten. Reg: 6 Apr 1836.

Page 268 - 20 Jan 1834. Isaac Phillips of Bedford Co., TN to Thomas Cheatham of Williamson Co., TN, land in Bedford Co., on waters of Wilson Creek. Borders lands of Newton Cannon, Thomas Elmore and Wiley Perry. Wit: Willis Perry, William Carter and John Halbrook. Reg: 9 Apr 1836.

Page 269 - 10 Apr 1833. John Whiteside of Bedford Co., TN, is bound unto Newton Jordan for 200 acres of land in Bedford Co., on waters of Sinking Creek, adjoining the land of John Combs, Thomas Greer and Griffin Randle and John Porter. Wit: Flour(Flower) Swift and Jacob W. Swift. Reg: 7 Apr 1836.

Page 271 - 13 Aug 1829. Lewis Hening(Henning) and Charlotte his wife of Hopkins Co., KY to John Sims of Bedford Co., TN, 110 acres in Bedford Co., on south side of Duck River including the mouth of Sugar Creek which land was willed Charlotte Hening by her father Caswell Powell, deceased, being her part of a tract granted to Dempsey Powel, deceased. Wit: Lewis A. Boyd and John Streater. Reg: 7 Apr 1836.

Page 271 - 3 Dec 1824. Walter B. Sorrels of Hardeman Co., TN to Alfred Jacobs of Bedford Co., TN, land in Bedford Co., on headwaters of one fork of the Garrison Fork. Borders John McBride, Samuel Hanner, Joel Dashiell, and the ridge that divides the waters of the Garrison Fork and McBrides Creek. 150 acres. Wit: Jeremiah Jacobs and Joseph Jacobs. Reg: 7 Apr 1836.

Page 272 - 7 Apr 1836. John Hall of Bedford Co., TN to Joseph Philips and Boyd McNairy of Davidson Co., TN, 100 acres of land in Bedford Co., on Sugar Creek. Borders lands of John Hall sold to him by Sarah Clift, Thomas Greer, lands that John Hall sold to Harman on 2 Jan 1816 and registered in Bedford Co., on 5 June 1816. Also a tract in Bedford Co. purchased from John Patton for 50 acres on waters of Sugar Creek. Borders John Patton and John Hall. Wit: William Gilchrist and William Murphree. Reg: 7 Apr 1836.

DEED BOOK "FF"

Page 274 - 5 Nov 1830. James Dillard and his wife Nancy Dillard formerly Nancy Gibson to Adam Rayburn, all of Bedford Co., TN, land in Bedford Co., on the Garrison Fork. Borders south side of a road known as the Dughollow Road, lands of John Sutton, the Garrison Fork, James Dillard and William Norton. 65 acres. Wit: A. Erwin, Jr., Abraham Frizzle and C. F. Sutton. Reg: 8 Apr 1836.

Page 276 - 2 Apr 1836. Simeon Marsh of Giles Co., TN to William London of Bedford Co., TN, land in Bedford Co. Borders lands of Alexander's and Osborne's line. 81½ acres. Wit: Thomas N. London, Henry Lipscomb, James C. Record and John B. Fowler. Reg: 8 Apr 1836.

Page 278 - 22 Mar 1830. James R. White and Catharine M. White his wife to Jordan C. Holt, all of Bedford Co., TN, land in Bedford Co., on waters of Sugar Creek. Borders Joseph A. Greer and Thomas Greer. 116½ acres. Wit: J. Newton and Joseph White. Reg: 8 Apr 1836.

Page 281 - 18 Sep 1834. Richard C. Hancock and his wife Elizabeth A. Hancock, Thomas W. Hancock and his wife Jane W. Hancock, all of Williamson Co., TN to Thomas P. Powell of Bedford Co., TN, land in Bedford Co., on Alexanders Creek which fell to them as legatees of John Guy and John W. Guy, deceased, formerly of Williamson Co., TN. 231 acres. Wit: George Jones and _. Worke. Reg: 11 Apr 1836.

Page 297 - 23 Apr 1836. Malcolm Gilchrist and Daniel Gilchrist of Lawrance Co., Alabama to Samuel W. Bingham, Mary S. Morris, Oliver H. Bingham, Margarett Scott, Moses S. Bingham, Elisha Bingham, Robert P. Bingham, Ursula P. Bingham and William N. Bingham, children and heirs and distributees of Robert Bingham, deceased. 631 acres in Bedford Co., TN. Borders William Murphree's land on which he now lives, the ridge dividing Duck River and Stones River, Malcolm Gilchrist and Joel Lawrence. Reg: 26 Apr 1836.

Page 298 - 13 Jun 1835. James Erwin of Fayette Co., KY by his Attorney Andrew Erwin, Jr. of Nashville, Davidson Co., TN sold to Elias Yates of Bedford Co., TN, land in Bedford Co., on South or Barren Fork. Borders Fergus Hall, William and Zachariah Cully and David Dobbs now owned by Willis Green. 51½ acres. Wit: John Dun(Dunn) and George W. Smith. Reg: 26 Apr 1836.

Page 299 - 13 Feb 1836. William Horsely of Maury Co., TN to Robert Arnold of Bedford Co., TN, land in Bedford Co., about two miles above the Town of Shelbyville. Bordered by the north side of Duck River, widow Coats, John G. Sims, the Georgia Road, Uriah Cross and Hamilton's Creek. 100 acres. Wit: E. J. Frierson and Uriah Cross. Reg: 27 Apr 1836.

Page 301 - 27 Jun 1831. John B. Pinson to John Blackwell, both of Bedford Co., TN, land in Bedford Co. of 200 acres, except one fourth of an acre whereon Mary Ann is buried, on the East Fork of Rock Creek. Borders Rock Creek, Joseph Porter, Jarman Woodard, W. D. Medearis, Thomas Smith and Anderson & Porter's line. Wit: George W. Cunningham, William _. and Humphrey Cunningham. Reg: 29 Apr 1836.

DEED BOOK "FF"

Page 301 - 1 Feb 1836. John Stewart to Michael Holt, both of Bedford Co., TN, land in Bedford Co., on south side of Duck River and on waters of Flat Creek, adjoining lands of Yates, Holt, Wiggins and others, being the one tenth of part or share of undivided interest and also Moore Smiley and wife of the same undivided land whereon William Stewart formerly lived of 127 acres. Wit: Jacob Allbright and Richard Burgess. Reg: 30 Apr 1836.

Page 302 - -- --- 1836. Peggy Stewart to Michael Holt, both of Bedford Co., TN, land in Bedford Co., on south side of Duck River and on waters of Flat Creek, adjoining lands of Yates, Holt and others, it being her interest and dower willed by her husband and also land on which he lived when he died. 127 acres. Wit: D. M. Smith, Richard Burgess and Jacob Albright. Signed by Margaret Stewart. Reg: 30 Apr 1836.

Page 303 - 12 Dec 1835. Hiram Harris to John T. Harris, land in Bedford Co., TN, adjoining lands of William Click and Thomas J. and Martin M. Lane, Thomas P. Deveraux, Gideon Panel and others. 170 acres. Wit: Thomas Hunter and Anna Harris. Reg: 30 Apr 1836.

Page 304 - 7 Dec 1835. Marquis D. Hix and Malinda his wife formerly Malinda Stewart and John Hix and Nelly his wife formerly Nelly Stewart and William Stewart, Sr. and William Stewart, Jr. and Joshua H. Stewart sold to Michael Holt, all of Bedford Co., TN, land in Bedford Co., on waters of Flat Creek and adjoining lands of Yates, Holt, Wiggins and others. Reg: 30 Apr 1836.

Page 322 - 1 Apr 1822. Samuel Musgrove of Morgan Co., Alabama sold to William Williams of Bedford Co., TN, land in Bedford Co., on waters of Big Flat Creek. Borders Sampson Sawyers. 5 acres. Wit: Andrew Hyles and Jacob Fuller. Reg: 23 May 1836.

Page 323 - 1 May 1822. Samuel Musgrove of Morgan Co., Alabama sold to William Williams of Bedford Co., TN, land in Bedford Co., on east waters of Big Flat Creek. Borders James Edde and Musgrove's line. 2 acres. Wit: Andrew Hyles and Jacob Fuller. Reg: 24 May 1836.

Page 324 - 1 Apr 1822. Samuel Musgrove of Morgan Co., Alabama sold to William Williams of Bedford Co., TN, land in Bedford Co., on headwaters of Big Flat Creek. Borders 50 acres on which Williams now lives. 5 acres. Wit: Andrew Hyles and Jacob Fuller. Reg: 24 May 1836.

Page 329 - 9 Aug 1833. Joel Rushing of Giles Co., TN to William Taylor of Bedford Co., TN, land in Bedford Co., on waters of Weakley Creek. Borders George Doherty survey, Evan Rushing, deceased, corner, and Caleb Cox. 45 acres. Wit: Joel Kimmons and Caleb Cox. Reg: 25 May 1836.

Page 333 - 18 Jan 1834. Lemuel H. Cole of Gibson Co., TN to Joshua White of Bedford Co., TN, land in Bedford Co., on waters of Wilson Creek. 300 acres. Wit: Jas. Wortham, William Wortham, Rich. Neese and Martin Neese. Reg: 26 May 1836.

Page 338 - 20 Oct 1835 - William London of Bedford Co., TN to William S. Bevins of Mecklenburg Co., NC, land in Bedford Co., on headwaters of the West Fork of Rock Creek. Borders Record's corner. 187¼ acres. Wit: Levi Cochran and John B. Fowler. Reg: 27 May 1836.

Page 341 - 22 Feb 1836. John McGregor and Judith McGregor his wife of Maury Co., TN to Robert McCrory of Bedford Co., TN, sold all their undivided interest as heirs at law of Robert and Sarah B. Jones, land in Bedford Co. Borders a corner formerly Marsh's corner. 50 acres, where Robert Jones now lives. Wit: John S. Weaver, William Emmerson and Alexander M. Weaver. Reg: 28 May 1836.

Page 342 - 26 Apr 1836. I, Hartwell Chandler of Pittsylvania Co., VA, appointed Henry Chandler of Bedford Co., TN, my Attorney, to dispose of all land in Bedford Co. 130 acres. Reg: 30 May 1836.

Page 342 - 1 Jun 1836. Hartwell Chandler of Pittsylvania Co., VA, by his Attorney sold to Enoch Trot of Bedford Co., TN, 75 acres of land in two surveys, one in Bedford Co., and on ridge dividing the waters of Thompson and Big Flat Creek and of 50 acres and bounded by Hezekiah Ray. Other tract of 25 acres and borders Hezekiah Ray and Thomas Martin. Reg: 1 Jun 1836.

Page 344 - 28 Nov 1831. Robert Cannon to Thompson Cannon, both of Bedford Co., TN, for natural respect and esteem I have for my brother Thompson Cannon, conveyed land in Bedford Co., on waters of Middle Fork of Rock Creek, it being a part of a tract of land granted originally to David Ross by the State of Tennessee. Borders Thompson Cannon's corner. 45 or 46 acres. Wit: George M. Cannon. Reg: 4 Jun 1836.

Page 345 - 31 May 1836. Robert Cannon of Bedford Co., TN and of Town of Shelbyville to Elizabeth Cannon, relict and widow of Thompson Cannon, deceased, and his children, George M. Cannon, Catharine Cannon, Susanna Cannon, David K. Cannon, Robert Cannon, Michael Cannon and Henry Cannon. Robert Cannon for the natural love and respect and esteem for his deceased brother Thompson Cannon, had made him a verbal gift in his lifetime, land. Borders James L. Woods, James Adams and Robert Cannon. 25 acres. Reg: 4 Jun 1836.

Page 346 - 29 Feb 1836. Preston Frazer of Mississippi to Minos Cannon of Shelbyville, Bedford Co. James Story sold under a Deed of Trust executed to him, said Story, and said Frazer by John Bradshaw, deceased, land in Bedford Co. Borders lands of Archibald Watkins now John Stewart's line. 200 acres. Wit: William Gilchrist and Thomas C. Whiteside. Reg: 4 Jun 1836.

Page 349 - 29 Dec 1829. John H. Kaighn of Loudon Co., VA to James Walker and Elias Gwyn of Bedford Co., TN, 160 acres in Bedford Co. Borders Donaldson's Grant, Isaac Muse's corner, J. Bradford, William Cooper, and Denison's tract. Wit: A. Erwin, Isaac Muse, Samuel Haggard and William P. Finch. Reg: 11 Jun 1836.

Page 350 - 20 Mar 1833. William Gwin of Bedford Co., TN to Elias Gwin of McGoopin Co., Illinois, land in Bedford Co., on waters of Wartrace Fork. Borders Stokley Donaldson's survey, lands whereon Isaac Muse now lives, John Bradford and James Walker. Wit: James L. Armstrong and D. M. Ragsdale. Reg: 11 Jun 1836.

Page 351 - 25 Apr 1836. John Sims to Richard H. Sims, both of Bedford Co., TN, for good will and affection for Richard H. Sims and for $1.00, sold all land in Bedford Co. that John Sims bought of Lewis Henning and his wife Charlotte, and William Robertson and Marcy P. Robertson his wife, except half of the spring, John Sims reserve to himself for his own use and benefit, the aforesaid land includes the mouth of Sugar Creek. Reg: 11 Jun 1836.

Page 351 - 8 Apr 1836. John Sims and Charlotte his wife of Bedford Co., TN, sold to Leonard P. Sims of Franklin Co., TN, for good will and affection for Leonard P. Sims and for $1.00, land in Bedford Co., on waters of Powels Creek. Borders Duck River and Mrs. Streater. 265 acres. Reg: 11 Jun 1836.

Page 352 - 2 Jun 1836. Logan Henderson of Rutherford Co., TN to John Ray of Bedford Co., TN, land in Bedford Co., on waters of Sinking Creek, adjoining lands of Humphrey Cunningham, William Patton, Lovett & Harper & Oliver, and John Gambill. 203 acres, it being a part of a tract granted to James Johnson and was conveyed to Logan Henderson. Wit: Aaron Gambel and George M. Ray. Reg: 11 Jun 1836.

Page 353 - 2 Jun 1836. Logan Henderson of Rutherford Co., TN to John Ray of Bedford Co., TN, land in Bedford Co., on waters of Sinking Creek, joining lands of Andrew Neil, Bratten & Thomas Moore. 82 acres. Wit: Aaron Bambel and William M. Russell. Reg: 11 Jun 1836.

Page 354 - 13 May 1836. Taylor Lane of Hardin Co., TN to James Proby of Bedford Co., TN, land in Bedford Co., on east waters of Little Flat Creek. Borders lands of William Dickson, it being the land now claimed by Joshua Townsend and James Carter. 18 acres. Wit: H. Conway and John Lane. Reg: 14 Jun 1836.

Page 354 - 5 Nov 1835. James Wilson of Rutherford Co., TN to John Thompson of Bedford Co., TN, land in Bedford Co., on north side of Duck River. Borders John Thompson and school land. 100 acres, it being the same tract granted by State of Tennessee to Daniel Parker assignee of Elisha Williams. Wit: Willie Snell and L. C. Thompson. Reg: 14 Jun 1836.

Page 355 - 8 Aug 1834. Alexander B. Reed and Violet Cathey to Hosea Mullins, all of Bedford Co., TN, land in Bedford Co., on waters of Rock Creek. 50 acres. Wit: James _. Ewing and John Orr. Reg: 14 Jun 1836.

Page 361 - 18 Dec 1832. Robert K. McGee of Ray Co., MO to Robert B. Maupin of Bedford Co., TN, land in Bedford Co., and known in the division of land among the heirs of William McGee, deceased, by Lot No. 1. Borders Giles Burditt's Mill, William Woods and Blann Maupin, deceased, heirs, and Duck River. 212 acres. Wit: E. W. Brown and D. P. T. House. Reg: 25 Jun 1836.

Page 362 - 14 Nov 1833. John Burns of Bedford Co., TN to Thornton C. Tulloss, J. B. Cooper, A. Mallard, Thornton Mallard, T. G. Watkins, A. Rolland, and Thomas P. Burns, Trustees for the use and purposes of the Methodist Episcopal Church of Bedford Co., TN, for $1.00, land in Bedford Co., on waters of Fall Creek. 1 acre and 8 poles. Wit: William S. Knott, Henry B. Missenheimer and E. J. Dodson. Reg: 25 Jun 1836.

Page 366 - Plat of land of David Vance. 100 acres. North Carolina Grant to David Vance, No. 88, Entry No. 803, land in Bedford Co., TN, on Rock Creek. Borders Tignal Jones, George Fisher's house and well. Surveyed 31 Aug & Sept 1, 1835. Reg: 28 Jun 1836.

Page 369 - 6 Jun 1836. David H. Williams and his wife Sydney Williams of Madison Co., Alabama to Lodwick Holt of Bedford Co., TN, land in Bedford Co., TN, on Barren Fork, east of Shipmans Creek, Lot No. 7 and containing 16 acres. Surveyed 28 Dec 1830. Borders widow's dowery, Barren Fork and Shipmans Creek, in the farm now occupied by Lodwick Holt. Wit: Blan Maupin and Robert B. Maupin. Reg: 9 Jul 1836.

Page 370 - 4 Jul 1836. John F. Couser of Lincoln Co., TN to John Brooks and Samuel Mitchell of Bedford Co., TN, land in Bedford Co., on the head of Shipmans Creek. 10 acres including a mill. Another tract of land bounded above 10 acres, for 100 acres. Another tract near the above 10 acres, for 30 acres. Wit: Robert M. Whitman and Robert G. Morgan. Reg: 9 Jul 1836.

Page 376 - 11 Sep 1835. James Erwin of Fayette Co., KY by his Attorney Andrew Erwin, Jr. of Bedford Co., TN sold to Nathan C. Johnson of Bedford Co., land in Bedford Co., on Knob Creek. Borders Old Stone Fort Road, Thomas Drake, Sr. and David Trammels. Wit: George W. Smith and John Dean. Reg: 19 Jul 1836.

Page 379 - 5 May 1836. Christopher Landers to Abel Landers, both of Bedford Co., TN, land of which Henry Landers, deceased, was in possession of at his death. 12½ acres, land now in the possession of Abel Landers, John Landers and others and located on waters of Thompsons Creek. Christopher Landers is holding the land as the legatees of Henry Land<u>is</u>, deceased. Wit: Jacob Shipman, Isam Ad<u>oris</u> and Benjamin Kimbro. Reg: 23 Jul 1836.

Page 382 - 26 Jul 1836. David Blessing to John Eakin, Spencer Eakin, William Eakin and Thomas Eakin, partners in trade and in the name of Eakin and Brothers, also Alexander Eakin and Robert Moffett, trading as partners in name of Eakin and Moffett indebted to Eakin & Brothers and Eakin & Moffett. Reg: 26 Jul 1836.

Page 387 - 16 Jan 1834. I, Joseph Grant of Columbis Co., GA (Richmond), appoint Andrew Erwin, Jr., of Bedford Co., TN, my Attorney to sell unto Theoderick Bradford of Bedford Co., land in Bedford Co., and known as David Adam's land, of 143 acres. Wit: Charles D. Williams and William W. Holt. Reg: 30 Jul 1836.

Page 388 - 25 Dec 1834. Joseph Grant of Augusta, GA by his Attorney Andrew Erwin, Jr., of Bedford Co., TN, sold to Theoderick Bradford of bedford Co., land in Bedford Co., on the Barren Fork and known as David Adam's tract and being the same that was conveyed by Joshua E. White and Steele White to James Erwin, dated 15 May 1819. Borders James Erwin, Barren Fork and David Adams. 143 acres. Wit: Jno. Green and J. M. C. Walker. Reg: 30 Jul 1836.

Page 390 - Tennessee Grant to James Erwin, 500 acres. No. 13545. Land of 500 acres, dated 14 Feb 1833 in bedford Co., TN, on north side of Barren Fork. Borders J. E. White, J. Erwin and Arrington and Barren Fork. Reg: 30 Jul 1836.

DEED BOOK "FF"

Page 391 - Tennessee Grant to James Erwin for 10½ acres. No. 13544. Land of 10½ acres, dated 15 Feb 1833 in Bedford Co., TN, on waters of Barren Fork. Borders Blount's grants and Samuel Jones. Reg: 30 Jul 1836.

Page 391 - May Term 1828. Thomas Claiborn vs Walter Sims and others. Davidson County, TN Circuit Court. Thomas Claiborn vs Walter Sims, Jr., Executor of Walter Sims, deceased, Elizabeth Scudder, Walter Sims, Walter, Ann, John and Boyd Sims, heirs at law of John G. Sims, deceased. 6 June 1828 - Judgement. Walter Sims, deceased, had interest in the Shelbyville Mills, commonly called the Sims Mills and 100 acres of land, it being bequeathed to Walter Sims, Jr. Sheriff ordered to sell said property to pay debts on 9 Feb 1829. Reg: 30 Jul 1836.

Page 394 - North Carolina Grant to John Gray and Thomas Blount, 5000 acres. No. 235. 10 lbs per 100 acres. Land on both sides of Duck River. Borders mouth of Wartrace Fork. Reg: 2 Aug 1836.

Page 395 - 13 Jul 1836. Herbert Owen and Martha A. R. Owen his wife of Williamson Co., TN to Preston Frazier of Bedford Co., TN, land in Bedford Co. of 5 acres. Borders James Brittain, Daniel McKisick, Skull Camp Ford Road. Including the mansion house and other buildings, the late residence of Robert C. Thompson, deceased, it being a part of the dower. (Martha A. R. Owen widow of Robert C. Thompson). The land adjoining the Town of Shelbyville. Reg: 2 Aug 1836.

Page 396 - 17 Aug 1835. John W. Houston and his wife Nancy and Robert McCrory, all of Tennessee, all undivided interest as heirs at law of Robert and Sarah B. Jones in and to a certain tract of land in Bedford Co., TN, on waters of West Rock Creek. 50 acres. Wit: Benjamin Williams and Dempsey Weaver. Reg: 3 Aug 1836.

Page 397 - 11 Aug 1835. Martha Jones and William C. Holbrook and his wife Mary, and Thomas H. Richardson and his wife Rebecca, heirs at law of Robert and Sarah B. Jones sold to Robert McCrory, all of Bedford Co., TN, 50 acres. Wit: Benjamin Williams, Thomas H. London and Robert M. Atkin. Reg: 3 Aug 1836.

Page 400 - 13 Dec 1834. George Cathey to Sarah Hamby, both of Bedford Co., TN, to hold land during her life and at her death to pass by this deed to her four sons, viz, John Walker Hamby, George Hamby, Hardin Hamby and Gabriel Williamson Hamby, each to have equal share. Land in Bedford Co., on waters of Caney Spring Creek. Borders Joshua Cherry. 55 acres. Wit: William Neill and James Walker. Reg: 3 Aug 1836.

Page 409 - 15 Oct 1832. John Gore, now deceased, executed to Edward Evans, a bond. I, John Gore of Bedford Co., TN, am bound unto Edward Evans of Lincoln Co., TN, for $800.00. Condition of above obligation, to 3 small tracts of land in all 90 acres. (1) Borders Gore, and of about 20 acres, (2) 47 acres, and (3) 23 acres, all on headwaters of Big Flat Creek. Wit: William Bearden and Edward Gore.
21 Jun 1836. John Long, administrator of John Gore, deceased, of Tallageda, Alabama, conveyed to William Russell of Bedford Co., TN, land dordering Kindred Pearson and Russell. 47 acres.

Another tract adjoining the above tract and Russel's field. 20 acres. Also another tract adjoining the last tract, of 23 acres. Wit: Nicholas Newton, Jr. and Needham King. Reg: 9 Aug 1836.

Page 412 - 3 Oct 1835. Thomas J. Lane and Martin M. Lane, Executors of Thomas Long, deceased, sold to Hiram Harris, land in Bedford Co., TN, on Duck River. Borders Joseph Click and Theophilus Hunter. 215 acres. Wit: John M. Lane and Samuel Winstead. Reg: 9 Aug 1836.

Page 414 - 8 Mar 1817. Green B. Dun of Williamson Co., TN sold to Richard Smith of Bedford Co., TN, land in Bedford Co., on waters of Clems Creek. Borders Abraham Boylers(Byler). Wit: Robert Wilson, Isaac Smith, James C. Fulton, James Smith and Hugh M. Gaunt. Reg: 10 Aug 1836.

Page 415 - 26 Jul 1836. James Floyd of Pope Co., Illinois to Samuel and Anthony Floyd of Bedford Co., TN, land in Bedford Co., on headwaters of Big Flat Creek. Borders lands of Michael Wommoc(Womack) now owned by David Floyd, and Nathan Hodge. 150 acres. Wit: James Finney and Spencer B. Floyd. Reg: 11 Aug 1836.

Page 419 - 24 May 1836. Robert Cannon of Bedford Co., TN to Erwin McAdams of Lincoln Co., TN, land in Bedford Co., on waters of the middle prong of Rock Creek, originally granted to David Ross by State of Tennessee. Borders James Adams and William D. Orr. 91 acres. Reg: 11 Aug 1836.

Page 423 - 6 Feb 1836. John Thompsonto Richardson Clardy in right of his wife Adaline Metilda, all of Bedford Co., TN, for $200.00 as part of a legacy to his daughter Adaline Metilda, now wife of Richardson Clardy, grants unto Richardson Clardy in right of his wife Adaline Metilda, a tract of land in Bedford Co., on headwaters of a north branch of Duck River running in near Thompson Ford. Borders school land, William Lemore and John Thompson. 100 acres. Wit: Joseph P. Thompson and W. D. Orr. Reg: 12 Aug 1836.

Page 426 - 17 Aug 1835. I, Thompson Thompson bequeathed to his son John F. Thompson and for $500.00, as a gift from his estate, land in Bedford Co., on south side of Duck River. Borders Jacob Lentz's land, Duck River, John F. Thompson's corner and Ben Lentz's corner. 74 acres. Wit: John Fisher and George W. Parsons. Reg: 13 Aug 1836.

Page 436 - 3 Aug 1835. John Morton, Sr. to Joseph T. Morton, John Morton, Jr. and Charles P. Morton, all of Bedford Co., TN, for love and affection John Morton, Sr. has for his sons, Joseph, John and Charles, granted unto them land in Bedford Co., on Duck River. Borders Joshua Nichols and John Webb, Duck River, Samuel McDaniel, Clark's corner, and where John L. Wood did reside. 200 acres. Wit: Joseph Headlee, William Mason, J. M. Riggs and Gabriel S. Morton. Reg: 19 Aug 1836.

Page 438 - 3 Aug 1836. Richard Smith of Williamson Co., TN to James Mankins of Bedford Co., TN, land in bedford Co., on Clems Creek. Borders Abram Byler. 121 acres. Wit: Hugh M. Gault and James Smith. Reg: 19 Aug 1836.

DEED BOOK "FF"

Page 439 - 23 Dec 1823. Zacheus Wilson of Sumner Co., TN to James Gammill of Bedford Co., TN, land in Bedford Co., on West Fork of Caney Spring Creek, it being part of 4096 acres granted to David Wilson, deceased, and by the Last Will and Testament of David Wilson left to Zacheus Wilson. Borders James Gammill and Sarah Long. 110 acres. Wit: Mark Dodd and Joseph Rossin. Reg: 19 Aug 1836.

Page 442 - 10 Aug 1836. John Thompson to Joseph P. Thompson, both of Bedford Co., TN, as a part of a legacy to Joseph P. Thompson his son, land in Bedford Co., on the north side of Duck River, on the headwaters of the first branch below Thompson's Old Ford. Borders John Thompson, William Wade and Lenore's tract. 137 acres. Wit: William N. Orr and William D. Orr. Reg: 22 Aug 1836.

Page 442 - 20 Dec 1834. Hugh Carothers of Maury Co., TN to John Oneal of Bedford Co., TN, 400 acres in Bedford Co., on south side of Duck River. Borders Wilson's line now John J. Lentz, Reynold's line now Michael Cleek's heirs and the original line of the old Roberson survey. Wit: Fielding Bell and James W. Bell. Reg: 22 Aug 1836.

Page 443 - 27 Oct 1826. James Lockhart, surviving Executor of John Strother, deceased, of Davidson Co., TN sold to Alfred Balch of Davidson Co., land in Bedford Co., TN, 926½ acres, it being residue of a tract of land of George Doherty. Borders school land, Thomas Thompson and Nathaniel Taylor. Wit: Robert C. Thompson, Joseph Kincaid and A. Byler. Reg: 23 Aug 1836.

Page 446 - 8 Sep 1836. George W. Heard to Eli Moss, both of Bedford Co., TN, land in Bedford Co. and Village of Rowesville, known as Town Lot No. 13. Borders Main Street. Wit: Moses P. Calahan and Sterling Edwards. Reg: 8 Sep 1836.

Page 446 - 1 Feb 1836. Atkinson Stewart of Limestone Co., Alabama and Mary M. Stewart formerly Mary M. Walker wife of Atkinson Stewart sold to W. Nunn of Williamson Co., TN, land in Bedford Co., on waters of Clems Creek which was granted by the State of Tennessee to Henry Miller, dated 11 Jul 1811. Borders John Doherty and Robert McCuistion's occupant claim. Reg: 18 Sep 1836.

Page 450 - 23 Aug 1836. Malcum and Daniel Gilchrist of Lawrence Co., Alabama to Thomas J. Purdee of Bedford Co., TN, land in Bedford Co., adjoining said Purdee. Borders George Doherty, R. M. McCuistion, Benjamin McCuistion and the Old Road leading from Shelbyville to Nashville. 45 acres. Wit: William Gilchrist and Clement Cannon. Reg: 9 Sep 1836.

Page 451 - 23 Aug 1836. Malcum and Daniel Gilchrist of Lawrence Co., Alabama to Gray Lynch of Bedford Co., TN, land in Bedford Co., on waters of Wartrace Fork. Borders Andrew Martin, Quinn's corner, and William Bingham. 15 acres. Wit: William Gilchrist and A. C. Yell. Reg: 9 Sep 1836.

Page 452 - 24 Aug 1836. Malcum and Daniel Gilchrist of Lawrence Co., Alabama to John Sutton, Jr. of Bedford Co., TN, land in Bedford Co., on the headwaters of Hurricane Creek. Borders John Sutton, Patton & Erwin land, and Blount brothers grant. 76 acres. Reg: 12 Sep 1836.

DEED BOOK "FF"

Page 453 - 23 Aug 1836. Malcum and Daniel Gilchrist of Lawrence Co., Alabama to William Blakely, Sr. of Bedford Co., TN, land in Bedford Co., on waters of Wartrace Fork. Borders the road from Shelbyville to Murfreesboro and called the McKain Road. 127½ acres. Reg: 12 Sep 1836.

Page 456 - 13 Sep 1836. I, John Low of Macon Co., Alabama, appoint my friend Thomas Coffey, Esq., of Bedford Co., TN, my Attorney to procure a division between myself, George Low and the heirs of William Low, of a division in the land in Bedford Co., on Rock Creek. 379 acres, the same being conveyed to Daniel Low, my father, by Robert Elliott and the same being by the Will of Daniel Low demised to his wife Patsey Low, and after her death to be equally divided between the said John, William and George Low. Patsey Low being now dead. The land descended to John, George and William Low, or to the heirs of the latter, he being dead. Reg: 14 Sep 1836.

Page 457 - 13 Sep 1836. Booker Sheppard of Lincoln Co., TN to John T. Neil of Bedford Co., TN, land in Bedford Co., in Town of Shelbyville and known as Lot No. 111. Wit: L. Shapard and Robert Mathews. Reg: 14 Sep 1836.

Page 457 - 4 Aug 1836. Jacob Harber of Gibson Co., TN to Christian Harber of Bedford Co., TN, land in Bedford Co., on Rich Creek and known by Lot No. 10 in plat of division. 19 acres. Wit: James Pyland and Joseph Cleek. Reg: 14 Sep 1836.

Page 459 - 3 Sep 1836. Jeremiah Hay and Elizabeth Hay his wife to Christian Harber, all of Bedford Co., TN, land in Bedford Co., on Rich Creek. Reg: 14 Sep 1836.

Page 460 - 22 Jul 1836. William Pollard of Wayne Co., TN to Thomas Berry Anderson of Bedford Co., TN, for love and affection for Thomas Berry Anderson and for $1.00, personal property, cattle &c. Property in possession of Thomas Berry Anderson who lives with John Owens and Elizabeth Owens his mother in Bedford Co., TN. Property is to remain with John and Elizabeth Owen so long as Thomas B. Anderson resides with them and when Thomas B. Anderson leaves or reaches lawful age, he or his guardian is to have full power to remove property or dispose of it in a manner to benefit Thomas B. Anderson. Reg: 20 Sep 1836.

Page 463 - 15 Jan 1835. George H. McCommons of Hardeman Co., TN to Gideon B. Cunningham of Bedford Co., TN, land in Bedford Co., on headwaters of Sugar Creek. Borders Samuel Cunningham and John Stuart. 337 acres. Wit: Robert E. Bradshaw and Samuel Cunningham and Charles Black. Reg: 29 Sep 1836.

Page 467 - 14 Sep 1836. Tabitha Warner widow of John Warner, Jr., deceased, of Bedford Co., TN to Richard Warner of Bedford Co., land in Bedford Co., on waters of Duck River and adjoining lands of George Earnhart and others, being the same tract of land purchased by John Warner, Sr. from George Earnhart. 200 acres. Wit: Elias Jones and George Neeley. Reg: 5 Oct 1836.

Page 469 - 28 Jul 1836. Mary Endsley, Executrix of John Endsley, deceased, of Bedford Co., TN, Alfred C. Anderson and Damaris his wife formerly Damaris Endsley of Lincoln Co., TN, John M. Endsley, Isaac N. Endsley, Willis Burgess and Cynthia his wife formerly Cynthia Endsley of Bedford Co., TN to Bedford Endsley of Bedford Co., for $750.00, being the sum to which the land, hereinafter described, was valued by William Williams, James Allison and William D. Orr, agreeable to the Will of John Endsley, deceased, released unto Bedford Endsley and his heirs, land in Bedford Co., on East Fork of Rock Creek, being Hardy Murphy survey. Borders John Medearis, Isaac N. Endsley, Murphy's Entry, J. M. Endsley and William C. Swanson. 150 acres. Wit: Thomas Cummings and Joseph McAdams. Reg: 6 Oct 1836.

Page 472 - 22 Mar 1833. Elias Gwynn of McGoupin Co., Illinois sold to Isaac Muse of Bedford Co., TN, land in Bedford Co., on waters of Wartrace Fork. Borders Muse's land and where he now lives, Bradford's line, Blount's survey, and Thomas Merritt. 100 acres. Wit: George Davidson and T. R. Anderson. Reg: 8 Oct 1836.

Page 479 - 19 Sep 1836. I, John Low of Macon Co., Alabama, appoint my friend Thomas Coffee, Esq. of Bedford Co., TN, my Attorney to procure a division between myself and the heirs of William Low of land in Bedford Co., on Rock Creek and of 379 acres, it being the same conveyed to Daniel Low, my father, by Robert Elliott and afterwards divided by the Will of Daniel Low to his wife Patsey Low and after her death to be equally divided between his three sons, myself, John Low, William and George Low. Patsey Low now being dead, desire the division of said land. Reg: 9 Nov 1836.

Page 483 - 19 Nov 1836. I, William Houston appointed my son Caleb P. Houston, both of Bedford Co., TN, my Attorney to bargain and purchase for my use, a tract of land from Robert McKenzie and wife Mary McKenzie. Land in Bedford Co., west of the Turnpike Road and north of the Dry Fork of Fall Creek, adjoining William Houston, Travis C. Nash, meanders of Fall Creek and Turnpike Road. Reg: 19 Nov 1836.

Page 486 - 9 Jan 1835. William Old of Lincoln Co., TN to Thomas W. Harper of Bedford Co., TN, land in Bedford Co. of 139 acres. Borders Patton & Erwin tract, Rogers & Hatley tract, ridge dividing Brown & Morton tract, and Lewis Medlin & school land, and Parrish Garner. Wit: John Armstrong and William Armstrong. Reg: 25 Nov 1836.

Page 487 - 18 Mar 1833. Henry Conway of Bedford Co., TN to Elias Gwynn of McGoupin Co., Illinois, land in Bedford Co., on waters of Wartrace Fork. Borders Thomas Owens, Gwynn's corner, and Henry Conway. 12 acres. Wit: R. H. Conway and William Trice. Reg: 26 Nov 1836.

Page 487 - 26 Nov 1836. We, Marinda Steele, Jane P. Steele, Volney H. Steele, Carlos D. Steele, John P. Steele, and Mary W. Neeley, all of Bedford Co., TN appointed our brother Price C. Steele of Bedford Co., our Attorney to convey all interest in the estate of Jas. C. Wilson, deceased, either real or personal (property) in Sumner Co., TN and Bedford Co., and through the administrator _____ Chambers. Jonathan Cooper and Elmore Hendly. Reg: 26 Nov 1836.

Page 488 - 14 Feb 1809. I, James Millikin, Sr. for love and affection for my daughter Jane Reynolds, both of Bedford Co., TN, conveyed one negro woman Cate and her child George. The negroes have already been delivered unto Jane Reynolds. Wit: James Millikin, Jr. and Anthony Reagor. Reg: 26 Nov 1836.

Page 489 - 28 Nov 1836. I, William S. Mayfield of Marshall Co., TN appointed Kenneth L. Anderson of Bedford Co., TN, my Attorney to expend the sum of $1274.62 which I have due 1 Jan 1838 drawn by O. Claiborne and accepted by Jno. S. Gouch, placed into hands of K. L. Anderson to purchase stock of merchandise for a suitable merchantile establishment in Town of Shelbyville. Wit: Michael Green and J. C. Burditt. Reg: 29 Nov 1836.

Page 494 - 30 May 1836. James C. Gambill and Martha Gambill his wife formerly Martha Stewart sold to Michael Holt, all of Bedford Co., TN, land in Bedford Co., on waters of Flat Creek. Bounded by Hundley Wiggins and Jacob Greer, Michael Holt, Joshua Yeates. 124 acres, land being the place of which the late William Stewart died seized and possessed and on which Peggy Stewart widow of William Stewart, deceased, lately resided. The land yet undivided to the heirs. Wit: William D. Orr, Clerk of Bedford County, TN. Reg: 2 Dec 1836.

Page 496 - 29 Dec 1835. Logan Henderson of Rutherford Co., TN to Wright Oliver of Bedford Co., TN, land in Bedford Co., on waters of Little Sinking Creek. Adjoining lands of John H. Gambill and Andrew Neil and borders James Neil. 166 acres. Wit: John H. Gambill and Thomas Gambill. Reg: 3 Dec 1836.

Page 498 - 18 May 1836. Nathan H. Schooler of Bedford Co., TN to George Davidson of Franklin Co., TN, land in Bedford Co., on waters of Fall Creek, it being a part of a 640 acre grant by State of Tennessee to John Payton and William Payton. Borders John and William Payton and Nowlin's land or Tillman's line. 153 acres. Wit: H. M. Davidson and G. W. Davidson. Reg: 3 Dec 1836.

Page 501 - 1 Dec 1834. Benjamin Fugit to Moses Cheves. For value received of Moses Cheves, I do hereby relinquish all the title, claim and interest that I have in 100 acres of land that my father Moses Fugit bought from Benjamin Penn. Wit: William A. Gaunt and Jacob H. Cheves. Reg: 5 Dec 1836.

Page 501 - 23 Jul 1835. Calloway Co., KY. Whereas William Reaves, deceased, late of Bedford Co., TN, owned a tract of land in Bedford Co., between Falling Creek and the North Fork, it being a part of a 4000 acre tract granted by North Carolina to Richard Trotter. Borders Eppes Taylor, land William Peach sold to William Reeves, deceased, belonging to the 7 heirs of William Reaves, deceased. Whereas we, Coleman Nichols and Rebecca Nichols his wife of Calloway Co., KY, one of the legatees hath an undivided land, appoint Absalom Reaves of Bedford Co., our Executor or Administrator, our Attorney to bargain and sell our share of the land. Wit: E. H. Curd. Reg: 5 Dec 1836.

Page 503 - 27 Jul 1835. Whereas William Reaves, deceased, of Bedford Co., TN, owned a tract of land in Bedford Co., between Falling Creek and North Fork of Duck River, it being a part of a North Carolina Grant to Richard Trotter. Borders Epps Taylor. Survey leaving 160 acres belonging to the heirs and legatees of William Reaves, deceased, there being seven in number and whereas Waitman Gullett of Pope Co., Illinois, one of the legatees hath an undivided land, appointed Abraham Reeves of Bedford Co., TN, as Executor or Administrator, my Attorney. Waitman Gullett and Elizabeth Gullett signed instrument. Reg: 5 Dec 1836.

Page 504 - 25 Jul 1836. Granville H. Frazer of Washington Co., Mississippi, now of Bedford Co., TN to Mrs. Jane Frazer of Bedford Co., land or Town Lot in Town of Shelbyville. Borders William Gilchrist and new street made by P. Frazer and Clement Cannon to the Square. Lot known as Lot No. 78. Wit: Mary Temple and J. S. Frazer. Reg: 5 Dec 1836.

Page 506 - 18 Apr 1834. James and Martha Wood to William Willis of Bedford Co., TN, land in Bedford Co., on waters of Falling Creek, the same being a part of a tract deeded to the heirs of Daniel Williams, deceased. 17 acres. Wit: James M. Williams and James Clanton. Reg: 6 Dec 1836.

Page 507 - 22 Oct 1836. Mary Worke to William Guy, both of Bedford Co., TN, land in Bedford Co., on waters of the North Fork and adjoining lands of William Guy and the main road leading from Shelbyville to Murfreesboro, said land was owned by Col. Alexander Worke, deceased, of North Carolina and descended to Mary Worke as one of his heirs and legatees. 190 acres. Wit: Robert S. Worke and William Weaver. Reg: 6 Dec 1836.

Page 509 - 13 Aug 1832. Robert Cannon to Leonard W. Marbury, both of Bedford Co., TN, land in Bedford Co., in Town of Shelbyville by part of Lot No. 69. Borders Brick Tavern now occupied by said Marbury, then west with the north side of a building lately built by Cannon and Marbury to center of the brick division wall in said building. Wit: H. Conway and J. S. Frazer. Reg: 6 Dec 1836.

Page 511 - 6 Oct 1836. John Eakin, Executor of Benjamin Strickler, deceased, to John S. Frazer and Mary Temple, bonds, lands in Bedford Co., TN, adjoining the Town of Shelbyville. Borders Spring Street, just north of the Old Corporation line, Turnpike Road, Gilchrist's line, north side of the Nashville Road, Robert P. Harrison and Ringstaff's line. 73+ acres. Reg: 7 Dec 1836.

Page 573 - 28 Oct 1834. James Erwin of Fayette Co., KY to Andrew Erwin, Jr. at present of Nashville, TN, land in Bedford Co. Borders the purchase of A. Erwin, Jr. of Rev. George Newton and also land purchased by Richard Ferrill of Vincent Smith on which Ferrill now resides, the Yeates place on which Mrs. McCullough now resides, land formerly owned by Matthew and Labon Jones and now by Mr. Cotner and the heirs of said Jones, and the Garrison Fork of Duck River and Adjoining lands of Jeremiah Cleveland. 150 acres. Wit: John P. Erwin and Frances L. Erwin, George W. Smith and G. G. Osborne. Reg: 8 Dec 1836.

Page 573 - 8 Oct 1830. Thomas Thompson of Hardeman Co., TN to Lewis Anthony of Williamson Co., TN, land in Bedford Co., TN, on Clems Creek. Borders school land, Clems Creek. 93 acres. Wit: George J. Poindexter and Wilson McAllen. Reg: 8 Dec 1836.

Page 516 - 3 Aug 1836. Jackson Lyles, Sr. to Jackson Lyles, Jr., his son, both of Bedford Co., TN, land in Bedford Co., on waters of Alexanders Creek, adjoining lands of Lain(Lane) & McClain and others. Borders land granted to William Alexander and Thomas McClain. 100 acres. Wit: Jas. H. Lile and William G. Hight. Reg: 12 Dec 1836.

Page 517 - 29 Nov 1836. Margaret Cunningham to John W. C. Cunningham, both of Bedford Co., TN, land in Bedford Co. Borders Margaret Cunningham, east side of Sinking Creek and G. W. Cunningham's corner. 50 acres. Wit: Thomas Coffey and Otheneil Freeman. Reg: 12 Dec 1836.

Page 519 - 29 Apr 1836. Joseph J. Marshall of Bedford Co., TN (or Marshall Co. as the case may be) to James Carson of Williamson Co., TN, negro boy Matt. Reg: 13 Dec 1836.

Page 521 - 23 Dec 1836. Michael Marsh to J. S. Frazer and Strickler & Cowan of Town of Shelbyville, and Alexander Eakin of Shelbyville of the third part. Michael Marsh is indebted to J. S. Frazer, Strickler & Cowan by two notes, sold unto Alexander Eakin, horses and personal property. Wit: J. S. Cooper and G. H. Frazer. Reg: 23 Dec 1836.

Page 523 - 19 Oct 1836. John B. Moss and his wife Nancy H. Moss, Hetty L. Alexander and Margaret Smith of Cabarrus Co., NC sold to Amos McAdams of Bedford Co., TN, land in Bedford Co., on waters of the South Fork of Fall Creek, about four miles north of Shelbyville, adjoining the lands of Demaricus Tune, Peyton H. Comb, Robert P. Harrison, McAdams, Martin Phifer's tract, Dr. Robert McKenzie, Farrar's lands, John Tune, and others. 833+ acres. Our interest being three shares of the tract, each share being one tenth part of the whole tract or about 83 acres a share, being our interest and share in the land described to us in right of our mother Esther Alexander who was one of the children of Caleb Phifer, deceased, being our interest. Wit: W. Phifer and Jno. F. Phifer. Certified 18 Oct 1836.

Page 526 - 30 Dec 1836. Joseph S. Cates and wife Sophia Cates, David K. Hime, David Hime, John Hime, Sophronia Hime, and Cynthia Hyme, heirs and distributees of Polly Hime, deceased, have in to said land as above described, be devisted out of said complainants and that the same be vested in John Wallace, his heirs and assignees forever. (Instrument not complete). Reg: 31 Dec 1836.

Page 528 - 1 Nov 1836. Malcome Gilchrist and Daniel Gilchrist of Lawrance Co., Alabama to Doctor William Houston of Bedford Co., TN, land in Bedford Co., on the North Fork of Fall Creek. Borders the west side of the Turnpike Road, north of the center of the first bridge north of the house where Capt. John Stone now lives, on a line between Doctor William Houston and Daniel Gilchrist, Malcom Gilchrist, land of widow Deason now lives, and Jesse Scott. 78 acres. Wit: Caleb P. Houston and William Houston. Reg: 2 Jan 1837.

Page 535 - 26 Dec 1835. Samuel McGuffin of Rutherford Co., TN to William R. Alford of Bedford Co., TN, land in Bedford Co., on waters of Alexanders Creek. Borders William Harrison. 65 acres. Wit: John L. Cooper and C. D. Cooper. Reg: 6 Jan 1837.

Page 535 - 13 Feb 1836. Samuel McGuffin of Rutherford Co., TN to William R. Alford of Bedford Co., TN, land in Bedford Co., on Alexanders Creek. Borders Joseph Sanders, Joseph Dickerson's grant, Thomas Primrose's corner. 7 acres. Wit: Thomas Williams, Harmon Adcock, Daniel T. Barnes and Thomas T. Bullock. Reg: 6 Jan 1837.

Page 542 - 4 Dec 1835. I, William Kinney of Jackson Co., Alabama, sold to William Potter of Bedford Co., TN, land in Bedford Co., on waters of Sinking Creek. Borders Sinking Creek, Humphrey Cunningham and William Potter. 100 acres. Wit: James Potter and Elijah Potter. Reg: 7 Jan 1837.

Page 542 - 27 Oct 1836. Malcom Gilchrist and Daniel Gilchrist of Lawrance Co., Alabama to Mansfield Whitehead of Bedford Co., TN, land in Bedford Co., on headwaters of Clems Creek. Borders a corner of Mansfield Whitehead land where he now lives, N. Taylor's land on which Mrs. Absalom Boiler (Byler) now lives, Mr. McKisick's purchase, land on which Squire Taylor now lives, and George Doherty's grant. 141 acres. Reg: 9 Jan 1837.

Page 546 - 29 Dec 1835. Logan Henderson of Rutherford Co., TN to David Dryden of Bedford Co., TN, land in Bedford Co., on Big Sinking Creek. Borders James Johnston, Onail(Oneal)'s line, and Harper's line. 98½ acres. Wit: Michael Moore and David Guest. Reg: 10 Jan 1837.

Page 548 - 13 Sep 1834. Joseph Steele of Bedford Co., TN to James G. Neeley and Mary P. Neeley, for love and affection for his son-in-law James G. Neeley and Mary P. Neeley his daughter and as a part of the estate of her father, conveyed unto them land in Bedford Co., on the waters of Falling Creek. Borders McElwrath's tract. 175 acres. Wit: C. D. Steele and John P. Steele. Reg: 10 Jan 1837.

Page 552 - 10 Jan 1837. Logan Henderson of Rutherford Co., TN to Thomas Moore of Bedford Co., TN, land in Bedford Co., on waters of Little Sinking Creek. Borders Jordan's and James Neil's land. 244 acres. Wit: Michael Moore and Andrew Vannoy. Reg: 11 Jan 1837.

Page 554 - 13 Jan 1837. Deed of Gift. 2 negroes. I, Malcolm Gilchrist of Bedford Co., TN, for respect for Malcolm Gilchrist Anderson, the son of Kenneth P. Anderson and also 50¢, negro woman Milly and negro girl Harriett. Wit: Robert Mathews and George Davidson. Reg: 13 Jan 1837.

Page 556 - 3 Oct 1836. Thomas J. Muse is indebted to John T. Muse, both of Bedford Co., TN, for $35.00. Wit: William H. Muse, Jacob C. Muse and J. C. Muse. Reg: 18 Jan 1837.

Page 560 - 9 Jan 1837. Logan Henderson of Ritherford Co., TN to Michael Moore of Bedford Co., TN, land in Bedford Co.,on both sides of Big Sinking Creek. Borders lands of David Dryden and Samuel Harper, James Johnston, and Briant's line. 100 acres. Wit: William H. Moore and Nancy E. Moore. Reg: 18 Jan 1837.

Page 563 - 8 Jan 1836. Absalom Reeves to Dudley Crutchfield, both of Bedford Co., TN, land in Bedford Co., on waters of Falling Creek, it being three seventh of a one hundred and six acres left by will of William Reaves, deceased, to his heirs. Borders Esquire Taylor. 106 acres. Wit: Evan Harris and G. T. Harris. Reg: 19 Jan 1837.

Page 563 - 23 Mar 1836. Alanson and Benjamin Oslin to Mansfield Whitehead, all of Bedford Co., TN, land in Bedford Co., on waters of Clems Creek. Borders the road leading from Shelbyville to Nashville, A. Bylers' line, and Walker's line. 100 acres. Wit: James T. Byler and William Elmore. Reg: 19 Jan 1837.

Page 565 - 2 Mar 1836. Isaac Raney to Mary Wells his daughter, both of Bedford Co., TN, all his interest &c in land in Bedford Co., on the north side of Duck River, it being a part of three tracts belonging to said Rainey. Borders A. C. Wilson, G. H. Allen, and B. G. Raney's line and J. N. Raney. 227 acres. Wit: Jos. Lillard and J. N. Rainey. Reg: 19 Jan 1837.

Page 565 - 13 Jan 1836. I, Isaac Raney of Bedford Co., TN, for love and affection for my daughter Rachel now the wife of William Lane, convey unto her a negro girl Susanna. Wit: J. N. Rainey and L. Rainey. Reg: 19 Jan 1837.

Page 560 - 29 Feb 1836. Isaac Raney to Isaac N. Rainey, both of Bedford Co., TN, 184½ acres. Two tracts in Bedford Co., on north side of Duck River. Beginning in the middle of the well in corner of B. G. Rainey's land near his gin, Cathey's corner and Isaac Rainey. Other tract borders James A. McCall's corner, A. C. Wilson's line, and Mary Well's line. 35 acres. Wit: Hugh McClelan and Jos. Lillard. Reg: 19 Jan 1837.

Page 569 - Dec Term 1831, Circuit Court of Bedford Co., TN. Mary Shuffield who sued by her next friend Richard Wright, obtained a decree divorcing the said Mary Shuffield from her husband Arthur Shuffield. Mary was allowed $10.00 quarterly as allimony for support of said Mary, which allimony is made out of the personal property and lands of Arthur Shuffield, sum of $180.00 due on 11 June 1836. John Shuffield appointed guardian of Arthur Shuffield. This 6 Dec 1836. Reg: 20 Jan 1837.

Page 573 - 2 Jan 1835. Reuben Reeves of Calloway Co., KY to Luddy Crutchfield of Bedford Co., TN, land in Bedford Co., on waters of Fall Creek, it being four sevenths of a one hundred and six acre tract left by the will of William Reeves, deceased, to his heirs. Borders Epps Taylor. 106 acres. Wit: William Anderson and Sion Damron. Reg: 20 Jan 1837.

Page 578 - 21 Jan 1837. I, John Scott of Bedford Co., TN, for love and affection I have to my daughter Elizabeth Sarah Singleton, convey unto her a negro girl Kitty. At the death of Elizabeth Sarah Singleton, the negro is to go to her children. Wit: Joshua P. Scott and John Eakin. Reg: 21 Jan 1837.

Page 581 - 19 Mar 1834. Richard D. McGee of Ray Co., MO to Dudley P. T. House of Bedford Co., TN, land in Bedford Co., on north side of Duck River and known as Lot No. 3 in the division of land among the heirs of William McGee, deceased. Borders center of a spring now used by John Howe and Jacob Ham on south side of Duck River, small tract called The Meeting House Tract (Three Forks C. P. Church), Charles Lucas, Mill Tract, and to the edge of Mill Race. 108 acres. Wit: William Jenkins and E. W. Brown. Reg: 25 Jan 1837.

DEED BOOK "FF"

Page 582 - 20 Jan 1837. Thomas Norville to William Brown, both of Bedford Co., TN, release to an estate claim, both real and personal estate of David Norville, deceased. Thomas Norville being one of the heirs at law of David Norville, deceased. Wit: Henry Brown and E. J. Frierson. Reg: 25 Jan 1837.

Page 586 - 15 Sep 1835. Martha Brown of Bedford Co., TN to her three children, William R. Brown, Charlotte E. Brown and George W. Brown of Bedford Co., for natural love and affection for her children, conveyed a certain portion of goods and chattles &c. Wit: Nathan Ivey and H. S. Wilson. Reg: 4 Feb 1837.

Page 587 - 3 Feb 1837. Jesse K. Webb of Bedford Co., TN to Uriah A. Clary of Phillips Co., Arkansas, conveyed all his interest to a certain preemption, being on the west bank of the Mississippi River in Phillips Co., Arkansas, known in the survey as the north half of Fractional Section No. 20, in the Township three south, in range five east. 192 acres. Also, the south east fractional quarter of Section 17, Township 3 south, and range 5 east. 112 acres. Wit: Robert P. Harrison. Reg: 4 Feb 1837.

Page 589 - 7 Feb 1837. James D. Norville to Samuel Phillips, for natural love he bears for his children and for $1.00, all right title, claim and interest which James Norville has in the estate of David Norville, deceased, as one of the legatees of David Norville, deceased, both real and personal property. Wit: Theoderick F. Bradford and Samuel Escue. Reg: 7 Feb 1837.

Page 590 - 17 Oct 1836. W. R. Nunn of Williamson Co., TN to John Boyce of Bedford Co., TN, land in Bedford Co., it being part of Grant No. 3199 granted by State of Tennessee to Henry Miller and bounded by David Lamb's line. 55 acres. Wit: W. D. Hill and Thomas McCuistion. Reg: 7 Feb 1837.

Page 592 - 1 Feb 1836. Samuel Walker of Bedford Co., TN one part and Peggy Stewart her lifetime and then John Stewart other part, land in Bedford Co., on the head of Sugar Creek. Borders lands of Nathaniel White, John Bradshaw, Cunningham and Leven McNutt's corner and McCommon's line. Wit: William Stewart and Isaac B. Holt. Reg: 7 Feb 1837.

Page 592 - 31 Jan 1837. William Yeates of Bedford Co., TN to Samuel Walker of Cole Co., Illinois, 11 acres of land in Bedford Co. Bounded by Nathan Evans, Bradshaw's line, mouth of a lane between Bradshaw and Walker, and between Bradshaw and the widow Evans. Wit: A. W. Morrison and J. B. Dryden. Reg: 8 Feb 1837.

DEED BOOK "GG" 1837 - 1838

Page 3 - 20 Dec 1836. The heirs of George W. Lynn, deceased. Bill for sale of land. Land sold at Court House in Shelbyville. George Pratt being highest bidder. Joseph Hasty and his wife Mary, Nathan Hubbard and Nancy Hubbard, heirs and children of Katharine Hubbard one of the heirs of Lynn, deceased. The land in Bedford Co., TN, on Big Flat Creek. Borders George Pratt's land, lands Valentine Kizer deeded to George Lynn, Sr., to land where George Pratt now lives, middle of Flat Creek, land Enoch Pratt deeded to George Pratt, and also land William Kizer deeded to Pratt. The land included the plantation where Lynn, Sr. lived at his death. 73 acres. Reg: 11 Feb 1837.

Page 12 - 17 Aug 1835. Isaiah Davis of Hardeman Co., TN to Erwin W. Tucker of Bedford Co., TN, land in Bedford Co., on south side of Duck River. Borders Davis' line and Marcum's line. 20 acres. Wit: William Tucker, John Rogers and Thomas Ballard. Reg: 16 Feb 1837.

Page 13 - 17 Aug 1835. Isaiah Davis of Hardeman Co., TN to Erwin W. Tucker of Bedford Co., TN, land in Bedford Co., opposite mouth of North Fork, it being a part of a 2000 acre tract granted to John Graham. Borders John Marcum, Thomas Cook and Duck River. 150 acres. Wit: William Tucker, John Rogers and Thomas Ballard. Reg: 16 Feb 1837.

Page 13 - 26 Oct 1836. Walton H. Payne of Augustine Co., Texas to Allen Knight of Bedford Co., TN, land in Bedford Co., on Barren Fork. Borders Zebediah Payne's land he purchased of Archibald Reaves, also land of Z. Payne which he purchased of Theoderick F. Bradford, and the mouth of a ditch dug by Z. Payne to divide his land from Allen Knight. Wit: Joel H. Still and Jacob Coble. Reg: 16 Feb 1837.

Page 16 - 4 Jun 1832. Andrew Davidson to Isaac Muse and Richard Muse, all of Bedford Co., TN, land in Bedford Co., on headwaters of Sugar Creek, part of a 1000 acre land granted by State of North Carolina to Anthony Sharp and Thomas Dugan, No. 69. Borders Dugan tract and Morris' tract. 200 acres. Wit: James L. Armstrong and M. C. Daniel. Reg: 17 Feb 1837.

Page 17 - 21 Feb 1836. William Burns of Williamson Co., TN to Edward Haley of Bedford Co., TN, land in Bedford Co., on waters of Parch Corn Creek. Bounded by Clardy's land and Phifer line. 80 acres. Wit: Thomas P. Burns and William Haley. Reg: 17 Feb 1837.

Page 18 - 17 Sep 1835. John T. Harmon of Henderson Co., TN & Adam Ralmage and James Ronaldson of City of Philadelphia, PA sold to Carey Nicholas, deceased, in his lifetime, for a Printing Press &c advanced by Ronaldson & Ralmage in year 1821 to said Nicholas & George Tunstall then residing in Territory of Florida. Wit: Jas. Neeley and Jno. Purdy. Reg: 21 Feb 1837.

Page 19 - 19 Sep 1836. Joseph Phillips of Rutherford Co., TN and Boyd McNairy of Davidson Co., TN to James Ronaldson and Adam Ramage of City of Philadelphia, PA, land in Bedford Co., TN, on Sugar Creek. Borders lands of John Hall purchased of Sarah Clift and Thomas Greer. 100 acres. Also, 50 acres in Bedford Co., on Sugar Creek. Borders John Patton's corner and John Hall's line. Another tract of 50 acres, borders George Martin and Patton's line. Wit: Francis B. Fogg, G. M. Fogg, Philip McNairy, Thomas J. Wharten and P. M. Sands. Reg: 21 Feb 1837.

Page 20 - 28 Jun 1836. I, James Ronaldson of Township of Philadelphia, PA, Type Founder & Cotton Spinner, appoint Ephraim H. Foster, Francis B. Fogg and Godfrey M. Fogg or either of them, my Attorneys to grant, bargain and sell his lands in Bedford Co., TN. Wit: Edward Hurst and J. R. Brognard (of Philadelphia, PA). Reg: 21 Feb 1837.

DEED BOOK "GG"

Page 21 - 25 Oct 1836. I, Adam Ramage of Philadelphia, PA, appoint Ephraim H. Foster, Francis B. Fogg and Godfrey M. Fogg or either of them, my Attorney, to grant, bargain and sell land in Bedford Co., TN, belonging to William Ronaldson and myself. Wit: Jno. Briggs and William P. Dilleker (PA). Reg: 21 Feb 1837.

Page 22 - 14 Feb 1837. James Ronaldson and Adam Ramage of Philadelphia, PA to John Harrison of Bedford Co., TN, land in Bedford Co., on Sugar Creek. Borders Sarah Clift and Thomas Greer. 100 acres. Also 50 acres in Bedford Co., on Sugar Creek and bordered by John Patton's corner and John Hall's line. Another 50 acres in Bedford Co., bordering George Martin's line, Greer's line, and Patton's line. Wit: Will S. Bailey and R. C. R. Martin. Reg: 21 Feb 1837.

Page 24 - 9 Feb 1836. Harrison Payne and his wife Peggy formerly Peggy Pearson of Bedford Co., TN to John Stephenson of Bedford Co., land in Bedford Co., on waters of Sinking Creek. Borders survey of Malcolme Gilchrist and his Blue Spring tract, and Jesse Mize. 40 acres. Wit: Green T. Neeley and Richard P. Stephenson. Reg: 22 Feb 1837.

Page 25 - 3 Feb 1837. Thomas Davidson of Marshall Co., TN to Margaret Price of Marshall Co., TN, land in Bedford Co., TN, on waters of Sinking Creek, being a part of the one third part of an entry of 640 acres in the name of Arthur Brooks and by grant No. 4583. Bounded by Resin Smith, Medlin's line and Doherty's line. 56 acres. Wit: Daniel Looney and James Dillard. Reg: 22 Feb 1837.

Page 27 - 1 Jan 1837. James Erwin of Davidson Co., TN to Samuel Escue of Shelbyville, TN, land in Bedford Co., TN and Town of Shelbyville and known as Lot No. 16. Reg: 28 Feb 1837.

Page 27 - 14 Feb 1837. James Erwin of Fayette Co., KY by his Attorney Andrew Erwin of Nashville, TN to Kinchen Stokes of Bedford Co., TN, land in Bedford Co., TN, on the Garrison Fork. Bounded by the Garrison Fork opposite the mouth of the Wartrace Fork, which is also the corner of one or two of the old grants from North Carolina to Blount brothers, Daniel Hooser and Cyrus Sharp's tract and now called the Mrs. McConnell tract, mouth of Roberts branch which is the lower corner on the Garrison Fork of the Brick House Tract. Wit: Edward Smith and Thomas J. Brown. Reg: 28 Feb 1837.

Page 29 - 31 Oct 1836. Malcum Gilchrist and Daniel Gilchrist of Lawrance Co., Alabama to Robert Clinkenbeard of Bedford Co., TN, land in Bedford Co., on headwaters of Fall Creek. Borders Joseph Loyd, Clinkenbeard's line, survey of Thomas Dougan, William Murphree. 54 acres. Wit: William Murphree and R. C. Clinkenbeard. Reg: 28 Feb 1837.

Page 31 - 6 Sep 1836. Thomas P. Powel of Bedford Co., TN to Dudley H. Lindsey of Rutherford Co., TN, land in Bedford Co., on Alexanders Creek. 231 acres. Wit: John L. Cooper and Jos. Lindsey. Reg: 28 Feb 1837.

Page 33 - 29 Jan 1836. Joseph Steele to John Steele, both of Bedford Co., TN, for love and affection for his son John Steele, as a part of his estate, given him land in Bedford Co., on waters of Falling Creek. Bounded by Falling Creek, Wilson Steele, McLewrath(McElwrath) corner and John McClain's line. Wit: David Orr and John Fisher. Reg: 1 Mar 1837.

Page 33 - 11 Jan 1836. Charles Ray sold to Samuel Crowel, Jr. land belonging to the heirs of William Ray, deceased, land in Bedford Co., TN, on south side of Duck River. Adjoining lands of Peter Crowel, Michael Fisher and James Paschal. Wit: Jos. Anderson, William Anderson and Benjamin Saxon. Reg: 1 Mar 1837.

Page 35 - 5 Jul 1830. Jefferson Haley Ake to Walter Mileham, both of Jackson Co., Alabama, sold an undivided inheritance that Jefferson Haley Ake is entitled to his father Joseph Ake, deceased, as an heir of Joseph Ake, deceased. 262 acres in Bedford Co., TN and whereon Joseph Ake, deceased and on the waters of the Wartrace Fork. Wit: C. B. H. Ake and Felix G. Ake. Reg: 6 Mar 1837.

Page 37 - 12 May 1827. John M. Bright, James Crow, Narcissa Crow his wife of James Crow formerly Narcissa Bright, all of Bedford Co., TN to George W. Bright of Franklin Co., Alabama, all of whom are heirs of William Bright, late of Bedford Co., TN. The parties of these presents are possessed and seized as co-partners in a treaty of land in Bedford Co., on east side of Rich Creek. Bounded by John H. Anderson and Josiah Davis. This land was granted to William Bright, deceased, by Tennessee Grant No. 1368. Wit: John T. Neil and J. B. Anderson. Reg: 10 Mar 1837.

Page 40 - 15 Dec 1835. Isaac James, Sr. to Theodocia H. Clardy, Executrix of Richard S. Clardy, deceased, all of Bedford Co., TN. I, Isaac James, Sr. sold to Theodocia H. Clardy a tract of land in Bedford Co., on waters of Wartrace Fork, it being a part of a 3000 acre grant to Tilman Dickson by State of North Carolina. Bounded by mouth of Cedar branch, a fork of the Oter (Otter) Fork of the Wartrace Fork, Dickson's corner and to what was formerly Peter Daniel's corner. 200 acres. Agreeable to the Last Will and Testament of Richard S. Clardy, deceased, wherein he made a special provision in said will authorizing his wife Theodocia H. Clardy at any time before a division took place according to the use of buying or purchasing another piece or tract of land. Wit: William J. Peacock and Burrell Featherston. Reg: 11 Mar 1837.

Page 45 - 16 Feb 1837. Julian Sharp (female) of Augusta Co., VA to James Scott of Augusta Co., VA, land in Bedford Co., TN, on waters of Duck River, on the Obion River, and on the Forked Deed River in Tennessee of which Alexander Worke of Iredell Co., NC, died seized, which lands passed by the will of said Alexander Worke, deceased, to the children of this deceased sister and brother. Julian Sharp is one of the daughters of Rebecca Scott of Augusta Co., VA who was a sister of said Alexander Worke. Wit: Thomas Thompson, George W. Baylor, William Thompson and Lewis Rhinehart. Reg: 17 Mar 1837.

Page 46 - 16 Feb 1837. James Scott and Ann his wife of Augusta Co., VA to John A. Davidson of Augusta Co., VA, land on Duck River, on the Forked Deer River, and on the Obion River in Tennessee of which Alexander Worke of Iredell Co., NC, died seized which passed by the will of Alexander Worke, deceased, to the children of his deceased sisters and brothers. James Scott is entitled by will, as one of the sons of Rebecca Scott of Augusta Co., VA, who was a sister of Alexander Worke, also James Scott is entitled by purchase of Julianne Sharpe widow and relict of Joseph Sharp, deceased, late Julianne Scott. Another of the children of Rebecca Scott to the half of another interest the said James Scott is entitled by purchase from John Scott, another of the children of Rebecca. And lastly to the one half of another interest said James Scott is entitled by purchase from Robert Berry and Rebecca his wife, late Rebecca Scott. Another of the children of Rebecca, the elder. Wit: Jefferson Kinney, J. N. Woodward and Nich. R. Trout. Reg: 17 Mar 1837.

Page 48 - 16 Feb 1837. John Scott of Augusta Co., VA to James Scott and John A. Davidson of Augusta Co., VA, land in Tennessee on Duck River on the Forked Deer River and on the Obion River, of which Alexander Worke of Iredell Co., NC died seized, which lands passed by the will of Alexander Worke, deceased, to the children of his deceased sister and brother. To one interest in which land the bargainer John Scott is entitled in virtue of said will. As one of the sons of Rebecca Scott of Augusta Co., VA, who was a sister of Alexander Worke, all this interest it is to be conveyed to James Scott and John A. Davidson. Wit: Thomas Thompson, Lewis Rhinehart, William Thompson and George W. Baylor. Reg: 17 Mar 1837.

Page 60 - 25 Jun 1835. John Deason, Sr. to Jesse Scott, Robert Clinkenbeard, Isaiah Webb, Thomas A. Peacock and John Deason, Commissioners, appointed to build a United Baptist Meeting House on the premises. John Deason granted unto the commissioners land in Bedford Co., TN, on waters of Fall Creek. Borders Malcum and Daniel Gilchrist and estate of Enoch Deason, east side of turnpike road between Shelbyville and Murfreesboro. Wit: Jesse Scott. Reg: 4 Apr 1837.

Page 61 - 9 Mar 1837. I, Nancy Cooper of Yalobusha Co., Mississippi, has appointed Lewis Fields of Bedford Co., TN, my Attorney to bargain and sell my interest in land in Bedford Co., it being the same which is known as a tract owned by the late William Cooper, deceased. Bounded by John McClure, Nathan Chaffin and E. H. Bigham. Reg: 4 Apr 1837.

Page 62 - 9 Mar 1837. Robert Brooks and Jane J. Brooks of Yalobusha Co., Mississippi to Elihugh H. Bigham of Rutherford Co., TN, land in Bedford Co., TN, being known as the tract owned by the late William Cooper, deceased. Bounded by John McClure, Nathan Chaffin and Elihugh H. Bigham. 30 acres. Wit: Lewis Fields and Anthony Clark. Reg: 4 Apr 1837.

Page 63 - 28 Jan 1837. Benjamin Kimbro and his wife Ann to Allen Knight, all of Bedford Co., TN, land in Bedford Co., on Barren Fork of Duck River. Bounded by Zebediah Payne's land purchased of Archibald Reaves and Theoderick F. Bradford. Wit: Charles G. McLean and C. W. Knight. Reg: 4 Apr 1837.

Page 64 - 1 Oct 1836. John Bond of Sumner Co., TN to Blann Maupin of Bedford Co., TN, land in Bedford Co., in Town of Rowesville and known as Lot No. 16 & 17. Bounded by Main Street and Barnett's line. Wit: Jas. _. Fowler and Sterling Edwards. Reg: 4 Apr 1837.

Page 65 - 27 Mar 1837. Nancy Cooper of Yalobusha Co., Mississippi to Elihu H. Bigham of Rutherford Co., TN, land in Bedford Co., TN, land in Bedford Co., known as tract owned by the late William Cooper, deceased. Bounded by John McClure, Nathan Chaffin and Elihu H. Bigham. About 35 acres. Wit: William W. Miller, H. Mason, Robert Clark and N. F. Neil. Reg: 4 Apr 1837.

Page 66 - 6 Dec 1828. Lecil Bobo of Franklin Co., TN to Kenneth L. Anderson of Bedford Co., TN, land in Bedford Co., adjoining Town of Shelbyville. Bounded on north side of town at middle of the end of Main Street which leads north from the west side of the Public Square of Shelbyville, corner of Dickson Academy land, and Martin Street. 2 acres. Wit: Robert Cannon and George Davidson. Reg: 5 Apr 1837.

Page 67 - 14 May 1836. I, Stephen White of Rutherford Co., TN, granted and given unto the heirs of Augustus H. White, Deed of Gift of negroes and property. The heirs of Augustus H. White are Stephen White, Jr., Thomas Davis White, and Elizabeth White and any other heirs that hereafter may be born unto Augustus H. White. I also give unto the heirs personal property. Wit: Newton Clark and William Norvell. Reg: 5 Apr 1837.

Page 68 - 24 Feb 1836. Thomas P. Payne of Province of Texas to Joseph Holt of Bedford Co., TN, land in Bedford Co., on the Barren Fork. Borders Holt's line and the bluff of the river. 12 acres. Wit: Allen Knight and Benjamin Kimbro. Reg: 5 Apr 1837.

Page 69 - 13 Dec 1836. George Davidson of Shelbyville, TN, Attorney for John W. Wilcox and wife of Evansville, Indiana to William Brown of Shelbyville, TN, land in Town of Shelbyville being south half of Lot No. 42. Borders Martin Street and Lot No. 54. Wit: William B. M. Brame and A. W. Young. Reg: 5 Apr 1837.

Page 69 - 28 Jun 1836. Robert McCuistion of Bedford Co., TN to William Little of Williamson Co., TN, land in Bedford Co., on waters of Wilsons Creek. Borders by Nancy Byler, William Poplin, Jesse Wheeler, Thomas McCuistion and James Garrett, J. C. Dever and William Collier, Jesse Daisy and widow Taylor and William Corbett. Wit: James Garrett and Chesley Williams. Reg: 5 Apr 1837.

Page 70 - 10 Aug 1835. Elliott Rucker of Bedford Co., TN to Jeremiah B. Boothe of Wilson Co., TN, land in Bedford Co., on waters of Alexander Creek, it being part of a grant to Ebenezer Alexander by North Carolina. Borders Wallace's line. Wit: Jacob Byler and Jesse Rucker. Reg: 5 Apr 1837.

Page 72 - 4 Feb 1837. Cyrus Simmons of Henderson Co., TN to Isaac B. Larue of Bedford Co., TN, land in Bedford Co., on waters of Rock Creek, it being land laid off and allotted to Cyrus Simmons and Adeline his wife in 1835. 175 acres. Borders John N. Hart, James H. McLaughlin, Thomas Hamilton and Lowe's land. Wit: H. B. Larue. Reg: 6 Apr 1837.

Page 73 - 21 Mar 1837. Henry C. Bradford to John M. Sehorn of Bedford Co., TN and Samuel McCarty of Lumpkin Co., GA. Deed of Trust. Reg: 6 Apr 1837.

Page 73 - 30 Mar 1837. I, John Scott of Bedford Co., TN, put into the possession of my daughter Elizabeth Sarah Singleton, a negro boy Westley and a negro girl Julia. Wit: J. W. Ragsdale and D. M. Ragsdale. Reg: 13 Apr 1837.

Pahe 78 - 16 Sep 1836. George E. Low of Tipton Co., TN to John Low of Macon Co., Alabama, conveyed to one of the heirs, John Low, land in Bedford Co., on waters of the East Fork of Rock Creek. Borders lands of Thomas Davidson, Isaac B. Larue, James Adams and Hart's and Simmons' line. 379 acres. Reg: 19 Apr 1837.

Page 79 - 8 Apr 1837. I, John Crawford of Marshall Co., TN sold to William H. Wisener of Bedford Co., TN, his interest in land in Marshall Co., on Flat Creek. Borders lands of John Laird, Esq., and others. Reg: 20 Apr 1837.

Page 79 - 26 Mar 1837. I, Kavanaugh Yancy of Bedford Co., TN, for love and affection for my son James Yancy and for $1.00, a negro girl Nancy. Reg: 20 Apr 1837.

Page 80 - 22 Mar 1837. Thomas J. Cooper of Florence, Lauderdale Co., Alabama one part and Elihu H. Bigham of Rutherford Co., TN second part, land in Bedford Co., TN, known as the late residence of William Cooper, deceased. Bounded by Weaver, Chaffin, Bigham, Epsey and McClure with the exception of one half acre known and designated The Grave Yard where the father of the said party of the first is buried and also with the exception of the dower of the mother of the said party of the first part, during her lifetime and at her death to be conveyed to Elihu H. Bigham. Also convey the dower of Mrs. McClure to the tract of land belonging to the heirs of William Cooper, deceased, unto Elihu H. Bigham. Wit: Lewis Fields and Anthony Clark. Reg: 20 Apr 1837.

Page 82 - 4 Feb 1837. Malcom Gilchrist and Daniel Gilchrist of Lawrence Co., Alabama to Elizabeth Cheves of Bedford Co., TN, land in Bedford Co., on waters of Big Sinking Creek. Borders a tract known as The Blue Spring tract and W. Hamel's tract. 40 acres. Wit: Calvin Cheves and Moses Cheves. Reg: 21 Apr 1837.

Page 83 - 15 Apr 1837. Jesse Gibson of Green Co., Alabama to John H. Laird of Bedford Co., TN, land in the Town of Shelbyville known as Lot No. 96. Reg: 21 Apr 1837.

Page 88 - 31 Oct 1836. Christopher Howard, Benjamin Howard, William Boone and Joseph Parker, heirs of the estate of William Howard, deceased, of Lincoln Co., TN to John Brooks and Samuel Mitchell of Bedford Co., TN, land in Bedford Co., on waters of Shipmans Creek. Borders east bank of Shipmans Creek now belonging to John Brooks and Samuel Mitchell about 35 yards below their mill and the road leading from Shelbyville to the mill, including the spring. 20 acres. Wit: Hosea H. Floyd and John F. Couser. Reg: 22 Apr 1837.

Page 90 - 10 Apr 1837. John A. Davidson of Augusta Co., VA to William Pollan of Bedford Co., TN, land in Bedford Co., on waters of North Fork. Bounded by John Thompson and the Sinking Creek. Reg: 28 Apr 1837.

Page 91 - 10 Apr 1837. John A. Davidson of Augusta Co., VA to James Clark of Bedford Co., TN, land in Bedford Co., on west bank of the lick branch which empties into the North Fork. Bounded by Thompsons Ford Road. 131 acres and known as Lot No. 5. Reg: 28 Apr 1837.

Page 92 - 10 Apr 1837. John A. Davidson of Augusta Co., VA to William Primrose of Bedford Co., TN, land in Bedford Co., on waters of North Fork. Borders Lot No. 5 (above instrument). 131 acres. Reg: 29 Apr 1837.

Page 93 - 10 Apr 1837. John A. Davidson of Augusta Co., VA to Barkley Tyler of Bedford Co., TN, land in Bedford Co., on waters of North Fork. Bounded by Lot No. 3 (see above instrument). 131 acres. Reg: 29 Apr 1837.

Page 93 - 10 Apr 1837. John A. Davidson of Augusta Co., VA to Dudley H. Lindsey of Bedford Co., TN, land in Bedford Co., on waters of North Fork. Bounded by Lot No. 6 (see above instrument). 118 acres. Reg: 29 Apr 1837.

Page 99 - 12 Feb 1837. Archibald C. Adams of Marshall Co., TN to Jabus Nowlin of Bedford Co., TN, land in Bedford Co., on East Fork of Rock Creek. Borders lands of Robert Montgomery and James Lowry, lands of Jabus Nowlin now owns and on which he lives, heirs of George _____, deceased, John Brown, and Thomas Nowlin. 152½ acres. Wit: Robert Montgomery and Thomas Nowlin. Reg: 3 May 1837.

Page 102 - 1 May 1837. Christeney (Christiana) and John F. Thompson, administrators, to John Blackwell. Bill of Sale for negro slave Nelson. Christeney and John F. Thompson, administrators of the estate of Thomas Thompson, deceased. Reg: 3 May 1837.

Page 105 - 24 Nov 1836. I, Ebenezer Wilson appoint Fordice Wilson, both of Bedford Co., TN, my Attorney to receive my property coming to me from the estate of James S. Wilson, deceased, late of Sumner Co., TN. Wit: J. Wortham. Reg: 6 May 1837.

Page 106 - 14 Apr 1837. George Davidson of Lawrence Co., Alabama to Philip Hodges of Bedford Co., TN, land in Bedford Co., of 152 acres. Bounded by Nowlin's corner and Watkins' field. Wit: Pinckney D. Woods and Jno. P. Davidson. Reg: 6 May 1837.

Pahe 107 - 22 Mar 1837. Joel F. Still and his wife Rutha to Allen Knight, all of Bedford Co., TN, land in Bedford Co., on the Barren Fork, being Lot No. 1 as laid off in the division of the estate of Zebediah Payne, deceased. Bounded by the Barren Fork and the Lot laid off to the widow's dowry. 8 acres. Wit: Benjamin Kimbro and Ann Kimbro. Reg: 6 May 1837.

Page 108 - 20 Mar 1837. Joel H. Still and his wife Rutha to Allen Knight, all of bedford Co., TN, land in Bedford Co., on the Barren Fork. Bounded by Zebediah Payne's land, and Allen Knight. Wit: Benjamin Kimbro and Ann Kimbro. Reg: 6 May 1837.

Page 117 - 9 Mar 1837. Relinquishment of Claim. We, relinquish our several claims to our part of our father's estate, the said H.(Hezekiah) Ray, to a colt. Signed by Jason Ray, William Ray, Solomon Ray and Jason Ray. Wit: Thomas R. Mullins and John Dean.

Reg: 26 May 1837.

Page 123 - 17 May 1837. James Young to William Young, his son, both of Bedford Co., TN, for love and affection for his son, conveyed unto him land in Bedford Co., on waters of Duck River. Borders near the mouth of east fork of Butlers Creek, Overton & Whiteside tract, and Mullins' corner. 174 acres. Reg: 2 Jun 1837.

Page 123 - 19 May 1837. Abraham Mayfield, Agreement &c. Agreement between me and my wife Martha before our marriage, that the property which she had at that time belong to her for life and at her death should be subject to her disposal and she was to claim no part of my estate at my death, which agreement has never been reduced to writing. She owned at the time of our marriage 111 acres of land in Bedford Co., TN, on Weakleys Creek, being the dower of Martha in the lands of her first husband William Lock, deceased, also 4 negroes and household furniture. Reg: 2 Jun 1837.

Page 124 - 29 May 1837. D. D. Arnold, Sheriff to Thomas Davis for 100 acres. Thomas Davis against the estate of Jesse McMahon on 3 Mar 1833. Attachment of property of Jesse McMahon being the place whereon Allice McMahon resides. Reg: 2 Jun 1837.

Page 128 - 26 May 1837. Frederick Anthony and wife Susannah to Robert L. Landers, all of Bedford Co., TN, land or portion of a tract of which Henry Landers, deceased, was in possession of at the time of his death. 12½ acres with one fourth over the whole tract of the deceased, of 125½ acres. Borders lands of Robert L. Landers. John Landis and others. Land on waters of Thompsons Creek. The 12½ acres of Frederick Anthony and wife Susannah holds as legatees of Henry Landers, deceased. Wit: Abel Landis, Jno. Harrison and Robert Harrison. Reg: 3 Jun 1837.

Page 130 - -- Apr 1837. I, John N. Hart of Henderson Co., TN sold to John Larue of Bedford Co., TN, land in Bedford Co. 181 acres. Borders John Larue, Adam's line, Simmonds corner now Isaac Larue's line, and McLaughlin's lot. Reg: 5 Jun 1837.

Page 131 - 15 Apr 1837. I, Alice McMahon of Bedford Co., TN, for $1.00, sold to my son Samuel McMahon, he being at this time and for years past my chief stay and comfort in enabling me to pass through life, conveyed unto him a negro girl Caroline, which is now in my possession. Also other property. Wit: James L. Armstrong and Abram McMahon. Reg: 5 Jun 1837.

Page 132 - 18 Nov 1836. Daniel L. Barringer and his wife Ann Barringer, late of North Carolina and now of Bedford Co., TN conveyed to Anna White, Elizabeth Felton, Susan White, Emma White, Sophronia White of City of Raleigh and Daniel L. Swain and his wife Eleanor Swain of Orange Co., NC, land in Bedford Co., on waters of Sugar Creek. Wit: J. H. Hayley and R. H. Hayley. Reg: 10 Jun 1837.

Page 134 - 22 May 1837. Joseph Wardlow of Township of London Grove in Chester Co., PA, Merchant, sold to Thomas Newsom of Bedford Co., TN, Town Lot No. 37 in Town of Shelbyville. Borders Martin Street. Wit: R. Palmer, Jr., and Joseph S. Tennery. Reg: 10 Jun 1837.

Page 136 - 19 Mar 1836. Charles Timmons of Lincoln Co., TN to Jesse Holt of Bedford Co., TN, land in Bedford Co. Borders the road leading from Shelbyville to Hillsboro where Mrs. Mary Ewell's line crosses the same, Lodwick Holt's line, and to Still and Lindsey's line. 63 acres. Wit: Larkin Holt, Jos. H. Thompson, G. W. Heard and T. J. Lindsey. Reg: 15 Jun 1837.

Page 140 - 28 May 1837. Charles Timmons of Lincoln Co., TN to George W. Heard of Bedford Co., TN, land in Bedford Co. Borders Erwin's line near the ford of Shipmans Creek, Lodwick Holt's line, J. S. Fowler's corner, R. M. Couser's corner, Isaac Barnett's shop lot, Old Hillsboro Road, William Shipman's old line, and T. J. Lindsey's dwelling house. 10 acres, be the same and known as Timmons Old Factory and Cotton Gin Lot. Wit: Thomas J. Lindsey and Jesse Holt. Reg: 20 Jun 1837.

Page 143 - 4 Mar 1837. Articles of Agreement. Lease for School House. John Phillips one part and we the undersigned citizens of Richmond and vicinity of other part, both of Bedford Co., TN, for $80.00 to be paid to Phillips in 6 months, which John Phillips is to teach commencing 1st day April next, has leased for 15 years to the citizens and vicinity, a lot or land in Bedford Co., in vicinity of Richmond. Bounded by Thomas W. Harper's field and Richmond & Shelbyville Road. 1 acre. Wit: William R. Looney and William H. Craig. Reg: 26 Jun 1837.

Page 143 - 2 Oct 1833. Robert Landers to Absalom Landers, both of Bedford Co., TN, for love and high esteem for his nephew Absalom Landers, has given unto Absalom Landers, land in Bedford Co., on Thompsons Creek. Bounded by Thompsons Creek. 22 acres. Wit: Abel Landers and John Smith. Reg: 26 Jun 1837.

Page 145 - 22 Aug 1827. Thomas Landers, administrators of estate of Abraham Landers, deceased, to Elliot Rucker, both of Bedford Co., TN, land in Bedford Co., on waters of Alexanders Creek. Bounded by Samuel Bell's tract which was originally granted to Ebenezer Alexander by State of North Carolina, Batt's line, and Joseph P. Morris. 50 acres. Wit: Joel Kimmins and James L. Hase. Reg: 29 Jun 1837.

Page 146 - 12 Nov 1836. Robert Allison of Bedford Co., TN to Travis C. Nash, Price C. Steele, John Rushing, John Thompson, Robert Allison, Thomas C. Rankins, and Joseph Williams, as Trustees for the Christian Religion, donate land to be build a Meeting House. Bounded by North Fork, road leading from Shelbyville to Nashville. 1 acre. Wit: John Thompson and James A. Keele. Reg: 3 Jul 1837.

Page 148 - 8 Jul 1829. Cyrus A. Alexander of Mecklenburg Co., NC to Joel Kimmons of Bedford Co., TN, land in Bedford Co., on waters of Weakley Creek. Borders Elliott Rucker. 20 acres. Wit: Samuel B. Watson and Elliott Rucker. Reg: 4 Jul 1837.

Page 150 - 17 Jun 1836. William Gilbert, Cintha Gilbert and Daniel Kimbro to John Smith, all of Bedford Co., TN, 14 acres in Bedford Co., on west side of Thompson Creek. Bounded by John Smith, Nicholas Anthony, John Kimbro, and lands whereon Cintha Gilbert and Daniel Kimbro now lives. Wit: Abel Landis and Charles Lucas. Reg: 10 Jul 1837.

Page 151 - 26 Feb 1835. James D. Anderson of Bedford Co., TN to William S. Anderson and Lorenzo B. Anderson of Bedford Co., his sons, for love and affection towards his sons William S. and Lorenzo B. Anderson, land in Bedford Co., on waters of Rock Creek. Bounded by John Blackwell, James Price, Alfred Anderson and William Swanson. 110 acres. Wit: Amzi D. Anderson and Alfred C. Anderson. Reg: 10 Jul 1837.

Page 162 - 1 Aug 1837. Abraham B. Cooper to William Brown, both of Bedford Co., TN, land whereon his mother Sarah Cooper now lives, land in Bedford Co. Bounded by John Sutton and Thomas McGuire. Abraham Cooper's interest and to the slaves belonging to his father's estate and now in the possession of his mother Sarah Cooper. Abraham B. Cooper is indebted to A. J. Goodrum for $385.00. Reg: 2 Aug 1837.

Page 163 - 2 Aug 1837. Larkin B. Orr and Martha Orr his wife to David Orr, all of Bedford Co., TN, for $1.00 to David Orr. Larkin B. Orr is indebted to David Orr for $50.00. Reg: 3 Aug 1837.

Page 164 - 28 Jul 1837. Patrick W. Williams and his wife Lucy (Lucinda) Williams of Madison Co., Alabama to Lodwick Holt of Bedford Co., TN, land in Bedford Co., on south side of Barren Fork, east of Shipmans Creek, Lot No. 6. 17¼ acres, it is the Lot laid off in the Mansion House Survey 28 Dec 1830. Bounded by Shipmans Creek. Reg: 4 Aug 1837.

Page 169 - 28 Nov 1836. John Oneal of Bedford Co., TN to George M. Gibson of Giles Co., TN, land in Bedford Co., on Sinking Creek. Bounded by Sinking Creek, John Bryans' spring, David Dryden, and William A. Gaunt. 101 acres. Wit: John M. Gibson and David Dryden. Reg: 8 Aug 1837.

Page 171 - 15 Apr 1831. Daniel Gilchrist to Percy Yell, Abraham Sriver (Shriver), Elijah Bomar, John Golothan, Daniel Gilchrist, Trustees of the Northern District of Captain Patterson's Company and their successors in office, for his interest and feels for the school in the Northern District, he conveyed unto the Trustees, the privilege of a tract of land in Bedford Co. Bounded by school land now used by the Trustees, to include the house and spring where the scholars now use water out of, for the purpose of keeping a school of the present kind. Wit: John R. Sriver (Shriver) and James Yell. Reg: 8 Aug 1837.

Page 172 - 26 Aug 1828. John L. Keele of Bedford Co., TN to Christopher Hoover of Rutherford Co., TN, 50 acres of land in Bedford Co., on waters of Alexanders Creek, it being originally granted by North Carolina to George Alexander. Bounded by John Rushing. Wit: John Rawlings and John L. Hoover. Reg: 8 Aug 1837.

Page 181 - 4 Feb 1837. James W. Bell of Marshall Co., TN to George Sharp of Bedford Co., TN, land in Bedford Co., on waters of Duck River, adjoining John Oneal and Joel Darnel. 75 acres. Wit: John Oneal and Fielding Bell. Reg: 12 Aug 1837.

Page 187 - 14 Aug 1837. I, Abigail Riggs in behalf of myself and heirs, relinquish all right title and interest which I have in David Riggs', my deceased husband's estate, to Adam S. Riggs and his heirs forever, for $89.00. Wit: William S. Jett and

J. Dixon. Reg: 18 Aug 1837.

Page 189 - 17 Aug 1837. Preston Frazer of Bedford Co., TN to Herbert Owen of Williamson Co., TN, dower interest in the name of Martha A. R. Owen the wife of Herbert Owen, land in Shelbyville. Borders James Brittain, Daniel McKisick, and the Scull Camp Road. 5 acres, including the mansion house &c, belonging to the late R. C. Thompson, deceased, house. Martha A. R. Owen was widow of R. C. Thompson, deceased. Reg: 21 Aug 1837.

Page 190 - Whereas by the Last Will and Testament of Andrew Morrison, deceased, dated 20 Oct 1832. Will proven. Will stated if necessary to sell 33 acres conveyed from Andrew M. Morrison to Andrew Morrison, deceased, on 16 Oct 1832, and whereas in the will, Jane H. Morrison wife of Andrew Morrison was appointed Executrix and Andrew M. Morrison Executor of said will. Andrew Morrison deceased, of Bedford Co., TN, Andrew M. Morrison of Washington Co., Arkansas, Executor sold to Joseph Adams of Bedford Co., TN, land in Bedford Co., on waters of Sugar Creek, being the tract sold by Andrew M. to Andrew Morrison, deceased. Borders Andrew Morrison's old tract and Nile (Neal) Norsworthy's line. 33 acres. Wit: Jesse Brown and William H. Craig. Reg: 21 Aug 1837.

Page 191 - 27 Sep 1833. William Younger and Wilson Abbott to Abraham Sriver (Shriver), G. M. Moore, B. B. Bomar, Thomas McFarling, Claiborne Coats, all of Bedford Co., TN, relinquish quit claim to above members as Trustees of the Methodist Church, a tract of land, it being on the east side of Horse Mountain and headwaters of Butlers Creek and south east corner of William Younger's 200 acres. Borders a cleared Camp Ground, including the New Camp Ground. Wit: Cornelius McGuire and William McFarlin. Reg: 21 Aug 1837.

Page 192 - Tennessee Grant to Joseph Hiles for 47+ acres. No. 13642. Tract of 47 acres and 78 poles, survey date 16 Feb 1827, in Bedford Co., TN, on waters of Flat Creek. Bounded by the Hile's corner, Russell's line, Williams' line, Cooper's line, and others. Reg: 21 Aug 1837.

Page 192 - 27 Auf 1835. John Patterson to Sanders J. Freeman. John Patterson of Bedford Co., TN and Sanders J. Patterson of Williamson Co., TN, sold all of a tract of land in Bedford Co. Bounded by Nathan Taylor, on which Abraham Byler and others lives. 153½ acres. Wit: Spias Ward and Henry W. Hayse. Reg: 22 Aug 1837.

Page 193 - 11 May 1834. George W. Bright of Williamson Co., TN to James Bell of Bedford Co., TN, land in Bedford Co., on the south side of Duck River and on east side of Rich Creek. Bounded by John H. Anderson's tract now belonging to John Oneal, and Josiah Davis. 92 acres. Wit: John Oneal and Fielding Bell. Reg: 22 Aug 1837.

Page 194 - 13 Nov 1830. I, Jonathan King of Bedford Co., TN to Alfred Ransom of Rutherford Co., TN, land in Bedford Co., on Clems Creek. 179 acres. Bounded by Thomas Powel, Thompson's line, and Cooper's line. Wit: John Byler and Thomas Maxwell and John Maxwell. Reg: 22 Aug 1837.

Page 194 - 31 Oct 1836. George W. Gibbs of Davidson Co., TN to Leonard C. Temple of Bedford Co., TN, land in Bedford Co., on south waters of Duck River. 300 acres. Bounded by lands of George Doherty and the school land. Wit: John C. Coldwell and Flower Swift. Reg: 22 Aug 1837.

Page 199 - 8 Feb 1836. Lemuel H. Cole of Gibson Co., TN to R. W. Fain of Bedford Co., TN, land in Bedford Co., on waters of Wilsons Creek. Adjoining lands of Joshua White. 150 acres. Wit: William Carlton and William M. C. Fain. Reg: 29 Aug 1837.

Page 200 - 8 Feb 1836. Lemuel H. Cole of Gibson Co., TN to William M. C. Fain of Bedford Co., TN, land in Bedford Co., on waters of Wilsons Creek. Bounded by lands of William Carlton, Allison's land, Holbrooks and others. 100 acres. Wit: R. W. Fain, Jas. Walker and William Carlton. Reg: 29 Aug 1837.

Page 201 - 1 Aug 1837. I, Susan Martin, daughter and one of the heirs of William Craig, deceased, sold to John Ray, all of Bedford Co., TN, my portion of William Craig's estate, which consists of a tract of land in Bedford Co., on waters of Rock Creek. Adjoining the lands of Solomon Dirret, Zachariah Davis and others. 200 acres. Wit: Stephen Freeman and J. P. Cunningham. Reg: 7 Sep 1837.

Page 204 - 22 Aug 1836. Deed of Gift. Polly Thorne of Bedford Co., TN to Patsey Thorne, her step-mother of Bedford Co., for love and affection she has for her step-mother Patsey Thorne, the widow of William Thorne, Sr., deceased, I have given all my property and claim in my father's estate, William Thorne, deceased. I, Polly Thorne in feeble condition. Patsey agrees to maintain me as long as I live. Wit: John Stephenson and David Bledsoe. Reg: 8 Sep 1837.

Page 205 - 5 Sep 1837. James G. Neely and Mary W. his wife of Bedford Co., TN, to Ursula J. Orr, David P. Orr, William C. Orr, Mary Ann Orr, Gilah Orr, Elizabeth Orr, Rebecca Orr, and Martha Orr, minor heirs of John Orr, deceased, by virtue of the power vested in them by the will of John Orr, deceased, that James G. Neeley and Mary W. his wife sold to the above heirs of John Orr, deceased, land in Bedford Co., on waters of Fall Creek. Bounded by David Keele's land, heirs of Joseph McElrath, and C. D. Steele's land. 50 acres. Reg: 8 Sep 1837.

Page 208 - 2 Jan 1836. John H. Laird sold to Greenville Cook, both of Bedford Co., TN, the Printing Press, types and furniture belonging to the office of the "Western Freeman", a newspaper published in the Town of Shelbyville, for $1400.00. Wit: J. T. Neil. Reg: 12 Sep 1837.

Page 211 - 13 Sep 1837. We, Alexander Davidson and Margaret Davidson sold to William Potter, land in Bedford Co., TN and District No. 19 & 20, both sides of Sinking Creek. 200 acres. Bounded by Daniel Hiney. Wit: Daniel Looney and Margaret Cunningham and G. W. Cunningham. Reg: 20 Sep 1837.

Page 212 - 14 Sep 1837. Daniel Gilchrist of Lawrence Co., Alabama to Charles Timmons of Lincoln Co., TN, land in Bedford Co., on west waters of Shipmans Creek. Bounded by George Blair, school land and Shipman's tract. 34 acres. Wit: James Stevens and Alfred Anthony. Reg: 20 Sep 1837.

Page 213 - 14 Sep 1837. Daniel Gilchrist of Lawrence Co., Alabama to William Blanton heirs of Bedford Co., TN, land in Bedford Co., on west waters of Shipman Creek. Borders school land, Timmon's land, and Andrew Erwin. 34 acres. Reg: 20 Sep 1837.

Page 214 - 13 Sep 1837 - George Wait of Bedford Co., TN to L. D. Campbell of Coffee Co., TN, land in Bedford Co. Borders Cleveland's land, Shelby's old line, and Jno. Bower's line. 204 acres. Wit: B. B. Bradford and William S. Watterson. Reg: 21 Sep 1837.

Page 215 - 2 May 1837. James G. Neeley and Mary W. Neeley of Bedford Co., TN to David Keele of Bedford Co., land in Bedford Co., on waters of Falling Creek. Borders T. C. Nash and the lands of John Orr, deceased. 60 acres. Wit: Jas. M. Johnson and John Tune. Reg: 21 Sep 1837.

Page 216 - 18 Sep 1837. Faniel Gilchrist of Lawrence Co., Alabama to Elijah Bomar of Bedford Co., TN, land in Bedford Co. Borders the mouth of a lane going from where Bomar now lives to the widow of David Norvill, and the heirs of D. Vaughan. 160 acres. Reg: 21 Sep 1837.

Page 217 - 18 Sep 1837. John B. Cooper of Madison Co., Alabama to William D. Orr of Bedford Co., TN. John B. Cooper is guardian of the minor heirs of Charles Cooper, deceased, which was taken upon himself in Bedford Co. while resident there. Wit: B. T. Moore. Reg: 23 Sep 1837.

Page 220 - 18 Mar 1837. Abel Landis to Robert L. Landis, both of Bedford Co., TN, land in Bedford Co., on Thompsons Creek, being a part of a tract of land granted by State of Tennessee. Phebe Landis widow and her legal representatives. 41 acres. Wit: Jeremiah Lee and Isom Adams. Reg: 27 Sep 1837.

Page 220 - 18 Mar 1837. Abel Landis to Robert L. Landis, both of Bedford Co., TN, land whereon Abel Landis now lives. 47 acres. Borders lands of the heirs of Christopher Landers, deceased. Wit: Jeremiah Lee and Isom Adams. Reg: 27 Sep 1837.

Page 221 - 18 Mar 1837. Abel Landis to Robert L. Landis, both of Bedford Co., TN. 25 acres, it being two shares of the lawful heirs of Henry Landis, deceased, to wit, Christopher Landis and Jacob Anthony and Phebe his wife, have deeded to Abel Landis and which Henry Landis, deceased, was in possession of at the time of his decease. The whole tract belonging to the heirs of the deceased. Adjoining lands of Robert L. Landis and others, on Thompsons Creek and Shipmans Creek. Wit: Jeremiah Lee and Isom Adams. Reg: 27 Sep 1837.

Page 222 - 26 Sep 1837. I, Samuel Woodfin of Bedford Co., TN, for love and affection for my children, Cicero and Sarah Woodfin, Deed of Gift, personal property. Other children: James, Elizabeth, Nicholas, Evelina, Jasper, Moses, John, Mariah and Mary Woodfin. When James, Elizabeth &c or either of them come of age, they are to receive their share. Reg: 27 Sep 1837.

Page 223 - 15 Sep 1837. Theoderick F. Bradford of Bedford Co., TN to Thomas Davis, in trust for Eliza J. Howe and her two children, Eliza Ann Howe and Cyntha Ann Howe, land in Bedford Co., on Cribbs Branch, a branch of the Barren Fork, except that part which was conveyed to the heirs of Hosea Garrett, deceased. 172 acres. Wit: William B. M. Brame and Thomas Knott. Reg: 27 Sep 1837.

Page 223 - 23 Sep 1837. Kenneth L. Anderson of Bedford Co., TN to William S. Watterson of Coffee Co., TN, Lots No. 25, 26, and 27 in Shelbyville. Wit: H. M. Watterson. Reg: 27 Sep 1837.

Page 224 - 28 Mar 1833. Amos Balch to Margaret Ann Docia Balch, Deed of Gift. I, Amos Balch of Bedford Co., TN, by Deed of Gift to Margaret Ann Docia Balch, daughter of James C. Balch of Rutherford Co., TN, a white cow that I purchased at the sale of James C. Balch's estate. Margaret Ann Docia Balch is grand daughter of Amos Balch, who is under age. When she comes of age the said property is to descend to David Lawson McCarver Balch. Wit: J. W. Patton, John Patton and B. F. Patton. Reg: 29 Sep 1837.

Page 225 - 7 Aug 1837. Benjamin Driver of Bedford Co., TN to Riland Birke and Richard Birke of Lincoln Co., TN, land in Bedford Co., on the ridge that forms the line between Bedford and Lincoln Counties. Bounded by James B. Gowen's line. 50 acres. Wit: Daniel Brown and Matthew P. Gowen. Reg: 30 Sep 1837.

Page 228 - 27 Sep 1837. I, William B. Anderson sold for $5.00 and other considerations, to Samuel Mitchell, one cast iron Printing Press together with all the types, cases, stands, ___ cuts, galleys, rollers, and all materials in my office (The Star). Reg: 2 Oct 1837.

Page 229 - 25 Sep 1837. John M. Stokes sold four negroes to Horatio Clagett. Negroes belonging to the heirs of Zachariah W. Waters, deceased, which third part of said negroes descending to my wife Rebecca G. Stokes former widow and relict of Z. W. Waters. Wit: W. F. Long and W. Haggard. Reg: 2 Oct 1837.

Page 231 - 29 Dec 1835. Logan Henderson of Rutherford Co., TN to Humphrey Cunningham of Bedford Co., TN, 60 acres in Bedford Co., on waters of Sinking Creek. Bounded by lands of his own and Potters, John F. Gambill's corner and Anderson's corner. Wit: G. W. Cunningham and William Cunningham. Reg: 3 Oct 1837.

Page 231 - 9 Jan 1837. Logan Henderson of Rutherford Co., TN to Samuel Harper of Bedford Co., TN, land in Bedford Co., on waters of Big Sinking Creek. Bounded by lands of Oliver and David Dryden. 98 acres. Wit: Elizabeth Harper and Eliza Gambill. Reg: 3 Oct 1837.

Page 232 - 22 Sep 1837. I, Jemima H. Light of Bedford Co., TN, appoint my friend James Adkinson of Halifax Co., VA, my Attorney to receive of James C. Bruce, Executor of James Bruce, Sr., deceased, late of Halifax Co., VA, my former agent and Attorney. He is to rent lands, hire negroes &c. I have confidence in my brother Melchisedek Brame of Bedford Co., I appoint him as my Attorney to receive of James Adkinson all my monies &c. Wit: Obadiah W. Knight and Gabriel B. Knight. Reg: 3 Oct 1837.

Page 234 - 25 Sep 1837. Cyntha Goodman and Jacob Goodman to Price C. Steele, all of Bedford Co., TN, land in Bedford Co., on waters of Duck River. Bounded by Richard Trotter's North Carolina Grant. 45 acres. Wit: Reason Gaither and Jackson Rackley. Reg: 9 Oct 1837.

Page 235 - 1 Sep 1837. Daniel Gilchrist of Lawrence Co., Alabama to Irea Barber of Bedford Co., TN, land in Bedford Co., on waters of Fall Creek. Bounded by Malcolm Gilchrist's grant now owned by Russell, Kent's corner, Tucker's field, McCuistion, and Steele's lines. 85 acres. Wit: William Murphree and Jesse Scott. Reg: 9 Oct 1837.

Page 237 - 7 Oct 1837. I, James Nowlin of Marshall Co., TN for love and affection for my children, Martha, Bryant W., Lucy, Fanny, Polley, Huldy E., Ann, Malvina S. and Thomas Nowlin, all of Bedford Co., TN, my wife has relinquished her right to land in Williamson Co., TN, have given unto the children, a tract of land in Bedford Co., on waters of Hurricane Creek. 122 acres, being the portion allotted to my wife Elizabeth out of the lands descended from her father George Tillman, also all my right &c in a tract adjoining the above tract. 108 acres, it being the tract I purchased of Stephen Nowlin and by him from Silas Tillman, also negroes. Wit: David Nowlin and E. J. Frierson. Reg: 13 Oct 1837.

Page 240 - 3 Oct 1836. William P. Johnson of Marshall Co., TN to Josiah Ely of Bedford Co., TN, land in Bedford Co., on south side of Falling Creek. Bounded by Trotter's line now P. C. Steele's corner and William Rowland. 100 acres. Wit: J. M. Johnson and Jane Johnson. Reg: 20 Oct 1837.

Page 246 - 18 Sep 1837. Daniel Gilchrist of Lawrence Co., Alabama to Theoderick F. Bradford of Bedford Co., TN, land in Bedford Co., on waters of Duck River. Bounded by land where Moses Nelson now lives. 133 acres. Reg: 21 Oct 1837.

Page 250 - 10 Oct 1837. I, Elizabeth Cheaves, for love and affection for my grandson Robert Cheaves, son of Jacob H. Cheaves, given a horse. Reg: 23 Oct 1837.

Page 250 - 11 Oct 1837. Marriage Contract. Caren Rutledge and John A. Lewis, both of Bedford Co., TN. Caren Rutledge is shortly to be married to John A. Lewis and is desirous of securing her property both real and personal, all the right title and claim to her father Jonathan Pierce's estate which has been paid to Grandison Sanders, her guardian, which consists of money and other personal property and other property in his possession consisting of household and kitchen furniture. Also dispose of the same by will at her death. Wit: W. F. Short, William D. Stone, William H. Wisener and G. W. Fogleman. Reg: 26 Oct 1837.

Page 251 - 25 Sep 1837. William S. Watterson of Coffee Co., TN to George Davidson of Bedford Co., TN, land in Bedford Co., known as being Lot No. 25, Lot No. 26, and Lot No. 27 in the Town of Shelbyville. Wit: Thomas C. Whiteside and William H. Wisener. Reg: 26 Oct 1837.

Page 252 - 27 Dec 1836. Josiah Nesbitt and Mary Jane Nesbitt of Rutherford Co., TN to Frederick Batte, Sr., of Bedford Co., TN, land in Bedford Co., on waters of Weakleys Creek. Bounded by William Allison, James Harris and Richard Bandy. It being their undivided interest in the tract of land decreed to the minor heirs of Henry Batte, deceased, of 27 acres. Wit: Frederick Batte, Jr., Robert C. Batte and John McCabe. Reg: 26 Oct 1837.

Page 253 - 31 Dec 1836. Josiah Nesbitt and Mary Jane Nesbitt his wife of Rutherford Co., TN to Frederick Batte of Bedford Co., TN, the dower tract of Rebecca Batte widow of Henry Batte, deceased, in Bedford Co., on waters of Weakleys Creek. Borders Jackson Lile, Edward Tarpley and the heirs of Henry Batte, deceased. Wit: John McCabe, Robert C. Batte, and Frederick Batte, Jr. Reg: 26 Oct 1837.

Page 257 - 14 Oct 1837. Frederick Batte, Jr. to Frederick Batte, Sr., both of Bedford Co., TN, land in Bedford Co., on waters of Weakleys Creek. Borders William Allison, James Harris, Jackson Lile and Richard Bandy, it being his undivided interest in the tract of land decreed to the minor heirs of Henry Batte, deceased, of 27 acres. Wit: Robert C. Batte. Reg: 4 Nov 1837.

Page 260 - 28 Oct 1837. Deed of Gift. John Stewart of Bedford Co., TN, given a sorrel mare and increase, to his four nieces, Adaline Helton, Frances Matilda Helton, Nancy Hannah Helton, and Narcissa Elizabeth Helton. Reg: 6 Nov 1837.

Page 262 - 1 Oct 1837. William and Archibald Gilchrist to Daniel Gilchrist, Power of Attorney. William and Archibald Gilchrist gives Power of Attorney to Daniel Gilchrist of Lawrence Co., Alabama, to sell all their lands in Bedford Co., TN. Wit: David Dobbins and Nancy Leech (both of Maury Co., TN). Reg: 11 Nov 1837.

Page 262 - 7 Nov 1837. Sophia W. Coldwell to Colbert Coldwell and others. Deed of Gift. Sophia W. Coldwell for her natural love and affection for her children, Colbert Coldwell, Orville Coldwell, Sarah C. Coldwell, Jane R. Coldwell and Mary B. Coldwell, given jointly a slave named Lucy, for life, said slave to be this day with four others conveyed to said children by William J. Peacock, administrator of John W. Peacock, deceased, divided between said children at the time they arrive at maturity, respectively. Reg: 11 Nov 1837.

Page 263 - 7 Nov 1837. William J. Peacock to Culbert Coldwell and others. Bill of Conveyance. John W. Peacock in his life time, by his obligation in writing, bound himself and others, to convey unto the heirs of Nathaniel E. Coldwell, deceased, certain slaves. I, William J. Coldwell, as administrator of John W. Peacock, deceased, do convey to Culbert Coldwell, Orville Coldwell, Sarah C. Coldwell and Mary B. Coldwell, heirs of N. E. Coldwell, deceased, slaves. Reg: 11 Nov 1837.

Page 263 - 1 Nov 1835. Joseph Robinson to James Robinson. 284 acres. Joseph Robinson of Williamson Co., TN to James Robinson of Bedford Co., TN, land being a part of a 1500 acre tract granted to Michael Robinson, deceased, of North Carolina. Land borders Fonville's land, John Robinson and Phifer's land. Wit: David Ray, Robert Ray, Benjamin Oslin, Jr., and Hugh Ray. Reg: 16 Nov 1837.

Page 269 - 19 May 1837. John W. Meeks to William S. W. Wakefield. Deed &c. I have a fee simple interest in remainder, to take effect and be united with the possession after the death of Sarah Putman, who has a life time estate in the same, land in Bedford Co., TN, District No. 19, of 100 acres to be laid off by the direction of the Will of Jesse Putman, deceased, out of the lands belonging to the estate, which land was willed to John W. Meeks, Minerva Calton and her heirs and Melissa Meeks and heirs, by Jesse Putman, deceased. Wit: W. M. H. Craig and William R. Looney. Reg: 21 Nov 1837.

Page 270 - 6 Sep 1837. Daniel Epps to Matthew Phillips and others. Trustees &c. Daniel Epps of Bedford Co., TN first part and Matthew Phillips, Uriah Cross and Thomas Wheeler, Trustees for the original Regular United Baptist Church called Elbethel of Bedford Co., other part. For sum of $5.00, Daniel Epps sold to the said Trustees and their successors forever, land in Bedford Co., on waters of Duck River and adjoining the Elbethel Tract of School Land on its south boundary line. Borders west side of Elbether School House. About one half acre. Wit: Alexander Sanders and Garret Phillips. Reg: 21 Nov 1837.

Page 290 - 21 Nov 1835. Deed of 100 acres. Benjamin D. Kelley and Nathan T. Kelley to Francis H. Keller, all of Bedford Co., TN, sold land in Bedford Co. It being a part of a 400 acre tract conveyed from Andrew Erwin and James Patton to Reuben Kelley, it being the said Benjamin D. and Nathan T. Kelley's equal part, fell to them by division with the heirs of Reuben Kelley, deceased. Wit: Joseph Keller and John M. Keller. Reg: 14 Dec 1837.

Page 292 - 27 Jan 1837. John Wood and others to Elihu H. Bingham. Deed of 150 acres. John Woods and Elizabeth Woods his wife of Bedford Co., TN, and Thomas J. Cooper of Lauderdale Co., Alabama and Nancy Cooper of Yalobusha Co., Miss., of one part and Elihu H. Bingham of Rutherford Co., TN other part, land belonging to the heirs of William Cooper, deceased. Borders land formerly owned by Jesse Chaffin, deceased, now in the name of Nathan Chaffin, borders William Weaver now in the name of Nathan Chaffin, John McLure (McClure), and old Patton & Erwin original line. With the exception of 35 acres in the north east corner of said tract, it being the widow's dower for life. Wit: John L(<u>S</u>). Cooper and Anderson Sharp. Reg: 16 Dec 1837.

Page 293 - 27 Jan 1837. John Wood and others to Elihu H. Bingham. Deed. John and Elizabeth Wood of Bedford Co., TN, and Thomas J. Cooper of Lauderdale Co., Alabama and Nancy Cooper of Yalobusha Co., Miss., one part, sold to Elihu H. Bingham of Rutherford Co., TN, all right claim they have unto a dower of 35 acres lying in the north east corner of said tract belonging to Misstress McClure her natural life, on the tract belonging to the heirs of William Cooper, deceased. Wit: John <u>S</u>(L). Cooper and Anderson Sharp. Reg: 16 Dec 1837.

Page 297 - 16 Jun 1837. Benjamin F. Craig to Joseph J. B. Crunk. Power of Attorney. To demand and receive from John Craig, administrator of William Craig, deceased, all my right to the estate. Wit: E. M. Temple and Fredr. R. Smith. Reg: 26 Dec 1837.

Page 297 - 6 Sep 1837. <u>Hurman</u> Maxfield and wife Judith to Martin Wheeler. Deed of 53+ acres. Hurman and Jusith Maxfield of Bedford Co., TN sold to Martin Wheeler, all of Bedford Co., TN, land borders mouth of Alexanders Creek, Susannah Sanders dower, bank of North Fork. Wit: Jackson Nichols and James D. Clark. Reg: 26 Dec 1837.

Page 306 - 1 Nov 1837. Thomas Harris of Charlotte, Mecklenburg Co., NC, appoint Caleb P. Houston of Bedford Co., TN, Power of Attorney for me, to redeem a certain tract of land in the vicinity of William Houston in Bedford Co., and sold. The said tract of land was formerly owned by the heirs of Robert Lock. Wit: William A. Todd and G. W. Coldwell. Reg: 27 Dec 1837.

Page 308 - 9 Dec 1837. Circuit Court of Bedford County, TN. The heirs of William Burgess. Bill for the sale of land. Exparte. That Richard Burgess became the purchaser of claims &c and interest of the heirs of William Burgess, deceased, land being an undivided part of said tract. Heirs of William Burgess, deceased, are, Mary J. Burgess, Elizabeth Burgess, Richard Burgess, Nancy Burgess, and Joseph L. Burgess. Land contained 67 acres in Bedford Co., on Big Flat Creek. Borders John B. Cummings, Newton Cannon, the Flat Creek and James Younger's old line. Reg: 29 Dec 1837.

Page 309 - 26 Dec 1837. George and Susanna Presgrove to Wilkison Fowler. Deed 43 acres. George and Susanna Presgrove of Bedford Co., TN sold to Wilkison Fowler of Monroe Co., Miss., 43 acres in Bedford Co., on waters of Alexanders Creek. Borders Joseph P. Morris' corner. Reg: 29 Dec 1837.

Page 310 - 22 May 1837. Mark Grady, Sr. to Martha Hartsfield. Deed of Gift. Mark Grady of Wake Co., NC, for love and affection for his daughter Martha Hartsfield of Bedford Co., TN, conveyed to her a negro boy Squire, now in the possession of John Hartsfield, her husband. Wit: Allen Rogers and Henry Brown and Quinting T. Holloway. Reg: 29 Dec 1837.

Page 314 - 8 Jun 1837. John Landers to Robert L. Landers. Deed. Land in Bedford Co., TN, on Thompsons Creek, District No. 25. One tract of 31½ acres, it being a part of a 200 acre tract granted by the State of Tennessee to Phebe, Henry, John, Abel, Jacob Jolly, Robert and Elizabeth Landers. Bounded by lands of Peter Graves and Henry Landers. Another tract of 18 acres, it being a part of the said 200 acre tract and bounded by lands of Robert L. Landers. Another tract of 50 acres in Bedford Co., on waters of Thompsons Creek and Shipmans Creek, borders the lands of Henry Landers, John Turner, Sarah Ann Nutt, John Stanfield. Also other property such as horse, mare, oxen, cows &c. Wit: Jno. Harrison and Isaac Barnett. Reg: 1 Jan 1838.

Page 322 - 19 Sep 1837. J. W. Ragsdale to Henry Davis. Deed for one half Town Lot in Coffeeville, Yalobusha, Miss. J. W. Ragsdale and Henry Davis both of Bedford Co., TN. Lot No. 63, fronting east side of the public square. Reg: 2 Jan 1838.

Page 326 - 20 Dec 1837 - K. Yancy to Alexander Yancy. Bill of Sale. Kavanaugh Yancy for love and affection for his son Alexander Yancy, both of Bedford Co., TN, conveyed unto him a negro boy named Jacob. Wit: J. Galbreath and Daniel McKisick. Reg: 2 Jan 1838.

Page 330 - 3 Jan 1838. Ephraim G. Meadows to John Wood. Bill of Sale. Both of Bedford Co., TN. Sold (9) slaves, which negroes are the property of the heirs of one Michael Meadows, deceased, subject to the life estate of one Jane Meadows, the widow of Michael Meadows, deceased. Reg: 4 Jan 1838.

Page 332 - 5 Jan 1838. William Hooper, Richard Bandy and Judah Hooper to William Houston Hooper. Bill of Sale for negro man Tom. Slave labor is to be for support &c for all of the heirs of William Hooper until William Houston Hooper is 21 years of age. This done in accordance to James Hooper, deceased, will. Wit: Thomas C. Rankin, E. A. Rushing and W. D. Hill. Reg: 6 Jan 1838.

Page 339 - 8 Jan 1838. John W. Meeks to William J. W. Wakefield. By the Last Will and Testament of Jesse Putman, deceased, William J. W. Wakefield (by marriage) and myself have derived an undivided interest in four slaves, which by said will, we are entitled to at the death of Sarah Putman, which we are equally entitled to by said will. I have now sold all my right title and claim and interest in to said negroes to said William J. W. Wakefield and his heirs. Wit: Thomas W. Harper and W. W. Mayes. Reg: 13 Jan 1838.

Page 340 - 19 May 1837. John W. Meeks to William J. W. Wakefield. Relinquishment Deed. My interest in land of Sarah Putman's dower of 100 acres in Bedford Co., TN, District No. 19, by will of Jesse Putman, deceased, and willed to John W. Meeks, Minerva Calton and her heirs, and Melissa Meeks and heirs. Wit: W. M. H. Craig and William R. Looney. Reg: 16 Jan 1838.

Page 341 - 29 Sep 1837. B. Fugit and C. Westerman and wife to Moses Cheves. Deed of 50 acres. Bedford Fugitt, Clifford Westerman and Fanny his wife of Bedford Co., TN, sold to Moses Cheves of Bedford Co. Fanny Westerman formerly Fanny Fugitt, daughter of Moses Fugitt, deceased, land in Bedford Co., on waters of Little Sinking Creek. Bounded by grant of Richard Martin. Also another tract in the name of Moses Fugitt by Grant No. 11240 granted 15 Aug 1829 and bounded by lands of Moses Fugitt, James Cheves, Josiah Hughes, Agness Hughes and Stephenson's land. Reg: 16 Jan 1838.

Page 344 - 22 Jan 1838. Robert Stephenson to Harrison Stephenson. Deed 95 acres. Both of Bedford Co., TN. Robert Stephenson sold Harrison Stephenson his interest in the undivided tract of land belonging to the heirs of his deceased father James Stephenson. His part being one tenth of the whole. Bounded by lands of Samuel Jones, Joseph Jones and William Eoff. Wit: William Wood. Reg: 23 Jan 1838.

Page 345 - 22 Jan 1838. Robert Stephenson to George Stephenson. Bill of Sale. Both of Bedford Co., TN. Robert Stephenson sold his interest in 2 negroes of his father's estate now living with his mother. Wit: William Wood. Reg: 23 Jan 1838.

Page 351 - 29 Sep 1836. Hezekiah Brown, Sr. to Hezekiah Brown, Jr. 39+ acres. Both of Bedford Co., TN. Land in Bedford Co., on waters of Big Flat Creek. Bounded by lands of John Casteel, Peter Raney, H. K. Raney. Land includes the cabins and improvement occupied by said Hezekiah, Jr. Wit: John W. Wilson and John Brown. Reg: 31 Jan 1838.

Page 354 - 13 Nov 1837. William Sharp to Anderson Sharp. Deed of Gift, 25 acres. William Sharpe, Sr. to Anderson Sharp, Jr., son of William Sharp. Land in Bedford Co., TN. Borders William Ditto, A. Sharp, James Cathey who is deceased, and William Sharp, Sr. Reg: 31 Jan 1838.

Page 357 - 16 Jan 1838. Sarah Smotherman and others to John Smotherman. Deed 50 acres. Sarah Smotherman, John Foster and Elizabeth Foster his wife, Edmund Lovvorn and his wife Sarah Lovvorn, and Thomas Smotherman, all of Bedford Co., TN and Samuel Smotherman, Hugh Smotherman and James Smotherman of Rutherford Co., TN one part and John Smotherman of Rutherford Co., TN other part. Land in Bedford Co., on Alexanders Creek. Wit: William H. Smotherman and William Smotherman. Reg: 31 Jan 1838.

Page 359 - 27 Jan 1838. William J. Peacock, administrator &c to Gabriel Blackwell. Deed 21 acres. Whereas Alexander Newton of Madison Co., Mississippi by deed dated 7 May 1834 and registered in Deed Book "EE", pages 31 and 32. Conveyed to John W. Peacock in Trust, land in Bedford Co., in the Town of Shelbyville, on the north and bounded by R. P. Harrison, and now owned by George Newton, land formerly owned by James Brittain. John W. Peacock has since died and William J. Peacock appointed administrator of his estate. Sold to Gabriel Blackwell. Wit: E. J. Frierson. Reg: 1 Feb 1838.

Page 360 - 16 Jun 1834. John Sutton, Sr. to John Sutton, Jr. Deed 531 acres. Both of Bedford Co., TN. John Sutton, Sr., for love and affection for his son John Sutton, Jr., land in Bedford Co., on waters of Fall Creek. Borders John Sutton, Sr., Erwin & Patton, Martin Phifer's land, south bank of Fall Creek, Charles Cooper's heirs, Daniel Gilchrist, and west side of Shelbyville - Murfreesboro Road. Also included one tract of 156¼ acres deeded to John Sutton, Sr., dated 13 Jan 1819. Also a tract 204+ acres, deeded to John Sutton, Sr., dated 7 Oct 1820. Also a tract of 75+ acres, dated 11 Sep 1820. Also about 90 acres on north side of the Hutchen's tract to John Sutton, Jr. Wit: I. T. Mayfield and Jiles Bowers. Reg: 1 Feb 1838.

Page 363 - 10 Jul 1833. Green County, Alabama. John and William Clinton to Joseph Clinton, Power of Attorney. Appointed Joseph Clinton of Green Co., Alabama, PA, to sell and dispose our part of a tract of land on Wilsons Creek in Bedford Co., TN, which land was the property of James Clinton, now deceased, which fell to us as the heirs of his body. Wit: Herbert M. Thompson and James M. Bannble(?). Reg: 5 Feb 1838.

Page 364 - 14 Oct 1834. Elvy and Sereny Clinton to Joseph Clinton, Power of Attorney. Elvy and Sereny Clinton of Sumpter Co., Alabama, appoint Joseph Clinton as PA to sell and dispose of their interest in land in Bedford Co., TN, on headwaters of Wilsons Creek. 200 acres, it being the tract whereon the widow Clinton formerly lived and was granted to James Clinton, deceased. Wit: G. W. Spin. Reg: 5 Feb 1838.

Page 371 - 28 Oct 1837. James N. Horn and others to Benjamin Nowlin. Deed 100 acres. James N. Horn, Loyal Brooks, Mary E. Brooks his wife, and Hugh McMurry and Margarett H. McMurry his wife, and George A. Horn, all heirs of George Horn, deceased, and Sarah Ewing late widow of the said George Horn, deceased, all of Marshall Co., TN, one part and Benjamin Nowlin of Bedford

Co., TN. Land in Bedford Co., on East Fork of Rock Creek. Same granted to George Horn by State of Tennessee on 20 July 1814. Bounded by Edward Bryant and the East Fork of Rock Creek. Wit: James Ewing and James H. Ewing. Reg: 12 Feb 1838.
Mary E. Brooks wife of Loyal Brooks, Margaret H. McMurry wife of Hugh McMurry, and Sarah E. Ewing wife of James Ewing.

Page 372 - 3 Feb 1838. Arbitration Award &c Dixon's to Mary Freeland. Whereas John Freeland, Mary Freeland and James Dixon, agreed and chosen John Barrett and Jacob Greer, with power vested in us to choose a third person, chose Andrew Reed, they agreed to stand by the final decision of John Barrett, in a tract of land of 200 acres which was willed to Mary Freeland, alias Mary Galbreath, former widow of Robert Dixon, deceased, of North Carolina, by her father William Galbreath, also between 200 and 300 acres that belonged to Robert Dixon, deceased, who died intestate. Also appointed James Dixon for himself and as guardian for Mary Dixon, an Idiot. Reg: 15 Feb 1838.

Page 375 - 22 Jan 1838. Robert McKenzie and Mary his wife to James M. Johnson. Deed 495 acres. Robert McKenzie and Mary McKenzie his wife of Hardeman Co., TN sold to James M. Johnson of Bedford Co., TN, land in Bedford Co., on waters of Fall Creek. Borders the south side of the bridge across the Dry Fork of Fall Creek on the Turnpike Road, and Martin Phifer, deceased, line. Wit: C. P. McKee and Moses McKinsy. Reg: 20 Feb 1838.

Page 380 - 19 Feb 1838. James Deery to Allen Phillips. Deed 50 acres. James Deery of Bedford Co., TN sold to Allen Phillips of Marshall Co., TN, land in Bedford Co., near Duck River. Borders land granted to Dempsey Powell. Wit: Christian Freeman and Joel Freeman. Reg: 21 Feb 1838.

Page 381 - 5 Feb 1838. James and Elizabeth M. Wortham to James G. Barksdale. Deed. Land in Bedford Co., TN, Town of Shelbyville, Lot No. 54. Borders John C. Coldwell and Minos Cannon's north east corner on the south boundary line of the Public Squire, and Martin Street. Reg: 21 Feb 1838.

Page 382 - 27 Jan 1838. Bradshaw's heirs to James M. Moore. 70+ acres. Land in Bedford Co., TN, on waters of Sugar Creek. Borders Yeates' corner, Sarah Evans, Margaret Stewart, and land where Mary Bradshaw now lives, Asenath Bradshaw, Louisa Bradshaw, and Rachel Bradshaw. Wit: William yeates and Andrew S. Bain. Reg: 24 Feb 1838.

Page 383 - 9 Feb 1838. William Brown to Henry Brown. Deed 54½ acres. Both of Bedford Co., TN, for love and affection for his sister Eveline Norville, and his nephews William H. Norville, Benjamin L. Norville, and an infant male child not yet named, also his niece, Sarah Jane Norville, all sons and daughter of Thomas Norville and the said Eveline Norville, granted unto Henry Brown, in trust for the only use of the above mentioned Eveline and children, property or land in Bedford Co., on north east of Shelbyville, being one of the divisions of David Norville's estate, deceased., No. 6. Borders Phillip's line, Bomar's line and crosses the McMinnville Road. Reg: 24 Feb 1838.

Page 386 - 25 May 1837. William Frizzel and Christiny Anna Frizzel to Henry Hays. Deed. William Frizzel and Christiny

DEED BOOK "GG"

Anna Frizzel his wife of Bedford Co., TN to Henry Hays of Bedford CO., land in Bedford Co., on waters of Wartrace Fork, containing one equal share, with all of the heirs of Peter Hays upon two tracts of land, granted to Peter Hays by State of Tennessee. Borders lane that divides farms of Hays and Jacob Whitworth, and M. Gilchrist. Other tract borders Jacob Whitworth's land and William Montgomery. Wit: Arch. Hays, Samuel Marr, William B. M. Brame, and Thomas Drake. Reg: 28 Feb 1838.

Page 388 - 25 Sep 1833. Orpha D. Smith and James P. Smith to Jacob Byler. All of Bedford Co., TN. Orpha D. Smith and James P. Smith sold their interest in three different tracts of land willed to them by their father, willed to Orpha D. Smith. Wit: James T. Byler and Thomas Drake. Orpha D. Smith wife of James P. Smith. Reg: 5 Mar 1838.

Page 437 - 31 Mar 1838. Freeman Burrow to William Burrow. Deed of Gift. Freeman Burrow for love and affection for his son William Burrow, conveyed to him all my interest, which will be coming to me, in four negro slaves for life. Wit: R. F. Arnold, T. F. Taylor and William Honea. Reg: 2 Apr 1838.

Page 438 - 22 Jan 1828. Robert McKenzie and wife to William Houston. Deed 355. Robert McKenzie and Mary McKenzie his wife of Hardeman Co., TN, to William Houston of Bedford Co., TN, land in Bedford Co., on waters of Fall Creek. Borders west side of the Turnpike Road, bridge on Dry Fork of Fall Creek, and land formerly owned by Caleb Phifer, deceased. Wit: C. P. McKee and Moses McKinley. Reg: 3 Apr 1838.

Page 439 - 7 Jul 1834. Edward and Charles Trabue to Charles G. McLean. Deed 75 acres. Edward and Charles Trabue of Davidson Co., TN to Charles G. McLean of Rutherford Co., TN, land in Bedford Co., TN, on the Barren Fork, in two tracts. (1) Borders junction of Barren Fork and Garrison Fork, Charles Lucas, a saw mill, in all 70 acres including saw mill. (2) Borders Blacksmith shop and spring, including Grist Mill, Cotton Gin, Screw and Blacksmith shop, in all about 50 acres. Reg: 3 Apr 1838.

Page 440 - 5 Jun 1837. Daniel L. Barringer and Ann Barringer to Thomas Stammers. Deed 486 acres. Daniel L. Barringer and Ann Barringer his wife of Bedford Co., TN to Thomas Stammers of Marshall Co., TN, land in Bedford and Marshall Counties, on waters of Wilson Creek. Borders James Rogers and Martin Adam. Reg: 3 Apr 1838.

DEED BOOK "HH" 1838 - 1839

Page 1 - 12 Mar 1838. James Adams and others to Robert and Thomas P. Adams. Deed 186½ acres. James Adams, Alexander D. Adams, James Harkness and his wife Eliza Harkness, and Samuel Woods and his wife Sarah Woods of Marshall Co., TN, and Julia Adams, Mary Adams and Thomas Dryden and Hannah his wife of Bedford Co., TN sold to Robert N. Adams their brother of Marshall Co., TN and Thomas P. Adams their brother of Bedford Co. James Adams and others for love and affection they have for their brothers, conveyed to them land in Bedford Co., on the East Fork of Rock Creek, it being part of a North Carolina Grant to James Hart (Iredell Co.). Borders Hart's corner. Wit: John Webb and John H. Larue. Reg: 7 Apr 1838.

Page 5 - 22 Nov 1837. David A. Weaver and Emily Ann Weaver to David Weaver, Sr. Bill of Sale. David A. and Emily Ann Weaver sold to David Weaver, Sr., their claim unto a negro boy named David. Wit: Murphey W. Jett and George Cortner. Reg: 10 Apr 1838.

Page 7 - 24 Nov 1837. Sidney Smith to Thomas C. Whiteside. Power of Attorney. Sidney Smith, Executor of Last Will and Testament of Jesse Whorton, late of Davidson Co., TN, deceased, appointed Thomas C. Whiteside, Esq. of Shelbyville, deliver a deed to Samuel Mitchell of Bedford Co., TN, land in Bedford Co., on Wartrace Fork. Reg: 12 Apr 1838.

Page 13 - 18 Dec 1837. James D. and Mary Clark to Little Berry Still. Deed 101 acres. James D. Clark and Mary Clark his wife of Bedford Co., TN to Little Berry Still of Rutherford Co., TN, land in Bedford Co., on west side of Alexanders Creek. Borders Harris' corner. Wit: John Thompson and Jason Winsett. Reg: 21 Apr 1838.

Page 15 - 19 Dec 1837. James D. Clark and Mary Clark to Nathan Wheeler. Deed 2½ acres. James D. Clark and Mary Clark his wife sold to Nathan Wheeler, all of Bedford Co., TN, land in Bedford Co., on west side of North Fork, it being a part of a tract that was divided between the heirs of John Sanders, deceased, it being a fraction of a lot adjoining the widow's dower on the east. Borders Dower's tract. Reg: 26 Apr 1838.

Page 16 - 6 Apr 1838. John Sutton to Colmore B. Sutton. Deed to part of Lot No. 40. Both of Bedford Co., TN. John Sutton for love and affection for his son Colmore B. Sutton, land in Town of Shelbyville, part of Lot No. 40. Borders house formerly belonging to John A. Marrs, deceased and now Harvey M. Watterson, Martin Street, and Lot belonging to the heirs of William B. Sutton, deceased. With the exception of the house and lot, it stands on formerly occupied as a Law Office by William B. Sutton, deceased, and now property of his heirs. Also Lot No. 22 in Town of Shelbyville. Wit: Charles F. Sutton and Alfred P. Gowen. Reg: 28 Apr 1838. Also (same page) land in Bedford Co., TN, on waters of Wartrace Fork. Borders lands of John Sutton and Drury Rogers. Same witnesses as above. Reg: 28 Apr 1838.

Page 19 - 19 Mar 1838. William Knight to Gabriel B. Knight and others, Trustees of the M. E. Church. 5 acres. William Knight of Bedford Co., TN and Trustees (unnamed) other part. William Knight for the love I bear for the Methodist Episcopal Church, I bequeath, make over, and confirm to Gabriel B. Knight, Obadiah W. Knight, Harberd Smith, Edward Stephenson, William Hammell, Joseph Adams, Richard H. Sims and Reuben Ellis, Trustees in Trust for the M. E. Church and their successors, land in Bedford Co., TN. Borders G. B. Knight's house. Wit: John N. Porter and Benjamin Adams. Reg: 5 May 1838.

Page 20 - 5 Dec 1836. Nathan H. Adams to Jasper Dazey. Relinquishment. Nathan H. Adams of Williamson Co., TN to Jasper Dazey of Bedford Co., TN. Quit Claim for benefit of Amanda Adams wife of Nathan H. Adams, on land in Mississippi. Wit: William Gilchrist and Hiram Adams. Reg: 7 May 1838.

Page 21 - 19 Apr 1838. Robert N., Thomas P. and Mary Adams to Thomas Dryden, all of Marshall Co., TN. Deed 91+ acres. Land in Bedford Co., TN, on waters of East Fork of Rock Creek, it being a part of land owned by Robert Adams, deceased. Wit: John Larue and John H. Larue. Reg: 7 May 1838.
Also (same page), 93¼ acres sold to John Larue of Bedford Co., TN. Wit: John H. Larue and Thomas Dryden. Reg: 7 May 1838.

Page 26 - 16 Aug 1837. Stephen Porter and others to Daniel Looney. Deed 67¼ acres. We, Stephen Porter, William Porter, Nathaniel Porter, Griffith J. Leonard and Mary has conveyed unto Daniel Looney, land in Bedford Co., in District No. 19. Wit: A. M. Loyd, William Robinson, William H. Craig and William R. Looney. Nancy E. Leonard wife of Griffith J. Leonard. Reg: 9 May 1838.

Page 27 - (Same as above) sold to John Ray. Deed of 100 acres. Land in Bedford Co., TN, District No. 19. Reg: 9 May 1838.

Page 43 - 19 Nov 1836. Anna White and others to Daniel L. Barringer. Deed undivided. Anna White, widow and relict of William White, deceased, late Secretary of State for the State of North Carolina and Elizabeth Felton, Susan White, Emma White and Sophronia White, daughters of William White, all of the City of Raleigh, NC one part and Daniel L. Barringer, late of Wake Co., NC and now of Bedford Co., TN other part. Land in Franklin Co., TN, on Elk River, also tract in Bedford Co., on Wilsons Creek, also tract in Madison Co., TN, on waters of Middle Fork of Forked Deer River, also tract in Humphreys Co., TN, on waters of South Fork of Turkey Creek, another tract in Humphreys Co., TN. All above tracts were granted to William White. Wit: J. H. Hayley and Richard H. Hayley. Reg: 26 May 1838.

Page 47 - 26 May 1838. Samuel Neeley to Eakin & brothers and others. Deed. Samuel Neeley of Bedford Co., TN sold to Eakin & brothers, Alexander and George Davidson, all of Bedford Co., sold two Town Lots in Shelbyville, No. 98 and No. 105. Reg: 31 May 1838.

Page 48 - 9 Feb 1838. John Sutton to Charles F. Sutton. Deed 407+ acres. Both of Bedford Co., TN. John Sutton for natural love and affection for his son Charles F. Sutton. If Charles F. Sutton dies without issue, it should go to John Sutton's two grandsons, John Sutton and Charles F. Sutton, minor heirs of my son John Sutton, deceased, conveyed land in Bedford Co., on waters of Wartrace Fork, it being the tract whereon Charles F. Sutton now lives. Borders road leading from Shelbyville to McMinnville, Benjamin Bradford's land, Charles F. Sutton's land purchased from James Cathey and Rebeckah Armstrong, John H. Newbil's line, McNutts Branch, Bradfords Branch, Arnold's line, William McGrew, and Baxter Ragsdale. Wit: C. B. Sutton and B. M. Bradford. Reg: 2 Jun 1838.

Page 54 - 15 May 1838. Cleveland L. Harrison to James Dillard. Mortgage. Land belonging to the heirs of William Craig, deceased, in Bedford Co., TN. Bounded by Widow Dawdy, Henry Haslett, Zachariah Davis, Solomon Durrett. Wit: C. S. Russell and John W. Dawdy. Reg: 5 Jun 1838.

Page 61 - 9 May 1836. John H. White to Nathaniel White. Power of Attorney. To sell land descended to the heirs of William White, deceased. Land in Bedford Co., TN of 50 acres. North Carolina, Cabarrus County Witnesses: John L. Beard and James G. Spears. Reg: 9 Jun 1838.

Page 62 - 9 Jun 1838. Hamlin Cook and wife to William H. Craig. All of Bedford Co., TN. Bounded by land Peter Garren conveyed to Solomon Durrett, John McAdams and land he bought of James Davis, land William Craig, deceased, made to Richard Standiford, Alfred Anderson, William C. Swanson and land made by William Craig, deceased, of Henry Tully. Hamblin Cook and Susannah Cook his wife, for and in consideration of the sum of $109.11, being an heir in common with James Craig, Cena Justice, John Craig, Hamblin Cook for Susannah Craig, Robert Craig, Martha Bradley, William M. Russell, Jr. for Roseller Craig, Cleveland C. Harrison for Julia Craig, Benjamin F. Craig and Flora Craig. Reg: 11 Jun 1838.

Page 65 - 23 Jun 1838. Charles S. Maddox and Sarah A. Maddox to Richard Sims. Relinquishment. Charles S. Maddox and Sarah A. Maddox his wife, both of Bedford Co., TN, sold to Richard Sims of Bedford Co., land in Bedford Co., on Powells Creek, which land now belongs to the heirs of John Stephens, deceased. Wit: John Streater and William M. Maddox. Reg: 28 Jun 1838.

Page 71 - 11 Jun 1838. Isaiah Atkinson to Meekey and Elizabeth Atkinson. Deed of Gift. 66 acres. For natural love and affection for Meekey and Elizabeth Atkinson, conveyed to them, my tract of land in Bedford Co., TN. Bounded by Evan Wallis and M. W. Morrison. Wit: George T. Landis and Philip Sprouse. Reg: 30 Jun 1838.

Page 81 - 25 Jun 1838. Theo. F. Bradford to the heirs of Robert Waite, deceased. 20 acres. Theo. F. Bradford sold to Gordentia Waite, Julia P. Waite, E. McLain and her husband Thomas McLean, and Artimetia Waite of Mississippi and Amanda M. Bradford, Susan Waite, Frances P. Waite, and Magdalene R. Waite, all of Bedford Co., TN, all of whom are heirs at law of Robert Waite, deceased. Land in Bedford Co., on west side of Wartrace Fork. Borders Henry B. Coffey, John Taylor, Patsey Cox, and Philip Coble. Wit: W. Galbreath and Thomas Davidson. Reg: 3 Jul 1838.

Page 85 - 4 May 1838. Martha Thompson to William S. Wade and John A. THompson. Deed. Martha Thompson sold to William S. Wade and John A. Thompson, all of Bedford Co., TN, some negro property which is in her possession which belongs to her during her natural life and having no horse or land and being old and infirm, the negroes do not obey her command. William S. Wade and John A. Thompson has taken to manage said property as Trustee in Trust. Martha Thompson has conveyed one negro woman Hannah and her three sons. The negroes are to remain on Elizabeth Thompson's plantation until 25 Dec 1839. Wit: James Thompson and Joseph P. Thompson. Reg: 6 Jul 1838.

Page 88 - 9 Apr 1838. Circuit Court. Decree for land. 144½ acres. Ruth H. Bernard, Walter Bernard and Virginia A. Norfleet, heirs of Thomas H. Bernard by their guardian James G. Barksdale. Their lands in Bedford Co., TN, between the forks of Duck River, known as the "Three Forks Tract". Bounded by A. Erwin, land conveyed by George Moore to Thomas H. Bernard, Garrison Fork of Duck River, Barren Fork, and Harman's Branch. Reg: 12 Jul 1838.

Page 92 - 5 Feb 1838. Thomas Harris to Joseph McCannaughey. Power of Attorney. Thomas Harris of Charlotte, Mecklenburg Co., NC, appointed Joseph McCannaughey of the same place, my Attorney, to sell my undivided interest in a tract of land of 700 acres, being one undivided half of said tract, in Bedford Co., TN. Land borders land of Johnston Houston and others and formerly owned by Robert Lock, deceased, of Rowan Co., NC. Wit: S. B. McComb and T. R. Hughes. Reg: 13 Jul 1838.

Page 93 - 9 Jan 1838. Joseph Clinton and others to Dorrington Garrett. Deed 6/11 of 200 acres. John Clinton, William Clinton, Sereny Clinton and Elvey Clinton and Joseph Clinton sold to Dorrington Garrett land in Bedford Co., TN, in District No. 10. Borders Wynn's land, James Hoskins and Jason Shuffield, William T. Tomerson and John G. Hall, and Matthew Dixon. Wit: Wilie Perry and THomas Cheatham. Reg: 13 Jul 1838.

Page 96 - 31 May 1838. James Womble and wife Joanna to John T. Neil. Deed in Trust. Slaves, now in the possession of Beckey Warren, agreeable to the Last Will and Testament of Edward Warren, deceased, to remain in her possession until her death, then to be equally divided between her ten children. Wit: James B. Dolby and Lydia T. Womble. Reg: 17 Jul 1838.

Page 102 - 16 Mar 1838. Mary Ann Means to Caleb P. Houston and Margarett Hutton. Deed 180 acres. Mary Ann Means of Marshall Co., Mississippi one part and Caleb P. Houston and Margarett Hutton, Executor and Executrix of John Hutton, deceased, of Bedford Co., TN other part. Land in Bedford Co., in District No. 5 and on the waters of Falling Creek, and on west side of the Nashville-Murfreesboro and Shelbyville Turnpike Road and about seven miles from Shelbyville. Bounded by William Houston, land of the heirs of John Houston, deceased, and Travis C. Nash. The land being the share allotted to Mary Ann Means in the portions of the lands of Barbary McRee, deceased. Wit: C. P. McRee and W. A. P. Jones. Reg: 21 Jul 1838.

Page 103 - 22 Jul 1836. Solomon Burrow and others to John Corsby. Solomon Burrow, Maddison Burrow, James Burrow, Jesse Burrow, Pierce Wilhoite and Hester Wilhoite and Letha B. Burrow of the one part and John Corsby of Guilford Co., NC other part. Land in Guilford Co., NC. Adjoining lands of Tobias Soots, Samuel Coble, Frederick Coble, Eli May and others. Wit: Jordan C. Holt and D. M. Smith. Reg: 21 Jul 1838.

Page 104 - 13 Jul 1838. Josiah Stephens to Richard Sims. Josiah Stephens of Gibson Co., TN conveyed my interest in a tract of land in Bedford Co., TN, on waters of Powel Creek, land of John Stephens, deceased. Wit: William M. Maddox and William M. Chinault. Reg: 26 Jul 1838.

Page 105 - 11 Jul 1838. James Stephens to Richard Sims. James Stephens of Perry Co., TN sold to Richard Sims, his interest in land in Bedford Co., TN, on Powels Creek and belonging to John Stephens, deceased. Wit: William M. Maddox and M. R. Fisher. Reg: 26 Jul 1838.

Page 116 - 28 Jul 1838. John Brooks to Leonard W. Marbury. Deed 15 acres and 34¼ acres. John Brooks of Talladega, Alabama one part and Leonard W. Marbury of Bedford Co., TN other part. Land in Bedford Co., on Duck River, one mile above Shelbyville and known as the Brooks Mill Tract. Borders Duck River. Another tract bordering Duck River where James Sharp built a mill, Wilson Coats, Sanders' line, another tract borbering Duck River to a lower part of an island in Duck River where Sanders built a mill, to including necessary ground for buttment to build a Mill Dam, 15 acres. Another tract on Duck River as divided among the heirs of Wilson Coats, deceased, Lot No. 7, S. Newsom's corner, 34¼ acres. Reg: 8 Aug 1838.

Page 117 - 25 Dec 1832. Thomas Whiteside to William Hoover. Deed 311 acres. Thomas Whiteside of Granger Co., TN one part and William Hoover of Bedford Co., TN, land in Bedford Co., on north side of Duck River below the "The Three Forks", it being part of land sold by the Blounts to John Overton and Jenkins Whiteside. Borders north bank of Duck River, and lands of Thomas Whiteside sold to Hugh Snelling. Wit: Thomas C. Whiteside and Erwin J. Frierson. Reg: In book "CC", page 415 on 7 Mar 1833.

Page 124 - 1 Dec 1836. John S. Booth to Elizabeth Haynes and heirs. Deed 56 acres. John S. Booth of Bedford Co., TN and Elizabeth Haynes and Harriet, Nancy, John, Thomas and Henry Haynes, they being the widow and children of John Haynes, dec'd, all of Bedford Co., TN. John Rushing and Elizabeth Haynes, Executor and Executrix of the Last Will and Testament of John Haynes, deceased. Will directed to purchase land for his wife and children during her lifetime or widowhood. In case of her death or marriage, should go to his five children. Land in Bedford Co., on waters of the North Fork. Borders James A. Keel and William McKay. Wit: John Larimer and Jacob Fisher. Reg: 10 Aug 1838.

Page 126 - 13 Mar 1838. James and Catharine Wortham to John C. Coldwell and Minos Cannon, Sr. Land in Bedford Co., Shelbyville, part of Lot No. 54. Borders lot James Brittain sold to Coldwell and Cannon, Thomas Davis, corner of Bank Alley, Martin Street, and Brittain's Counting Room. Catharine M. Wortham wife of James Wortham. Reg: 11 Aug 1838.

Page 128 - 1 Aug 1838. Peggy Clifft and James Clifft to William H. Stephenson. Deed 50 acres. Peggy Clifft and James Clifft her son of Bedford Co., TN, one part and William H. Stephenson of Bedford Co., other part. Land in Bedford Co., on Little Sinking Creek. Borders Richard Martin, Jr. Wit: Edward Stephenson and Daniel G. Stephenson. Reg: 13 Aug 1838.

Page 136 - 13 Nov 1835. Mary E. Sims and Walter Sims to Boyd McNairy. Mortgage. 420 acres. Mary E. Sims and Walter Sims of Davidson Co., TN one part and Boyd McNairy of Davidson Co.,TN, land in Bedford Co., TN, on Duck River between Spring Creek and Wilson Creek, it being the same conveyed by Deed of Gift from Rebecca Sims to Mary E. Sims on 4 Nov 1834 and recorded in book "EE", page 417 & 418. Mary E. Sims wife of Walter Sims. Reg: 17 Aug 1836.

Page 141 - 6 Jun 1837. Pearce Wilhoite and Mary Wilhoite to James Jones. Mary Wilhoite and Pearce Wilhoite one part and

James Jones, all of Bedford Co., TN, other part. Land in Bedford Co., on waters of the Big Flat Creek, which in the division of the lands of Jacob Wilhoite, deceased, amongst his heirs fell to Willie Wilhoite since deceased, it being two sevenths of the land of Willie Wilhoite, deceased. Wit: John F. Norman and Samuel Hawkins. Reg: 20 Aug 1838.

Page 142 - 2 Dec 1836. Jacob Cheves and others to Moses Cheves. 50 acres. Jacob H. Cheves and Calvin Cheves and William Oneal and Nancy Oneal formerly Nancy Cheves, Witheal Oneal and Polly Oneal formerly Polly Cheves, and Elizabeth Cheves wife of James Cheves, deceased, and Thomas Cheves and Rebeckah Cheves, all of Bedford Co., TN one part and Moses Cheves of Bedford Co., land in Bedford Co., on waters of Little Sinking Creek. Borders lands owned by the heirs of Moses Fugit, deceased, and Hughes' land. Wit: C. D. Westerman and James Clift. Reg: 23 Aug 1838.

Page 144 - 6 Jun 1837. James M. and Polly Jones to Pearce Wilhoite. 105 acres. James M. Jones and Polly his wife sold to Pearce Wilhoite, all of Bedford Co., TN, land in Bedford Co., on waters of Big Flat Creek. Borders William Boone, Thomas Dean, Hurst's tract. The land being the same which fell to James and wife as heirs to the estate of Jacob Wilhoite, dec'd. Wit: John F. Norman and Samuel Hawkins. Reg: 23 Aug 1838.

Page 146 - Plat of the survey and division of Martin Phifer's land. 4966 acres, 5 Lots.
Page 148 - Martin Phifer of Cabarrus Co., NC, directed his grandsons, John F. Phifer and Caleb Phifer to divide the land in Bedford Co., TN, on waters of Falling Creek. John F. and Caleb Phifer are sons of Martin Phifer's son John Phifer. Lot No. 2, assigned to the children of my son George Phifer, Lot No. 1, to my daughter Margarett, Lot No. 3, to my daughter Anne, Lot No. 4, my daughter Mary and her children of William Crawford, Lot No. 5, to James Childress' jis children by former wife. Wit: Margaret Rodgers and John Rodgers. Reg: 25 Aug 1838.

Page 149 - 8 Feb 1837. Ann Huff and others to Andrew Reed. 169 acres. We, Anne Huff, Catharine McKamey, Mary Freeland and Elizabeth Cunningham wife of Matthew Cunningham, sold to Andrew Reed, land in Bedford Co., TN, on Big Flat Creek. Borders Wiggin's line. Wit: Robert Reed and J. N. Reed. Reg: 30 Aug 1838.

Page 150 - 24 Aug 1838. Henry Hays to James Frizzell. Henry Hays sold to James Frizzell, land that I purchased of William Frizzell, it being the full share of William and Christine Frizzell, that they had in a tract of land belonging to Peter Hays, deceased. Wit: N. L. Majors and Arah Hays. Reg: 3 Sep 1838.

Page 155 - 5 Sep 1838. George W. Morris to David J. Norville. 53 acres. George W. Morris of Rutherford Co., TN one part and David J. Norville of Bedford Co., TN other part. James D. Norville one of the legal heirs of David Norville, deceased, did on 7 Feb 1837 make a Trust Deed to Samuel Phillips of Bedford Co.,conveying full power to Phillips to transact all things in his behalf concerning his interest in his father's estate, for the interest and benefit of James D. Norville and his children. Reg: 8 Sep 1838.

Page 159 - Peter Singleton Will.
I, Peter Singleton of Bedford Co., TN, being fully impressed with the uncertainty of human life, and being now at an advanced age of life, but of sound mind and memory, I do constitute and appoint this to be my Last Will and Testament.
Item 1. All debts be paid.
Item 2. Emancipate all the slaves of which I was possessed at the death of my wife Sally Brooks Singleton.
Item 3. Executor to emancipate my slaves at my wife's death.
Item 4. Will all his stock &c to his slaves after they are emancipated.
Item 5. The slaves are to get stocks &c if they cannot be emancipated. All the real estate to my friend Wiley F. Daniel.
Item 6. Wiley F. Daniel to get several slaves.
Item 7. Desires the Will to be take action on only after the death of his wife.
Item 8. Appoint my friend Wiley F. Daniel my Executor.
Wit: Wilkins Blanton, Robert Matthews and George Davidson. Reg: 20 Sep 1838.

Page 166 - 17 Sep 1838. William D. Warner to Eunice Warner. Relinquishment Deed. The Last Will and Testament of John Warner, Jr., deceased, William D. Warner has interest in remainder to take effect and be united with the possession after the death of my mother Eunice Warner, who has a life estate in two tracts of land in Bedford Co., TN, in District No. 21 of 250 acres. The other whereon Eunice Warner now lives of 250 acres. Also one Town Lot in Shelbyville, also negroes and personal property that did belong to John Warner, deceased. Sold to Eunice Warner all interest in the above mentioned property. Wit: Henry Earnhart and Hilliard Dixon. Reg: 26 Sep 1838.

Page 169 - 4 Oct 1838. William Deason to Jemima Ray and children. Deed of Gift. For love and affection for my daughter Jemima Ray, my oldest daughter, give to her and her children, a negro girl Viana. Wit: Thomas C. Rankin, James Harris and Thomas COllins. Reg: 4 Oct 1838.

Page 170 - 20 Apr 1833. John Byler and others to Isaac D. Maxwell. 70 acres. John Byler, William L. Byler, Jacob Byler, Thomas Black, James T. Byler, John H. Maxwell and James P. Smith one part and Isaac D. Maxwell other part. Land in Bedford Co., TN, on waters of Clem Creek. Bounded by A. Byler. Wit: Benjamin Oslin and Thomas B. Carlton. Reg: 8 Oct 1838.

Page 172 - 21 Jul 1838. Newcum Thompson, Sr. and Newcum Thompson, Jr. to William Word. Deed 20 acres. All of Bedford Co., TN, land in Bedford Co., on waters of Big Flat Creek. Borders William Heaslett's land, school land, and Mrs. Hubbard's land. Wit: Jo. Thompson and Henry Cannon. Reg: 8 Oct 1838.

Page 174 - 5 Aug 1837. John Mullins to Clayborn Bowles, dec'd, heirs. 54 acres. John Mullins of Bedford Co., TN one part and Clayborn Bowles, deceased, Sarah T. Bowles, Lousiannah C. Bowles, Elijah T. Bowles, Nancy S. Bowles, Elbourn Bowles, Claybourn Bowles, Sadusein(?) Ann Bowles, Elvira Bowles, John F. W. Bowles, and Amanda Belvina Bowles of Bedford Co., other part, land in Bedford Co., on north side of Duck River, being part of the Blount grant and surveyed to John Overton and Jenkins Whiteside. Borders James Young, road leading from Shelbyville to M. Mullins Mill on the Garrison Fork, where widow Bowles now lives, and Peter Miller. Reg: 9 Oct 1838.

Page 177 - 21 Mar 1838. John and Margaret Morgan to Andrew Presgrove. 49+ acres. John Morgan and Margarett Morgan sold to Andrew Presgrove, all of Bedford Co., TN, land in Bedford Co. Bounded by the bank of North Fork and Robert Allison. Margaret Morgan wife of John Morgan. Wit: H. S. Wilson and Jesse A. Morgan. Reg: 13 Oct 1838.

Page 182 - 22 Oct 1838. David J. Norville to John W. Norville. Undivided interest, 285 acres. David J. Norville conveyed to John W. Norville, both of Bedford Co., TN, all his interest in land in Bedford Co., it being the place whereon his mother Elizabeth W. Norville now lives, it being her dower land as laid off to her out of the estate of his father David Norville, deceased. Reg: 22 Oct 1838.

Page 189 - 26 Oct 1838. John Davidson to George Davidson. 500 acres. John Davidson, for love and affection for George Davidson, both of Bedford Co., TN, conveyed unto him land in Bedford Co., on Knob Creek. Bounded by E. Hord, east side of a wagon road, Kelly's corner, Elias Yeates' old place, and Vincent Smith. Also conveyed to George Davidson several negro slaves. Wit: Thomas B. Flintham and William Pepper. Reg: 12 Nov 1838.

Page 191 - 3 Nov 1838. Roger Snell to Keziah Galbreath. Obligation. Roger Snell is firmly bound unto Keziah Galbreath of Bedford Co., TN, for $10,000.00. The condition of the above obligation is such that whereas I have agreed to attend to and manage the affairs of Keziah Galbreath, when she desires it and to take care of her during her natural life and when she wishes to build her a comfortable house in my yard and remove her to it and furnish her with every convenience and necessary suitable to her age and not to remove or take possession of any property during her lifetime that she had given to him. Wit: Jacob Greer and Adam S. Riggs. Reg: 12 Nov 1838.

Page 192 - 3 Nov 1838. Keziah Galbreath to Roger Snell. Deed of Gift. Keziah Galbreath for the friendship and esteem for Roger Snell, both of Bedford Co., TN, and also in consideration that he will take care of her for her lifetime, conveyed unto him land in Bedford Co., on waters of Big Flat Creek, it being the land where she now lives and which she purchased from William Dixon. Also all her negroes (11), all her stock and furniture and all the property. At the death of Roger Snell, it is to go to his children by his last wife, the present wife. Wit: Jacob Greer and Adam S. Riggs. Reg: 12 Nov 1838.

Page 194 - 9 Nov 1838. Horace Blanton to Sarah Blanton. Deed of Relinquishment. Horace Blanton of Jackson Co., Alabama sold to Sarah Blanton of Bedford Co., TN, all his interest &c in the estate of William Blanton, deceased, as one of the distributees of William Blanton. Reg: 22 Nov 1838.

Page 199 - 21 Nov 1838. Samuel G. Dyer to William H. Dyer. 200 acres. Whereas by descent from James Dyer, deceased, our father, we, William H. Dyer and Esther G. Dyer, and John Dyer and Elizabeth Dyer and Joseph G. Dyer and James M. Dyer and Gibson J. Dyer and myself (Samuel G. Dyer) hold equal and undivided interest in land in Bedford Co., TN, in District No. 20. Bounded by Martha Dyer where she now lives and James Dyer.

Wit: John Barrett and Samuel Garrison. Reg: 24 Nov 1838.

Page 200 - 22 Nov 1838. Joseph G. Dyer to William H. Dyer. Deed 200 acres. (Same as above). Wit: Newcum Thompson and William Gammill. Reg: 24 Nov 1838.

Page 201 - 26 Nov 1838. John Scott to E. S. Singleton. Deed of Gift. John Scott for love and affection for my daughter Elizabeth Sarah Singleton and for her better support and comfort, conveyed two negroes now in her possession, a boy Wesly and a girl Julia. Reg: 26 Nov 1838.

Page 201 - 1 Oct 1838. William Gilchrist to Erwin J. Frierson. Deed to Lot No. 77. William Gilchrist of City of Little Rock, Pulaski Co., Arkansas sold to E. J. Frierson of Shelbyville, Lot No. 77. Reg: 30 Nov 1838.

Page 204 - 28 Nov 1838. John Dyer to William H. Dyer. (Same as on pages 199 and 200). Reg: 1 Dec 1838.

Page 209 - 26 Nov 1838. Mary Dixon alias Mary Freeland to James Dixon. 200 acres. Mary Dixon alias Mary Freeland sold to James Dixon, both of Bedford Co., TN, for and consideration of the following items, to wit, $25.00 allowed me by John Barrett, Jacob Greer and Andrew Reed the arbitrators to which was referred the matter sometime last winter to be paid to me annually during my natural life, also, I am to live with my daughter Nancy and be paid for my trouble in taking care of Nancy and her children as I have been heretofore, out of the rents of Nancy's part of the land, has granted and sold to James Dixon all her right title &c in land willed to her (Mary Dixon) by my father William Galbreath. Land in Bedford Co., on waters of Big Flat Creek. Borders lands formerly owned by Francis McKame, Hundley Wiggins, and James W. Patton, William Dixon's land willed to him by William Galbreath, and lands of Holt and Hix. Wit: Jacob Greer and James W. Patton. Reg: 3 Dec 1838.

Page 210 - 29 Aug 1838. Joseph McConnaughey and wife and Thomas Harris and wife to Theoderick F. Bradford. Deed 775 acres. Joseph McConnaughey and wife Mary and Thomas Harris and wife Elizabeth of Mecklenburg Co., NC one part and Theoderick F. Bradford of Bedford Co., TN, other part, land in Bedford Co., it being part of a grant to Matthew Lock and which fell to Robert Lock. Wit: Henry C. Owens. Reg: 4 Dec 1838.

Page 212 - 3 Dec 1838. Andrew Davidson to Lorenzo C. Elliott. Deed in Trust. For love and affection for my grandchildren, Andrew Elliott, Samuel Elliott, Malinda Elliott, Isabella Elliott, Thomas Elliott, and Cannon Elliott, minor children of my son-in-law Lorenzo C. Elliott, in Trust for the grandchildren until they arrive at age, conveyed a negro girl Mary Ann. Wit: W. D. Orr. Reg: 6 Dec 1838.

Page 213 - 11 Jan 1837. Hiram Hays and others to A. H. White and Clarke. 188 acres, undivided interest. Hiram Hays and Jane Hays and Henry Hays and Archibald Hays and William Brookshear and his wife Sarah Brookshear, all of Bedford Co., TN and heirs of Peter Hays, deceased, one part and B. G. White and Newton Clark and Augustus H. White other part, their interest in the estate of Peter Hays, deceased, land in Bedford Co., on Wartrace Fork. Bounded by James H. Clark, Gray Linch, Noble

L. Majors, John Eoff, John Robinson, Jr., James Sutton, and James Haile. Wit: James Frizzell and N. L. Majors. Reg: 6 Dec 1838.

Page 214 - Tennessee Grant to William and Archibald Gilchrist, 880 acres. No. 3843. For 12½ cents per acre. Entered 5 Jul 1824, dated 29 Aug 1824, on waters of east waters of Rock Creek and on Sinking Creek. Borders William Poston, Edward Bryeans, school land, James Johnson, Joseph Dobbs, John Bryeans, Malcom Gilchrist, William Brown, and James Hart. Reg: 11 Dec 1838.

Page 217 - 24 Oct 1836. John Cross to R. Denniston. Deed undivided. John Cross of Randolph Co., MO one part and Robert Denniston of Bedford Co., TN, other part. Land in Bedford Co., on Sally's Branch, a branch of the Garrison Fork. Borders lands of John L. Neill, William Thomas and Alexander Lee. It being land which Jacob Cross, deceased, purchased of Andrew Erwin and was deeded to the heirs of Jacob Cross. Wit: Samuel Mitchell and J. W. Norvill. Reg: 12 Dec 1838.

Page 220 - 8 Dec 1838. Sarah Gollerthan and others to Phereba Ditto. Relinquishment. We, Sarah Gollerthan, Cyntha Cathey and Mary McGuire relinquished unto Phereba Ditto guardian of our brother John Ditto, all the profits that may arise from his hands and negroes and other property during his natural life, binding Phereba Ditto to take care of said John Ditto and not to diminish his property in any way. Wit: J(?). T. Mayfield and Peter Lee and Samuel Phillips. Reg: 13 Dec 1838.

Page 228 - 29 Aug 1837. Elliott Rucker to William Rucker. 75 acres. Elliott Rucker one part and William Rucker and Elizabeth Kimmons, Executor and Executrix, with will annexed of Joel Kimmons, deceased, all of Bedford Co., TN, conveyed unto the Executors of Joel Kimmons, deceased, for special use and benefit of the widow and orphans of Joel Kimmons, deceased, a tract of land in Bedford Co., on the dividing ridge between Alexander and Weakleys Creeks. Borders land whereon Elliott Rucker now lives, land Elliott Rucker purchased of Evan Wallace, George Landers and John Morrison. Wit: A. Litle, William Taylor and James Harris. Reg: 26 Dec 1838.

Page 228 - 13 Dec 1838. James Lambert and others to Samuel Mitchell. Whereas by purchase from several of the heirs of Robert Wallace, deceased, and we by descent Samuel Mitchell and ourselves have derived title to and now hold an undivided interests in a tract of land in bedford Co., TN, District No. 4. Bounded by Mrs. Merritt, John Norville, William Waite, Samuel Mitchell's land purchased by the heirs of John Gowen and Norville McGee. The land being whereon Robert Wallace, deceased, died seized and possessed. We convey all rights &c we now have and all we have in the death of the widow Elizabeth Wallace, to Samuel Mitchell. Signed by: James Lambert, Elizabeth Lambert and Nancy Wallace. Elizabeth Lambert wife of James Lambert. Reg: 26 Dec 1838.

Page 244 - 16 Jan 1838. James Adams to Archibald Adams. 164 acres. James Adams of Marshall Co., TN to Archibald Adams of Bedford Co., TN, for love and affection he bears for Archibald Adams, his son, conveyed land in Bedford Co., bordering Cook's Spring, Thomas Ellison, Martin Smith, and David Patrick. Wit: Thomas Coffey and James W. Coffey. Reg: 7 Jan 1839.

DEED BOOK "HH"

Page 244 - 10 Dec 1838. Phillips and Margaret Burrow to Nimrod Burrow. Relinquishment. Phillip and Margaret Burrow his wife of Carroll Co., TN relinquished to Nimrod Burrow of Bedford Co., TN, all rights &c in undivided nineth part of a tract of land, which by the Last Will and Testament of Martin Shofner, deceased, falls to us, Phillip Burrow and Margaret Burrow, lawful legatees named in said will, land on Thompsons Creek in District No. 25. Adjoining lands of Robert Harrison, John Smith and Adam Phillips. Wit: H. Holt and Austin Shofner. Reg: 7 Jan 1839.

Page 246 - 23 Apr 1838. Chancery Court at Franklin. Thomas E. Dobyns and others, Compl. and John Thompson and others, Deft. It appears to the Court that the Clerk made a report, to wit, exposed to sale at the Market house in Nashville, a negro boy, sold to Jesse Collins and negro girl sold to Levi Dobyns, another negro girl sold to James Stevens and another negro child sold to John Thompson, another negro sold to Benjamin Litton. Reg: 8 Jan 1839.

Page 248 - 8 Jan 1839. Peter Raney to Eakin & brothers. Deed in Trust. Peter Raney of Bedford Co., TN sold to John Eakin, Spencer Eakin, William Eakin and Thomas Eakin, trading under the firm of Eakin & brothers. Personal property &c. Reg: 8 Jan 1839.

Page 250 - 8 Jan 1839. D. D. Arnold, Sheriff to William H. Craig. Darling D. Arnold, Sheriff of Bedford Co., TN one part and William H. Craig of Bedford Co., other part, to sell at public sale, all rights &c that James Craig had in land of about 200 acres belonging to the heirs of William Craig, deceased. Land in Bedford Co., on waters of East Fork of Rock Creek and where the widow of William Craig, deceased, now lives. Reg: 11 Jan 1839.

Page 258 - 25 Oct 1838. James B. Brown and Sally Brown and Amelia Earls to Charles Ray. 38½ acres. Amelia Earls, James B. Brown and Sally Brown his wife one part and Charles Ray other part, sold land in Bedford Co., TN on north side of Duck River. Borders lands of John Capley's heirs. Wit: Jos. Anderson and Z. B. Smith. Reg: 18 Jan 1839.

Page 261 - 18 Jan 1839. William B. Gowen to John Tillman. 4 acres. Whereas John Blessing by deed dated 19 Jul 1836 conveyed to William B. Gowen, in Trust, land near Town of Shelbyville, on east side of town and adjoining the lands of William F. Long, being the place where John Blessing resided at the time of the execution of the deed. Reg: 21 Jan 1839.

Page 262 - 22 Jan 1839. John Blessing to James Coats. For a debt to James Coats, transfers all his interest in negroes belonging to the estate of Wilson Coats which are now in the possession of Celia Coats, also all my interest in land known as Lot No. 10 of Wilson Coats division. Reg: 22 Jan 1839.

Page 266 - 11 Oct 1838. James Wortham and wife to Clement Cannon. Deed 28 acres. Robert Y. Cannon, James Wortham and Catharine M. his wife formerly Catharine M. Cannon one part and Clement Cannon other part, all of Bedford Co., TN, land in Bedford Co., being the one third part to which Robert Y. and the one third part to James and Catharine M. Wortham are entitled of a 28 acre tract of land which descended to them as heirs of Minos Cannon, deceased, it being a part of a 100 acre tract by Grant No. 465. Bounded by Walter Galbreath and Duck River. Reg: 28 Jan 1839.

Page 268 - 9 Oct 1820. John Atkinson, John Lane and Howel Dawdy surviving Commissioners for fixing the Seat of Justice in Bedford Co., TN one part and John H. Anderson of Bedford Co. other part. Land in Bedford Co., Town of Shelbyville and known as Lot No. 100. Wit: Jas. McKisick and John Wortham. Reg: 28 Jan 1839.

Page 274 - 7 Mar 1838. William Ellison to Zachariah Cully. 188½ acres. William Ellison, Sr. and William Ellison, Jr., both of Marion Co., TN one part and Zachariah Cully of Bedford Co., TN other part. Land in Bedford Co., on waters of the South or Barren Fork of Duck River. Borders Elijah Holt, Barren Fork of Duck River, and Mrs. Howe's corner. Reg: 29 Jan 1839.

Page 277 - 18 Jan 1839. Eunice Warner to Richard Warner. Deed. By the Last Will and Testament of John Warner, Jr., deceased, William Dixon Warner had interest in remainder to take effect and to take possession after the death of his mother Eunice Warner, in two tracts of land in Bedford Co., TN. One tract in District No. 21 containing 250 acres, other tract is where Eunice Warner now lives, containing 250 acres and one town lot in Shelbyville. William Dixon Warner also has interest in the negroes and in all the personal property to take effect at the death of Eunice Warner. William Dixon Warner on 20 Sep 1838 convey to Eunice Warner all his interest in above estate. Wit: Ro. P. Harrison and E. J. Frierson. Reg: 30 Jan 1839.

Page 282 - 12 Jan 1839. Sarah Burditt to Nathan Ivy. 10 acres. Sarah Burditt widow of William Burditt, Jr., deceased, one part and Nathan Ivy other part, both of Bedford CO., TN, one undivided half of the land in Bedford Co., on Noah's Fork. Borders road leading from Shelbyville to McMinnville, Samuel Bird's line, and Crain's Mill Pond. It included the Saw & Grist Mills. Wit: Edward B. Popejoy, William Cavin and W. R. Burditt. Reg: 31 Jan 1839.

Page 284 - 7 Nov 1838. Benjamin Coats to James Coats and John Reed. Power of Attorney. Benjamin Coats of Polk Co., MO, appointed either James Coats or John Reed or both to be my Attorney, for me to sell and convey his part of Lot No. 10, in Bedford Co.,formerly owned by Baity W. Coats, deceased, and now owned by the heirs of Baity Coats. Land borders Lot No. 9, containing 17 acres. Wit: Thomas Davis and William Brown. Reg: 31 Jan 1839.

Page 285 - 16 Nov 1838. James G. Neely and wife to John Overcast. Deed 57½ acres. James G. Neely and Mary his wife of Bedford Co., TN, one part and John Overcast of Bedford Co., other part, land in Bedford Co., on waters of Fall Creek. Borders lands of the heirs of Joseph McElwrath, deceased, land of the heirs of Thomas P. Burns, deceased, and C. D. Steele. Wit: James M. Johnson. Reg: 31 Jan 1839.

Page 290 - 28 Jan 1839. Edward M. B. Norville to John W. Norville. Undivided interest in 185 acres. Edward M. B. Norville of Bedford Co., TN, sold to John W. Norville, all his interest

&c in land in bedford Co., TN in District No. 3, it being the land whereon my mother Elizabeth W. Norville now lives, it being her dower of land out of the estate of my father David Norville, deceased. Feb 1 Feb 1839.

Page 290 - 28 Jan 1839. Alexander S. Norville to John W. Norville. Undivided interest &c. (Same as above, Alexander S. Norville son of Elizabeth W. Norville and David Norville, dec'd). Reg: 1 Feb 1839.

Page 293 - 2 Jan 1838. Thomas Coffee, Attorney for John Low to David Patrick. Deed 152 acres. THomas Coffee, Agent and Attorney, for John Low of Montgomery Co., Alabama one part and David Patrick of Bedford Co., TN, other part. Land in Bedford Co., on East Fork of Rock Creek, being a part of a 1200 acre survey of William Brown and late the lands of Daniel Low, dec'd, and one of the three division made by the Commissioners appointed at Feb Term 1837. Land bounded by near the grave of Daniel Low, deceased, center of Shelbyville and Pulaski Road, near where James Harbin once lived, J. Darnall's Still House, and Larue's land. Wit: James Adams and James W. Coffey. Reg: 4, Feb 1839.

Page 295 - 4 Feb 1839. John Meadows to Thomas Lipscomb. John Meadows one part and Thomas Lipscomb other part, both of Bedford Co., TN. John Meadows one of the heirs of Michael Meadows, deceased, sold his interest in a family of negroes (10), belonging to Jane Meadows during her natural life or widowhood. Jane Meadows is widow of Michael Meadows, deceased. Reg: 4 Feb 1839.

Page 311 - 3 Dec 1821. Thomas S. Cates to Joseph Hastings. Relinquishment Deed. Thomas S. Cates sold to Joseph Hastings, both of Bedford CO., TN, all my interest in the estate of Susannah Hastin(g), widow of Joseph Hastin(g), deceased, all my part that may come into the lands of Susannah Hastin(g) by heirship in the State of North Carolina or otherwise. Wit: Henry Hastings and John Hastings. Reg: 12 Feb 1839.

Page 311 - 3 Jul 1833. Stephen Hastings to Joseph Hastings. Relinquishment Deed. Stephen Hastings sold to Joseph Hastings, both of Bedford Co., TN, all my interest in the estate of Susannah Hastings, widow of Joseph Hastings, deceased, and my part that may come into the hands of Susannah Hastings by heirship in State of North Carolina, or otherwise. Wit: Jno. Hastings and William N. Fuller. Reg: 13 Feb 1839.

Page 326 - 28 Sep 1835. Dolly Burnett to Nathaniel Brown. Deed of Gift. Dolly Burnett of Bedford Co., TN one part and Nathaniel Brown, her nephew, of Bedford Co., other part. For natural love and affection for her nephew Nathaniel Brown, and for caring for her during her natural life, has given him personal property. Negroes and stock, all in possession of Dolly Burnett. Wit: Samuel Escue and George W. Hoover. Reg: 19 Feb 1839.

Page 336 - 2 Feb 1839. Heirs of Thomas Nash, deceased, to John Wood. Deed 112 acres. Dennis Holden and Sarah Holden his wife, John B. Nash, William W. Nash, and George W. Nash of Rutherford Co., TN and William R. Stewart and Mary Ann Stewart of Warren Co., TN, heirs of Thomas Nash, deceased, of Rutherford Co., TN one part and John Wood of Bedford Co., TN other part. Land in Bedford Co., TN, on waters of Falling Creek. Borders mouth of Hurricane Creek and Falling Creek. The land being a part of land granted by State of North Carolina to Richard Trotter. Wit: George Roberts. Reg: 20 Feb 1839.

Page 341 - 18 Feb 1839. Jackson Jordan to Jefferson F. Jordan. Deed, undivided. Jackson Jordan sold to Jefferson F. Jordan, land in Bedford Co., TN, land in Bedford Co., in District No. 18, of about 200 acres. The land whereon Zachariah Jordan, deceased, formerly lived and whereon Tabitha Jordan now lives. Land adjoins lands of P. L. Doty, James Gambill, Moses Cheves and Thomas Moore. Jackson Jordan had one sixth part of the individed interest. Reg: 22 Feb 1839.

Page 342 - 23 Feb 1839. William R. McFarland and wife to William F. Long. 14¼ acres. William R. McFarland and wife Elzira McFarland of Bedford Co., TN, one of the heirs of Wilson Coats, deceased, sold to William F. Long, land in Bedford Co., being Lot No. 6 in the division of lands of Wilson Coats, dec'd. Borders Lot No. 5, belonging to said Long and where Long now lives, and Coldwell's line. Wit: John Blessing and W. T. McGrew, Reg: 23 Feb 1839.

Page 343 - 23 Feb 1839. Zadoc Wood to Ephraim B. Jones. 50 acres. Zadoc Wood for natural affection for my daughter Mary B. who intermarried with Ephraim B. Jones, conveyed land in Bedford Co., TN, on waters of Wartrace Fork. Borders lands of his son William Wood, John Bowers, deceased, land, and heirs of Robert Waite, deceased, the same place where the widow now lives, Isaac Muse. It being that part of my original tract remaining to said Wood after his division of land to his son William Wood, it being land originally bought by Zadoc Wood from John Hinton, dating 28 Sep 1818, and it being the same whereon Z. Wood now lives. Zadoc Wood's wife Rhoda Wood live on their property during their natural lifetime. Wit: G. G. Osborne and J. E. Couch. Reg: 23 Feb 1839.

Page 351 - 9 Feb 1839. Thomas and J. S. Davis to James McMichael. Deed, Lot No. 26, Fairfield. Thomas Davis and John S. Davis, Executors of Henry Davis, deceased, of Bedford Co., TN one part and James McMichael of Coffee Co., TN other part. Wit: Robert Hurst and Thomas A. Hime. Reg: 2 Mar 1839.

Page 362 - Dec Term 1838, Bedford County Circuit Court. Bill for the sale of land. 233 acres. Caroline, Lucilla, Josiah, James, Leander and Newton Peacock by their guardian William J. Peacock. Land in Bedford Co., six slaves, which descended from their ancestor John Peacock, deceased, as his six heirs, made Jan Term 1824. Caroline Peacock to Lot No. 1, James Peacock to Lot No. 5, Josiah Peacock to Lot No. 6, Lucilla to Lot No. 8, Leander Peacock to Lot No. 9, and Newton Peacock to Lot No.11. Each Lot of 15 acres. Reg: 9 Mar 1839.

Page 365 - 15 Oct 1837. Eve and Jesse Burrow, Executors &c to John W. Raney. Deed of 60 acres. Eve Burrow, Executrix and Jesse Burrow, Executor, of estate and will of Ephraim Burrow, deceased, one part and John W. Raney other part, all of Bedford Co., TN, on waters of Big Flat Creek. Bounded by Joseph Parker, Spring of William Burrow, top of ridge near Amelia Bruton's line. Including the cabins &c, whereon Raney now lives. Wit: Peter Raney and Henry Hart. Reg: 9 Mar 1839.

DEED BOOK "HH"

Page 381 - 1 Oct 1838. Isaac D. Maxwell and Nancy his wife to Thomas Carlton. Deed, 74 acres. Land in Bedford Co., TN, in District No. 10. Reg: 2 Apr 1839.

Page 405 - 2 Apr 1839. James and Jane Ogilvie to Nathan Wheeler. Deed 30 acres. James Ogilvie and Jane Ogilvie his wife and formerly Jane Locke, sold to Nathan Wheeler, land in Bedford Co., TN, in District No. 11. Bounded by Putman's line, the heirs of Covington. Reg: 13 Apr 1839.

Page 406 - 22 Feb 1839. Mary Sugg to John Thompson. Power of Attorney. Mary Sugg formerly Mary Roadsmith, appointed John Thompson, Sr. her Attorney to receive from George Roadsmith a judgement of $25.91½. Judgement dated Dec Term 1824 wherein Mary Petitioned for a divorce. Wit: Jos. Anderson, A. Wilson and W. Perry. Reg: 15 Apr 1839.

Page 407 - 1 Nov 1837. Joel B. McMahan and Jas. McMahan to Baxter H. Ragsdale. Deed, 100 acres. Joel B. McMahan and James McMahan of Bedford Co., TN one part and Baxter H. Ragsdale of Rutherford Co., TN, other part. Land in Bedford Co., on waters of the Garrison Fork, it being the same land on which Joel B. and James McMahan and their mother now lives. Borders John Tillman and Armstrong's land. Wit: Jas. L. Armstrong and James Vaughan. Reg: 15 Apr 1839.

Page 409 - 6 Apr 1839. Decree of Title to Roger Snell to 240 acres from Thomas Greer and others. Land of Thomas Greer, Jr., Thomas G. Williamson, Joseph M. Williamson and Caroline Williamson, the last three are the minor children of Richard S. Williamson. Land sold to Roger Snell on 4 Jun 1836. Reg: 17 Apr 1839.

Page 409 - 15 Apr 1839. William J. Wakefield and wife to William H. Wisener. Bill of Sale. William J. W. Wakefield and wife Malissa F., sold to William F. Wisener, slaves. Reg: 17 Apr 1839.

Page 411 - 2 Mar 1839. Nathan and Jemima Roberts to Richard Muse. Relinquishment. Nathan and Jemima Roberts sold to Richard Muse, all of Bedford Co., TN, all their interest sue us from the estate of Michael Meadows, deceased. Wit: J. Cleveland and Henry B. Coffey. Reg: 17 Apr 1839.

Page 421 - 7 Apr 1838. Sparrell and Bartlett Bird to John Jakes. 75 acres. Sparrell and Bartlett Bird sold to John Jakes, all of Bedford Co., TN, for $90.00 paid to our father Samuel Bird in his lifetime, for our interest in a tract of land, sold to John Jakes the undivided interest, that being two fifths of one half of an undivided tract of land, which descended to them by the Will of their grandfather John Jakes, deceased. Borders Bradford Merville and tract called Henry's. Wit: Orville Muse and John S. Davis. Reg: 25 Apr 1839.

Page 421 - 28 Dec 1838. Stephen White to the heirs of A. H. White. Deed of Gift. Stephen White conveyed unto the heirs of Augustus H. White, negroes. The heirs of Augustus H. White is Stephen White, Jr., Thomas Davis White and Susan White. Wit: J. M. Sehorn and S. W. Jameson. Reg: 3 May 1839.

Page 426 - 24 Apr 1839. Patsy Oneal, Jeremiah Forbes and wife Edy to William Heaslett. Bill of Sale. Patsy Oneal, Jeremiah Forbes and Edy Forbes his wife sold to William Heaslett, a negro boy Jack. Wit: John T. Neil and John Oneal. Reg: 6 May 1839.

Page 426 - 8 Mar 1839. Francis Locke and Sarah Locke to Joseph R. McKinley. Deed, undivided interest. Francis Locke and his wife Sarah Locke formerly Sarah Alexander and daughter of Nathaniel Alexander, late of Cabarrus Co., NC, of Montgomery Co., NC one part and Joseph R. McKinley of Bedford Co., TN other part. Land in Bedford Co., which it includes one undivided tenth part of a tract of land known as the Alexander land, having descended from Nathaniel Alexander to his heirs at law. Wit: Jas. L. Gaines. Reg: 6 May 1839.

Page 448 - 16 May 1839. Price C. Steele to the Methodist E. Church. Deed 2 acres. Price C. Steele one part and John L. Cooper, J. J. Cooper, John Taylor, V. M. Hamilton and Wilson Turrentine, other part, all of Bedford Co., TN. Price C. Steele for the respect and regard for his religion, conveys to the Trustees for the use and benefit of the Methodist Episcopal Church, land in Bedford Co., on waters of Falling Creek. Bounded by Falling Creek, and the Church. They are to establish a Campground. The land can never be sold. Should the church cease to operate, the land is to return to Price C. Steele or his heirs. The Old Presbyterian denomination shall have the privilege to worship on said ground and hold Camp Meetings when not occupied by the Methodist. Wit: C. D. Steele. Reg: 30 May 1839.

Page 450 - 24 May 1839. Richard Cunningham to Giles R. Bowers. Deed Relinquishment. Richard Cunningham sold to Giles R. Bowers, both of Bedford Co., TN, all his share of his father's estate now held by John Cunningham his father in Warren Co., TN, that he may leave by will or by gift, or by heirship at the death of John Cunningham. Wit: Henry T. Frazer and G. H. Frazer. Reg: 3 Jan 1839.

Page 454 - 29 May 1839. Catharine Shofner to John Shofner and others. Relinquishment. Catharine Shofner for $1,000.00, sold to John, Frederick and Austin Shofner, the heirs of Christopher Shofner, Phillip Burrow and his wife Peggy, Adam Eulis and Dorothy his wife, Eve Holt, John Dean and Sally his wife, and Polly Brown, release to them all right title and interest to the estate of the late Martin Shofner, my husband. Wit: Jacob Coble and Benjamin Kimbro. Reg: 4 Jun 1839.

Page 459 - 12 Mar 1839. Matt Martin and Elizabeth Martin. Agreement or obligation. Matt Martin and Elizabeth Martin his daughter in law, widow of his son Abram Martin, deceased, entered into an obligation. Matt Martin agrees for the love for his daughter in law Elizabeth Martin. She shall have the plantation on which she now resides, to live on during her natural life and she is to pay him $1.00 each year for rent. She is also to have the work and labor of two negroes now in his possession. Wit: Lewis Tillman and R. C. C. P. Shaw. Reg: 12 Jun 1839.

Page 485 - 29 Dec 1837. Robert Allison, Sr. to Robert Allison, Jr. 96½ acres. Robert Allison, Sr. for consideration of a legacy and part of the estate of the said Robert, Sr., to his son Robert, Jr., conveyed land in Bedford Co., TN, on waters of Weakleys Creek. Borders Morrison's line and William Allison. Wit: John Morgan and John A. Morgan. Reg: 1 Jul 1839.

Page 486 - 19 Apr 1839. Thomas M. Nash to John Wood. 112 acres. Thomas M. Nash of Walker Co., GA, Amos West and Nancy West his wife of Rutherford Co., TN, heirs of Thomas Nash, deceased, one part and John Wood of Bedford Co., TN other part. Land in Bedford Co., on waters of Falling Creek, it being an undivided tract. Borders near mouth of the Hurricane Creek, and Falling Creek. The land being a part of a tract granted by State of North Carolina to Richard Trotter for 1000 acres and deeded by Thomas G. Polk and Mary E. Polk to Dennis Springer and by Springer to the heirs of Thomas Nash, deceased. Wit: T. C. Nash and Levi C. Johnson. Reg: 1 Jul 1839.

Page 489 - 27 Dec 1838. Newton F. Neil to John T. Neil. 50 acres. Newton Franklin Neil one part and John Thompson Neil other part, both of Bedford Co., TN, land in Bedford Co., on Bryeans Creek, it being the tract of land devised to N. F. Neil by his father Joseph Neil, deceased, and is described in his Last Will and Testament. Bounded by land bequeathed by Joseph Neil to John Thompson Neil, land bequeathed by Joseph Neil, deceased, to his grandson Joseph F. Neil, land of James Harris, land of William Oneal, and Martin Sims. Wit: W. Galbreath and William Eakin. Reg: 2 Jul 1839.

Page 492 - 11 Apr 1839. Noah Scales. Copy of Decree. Circuit Court. James G. Whitney, Joseph A. Whitney and Jane G. Whitney, minors by their next friend James McKisick. Exparte. Bill for Sale of land, 290 acres. Land borders Sugar Creek and Harrell Wiggins. Plat on page 492. Reg: 11 Jul 1839.

Page 495 - 25 Feb 1824. John McIntosh and Susan McIntosh to John Sims. Deed. John McIntosh and Susan his wife, she being appointed Executrix by Green D. House, deceased, to his Last Will and Testament and now of Robertson Co., TN one part and John Sims of Bedford Co., TN other part. Land on east side of Sinking Creek. Another tract bordered William Hartsfield. Another tract bounded by William Hamblin and William Hartsfield. Wit: William Hodges and John Hartsfield. Reg: 17 Jul 1839.

Page 497 - 29 Oct 1836. The heirs of Robert Allison to Nathaniel Walker. 175 acres. William Allison, Thomas Allison, Robert Allison and Kimbrough Allison of Bedford Co., TN and James Williams and his wife Sarah (Sally), and William Williams and his wife Elizabeth, and James Allison of Marshall Co., TN, and John Allison of Williamson Co., TN one part and Nathaniel Walker of Smith Co., TN other part. The above named heirs of Robert Allison, deceased. Land in Bedford Co., on Wilsons Creek. Borders Wilsons Creek and Kimbrough Allison. Including the place where Moses Couch now lives. Another 10 acre tract on Wilson Creek. Borders William Clark, Robert Allison and Jonas Sykes where he now lives. Another tract of 8 acres on Wilsons Creek. Borders where Jonas Sykes now lives, land where Jesse Atkinson now lives, lands of Matthew Russell, and William Clark. Wit: William M. Fain, Jas. Walker, R. W. Fain, Albert Anderson and Thomas H. Allison. Reg: 19 Jul 1839.

Page 509 - 2 Aug 1839. William and Patience Cavin to Thomas B. Moseley. Agreement. 135 acres. William Cavin and Patience Cavin his wife one part and Thomas B. Moseley other part, convey unto Moseley all their undivided interest in a tract of land willed and bequeathed to them by William Burditt, Sr., deceased, first to Sarah Burditt the widow of William Burditt, Jr., son of William Burditt, Sr. and after her death or marriage to the heirs of William, Jr. and Sarah his wife. The said will was made 13 Oct 1835. The tract of land in Bedford Co., TN, adjoining the lands of Samuel Bird, deceased, and on waters of the Garrison Fork. Wit: George M. Bedford and Rachel P. C. Lane. Reg: 5 Aug 1839.

Page 514 - 5 Aug 1839. Wilson B. McElroy and Milley McElroy to Uriah Cross. Deed, 28 acres. Wilson B. McElroy and Milley McElroy of Hardeman Co., TN one part and Uriah Cross of Bedford Co., TN other part, sold their undivided interest in a tract of land that George Crews owned at the time of his death. Land on north west side of Hamiltons Creek and south of the road from Shelbyville to Rowesville. Borders Hamiltons Creek and mouth of a lane where an Old Still House formerly stood. Wit: W. R. Burditt, Henry B. Coffey, Piercy Yell and Thomas Holden. Reg: 6 Aug 1839.

Page 517 - 4 Nov 1824. Walter B. Sims and John S. Green to John G. Sims, administrator &c. Walter B. Sims and John S. Green of Bedford Co., TN one part and John G. Sims, administrator with will annexed of Walter Sims, deceased, of Davidson Co., TN other part. Conveyed undivided tract of land in Giles Co., TN, it being granted by State of North Carolina to Stokley Donalson, Grant No. 155, 5000 acres. Another tract of land in Bedford Co., TN of 400 acres, it being part of a grant to James Grant No. 196, part laid off by Commissioners for that purpose appointed to Elizabeth Scudder, adjoining land that belonged to Jonathan Graves, Elizabeth Scudder, River bank, opposite Sims Mill on Duck River, a Saw Mill and Grist Mill and other buildings. Another tract in Bedford Co., bordering Joseph Hamilton's land he sold to John S. Green, Phillip J. Scudder. Also a tract devised by will of David Sims and David conveyed to John G. Sims. Also another tract. Wit: O. B. Hayes and Jno. Bell. Reg: 8 Aug 1839.

Page 525 - 16 Mar 1839. William Eoff to John and George W. Jakes. Deed, 235 acres. William Eoff one part and John Jakes and George W. Jakes, infant son of John and grandson of William Eoff, other part, all of Bedford Co., TN. For natural love and affection he bears to his grandson George W. Jakes, conveyed land in Bedford Co. Borders James Morrow's field on Scotts Branch, Bedford and Rutherford Counties line, William Keele, where Pinkney Shaw now lives, and land where William Eoff now lives. Wit: Jas. L. Armstrong and William Wood. Reg: 9 Aug 1839.

DEED BOOK "JJ" 1839 - 1840

Page 1 - 1 Jan 1839. Thomas and John S. Davis, Executors to Jeremiah Cleveland. Deed. Thomas Davis and John S. Davis, Executors of Henry Davis, deceased, of Bedford Co., TN one part and Jeremiah Cleveland of Bedford Co., other part, land in Bedford Co., in the Town of Fairfield. Wit: J. W. Ragsdale and Newton McQuiddy. Reg: 12 Aug 1839.

DEED BOOK "JJ"

Page 3 - 12 Aug 1839. William W. Wilson to Andrew Reed. 39 acres. William W. Wilson sold to Andrew Reed for $90.00 paid to William W. Wilson's wife Edy Wilson and Joseph H. McCamy, his part of a tract of land which he holds in right of his wife Edy, in Bedford Co., TN, on Big Flat Creek. Borders Big Flat Creek and Reed's land. Reg: 12 Aug 1839.

Page 35 - 4 Jul 1827. E. W. Brown and others to Nicholas Anthony. 81+ acres. Ezekiel W. Brown, Franklin M. Brown and Katharine Brown one part and Nicholas Anthony other part, all of Bedford Co., TN, sold land in Bedford Co., on Thompsons Creek, it being a part of a grant from State of Tennessee to Newton Cannon, and by Cannon to Samuel Brown the father and husband of the above named Ezekiel, Franklin and Katharine Brown on 3 Sep 1810. The land bwqueathed to E. W., Franklin and Katharine Brown by the Last Will and Testament of Samuel Brown, deceased. Borders Clement Neeley. Wit: Frederick Anthony and Jacob Anthony. Reg: 6 Sep 1839.

Page 40 - 7 Sep 1839. Alfred Kimery and others. Division of land and conveyances to each other. 248 acres. As heirs of Frederick Kimery, the following, Alfred Kimery, Edwin Kimery, Mary now the wife of Jesse Koonce, and Margaret now the wife of Henry Lynn, hold title to and now hold undivided interest in land in Bedford Co., TN, on both sides of Big Flat Creek. Borders Jacob Kizer and George Pratt. The land whereas Henry Lynn and wife Margaret hath by deed dated -- Sep 1839 conveyed to Alfred Kimery and Edwin Kimery. Reg: 19 Sep 1839.

Page 42 - 7 Sep 1839. Henry and Margaret Lynn his wife to Alfred and Edwin Kimery. 248 acres. Land in Bedford Co., TN, on both sides of Big Flat Creek. Bounded by Jacob Kizer, Robert Reed, and George Pratt. The same being land that Frederick Kimery, deceased, formerly lived on and where Turley Kimery now lives. Reg: 20 Sep 1839.

Page 46 - 17 Sep 1839. Andrew J. Caughran to James Deery. Deed. Both of Bedford Co., TN, land in Bedford Co., and it being a part of the land of which John McClintick died seized and possessed. Conveyed to James Deery, includes the shares of land belonging to John McClintick and which was set apart from James McClintick and George McClintick in the division of said land, on which Caughran now lives, also two fifths of that part set apart in the division to Elizabeth McClintick. Reg: 21 Sep 1839.

Page 47 - 17 Sep 1839. Joseph and Jane Couch to Thomas Lipscomb. Bill of Sale. Joseph and Jane Couch his wife sold negroes to Thomas Lipscomb, undividedeleventh part of the remainder interest in negroes after the termination of the life estate of Jane Meadows bequeathed to her by Michael Meadows, deceased. Wit: G. H. Stewart. Reg: 24 Sep 1839.

Page 48 - 21 Sep 1839. William Walker and wife to Thomas Lipscomb. Bill of Sale. William Walker and his wife Rebecca Walker conveyed unto Thomas Lipscomb, all their interest &c in 10 negroes, which interest is undivided eleventh part of the remainder interest in the negroes after the termination of the life estate of Jane Meadows bequeathed to her by Michael Meadows, deceased. Wit: James Gaither and James P. Couch. Reg: 24 Sep 1839.

Page 49 - 24 Apr 1839. Patsey Oneal and others to John T. Neil. 4+ acres. Patsey Oneal, Jeremiah Forbes and his wife Edy Forbes one part and John T. Neil other part, all of Bedford Co., TN, land in Bedford CO., on Bryeans Creek in District No. 18. Bounded by lands of John T. Neil, land formerly owned by William Oneal, Martin Sims, and Bryeans Creek. Wit: John Oneal and J. B. Anderson. Reg: 24 Sep 1839.

Page 54 - 16 Aug 1839. Patsey Oneal and others. Articles of Agreement. Patsey Oneal the widow of William Oneal, deceased, one part and Jeremiah Forbes and Edy Forbes his wife of the other part, all of Bedford Co., TN. Patsey Oneal is entitled to a dower which is one third part of all the lands that William Oneal died possessed of, as long as she lives and then return to the legal heirs. All heirs are of legal age. Land borders Martin Sims. Another tract of 50 acres borders lands formerly belonging to John H. Anderson, and Benjamin Coffee. Wit: Walter Sims and John Oneal. Reg: 28 Sep 1839.

Page 65 - 26 Aug 1839. John Stephens to Richard H. Sims. Deed. John Stephens sold to Richard H. Sims, his interest in the lands devised to him and others by the Last Will and Testament of John Stephens, deceased, late of Bedford Co., TN. Lands in Bedford Co., on Powell Creek about five miles below Shelbyville. McCracken Co., KY, Town of Paducah. Reg: 7 Oct 1839.

Page 71 - 9 Oct 1839. Joseph S. and Sophia Cates to William H. Hymes(Himes). 46 acres. Joseph S. Cates and Sophia Cates his wife conveyed to William H. Himes, all of Bedford Co., TN, land in Bedford Co. Borders the dower of Mary Ann Himes. Reg: 23 Oct 1839.

Page 77 - 1 Aug 1839. John Davidson to Trustees of Union Meeting House and Camp Ground. Whereas the late Edmund Hord did on 22 Aug 1833, execute his deed convey to Trustees and that it appears that Edmund Hord had been mistaken as to where the lines of his lands were and that he made a title to same part that is conveyed and described in said deed that his title does not cover, but that the lines of John Davidson included that part of the land which Edmund Hord conveyed. John Davidson being desirous for the spread of the Gospel and a universal acceptance of it by all people, is willing to convey that part and more as a whole lot. The Trustees, William M. Galleghy has removed away and H. C. Ferguson is expected to do so and that David Williams has refused an appointment as a trustee, it is the desire of John Davidson that Andrew Vannoy take the place of Galleghy for the Separate Baptist Church, that William P. Campbell take it for the Cumberland Presbyterian Church, that Capt. Burrell Featherston act in behalf of the Methodist Church to succeed David Williams, Dr. Jas. L. Armstrong for the Protestant Methodist Church, that Francis H. Keller act for the United Baptist Church, that Hugh Davidson, Jr. act for any other Churches herein not named, and Samuel Vance in behalf of the Presbyterian Church. They are to assign each profession that may wish to worship at that place, a day to worship. Trustees are Andrew Vannoy, Burrell Featherston, William P. Campbell, Jas. L. Armstrong, Francis H. Keller, Hugh Davidson, Jr., and Samuel Vance of the Union Meeting House and Camp Ground. The land is between the waters of the Barren Fork and the Garrison Fork of Duck River. Adjoining lands of the heirs of Edmond Hord. Wit: J. Anderson, William P. Campbell, E. B. Hord, and

J. Walker. Reg: 24 Oct 1839.
NOTE: Located on the ridge between the Barren Fork and the Garrison Fork of Duck River at Union Ridge Community.)

Page 84 - 4 Nov 1839. Joshua H. Stewart to Benjamin Phillips. Joshua H. Stewart sold to Benjamin Phillips, his interest he has under the Will of Joshua Holt, deceased, in a tract of land surveyed and plotted during the life time of Joshua Holt, dec'd, for daughter Eleanor Nease and willed by him to the children of Eleanor for her lifetime, in Bedford Co., TN, in District No. 22, sold to Benjamin Phillips. Wit: Joseph Morton and Christian Freeman. Reg: 5 Nov 1839.
NOTE: Another instrument of same on page 84 & 85. Reg: 6 Nov 1839.

Page 90 - 13 Nov 1839. Henry F. Hastings to Joseph Hastings. Relinquishment. Henry F. Hastings to Joseph Hastings, both of Bedford Co., TN, conveyed unto him all my interest in the estate of Susannah Hastings widow of Joseph Hastings, deceased, also all that may come to him from Susannah Hastings by her heirship in North Carolina or otherwise. Wit: Martin F. Wade and Flower Swift. Reg: 22 Nov 1839.

Page 92 - 18 Nov 1839. Edward Maxwell to Mary E. Holder. Deed of Gift. For love and affection for Mary Elen Holder, convey unto her a heifer. Reg: 22 Nov 1839.

Page 93 - 10 Nov 1831. William Coats to Joseph Alexander. Power of Attorney. William Coats of Monroe Co., Miss., appointed Joseph Alexander, Power of Attorney, to sell or convey all the rights and interest he has as one of the heirs at law of Bailey W. Coats and John B. Coats, late of Bedford Co., TN, land in Bedford Co., near the Town of Shelbyville, one of which is about 14 acres and other about 21 acres, being of the divided part or portion of Bailey W. Coats and John B. Coats in the real estate of Wilson Coats, late of Bedford Co., deceased. Reg: 26 Nov 1839.

Page 93 - 10 Jul 1839. Dennis Hemby to Joseph Hemby. Deed of Gift. For love and affection for his son Joseph Hemby, convey unto him two tracts of land in Bedford Co., TN, near the waters of Shipmans Creek in District No. 25. First tract of about 60 acres and bordered by road leading from Three Forks of Duck River to Winchester, Robert Brinkley's improvement, it included the improvements claimed by Robert Brinkley and which was granted to Robert Harrison by State of tennessee, Grant No. 1164. Another tract of 50 acres and bordered by R. P. Harrison. It including the house then occupied by Robert Brinkley. Wit: John Hemby and Timothy Long. Reg: 26 Nov 1839.

Page 96 - 8 May 1839. Hetty Scott and Sarah Dinkins to Theo. F. Bradford. 390 acres. Hetty Scott and Sarah Dinkins, both of Rowan Co., NC one part and Theoderick F. Bradford of Bedford Co., other part, land in Bedford Co., being part of a tract of land allotted to James Locke, deceased, and devised by him in his Last Will and Testament to his two daughters, Eliza and Hetty Locke and Sarah his wife. Land borders Matthew Locke which is divided amongst his several sons. Wit: Alexander W. Brandon and James L. Scott. Reg: 28 Nov 1839.

Page 104 - 3 Sep 1838. Andrew Reed and others to Sterling Newsom. 28½ acres. Andrew Reed in right of his wife Malinda, John Blessing in right of his wife Matilda, David Blessing in right of his wife Polley, John N. Reed in right of his wife Lovicey, Claiborn W. Coats and James Coats, Eliza Coats and Benjamin Coats and Henry C. Coats and William Coats by Joseph Alexander, Attorney, has sold and conveyed unto Steling Newsom, their interest as heirs in a tract of land of John B. Coats, deceased, a minor heir of Wilson Coats, deceased. Land in Bedford Co., on waters of Duck River and east of Shelbyville. Borders Newsom's land. Reg: 30 Nov 1839.

Page 105 - 28 Nov 1839. Mary Scruggs to John E. Scruggs. 300 acres. Mary Scruggs for love and affection for her son John E. Scruggs, all rights and interest in the land whereon John E. Scruggs lives, during her natural life. The land being same that Mary Scruggs purchased of Theo. F. Bradford and W. P. Finch. She deeded the land to J. E. Scruggs on 8 Mar 1834. Wit: G. G. Osborne and William P. Finch and J. W. Ragsdale. Reg: 2 Dec 1839.

Page 106 - 13 Nov 1839. Mary Scruggs to William P. Finch and others. Deed of Gift. Mary Scruggs for love and affection she has for her children, Betsey Finch wife of William P. Finch, John E. Scruggs, Susan Fugitt wife of Benjamin Fugitt, James Scruggs, and the children of hy daughter Edney Finch, deceased, former wife of Thomas Finch. She conveys to daughter Betsey Finch a negro boy Buff and $300.00, to son John E. Scruggs land whereon he lives at this time and three negroes, Joe, Charles and Bungy, to my daughter Susan Fugitt a negro girl Clara and a note held on her husband Benjamin Fugitt, to son James Scruggs $1100.00 which is made up of the part of land he sold his brother J. E. Scruggs and also the amount he owed his brother Matt Scruggs, deceased, which has already given to him, to the six children of my daughter Edney Finch gets $70.00. She also handed Mary C. March one of same and $730.00 to be equally divided between them, my negro girl Mattey. The property coming to Mary Scruggs from her father John Elam, deceased, estate in Edgefield District, South Carolina, also of my stepmother Mary Elam which I inherit at her death to be equally divided among my children. Wit: G. G. Osborne and J. N. Ragsdale. Reg: 2 Dec 1839.

Page 108 - 30 Nov 1839. William P. Finch and others to Mary Scruggs. Obligation. Agreement between William P. Finch for his wife Betsey Finch, John E. Scruggs, Benjamin Fugitt for his wife Susan Fugitt, James Scruggs, and Thomas Finch for his six children by his wife Edney Finch, deceased, one part and Mary Scruggs of the other part, all of Bedford Co., TN. Mary Scruggs is about to marry and that if Mary Scruggs should marry and afterwards become a widow again, the above named are to refund in part or whole the amount Mary Scruggs has given to them by Deed of Gift, dated 30 Nov 1839. Wit: G. G. Osborne and J. W. Ragsdale. Reg: 2 Dec 1839.

Page 113 - 27 Nov 1839. Thomas Holland, Sr. to Rufus C. Holland. 52½ acres. Thomas Holland, Sr. for the regard he has for his grandson Rufus C. Holland, conveyed unto him land in Bedford Co., TN. Bounded by Spring, half of which belongs to Robert Moffatt, Wilson Coats, and Harris Graham. Reg: 4 Dec 1839.

DEED BOOK "JJ"

Page 118 - 20 Feb 1839. J. Blessing and wife to James Coats. 17 acres. John Blessing and wife Matilda conveyed to James Coats, for $20.00, in part of a debt that they owe Coats, their interest in a tract of land in Bedford Co., TN, known in the division of Wilson Coats, deceased, as Lot No. 10. The said land belonged to Bailey W. Coats, deceased. Wit: Robert G. Morgan and J. N. Reed. Reg: 10 Dec 1839.

Page 125 - 22 Nov 1839. William Poplin to William J. Montgomery. Deed of Gift. William Poplin for love and affection for his grandson William J. Montgomery, conveyed unto him a sorrel mare. Wit: H. Martin and A. Poplin. Reg: 17 Dec 1839.

Page 130 - 31 May 1839. Benjamin Blankenship to the Methodist E. Church. Deed 1 acre. Benjamin Blankenship of Bedford Co., TN one part and John L. Cooper, Edward Tarpley, James P. Shapard, D. F. Lindsey and Benjamin Blankenship, all of Bedford Co., Trustees of the other part. Conveyed to Trustees for the benefit of the Methodist Episcopal Church, land in Bedford Co., on the North Fork near the Rutherford Co., TN line. Bounded by Thomas Sanders and Blankenship's line. The land whereon they have built a church. Reg: 31 Dec 1839.

Page 135 - 6 Nov 1839. John Maxwell and others to Olive Bullock. Deed 75 acres. John Maxwell, Keziah Rushing and Mesheck Haile as Attorney in fact, for Solomon Maxwell, Daniel Maxwell, Thomas Maxwell, Jonathan King and his wife Jemima King, Elizabeth Haile of Bedford Co., TN one part and Olive Bullock of Bedford Co., other part, land in Bedford Co., on west side of Clems Creek in the 10th District. Borders Clems Creek. Wit: J. C. Rushing and A. Poplin. Reg: 25 Dec 1839.

Page 142 - 6 Jan 1840. Stephen Hastings and Henry F. Hastings to Joseph Hastings. Stephen Hastings of Marshall Co., Alabama and Henry Hastings of Bedford Co., TN sold to Joseph Hastings of Bedford Co., their rights and interest in the property which was allotted to Susannah Hastings, our mother, for her portion of our fathers estate. Reg: 6 Jan 1840.

Page 155 - 18 Jan 1840. Felix B. Norville to John W. Norville. Deed 285 acres. Felix B. Norville conveyed to John W. Norville, all his right title and interest in a tract of land in Bedford Co., TN in District No. 3, it being the lands whereon my mother Elizabeth W. Norville now lives and it being her dower of land of estate of my father David Norville, deceased. Reg: 18 Jan 1840.

Page 156 - 18 Jan 1840. Henry C. Coats to Wilie B. Watkins. Deed 17 acres. Both of Bedford Co., TN. Henry C. Coats sold to Wilie B. Watkins, all his right title and interest in land lying east of Shelbyville, which land formerly belonged to Wilson Coats, deceased, and descended to Bailey W. Coats, my brother, who is now deceased, which lot or land belonging to my deceased brother. Reg: 18 Jan 1840.

Page 165 - 17 Oct 1838. Bradshaw heirs to George Waite. Relinquishment Deed, 18 acres. The heirs of John Bradshaw, deceased, do relinquish all rights in tract of land in Bedford Co., TN, on the headwaters of Sugar Creek. Adjoining the lands of George Waite, Nathan Evans and William Yateson. Wit: Jacob Albright and James B. Dolby. Signed by the heirs and representatives

Mary Bradshaw, O. W. Bradshaw, Asenath Bradshaw, Jas. Bradshaw, Louisa Bradshaw, Rachel Bradshaw, Mary C. Bradshaw, John A. Bradshaw, Adaline Bradshaw, Clarinda Bradshaw, and Sophia C. Bradshaw. Reg: 21 Jan 1840.

Page 181 - 24 Jan 1840. David Blessing and wife to Thomas Lipscomb. Deed 17 acres. David Blessing and Polley Blessing his wife sold to Thomas Lipscomb, all of Bedford Co., TN, it being the undivided interest that David Blessing and wife Polley, land in Bedford Co., TN, it being the land allotted to Bailey W. Coats, out of the estate of Wilson Coats and known as Lot No. 10. Borders the lands of Graham, and Henry C. Coats. Reg: 30 Jan 1840.

Page 183 - 7 Dec 1839. William and D. Glenn to George C. Armstrong. Relinquishment Deed, 77½ acres. For love and affection William and Dancy Glenn and Nelly Cathey has for their brother George C. Armstrong, conveyed unto him their undivided interest in a tract of land in Bedford Co., TN, on Wartrace Fork, which descended to them by the death of their father Robert Armstrong, deceased. Land borders Newbill's land, I(?). T. Mayfield, D. H. Williams and C. S. Sutton. Wit: A. C. Armstrong and William Armstrong. Reg: 31 Jan 1840.

Page 184 - 4 Dec 1839. Robert Armstrong to George C. Armstrong. Deed 70 acres. Robert Armstrong conveyed to George C. Armstrong, both of Bedford Co., TN, land in Bedford Co., his undivided interest in a tract of land on waters of Wartrace Fork. Bounded by J. H. Newbill, C. F. Sutton, D. H. Williams and I(?). T. Mayfield. Said land belonging to his father Robert Armstrong, deceased, at his death and descended to him. Wit: John H. Newbill and Allen Wallis. Reg: 31 Jan 1840.

Page 191 - -- --- 1839. William Armstrong to George C. Armstrong Deed 77½ acres. William Armstrong of Marshall Co., TN one part and G. C. Armstrong, his brother, of Bedford Co., TN other part. For love and affection William Armstrong has for his brother George C. Armstrong conveyed unto him land in Bedford Co., on waters of Wartrace Fork. Bounded by John H. Newbill, C. F. Sutton, D. H. Williams and I(?). T. Mayfield. It being the land descended to him by his father Robert Armstrong, deceased. Reg: 3 Feb 1840.

Page 191 - 3 Feb 1840. John Tillman, Executor to Moses Neeley. Deed 86+ acres. John Tillman, Executor of the Last Will and Testament of Samuel Escue, deceased, sold to Moses Neeley a tract of land or lot known as Robert T. Cannon's portion laid off to him by his father's estate, in Bedford Co., TN, on Duck River. Bounded by Carter's or R. Cannon's line in channel of Duck River. To defend it against a lawful claim, reserving about two acres on which the Tanyard is situated and for which he is bound to deed to Matthew Cunningham. Reg: 4 Feb 1840.

Page 194 - 10 Oct 1839. James M. Moore to William Yeates. Relinquishment Deed. James M. Moore sold to William Yeates, both of Bedford Co., TN, his interest as a legatee share in all the personal property belonging to his mother Mary Moore. Wit: John Patton and Samuel Stewart. Reg: 8 Feb 1840.

Page 195 - 10 Oct 1839. James M. Moore to William Yeates. Deed 96 acres. Whereas by descent from James Moore, deceased,

William Yeates, Martha D. McClure, E. H. Moore, Nancy J. Hart, Caroline D. Moore, Harriet E. Moore and himself James A. Moore, has derived title to and now hold equal and undivided interest in land in Bedford Co., TN. Borders Greer's line, McKisick's corner and Templeton's corner. Wit: John Patton and Samuel Steward. Reg: 8 Feb 1840.

Page 197 - 4 & 5 Dec 1839. Jordan C. Holt and Herod F. Holt, Executors, to Hiram and Eleanor Holt. Deed 75 acres. In the Last Will and Testament of Joshua Holt, deceased, the Executors to lay off to Hiram Holt, land in Bedford Co., TN, on waters of Big Flat Creek, being part of 173 acres purchased by the deceased from Joseph Greer and bounded by John C. Hix, Salley Hix and Elijah Lacy. Also laid off for Eleanor Holt the widow of the deceased, 200 acres, including the dwelling house where the deceased lately lived, also the out houses,)excepting the Still House and half of the large double barn) and other lands. William Boone, Surveyor. Reg: 10 Feb 1840.

Page 199 - 16 Jan 1839. Richard Haggard and wife to Henry Green. Deed 107 acres, undivided interest. Richard Haggard and Syntha Haggard, formerly Syntha Meadows, sold their undivided eighth part of a tract of land in Bedford Co., TN, in District No. 3. Bounded by Henry Holt, Theo. F. Bradford, William Ditto, dec'd, and Robert Chambers which belonged to Michael Holt. Reg: 13 Feb 1840.

Page 201 - 13 Feb 1840. William S. Wade to James Thompson. Deed in Trust. 98 acres. William S. Wade sold to James Thompson land in Bedford Co., TN, in District No. 11. Adjoining the lands of James Thompson, John J. Lintz, Joseph P. Thompson, Elizabeth Thompson widow of Joseph Thompson, deceased. Also negroes and other personal property. reg: 13 Feb 1840.

Page 203 - 12 Dec 1837. Feliz G. Ake to Burrell Featherston. Deed 262½ acres. Feliz G. Ake one part and Burrell Featherston, both of Bedford Co., TN, land in Bedford Co., on Bell Buckle Creek, it being part of a North Carolina Grant to Tillman Dickson and also part of a tract sold by Tillman Dickson to Joseph Ake, Sr., deceased. Borders Tarwick Frazer, William P. Elkins, the Bell Buckle Creek, Otter Fork, Featherston's line and Theodocia H. Clardy. Wit: John Davis and C. M. Norville. Reg: 13 Feb 1840.

Page 206 - 13 Feb 1840. James Neill to Thomas Davidson. Deed in Trust, 60 acres. James Neill sold to Thomas Davidson, land in Bedford Co., TN, in District No. 18 and bounded by lands of James Neill son of Andrew Neill, Andrew Neill, Thomas Moore, Wright Oliver. Sold also personal property. Reg: 14 Feb 1840.

Page 231 - 3 Mar 1840. James Wortham to Robert T. Cannon. Deed in Trust, 110¼ acres. James Wortham sold to Robert T. Cannon, land in Bedford Co., on south side of Duck River, being a part of a tract on which the late Minos Cannon, deceased, lived last before his death. Bounded by Lot No. 2 in the division of the original tract, Reed's old line, Dower lot allotted to the widow of Minos Cannon, deceased, Lot No. 1 in the division of original tract in the middle of Duck River, and Duck River opposite the mouth of the Sulphur Spring Branch. Reg: 3 Mar 1840.

Page 232 - 16 Dec 1839. Circuit Court Decree to Elliott Rucker and others. 140 acres. Stephen B. Johns, James Rucker and his wife Mary N., Clement Johns and Edmund G. Johns. Decree Exparte. Land had been sold to Elliott Rucker. Land in Bedford Co., TN, on Bylers Branch, the waters of Weakleys Creek. Borders land granted to John Byler, grant of E. Alexander, and Bylers Branch. The land being the tract conveyed to John Johns, dec'd, by William Wheeler and registered in book S(L), page 102 and 103. Excepting one acre which is to remain for the use of a Meeting House and Burying Ground. Other purchasers of land were William Brown, land being the tract conveyed to John Johns, deceased, by Abraham Byler by deed. (Book R, pages 287 & 288) James Hooper who purchased one of the tracts has since departed this life and the Executor and Executrix has paid for said land and reports to have been sold to James Hooper. The Executor and Executrix of the Last Will and Testament of James Hooper, deceased, filed for the sale of slaves which was sworn by Richard Bandy, William Hooper, Joseph Hooper, and George Hooper who are the only heirs at law of James Hooper. Reg: 4 Mar 1840.

Page 236 - 4 Mar 1840. William P. Bowers to Jesse P. Bowers. William P. Bowers of Blount Co., Alabama one part and Jesse P. Bowers other part, land in Bedford Co., TN, which legacy was willed and bequeathed to him by his father's Last Will and Testament, which is recorded in Shelbyville. His father John Bowers, deceased, did give unto him also negroes and money and property. Wit: Solomon Bowers and David Bowers. Reg: 10 Mar 1840.

Page 246 - 21 Mar 1840. John Tillman to Matt Martin. Deed for slaves. For $2000.00 loaned to him for two years and not charged interest by eight of the children of Matt Martin and for enabling Martin to divide the negroes for life amongst his children and grandchildren. He gives all rights and interest in all the slaves (46, named) which he purchased of Rachel Martin for her life time. Slaves belonging to the estate of Barkley Martin, deceased. Rachel Martin widow of Barkley Martin, deceased. Reg: 23 Mar 1840.

Page 247 - 21 Mar 1840. Rachel Martin to Matt Martin. Deed for slaves. Rachel Martin of Bedford Co., TN, and the widow of Barkley Martin, deceased, for love and affection she has for the children and grandchildren of Matt Martin and for him to divide the negro slaves amongst the children and grandchildren. Wit: John Scott, J. Cleveland and W. Pepper. Reg: 23 Mar 1840.

Page 247 - 21 Mar 1840. Matt Martin to Lucy G. Bradford. Deed of Gift. Matt Martin for love and affection for his daughter Lucy G. Bradford wife of Theoderick F. Bradford, all of Bedford Co., TN, delivered and sold to John Scott, Esq., of Bedford Co., negroes for life. To all the children of Lucy G. Bradford then living, to wit, Barclay M. Bradford, Caroline M. Bradford, Louisa R. Bradford, Lucy G. Bradford, Theoderic F. Bradford, William F. Bradford and Elizabeth M. M. Bradford, they are to get slaves for life. Wit: J. Cleveland and W. Pepper. Reg: 23 Mar 1840.

Page 258 - 26 Mar 1840. Matt Martin to Polly C. Marshall. Matt Martin of bedford Co., TN, for love and affection for his daughter Polly C. Marshall, given to Rachel Martin, acting friend and agent for Polly C. Marshall and for her benefit, negroes (4) which came from estate of Barkley Martin, deceased. Wit: Matt Martin, Jr., and M. M. Neill. Reg: 27 Mar 1840.

Page 259 - 23 Mar 1840. Matt Martin, Sr. to John L. Neill and wife. Matt Martin for love and affection for his daughter Sally Neill wife of John L. Neill, give unto her slaves (4), slaves comes from estate of Barclay Martin, deceased. Wit: R. C. C. P. Shaw and Matt Martin, Jr. Reg: 27 Mar 1840.

Page 259 - 26 Mar 1840. Matt Martin to Thomas B. Moseley and wife. Matt Martin for love and affection for his daughter Rebeckah Moseley wife of Thomas B. Moseley, give slaves (4), which came from estate of Barclay Martin, deceased. Wit: Matt Martin, Jr., and M. M. Neill. Reg: 27 Mar 1840.

Page 260 - 25 Mar 1840. Matt Martin to Edward A. Moseley and wife. Matt Martin for love and affection for his daughter Betty M. Moseley wife of Edward A. Moseley, slaves (4), which came from estate of Barclay Martin, deceased. Wit: R. C. C. P. Shaw and Matt Martin, Jr. Reg: 27 Mar 1840.

Page 260 - 25 Mar 1840. Matt Martin to Matt Martin, Jr. Matt Martin for love and affection for his son Matt Martin, Jr., fives slaves (4), which came from estate of Barclay Martin, deceased. Wit: Edward A. Moseley and R. C. C. P. Shaw. Reg: 27 Mar 1840.

Page 261 - 21 Mar 1840. Matt Martin, Sr. to Matt Martin, Jr. In Trust. Matt Martin of bedford CO., TN, for love and affection for his daughter Rachel Tillman wife of John Tillman of Bedford Co., given slaves (4), which came from estate of Barclay Martin, deceased. At Rachel's death, the slaves are to go to her children, Rachel Tipton, Lewis Tillman, Barkley Tillman, Anna Tillman, Abram Tillman and Lucy R. Tillman. Wit: R. C. C. P. Shaw and M. M. Neill. Reg: 27 Mar 1840.

Page 265 - 23 Jan 1840. John Phifer, Executor of Martin Phifer, deceased, to Mary Childers and others. Deed. Martin Phifer, late of Cabarrus Co., NC now deceased, by his Last Will and Testament, authorized John Phifer, his Executor, to sell lands one part and Mary Childers, James Childers, Susan formerly Susan Childers a daughter of Mary, and Ann formerly Ann Childers also a daughter of Mary, of the State of Alabama other part, sold land in Bedford Co., TN, except for 400 acres devised by William Phifer to William and Elizabeth Crawford, children of William Crawford, deceased, which was to be allotted to them and has yet to be allotted to them. One tract is bounded by South Fork of Fall Creek, Caleb Phifer's lane, McAdam's line, crosses the McMinnville Road. Containing in all 1413 acres. Also undivided fifth part of another tract in bedford Co., above the mouth of Fall Creek, about 15 or 16 acres. Wit: Jas. E. Morrison and L. B. Krommins, Jr. and John Rogers. Reg: 7 Apr 1840.

Page 270 - 8 Feb 1840. Willie Perry to Thomas Cheatham. By deed of William G. Adams to Eleanor A. Adams his wife, Willie Perry is lawfully seized of a life estate in a tract of land in bedford Co., TN, District No. 10, of 50 acres and bounded by Wilson Creek, Thomas Cheatham, Jesse Atkinson, lands willed by Isaac Phillips to W. G. Adams and wife Eleanor A. Adams, Stammer's line, Osteen's corner, and to Bigger's fence. Reg: 8 Apr 1840.

Page 297 - 1 May 1840. Melch. Brame to Grandchildren. Deed of Gift. Melchezedeck Brame of Bedford Co., TN, for love and affection for his grandchildren, Washington B., Virginia, Ann O., and William B. Fonville, conveys negroes (7) for life. Reg: 2 May 1840.

Page 300 - 15 Jan 1839. William M. Russell and Rosella Russell to William H. Craig. 202 acres. Whereas by descent from William Craig, deceased, Hamblin Cook and Susannah his wife, James Craig, Cena Justice, minor heirs of Thomas Justice, Martha Bradley minoe heir of Joel Bradley. (Nancy Justice wife of Thomas Justice and Martha Bradley wife of Joel Bradley, being dead), John Craig, Cleveland C. Harrison and Julia his wife, Robert Craig, Benjamin F. Craig, Flora Craig, and myself William M. Russell and Rosella my wife, have derived title to an equal and undivided interest in a tract of land in Bedford Co., in District No. 19 and bounded by Solomon Durrett, John McAdams, Jr., lands of Richard Santifer purchased of William Craig, dec'd, in his life time, Henry Heaslett's land purchased of Alfred Anderson, James Adams, and where Henry Heaslett now lives. Wit: William R. Looney and C. N. Allen. Reg: 5 May 1840.

Page 301 - 17 Oct 1839. C. S. Harrison and wife and Jas. Dillard to William H. Craig. 200 acres. By descent from William Craig, deceased, we have an equal and undivided one tenth of a tract of land in Bedford Co., TN, District No. 19. Bounded by John W. and H. M. Dawdy, Solomon Durrett and others, Zachariah Davis and Henry Heaslett and James Adams, Sr. Wit: James H. Harrison and J. M. Gibson. Reg: 5 May 1840.

Page 309 - 29 Oct 1838. The heirs of John Bradshaw to Minos Cannon. 130 acres. Heirs of John Bradshaw sold to Minos Cannon land in Bedford Co., TN, in District No. 12. Borders Yeates' line, James More (Moore), and Bradshaw's old corner. Signed by Mary Bradshaw, J. N. Bradshaw, Asenath Bradshaw, Rachel Bradshaw, Louiza Bradshaw, Mary C. Bradshaw, Adaline Bradshaw, Sophia Bradshaw, O. W. Bradshaw and Arrenda Bradshaw. Wit: Samuel Stewart and John Stewart. Reg: 13 May 1840.

Page 311 - 24 Jul 1833. Richard Allen, Rosalinda Allen and Sareny Brown to Rezin Smith. Deed 85 acres. Richard Allen, Rosalinda Allen and Sareny Brown one part and Rezin Smith other part, sold their two sixths part of an undivided interest in tract of land in Bedford Co., TN, on headwaters of Sinking Creek. Bounded by John Smith, Jr., lands of George Doherty, Philip Phillips and Michael Campbell. Wit: Thomas S. Brown and Joseph Wallace. Reg: 16 May 1840.

Page 313 - 18 May 1840. Eve Holt to John Dean. 120 acres. For love and affection that Eve Holt has for her children (10), Rachael Jones, Katy Holt, Polly Heathcock, Christopher Holt, Peggy Jones, Enoch, Milly, Sally, Dolly and Nancy Holt, conveyed unto John Dean land on Thompsons Creek, it being the same land given to her by her father Martin Shofner and on which she now resides. Also a negro girl Amanda and a negro boy Brook. Reg: 18 May 1840.

Page 317 - 21 May 1840. Robert M. Foster to Robert Foster, Sr. Deed 50 acres. Robert M. Foster and Robert Foster, Sr., his father, both of Bedford Co., TN, land in Bedford Co., on North Fork and bounded by Abel Rushing and E. Head. Wit: Moses

Williams and Wiley Foster. Reg: 23 May 1840.

Page 319 - 24 Mar 1840. City of New Orleans, Louisiana. James Erwin to John P. Erwin. Power of Attorney. 950 acres. James Erwin of New Orleans, LA, appointed John P. Erwin of Nashville, TN as his Attorney, to sell and convey to Andrew Erwin of Bedford Co., TN, land on the Garrison Fork and now occupied by Andrew Erwin and commonly called The Brick House Tract. Borders the Garrison Fork, Kinchen Stokes, John B. Bates and Moses Payne, Norman Wallace and John Q. Davidson, and William Pepper and others. Wit: Robert Woods and Elisha S. Hall. Reg: 28 May 1840.

Page 320 - 23 Apr 1840. James Erwin by his Attorney in Fact, John P. Erwin to Andrew Erwin. 950 acres. (Same as above instrument) Conveyed land in Bedford Co., TN, on which Andrew Erwin now resides and commonly called The Brick House. Reg: 28 May 1840.

Page 321 - 9 Feb 1839. William H. Miles to School Commissioners. Deed one-fourth acre. For love and affection for the neighborhood and the rising posterity, he gives and conveys unto James McGill, Mt. Cunningham, John Dunaway, D. D. Hix, and John Hastings, the five Commissioners for School Land, for the 23rd District in Bedford Co., TN. Where William H. Miles now lives. Wit: John Wallis and Willie B. Snell. Reg: 28 May 1840.

Page 348 - 12 Jun 1840. John S. Cates and Elizabeth Cates to Joseph Hastings. 25 acres. John S. Cates and his wife Elizabeth Cates, all of Bedford Co., TN, land in Bedford Co., on waters of Big Flat Creek and bounded by Joshua Woosley, Doherty's line and Mrs. Himes' dower line. Reg: 13 Jun 1840.

Page 352 - 1 Jun 1840. Benjamin F. and William P. Bowers to Rice Coffey. Bill of Sale. It was decreed that the Executors of John Bowers, deceased, should sell a negro man Isham, belonging to the estate of John Bowers, deceased. Rice Coffey purchased the negro man. Benjamin F. and William P. Bowers are Executors of John Bowers, deceased. Reg: 18 Jun 1840.

Page 357 - 28 Oct 1833. John McMichael to Alexander, James and William McMichael. Relinquishment. John McMichael of Pike Co., MO, conveyed unto Alexander, James and William McMichael of Bedford Co., TN, all his right title and interest in 180 acres on Noahs Fork, being the tract of land whereon the McMichaels now lives and whereas as one of the legal heirs. Wit: Andrew Vannoy and J. Cleveland, Jr. Reg: 20 Jun 1840.

Page 359 - 7 Jan 1837. Lettitia C. Dickerson to William Hooser. 100 acres. Lettitia C. Dickerson sold to William Hooser, both of Bedford Co., TN, land in Bedford Co., known as Lot No. 3 of the division of land made by Daniel Gilchrist, between Lettitia C. Dickerson and others as heirs of William Dickerson, deceased. Land borders William Hooser and the land formerly owned by Daniel Johnson. Wit: Maria E. Hooser, Jas. W. Dickerson and James J. Miller. Reg: 22 Jun 1840.

Page 375 - 2 Jul 1840. Benjamin F. Bowers to John W. White. Bill of Sale. For $625.00, Benjamin F. Bowers sold to John W. White, the Presses and Type and all the materials on which The Whig Advocate is now printed in Town of Shelbyville, including office furniture. Wit: William H. Wisener. Reg: 7 Jul 1840.

Page 375 - 6 Jun 1840. William H. Cates and others to Joseph Hastings. Relinquishment. William F. Cates, Joseph S. Cates, Robert Pollock and Susanna Pollock his wife, Andrew Morgan and Tempy Morgan his wife, Jacob Hershaw and Mary Hershaw his wife, all of Bedford Co., TN, conveyed to Joseph Hastings all their interest in the estate of their grandfather Joseph Hastings, deceased. Wit: A. C. Wood, H. Holt and Jno. Hastings. Reg: 7 Jul 1840.

Page 378 - 6 Apr 1840. George Jakes and others to John Jakes. 75 acres. George Jakes and James Drake and Judith Drake his wife one part and John Jakes other part, all of Bedford Co., TN, land which descended to them by the will of their grandfather John Jakes, deceased, the tract borders the Blount Grants. Wit: William Wood and Samuel McMahan. Reg: 9 Jul 1840.

Page 379 - 22 Jun 1840. Heirs of William Blanton, deceased. Exparte. 109 acres. Land which descended from William Blanton, deceased, to Wilkins Blanton, Willis Blanton, Charles Blanton, Smith Blanton, Horace Blanton, Elizabeth P. Blanton, Henson G. Blanton, Jasper N. Blanton and Susan wife of Leighton Ewell, and Mary wife of James Nichols, and Sarah Blanton who accepts a share or child's part of purchase money in lieu of her dower the land. The land borders B. Maupin, Duck River. Another tract of 50¼ acres. Reg: 9 Jul 1840.

Page 383 - 30 May 1840. Low Harmon and wife to William Brown. One half Lot No. 42. Low Harmon and Harriett B. Harmon his wife formerly Harriett B. Younger and Lucy Younger of one part and William Brown other part, all of Bedford Co., TN, Town Lot of Shelbyville, on east side of Martin Street (now Main Street). Borders Lot No. 42. Reg: 16 Jul 1840.

Page 393 - 15 Jul 1840. Alfred Y. Wallis and wife to William Hooser. Bill of Sale. Negro. Alfred Y. Wallis and Cyntha Wallis his wife sold William Hooser a negro man Ned. Wit: Samuel Phillips, Allen Wallis and John Snelling. Reg: 21 Jul 1840.

Page 401 - 28 Jul 1840. William Dwyer to Shadrack Brown. 100 acres. William Dwyer sold to Shadrack Brown, both of Bedford Co., TN, his interest in a tract of land in Bedford Co., about two miles northwest of Shelbyville near the road from Shelbyville to Columbia, being the land on which the late Daniel Dwyer, deceased, resided at the time of his death and my interest being one eighth. Reg: 30 Jul 1840.

Page 402 - 27 Jul 1840. Henry C. Coats to Charles Phelps. Henry C. Coats sold to Charles Phelps land in Town of Shelbyville, part of Lot No. 4 in the division of land, line passsing over the center of the well in the Town of Shelbyville formerly belonging to John B. Coats a minor heir of Wilson Coats, dec'd. Reg: 30 Jul 1840.

Page 403 - 26 Feb 1840. William Hooper and George Hooper to Washington F. Short. A negro girl Sublena, their interest as heirs of James Hooper, deceased. Wit: Richard Bandy and William Rucker. Reg: 31 Jul 1840.

DEED BOOK "JJ"

Page 406 - 1 May 1840. Isreal Fonville to his children. Deed of Gift. Isreal Fonville of Bedford Co., TN, for love and affection for his children, Washington B., Virginia, Ann O., and William B. Fonville, conveyed all his interest in negroes. Wit: O. W. Knight and William Brame. Reg: 3 Aug 1840.

Page 419 - -- Aug 1840. John S. Dwyer to Shadrack Brown. Deed, undivided interest. 100 acres. John Dwyer to Shadrack Brown, both of Bedford Co., TN, being one undivided eighth in land in Bedford Co., near the road from Shelbyville to Columbia and on the north side of Duck river about two miles from Shelbyville, it being the tract owned by the late Daniel Dwyer and it being where Daniel Dwyer lived at the time of his death. Reg: 10 Aug 1840.

Page 419 - 10 Aug 1840. Richard Muse to Thomas Lipscomb. Bill of Sale. Both of Bedford Co., TN. Richard Muse sold all the interest that may come to him from the estate of Michael Meadows, deceased, it being the interest of one legatee in the estate or the eleventh part thereof, also all his interest he purchased of Nathan Roberts and Jemima Roberts his wife. Reg: 10 Aug 1840.

Page 424 - 23 Jan 1840. Thomas F. Harrison to James H. Harrison. Deed 188½ acres. Whereas by descent from Jonathan Harrison, deceased, Thomas F. Harrison, Cleveland S. Harrison, William T. Harrison, James F. Harrison, Polly Ann Harrison, Peggy Perthenia Harrison and Susanna Elvira Harrison sold to James H. Harrison land in Bedford Co., TN in District No. 19. Bounded by Thomas Harper's purchased of James Dillard, James Dillard's purchase of William Williams, Margaret Price, Nathaniel Porter, Green Lovett a minor heir of Lancaster Lovett, deceased, and J. M. Gibson. Another tract of 60 acres purchased from Lewis Medlin, second 122 acres from Owen Medlin deed to Mary Harrison, Executrix of Jonathan Harrison, deceased. Wit: T. W. Harper and W. W. Mayes. Reg: 13 Aug 1840.

Page 425 - 6 Mar 1840. C. S. Harrison to James H. Harrison. Deed Release. 188½ acres. Whereas by descent from Jonathan Harrison, William T. Harrison, Thomas F. Harrison, James H. Harrison, Polly Ann Harrison, Peggy Parthena Harrison, Susanna Elvira Harrison and C. S. Harrison received title to an unequal and undivided interest in a tract of land in Bedford Co., TN, in District No. 19, on waters of Rock and Sinking Creeks and borders lands made by Thomas Harper of James Dillard, made by James Dillard of William Williams in about 1834, Margaret Price, Nathaniel Porter, lands of Green Lovett minor heir of Lancaster Lovett, deceased. This land being bought in two purchases. First, a 60 acre tract from Lewis Medlin and second, a 122½ acre tract from Owen Medlin, deeded to Mary Harrison, Executrix of Jonathan Harrison, deceased. Wit: W. W. Mayes and Green Lovett. Reg: 13 Aug 1840.

Page 426 - 10 Apr 1840. James McMinn to Thomas P. Powell. 40 acres. James McMinn of Hickman Co., TN one part and Thomas P. Powell of Bedford Co., TN other part, land in Bedford Co., on waters of North Fork, being a part of a tract of land originally granted to Alexander Worke and being divided among his heirs, and it being a part which was the share of Richard Brandon one of the heirs of A. Worke. Borders land whereon William Guy now lives. Wit: Samuel Woodfin and John Naler. Reg: 13 Aug 1840.

DEED BOOK "JJ"

Page 434 - 7 Aug 1840. Shurwood and Sarah Lisenby to Robert Clinkenbeard. Deed 53 acres. Shurwood Lisenby and Sarah Lisenby his wife one part and Robert Clinkenbeard other part, all of Bedford Co., TN. Sarah Lisenby the daughter of John Jones, deceased. Land in Bedford CO., their three fourth part of a tract of land, as the lawful heirs of John Jones, deceased, which tract John Jones purchased of John Coffee. Bounded by Martin Phifer's line, William P. Anderson, Thomas Doogan. It being the land Mrs. Sarah Jones, the mother of Sarah Lisenby, will be entitled to the rent and possession of all buildings with the use of the spring and grass lots during her natural life, then the entire right will be to Robert Clinkenbeard. Reg: 27 Aug 1840.

Page 435 - 28 Jul 1840. Martha W. Dillard to Robert Clinkenbeard. Deed 53 acres. Martha W. Dillard wife of Joel Dillard, deceased one part and Robert Clinkenbeard other part, all of Bedford Co., TN, land being the one fourth interest in land as one of the heirs of John Jones, deceased. (Same as above instrument) Wit: David W. Anglin and Sherwood Lisenby. Reg: 27 Aug 1840.

Page 442 - 11 Oct 1838. James Wortham and others to Clement Cannon. Deed 28 acres. Robert T. Cannon, James Wortham and Catharine M. his wife formerly Catharine M. Cannon, one part and Clement Cannon other part, all of Bedford Co., TN, land in Bedford CO., it being the one third part of which Robert T. and the one third part to James and Catharine M. Wortham. The tract which descends to them as heirs of Minos Cannon, deceased, the same being part of 100 acre tract by Grant No. 465. Borders Walter Galbreath and the bank of Duck River. Reg: 3 Sep 1840.

Page 444 - -- Aug 1840. William P. Sample to John Marsh, B. Featherston and others. Deed 4 acres. William P. Sample of Bedford Co., TN one part and John Marsh, Burrell Featherston, Farwick Frazer, John Norville and Charles F. Sutton, Trustees in Trust and their successors for Methodist Episcopal Church other part, for $10.00, sold land in Bedford Co., on waters of Wartrace Fork. Bounded by Farwick Frazer and Elkin's line. The land they shall erect and build a house or place of worship for the members of the Methodist Episcopal Church. Reg: 7 Sep 1840.

Page 445 - 17 Jul 1840. J. G. Philpot and Mary Ann Philpot to Charles T. Philpot. Deed. John G. Philpot and Mary Ann Philpot his wife of Bedford Co., TN sold to Charles T. Philpot of Bedford Co., a distributive or child's share of the estate of William Hix, deceased, which they are entitled to agreeable to the Last Will and Testament of William Hix, deceased, which they are entitled to by the death or marriage of Sally Hix the widow of William Hix, deceased. Reg: 7 Sep 1840.

DEED BOOK "KK" 1840 - 1841

Page 11 - 19 Sep 1840. Thomas Cummings to Edward Johnson. 70 acres. Thomas Cummings given and donated to Edward Johnson, both of Bedford Co., TN, in behalf of his wife Sally, daughter of Thomas Cummings, land in Bedford Co., on east side of East Fork of Rock Creek. Borders lands of John Dawdy, Gabriel Blackwell, Brown's line now Dawdy's land, and James Allison. Wit:

John B. Cummings and George Cummings. Reg: 21 Sep 1840.

Page 13 - 24 Sep 1840. Giles R. Bowers to Martha Cunningham and others. Giles R. Bowers conveyed unto Mrs. Martha Cunningham and James Cunningham and Angeline Cunningham all the property real and personal conveyed to him by Robert Cunningham which came to him from John Cunningham of Warren Co., TN by deed dated 24 May 1839 and registered in Bedford Co., TN in Book "HH", page 450. Reg: 24 Sep 1840.

Page 13 - 27 Jul 1831. Richard Ferrill to Vincent Smith. Obligation. Richard Ferrill of Bedford Co., TN bound himself to keep Vincent Smith and his wife Anna, in peaceable possession of the largest room of the house that stands on the land that Smith sold to Terrill, and the use of the lots and orchard during Smith's and his wife's natural life time. Wit: Edward Smith. Reg: 26 Sep 1840.

Page 14 - 23 Sep 1840. Vincent Smith and Mary Ferrill. Agreement. Vincent Smith one part and Mary Ferrill other part, both of Bedford Co., TN. Mary Ferrill on 22 Sep 1838 at the sale of perishable property of her husband Richard Ferrill, deceased, purchased various articles of property. Vincent Smith was the administrator of the estate. Mary not able to pay for property sold same to Vincent Smith. Wit: Andrew Vannoy and Edward Smith. Reg: 26 Sep 1840.

Page 14 - 25 Jul 1839. Lucinda Barrett to Michael Holt. Deed. Whereas by descent from William Stewart, deceased, my grandfather Benton C. Barrett and myself, Lucinda Barrett, hold undivided equal part of a tract of land in Bedford Co., TN. Bounded by Hunly Wiggins, Joshua Holt, Sr., Joshua Yates on waters of Big Flat Creek, sold all her interest in said land to Michael Holt. Wit: John Barrett and Samuel Stewart. Reg: 3 Oct 1840.

Page 18 - 2 Oct 1840. Rachel Martin to Ann Pauline Butler. Deed of Gift. Rachel Martin, for love and affection for Ann Pauline Butler of New Orleans, LA, niece of Rachel Martin, convey unto her a negro woman Lear. Wit: Thomas B. Moseley, N. W. Butler, John Tillman and T. B. Moseley, Jr. Reg: 6 Oct 1840.

Page 19 - 26 Jan 1820. Contract between John G. Sims and others and Elizabeth Scudder and Phillip J. Scudder. Whereas Walter Sims, late of Davidson Co., TN, deceased, by his Last Will and Testament, bequeathed in favor of his daughter Elizabeth Scudder, which are as follows: Item 20: It is my will that the land certificates to the amount of five thousand acres now in the hands of Capt. John A. Rogers of Hawkins Co., TN, when they shall be received from him, and when my account with the heirs of G. Dennison is settled, the portion of the said warrants which cannot be less than twenty five hundred acres, shall be divided between my son Walter B. Sims and my daughter Elizabeth each one half. Whatever the amount may be. Item 24: It is my will and I bequeath to my daughter Elizabeth Scudder the one half of my tract of land in Bedford Co., known by the name of Skull Camp Tract, the other half having been bequeathed to my son David in Item 23, the tract to be equally divided between my son David and daughter Elizabeth &c. Item 25: It is my will and I bequeath to my daughter Elizabeth Scudder all my interest in my tract of land in bedford Co., known by the name of the Fishing Ford Tract, except 400 acres, which I hereafter bequeath. Item 27: It is my will that my lands in Hawkins Co., TN may be sold by my Executors as soon after my death as can be done with advantage to my estate, and that the debt dur me from the estate of Gideon Dennison may be collected, and when the said lands shall be sold and the said debt shall be collected that the proceeds shall be divided, share and share alike amongst my children, John G. Sims, Walter B. Sims, David Sims, and Elizabeth Scudder. Item 28: It is my will that the debt due me from the estate of Nicklin and Griffith shall be attended to, about $40,000.00. When recovered it is to be divided amongst my sons. Walter B. Sims to receive one fourth, David Sims gets one fourth, and my daughter Elizabeth Scudder gets one half of the proceeds of the debt. Item 33: It is my will and I give and bequeath at the death of my wife, $5000.00 of the last mentioned bond to my daughter Elizabeth for $10,000.00 executed by Walter B. Sims and John S. Green. Item 35: It is my will that at the death of my wife, all my slaves and increases, to be equally divided between my daughter Elizabeth and my son William, except my slave Jefferson which is now the property of my son William, and whereas said Elizabeth Scudder departed this life before Walter, by which the legatees became lapsed, and the property will vest or invested in John S. Sims, Walter B. Sims and David Sims, the remaining legatees in the will mentioned, and whereas Elizabeth Scudder died leaving a daughter also named Elizabeth for whom John G., Walter B., and David Sims are desirous of making some provision, and in the event the child should die before she attain the age of 21 years without issue living at her death, they are also desirous of giving a testimonial of their esteem for her father Philip J. Scudder. Land of 3 Lots in Shelbyville. Reg: 10 Oct 1840.

Page 22 - 24 Jul 1837. Benton C. Barrett to Michael Holt. Deed undivided interest. Whereas by descent from William Stewart, deceased, my grandfather, Lucinda Barrett and myself, Benton C. Barrett have derived title now hold equal undivided interest in land in Bedford Co., TN. Bouded by Hunly Wiggins, Joshua Holt, Sr., Joshua Yeates, on waters of the Big Flat Creek. Sold said land. Wit: William Baily and J. W. B. Moore. Benton C. Barrett of Warrick Co., Indiana. Reg: 10 Oct 1840.

Page 40 - 15 Sep 1840. Joel Lawrance and wife to John Fisher. Bill of Sale. John Lawrance and his wife Mary sold to John Fisher a negro woman Tempy and her child. Wit: John Thompson and William N. Orr. Reg: 28 Oct 1840.

Page 43 - 17 Aug 1840. Jane J. Mahew (Mayhew) and others to Joseph McKenley. Deed 140 acres. Jane J. Mayhew and Presley Mayhew her husband of Iredell Co., NC and Ann W. Lanier and her husband Robert Lanier of Mecklenburg Co., NC one part and Joseph McKenley of Bedford Co., TN other part, land in Bedford Co., on waters of North Fork, it belonging to the heirs of Alexander Worke, Jr., a devisee of Alexander Worke, late of Iredell Co., NC, their interest. Wit: Jas. E. Godbey and P. R. Gaither. Reg: 2 Nov 1840.

Page 48 - 22 Oct 1840. Joseph S. Cates and Sophia Cates to William H. Himes. Deed 46 acres. Joseph S. Cates and his wife Sophia Cates sold to William H. Himes, all of Bedford Co., TN, land in Bedford Co. Reg: 7 Nov 1840.

Page 53 - 16 Nov 1840. Charles and Jane Dement and Owen O. Briant and wife to Mansfield Whitehead. 160 acres. Charles Dement and Jane Dement of Williamson Co., TN and Owen O. Briant and Ann O. Briant his wife, late Ann Johnson, of Bedford Co., TN, land in Bedford Co., in District No. 10. The land being deeded by Thomas Powell of Mississippi to Jose M. Davis. Bounded by Mansfield Whitehead, Elizabeth Davis and Alfred Ransom and Crawford Carlton. Reg: 19 Nov 1840.

Page 63 - 23 Nov 1840. Archibald Dobson and wife Mary to Robert T. Cannon. Archibald Dobson and Mary Dobson his wife one part to Robert T. Cannon other part, for love and affection they bear unto Justina Ashburn, Mary T. Ashburn, Hazard T. Ashburn and Clement Ashburn, children of Mary Dobson by her former husband Thomas F. Ashburn, sold to Robert T. Cannon, land in Bedford Co., TN, on both sides of Duck River, adjoining the land of Clement Cannon, Andrew Reed and Keziah Galbreath, deceased. It being the dower for life of Mary Dobson in a tract of land belonging to her first husband Minos Cannon and the place on which Washington Goodwin now lives. Also conveyed negro woman Sally, a negro man Nelson and others. Also, Lots in Shelbyville known as Lot No. 33 and Lot No. 34. Also, other personal property. Wit: Thomas J. Purdie and THomas C. Whiteside. Reg: 23 Nov 1840.

Page 65 - 20 Nov 1840. Hiram Holt to Herod F. Holt. Hiram Holt conveyed all his interest in the estate of Eleanor Holt at her decease, left to him by the will of his father. Wit: Jordan C. Holt and D. M. Smith. Reg: 24 Nov 1840.

Page 67 - 1 Jul 1833. Thomas Hamilton to Masedora B. Hamilton and others. Deed 160 acres. Thomas Hamilton one part and Masedora B. Hamilton, James M. Hamilton, George W. Hamilton, Mary E. Hamilton, Sarah Hamilton, Silas E. G. Hamilton, other part, all of Bedford Co., TN, land in Bedford Co., on waters of West Fork of Rock Creek. Borders lands of William Martin's grant. The land belonging to John Hamilton. Reg: 26 Nov 1840.

Page 69 - 30 Nov 1840. Sarah Cooper to L. B. Knott. Deed in Trust. Sarah Cooper sold to L. B. Knott her interest in the tract of land on which she now reside, land in Bedford Co., TN, on the upper Murfreesboro Road about 5½ miles from Shelbyville and being the tract of land on which her late husband Charles Cooper resided at the time of his death. Also, sold her interest in negro slaves and other personal property. Reg: 30 Nov 1840.

Page 73 - 8 Jul 1840. Pherebe Ditto and others to Cyntha Wallis. Bill of Sale. Division of negro property of John Ditto, dec'd, negro man Ned goes to Cyntha Wallis. John McGuire and William Mullins, administrators of heirs of Mary McGuire, deceased. Wit: E. J. Frierson, Peter Lee, William Meadows and William Dean. Reg: 7 Dec 1840.

Page 85 - 19 Nov 1840. Cyntha McNeeley to Allen Wallis. Power of Attorney. Cyntha McNeeley appointed Allen Wallis Attorney to receive from George C. Armstrong, my former guardian or Quarles T. Mayfield, having possession of my distributive share of money or property descended to her from her father Isaac McNeeley, deceased, late of Bedford Co., TN. Wit: Alfred Y. Wallis and Archibald Pruit. Reg: 9 Dec 1840, 2:15 PM.

Page 86 - 10 Dec 1840. John W. Hooker. Revocation Power of Attorney &c. John W. Hooker of Bedford CO., TN revoke of Power of Attorney by Cyntha Ann McNeeley now my wife, to Allen Wallis. Reg: 10 Dec 1840.

Page 97 - 16 Dec 1840. William C. Gregory and Lucinda P. Gregory to James Dixon. 18 acres. William C. Gregory and Lucinda P. Gregory his wife sold to James Dixon, land in Bedford Co., TN, District No. 21, it being their fifth part of tract of land belonging to the heirs of John McKamy, deceased. Wit: Thomas C. Whiteside and Jacob Greer. Reg: 23 Dec 1840.

Page 111 - -- Sep 1840. Mary Gaunt to William A. Gaunt. Deed of Gift. Mary Gaunt for love and affection for William A. Gaunt her son, conveys all her personal property. Wit: Jacob B. Morgan and Jacob H. Cheves. Reg: 5 Jan 1841.

Page 112 - 24 Nov 1840. James L. Armstrong to Edward A. Moseley. Deed 120 acres. Both of Bedford Co., TN, land in Bedford Co., on waters of the Garrison Fork, it being the land on which B. H. Ragsdale now lives. Bounded by where James L. Armstrong lives and Mrs. Rachel Martin. With the exception of one acre of land laid off to include the school house called Rural Academy with the right of way to the spring and for which B. H. Ragsdale who formerly owned the land hath given his bond to certain Trustees. Wit: G. G. Osborne and Matt Martin. Reg: 5 Jan 1841.

Page 129 - 16 Nov 1840. Amos West and wife Nancy to John Wood. Deed one tenth of 112 acres, undivided. Amos West and Nancy West his wife of Rutherford Co., TN one part and John Wood of Bedford Co., TN other part, land in Bedford CO. Bounded by lands of John Wood, Dennis Springer, Edmund Whitman and Thornton Mallard. It being on waters of Hurricane Creek and Fall Creek. The land belonging to the estate of Thomas Nash, deceased. Reg: 14 Jan 1841.

Page 131 - April Term 1840. Circuit Court Decree to Jonathan Cooper. 226 acres. Caleb Houston, administrators of Jane Worke, deceased. Jane Worke, deceased, land in Bedford Co., TN, on waters of North Fork and being Lot No. 2 of the division amongst the heirs of Jane Worke, deceased, made and returned to Bedford Co., TN Court at Nov Term 1829, was sold by Caleb Houston, adminr. and he made his report at April Term 1838, saying that the said land was bid-off and purchased by Jonathan Cooper. Reg: 14 Jan 1841.

Page 142 - 9 Feb 1835. James Gaunt and others to Benjamin Broughton. Deed 158 acres, 3 tracts. John Gaunt, James Gaunt, John Ray and his wife Patsey formerly Patsey Gaunt, and Mary Gaunt widow of Lewis Gaunt, Sr., deceased, of Bedford Co., TN, and Jesse B. Gaunt of Hardin Co., TN, and Absalom B. Gaunt of Wayne Co., TN, and Samuel Herber and his wife Nancy Herber of Hardin Co., TN, and John Aldrige and his wife Margarett formerly Margarett Gaunt of Lawrance Co., Alabama, and James Aldrige of Lawrance Co., Alabama of one part and Benjamin Broughton of Bedford Co., other part, land in Bedford Co., on Little Sinking Creek. Borders lands of Johnston. Another tract borders Johnston, and another tract borders James Clifft, Little Sinking Creek. Wit: J. T. Neil, William A. Gaunt, Lewis Gaunt and John A. Gaunt. Reg: 22 Jan 1841.

Page 149 - 14 Aug 1840. Michael Holt to John H. Rives and others. 9 acres. Michael Holt of Bedford Co., TN one part and John H. Rives, Benjamin Rives, George Pratt, Joshua Parkes and Wiley B. Snell, Trustees, of Bedford Co., other part, conveyed unto the Trustees, land in Bedford Co., and bounded by Eleanor Nease, Jordan C. Holt, The Campground, bluff of the creek, and east of the graveyard. Reg: 26 Jan 1841.

Page 168 - 8 Feb 1841. Absalom Arnold and wife Mary to Robert L. Landers. Deed in Trust. Absalom Arnold and wife Mary conveyed Robert L. Landers and Robert P. Maupin and Dudley P. T. House, all his interest which he is entitled to as an heir at law in the estate of Jacob Coble, Esq., deceased. Wit: William Jenkins and A. L. Landis. Reg: 9 Feb 1841.

Page 173 - 5 Feb 1841. Austin Shofner to John Shofner and William Jenkins. Deed &c, 4 acres. Austin Shofner of Bedford Co., TN one part and John Shofner and William Jenkins, in Trust for the Evangelical Lutheran Church other part, conveyed to Trustees, for the affection for the congregation which worship at the Meeting House, known as Shofners Church, land in Bedford Co., in District No. 25, and upon which the Lutheran Church is built. Borders Austin Shofner's Spring Branch near the Meeting House Spring. For proper use of Lutheran Congregation. Wit: George Cortner and Jos. H. Cooper. Reg: 10 Feb 1841.

Page 174 - 9 Feb 1841. Pinkney H. Thompson and wife to Louvicia Covington. Deed &c, 161 acres and negroes. Pinkney H. Thompson and Manervia C. Thompson his wife sold to Louvicia Covington, all interest in an undivided interest in the estate of Jesse Covington, deceased, in negroes now belonging to the estate. Also land in District No. 11 of Bedford Co., TN, on waters of Weakleys Creek near the Village of Unionville. Borders lands of William Ogilvie and others. Wit: Thomas Wheeler and David J. Wheeler. Reg: 10 Feb 1841.

Page 190 - 5 Feb 1841. John R. Proby to William Pepper and George Davidson. Bill of Sale. John R. Proby sold and delivered to William Pepper and George Davidson, negro slaves (14), belonging to the estate of the late Richard Daniel formerly of Halifax Co., VA. My interest accreed in conveyance of my intermarriage lawfully with Sarah Daniel one of the children of Richard Daniel, the share of Sarah to which I have succeeded by intermarriage. Wit: William T. Edmonson and Wiley Daniel. Reg: 15 Feb 1841.

Page 192 - 16 Jan 1841. James Mullins, Sheriff, to Gabriel Blackwell. Deed. Whereas John J. Snead, administrator, and Martha McAdoo, administratrix, of John McAdoo, deceased, received a judgement against Ruthy Whitney of Bedford Co., TN, on 11 Dec 1837. No personal property to be found. Reg: 15 Feb 1841.

Page 198 - 29 Jan 1841. Jesse Gurley and Jemima his wife to Michael Holt. Deed 11½ acres. Jesse Gurley amd Jemima his wife both of Marshall Co., Mississippi, one part and Michael Holt of Bedford Co., TN, other part, their interest as heirs of William Stewart, land in Bedford Co., on waters of Little Flat Creek. Borders lands of Joshua Holt, Jacob Greer, Joshua Yeates. Wit: William Gurley and Joseph Gurley. Reg: 16 Feb 1841.

Page 202 - 20 Feb 1841. Lowe Harmon and wife to Samuel Thompson. Lowe Harmon and his wife Harriet B. Harmon sold to Samuel Thompson, all of Bedford Co., TN, land in Bedford Co., in District No. 21, on road leading from Shelbyville to Fayetteville and about two miles from Shelbyville. Bounded by Flat Creek, Andrew Johnson and John Blackwell. Land being the tract on which James Younger, deceased, resided at the time of his death. Reg: 20 Feb 1841.

Page 204 - 28 Jan 1841. Polly G. Boyd and others to William Boyd. Power of Attorney. Polly G. Boyd, Christopher C. Gwin and Levina J. Gwin his wife, and Tennessee A. Pinkston. Polly G. Boyd being the wife of William Boyd and late widow of William Pinkston, deceased, formerly of Bedford Co., TN. Levina J. Gwin and Tennessee A. Pinkston being the daughters and only heirs of William Pinkston, deceased, appointed William Boyd of Lawrence Co., Alabama, as Power of Attorney, to receive or sell their interest in what they are to receive of William Pinkston, deceased. Reg: 22 Feb 1841.

Page 206 - 20 Feb 1841. William Boyd and others to Alex. and John P. Moon. Deed, 1 acre. William Boyd and wife Polly G. Boyd late the widow of William Pinkston, deceased, and Christopher C. Gwin and wife Levina J. his wife, and Tennessee A. Pinkston, all of Lawrence Co., Alabama of one part and Alexander B. Moon and John P. Moon, of Bedford Co., TN, sold to Alex. B. Moon, assignee and heirs in Trust for Polly H. Jeffries wife of Thomas B. Jefferies of bedford Co., during her natural life and at her death for her children. John P. Moon to get land or mill site on North Fork formerly Pinkston Mill in District No. 11. Bounded by John Moon, Clark's corner. Wit: Thomas C. Whiteside and E. J. Frierson. Reg: 22 Feb 1841.

Page 208 - 20 Feb 1841. William Boyd and others to John P. Moon. Deed, 34 acres. William Boyd and Polly G. his wife, late widow of William Pinkston, deceased, Christopher C. Gwin and Levina J. his wife, and Tennessee A. Pinkston, all of Law=rence Co., Alabama one part and John P. Moon of Bedford Co., TN other part, land in Bedford Co., on waters of Weakleys Creek. Bounded by North Fork, Ford at the mill, Moon's line. Wit: Thomas C. Whiteside and E. J. Frierson. Reg: 23 Feb 1841.

Page 209 - 20 Feb 1841. William Boyd and others to Alexander B. Moon. Deed 191 acres. (Same as the above instrument). Wit: Thomas C. Whiteside and E. J. Frierson. Reg: 23 Feb 1841.

Page 210 - 20 Feb 1841. William Boyd and others to William B. Jones. Deed, 31 acres. (Same as above instrument). Reg: 23 Feb 1841.

Page 211 - 20 Feb 1841. Harrell Wiggins to John W. Wiggins. Bill of Sale. Harrell Wiggins of Bedford Co., TN, for love and affection for his daughter Harriett Evans, conveyed a negro girl Aggy. Reg: 23 Feb 1841.

Page 212 - 11 Dec 1840. Court Decree to Herbert Smith. Hubert Smith and Mildred his wife, formerly Mildred Stephens, John A., Margaret J., William S., and Leonard Stephens, minor heirs of Willis Stephens, deceased, who sue by their guardian Herbert Smith. Exparte. Bill for sale of land. Reg: 23 Feb 1841.

Page 213 - 24 Feb 1841. John Williams to William E. Jones. Power of Attorney. John Williams of Bedford Co., TN, an heir and legal representative of Martha Dixon, deceased, the widow of Henry Dixon who was a Lieutenant Colonel of the Third Regiment of the North Carolina Continental Line in the War of the Revolution and died whilst in service of the United States on the 17th day of July 1782, appointed William E. Jones of Smith Co., TN, his Attorney to prosecute a certain claim for him to seven years half pay before the Congress of the United States or elsewhere which the claims is coming to him as an heir of Martha Dixon, deceased, widow of Lt. Col. Henry Dixon. Wit: Michael Marsh and Pleasant Hart. Reg: 24 Feb 1841.

Page 220 - 9 Feb 1841. Martha Oneal to William O. Forbes. Deed of Gift. Martha Oneal of Bedford Co., TN, for love and affection for William O. Forbes the grandson of her late husband William Oneal, has granted and conveyed unto him a negro man Riley and other property. Wit: John Oneal and M. H. Sims. Reg: 27 Feb 1841.

Page 221 - 26 Feb 1841. A. Y. Wallace and wife to James H. Bomar. Bill of Sale. A. Y. Wallis and Cynthia Wallis his wife sold James H. Bomar a negro girl Julian. Wit: Allen Wallis and Joel A. Wallis. Reg: 1 Mar 1841.

Page 231 - 8 Jul 1840. Sarah Gollathan and others to Phereby Ditto. Relinquishment. By sonsent of parties, a division of negro property of the estate of John Ditto, deceased, has taken place, a negro woman Lucy and her child fell to Phereby Ditto. Wit: E. J. Frierson and Peter Lee. Signed by: Sarah Gollathan, A. Y. Wallis, Cynthia Wallis, John McGuire, and William Mullins. Reg: 8 Mar 1841.

Page 231 - 8 Jul 1840. Pherebe Ditto and others to Sarah Gollathan. Relinquishment. Division of negro property of the estate of John Ditto, deceased, two negro girls Judy and Sophia fell to Sarah Gollathan. The undersigned: John McGuire and William Mullins, guardian for the heirs of Mary McGuire, dec'd. Wit: E. J. Frierson and Peter Lee. Signed by: Pherebe Ditto, A. Y. Wallis, Cynthia Wallis, John McGuyre, and William Mullins. Reg: 8 Mar 1841.

Page 238 - 10 Mar 1841. Mary Temple, Preston Frazier and William F. Long. Marriage Agreement. William F. Long of Talledga Co., Alabama first part, Mary Temple of Bedford Co., TN second part and Preston Frazier of Bedford Co., third part. Whereas a marriage is shortly intended between William F. Long and Mary Temple and it being the desire of each party of the first and second parts of this indenture, that the property now owned by one shall not become responsible for the debts or contracts of the other, also each may be restrained from using and exercising the same control which they now own. They entered into the marriage contract. Wit: M. A. Long and W. R. Mann. Reg: 11 Mar 1841.

Page 248 - 20 Jul 1839. Lewis F. Thompson and wife Minerva to G. W. Bright. Deed, one half of 60 acres. Lewis F. Thompson and his wife Minerva, J. Thompson of Obion Co., TN one part and G. W. Bright of Obion Co., TN other part, land in Bedford Co., on south side of Duck River, being part os a 2000 acre tract granted by North Carolina to Alexander Robertson and it being part of undivided interest in a 60 acre tract conveyed by James Croe (Crow) to Polly L. Turnage. Borders lands of Samuel H. Card. Wit: Right T. Daniel and Jesse Farmer. Reg: 18 Mar 1841.

Page 252 - 2 Dec 1840. Sarah Springer to Price C. Steele. Deed 8/214 acre. Sarah Springer sold to Price C. Steele all her interest in and to a tract of land in Bedford Co., TN, in District No. 5, her part being eighth part of a tract of land that James Cooper willed to his wife Elizabeth during her natural life and then to his eight youngest children, to wit, Sarah Springer, Jane Cooper now Jane Harris, Washington B. Cooper, Elizabeth B. Steele, Catharine Steele, Jonathan Cooper, William A. Cooper, and Malinda Cooper now Malinda Puckett. Wit: John Crook and James Claxton. Reg: 19 Mar 1841.

Page 258 - 20 Mar 1841. Lucy C. Low to George E., Daniel J., and Semor Low. Deed of Gift. For love and affection for her three sons, conveys all her dower in land in Bedford Co., TN, in District No. 19, adjoining the lands of Isaac B. Larue, Thomas Davidson, David Patrick, land belonging to the heirs of Lucy C. Low's late husband William Low, deceased. Including the dwelling house, also her household furniture and cattle &c. Wit: Thomas Coffey and Albert Anderson. Reg: 26 Mar 1841.

Page 262 - 5 Jan 1841. William Sugg to Nehemiah Sugg. 178½ acres. William Sugg one part and Nehemiah Sugg other part, both of Bedford Co., TN. William Sugg sold his undivided half in a tract on which he lives, the other half being sold by him to Nehemiah Sugg on 4 Aug 1834. Bounded by Wartrace Fork, Mill Pond near the Mill House, top of the ridge, Gilmore's line, William Sugg's line of his old 170 acre tract, near Davis Smith's shop, and the school land. William to keep possession of the houses which he now occupies and the field on the south side of the apple orchard &c during William's lifetime also during the natural life of his wife Jemima Sugg should she outlive William and live as his widow. Wit: G. G. Osborne and Jesse M. Davis. Reg: 26 Mar 1841.

Page 276 - 16 May 1834. Samuel Bingham and others to Daniel Putman. Deed 14 acres. Samuel Bigham, Hugh B. Bigham, Nancy Bigham, Margaret S. Bigham, Maria C. Bigham, James Bigham, and Sarah Bigham, all of Bedford Co., TN and James Clarke of Rutherford Co., TN, and William Bigham of Mecklenburg Co., NC, all heirs of John Bigham, deceased of one part and Daniel Putman of Bedford Co., other part, land in Bedford Co., on North Fork. Bounded by Weakleys Creek. Wit: Thomas McKnight and Robert McCrory. Reg: 7 April 1841.

Page 279 - 9 Feb 1841. Blackman C. Dobson to Martha W. Whitney. Blackman C. Dobson of Johnson Co., Illinois one part and Martha W. Whitney of Bedford Co., TN other part, sold all his claim and right to the estate of which Archibald Dobson, a brother of Blackman C. Dobson, died seized of. Recorded in Pope Co., IL. Reg: 7 Apr 1841.

Page 284 - 19 Mar 1841. Alexander McCorkle and wife Mary to Joseph McKinley. 1/7 of 140 acres, 20 acres. Alexander McCorkle and Mary McCorkle his wife formerly Mary Worke of Pope Co., IL one part and Joseph McKinley of Bedford Co., TN other part, land in Bedford Co., it being the one seventh part of 140 acres of land which Alexander Worke, father to Mary McCorkle, died seized. Reg: 10 Apr 1841.

Page 286 - 10 Oct 1840. Joseph Galleghy and others to Jesse and John Cawthron. 127 acres. Joseph M. Galleghy, James D. Galleghy, William M. Maxwell and Harriet L. Maxwell his wife formerly Harriet L. Galleghy, all of Wilson Co., TN, sold to Jesse and John Cawthron of Bedford Co., TN, land in Bedford Co., in District No. 2, on the headwaters of Strait Creek, formerly known by the name of Ephraim Galleghy tract and sold by John S. Wood to William P. Finch and by Finch to Reuben Couch and by Couch to Jesse and John Cawthron. Bounded by lands formerly owned by Thomas Drake, Sr., John Anderson, E. Haynes, Jacob Anderson and Robert Thogmorton. The part they sell being one tenth of a tract which they inherit as heir of Gardner Galleghy who was a brother of Ephraim Galleghy and Ephraim dying without children. Wit: G. G. Osborne and William P. Finch. Reg: 10 Apr 1841.

Page 287 - 23 Nov 1835. William Ward and wife to F. G. Ake. 1/10 of 262 acres. William Ward and Leah Ward his wife of Franklin Co., TN one part and F. G. Ake of Franklin Co., TN other part, all their interest which is one tenth, to land in Bedford Co., TN, on waters of the Wartrace Creek. Bounded by James' land, Burrell Featherston, Elkin's line and William Sample and others. Wit: Jethro Goodman and Walter Mileham. Reg: 12 Apr 1841.

Page 288 - 21 Feb 1837. John E. Price and Nancy C. Price to Felix G. Ake. 262 acres. John E. Price and his wife Nancy C. Price of Hamilton Co., TN one part and Felix G. Ake of Franklin Co., TN other part, their undivided inheritance, is entitled to as heirs at law of the estate of Joseph Ake, deceased, of land in Bedford Co., TN, whereon Joseph Ake, deceased, and on the waters of the Wartrace Fork. Wit: Walter Mileham, William J. Peacock, Henry A. Rains and E. M. Tatum. Reg: 19 Apr 1841.

Page 289 - 8 Oct 1839. C. B. H. Ake and others to F. G. Ake. 262 acres. C. B. H. Ake, William Ake, and Joseph H. Ake of Crawford Co., Arkansas one part and F. G. Ake of Crawford Co., Arkansas other part, land in Bedford Co., TN, on waters of the Wartrace Fork, now occupied by Thomas Peacock. Bounded by B. Featherston, widow Clardy, William Samples, and James and others. Wit: E. M. Tatum and Castleton Ake. Reg: 12 Apr 1841.

Page 290 - 18 Oct 1839. Walter Mileham and Elizabeth Mileham to F. G. Ake. 262 acres. Walter Mileham and his wife Elizabeth sold their one tenth of an undivided tract of land in Bedford Co., TN, in District No. 4, it being the tract of which Joseph Ake, deceased, died seixed and it being the distributive shares of Jefferson Jackson H. Ake and Elizabeth Mileham, heirs of Joseph Ake, deceased. Borders Farwick Frazer, William P. Elkins, William P. Sample, Theodocia H. Clardy, Robert H. Majors, and Burrell Featherston. Wit: H. L. Davidson and John Bell. Reg: 12 Apr 1841.

Page 292 - 24 Mar 1841. Robert K. and Mary B. Haley to Burrell Featherston. Robert K. Haley and his wife Mary B. Haley of Franklin Co., Alabama, one tenth of an undivided tract of land in Bedford Co., TN, in District No. 4, it being the tract that Joseph Ake, deceased, died seized of, the one tenth being the share of Robert K. Hailey and his wife Mary B. Haley, as heirs of Joseph Ake, deceased. Bounded by Farwick Frazer, William P. Elkins, Styras A. Mash, Theodocia H. Clardy and Burrell Featherston. Wit: Robert H. Majors and William J. Peacock. Reg: 13 Apr 1841.

Page 297 - 27 Aug 1840. James A. Wilson and wife Nancy to Isaac Noblitt. 164 acres. Whereas by descent from John Noblitt, deceased, James A. Wilson and Nancy Wilson his wife, now hold equal and undivided interest in land in Bedford Co., TN. Borders Jordan Mullins, Isaac Noblitt, Peterson Grammer, Thomas Conwell and Henry Dean. Land included land whereon the widow Sarah Noblitt now lives. Wit: Henry Dean, Thomas Morris, L. W. Barrett and John Grammer. Reg: 15 Apr 1841.

Page 298 - 23 Mar 1841. Mosby Harris to Newton C. and Rebecca S. Harris. 100 acres. All of Bedford Co., TN, land in Bedford Co., on Wartrace Fork, except he reserves in the foregoing lands and a home and a descent support for himself and his belobed wife Judith during their lifetime. Wit: F. D. Haggard and Granville H. Frazer. Reg: 19 Apr 1841.

Page 301 - 17 Apr 1841. Jemima H. Light to Samuel Carter. Power of Attorney. Jemima H. Light of Bedford Co., TN appointed Samuel Carter of Halifax Co., VA, as her Attorney, to receive any monies, rents &c. Also appointed her brother Melchezedeck Brame of Bedford Co., TN to receive any monies &c of Samuel Carter. Wit: William B. M. Brame and Gabriel B. Knight. Reg: 21 Apr 1841.

Page 302 - 2 Apr 1841. Tabitha Jordan to Winston W. Jordan. 200 acres. Tabitha Jordan sold to Winston W. Jordan, all her interest in land in Bedford Co., TN, in District No. 18, it being the land whereon Zachariah Jordan formerly lived and dec'd and where Tabitha Jordan now lives. Borders lands of P. S. Doty, James C. Gambill, Moses Cheves, Thomas Moore and Tabitha Jordan's land. Wit: Thomas C. Williams and Ethen L. Jordan. Reg: 21 Apr 1841.

Page 320 - 4 May 1841. James H. Arnold to Peter Lee. Deed in Trust. Whereas by the death of Hugh Snelling, the grandfather of James H. Arnold's wife Louisa H., she became entitled as distributee of Snelling and as an heir at law to a portion of the estate of Snelling which estate has not yet been divided, Jas. H. Arnold sells to Peter Lee all rights &c to the estate of negroes and lands of the estate. Reg: 4 May 1841.

Page 341 - 24 Mar 1841. Nancy Dorrell to Martha Beasley. Deed of Gift. Nancy Dorrell, for love and affection for Martha Beasley, conveyed unto her two negroes Manuel and Amy and other personal property. Wit: George Cortner and Isaac Keck. Reg: 22 May 1841.

Page 347 - 1 Jan 1839. Thomas Davis and John S. Davis, Executors &c to E. H. Popejoy, Jr. Thomas Davis and John S. Davis, Executors of H. Davis, deceased, of Bedford Co., TN one part and Edward H. Popejoy of Bedford Co., TN other part, land in Bedford CO., in the Town of Fairfield and known as Lot No. 21 and No. 29. Wit: J. W. Ragsdale and James L. Armstrong. Reg: 31 May 1841.

Page 348 - 31 May 1841. Thomas and John S. Davis to Thomas Stephens. Deed. Thomas Davis and John S. Davis, Executors of Henry Davis, deceased, of Bedford Co., TN one part and Thomas Stephens of Bedford Co., other part, land in Town of Fairfield and known as Lot No. 25. Wit: Richard H. Sims and H. T. Blanton. Reg: 31 May 1841. (Also see page 353). Sold Lot No. 22 in Fairfield. Wit: William B. Gowen and Minos Cannon, Jr. Reg: 3 Jun 1841.

Page 355 - 15 Aug 1836. Robert W. Mitchell and Isabella Mitchel to Thomas McCall. Deed 97½ acres. Robert W. Mitchell and Isabella Mitchell of Hardeman Co., TN one part and Thomas McCall of Bedford Co., TN other part, land in Bedford Co., on Wilsons Creek. Wit: J. B. Shuffield, John Little and Daniel Little. Reg: 7 Jun 1841.

Page 357 - 3 Jun 1841. William B. Phillips and Malinda Ann his wife to William F. Cooper. Deed 174½ acres. William B. Phillips, Jr. and Malinda Ann his wife one part and William F. Cooper other part, all of Bedford Co., TN, whereas two judgements against William F. Cooper and John S. Cooper, judgements in favor of C. F. Sutton and Samuel Phillips, guardians of the minor heirs of John Sutton, deceased, William B. and Malinda A. Phillips sold their undivided interest in land belonging to the estate of Charles Cooper, deceased, land in Bedford Co., on Fall Creek. Also sold slaves. Wit: Samuel P. Phillips and James B. Phillips. Reg: 7 Jun 1841.

Page 361 - 1 May 1841. Allen Chandler and Frances Chandler to John A. Chandler. Deed 330 acres. Allen Chandler and Frances Chandler his wife, conveyed to John A. Chandler, land in Pittsylvania Co., VA. Reg: 8 Jun 1841.

Page 370 - 8 Jun 1841. Samuel Mitchell to Catharine H. T. Davis and others. Deed of Gift. Samuel Mitchell of Arkansas Co., Arkansas, for love and affection for Catharine H. T. Davis, Henrietta S. Davis, Caroline M. M. Davis and William John Davis, children of John and Catharine Davis of Bedford Co., TN. They received personal property, stock &c. Wit: Thomas J. Peacock and Farwick Frazer. Reg: 9 Jun 1841.

Page 377 - 14 Jun 1841. George Davidson to William Pepper. Deed, ½ of 500 acres. George Davidson sold to William Pepper, both of Bedford Co., TN, land in Bedford Co., reserving the dwelling house, out houses &c during the life of John Davidson, Jr., the father of George Davidson. Land on Knobb Creek. Borders E. Hord, Kelly's corner, Elias Yeates' old place, and Vincent Smith. Wit: William B. M. Brame and Wilkins Blanton. Reg: 15 Jun 1841.

Page 383 - 15 Sep 1840. John P. Steele to the heirs of Thomas P. Burns, deceased. Deed 106 acres. John P. Steele of Bedford Co., TN one part and William Burns, John H. Burns, Robert S. Burns, Thomas K. Burns and James P. Burns, children and heirs of Thomas P. Burns, deceased, of Bedford Co., land in Bedford Co., on Falling Creek, in District No. 8. Bounded by the heirs of Joseph McElwrath, deceased, John Overcast, lands formerly owned by John McClain, deceased, lands of Wilson Steele, dec'd., and John Woods. The land being the tract whereupon Thomas P. Burns resided at the time of his death. Wit: James M. Johnson and William Houston, Jr. Reg: 17 Jun 1841.

Page 387 - 21 Jun 1841. Larkin B. and Martha orr to David Orr. Larkin B. Orr and Martha Orr his wife sold to David Orr, all of Bedford Co., TN, their interest in the estate of William Carter, deceased, in right of Martha Orr who is one of the children heirs. Reg: 21 Jun 1841.

Page 398 - 29 Jun 1841. John B. Read to James S. Childress. Power of Attorney. John B. Read of Maringo Co., Alabama, owns one fourth part of a tract of land about four miles north of Shelbyville, Bedford Co., TN, it being belonging to Mary Childress, James S. Childress, E. Walker and himself, John B. Read. John B. Read appointed James S. Childress my Attorney to sell his interest in said tract. Reg: 29 Jun 1841.

Page 399 - 13 Apr 1841. Mary Childress to James S. Childress. Power of Attorney. (Same as above instrument). Reg: 29 Jun 1841.

Page 399 - 1 May 1841. James S. Childress to John C. Coldwell. Deed 983 acres. James S. Childress inbehalf of himself and John B. Read and Mary Childress of Tuscaloosa Co., Alabama one part and John C. Coldwell of Bedford Co., TN other part, land in Bedford Co., on Falling Creek about four miles north of Shelbyville. Bounded by the heirs of Charles Cooper, deceased. Wit: Thomas P. Mitchell, J. G. Carroll, William H. Wisener and James M. Johnson. Reg: 29 Jun 1841.

Page 403 - 30 Jun 1841. John Muse to Eve Muse his wife. Deed of Settlement. John Muse of Bedford Co., TN, for regards for his wife Eve and inconsideration that the property which he now owns belonged to Eve Muse before her marriage with John Muse and that they, John and Eve, cannot live together, sell land to Austin Shofner of Bedford Co., all his property. Wit: John Shofner and William H. Wisener. Reg: 30 Jun 1841.

Page 404 - 3 Jul 1841. Thomas Brown and Sarah his wife to Thomas J. Brown. Deed 100 acres. Thomas Brown and Sarah Brown his wife of Bedford Co., TN one part and Thomas J. Brown of Bedford Co., other part. Sold all their undivided interest in a tract of land in Bedford Co., near the road that leads from Shelbyville to Columbia, about two miles from Shelbyville, it being land owned by the late Daniel Dwyer and upon which he lived at the time of his death. Reg: 5 Jul 1841.

Page 417 - 5 Jun 1841. Moses Woodfin and others to John D. Gilmore and Benjamin Brothers. Power of Attorney. We, Moses Woodfin and Rebecca Woodfin of Gibson Co., TN and John Woodfin of Fayette Co., TN, appointed John D. Gilmore of (blank) Co., and Benjamin Brothers of Rutherford Co., TN, or either of them, as our Attorney for the purpose, to wit, at the death of Nicholas Woodfin of Bedford Co., TN, the widow and children of Nicholas Woodfin, deceased, are seized of and are equal owners in land on which Nicholas Woodfin lived and died in Bedford Co. The land may be sold and proceeds equally divided among widow and heirs. Reg: 23 Jul 1841.

Page 421 - 16 Mar 1841. Peter F. Brumfield to William Stewart. Relinquishment, 51 acres. Peter F. Brumfield of Bedford Co., TN, relinquished all rights &c to land on waters of Big Flat Creek, willed by his father Joseph Brumfield to Anna Brumfield and at her death to be equally divided among all of his heirs.

Wit: Robert Snoddy and Ezekiel Sisk. Reg: 8 Jul 1841.

Page 424 - 16 Mar 1841. David Brumfield to William Stewart. Relinquishment, 50 acres. David Brumfield of Bedford Co., TN, relinquished his interest &c in land in Bedford Co., on waters of Big Flat Creek, willed from his father Joseph Brumfield to Anna Brumfield and at her death to be equally divided among his heirs. Wit: J. F. Norman and A. C. Wood. Reg: 31 Jul 1841.

Page 441 - 21 Jul 1841. H. Austin and A. Bruton to A. W. Reagor. Deed 11 acres. Harris Austin and Amelia Bruton one part and A. W. Reagor other part, all of Bedford Co., TN, sold land in Bedford Co., on waters of Big Flat Creek, being part of the lands which Bruton inherited of her father's estate, John Bruton interest in same having been sold for debt, Austin purchaser. Land borders Reagor's land, Peter Raney, William Boone, Henry Hart's corner. Wit: William Boone and James Wilson. Reg: 6 Aug 1841.

Page 446 - 23 Nov 1838. George Nease, Sr. to Jacob Albright. Bill of Sale. George Nease, Sr. of Bedford Co., TN (Orange Co., NC), sold to Jacob Albright, his son in law of distributing Nease's property amongst his children, negro slaves. Wit: George Noah and William Sharp. Reg: 11 Aug 1841.

DEED BOOK "LL" 1841 - 1842

Page 8 - 16 Aug 1841. J. F. Norman to William Heaslett. Bill of Sale. John F. Norman of Bedford Co., TN sold to William Heaslett all interest &c in a negro girl Ealsy and three children Ann, Toney and Martha, now in the possession of the widow Sarah Hubbard. Wit: H. Edde and Elijah Crier. Reg: 23 Aug 1841.

Page 10 - 11 Nov 1839. James Mullins, Executor to Gable Blackwell. John B. Pinson, now deceased, sold to John W. Hamlin, a Town Lot No. 86 in Shelbyville, and whereas John B. Pinson has departed this life before he made any title deed and I, James Mullins, was appointed his Executor, issue Gabriel Blackwell title to same. Reg: 24 Aug 1841.

Page 13 - 23 Aug 1841. Thomas Allison to M. S. Sims. Deed of Gift. For love and affection Thomas Allison has for Matilda S. Sims, his daughter and the wife of Brigg G. Sims, give unto her one negro boy George. Wit: William Collins and Bennet Pyland. Reg: 15 Aug 1841.

Page 13 - 25 Oct 1840. James Burrow and Margaret Burrow to James M. Jones. James Burrow and Margaret Burrow his wife one part and James M. Jones other part, all of Bedford Co., TN, on waters of Big Flat Creek, in the division of the lands of Jacob Wilhoite, deceased, amongst his heirs, fell to Willis Wilhoite, deceased, it being one seventh of the land of Willie, deceased. Wit: G. H. Phillips and Philip Phillips. Reg: 25 Aug 1841.

Page 14 - 25 Sep 1840. James M. Jones and wife to William Dwyer. 170 acres, 1/5 of. James M. Jones and Mary Jones his wife to William Dwyer, all of Bedford Co., TN, land in Bedford Co., on waters of Big Flat Creek, it being the lot which fell to Willie Wilhoite, deceased, in the division of lands of Jacob

Wilhite, deceased. Wit: William Bateman and Samuel Morris. Reg: 25 Aug 1841.

Page 29 - 11 Sep 1841. Alexander Greer to John Moseley. A. Greer sold to John Moseley all his interest to an undivided share of the estate of Frances Greer, deceased, mother of Alexander Greer. Reg: 11 Sep 1841.

Page 30 - 18 May 1841. William Guy, Trustee to James and Elizabeth Bell. 131 acres. William Guy one part and James Bell and Elizabeth Bell other part, all of Bedford Co., TN. Whereas on 10 Apr 1837, William Patton executed a certain deed in trust to William Guy, a Trustee to secure payment of a certain note to John A. Davidson, a tract of land in Bedford Co., on waters of North Fork. Bounded by lands devised by Alexander Worke, late of North Carolina, to the heirs of James Scott, deceased. Wit: Sebastian Patton and Joseph Payton. Reg: 11 Sep 1841.

Page 33 - 7 Sep 1841. Mary Biggers to James M. Robinson. Mary Biggers sold James M. Robinson, her undivided interest as one of the heirs at law of John Robinson, Sr., deceased, to all the lands which belonged to John Robinson, Sr., at the time of his death. Land in Bedford Co. Wit: Joseph Robinson and Joseph M. Burnett. Reg: 14 Sep 1841.

Page 33 - 1 Sep 1841. Hundley Wiggins to Sarah Wiggins. Bill of Sale. Hundley Wiggins of Bedford Co., TN, for love and affection for Sarah Wiggins wife of Harrell Wiggins, a negro girl Almira and at her death to go to her two sons David and Herbert Wiggins, being her two youngest sons. Reg: 14 Sep 1841.

Page 36 - 11 Sep 1841. James Coats to David Blessing, for the use of Elzira McFarling. Inconsideration of love and affection for his sister Elzira McFarling, conveyed a negro girl Rebecca. Reg: 21 Sep 1841.

Page 36 - 20 Aug 1839. Elias Yeates to Ibby Meadows. Deed of Gift, 122 acres. Elias Yeates for love and affection for his daughter Ibby Meadows, conveyed land in Bedford Co., TN, on waters of the Barren Fork. Borders Allen Knight, Zachariah Culley, Fergus Hall and Samuel Yeates. Wit: Allen Knight, James Thompson, James Murrell and Thomas Murrell. Reg: 23 Sep 1841.

Page 39 - 23 Sep 1841. Green Bowers to Benjamin F. Bowers. Release. Received of Benjamin F. Bowers, one of the heirs of John Bowers, deceased, $100.00 in full of his distributive share of his interest in a tract of land left his mother by his father during her life, conveyed to Benjamin F. Bowers. Reg: 27 Sep 1841.

Page 42 - 30 Sep 1841. Johnathan Moseley to Elizabeth Blackwell. Whereas by my Last Will and Testament, I have bequeathed to Elizabeth Blackwell, wife of John Blackwell, during her life, negroes, Eliza, Capey, Peggy and Mary. Reg: 30 Sep 1841.

Page 42 - 27 Sep 1841. James D. Davis to George Marion Davis. Deed of Gift. For love and affection for George Marion Davis, conveyed a mare. Reg: 30 Sep 1841.

Page 45 - 14 Nov 1840. Andrew Reed and others to Thomas Holland. Deed, 17 acres. We, Andrew Reed and wife Malinda, John Reed and wife Lovicey, William McFarling and wife Elzira, James Coats, Claborn W. Coats, Thomas Lipscomb, Willie B. Watkins, William Coats, Benjamin Coats, conveyed ti Thomas Holland, Jr. and his heirs, our undivided interest in land in Bedford Co., TN, in a certain lot of land known in the division of the lands of Wilson Coats, deceased, as Lot No. 10. Said land formerly owned by Balie W. Coats, deceased, in said division. Signed by Andrew Reed, Malinda Reed, J. N. Reed, Lovicia Reed, James Coats, Thomas Lipscomb, Joseph Alexander, Attorney in fact for William Coats, W. B. Watkins, Claiborne W. Coats, Benjamin Coats, by his Attorney J. N. Reed, William R. McFarling and Elzira McFarling. Reg: 2 Oct 1841.

Page 54 - 10 Jul 1841. Dudley H. Lindsey to Joseph Lindsey. Bill of Sale. D. H. Lindsey conveyed to Joseph Lindsey, his interest in the estate of Caleb Lindsey, deceased, negroes. Negroes willed by Caleb Lindsey, deceased, to Temperance Lindsey his wife during her natural life and at her death or marriage, to go to the legatees of Caleb Lindsey, deceased. Wit: John Leiper and William F. Leiper. Reg: 7 Oct 1841.

Page 59 - 9 Oct 1841. Eveline and Andrew Hartsfield to Joshua Hall. Bill of Sale. Sold slave Jane. Wit: John Hartsfield and William Solomon. Reg: 9 Oct 1841.

Page 61 - 15 Oct 1841. Alexander Greer to John Moseley. Deed 107 acres. Alexander Greer of Green Co., Alabama and John Moseley of Bedford Co., TN, land in Bedford Co., TN, on waters of Sugar Creek, being a part of a tract of land, late the property of Joseph A. Greer, deceased, and known in as in the division of land among the heirs of Joseph A. Greer, as Lot No. 2. Bounded by Benjamin Moseley, William Gammill, Thomas Alexander Greer and Henry Turpin. Reg: 15 Oct 1841.

Page 62 - 15 Oct 1841. Alexander Greer to John Moseley. Alexander Greer conveyed to John Moseley his interest in undivided share of estate of Frances Greer, deceased. Frances Greer is my mother. Reg: 15 Oct 1841.

Page 64 - 18 Oct 1841. Samuel Phillips and Gordentia Waite, Administrators vs Julia P. Waite and others. Copy of Decree. April Term 1838. Samuel Phillips and Gordentia Waite, administrators of Robert Waite, deceased vs Julia P. Waite and others, heirs at law of Robert Waite. Bill for sale of land. Land being three fourth mile north of Shelbyville. Bounded by the Nashville, Murfreesboro and Shelbyville Turnpike Road, John Eakin, Thomas J. Purdy, Daniel Gilchrist, sold off to John Blessing. Reg: 21 Oct 1841.

Page 67 - 12 Oct 1833. James Erwin by A. Erwin, Attorney &c to Martha Slaton. Deed 2+ acres. James Erwin of Fayette Co., KY by his Attorney in fact Andrew Erwin, Jr. of Bedford Co., TN one part and Mrs. Martha Slaton widow of the late James Slaton, deceased, of Bedford Co., other part, land in Bedford Co., on waters of Strait Creek. Borders Mrs. Slaton's spring, Crittendons' corner, William P. Finch, tract whereon Mrs. Slaton now lives. Wit: John F. Hall and Jas. Searcy. Reg: 22 Oct 1841.

Page 68 - 1 Oct 1841. Jonathan Moseley to Theresa Curtis. Deed of Gift, negroes. Whereas by my Last Will and Testament, I have bequeathed to my daughter Theresa Curtis wife of James Curtis, negroes, for life. Reg: 22 Oct 1841.

Page 69 - 20 Sep 1841. Lemuel Snelling and others to L. H. Arnold. Deed 164½ acres. Lemuel Snelling, John Snelling, Susannah Searcy, James H. Arnold and his wife L. H. Arnold, R. S. McConnell and his wife Frances, and Elizabeth Snelling, the heirs of Hugh Snelling, deceased, all of Bedford Co., TN. They are heirs to a tract of land in Bedford Co., on the waters of the Garrison Fork of Duck River. Adjoining lands of William Hooser, Peter Lee, Matthew Mullins, Lemuel Snelling, N. Noble, A. Mullins, and Brandon King, Frances King, bank of the Garrison at the mouth of the Wartrace Fork, Pannel tract. Wit: George Cortner, Peter Lee, A. E. Mullins and Neeley Coble. Signed by John Snelling, Susannah Searcy, Robert S. McConnell, Frances McConnell, E. Snelling by her guardian J. A. Moore, and Lemuel Snelling. Reg: 22 Oct 1841.

Page 70 - 20 Sep 1841. John Snelling and others to Lemuel Smelling. Deed 238½ acres. Lemuel Snelling, John Snelling, Susannah Searcy, James H. Arnold and his wife L. H. Arnold, R. S. McConnell and his wife Frances, and Elizabeth Snelling, the heirs of Lemuel Snelling, deceased, all of Bedford Co., TN, land in Bedford Co., on waters of the Garrison Fork, adjoining lands of William Hooser, Peter Lee, Matthew Mullins, Lemuel Snelling, N. Coble, A. Mullins, and Brandon King. Wit: George Cortner and Peter Lee. Signed by John Snelling, L. H. Arnold, Jas. H. Arnold, Susannah Searcy, Frances McConnell, Robert S. McConnell, and Elizabeth Snelling by her guardian J. A. Moore. Reg: 22 Oct 1841.

Page 72 - 20 Sep 1841. Lemuel Snelling to R. S. McConnell. 125½ acres. (Same as above instrument) Reg: 22 Oct 1841.

Page 74 - 20 Sep 1841. Lemuel Snelling and others to Susannah Searcy. 199½ acres. (Same as above instrument) Reg: 23 Oct 1841.

Page 75 - 20 Sep 1841. Lemuel Snelling and others to Elizabeth Snelling. Deed 150 acres. (Same as above instrument) Reg: 23 Oct 1841.

Page 76 - 20 Sep 1841. Lemuel Snelling and others to John Snelling. Deed 123½ acres. (Same as above instrument) Reg: 23 Oct 1841.

Page 89 - 1 Nov 1841. Gabriel Blackwell to Nancy Jane Edgar. Relinquishment. Gabriel Blackwell relinquishes all claim to Nancy J. Edgar, to land whereon Nancy J. Edgar now lives, about 30 acres, about one mile of Shelbyville, deeded to him by John Edgar. Reg: 2 Nov 1841.

Page 94 - 4 Nov 1841. Turner Wilhoite and Sophronia Wilhoite to Samuel B. McCuistion. 100 acres. Turner Wilhoite and Sophronia formerly Sophronia Dwyer, conveyed to Samuel B. McCuistion, land owned by Daniel Dwyer, deceased. Reg: 5 Nov 1841.

Page 95 - 21 Oct 1841. Joseph Kincaid and Arey E. Kincaid to John C. Coldwell. Deed. Joseph Kincaid and Arey E. Kincaid his wife of Bedford Co., TN, sold to John C. Coldwell of Bedford Co., land, being one fourth of a 32 acre tract on north side of Duck River. Borders lands of Amos Balch, Banjamin McCuistion, Warner's road and Howel Tatum. Reg: 5 Nov 1841.

Page 96 - 21 Oct 1841. James H. Kincaid and Caroline C. Kincaid to John C. Coldwell. Deed 32 acres. James H. Kincaid and Caroline C. Kincaid of Platt Co., MO sold to John C. Coldwell land on north side of Duck River of Bedford Co., TN. Borders Amos Balch, Benjamin McCuistion, Warner's road, and Howel Tatum. Reg: 6 Nov 1841.

Page 97 - 15 Oct 1841. William E. Suiter and Nancy E. Suiter to Isaac West. Deed 48 acres. Land in Bedford Co., TN, in District No. 3. Borders Charles Harryman and Gannaway's line. Wit: Peter Lee and Levi Thronburg. Reg: 6 Nov 1841.

Page 98 - 21 Oct 1841. John Thompson to Joseph R. McKinley. Deed 47 acres. All interest in a tract of land in Bedford Co., TN, in District No. 5, on waters of North Fork. The lot of said lot containing 190 acres belonging to the heirs of Sarah Guy. John Thompson's wife a devisee of Col. Alexander Worke, late of Iredell Co., NC, all his interest about 47 acres undivided. Reg: 6 Nov 1841.

Page 102 - 8 Nov 1841. Joshua Hall to Evalina Hartsfield. Agreement. Evalina Hartsfield is to take a negro girl Jane and keep her until Joshua Hall pays G. E. Hartsfield $220.28. Wit: John Hartsfield and Mary Hartsfield. Reg: 11 Nov 1841.

Page 102 - 11 Nov 1841. William Pratt and Mary A. C. Pratt to Minos Cannon. 40 acres. Land in Bedford CO., TN, in District No. __. Borders lands of Minos Cannon, deceased, of David Sims and Edmund Green. Reg: 13 Nov 1841.

Page 118 - 30 Nov 1841. Jane Eakin and others to John Eakin and others. Deed. Whereas Spencer Eakin, late of Nashville, TN, lately departed this life intestate, and without issue, leaving John, William and Thomas Eakin, and the undersigned, Jane and Mary Eakin, Sarah and Jane Cowan, Alexander Eakin and Eliza McClellans, his heirs at law and distributees and leaving a large personal property. Thomas Eakin, Administrator of Spencer Eakin. Signed by Jane Eakin, Mary Jane Eakin, John W. Cowan, Jane Cowan, William G. Cowan, Sarah Cowan, James J. McClelland, Eliza McClelland and Alexander Eakin. Reg: 2 Dec 1841.

Page 120 - 1 Dec 1841. John Scott to Mary Scott Yell. Deed of Gift. John Scott of Bedford Co., TN, for love and affection for his granddaughter Mary Scott Yell, conveyed a mulatto girl Eliza. Reg: 6 Dec 1841.

Page 121 - 4 Dec 1841. Benjamin Braughton and wife to William A. Gaunt. Benjamin Braughton and his wife Mary Braughton formerly Mary Gaunt, sold to William A. Gaunt, land and town lots, being part of John Gaunt, deceased, estate left to his heirs. Wit: John Stephenson and John Wise. Reg: 6 Dec 1841.

Page 124 - 20 Nov 1841. Jane Eakin and others to Thomas Eakin. In Trust for Nancy Nevins. Whereas Spencer Eakin, late of Nashville, TN, lately died intestate, and without issue, leaving a sister Nancy Nevins in Ireland, who by the laws of this State is incapable of inheriting property. Reg: 6 Dec 1841.

DEED BOOK "LL"

Page 125 - 30 Nov 1841. Thomas Eakin to Jane Eakin and others. Obligation. In consideration that his mother Jane Eakin and my brothers John, Alexander and William, and my sisters Mary, Sarah and her husband William G. Cowan, Jane and her husband John W. Cowan, and Eliza and her husband James J. McClelland, conveyed to Thomas Eakin as Trustee for his sister Nancy Nevins in Ireland $888.88 each. Reg: 6 Dec 1841.

Page 126 - 3 Dec 1841. Dennis Bryant and wife to Edmund Word. 91 acres. Dennis Bryant and wife Elizabeth of Bedford Co., TN sold to Edmund Word, their interest in the tract of land of which Willis Hastings died seized of in Bedford Co., adjoining Sarah Hastings and others. Said land is where Dennis Bryant and wife Elizabeth now lives. Elizabeth being the dower intrest as the wife of Willis Hastings who was her former husband. Reg: 6 Dec 1841.

Page 134 - 27 Oct 1841. Elliott Rucker to William Rucker. 120 acres. Land in the 10th District of Bedford Co., TN, on Bylers Branch, a branch of Weakleys Creek. Bounded by John Byler and Byler's Branch, without including one acre set apart for the use of the Meeting House (Enon) and Burying Ground. Also a small piece of ground which he reserves and set apart for the purpose of burying myself and family. Beginning at the south east corner of the acre of ground set apart for the use of the Meeting House and Burying Ground, running south 15 feet to the corner of the pailing around Doc Church's grave, thence east 40 feet to east boundary line of the Meeting House tract, thence south to the beginning. Wit: Anderson Rucker and George T. Landis. Reg: 8 Dec 1841.

Page 140 - 19 Nov 1841. John H. Anderson and wife to Gabriel Blackwell. Lot No. 91. John H. Anderson and Elizabeth Anderson his wife of one part sold to Gabriel Blackwell, all of Bedford Co., TN, Lot No. 91 in Shelbyville. Wit: John T. Neil. Reg: 10 Dec 1841.

Page 141 - 10 Dec 1841. David Weaver to Sarah Lasater and Trena Weaver. Deed of Gift, 120 acres. Land in Bedford Co., TN, on West Fork of Gages Creek, it being where David Weaver, Sr. now lives. Borders Zephanial Weaver, David Weaver and John Keck. Conveyed to my daughters Sarah Lasater and Trena Weaver all my land. Wit: M. W. Nutt and A. J. Green. Reg: 10 Dec 1841.

Page 149 - 19 Nov 1841. Gabriel Blackwell to Thomas Lipscomb. Deed in Trust. Lot No. 75 in Shelbyville, in trust for the benefit of Elizabeth Anderson at the exclusion of her husband John H. Anderson and at her death to go to her children. Reg: 11 Dec 1841.

Page 158 - 23 Jan 1839. B. G. White to Robert Denniston. Deed 443 acres. B. G. White and Stokely White of Rutherford Co., TN sold to Robert Denniston of Bedford Co., TN, land in Bedford Co., upon the Wartrace Fork of Duck River. Bounded by lands formerly owned by Norville McGee, the mouth of Bell Buckle, lands of John Gowen and James Petty, William McGrew, Charles Sutton and land formerly owned by Jesse Davis. Wit: William Wood and Smith Bowlin. Reg: 16 Dec 1841.

Page 159 - -- --- 1841. John T. Muse to Richard Anderson and others, Trustees to Friendship Church. 2 acres. John T. Muse of Bedford Co., TN one part and Richard Anderson, Melchesidec Brame, Thomas Smith, John Strator and Jacob C. Muse, all of Bedford Co., Trustees &c of the other part. For $1.00, granted unto the Trustees and their successors, a tract of land in Bedford Co., and being on the waters of Sugar Creek, adjoining the land of John Strator and bounded by the lands of said Strator and the Columbia Road. For the purpose of building a Meeting House, for the Friendship Missionary Baptist Church. Wit: William Brame and Sarah Brame. Reg: 16 Dec 1841.

Page 170 - 25 Dec 1840. Circuit Court Decree to Washington P. Goodwin and others. Benjamin F. Bowers and William P. Bowers, Exparte. Report. To sell the four slaves belonging to the estate of John Bowers, deceased. Washington P. Goodwin, William McGrew, William Sutton and Martin Hancock purchased a slave each. Also James R. Terry purchased negro man Miles. Reg: 3 Jan 1842.

Page 174 - 1 Nov 1841. James P. P. Parkes and others to Sarah Parkes. Quit Claim. Whereas Joshua Parkes by his Last Will and Testament, devised to his wife Sarah Parkes, for life, the plantation on which he resided at the time of his death and as there was only one witness to the Will, makes the disposition of the land void. The undersigned are desirous that said land be sold. They relinquish and quit claim all their right and interest to said Sarah during her natural life. Signed by: James P. P. Parkes, William Gammill, Eleanor Gammill, Margaret A. Fonville, Robert Parkes, Jefferson Parkes, Cynthia S. Brown, Sarah C. Parkes and F. F. Fonville. Reg: 3 Jan 1842.

Page 179 - 4 Jan 1842. Newton C. Thompson to William G. Cowan. Bill of Sale. By virtue of a Power of Attorney, executed 2 Jan 1842 by Elizabeth Thompson, Calvin Thompson, William S. Wade and J. H. Locke, heirs and distributees of John A. Thompson, deceased, to sell, mortgage or dispose to William G. Cowan, a negro boy Jerry, for the purpose to raise money to pay off all claims against the estate of John A. Thompson, deceased. Reg: 6 Jan 1842.

Page 185 - 29 Dec 1841. Jonathan J. Cooper to Price C. Steele. Deed 1/8 of 214 acres. J. J. Cooper sold all his interest in and to land in Bedford Co., TN, in District No. 5 and 8, it being land that James Cooper willed to his wife Elizabeth Cooper during her natural life and then to his eight youngest children, to wit, Sarah Springer, Jane Cooper now Jane Harris, Washington B. Cooper, Elizabeth B. Steele, Catharine Steele, Jonathan Cooper, William Cooper, and Malinda Cooper now Malinda Puckett. Wit: V. M. Hamilton and Taliaferro Berryman. Reg: 8 Jan 1842.

Page 191 - 11 Mar 1840. Jackson C. Devore and wife Permela to James W. Devore. 25 acres. Jackson C. Devore and Pamela Devore his wife, sold to James W. Devore, land in Bedford Co., TN. Borders Presley Jones, Collin's line and Little's line. Reg: 12 Jan 1842.

Page 194 - 18 Aug 1841. James H. Claunch and wife to Nathan Bearden. Deed of Release. James H. Claunch and Charlotte Claunch his wife of Bedford Co., sold all interest in land in Bedford Co., TN, on waters of Big Flat Creek, it being the tract of land where Nancy Bearden now lives. Reg: 25 Jan 1842.

Page 198 - 21 Jan 1842. R. F. P. Jones to the heirs of J. J. Marshall. Deed of Gift. A gift to the heirs of J. J. Marshall, viz, Nancy, Hannah, John A., Richard E., Martha P., William, Jasper N., Thomas H., and James A. Marshall, personal property and other household furniture. Wit: Zeph. Anglin and W. Jones and S. Venable. Reg: 26 Jan 1842.

Page 199 - 24 Jan 1842. Solomon Ramsey to Solomon T. Ramsey. Deed of Gift, 101 acres. Solomon Ramsey for love and affection for his son Solomon T. Ramsey, conveyed land in Bedford Co., TN and being the place whereon Solomon Ramsey now resides , on the waters of Sinking Creek, in Civil District No. 18. Bounded by Sinking Creek, near John Briant's spring, David Dryden and William A. Gaunt. Wit: Jonathan England and John D. Neill. Reg: 24 Jan 1842.

Page 207 - 7 Jan 1842. Sidney S. Norville to John W. Norville. Deed 285 acres. Sold land in Bedford Co., TN, in District No. 3, it being the land whereon my mother Elizabeth W. Norville now lives, it being her dower of land, as laid off to her out of the estate of my father David Norville, deceased. Reg: 31 Jan 1842.

Page 211 - 18 Dec 1840. John W. Dawdy to William H. Craig. Deed 100 acres. By the Last Will and Testament of John Dawdy, deceased, one H. M. Dawdy and John W. Dawdy derived title to a tract of land. Bounded by Edward Johnston, Rezin Smith, and the heirs of William Craig, deceased, Henry Hazelett, Albert Anderson. The said land H. M. and John W. Dawdy has been divided. John W. Dawdy's interest in his lands is in District No. 19 of Bedford Co., being the north half of 200 acres, subject however to the life estate of Mary Dawdy. Wit: W. R. Looney and C. N. Allen. Reg: 7 Feb 1842.

Page 212 - 7 Feb 1842. P. C. Steele to Caswell Puckett. Bill of Sale. P. C. Steele sold to Caswell Puckett a family of negroes, belonging to the estate of James Cooper, deceased, which were bequeathed by him at the death of his wife, to his children, his interest in right of his wife being one eighth part of said negroes. Reg: 7 Feb 1842.

Page 216 - 8 Jan 1841. William Cooper to Price C. Steele. Deed, undivided interest. William Cooper sold to P. C. Steele land in Bedford Co., TN, in Districts No. 5 and No. 8, about 214 acres, his part being the one eighth part and it being the land that James Cooper willed to his wife Elizabeth Cooper during her natural life and then to his eight youngest children, to wit, Sarah Springer, Jane Cooper now Jane Harris, Washington B. Cooper, Elizabeth B. Steele, Catharine Steele, Jonathan Cooper, William Cooper and Malinda Cooper now Malinda Puckett. Wit: J. J. Cooper and William D. Murphree. Reg: 7 Feb 1842.

Page 218 - 4 Dec 1841. Elizabeth Cooper to Price C. Steele. Obligation &c. Elizabeth Cooper rented to Price C. Steele, her farm and land which was willed to her by her husband James Cooper, deceased, land of 214 acres. Wit: Allsea Harris and Caswell Puckett. Reg: 9 Feb 1842.

Page 219 - 4 Dec 1841. W. B. Cooper to Price C. Steele. 1/8 of 200 acres. Land in Bedford Co., TN and whereon Mrs. Elizabeth Cooper now lives. Borders Josiah Springer and Dixon's line. Wit: Allsea Harris and Jane Harris. Reg: 9 Feb 1842.

Page 219 - 12 Jan 1841. Allsea Harris and wife to Price C. Steele. 1/8 of 214 acres. Allsea Harris and Jane Harris his wife, sold to Price C. Steele, their interest in 1/8 of 214 acres in Bedford Co., TN, in Districts No. 5 and No. 8, it being land willed by James Cooper, deceased, to his wife Elizabeth Cooper and then at her death to the eight youngest children, to wit, Sarah Springer, Jane Cooper now Jane Harris, Washington B. Cooper, Elizabeth B. Steele, Catharine Steele, Jonathan Cooper, William Cooper and Malinda Cooper now Malinda Puckett. Wit: George Comer and Charles Holden. Reg: 9 Feb 1842.

Page 220 - 7 Feb 1842. Caswell Puckett and wife to P. C. Steele. 1/8 of 214 acres. Caswell Puckett and Malinda his wife, sold to P. C. Steele. (Same as above instrument) Reg: 9 Feb 1842.

Page 231 - 14 Feb 1842. John Wray to Samuel Wray. Bill of Sale. John Wray is indebted to his son Samuel Wray, both of Bedford Co., TN. Whereas Samuel Wray, deceased, formerly of Giles Co., TN, by his Last Will and Testament, bequeathed to his son Samuel Wray, some negroes, which was put into John Wray's hands for safe keeping for his son, to be delivered to him whenever he arrives at age of 21 years. Sold and conveyed away one of the negroes, Bartlett. Conveyed to his son Samuel Wray a negro boy, Cesar. Reg: 16 Feb 1842.

Page 239 - 10 Dec 1841. Circuit Court. Final Decree. To Sherwood Lisenby. William D. Baird, administrator of all and singular, the goods and chattles, rights and credits of Lewallen Jones, deceased vs John Jones, Sarah Jones, George Jones, and Mary Jones, minor heirs of Lewallen Jones, deceased. Defts. has in one undivided third part of land in Bedford Co., TN, on headwaters of Falling Creek. Borders Martin Phifer's line, William P. Anderson and Thomas Dougan. Said land was granted by State of Tennessee to John Coffee, dated 16 Aug 1816. Land a undivided part descended from John Jones at his death to Lewallen Jones and from Jones to said Defendants. Reg: 21 Feb 1842.

Page 240 - 14 Jan 1842. James M. Johnson, surviving partner &c to Martha Beasley's heirs. 4 acres. James M. Johnson and Daniel Johnson transferred to Martha Beasley and her heirs, land in Bedford Co., TN. Borders George W. Heard's lot formerly known as Heard and Lindsey's lot, center of a road, and crossfence between the house lot and field. The above property is to be for the use of Nancy Dorrell, so long as she may live and proceeds arising therefrom, it being purchased with debts due Nancy Dorrell and she made a Deed of Gift to Martha Beasley and the debts was to be put to Nancy Dorrell's use as long as she lives. Nancy Dorrell agreed the property to be purchased with said debts. Wit: C. C. Carter and A. L. Landis. Reg: 21 Feb 1842.

Page 241 - 22 Feb 1842. John Blackwell to the children of S. B. Blackwell. Deed of Gift. For love and affection for the children of my son S. B. Blackwell, who is under embarrassment, and in view of keeping the children from want and distress, John Blackwell conveys unto the children, Zeno Blackwell, Robert

Blackwell, Sumner Blackwell, the following property, furniture, personal property, cattle &c. The said property is in the possession of son S. B. Blackwell where he desires it to stay for their benefit. Reg: 25 Feb 1842.

Page 251 - 4 Feb 1842. Theodocia H. Clardy to Robert H. Majors. Deed, 57 acres. Theodocia H. Clardy sold to Robert H. Majors, both of Bedford Co., TN, land in Bedford Co., it being part of a tract that Theodocia H. Clardy, Executrix of Richard J. Clardy, deceased, bought of Isaac James, Sr. Land bounded by Robert H. Majors and Elnathan Davis. Wit: A. H. White and William W. Miller. Reg: 2 Mar 1842.

Page 259 - 7 Mar 1842. Thomas Holland, Sr. to John Thomas Holland. Deed of Gift. Thomas Holland, Sr. of Bedford Co., TN, for love and affection for his grandson John Thomas Holland, of Bedford Co., a negro boy William. Reg: 7 Mar 1842.

Page 259 - 8 Mar 1842. Edmund W. Tipton and Rachel M. Tipton to John Tillman. Deed, Dower Lot. Edmund W. Tipton and Rachel M. Tipton his wife of Obion Co., TN, sold to John Tillman, land in Bedford Co., on waters of Duck River, about three and one-half miles below Shelbyville, on north side of said river. It being the land formerly owned by Samuel Escue and purchased by him from Leonard C. Temple. Reg: 11 Mar 1842.

Page 264 - 16 Mar 1842. Blan Maupin to Gabriel Maupin. 48 acres. Blan Maupin sold to Gabriel Maupin, both of Bedford Co., TN, land in Bedford Co., on south side of the Barren Fork, it being one-half of six shares of the widow Sarah Maupin's dower. The dower was 114 acres. The half of the six part was 48 acres. Reg: 19 Mar 1842.

Page 267 - 17 Mar 1842. Moses Payne and Blan Maupin to Robert B. Maupin and others. Deed Trust. Moses Payne and Blan Maupin sold to Robert B. Maupin, George Davidson and Warner Wallace, all of Bedford Co., TN, land in Bedford Co., near Three Forks including the mills commonly known by Three Forks Mills. Borders Garrison and Barren Forks and Charles Lucas. Another tract borders road near an old smith-shop and spring and the Duck River. Another tract borders Barren Fork and the Tanyard tract. Another tract bounded by A. Erwin, Thomas H. Bernard, Garrison Fork, Barren Fork, Harmons Branch. Another tract of 8 acres includes the whole Bernard tract and bounded by Daniel Hooser, & John Bramlett. Reg: 21 Mar 1842.

Page 273 - 22 Mar 1842. Wilson G. Fuller to Daniel Dean. 50 acres. Land in Bedford Co., TN, the tract willed to W. G. Fuller by his grandfather Jacob Fuller at his wife Mary Fuller's death. Wit: J. H. Scott and C. T. Philpot. Reg: 26 Mar 1842.

Page 278 - 31 Mar 1842. Sarah Noblitt to Henry Dean and Thomas Dean. Deed to dower, 60 acres. Sarah Noblitt has a life estate in Bedford Co., TN, in District No. 22. Bounded by Cave Spring, entry to John Noblitt and Henry Dean. Wit: Isaac Noblitt and P. Grammer. Reg: 31 Mar 1842.

Page 279 - 31 Mar 1842. John Norman and Elizabeth Norman to Peterson Grammer. 1/10 of 183 acres. John Norman and Elizabeth Norman his wife and formerly Elizabeth Noblitt, sold to Peterson Grammer 1/10 of 183 acres of land in Bedford Co., TN, on Big

Flat Creek in District No. 22. Bounded by Jordan Mullins and Henry Dean, Peterson Grammer and Thomas Conwell. Wit: Thomas Dean and Henry Dean. Reg: 2 Apr 1842.

Page 301 - 27 Dec 1841. Josiah Hastings to Robert Hastings. Trust Deed, 26 acres. Josiah Hastings sold to Robert Hastings, Jr., land in Bedford Co., TN, on waters of Big Flat Creek, it being a tract allotted to Robert Hastings, Jr. by the Commissioners appointed to divide the lands of Robert Hastings, Sr., deceased, known as Lot No. 3. Reg: 12 Apr 1842.

Page 307 - 12 Apr 1842. William Warren to William Guy. Deed in Trust, 270½ acres. William Warren sold to William Guy, both of Bedford Co., TN, land from John Tilford, Executor and Trustee of the Last Will and Testament of Sarah Trotter, deceased, of Fayette Co., KY, land in Bedford Co., it being the same tract of land allotted to Sarah Trotter and her brother William Scott, deceased, as devises of the late Alexander Worke of Iredell Co., NC. The interest of William Scott having been conveyed to Sarah Trotter by his (william Scott) devisee Jefferson Scott of Bourbon Co., KY. Wit: Preston Frazer and William Walker. Reg: 18 Apr 1842.

Page 310 - 25 Sep 1841. Samson Nease and Eleanor his wife to Jordan C. Holt. Deed, 233 acres. Samson Nease and Eleanor Nease his wife sold to Jordan C. Holt, land in Bedford Co., TN in District No. 22 (willed to the aforesaid Eleanor Nease by Joshua Holt, deceased, for her use during her natural life). Borders Michael Holt, Jordan C. Holt, and the Fayetteville Road. Signed by Samson Nease and Neely C. Nease. Wit: Henry Blagg and B. Phillips. Reg: 18 Apr 1842.

Page 310 - 4 Oct 1841. Benjamin Phillips to Jordan C. Holt. Deed, undivided interest &c, 233 acres. Benjamin Phillips sold to Jordan C. Holt, land in Bedford Co., TN, in District No. 22, it being the land willed by Joshua Holt, Sr., deceased, to the heirs of Eleanor Nease. Phillip's interest being the interest of William H. Stewart and Joshua H. Stewart and Jarrel B. Smith, heirs of said Eleanor Nease. Wit: D. M. Smith and Bluford Davidson. Reg: 19 Apr 1842.

Page 311 - 1 Mar 1842. B. Phillips to J. C. Holt. Also sold property consisting of negroes, horses, cattle and household furniture, willed by George Nease, late of Orange Co., NC, to his wife Polly Nease, during her natural life. Wit: Henry Blagg and H. F. Holt. Reg: 19 Apr 1842.

Page 318 - 30 Jan 1841. Elizabeth Cheaves to Thomas Cheaves. Deed of Gift. For love and affection Elizabeth Cheaves has for her son Thomas Cheaves, conveys to him, land and stock of all kind, her entire estate. Thomas Cheaves is to pay all her debts and support her during her lifetime. Also after 12 months after her death, Thomas Cheves is to pay to Jacob H. Cheves and Moses Cheves and Calvin Cheves, and to Nancy O'Neal formerly Nancy Cheves, and Polly Oneal formerly Polly Cheves, and Rebecca Hughes formerly Rebecca Cheves, eight dollars each, all in Bedford Co., TN. Land of 43 acres on east waters of Big Sinking Creek. Bounded by the Blue Spring tract. Including 43 acres. Wit: William A. Gaunt and Absalom Trolinger. Reg: 28 Apr 1842.

DEED BOOK "LL"

Page 325 - 11 Apr 1842. G. H. Kyle, Trustee &c to Thomas D. Connally and brother. 152 acres. Whereas Calvin Thompson, by deed dated 29 Mar 1841, conveyed to him in trust, land in Bedford Co., TN, sold all interest that Calvin Thompson has in Lots No. 1 and No. 4, known as such in the division of the lands of Joseph Thompson his father and his interest in the widow's dower. Reg: 11 May 1842.

Page 328 - 13 May 1842. Shadrack S. Brown to Richard Warner. Deed of Gift in Trust &c. Shadrack S. Brown, for love and affection for maomi Tilford wife of David Tilford and her children, paid by Richard Warner of Marshall Co., TN, conveyed to said Warner, a negro girl Caroline. Reg: 16 May 1842.

Page 330 - 18 Sep 1841. William T. Harrison to James H. Harrison. Deed, undivided interest &c. Whereas by descent from Jonathan Harrison, deceased, Thomas F. Harrison, Cleveland S. Harrison, James H. Harrison, Polly Ann Harrison, Peggy Parthenia Harrison, Susanna Elvira Harrison, and myself, William T. Harrison, received title to an unequal and undivided interest in and to a tract of land in Bedford Co., TN, District No. 19, on waters of Rock and Sinking Creek. Borders T. W. Harper bought of James Dillard, James Dillard of William Williams, Margaret Price, Nathaniel Porter and Green Lovett, J. M. Gibson and Thomas Harper. 188½ acres. This land being in two purchases from Lewis Medlin and Owen Medlin, deeded to Mary Harrison, Executrix of Jonathan Harrison, deceased. Reg: 17 May 1842.

Page 333 - 4 May 1842. A. G. and Cyntha Wallis to David Hunter. Bill of Sale. A. Y. and Cyntha Wallis sold to David Hunter, a negro girl Rebecca Jane. Wit: Samuel Phillips and James M. Hunter. Reg: 17 May 1842.

Page 352 - 31 May 1842. Jacob Wilhoite to Pearce Wilhoite. Deed, 121 acres. Jacob Wilhoite sold to Pearce Wilhoite, both of Bedford Co., TN, all his undivided interest in a tract of land, being in Bedford Co., on waters of Flat Creek, it being the lot allotted to Willis Wilhoite in the division of the lands of Jacob Wilhoite, Sr., deceased, and known as Lot No. 3. It being my interest, being one seventh. Reg: 1 Jun 1842.

Page 353 - 7 Jun 1842. Carlos D. Steele and Catharine Steele to Price C. Steele. Deed, 214 acres. Carlos D. and Catharine Steele conveyed to Price C. Steele, land in Bedford Co., TN, in Districts No. 5 and No. 8. One part of tract being one eighth of a tract of land that James Cooper willed to his wife Elizabeth Cooper during her natural life and then to his eight youngest children, to wit, Sarah Springer, Jane Cooper now Jane Harris, Washington B. Cooper, Elizabeth B. Steele, Catharine Steele, Jonathan Cooper, William Cooper, and Malinda Cooper now Malinda Puckett. Reg: 8 Jun 1842.

Page 355 - 4 Jan 1840. Thomas D. Wilson to John A. Holland. Power of Attorney. Thomas D. Wilson of Caddo Parish, Louisiana, appointed John A. Holland of Williamson Co., TN, his Attorney, to sell and convey all his undivided interest in a tract of land in Bedford Co., TN, it being the same which he inherited as the heir of "my" son Walter Sims Wilson, who inherited same as the only heir of mother, one of the heirs of John G. Sims, deceased. Wit: James H. Wilson and Jason H. Wilson. Reg: 9 Jun 1842.

DEED BOOK "LL"

Page 356 - 9 Jun 1842. Mary C. Brame to Fanny J. Clay. Deed. Mary C. Brame of Bedford Co., TN, for love and affection for her sister Fanny J. Clay, conveyed to Anderson T. Clay of Bedford Co., negroes, stock and furniture. After the death of Fanny J. Clay, to go to her living children. Wit: G. B. Knight and O. W. Knight. Reg: 15 Jun 1842.

Page 358 - 9 Mar 1842. Alexander Bryant and Anna Briant to Americus Gifford. Alexander Bryant and Anna Bryant his wife, sold to Americus Gifford, all the right title and in to that Alexander and Anna Bryant has in to one eighth part of the sales of all the land belonging to the heirs of John Gaunt, deceased. Anna Bryant formerly Anna Gaunt. Wit: Jesse Phillips and Jahugh Blagg. Reg: 15 Jun 1842.

Page 361 - 15 Jun 1842. Marriage Contract between Samuel Thompson and Mary Davis. Samuel Thompson and Mary Davis, both of Bedford Co., TN, whereas a marriage is shortly intended between Samuel Thompson and Mary Davis, and they being desirous that the property which they own, at the time of marriage, shall be inherited by their respective families as if no marriage had taken place. Samuel Thompson is not to use Mary Davis' property for his debts &c. If Mary should survive Samuel Thompson, relinquishes all right to Samuel Thompson's property with the exception of a dower which is one third. Reg: 16 Jun 1842.

Page 363 - 11 Jun 1842. John A. Holland, Attorney in Fact for Thomas D. Wilson to John G. Sims and others. Deed. (4 tracts) Thomas D. Wilson of Caddo Parish, Louisiana, sold to John G. Sims, Walter H. Sims and Boyd M. Sims of Williamson Co., TN. Whereas in October 1836, John G., Walter H., and Boyd M. Sims and their sister Ann H. Sims, were as heirs of their father John G. Sims, deceased, seized of certain land in Bedford Co., TN, on Duck River. Two tracts, borders Arnold's corner, Dawdy's corner, Moors and Sutton's line, Holland's corner and Hamilton's Branch. 2nd tract, south banks of Duck River. 3rd tract, Bluff of Duck River. 4th tract, Dunaway's corner and Reaves' corner. and Whereas Thomas D. Wilson intermarried with Ann H. Sims in October 1836 and she had one child, the issue of said marriage born in October 1837 and Ann H. died in November 1837 and her child died in February 1839, Thomas D. Wilson inherited one fourth of estate. Wit: H. Nunkey and R. S. Wilson. Reg: 18 Jun 1842.

Page 366 - 17 Jun 1842. William R. McFarlin and wife Eliza to James Coats. Deed. William R. McFarlin and wife Eliza sold to James Coats, land in Bedford Co., TN, it being the tract of land owned by Wilson Coats, deceased, now the dower of Celia Coats the widow of Wilson Coats, her life time. Wit: J. N. Reed and H. C. Blessing. Reg: 18 Jan 1842.

Page 370 - 21 May 1842. Helen M. Newton to Ebenezer Newton and others. Transfer. Helen M. Newton of Bedford Co., TN, for and inconsideration that Ebenezer Newton, James Bell and wife Eliza, and Richard S. Arrington and wife Jane M., have agreed to withdraw all opposition to the establishment of the Last Will and Testament of George Newton, deceased, a contest which is pending in Circuit Court of Marshall Co., TN, by change of venue from Bedford Co., TN. She sold and conveyed to Ebenezer Newton and others, the Executors and Administrators, 3/4 of the property both real and personal devised to her by George

Newton, deceased, last Will and Testament. She reserves a life estate in all property except the slaves (5). Wit: Robert P. Harrison and William Galbreath. Reg: 20 Jun 1842.

Page 370 - 20 Jun 1842. John Ray to William Ray. Deed, 98 acres. For love and affection for his son William R. Ray, conveyed to him land in Bedford Co., TN, on waters of Sinking Creek in District No. 19. Borders Alexander Ray, Jane Ray's dower tract, Davis' line and James Davis. Reg: 20 Jun 1842.

Page 375 - 25 Jun 1842. James R. Neill and George W. Neill to Thomas Greer. Whereas by descent from the estate of William Neill, deceased, we have derived equal and undivided interest in to a certain tract of land in Bedford Co., TN, on the waters of Sinking Creek. Borders James Neill, Sr., deceased, survey, Gaunt's heirs' land, David Dryden, Henderson's land, Andrew Neill and Gilchrist's line. Wit: Andrew A. Harper and Benjamin B. Harper. Reg: 25 Jun 1842.

Page 382 - Tennessee Grant No. 9299 to Dempsey P. Temple. 100 acres. Entered on 5 Jul 1824 by No. 229. Land on south side of Duck River, on waters of Rich Creek. Borders William Chapman. Recorded in Register's office 5 July 1829. Reg: 13 Jul 1842.

Page 383 - Tennessee Grant No. 9201 to Dempsey P. Temple. 50 acres. Entered 14 Apr 1827 by No. 753. Land in Bedford Co., TN, on waters of Rock Creek. Borders William Cook. Reg: 13 Jul 1842.

Page 384 - 11 Jul 1842. Mary Temple to Robert H. Temple and others. Deed. 3 tracts of land. Mary Temple sold to Robert H. Temple, William P. Temple, and Jane T. Temple and Hannah M. Temple, all of Bedford Co., TN, for love and affection for the minor heirs of Dempsey P. Temple, deceased. One tract whereon Mary Temple now lives, in Bedford Co., TN, on north side of Duck River and below the mouth of Sugar Creek, it being part of a 1900 tract granted to Dempsey Powell and deeded by Jesse Powell to Elizabeth Temple and by her to her two sons and deeded by Leonard C. Temple and Dempsey P. Temple and willed by Dempsey P. Temple' s Last Will and Testament to Robert H. Temple and William P. Temple and Jane T. Temple and Hannah M. Temple, the land being on north side of Duck River. 95 acres. 2nd tract, in Bedford Co., on waters of Rich Creek and borders William Cook. 50 acres, to above heirs. 3rd tract, 100 acres in Bedford Co., on south side of Duck River, on waters of Rich Creek and borders William Chapman. 4th tract, sold all household and kitchen furniture and farming tools and all stock, Crops &c, willed by Dempsey P. Temple to his four children, Mary Temple reserves a descent and support out of above lands &c during her natural life. Wit: Granville H. Frazer. Reg: 13 Jul 1842.

Page 404 - 14 Aug 1841. John Stone to James B. Reagor. Deed 290 acres. John Stone sold to James B. Reagor, both of Bedford Co., TN, land in Bedford Co., on both sides of Big Flat Creek, it being the tract whereon P. H. Prewit formerly lived, a 175 acres of which was willed to P. H. Prewitt by his father Michael Prewitt, deceased, the balance 120 acres that P. H. Prewit purchased from John G. Brown. Land borders James Cheshire, Henry Lynn and where he now lives, D. D. Hix, the Stage Road, the edge of Big Flat Creek, Hugh C. Hurst, Martin Friddle and William Stewart. Including the plantation and buildings where P. H.

Prewitt formerly lived and the plantation and house where John G. Brown once lived. Wit: William Boone, B. G. Tucker, William Stewart, and Abm. Reagor. Reg: 1 Aug 1842.

Page 410 - 10 Nov 1841. John A. Cathey and Narcissa C. Cathey to George W. Bright. Deed. Land in Bedford Co., TN, on south side of Duck River. Reg: 3 Aug 1842.

Page 412 - 26 May 1842. William Brown and Nancy Frost. Marriage Contract. William Brown of Lincoln Co., TN and Nancy Frost of Bedford Co., TN, agreed to unite in Holy estate of Matrimony. Nancy Frost shall stil retain to herself after her marriage with William Brown. She may dispose of her property as she desires. Wit: L. Broadaway and Walter Watson. Reg: 3 Aug 1842.

Page 416 - 4 Aug 1842. Elnathan Davis to Mary E. and Sarah J. Davis. Deed of Gift. For love and affection for his grand-daughters, Mary E. Davis and Sarah Jane Davis, the children of his son Jesse S. M. Davis, Elnathan Davis conveys to them and to the interest of their mother for their benefit, personal property, stock &c. Reg: 4 Aug 1842.

Page 423 - 25 Dec 1841. Joseph Trice to John Trice. Relinquishment, Deed in estate. Joseph Trice of Blount Co., Alabama, conveyed to John Trice, all rights and title to the estate of Eleanor Trice, late of Bedford Co., TN. Wit: Joseph Trice, Jr. and William R. Trice, Jr. Reg: 8 Aug 1842.

Page 442 - 13 Aug 1841. Circuit Court. Stephen B. Johns, James Rucker and his wife Mary N., and Clement Johns and Edmund G. Johns. Exparte - Report. Sold several tracts of land in Bedford Co., TN. Oliver Bullock purchased one tract of 50 acres, on waters of Weakley Creek of Bedford Co., bordering William Wheeler, Cooper's land, and A. Byler, it being conveyed to John Johns, deceased, by Henry Haynes. Reg: 18 Aug 1842.

Page 443 - 17 Aug 1842. Burwell Blanton and Sanford C. Blanton to Robert P<u>reyer</u>. Burwell Blanton and Sanford C. Blanton, both heirs and legatees of William Blanton, deceased, and whose names are omitted in the Deed of Conveyance made to Robert P<u>reyear</u> of land belonging to the estate and which was sold on 22 Jun 1840. Reg: 18 Aug 1842.

Page 451 - 23 May 1842. John Blackwell to Zeno Blackwell and others. Deed of Gift. John Blackwell, Sr., one part conveyed to Zeno, Robert, Sumner, Elizabeth, David, Mary Jane, Lafayette, and Isaac Blackwell, children of Shrewsberry Blackwell of other part, all of Bedford Co., TN. John Blackwell, Sr. for love and affection for the above named children of his son Shrewsberry Blackwell, land in Bedford Co., in District No. 19, on East Fork of Rock Creek, being the place whereon Shrewsberry Blackwell now lives and is bordered by Benjamin W. H. Medearis now James Sheppard's, Anderson's line now James Price's land, Woodard's line, Andrew E. Cummings, and near Joseph B. Porter's Lot of 600 acres, and others. Reg: 24 Aug 1842.

DEED BOOK "MM" 1842 - 1843

Page 7 - 27 Mar 1842. Nancy Spraggin to Elizabeth Smith. Deed, 1 acre. Nancy Spraggin for love and affection for Elizabeth

Smith, both of Bedford Co., TN, conveyed one tract of land in Bedford Co. Borders Nancy Spraggins and Dr. Thomas Lipscomb. Wit: N. O. Blake and David Green. Reg: 30 Aug 1842.

Page 28 - 23 Jan 1840. James Morris and wife to O. H. Bigham. Obligation. 631 acres. James Morris and Mary A. S. Morris his wife sold to O. H. Bigham, undivided interest in land in Bedford Co., TN, it being deeded by M. and D. Gilchrist to the heirs of Robert Bigham, deceased. Wit: Moses S. Bigham and Sherwood Lisenby. Reg: 13 Sep 1842.

Page 29 - Joseph Kincaid to Robert Clark and others. School land in Wartrace, Bedford Co., TN.

Page 30 - 9 Sep 1839. Alfred Kimmery to Turley Kimmery. Obligation. 248 acres. Whereas by the statutes of dower, my mother Turley Kimmery is seized with a life estate of land, late estate of Frederick Kimmery, my father, in Bedford Co., TN, and bounded by Jacob Kizer and George Pratt. My mother Turley Kimmery relinquishing her right to dower to the heirs of Frederick Kimmery. She should enjoy peaceably the mansionhouse and other out houses and use of 20 acres of land on east side of Flat Creek. Wit: Edwin Kimmery and Henry Lynn. Reg: 16 Sep 1842.

Page 32 - 15 Sep 1842. Thomas C. Ryall and wife Elizabeth S. to Daniel B. Ryall. Mortgage on land, 620 acres. Thomas C. Ryall and wife Elizabeth S. Ryall of Bedford Co., TN sold to Daniel B. Ryall of Monmouth Co., New Jersey, land on south side of Duck River in Bedford Co. Bordered by Duck River and John G. Sims. It being land entered in the name of Walter Sims and laid off for Elizabeth Scudder. Wit: Thomas H. Coldwell. Reg: 20 Sep 1842.

Page 37 - 4 Jun 1841. Elisha Arnold, Executor &c to Thomas Black. Deed 58 acres. Elisha Arnold, Executor of Joseph A. Arnold, deceased, sold to Thomas Black, according to the Last Will and Testament, land in Bedford Co., TN, in District No. 10. Borders William Mallard, Thomas Black, George Daugherty and John McGowen. Wit: William L. Mayfield and James C. Wortham. Reg: 23 Sep 1842.

Page 37 - 3 Feb 1840. Nancy and Daniel Kizer to Henry Lynn. Deed 17 acres. Nancy Kizer and Daniel Kizer sold to Henry Lynn land in Bedford Co., TN, on waters of Big Flat Creek. Bounded by Nancy and Daniel Kizer's tract on which they live, and D. D. Hix's corner. Wit: D. D. Hix and Zacheus Cheshire. Reg: 24 Sep 1842.

Page 48 - 25 Aug 1842. Isaac Smith and Margaret Smith to James H. Harrison. Deed 28 acres. Isaac Smith and Margaret Smith sold to James H. Harrison, land being a part of an entry made by Arthur Brooks granted and No. of Grant 4583, it being in Bedford Co., TN, on waters of Sugar Creek. Borders Rezin Smith, Mary Harrison and Benjamin Hazlett. The land being deeded to Margaret Price by Jas. Davidson before her union with Isaac Smith. Wit: T. S. Mays and Reuben C. Hale. Reg: 11 Oct 1842.

Page 49 - 4 Oct 1842. Zebediah Payne to W. E. Venable and H. S. Emmerson and B. H. Emmerson. Deed 17 acres. Zebediah Payne sold and conveyed to William Edward Venable, Hiram S. Emmerson and Burr H. Emmerson, land in Bedford Co., TN. Bounded by Duck

River, Loddy Holt, Isaac Troxler and the lands of Poindexter Payne, being the same inherited by Zebediah Payne from his father Zebediah Payne, deceased. Wit: W. D. Maddox and John Coltort(?). Reg: 11 Oct 1842.

Page 50 - 10 Oct 1842. Jacob Bledsoe to John Hall. Deed of Gift, 120 acres. Jacob Bledsoe for love and affection for John Hall, conveyed unto him, land whereon Jacob Bledsoe now lives in Bedford Co., TN. Bounded by Benjamin Dorman and William Hamills. Wit: Jacob Hall and David Bledsoe. Reg: 13 Oct 1842.

Page 57 - 23 Jun 1842. Mary Hord and others to Amzi Bradshaw. Deed, 2 acres. Mary Hord, Edwin B. Hord, Coleman F. Hord, William M. Hord and James A. Hord, sold to Amzi Bradshaw, all of Bedford Co., TN, land in Bedford Co., on the ridge between the waters of the Garrison and Barren Forks of Duck River. Bounded by the head of Bear Wallow Hollow, being the corner of a tract of land belonging to the heirs of Edmund Hord, dec'd. Wit: William Hutton and Edwin L. Bryan. Reg: 19 Oct 1842.

Page 60 - 11 Oct 1842. Willie B. Jones and Nancy Jones his wife to George Davidson. Interest in estate. Willie B. Jones and his wife Nancy Jones of Bedford Co., TN, sold to George Davidson of Bedford Co., the undivided interest of Willie B. and Nancy Jones, in the estate of Mark Whitaker, deceased, late of Lincoln Co., TN, it being 1/5 of one undivided share derived as follows: the said Willie B. and Nancy Jones being entitled to the same, the said Willie B. by virtue of his marital rights, and the said Nancy as the daughter of Mary Lucas, daughter of said Mark Whitaker and wife, Charles Lucas, the said Charles and the said Mary having died before the said Mark Whitaker. Theinterest being both real and personal estate of Mark Whitaker. Reg: 22 Oct 1842.

Page 62 - 4 Feb 1842. Enoch Head to James Head. Deed, 40 acres. Enoch Head sold to his son James Head, land in Bedford Co., TN, in District No. 8. Wit: John Thompson and Lafayette Mason. Reg: 26 Oct 1842.

Page 75 - 5 Nov 1842. Terrill Griggs and wife to Wilkins Blanton. Interest in land, 53 acres. Terrill Griggs and wife Melissa Griggs formerly Melissa Holt, sold to Wilkins Blanton, land in Bedford Co., TN, it being the interest of Griggs and wife in the lands of Michael Holt, deceased, being the part set aside to them by the division recently made between the heirs and the widow of Michael Holt. Bounded by John McGuire, Daniel Gilchrist, Moses Nelson, other heirs of Michael Holt. Wit: L. Shapard and Jas. H. Graham. Reg: 7 Nov 1842.

Page 78 - 3 Nov 1842. C. T. Philpot to John H. Scott. Deed, interest in estate. Charles T. Philpot sold to John H. Scott, both of Bedford Co., TN, the interest conveyed to Charles T. Philpot by John G. Philpot and Mary Ann Philpot his wife, dated 17 July 1840, which was conveyed to C. T. Philpot as a child's part of the estate of William Hix, deceased. Reg: 7 Nov 1842.

Page 88 - 14 Feb 1842. Pearson Terrill and wife Rachel to William S. Wallace. Deed for Lot No. 17 in Shelbyville. Pearson Terrill of Philadelphia, a merchant, and Rachel his wife, sold to William S. Wallace of Shelbyville, Bedford Co., TN, Lot No. 17 in Shelbyville. The lot being sold to Pearson Terrill by Nathaniel E.

Coldwell, dated 10 Jun 1833. Wit: J. S. Terrill and Henry S. Terrill. Reg: 19 Nov 1842.

Page 103 - 5 Dec 1842. James P. Smith to Thomas Black. Deed in Trust &c. James P. Smith sold to Thomas Black all his undivided share or interest being the 1/9th part, in the real and personal property which Abram Byler, deceased, devised and bequeathed to his wife Nancy Byler during her life, remainder to his heirs, by wife Orpha D., daughter of Abram and Nancy Byler, the said Nancy also being recently departed this life. Reg: 6 Dec 1842.

Page 104 - 1 Jun 1842. Frances Parker to Nicholas Anthony. Deed, 101½ acres. Frances Parker sold to Nicholas Anthony, land in Bedford Co., TN, in District No. 21, it being her dower for life where she now lives and being a part of the lands whereon Jonathan Parker, deceased, formerly lived and adjoining the lands of Frederick Anthony, Adam Euless, Nicholas Anthony and others. Wit: R. L. Landers and Jesse Nutt. Reg: 7 Dec 1842.

Page 105 - 5 Dec 1842. Moriah Wheeler to Martin Wheeler and others. Deed, about 600 acres. Whereas by the statue of dower, Moriah Wheeler has a lifetime estate in land in Bedford Co., TN, in Districts No. 8 and No. 11, on the North Fork and on the waters of Weakleys Creek, it being her third part or dower undivided of Nathan Wheeler, deceased, sold to Martin Wheeler and Absalom Reeves and David W. Thompson and J. Nichols. Wit: Alexander B. Moon and John A. Moor. Reg: 7 Dec 1842.

Page 109 - 13 Sep 1842. Allen Wallis to Joel Wallis. Title Bond. Allen Wallis bought of Alfred Y. Wallis on 17 May 1842, land, which said land is being sold to Joel Wallis by Allen Wallis. Alfred Y. Wallis acquired land in right of his wife formerly Cyntha Cathey and to a dower in 67 acres owned by Jas. S. Cathey at his death, it being 1/3. Another parcel of land is the 1/3rd part of land allotted to Mrs. Ditto as her dower out of the lands of William Ditto, deceased, which wil decree to the said Cyntha Wallis, now, at the death of her mother Mrs. Ditto, the dower near 100 acres, sold to Joel Wallis. Wit: Samuel Phillips and William B. Armstrong. Reg: 8 Dec 1842.

Page 110 - 1 Oct 1842. Thomas S. Cates to Joseph Hastings. Relinquishment. Thomas S. Cates of Bedford Co., TN intended to convey unto Joseph Hastings all his right and interest to negroes belonging to the estate of Joseph Hastings, deceased, but then in the possession of Susannah Hastings, widow of said Joseph Hastings, dated 3 Dec 1821, but the deed is described as the estate of Susannah and wherein doubts have arisen whether in law the conveyance will embrace the property intended to be conveyed. Wit: D. D. Hix and Daniel Kizer. Reg: 9 Dec 1842.

Page 112 - 7 Dec 1842. James Elkins to James Mullins. Relinquishment. James Elkins sold to James Mullins all his interest in the estate of David E. Elkins, deceased, both real and personal. He warrants and defends the title to said interest to Mullins, his interest in 1/5 of the share in the estate to which his mother if living would habe been entitled. Reg: 9 Dec 1842.

Page 116 - 14 Nov 1842. Lucy A. Younger to Abraham Whinnery. Power of Attorney. Lucy A. Younger of Benton Co., Arkansas appointed Abraham Whinnery of same County and State, her Attorney, to receive from David M. Jarret, her late guardian, all her estate both real and personal, which he has in his hands, whether the same came to her as one of the heirs of James Younger, late of Bedford Co., TN. He is to sell all lands in Bedford Co., also all the slaves that is to come to her from the estate of James Younger, deceased. Wit: W. B. Wooddy and L. Harmon. Reg: 12 Dec 1842.

Page 117 - 12 Dec 1842. P. C. Steele to Mary Steele. Deed of Gift. For love and affection for his niece Mary Steele, daughter of his deceased brother Wilson Steele, conveys unto her property of which is now at the residence of Mary Steele, the mother of the said Mary Steele, niece as above, and which was lately sold as the property of the said Mary Steele by the authority of an execution against her in favor of J. and W. Elkins and bought by P. C. Steele. Reg: 12 Dec 1842.

Page 120 - 10 Jan 1842. George W. Nease to Jordan C. Holt. Deed, interest in land, 233 acres. George W. Nease sold to Jordan C. Holt, all the right title and interest that he had under the will of Joshua Holt, Sr., deceased, in a tract of land surveyed for his daughter Eleanor Nease and willed by him to the heirs of Eleanor Nease for her lifetime, in Bedford Co., TN, in District No. 22. Bounded by Jane Higinbotham, Michael Holt, Jordan C. Holt, the Fayetteville Road and Joshua Holt. Wit: Michael Holt, D. M. Smith and H. F. Holt. Reg: 17 Dec 1842.

Page 122 - 11 Aug 1841. Thomas Rucker, Sr. to Salley Ann Porter. Deed of Gift. Thomas Rucker, Sr. of Rutherford Co., TN, for natural love and affection for his grand daughter Sally Ann Porter and for $1.00 paid by John N. Porter of Bedford Co., TN, negroes (7). Wit: Isabella P. Rucker, Thomas O. Rucker and E. P. Rucker. Reg: 19 Dec 1842.

Page 123 - 11 Aug 1841. Thomas Rucker, Sr. to Thomas N. Porter. Deed of Gift. Thomas Rucker, Sr. of Rutherford Co., TN, for love and affection for his grand son Thomas Nathaniel Porter, conveyed unto him slaves (8). Wit: Isabella P. Rucker and Thomas O. Rucker. Reg: 19 Dec 1842.

Page 123 - 11 Aug 1841. Thomas Rucker, Sr. to Kitty M. Porter. Deed of Gift. Thomas Rucker, Sr. of Rutherford Co., TN, for love and affection for his grand daughter Kitty Miranda Porter, slaves (7). Wit: Isabella P. Rucker and Thomas O. Rucker. Reg: 19 Dec 1842.

Page 124 - 11 Aug 1841. Thomas Rucker, Sr. to Mary Harriett McCutchen. Deed of Gift. Thomas Rucker, Sr. of Rutherford Co., TN, for love and affection for his grand daughter Mary Harriett McCutchen, slaves (6). Wit: Isabella Rucker and Thomas O. Rucker. Reg: 19 Dec 1842.

Page 124 - 6 Dec 1842. Samuel Ingram to John J. Fuqua. Deed. Whereas some years ago Samuel Ingram sold unto John J. Fuqua, the one half a Lot in Shelbyville, Bedford Co., TN, it being the north half of the Lot on which the Methodist Church now stands and one fourth of a Lot adjoining thereto, the No. of the 1st Lot he supposes to be No. 58 and the 2nd Lot being the No. which has been lost or mislaid before it was registered.

He now makes title to John J. Fuqua. Reg: 19 Dec 1842.

Page 125 - 16 Dec 1842. John J. Fuqua and Eliza A. his wife to Samuel Doak. Deed. John J. Fuqua and Eliza A. his wife of Madison Co., Alabama, sold to Samuel Doak of Bedford Co., TN, land in Shelbyville, Bedford Co., it being the north half of Lot No. 58 and east one fourth of Lot No. 66. Wit: Jarret B. Huffman and I. S. Brasfield. Reg: 19 Dec 1842.

Page 125 - 19 Dec 1842. Terrell Griggs and wife to Wilkins Blanton. Deed, 53 acres. Terrell Griggs and Melissa Griggs his wife, conveyed to Wilkins Blanton, land in Bedford Co., TN. Borders land where Moses Nelson now lives. Being the share of real estate which descended from Michael Holt, deceased, to his daughter, Melissa Holt now Melissa Griggs. Land about three miles from town, a little north of east from town. Reg: 22 Dec 1842.

Page 126 - 10 Aug 1842. Hawley Williamson to Jordan C. Holt. Deed, interest in money &c. Hawley Williamson of Madison Co., Alabama sold to Jordan C. Holt of Bedford Co., TN, his interest on a fund, now in the hands of John T. Neil, Clerk of the Circuit Court of Bedford Co., amounting to $2,930.55 which originated from a sale of a tract of land in Bedford Co., upon the petition of Thomas Greer, Sr., and Thomas G. Williamson and Caroline Williamson, children and heirs of Richard S. Williamson and who being minors, petitioned by their guardian, which land originally belonged to Richard S. Williamson during his life time, remainder over to the children and heirs of Richard S. Williamson. Hawley Williamson became entitled to the interest by purchase and the fund of $2,930.55 being the net proceeds of the sale of the entire estate. Wit: D. M. Smith and J. Hall. Reg: 22 Dec 1842.

Page 132 - 22 Dec 1842. William J. Bryeans to Jabus Nowlin. Deed, 300 acres. William J. Bryeans of Humphreys Co., TN, sold to Jabus Nowlin of Bedford Co., TN, all rights and title and estate, in land in Bedford Co., on East Fork of Duck River. 4 tracts of 300 acres. Granted by State of Tennessee to Edward Bryeans, one for 100 acres, one for 90 acres, one for 60 acres and one for 50 acres, the interest and estate of the above being one third part of the lands which said William J. Bryeans now holds by descent from his father Edward Bryeans with the other heirs of Edward Bryeans. Wit: Joel Stallings and Richard Musgrave. Reg: 24 Dec 1842.

Page 133 - 8 Dec 1842. James Sadler to Alexander Allen. Deed in Trust. James Sadler one part sold to Alexander Allen of second part, and Richard F. Sadler and James H. Sadler, children of James Sadler of third part, all of Bedford Co., TN. James Sadler for love and affection for his children, Richard F. and James H. Sadler, sold to Alexander Allen, negroes (2) and colts, in special trust. Allen shall retain the above property until Richard T. and James H. Sadler arrive at age of twenty one. Wit: J. M. H. Coleman and Alexander W. Allen. Reg: 26 Dec 1842.

Page 135 - 23 Dec 1842. Keziah Rushing to Martha Poplin. Deed of Gift. For love and affection Keziah Rushing has for her daughter Martha Rushing, now Martha Poplin, conveys a negro girl Eliza. Wit: Jno. H. Lane and G. W. Lain(Lane). Reg: 27 Dec 1842.

Page 135 - 23 Dec 1842. Keziah Rushing to Amiline Deason. Deed of Gift. For love and affection Keziah Rushing has for her daughter Amyline Rushing now Amyline Deason, conveys a negro girl Judah. Wit: Jno. H. Lane and G. W. Lane. Reg: 27 Dec 1842.

Page 136 - 23 Dec 1842. Keziah Rushing to Jemima Lane. Deed of Gift. For love and affection Keziah Rushing has for her daughter Jemima Rushing now Jemima Lane, a negro girl Milly Ann. Wit: Jno. H. Lane and G. W. Lane. Reg: 27 Dec 1842.

Page 139 - 27 Dec 1842. John Blackwell, Sr. to Jane Wakefield. Marriage Contract. A marriage contract between John Blackwell, Sr. of Bedford Co., TN and Jane Wakefield of Marshall Co., TN, whereas a marriage is intended shortly to be had and solemnized between them and whereas they are desirous that each of them should separately have, hold and enjoy the property they are seized and possessed at the time of their intermarriage, free from the right, title, claim or interest of the other party. Wit: Thomas Coffey, Daniel Davis and William J. W. Wakefield. Reg: 29 Dec 1842.

Page 161 - 21 Jun 1842. Samuel McGowen and wife to Frederick Batte. Deed 27 acres. Samuel G. McGowen and Rebecca his wife sold to Frederick Batte, Sr., all of Bedford Co., TN, land in Bedford Co., on Weakley Creek and adjoining lands of William Allison, James Harris and Richard Bandy, deceased by the Circuit Court. Wit: D. A. Ozment, Robert C. Batte and Josiah Nisbitt. Reg: 7 Jan 1843.

Pahe 163 - 18 Jan 1842. Andrew W. Johnson and Henry H. Collins. Contract. Andrew W. Johnson sold to Henry H. Collins, his Wool Carding Machine with all the implements and Collins executed a note. Collins is to build a house to live in. Wit: L. Shapard and William H. Pearson. Reg: 7 Jan 1843.

Page 181 - 12 Jan 1843. E. A. Covington to Lovice Covington. Relinquishment Deed. E. A. Covington relinquishes all his right title &c to an undivided interest in the estate of Jesse Covington, including slaves that may come to him and all interest in land in Bedford Co., TN, in District No. 11, on Weakley Creek near the Village of Unionville and it adjoining the lands of William Ogilvie and others. Wit: Ed. Wortham and J. M. Wheeler. Reg: 13 Jan 1843.

Page 182 - 3 Jan 1843. Joseph P. Thompson to John Thompson. Deed in Trust. Joseph P. Thompson one part of Bedford Co., TN, and Minos F. Thompson and William N. Orr of Bedford Co., other part. Joseph P. Thompson is indebted to John Thompson. Notes remains on that John Thompson has granted unto Minos F. Thompson and William N. Orr, 1/5 part of a negro girl Harriett and 1/5 part of the money that will be due from the estate of Robert Allison, deceased, to Prudence Thompson and her children. Reg: 13 Jan 1843.

Page 193 - 18 Jan 1843. William C. Gordon and wife Sarah to William Jenkins. Deed &c. William C. Gordon and Sarah his wife sold to William Jenkins their security, all their interest in the estate of Jacob Coble, deceased, being a legal heir and entitled to a share of the estate. Also to receive from Mary Coble, administratrix of Rachel Elizabeth Coble, deceased, their share in the said estate. Reg: 18 Jan 1843.

Page 209 - 28 Jan 1843. Lemuel Loyd to his Granddaughter L. J. M. Elkins &c. Lemuel Loyd one part and Lively Jane Mary Frances, a daughter of James Elkins of other part, all of Bedford Co., TN. Lemuel Loyd for his love and affection for his granddaughter Lively Jane Mary Frances, being the child of his daughter Margaret Loyd now Margaret Elkins, conveyed unto her personal property and cattle &c. Reg: 30 Jan 1843.

Page 211 - August Term 1841. Circuit Court Decree to Redding Stephens. Final Decree. James P. Ervin, Malissa F. Ervin and Chapman B. Davis. Sold the lands of which Josiah Davis died seized and possessed, one tract of 80 acres and another of 50 acres. Redding Stephens being the purchaser. Reg: 31 Jan 1843.

Page 213 - 4 Feb 1843. John Blackwell, Sr. to Nathan Blackwell and others, his grandchildren. John Blackwell of Bedford Co., TN, for love and affection for his grandsons Nathan Blackwell, John Blackwell and James K. Blackwell, the sons of his son Brice M. G. Blackwell, grant and deliver unto them a negro boy Jordan. Reg: 4 Feb 1843.

Page 220 - 15 Feb 1842. James M. Dyer to William H. Dyer. Deed 200 acres. Whereas by descent from James Dyer, our father, we, William H. Dyer, Joseph G. Dyer, Esther G. Dyer, Elizabeth Dyer, John Dyer, Samuel G. Dyer, Gibson J. Dyer and himself, James M. Dyer, lave derived title to and now hold equal and undivided interest in land in Bedford Co., TN, District No. 20. Borders Martha Dyer's land which she now lives on and James Dyer's line. Sold to William H. Dyer. Reg: 11 Feb 1843.

Page 221 - 15 Feb 1842. Elizabeth and J. W. Davidson to William H. Dyer. Deed, 200 acres. Whereas by descent from James Dyer, our father, we, William H. Dyer, Joseph G. Dyer, Esther Dyer, John Dyer, Samuel G. Dyer, James M. Dyer, Gibson J. Dyer, and herself, Elizabeth Davidson, have derived to and now hold equal and undivided interest in land in Bedford Co., TN, in District No. 20. Bounded by Martha Dyer's land which she now lives on, sold to William H. Dyer. Wit: Jas. M. Dyer and Samuel G. Dyer. Reg: 11 Feb 1843.

Page 222 - 31 Jan 1843. Sarah Springer to Price C. Steele. Bill of Sale. Sold to Price C. Steele, all her undivided interest in a family of negroes (8), willed by James Cooper to his wife Elizabeth Cooper during her lifetime and then to his eight youngest children, to wit, Sarah Springer, Jane Cooper now Jane Harris, Washington B. Cooper, Elizabeth B. Steele now deceased, Katharine Steele, Jonathan Cooper, William Cooper, and Malinda Cooper now Malinda Puckett. Wit: Josiah Springer and Thomas Hart. Reg: 16 Feb 1843.

Page 233 - 24 Mar 1815. Roger Snell and Elizabeth Snell to the Methodist Church. Deed, 2 acres. Roger Snell and Elizabeth Snell of Bedford Co., TN, one part to Bennet Phillips, David Owen, Jesse Mise, William Wise and Daniel Barcroft, Trustees of Methodist Church, other part. For $10.00, conveyed unto the Trustees, land in Bedford Co. Borders Bennet Phillips. Said Lot or Meeting House to be known in the Elk Circuit by the name of Mount Zion. Two acres, including the house, woods, waters &c. Wit: George W. Gray and Joshua Parkes. Reg: 25 Feb 1843.

Page 235 - 24 Dec 1842. Mary Carroll to Sterling Carroll. Power of Attorney. Chatham Co., NC. Mary Carroll of Chatham Co., NC one of the legal heirs of Edward Warren, Sr., deceased, late of Bedford Co., TN, appoint Sterling Carroll of Marshall Co., TN, her Attorney, to recover from George Waite, Executor of Edward Warren, Sr., deceased, or from the Executors of Edward Warren, Jr., deceased, late of Mississippi, as descended by the Last Will and Testament of the said deceased. Wit: Thomas E. Glass of Chatham Co., NC. Reg: 2 Mar 1843.

Page 250 - 6 Jul 1841. Elizabeth and Matthew Cunningham to John Stanfield. Deed, 80 acres. One Ann Huff purchased a tract of land at a Sheriff's Sale in Bedford Co., TN. Ann Huff has since died and by her will, admitted to probate at the June Term 1842 of County Court of Bedford Co, devised the land to Elizabeth Cunningham, during her natural life, remainder to Matthew Cunningham and his heirs, subject to the right of redemption allowed by the laws of State of Tennessee and whereas John Stanfield of Bedford Co., is a judgement creditor of William H. Miles, the person for whose debt the land was sold and purchased by Ann Huff and is therefore entitled to redeem the land from the devises of Ann Huff. Land sold to John Stanfield. Borders Joshua Woosley, Willie B. Snell, William S. Caruthers, D. D. Hix, and William Kizer. Wit: L. D. Walker and B. G. Andrews. Reg: 8 Mar 1843.

Page 251 - 8 Mar 1843. John Blackwell to John and William Blackwell. Deed of Gift. John Blackwell, Sr. of Bedford Co., TN, for love and affection for his two grandsons John Blackwell and William Blackwell, sons of his son James Blackwell, given and conveyed unto them a mare, colt and other items. Reg: 8 Mar 1843.

Page 261 - 26 Nov 1842. Andrews and wife to Wade H. Naler. Deed, undivided interest in 200 acres of land. Andrew S. Edwards and Mary Edwards his wife and daughter of Nicholas Woodfin, deceased, sold to Wade H. Naler their undivided interest in all the estate of Nicholas Woodfin, deceased. Wit: Woodfin Naler, Levi C. Anderson, and Newton Clark. Reg: 15 Mar 1843.

Page 261 - 26 Dec 1842. Elizabeth Reaves to Tarlton J. Reaves and others. Bill of Sale. Elizabeth Reaves sold to Tarlton J. Reaves, Alexander J. Reaves, Benjamin S. Reaves, Moses Reaves and Pleasant H. Reaves, a negro girl Eliza and her child. Wit: Lewis Wilhoite and Thomas T. Rives. Reg: 15 Mar 1843.

Page 273 - 16 Mar 1843. James M. Robinson to Joseph Robinson. Deed. James M. Robinson sold to Joseph Robinson, all his undivided interest in the land John Robinson, deceased, died seized and possessed of in Bedford Co., TN. James M. Robinson being one of the heirs at law of John Robinson, deceased, and also, all the right and interest that Mary Biggers had as one of the heirs of John Robinson, deceased, whereon John Robinson lived at the time of his death. Mary Biggers transferred her interest to me, James M. Robinson, by deed on 7 Sep 1841. Reg: 20 Mar 1843.

Page 277 - 22 Mar 1843. Tarlton J. Reaves to Alexander S. Reaves. Bond for Title. Tarleton J. Reaves of Bedford Co., TN is bound to Alexander S. Reaves of Bedford Co., for judgement. Obligation is that Tarleton J. Reaves agreed to sell to Alexander

S. Reaves their undivided eighths of a tract of land of about 128 acres, subject however to the life estate of Elizabeth Reaves, widow of Archibald Reaves, deceased, and it being the land Archibald Reaves lived at the time of his death. Reg: 23 Mar 1843.

Page 282 - 1 Nov 1842. Willis Bearden to John T. Bearden. Deed. Willis Bearden sold to John T. Bearden, land in Bedford Co., TN, on waters of Big Flat Creek and whereon Nancy Bearden now lives. Wit: D. D. Arnold, Wynn Bearden and Samuel S. Haile. Reg: 29 Mar 1843.

Page 284 - 28 Mar 1843. John Tillman to William Gosling. Deed, interest in Factory &c. John Tillman sold to William Gosling, all his interest &c in a Lot in Shelbyville, on north bank of Duck River, on which lot there is a Brick Factory House erected. Lot borders Martin Street, Duck River, Lots of Clement Cannon sold to Robert Cannon and Archibald Yell. It being the same piece of ground on which Clement Cannon's Grist Mill on the north bank formerly stood and also the Brick Factory House and Alco machinery in said house, the dam across Duck River to said house attached, also much of the waterpower now existing from the lowest point of Lot No. 108. Wit: Thomas C. Whiteside. Reg: 29 Mar 1843.

Page 296 - 3 Apr 1843. Isaac and Margaret Smith to William C. Swanson. Deed. Isaac and Margaret Smith sold to William C. Swanson, land in Bedford Co., TN, on waters of Sinking Creek. Bounded by lands of Mary Harrison, Executrix of Jonathan Harrison deceased, Doherty's line, Smith's line, and Hazelett's line. It being a part of a purchase by Margaret Price before her union with Smith of Thomas Davidson. Wit: G. W. Cunningham and William Potter. Reg: 4 Apr 1843.

Page 307 - 20 Jul 1842. William H. Craig to William R. Looney. Deed, 188 acres. William H. Craig sold to William R. Looney, both of Bedford Co., TN, land in Bedford Co., on waters of Rock Creek. Borders lands whereon Mary Davis now lives. Another tract borders lands of Zachariah Davis and Henry Hazelett. Also borders lands of Solomon Durrett, the same belonging to the heirs and representatives of William Craig, deceased, and on which he lived at the time of his death, also out of which Polly Craig, widow of the deceased has had a dower of 64 acres in which dower Flora Craig has had an undivided interest of 1/10th in which also the heirs of John Craig, deceased, has an undivided interest of 1/10th, the balance having been purchased by William H. Craig from James Craig, Leona Justice, Hamlin Cook, William M. Russell, Joel Bradley, Robert Craig, C. L. Harrison and Benjamin F. Craig, heirs at law of the deceased, as well as the undivided interest of Flora Craig and the heirs of John Craig, deceased, out of the dower, from R. P. Harrison, Clerk and Master. Wit: J. H. Curtis, Jr. and Alexander Freeman. Reg: 6 Apr 1843.

Page 310 - 31 Dec 1842. Powel Kimbro and wife to Willis D. Johnson. Relinquishment. Powel Kimbro and Rebecca Ann Kimbro his wife, relinquishes all rights in the estate of Daniel Johnson deceased, to Willis D. Johnson. Wit: David B. Johnson and Andrew J. Franklin. Reg: 8 Apr 1843.

Page 325 - 8 Apr 1843. Patsy Thorn to Jeremiah Dobbs and G. T. Neely. Deed in Trust. Patsy Thorn is guardian for the minor heirs of her husband William Thorn, deceased, appointed in August 1842 and made bond. She granted unto Jeremiah Dobbs and G. T. Neely, property and estate. Land on which Patsy Thorn now lives of 85 acres. Bounded by Henry Pickle and Moses Aaron. Also her lifetime dower and one child's part of 115 acres (in two tracts). One child's part to the land was gifted by Polly Thorn to her stepmother Patsy Thorn and registered in Book "GG" on 8 Sept 1837. Reg: 17 Apr 1843.

Page 326 - 15 Apr 1843. William C. Freeman to Abner Freeman. Deed, 26 acres. Whereas by the Last Will and Testament of William Higginbotham, deceased, William C. Freeman is lawfully seized of a life estate in a tract of land in Bedford Co., TN, in District No. 22. Borders Jacob Albright, Lewis Wilhoite, land belonging to the minor heirs of James Higginbotham, deceased and near the school land. Wit: J. A. Simmons and William S. Lee. Reg: 17 Apr 1843.

Page 329 - 17 Sep 1842. Jane Matheny and Elizabeth Grim to William Matheny. Power of Attorney. Jane Matheny wife of William Matheny and mother of Chesly K. Rolley and Elizabeth Grim of Harrison Co., VA, appointed William Matheny of Harrison Co., VA, their Attorney to take possession of all real and personal estate in the interest as heirs of Chesly K. Rolley. Harrison Co., VA, Elizabeth Grim, Jr. appeared before the Justices and made bond that said Elizabeth Grim named in the Power is the grandmother of Chesly K. Rolley. Reg: 18 Apr 1843.

Page 330 - 7 Mar 1843. E. D. Rushing to William Bullock. Deed of Gift. E. D. Rushing of Bedford Co., TN, for respect and love for William, son of Olive Bullock of Bedford Co., granted unto him, nine sheep. Reg: 18 Apr 1843.

Page 343 - 15 Apr 1843. Nathaniel Porter and Sally A. Porter to George Porter. Bill of Sale. Nathaniel Porter sold to George Porter, all of Bedford Co., TN, a negro girl Manerva. Wit: Jno. Eakin, Alexander Eakin, Daniel Looney and Noah W. Looney. Reg: 1 May 1843.

Page 345 - 4 May 1843. Nancy, Daniel and Enoch Kizer to Jacob Kizer. Deed, 24 acres. Nancy Kizer, Daniel Kizer and Enoch Kizer sold to Jacob Kizer, land in Bedford Co., TN, on waters of Big Flat Creek. Borders D. D. Hix, the lands willed to Nancy Kizer and Daniel Kizer by Valentine Kizer, deceased, and Jacob Kizer's corner. It includes the cabins and some improvements where Daniel Kizer now lives. Wit: J. W. Tribble and Edward A. Williams. Reg: 8 May 1843.

Page 351 - 29 Dec 1842. John Byler and others to Thomas Black. Bill of Sale. John Byler, William L. Byler, Jacob Byler, James T. Byler, John H. Maxwell guardian of the minor heirs of Elvira his wife, Isaac D. Maxwell guardian for the minor heirs of Nancy L. his wife, James P. Smith in right of his wife Orpha D., the receipt whereof is hereby acknowledged by John Byler and above named, sold a negro man Charles. Wit: E. D. Rushing and Noah Putman. Reg: 17 May 1843.

Page 352 - 29 Dec 1842. John Byler and others to Abraham Byler. Bill of Sale. John Byler, William L. Byler, Jacob Byler, James

T. Byler, John H. Maxwell guardian of the minor heirs of Elvira his wife, deceased, Thomas Black in right of his wife Mary T., Isaac Maxwell guardian of the minor heirs of Nancy L. his wife, deceased, and James P. Smith in right of his wife Orpha D., sold unto Abraham Byler a negro boy Frank. Wit: E. D. Rushing and Noah Putman. Reg: 17 May 1843.

Page 353 - 4 May 1843. Haiden Trigg to Mary Ann Trigg and children. Deed of Gift. Haden Trigg, Sr. of Bedford Co., TN, for love and affection for my grand daughter in law Mary Ann Trigg wife of William H. Trigg and the children of Mary Ann and William H. conveyed unto them a negro boy Jack. Wit: George N. Whitson, C. G. McLean and John Smith. Reg: 22 May 1843.

Page 355 - 29 Dec 1842. J. and J. T. Byler and others. Receipt. Securities of Nancy Byler &c, received of John H. Maxwell, Thomas Carlton, James T. Byler, William Wright and Allen Perry as securities of Nancy Byler, Executrix of Abraham Byler, deceased, our distributive share of said estate as legatees. Signed by J. and J. T. Byler representatives of William L. Byler, Jacob Byler, Thomas Black, James T. Byler, John Byler, James T. Byler guardian of Abraham Byler, James P. Smith, J. H. Maxwell and Isaac D. Maxwell. Wit: E. D. Rushing and Noah Putman. Reg: 26 May 1843.

Page 357 - 24 May 1843. Susanna Parkes to Andrew Vannoy. Power of Attorney. I, Susanna Parkes of Bedford Co., TN, being now about to travel a journey to South Carolina to remain for a season, not knowing how long, and whereas I am about to leave my negro property in Bedford Co., to remain till I shall return, I do hereby appoint Andrew Vannoy my Attorney, to transact my business &c. Wit: John C. McCuistion and William S. Watkins. Reg: 27 May 1843.

Page 360 - 1 Jun 1843. William Throgmorton and wife to Daniel Stephens. Deed, 96 acres. William Throgmorton and Elizabeth his wife sold to Daniel Stephens, all of Bedford Co., TN, land in Bedford Co., on headwaters of Knob and Straight Creeks. Borders lands of Burns Eaton. Reg: 2 Jun 1843.

Page 368 - 5 Jun 1843. Jordan C. Holt, Jr. to Jordan C. Holt, Sr. Deed, 274 acres. I, Jordan C. Holt, the 2nd son of Nimrod B. Holt, deceased, sold to Jordan C. Holt, Sr., land in Bedford Co., TN, in District No. 22. Borders lands of original survey of Joshua Holt, deceased, middle of the Fayetteville Road, and Jordan C. Holt, Sr. This land being the tract of land willed to me by my grandfather Joshua Holt, deceased. Wit: D. M. Smith and H. H. Holt. Reg: 12 Jun 1843.

Page 369 - 12 Jun 1843. Flower Swift to Jane Oneal. Loan of property. Flower Swift lends to his daughter Jane Oneal, property. Reg: 12 Jun 1843.

Page 386 - 10 Jul 1843. William S. Jett to Elizabeth Arnold. Deed, 45 acres. William S. Jett sold to Elizabeth Arnold formerly Elizabeth Sharp, all of Bedford Co., TN, land in Bedford Co., it being the place once owned by Josiah Marbury and on which D. D. Arnold lived in 1840 and being more fully described in a deed from Robert Cannon and registered in Deed Book "JJ", pages 340 and 341. Another tract described in Deed Book "JJ", page 326, it being formerly the estate of William Carter, dec'd.

Reg: 12 Jul 1843.

Page 393 - 24 Jul 1843. John Blackwell, Sr. to Margaret Cortner and Anthony Sharp. John Blackwell, Sr. of Bedford Co., TN, for love and affection for his daughter Elizabeth Arnold and her two children, Margaret Cortner and Anthony Sharp, conveyed unto Margaret Cortner and Anthony Sharp, a negro woman Mariah and her two children. Reg: 26 Jul 1843.

Page 398 - 3 Aug 1843. John Hull to William H. Stephenson and others, Trustees of Meeting House. Deed 1 acre. John Hull of Bedford Co., TN sold to the Trustees in Trust for the Methodist Episcopal Church, for $2.50, Hull conveyed unto William H. Stephenson, William Hummel, Edward Stephenson, Harbert Smith, Gabriel B. Knight, Obadiah W. Knight and Henry Pickle, Trustees in Trust for the M. E. Church and their successors, land in Bedford Co., on waters of Sinking Creek. Bounded by lands of William Hummel. Reg: 4 Aug 1843.

Page 413 - 18 Jan 1843. James H. McLaughlin to John Ramsey. Power of Attorney. Iredell Co., NC. James H. McLaughlin of Iredell Co., NC, appointed John Ramsey of Marshall Co., TN, his Attorney to make and execute a Warrantee Title to Hugh A. Hall of Marshall Co., TN, land in Bedford Co., TN, on East Fork of Rock Creek. It adjoins lands of John and Isaac Larue and others, it being the part of the Hart tract that descended to James H. McLaughlin's mother Margaret McLaughlin from the estate of her father James Hart, deceased. Land of about 200 acres. Wit: Milton Campbell and Robert White. Reg: 14 Aug 1843. (Also see page 418 for another deed of 150 acres.)

Page 419 - 30 May 1843. John B. Vancleave and Esther Lamb. Agreement &c. John B. Vancleave and Esther Lamb, both of Bedford Co., TN, agrees that Esther Lamb has hired her son Longshon Lamb to John B. Vancleave on 27 Jan 1843 and is to work until 25 Dec 1843 or unless sooner dismissed. John B. Vancleave is to pay Longshon Lamb on 25 Dec 1843. Wit: William Lamb and James Mankins. Reg: 15 Aug 1843.

Page 420 - 1 May 1843. Mills Manor to Rhoda Wilson. Deed of Gift. For love and affection Mills Manor has for his daughter Rhoda Wilson, he has conveyed unto her, negroes for life. Wit: H. Yoakum and John E. Droomgoole. Reg: 19 Aug 1843.

Page 422 - 28 Feb 1828. Thomas Alford and Robert Powell to Abraham Landers and others. Deed for Meeting House. Thomas Alford and Robert Powell, both of Bedford Co., TN, conveyed unto Abraham Landers, Moses Guess and John Taylor of Bedford Co., being chosen Trustees for the purposes following: To promote the cause of religion and to facilitate seminaries of learning in their neighborhood, conveyed about two acres to build a house for preaching and teaching of different denominations. Land in Bedford Co., on waters of Alexanders Creek. Borders McCorkle's line. Wit: John W. Nelson, James Alexander and Moses B. Clark. Reg: 19 Aug 1843.

Page 425 - 22 Aug 1843. William Allison to Thomas D. Tarpley. Deed, 277 acres. William Allison sold to Thomas D. Tarpley, his undivided interest in a tract of land which was decreed to Robert Batte, Jr. by the Curcuit Court of Bedford Co., TN, he being one of the minor heirs of Henry Batte, deceased, land in Bedford Co., TN. Borders Allison's land. The land all of which with the exception of that allotted to Rebecca Batte his mother as her dower, all the balance is conveyed and sold to said Tarpley. Wit: Thomas Foster and Frederick Batte, Jr. Reg: 25 Aug 1843.

Page 425 - 10 Aug 1843. Josiah Nisbitt and wife Mary Jane to Frederick Batte, Sr. Deed. Josiah Nisbitt and Mary Jane his wife sold to Frederick Batte, Sr. all of Bedford Co., TN, land decreed to the heirs of Henry Batte, deceased. The land adjoins lands of William Allison, John T. Harris, Richard Bandy and others. Wit: Samuel Nisbitt, J. D. Stovall, William Allison and THomas D. Tarpley. Reg: 25 Aug 1843.

Page 431 - 25 Aug 1843. Rachel Martin to Thomas B. Moseley. Deed of Gift, 200 acres. For love and affection Rachel Martin has for Thomas B. Moseley, Sr., conveys her tract of land in Bedford Co. Borders on east bank of Sailing Creek and east of the building on said tract, Matt Martin's tract he purchased of Samuel Rucker, lands of Thomas B. Moseley, and Edward A. Moseley. The land being the tract on which Rachel Martin now lives, the same being purchased by Rachel Martin of John Tillman. Wit: William Thomas and A. M. Hughes. Reg: 28 Aug 1843.

Page 431 - 25 Aug 1843. Rachel Martin to Thomas B. Moseley. Deed of Gift on 6 negroes. For love and affection, Rachel Martin has for her niece Rebecca Moseley, conveyed to Thomas B. Moseley, a Trustee, negroes (6). Wit: William Thomas and A. M. Hughes. Reg: 28 Aug 1843.

Page 434 - 24 Aug 1843. Rachel Martin to Samuel E. Gilliland. Deed of Gift for slaves in Trust &c. For love and regard Rachel Martin has for Eliza M. S. Marshall the wife of her relation Matt M. Marshall and their children, conveys slaves in Trust to S. E. Gilliland, Trustee. Wit: T. B. Moseley, Sr. and Thomas B. Moseley, Jr. Reg: 31 Aug 1843.

Page 436 - 26 Aug 1843. Josiah Nisbitt to Frederick Batte, Sr. Power of Attorney. Josiah Nisbitt appointed Frederick Batte, Sr., his Attorney, to receive a legacy bequeathed to my wife as a distributive share which has descended to him by Gardner Batte, deceased, late of Giles Co., TN. Wit: Samuel Nisbitt and J. S. Stovall. Reg: 2 Sep 1843.

Page 440 - 6 Aug 1842. Circuit Court Decree Title &c to Susanna Kerby. Bill for the Sale of land, 148 acres. John Miles and James H. Miles, administrators of John Kerby. Exparte. Susannah Kerby has paid all the purchase money of a tract of land. The lands on waters of Little Flat Creek. It being the place whereon Peter Kerby formerly resided. Borders Tillman Shipp. The said tract was sold as the property of the estate of John Kerby, deceased. It is therefore ordered and decreed by the Court that all the right, title, claim and interest of the heirs at law of the said John Kerby, deceased, to wit, James Anderton and Martha his wife, John Stanfield and Mary his wife, John Evans and Nancy his wife, Temperance Miles, James H. Miles and Harriett his wife, Henry Kerby and the heirs of Alvis Kerby be and the same is hereby divested out of them and their heirs forever and vested in the said Susannah Kerby and her heirs. Reg: 4 Sep 1843.

DEED BOOK "MM"

Page 446 - 14 Sep 1843. Thomas R. Wynn to Samuel A. Bell. Bill of Sale &c. Thomas R. Wynn sold all his right title and interest in the estate of his mother Frances Wynn, which was bequeathed to Frances Wynn by Thomas Miles, deceased. Thomas R. Wynn's share is 1/8th part of 6 slaves. Wit: G. W. Brown and J. A. Blakemore. Reg: 14 Sep 1843.

Page 447 - 2 Sep 1843. Isaac West to Tabitha Jones. Deed of Gift. For love and affection Isaac West has for his daughter Tabitha Jones, conveyed to her a sorrel filly. Levi Jones the husband of Tabitha Jones shall have no right to or interest in said filly. Reg: 18 Sep 1843.

Page 447 - 21 Feb 1843. Nathan W. Sanders and others to Martin Wheeler. Deed, 43 acres. Nathan W. Sanders and Elbert Clark and his wife Elizabeth Clark, sold unto Martin Wheeler, land in Bedford Co., TN, in District No. 8. Wit: W. B. Wheeler and D. J. Wheeler. Reg: 18 Sep 1843.

Page 449 - 18 Sep 1843. Thomas Shearin to Elizabeth Ledbetter. Deed of Gift. Thomas Shearin of Bedford Co., TN, conveyed to his daughter Elizabeth Ledbetter of Marshall Co., TN, for love and affection, a negro woman Lurena, and at her death to her heirs by P. M. Ledbetter. Wit: John K. Lawwell and William Shearin. Reg: 18 Sep 1843.

Page 450 - 18 Sep 1843. James W. Lawrance to William Guy. Deed. James W. Lawrance sold unto William Guy, both of Bedford Co., TN, all his right title and interest in land in Bedford Co., in District No. 5, it being the tract which descended from Margaret Lawrance to her heirs, five in number. The whole tract is bordered by Capt. Z. B. Dozier, William Warren and William Guy. Reg: 21 Sep 1843.

DEED BOOK "NN" 1843 - 1848

Page 1 - 25 Sep 1843. James H. Muse to Obadiah Knight. Deed in Trust on land, 2 acres. James H. Muse sold to Obadiah Knight all his undivided interest in a tract of land in Bedford Co., TN, which descended from Andrew Hartsfield to his heirs, one of which Mary G. intermarried with James H. Muse. The land being in Bedford Co., on waters of Powell Creek, adjoining the lands of John Muse, Hugh Doak, school land, Daniel Gilchrist. There are five heirs, sold 1/5th of the whole to Obadiah Knight. Reg: 25 Sep 1843.

Page 2 - 26 Sep 1843. Green Lovett to James A. Gaunt. Deed in Trust, 150 acres. Green Lovett sold to James A. Gaunt, land in Bedford Co., TN, being the land that was conveyed to Green Lovett by his father Lancaster Lovett as appears in Deed Book "AA", page 44. Borders lands owned by Lancaster Lovett during his lifetime, an apple orchard, and William Kinney. Reg: 28 Sep 1843.

Page 6 - 20 Feb 1841. Thomas Fisher to John F. Thompson. Bill of Sale. Thomas Fisher one of the heirs of Silas Tillman, deceased, sold unto John F. Thompson 1/7th part of a negro woman Jane. Wit: Jacob Fisher and Michael F. Parsons. Reg: 2 Oct 1843.

Page 9 - 7 May 1842. Anderson Landers to Union Grove Meeting and School House. Deed. Anderson Landers of Bedford Co., TN conveyed to William Allison, James Harris, Ziza Moore, Anderson Landers, and Anderson Rucker, Trustees for Union Grove Meeting and School House of Bedford Co., a tract of land. Borders Elizabeth Kimmons. Wit: William Straten and George Landers. Reg: 9 Oct 1843.

Page 17 - 13 Dec 1841. Newton K. Shofner and Mary Ann Shofner to James Fulkerson. Deed, 58 acres. Newton Shofner and wife Mary Ann Shofner, sold to James Fulkerson, land in Bedford Co., in District No. 24, on Thompson Creek or Lot No. 3 in the division of the lands belonging to the heirs of Thomas Bomar, deceased. Borders Lot No. 1, being the part that falls to Nancy J. Bomar and school land. Wit: James Anderton and John Anderton. Reg: 18 Oct 1843.

Page 27 - 25 Oct 1843. Marriage Contract between Robert Taylor and Keziah Rushing. Robert Taylor of Williamson Co., TN and Keziah Rushing of Bedford Co., TN, agreed to marry and to make a marriage contract. Robert Taylor has a quanity of negroes (20 or more) and land from five to six hundred acres and he is to have exclusive right to dispose of the whole property to benefit his legal heirs. Keziah Rushing has a negro woman and her three children and forty four acres which is to be disposed of according to the will of her former husband Evan Rushing, deceased. The negro woman and her three children is to go with Keziah Rushing to Robert Taylor's house. Wit: William J. Lane and A. Poplin. Reg: 26 Oct 1843.

Page 29 - 27 Oct 1843. Lemuel Snelling to James W. Dickerson. Deed, 100 acres. Lemual Snelling sold to James W. Dickerson, land in Bedford Co., TN, on the waters of the Garrison Fork of Duck River, a part of a tract of land formerly owned by William Dickerson and devised to Rebecca Wood formerly Rebecca Dickerson. Borders the Garrison Fork, William Hooser, and the original Dickerson tract. Reg: 27 Oct 1843.

Page 33 - 28 Sep 1843. Elizabeth Lile to Rebecca Bullock. Deed of Gift. Elizabeth Lile bequeathed unto her daughter Rebecca Bullock, both of Bedford Co., TN, property for life and at her death devises the property of beds and furniture be divided equally between her two eldest daughters, Ann and Jane Bullock. Wit: A. W. Caruthers and Thomas J. Nelson. Reg: 30 Oct 1843.

Page 39 - 2 Nov 1843. Hiram Sutton and wife to Michael Holt. Deed, 24 acres. Hiram Sutton and Nancy Sutton his wife, conveyed to Michael Holt, land in Bedford Co., TN, in District No. 23. On Big Flat Creek and borders Hiram Holt. Wit: John C. Hix and William C. Hix. Reg: 6 Nov 1843.

Page 51 - 13 Nov 1843. John M. Keller to Ann Keller. Deed in Trust. John M. Keller conveyed to Ann Keller, his interest in a 250 acre tract in Bedford Co., TN, District No. 2, the place on which Ann Keller now lives, his interest being one-thirteenth part of said tract, about 2 acres of hemp standing in the shock and other property. Reg: 13 Nov 1843.

Page 58 - 8 Aug 1842. N. Woodfin's heirs. Agreement. The heirs and widow of Nicholas Woodfin, deceased, late of Bedford Co., TN, now desiring an equal division of all the landed estate of Nicholas Woodfin and whereas there is in the possession of Hannah Woodfin, one of the undersigned, an instrument of writing signed by the undersigned bearing date 4 Oct 1833 granting to Hannah the rents of said landed estate during her lifetime. John D. Gilmore and John L(S). Cooper were appointed surveyor to lay off and divide the estate equally to the following heirs, to wit, Hannah Woodfin, Samuel Woodfin gets where he lives, Elizabeth McMinn, Sally Naylor, Polly Edwards, Phebe Swann, Mary Woodfin, Rebecca Woodfin, John Woodfin, and Hannah Hall, all that one acre including the family burying ground to be left out of the division for a family burying ground fore-ever. Signed by John Woodfin, Hannah Woodfin, Thomas Haile, Hannah Hale, Samuel Woodfin, John Naler, Sally Naler, M. Woodfin, Rebecca Woodfin, Phebe Swann, Thomas Swann, M. H. Naler, James McMinn and Elizabeth McMinn. Wit: Thomas Hale, John Woodfin, J. Naler, J. Woodfin and Robert Swann and W. H. Naler. Reg: 16 Nov 1843. Plat on page 59.

Page 64 - 13 Nov 1843. Circuit Court, April Term 1843. James Reynolds, John Reynolds, Henry Reynolds, David Reynolds, Richard Reynolds, Andrew Reynolds, Moses Reynolds and Arthur Campbell and wife. Bill to sell land. Reg: 17 Nov 1843.

Page 78 - 17 Nov 1843. George Clanton to Thomas W. Clanton. Deed of Gift, 50 acres. For love and affection George Clanton has for Thomas W. Clanton, all his land in Bedford Co., TN. Bounded by Joseph Steele, David Frizell and William Stammers. Wit: P. C. Steele and Ira Barber. Reg: 4 Dec 1843.

Page 88 - North Carolina Grant to Caleb Phifer. No. 102. Copy of Record. 10 lbs for every 100 acres. 5000 acres on Falling Creek. Borders Richard Trotter's corner and Martin Phifer's corner. Plat on page 89. Reg: 13 Dec 1843.

Page 100 - 14 Aug 1843. Robert E. Gray and others to Robert S. Worke. Deed, 130 acres. Robert E. Gray of City of Philadelphia, PA, brewer and Maria C. his wife late Maria C. Scott widow of Thomas Scott, deceased, Sophia D. Scott of said city, single woman, John G. Scott of Kentucky, farmer, now in the said city, and Thomas J. Scott of the same city, merchant, one part and Robert S. Worke of Bedford Co., TN other part, farmer. Sold land in Bedford Co., marked in the plan of partition of lands among the heirs of James Scott, deceased. Reg: 21 Dec 1843.

Page 106 - 23 Dec 1843. Josiah Nisbitt and Mary J. Nisbitt to Frederick Batte, Jr. Josiah Nisbitt and Mary Jane his wife of Rutherford Co., TN, sold to Frederick Batte, Jr. of Giles Co., TN, land in the dower of Rebecca Batte widow of Henry Batte, deceased, in Bedford Co., on waters of Weakleys Creek and adjoining lands of Jackson Lile, Edward Tarpley and the heirs of Henry Batte, deceased. Wit: Samuel Nisbitt and Thomas D. Tarpley. Reg: 25 Dec 1843.

Page 109 - 26 Dec 1843. Jacob Greer to Jane H. Wiggins. Deed of Gift, 50 acres. For love and affection for his daughter Jane H. Wiggins, conveyed unto her land on which she now lives and was deeded to Jacob Greer by Herod F. Holt on 29 Apr 1843 in Bedford Co., TN, District No. 22. Jane H. Wiggins wife of Benjamin F. Wiggins. Wit: Robert Parkes and Jackson Greer. Reg: 27 Dec 1843.

Page 110 - 18 Dec 1843. Joseph McCamy to James Dixon. Deed, undivided interest &c, 90 acres. Whereas by descent from John McCamie, William McCamie, Lucinda McCamie, Catharine McCamie, Ellen McCamie and Joseph McCamie has derived title to and now hold equal interest in a tract of land in Bedford Co., TN, in District No. 21. Borders lands of James Dixon. Reg: 27 Dec 1843.

Page 120 - 25 Nov 1843. Martha Oslin to Eady Augustine Wheeler and others. Deed of Gift. For love and affection Martha Oslin has for Eady Augustine Wheeler, Lucy Engline Wheeler, and Sarah B. Frances Wheeler, conveyed unto Eadt Augustine Wheeler a cow and calf, to Lucy Engline Wheeler a cow and calf, to Sarah B. Frances Wheeler one heifer. Wit: Willis B. H. Clements, Columbus A. Craine, and David P. Wheeler. Reg: 9 Jan 1844.

Page 122 - 6 Jan 1844. Kary Kennedy to John M. Kennedy and others. Deed of Gift. For love and affection Kary Kennedy has for her three children, John M. Kennedy, William H. Kennedy, and Willie G. Kennedy, conveys unto them household items. Wit: James Mullins and Alsey Arnold. Reg: 9 Jan 1844.

Page 130 - 8 Jan 1844. George Campbell and Ann Campbell to James McConnell. Bill of Sale. George Campbell and Ann Campbell his wife of Bedford Co., TN, sold to James McConnell of Marshall Co., TN, three negroes. Wit: James Campbell, Samuel Anderson and Benjamin Gambill. Reg: 12 Jan 1844.

Page 133 - 13 Jan 1844. James Christian and wife to William Hime. Deed, 28 acres. James Christian and Sophronia Christian his wife formerly Sophronia Hime, sold to William Hime, land in Bedford Co., TN, being the land allotted to Sophronia in the division of the lands of John Hime, deceased, out of a 100 acre tract. Bounded by Pratt's line. Reg: 13 Jan 1844.

Page 148 - 25 Jan 1844. James Harris to John N. Hill. Deed of Gift. James Harris, Sr. of Bedford Co., TN, conveyed unto John N. Hill of Henry Co., TN, and for love and affection for his grandson William James Hill, son of his daughter Almeida Hill and John N. Hill, a negro girl Mary. William James Hill is under age of twenty one years. Reg: 27 Jan 1844.

Page 149 - 18 Jan 1844. Josiah Hastings and wife to William S. Wisdom. Deed, interest in estate. Josiah Hastings and his wife Sally Hastings of McNairy Co., TN one part and William S. Wisdom of McNairy Co., TN other part. Josiah Hastings and Sally Hastings being heirs at law of Culberth Word, deceased, and being entitled to one seventh part of Culberth Word's estate at the death of his wife Jane Word who is entitled to the estate during her natural life. Sally Hastings who was Sally Word before marriage and daughter of Culberth Word, deceased. Wit: Maclin Cross. Reg: 29 Jan 1844.

Page 159 - 25 Jan 1844. Stephen Austin to Lebinda B. Austin. Deed of Gift. Whereas sometime in the year of 1830 or 1831, George Parrish and his wife Mary Parrish gave to Stephen Austin's wife Rebecca Austin and his daughter Lebinda B. Austin, a negro girl Molly. Now for love and affection Stephen Austin has for his daughter Lebinda B. Austin, all his interest in negro woman Molly and her infant child. Wit: Joseph Kincaid and J. Sively. Reg: 3 Feb 1844.

Page 159 - 25 Jan 1844. Stephen Austin to Lebinda B. Austin. Deed of Gift. Whereas somrtime in the year of 1830, George Parrish and his wife Mary Parrish gave to Stephen Austin's wife Rebecca Austin and his daughter Lebinda B. Austin, a negro girl Molly. Now for love and affection he has for his daughter Lebinda B. Austin, gives to her all his interest in said negro woman Molly and her infant child. Wit: Joseph Kincaid and J. Sively. Reg: 3 Feb 1844.

Page 160 - 28 Dec 1843. John Garrett to Wilson Garrett. Deed, 46 acres. John Garrett of Perry Co., TN sold to Wilson Garrett, land in Bedford Co., TN, on waters of Little Flat Creek, it being the land on which Polly Harrett died. Borders William Shook, Samuel Coldwell and James Tribble. Wit: William B. Jones and Moses Oneal. Reg: 5 Feb 1844.

Page 161 - 21 Dec 1843. Joseph Hemby to Dennis Hemby. Deed, 125 acres. Joseph Hemby sold to Dennis Hemby, his father, both of Bedford Co., TN, for love and affection Joseph has for his father Dennis Hemby, land in Bedford Co., on waters of Shipman Creek. Borders lands of Dennis Hemby, Low's land, Adam Anthony, Brinkley's line, R. P. Harrison and Micajah Scruggs. Wit: Wiley Harp and James Spears. Reg: 6 Feb 1844.

Page 162 - 11 Sep 1843. Mary Friddle and Martin Friddle. Agreement Mary Friddle one part and Martin Friddle other part, both of Bedford Co., TN, state that on 11 Sept 1843 that Martin Friddle bind himself of $600.00 to be paid and if he refuses or fails to provide for Mary Friddle, her natural life and Mary Friddle will agree to deliver the note she holds on Martin Friddle for $300.00, and interest. The note is in possession of Henry Lynn for safe keeping. Wit: H. C. Hurst, Jos. Woosley and Thomas Dean. Reg: 6 Feb 1844.

Page 163 - 27 Dec 1841. George Jones and wife Susan to Farwick Frazer. Deed. George Jones and Susan his wife of Bedford Co., TN, sold to Farwick Frazer of Bedford Co., their 12th part of an undivided tract of land in Bedford Co., on the Bell Buckle Fork of the Wartrace Fork. They being of the heirs of John Culver, deceased, to whom Martin Murphree has made a deed of said land of 99½ acres. Borders Andrew Bailey and Wesley Mash, Bell Buckle Fork, mouth of Sugar Camp Branch and spring, Tillman Dixon, Edward Cages, Coldwell tract. Reg: 6 Feb 1844.

Page 164 - 6 Feb 1844. John Baker and Vilsey Baker to Jordan C. Holt. Deed in Trust. John Baker and Vilsey Baker his wife conveyed to Jordan C. Holt, in Trust in three tracts of land in Bedford Co., TN, they being the lands William Burgess died seized and possessed of and our interest in the dower of Vilsey the widow of William Burgess in the three tracts of land. Lands borders George Waite, McKisick's old line, Bennett's line for one tract and whereon Baker now lives. Also, one half of another tract on headwaters of Sugar Creek in the Dailey Hollow and borders Andrew Evans. Another tract on Flat Creek, bordering John B. CUmmings, Newton Cannon and the Flat Creek in James Younger's old line. Reg: 7 Feb 1844.

Page 173 - 10 Feb 1844. James Mullins, Sheriff, to Brittain Phelps. Deed. Brittain Phelps recovered a judgement against Hiram Edde in the Circuit Court on 11 Aug 1842 and came into the hands of the Sheriff on 6 Dec 1843 and there not being any personal property of Hiram Edde sufficient to satisfy the execution. He levied on a tract of land as the property of Hiram Edde. Land in Bedford Co., TN, in District No. 22, it being the lands which Joshua Holt, Sr. willed and bequeathed to his daughter Candis now the wife of Hiram Edde and adjoining the lands of the widow of Joshua Holt, deceased and on the road leading from Jordan C. Holt's store to Thomas Newsom's store. On 10 Feb 1844 sold to Brittain Phelps. Reg: 12 Feb 1844.

Page 187 - 15 Mar 1843. Martin Sims and wife to Jabus Nowlin and wife. Deed. Martin Sims and his wife Charlotte formerly Charlotte Bryeans one part and Jabus Nowlin and his wife Mary L. formerly Mary L. Bryeans other part, all of Bedford Co., TN. The above parties at the demise of Edward Bryeans, late of Bedford Co., became possessed as tenants in common as the heirs &c of Edward Bryean of four tracts of land in Bedford Co., on East Fork of Rock Creek, granted by the State of Tennessee to Edward Bryeans, of 340 acres. Jabus Nowlin being entitled to one third in right of his wife and one third by Deed of Conveyance from William J. Bryeans as the other and only remaining legatee. Land borders lands of Walter Sims' lot near the graveyard in Baker's, now Larue's line, and Garrens' corner. Wit: Josiah Wheat and William Person. Reg: 24 Feb 1844 (also, see deed in Book "NN", page 199).

Page 195 - 5 Mar 1844. R. C. C. P. Shaw to C. G. W. B. Shaw. Deed, interest in land. R. C. C. P. Shaw sold to C. G. W. B. Shaw his undivided interest in a tract of land in Bedford Co., TN, in District No. 1, it being the place whereon Mary Shaw now lives, which was bequeathed to her by the Will of my father Christopher Shaw, for her use during her natural life, also R. C. C. P. Shaw's interest being one third part of said land. Reg: 5 Mar 1844.

Page 196 - 27 Feb 1844. John A. Head to Edward Whitman. Power of Attorney. John A. Head appointed Edward Whitman his Attorney to receive for him from P. C. Steele, Esq., or any other person having possession of or liable for the same, a legacy or a share which descented to him from Enoch Head, now deceased, late of Bedford Co., TN. Wit: H. S. Wilson and J. P. Tucker. Reg: 6 Mar 1844.

Page 205 - 25 Dec 1843. Circuit Court Decree to William Gaston and wife and others. William Gaston and wife Elizabeth, Harrison Gaston and wife Nancy, John Sutton and wife Jane, Samuel Morrow, Mary Morrow, Catharine Morrow, Margaret Caroline Morrow, and Sarah Parthena Morrow, the last five being minors and petition by their next friend William Gaston, all being heirs of James Morrow, deceased, and Margaret Morrow widow of James Morrow, deceased. Exparte. John Jakes was the purchaser of 107 acres of land in Bedford Co., TN. Borders William Sharp, William Stephens, William Eoff, John Jakes and James Morrow's widow. Reg: 12 Mar 1844.

Page 214 - 7 Dec 1841. Thomas B. Anglin and wife Edith to Farwick Frazier. Deed, 1/12th part of 99½ acres. Thomas B. and wife Edith Anglin of Rutherford Co., TN, sold to Farwick Frazier of Bedford Co., TN, land in Bedford Co., on the Bell Buckle. They being heirs of John Culver, deceased, to whom Martin Murphree made a deed for the land. Borders Andrew Bailey and Wesley Mash, the Bell Buckle Branch, mouth of Sugar Camp

Branch, Tillman Dixon, and Edward Cages. Wit: D. W. Anglin and W. P. Sample. Reg: 19 Mar 1844.

Page 216 - 15 Mar 1844. Charlotte Head and others to Jesse P. Tucker. Deed+ acres. Charlotte Head, John A. Head, James W. Head, Lyttleton Averett and his wife Sally formerly Sally Head, Isreal Harris and his wife Martha formerly Martha Head of one part and Jesse P. Tucker and his wife Elizabeth formerly Elizabeth Head of other part. The above named parties being the heirs and distributees of Enoch Head, deceased, late of Bedford Co., TN, and borders Eben Wilson, Isreal Harris and his wife, Ed. Whitman's corner and the land conveyed by Jacob Fisher to Enoch Head. Reg: 19 Mar 1844.

Page 217 - 13 Mar 1844. Charlotte Head and others to John A. Head. Deed, 48 acres. Charlotte Head, James W. Head, Lyttleton Averett and wife Sally formerly Sally Head, Isreal Harris and wife Martha formerly Martha Head, Jesse P. Tucker and wife Elizabeth formerly Elizabeth Head one part and John A. Head of other part. Lands descended from Enoch Head, deceased. Charlotte Head the widow waiving her right to her dower and receiving a child's part or one seventh part of estate. Land to John A. Head is land known as the Foster place and borders north west bank of Falling Creek. Reg: 20 Mar 1844.

Page 218 - 13 Mar 1844. Charlotte Head and others to James W. Head. Deed 60+ acres. (Same as above heirs) sold to James W. Head, a child's part of Enoch Head's estate, land in Bedford Co., TN, on north side of Falling Creek and bounded by James W. Head's home tract, James Claxton, the corner of Charlotte Head's lot, and Daniel Capps' line. Reg: 20 Mar 1844.

Page 219 - 13 Mar 1844. Charlotte Head and others. Joint Deed &c. Whereas the heirs and distributees of Enoch Head, deceased, has agreed to make division of the lands among themselves, all of lawful age. That whereasCharlotte Head the widow of Enoch Head, deceased, agrees to relinquish and quit claim to the other heirs all her right that she has to her dower interest, she is to receive a child's part. Reg: 20 Mar 1844.

Page 222 - 13 Mar 1844. Charlotte Head and others to L. Averett and wife. Deed 102½ acres. (See above instruments for the names of the heirs of Enoch Head, deceased) Land to go to Littleton Averett and wife Sally formerly Sally Head. Land borders east bank of Falling Creek, Jesse P. and Elizabeth Tucker, Whitman's corner and Phifer's line. Reg: 21 Mar 1844.

Page 224 - 13 Mar 1844. Charlotte Head and others to Isreal Harris and wife. Deed 67¼ acres. (See above instruments for names of Enoch Head, deceased) Land in Bedford Co., TN, on both sides of Falling Creek. Borders E. Wilson, widow Head's lot, Fisher's tract, and others. Reg: 23 Mar 1844.

Page 232 - 27 Mar 1844. John T. Minter to George W. Minter and others. Deed of Gift, in Trust. For love and affection for his daughter Martha A. Key, John T. Minter conveyed to his three sons, to wit, George W. Minter, Jeptha Minter and Franklin Minter, in Trust for their sister Martha A. Key, a servant boy Jerry. (John T. Minter of Davidson Co., TN) Reg: 2 Apr 1844.

Page 233 - 26 Feb 1844. Thomas Lenoir, Executor &c to Newcum Thompson, Sr. Deed 1500 acres. Thomas Lenoir as Executor of William Lenoir, deceased, late of Wilkes Co., NC one part and Newcum Thompson of Bedford Co., TN other part. Sold land in Bedford Co., on both sides of Falling Creek. Borders the bank of Duck River at upper end of a rock bluff and including mouth of Falling Creek. William Lenoir's land issued by State of North Carolina by a grant, dated 10 July 1788. Wit: A. McMillan, George H. Hamilton and L. Martric of Ash Co., NC. Reg: 2 Apr 1844.

Page 236 - 28 Aug 1843. J. E. Couch to James M. Black. Deed, 9½ acres. Sold his share of a tract of land, it being a part of an undivided tract of land belonging to the heirs of James Couch, deceased, land on waters of Mulberry Creek in Lincoln Co., TN. Wit: Daniel Stephens. Reg: 3 Apr 1844.

Page 247 - 4 Apr 1844. John A. Davidson to Jane Davidson. Bill of Sale. A negro boy Grandison was sold to Mrs. Jane Davidson for her life time and at her death is to go to the heirs of Hugh Davidson, deceased, according to the Last Will and Testament. Reg: 8 Apr 1844.

Page 250 - 12 Apr 1844. David G. Deason to Louisa M. Rankin. Deed, undivided interest. David G. Deason sold to Louisa M. Rankin, all his interest in the real estate of Thomas C. Rankin, deceased, late of Bedford Co., TN. The land conveyed being one child's part of sundry tracts which Thomas C. Rankin died seized and possessed and which has never been divided among the minor heirs of Thomas C. Rankin, deceased. The interest being conveyed is the part that David G. Deason acquired by marriage with Margaret L. Rankin, one of the heirs of Thomas C. Rankin, deceased. Reg: 12 Apr 1844.

Page 251 - 1 Dec 1835. Jesse Scott, Administrator &c to Simon Willeford. Deed 14 acres. Jesse Scott of Bedford Co., TN, administrator of Jeremiah Dial, deceased, estate, conveyed unto Simon Willeford, land. Borders lands formerly owned by Jeremiah Dial, lands formerly owned by Dugans, Mosby Harris' line, and John Stevenson. Wit: Malinda Scott, Susannah Scott, A. S. Lawrance, and Joseph Loyd. Reg: 16 Apr 1844.

Page 255 - 2 Dec 1843. John Bennett and others to George Waite. Deed, 20¼ acres. John Bennett, Margaret Bennett, Thomas J. Bingham and his wife, Sally Nancy Bennett, Polly Harrison Bennett, and Margaret Ann Bennett of one part sold to George Waite other part, land in Bedford Co., TN, in District No. 22. Bounded by Waite's corner, Burgess' corner and Jacob Allbright's corner. Wit: Daniel Bartlett, Thomas J. Bingham and Jerome Albright. Reg: 20 Apr 1844.

Page 261 - 11 Mar 1844. Banks M. Burrow to N. B. Burrow. Deed, Town Lot. For natural love and affection for his son Napoleon B. Burrow of Bedford Co., TN, Banks M. Burrow of Bedford Co., conveyed unto him one equal third part of a tract of land, being in the Town of Shelbyville, in the north east corner of the Public Square fronting on the Public Square and known as the lot upon which the Old Globe Tavern formerly stood and it being the same interest conveyed to him by John Dickson. The said lot was conveyed by Marmaduke Mitchell to John Dickson. Reg: 1 May 1844.

DEED BOOK "NN"

Page 271 - 22 Jan 1844. Sally M. Freeman to William R. Looney and Joel C. Russell. Deed in Trust. Sally Malinda Freeman sold unto William R. Looney and Joel C. Russell, a negro girl Hulda. Sally Malinda Freeman is one of the legatees of William M. Russell, deceased. Wit: Jeremiah Whitsell, J. Hall and John Robinson. Reg: 11 May 1844.

Page 271 - 13 Mar 1844. William Thompson and others to Samuel G. Thompson. Deed, 35 acres. William Thompson of Desoto Co., Mississippi and Jane S. Thompson and Joseph R. McKinley of Bedford Co., TN sold to Samuel G. THompson of Bedford Co., land on both sides of North Fork and adjoining the lands of William Guy, Esq., Worke, and known as the Sarah Thompson, (blank) lot in the division of Alexander Worke's land. Borders William Thompson's lot, Mrs. Worke's line. Wit: William D. Orr and R. S. Worke. Reg: 15 May 1844.

Page 273 - 13 Mar 1844. William Thompson and others to Joseph R. McKinley. Deed, 50 acres. (See above names) Sold to Joseph R. McKinley of Bedford Co., TN, land in Bedford Co., on both sides of the North Fork and known as Sarah Thompson's lot of Alexander Worke's land. Wit: William D. Orr and R. S. Worke. Reg: 10 May 1844.

Page 275 - 13 Mar 1844. William Thompson and others to Jane S. Thompson. Deed, 57 acres. (See above instruments for names) Conveyed land in Bedford Co., TN, on both sides of North Fork and known as Sarah Thompson's lot in the division of Alexander Worke's land. Wit: W. D. Orr and R. S. Worke. Reg: 15 May 1844.

Page 275 - 13 Mar 1844. Samuel G. Thompson and others to William Thompson. Deed, 46 acres. (See above instruments for names) Land in Bedford Co., TN, on both sides of North Fork and known as Sarah Thompson's lot of Alexander Worke's land. Wit: William D. Orr and Robert S. Worke. Reg: 15 May 1844.

Page 283 - 3 Feb 1844. Newton C. Harris to Charles F. Wilkes and others. Deed of Gift. Newton C. Harris of Bedford Co., TN, for love and affection for his nephews and nieces, to wit, Charles F. Wilkes, William P. Wilkes, Eliza J. Wilkes, Elizabeth J. Wilkes, Lazina D. Wilkes, Martha C. Wilkes, Sarah F. Wilkes, Tallitha W. Wilkes, Almeda B. Wilkes, and Susanna M. Wilkes, conveyed personal property. Reg: 1 Jun 1844.

Page 286 - 27 Sep 1843. D. H. Rozar and others to George Waite. Deed, 2/5 of 130 acres. Between Holliday Rozar and for his wife Mary Jane, and William Balch and for his wife Elizabeth, sold to George Waite, land in Bedford Co., TN, in District No. 22 and on head of Sugar Creek. Bounded by lands of Waite and Bennett's line and McKisick's old line. It being the tract William Burgess died seized and possessed of. Wit: David Rozar, M. S. Rozar, D. M. Smith and John Baker. Reg: 4 Jun 1844.

Page 287 - 27 May 1844. Stephen Culp to John M. Warner. Deed, 107½ acres. Stephen Culp sold to John M. Warner, land in Bedford Co., TN, on south side of Duck River, it being a part of 1000 acres conveyed to Oliver B. Hays to George Earnhart. Borders bluff of Duck River, George Burgess and Russell Freeman. The said land to have and to hold at the death of Stephen Culp's mother Abigail the wife of his father Adam Culp. Wit: Hiram

Harris and Samuel J. Warner. Reg: 4 Jun 1844.

Page 292 - Circuit Court Decree. Title to Matt S. Finch. Apr 1844. Petition to sell land. John Bird and others, heirs at law of Samuel Bird, deceased, Exparte. 174 acres. Land was sold to Matt S. Finch by John Bird, Spiral Bird, Bartlett Bird, Mary Bird, Parnetta Bird, and Samuel Bird. Land in Bedford Co., TN, on waters of Noahs Fork. Borders south bank of Noahs Fork, land formerly belonging to A. W. Slaton, deceased, A. Crain and Haynes' line. Reg: 12 Jun 1844.

Pagw 294 - 15 Jun 1844. James H. Muse and wife to John B. Smith. Deed. James H. Muse and wife Evaline formerly Evaline Hartsfield conveys to John B. Smith all their interest in which Andrew Hartsfield lived at the time of his death, except the life estate which James H. Muse has one fourth of said tract of land in right of his former wife now deceased. Reg: 15 Jun 1844.

Page 295 - 17 Jun 1844. Enoch Kizer to John Wallace. Interest in estate. Enoch Kizer sold to John Wallace all his right title and claim to the estate of Volunteer Kizer, deceased. Wit: Horatio N. Manning and William Kizer. Reg: 22 Jun 1844.

Page 297 - 26 Jun 1844. Sarah Houston to Caleb P. Houston. Deed of Gift, 366 acres. For love and affection for Caleb P. Houston, Sarah Houston conveyed to him a tract of land in Bedford Co., TN, in District No. 5, it being part of the land willed to her by her father Caleb Phifer. Borders her father's lnad and the Turnpike. Reg: 29 Jun 1844.

Page 298 - 26 Jun 1844. Sarah Houston to William Houston. Deed of Gift, 422 acres. For love and affection for William Houston, Sarah Houston conveys unto hin land in Bedford Co., TN, it being part of the land willed to her by her father Caleb Phifer. Borders Turnpike and land whereon her late husband lived and now belongs to Louisa Steele. Reg: 29 Jun 1844.

Page 299 - 26 Jun 1844. Sarah Houston to Mary Ann Houston. Deed of Gift, 63 acres. For love and affection for Mary Ann Houston, Sarah Houston conveys unto her a tract of land in Bedford Co., TN, it being a part willed to her by her father Caleb Phifer. Reg: 29 Jun 1844.

Page 311 - 3 Feb 1836. Alfred Campbell to Daniel or Nancy Kizer. Deed, 1 acre. Alfred Campbell sold to Daniel Kizer or Nancy Kizer his mother, all of Bedford Co., TN, land in Bedford Co., on waters of Big Flat Creek. Borders Daniel Kizer's original line and willed to Daniel by Voluntine Kizer, deceased. Wit: William Stewart and William H. Cates. Reg: 2 Aug 1844.

Page 312 - 17 Jan 1844. John Webb and wife to Ezekiel H. Hazlett and wife. Deed, 100 acres. John Webb and wife Manerva Webb in exchange of land being the lands of which James Adams died seized and possessed have for and consideration of Lot No. 6, the title of which has been caused by Ezekiel H. Hazlett and his wife to be made to us by James H. Adams, exchanged and do hereby convey unto Ezekiel H. Hazlett and his wife Mary Hazlett Lot No. 8. Borders John Dawdy's line, William Craig's line, D. Anderson and Thomas Coffey. Reg: 2 Aug 1844.

Page 317 - 18 Jul 1844. John and Elizabeth Woodard to R. M.

Whitman and William Walker. Deed in Trust. John Woodard delivered to Robert M. Whitman of Lincoln Co., TN and William Walker of Bedford Co., TN, stock &c and their right to land in Bedford Co., of about 50 acres. Land adjoining George Woodard, Garrett, Phillips and others. Elizabeth Woodard on her part, land whereon she now lives, about 30 acres, in order to assist her brother. The land borders the same as above. Wit: Martin Collins and Daniel C. King. Reg: 6 Aug 1844.

Page 319 - 5 Aug 1844. Hugh Ray to Robert Ray. Bill of Sale. Negro boy Harry. Hugh Ray of Marshall Co., TN, sold to Robert Ray of Bedford Co., TN, a negro boy Harry. Wit: Jos. Anderson and William C. Ray. Reg: 7 Aug 1844.

Page 320 - 13 Jun 1844. William S. Anderson and Isabella Anderson to James W. Coffey. Deed, 110 acres. William S. Anderson and Isabella Anderson of Marshall Co., TN, sold to James W. Coffey of Bedford Co., TN, land in Bedford Co. Borders John Blackwell, James Price, Henry Haslett and Newcum Thompson. Wit: Thomas Coffey and James Price. Reg: 8 Aug 1844.

Page 327 - 5 Aug 1844. Isaac Parish and wife and others to Robert Matthews. Power of Attorney. Isaac Parrish and Sarah R. his wife, Helen G. Longstreth, Meirs Fisher Longstreth and Mary T. his wife, Lydia W. Longstreth, and Sidney E. Longstreth, heirs of the estate of Samuel Longstreth, appointed Robert Matthews as their Attorney to grant, bargain and sell all the land in Bedford Co., TN below Shelbyville. Borders lands now or late owned by Daniel Turrentine and sold to him by James L. Armstrong, Balch's old line, Wilhoite's line. 71 acres. Signed by Isaac Parrish, Sarah R. Parrish, Helen G. Longstreth by her attorney M. Fisher Longstreth, M. Fisher Longstreth, Mary T. Longstreth, Lydia W. Longstreth and Sidney E. Longstreth. Wit: Nathan T. Clapp and S. Badger. NOTE: Samuel Badger of Philadelphia, PA. Reg: 22 Aug 1844.

Page 328 - 12 Feb 1844. Jackson Nichols and wife to Absalom Reaves. Deed, 82 acres. Jackson Nichols and Nancy Nichols his wife sold to Absalom Reaves, land in District No. 11, on the North Fork, in Bedford Co., TN. Borders North Fork, crosses the Shelbyville to Franklin Road. Wit: R. W. Locke and David W. Thompson. Reg: 22 Aug 1844.

Page 329 - 19 Aug 1844. Isaac Parrish and others, by Attorney, to Thomas Pettis. Deed, 71 acres. Isaac Parrish, Sarah R. Parrish, Helen G. Longstreth, M. Fisher Longstreth, Mary T. Longstreth, Lydia W. Longstreth, and Sidney E. Longstreth, all of Pennsylvania, sold to Thomas Pettis of Bedford Co., TN, land in Bedford Co., below Shelbyville. Bounded by W. B. Sutton, Thomas Pettis, E. Kimmons, the Duck River, and Wilhoite's line. It being the place purchased by Samuel Longstreth, deceased, of James L. Armstrong. Reg: 23 Aug 1844.

Page 330 - 17 Aug 1844. Boyd M. Sims to Walter H. Sims. Deed. Boyd M. Sims conveyed to Walter H. Sims whatever interest was conveyed to him by Thomas O. Wilson, being one third of his life estate in one fourth of all the lands in Bedford Co., TN, which formerly belonged to Boyd M. Sims, Walter H. Sims, John G. Sims and Ann H. Sims, subsequently married to Thomas O. Wilson. Reg: 26 Aug 1844.

DEED BOOK "NN"

Page 331 - 9 Aug 1844. Benjamin F. Whitworth to Baptist and Presbyterian Churches. Deed. For love and affection, B. F. Whitworth conveys to the following religious denominations, to wit, Cumberland Presbyterians, and Missionary or Separate Baptist, for the purpose of building a church for the worship of God, the land lay in Bedford CO., TN, on the road leading from Shelbyville to Middleton. Borders Michael Shofner. Methodist of all kinds, Presbyterians of all kind, and Baptist and Episcopalians of all kind, to hold public worship in the Meeting House. Reg: 28 Aug 1844.

Page 332 - 29 Aug 1844. Robert F. Elkins and Phereba Ditto. Marriage Contract. Phereba Ditto and Robert F. Elkins, both of Bedford Co., YN, stated that a marriage is shortly intended between them. Phereby Ditto is possessed of property and estate which she is desirous to secure to her sole and separate use during her lifetime. Her estate is a life estate is land in Bedford Co., TN of 103 acres and being the dower tract assigned to her as dower of her deceased husband, William Ditto, also slaves from same estate and other property. Reg: 31 Aug 1844.

Page 334 - 2 Feb 1844. Samuel G. McGowen and wife to Frederick Batte, Jr. Deed. Samuel G. McGowen and Rebecca J. his wife of Rutherford Co., TN, sold to Frederick Batte, Jr., land in the dower of Rebecca Batte, widow of Henry Batte, deceased, in Bedford Co., TN, on waters of Weakley Creek and adjoining lands of Jackson Lile, Edward Tarpley and the heirs of Henry Batte, deceased. Wit: Frederick Batte, Sr. Reg: 2 Sep 1844.

Page 335 - 18 Nov 1836. Robert Batte, Jr. to Frederick Batte, Jr. Deed 7½ acres. Robert Batte, Jr. of Rutherford Co., TN to Frederick Batte, Jr. of Bedford Co., TN, land or part of a parcel of land in his mother's dower decreed to the heirs of Henry Batte, deceased, it being his part of the dower in Bedford Co., on waters of Weakleys Creek, adjoining lands of Jackson Lile, Sr., Ned Tarpley and Frederick Batte, Sr., and the heirs of Henry Batte, deceased. Wit: Frederick Batte, Sr. and Robert C. Batte. Reg: 2 Sep 1844.

Page 335 - 13 Oct 1837. T. Batte to Frederick Batte, Jr. Deed, 7½ acres. T. Batte, Jr. of Rutherford Co., TN, sold to Frederick Batte, Jr., land in his mother's dower decreed to heirs of Henry Batte, deceased, adjoining lands of Jackson Lile, Sr., and Edward Tarpley and the heirs of Henry Batte, deceased. Wit: Robert C. Batte and Frederick Batte, Sr. Reg: 2 Sep 1844.

Page 336 - 23 Dec 1843. Frederick Batte, Sr. and wife Eliza Ann to Frederick Batte, Jr. Deed, 7½ acres. Frederick Batte and Eliza Ann Batte his wife of Bedford Co., TN, sold to Frederick Batte, Jr. land deeded to Frederick, Jr., land, but finding the same not satisfactory to the said Frederick Batte, Jr. because Eliza Ann Batte had not signed the deed. The land being in Bedford Co., deeded to the heirs of Henry Batte, deceased and it being a part of the dower of Rebecca Batte his wife's mother. Wit: Robert C. Batte. Reg: 3 Sep 1844.

Page 337 - 23 Dec 1843. Robert C. Batte and wife Martha P. to Frederick Batte, Jr. Deed 7 acres. (Same as above instrument) Wit: Robert Batte, Jr. and Thomas D. Tarpley. Reg: 3 Sep 1844.

DEED BOOK "NN"

Page 340 - 30 Aug 1844. William G. Cowan to Thomas F. Webb. Deed. William G. Cowan sold to Thomas F. Webb, both of Bedford Co., TN, land in Bedford Co., in District No. 5, being the portion which Jordan Loyd inherited at the death of his father Joseph Loyd. Reg: 4 Sep 1844.

Page 341 - 13 Aug 1844. Charles Ready to Robert N. Strong and others. Deed of Gift. For the friendship and esteem for his brother in law Joseph C. Strong and his wife Sophronia, all of Bedford Co., TN and for their four children, Robert N., John M., Martha Jane and Joseph C. Strong, personal property &c. Reg: 7 Sep 1844.

Page 342 - 9 Nov 1843. James T. and Ann B. Crain to Collins & Perry. Deed, 1/13 of 175 acres. James T. Crain and Ann B. Crain his wife and daughter of Caleb Cox, deceased, sold to Collins & Perry, one undivided interest, being one thirteenth portion of a tract of land that Caleb Cox died seized and possessed of in Bedford Co., TN, on waters of Weakleys Creek. Borders John Jackson, Joseph Rushing, Mr. Natt, John T. Harris, and Richard Bandy. Wit: Nancy Cox, Marthiny Rushing and A. B. Moon. Reg: 10 Sep 1844.

Page 343 - 10 Sep 1844. James L. Armstrong to John S. Frazier. Agreement. Agreement between John S. Frazier, guardian of Robert H. Temple, William P. Temple, Jane T. Temple, and Hannah M. Temple, minor heirs of Dempsey P. Temple, and James L. Armstrong on behalf of himself and wife Mason P., relative to a judgement obtained by them as joint plaintiff in the name of James K. Polk, Governor, for the time being, who sued for the use of the above named parties against C. D. Steele, J. A. Blakemore, W. H. Wisener, George W. Fogleman and John Tillman, Executor of Samuel Escue, deceased, &c. Reg: 10 Sep 1844.

Page 344 - 4 Jan 1840. Thomas D. Wilson to John A. Hallan. Power of Attorney to sell land. Thomas D. Wilson of Caddo Parish, Louisiana, appointed John A. Hallen of Williamson Co., TN, his Attorney, to sell all his undivided interest in land in Bedford Co., TN, the same which he inherited as the heir of my son Walter Sims Wilson, who inherited the same as the only heir of his mother, one of the heirs of John G. Sims, deceased, or in right of his late wife, Ann H. formerly Ann H. Sims. Wit: James H. Wilson and Jason H. Wilson. Reg: 14 Sep 1844.

Page 348 - 18 Sep 1844. Edward Martin and wife Susanna to Thomas Hastings. Deed, 20 acres. Edward Martin and wife Susanna Martin, sold to Thomas Hastings, land in Bedford Co., TN, on the waters of Big Flat Freek. A part of a 130 acre tract, the same fell to them by kinship from the estate of Robert Hastings, deceased, the father of Susannah Martin. Borders Minos Cannon and Jane Hastings. Reg: 20 Sep 1844.

Page 349 - 24 Aug 1844. Isreal Harris and others to James W. Head. Deed, 80 acres. Jesse P. Tucker and Elizabeth his wife, and Isreal Harris and wife Martha, and John A. Head of one part sold to James W. Head, Charlotte Head and Sarah Averett other part, land in Bedford Co., TN, on waters of Fall Creek, in District No. 8. Bounded by Daniel Capps, Wilson Turrentine, Hartwell Freeman, James W. and Charlotte Head. Reg: 21 Sep 1844.

Page 350 - 5 Oct 1843. Washington B. Cooper to Jonathan J. Cooper. Deed of Gift, 94 acres. Washington B. Cooper of Nashville, Davidson Co., TN, for love and affection for Jonathan J. Cooper of Bedford Co., TN, land in Bedford Co., TN, in District No. 5 and on waters of Falling Creek. Borders P. C. Steele and W. B. Cooper. Sale of land to benefit William A. Cooper and James Cooper, sons of J. J. Cooper and also for the benefit of Mary Anne, wife of J. J. Cooper (Jonathan J.). Wit: John Tune and A. Dunlap. Reg: 24 Sep 1844.

Page 351 - 14 Sep 1844. Spencer and Henry Brown to Daniel Kizer. Deed. Spencer and Henry Brown were the purchasers of the property of Enoch Kizer, Nancy Kizer and Daniel Kizer. Now they sell same to Daniel Kizer. Reg: 24 Sep 1844.

Page 353 - 3 Oct 1844. Joshua M. Hix to Thomas Hastings. Deed. Joshua M. Hix sold to Thomas Hastings, land in Bedford Co., TN. Borders lands of Thomas Hastings and Robert Hastings from their father Robert Hastings, deceased, James Hastings and Jane Hastings. Reg: 7 Oct 1844.

Page 356 - 30 May 1843. William Keele to Matt Martin. Deed, 60 acres. William Keele sold to Matt Martin, Jr., land in Bedford Co., TN, in District No. 1, the undivided interest of William H. Rowton in and to a tract of land belonging to the heirs of A. B. Rowton, deceased, adjoining lands of Matt Martin, Jr., William Norton and others, it being the land whereon Nancy Rowton, widow of A. B. Rowton, now lives. Wit: R. C. C. P. Shaw and James Jakes. Reg: 8 Oct 1844.

Page 361 - 8 Oct 1844. J. H. Cobb and wife Sarah Cobb to Mary Kimbro. Deed of Gift, negro Aggy. For love and affection J. H. Cobb and his wife Sarah Cobb has for Mary Kimbro, conveyed a negro girl Aggy. Mary Kimbro wife of Allen Kimbro. Wit: Alexander Kimbro and Mary Stallard. Reg: 15 Oct 1844.

Page 362 - 8 Oct 1844. J. H. Cobb and Sarah Cobb to Moriah Hitt. Deed of Gift. For love and affection J. H. Cobb and Sarah Cobb his wife, has for Moriah Hitt, conveys a negro girl Nancy. Wit: Alexander Kimbro and Mary Stallard. Reg: 15 Oct 1844.

Page 362 - 8 Oct 1844. J. H. Cobb and wife Sarah to Susan Hitt. Deed of Gift. For love and affection they have for Susan Hitt, conveys a negro girl Emily. Emily Hitt wife of D. D. Hitt. Wit: Alexander Kimbro and Mary Stallard. Reg: 15 Oct 1844.

Page 363 - 7 Oct 1844. Payton Still and wife Sarah to George D. Stephenson. Deed, 1/10 of 95 acres. Payton Still and his wife Sarah Jane Still sold to George D. Stephenson, all of Bedford Co., TN, land in Bedford Co., belonging to the heirs of James Stephenson, deceased. Bounded by Samuel McMahan, William Eoff, and James Hoover. Wit: George Gill and Mead J. Hale. Reg: 16 Oct 1844.

Page 367 - 21 Oct 1844. Elijah Woosley to Joshua and William Woosley. Deed of Gift, 125 acres. For love and affection he has for his two sons Joshua and William Woosley, conveyed unto them, all his lands he now possess in Bedford Co., TN, whereon he now lives. Reg: 21 Oct 1844.

Page 368 - 23 Oct 1844. John McCuistion and William A. Young to Claiborn McCuistion. Deed of Gift, Trust. John McCuistion and William A. Young for love and affection for Susan Young the daughter of John McCuistion and wife of William A. Young, conveyed a negro woman Matilda and her two children. Reg: 24 Oct 1844.

Page 368 - Dec Term 1843. Circuit Court Decree to Thomas Wood and William G. Hight. Title to land, 159 acres. Travis C. Nash, administrator vs Mary V. West and others, at law of Amos West, deceased. The land in Bedford Co., TN, on head waters of Weakley and Alexander Creek. Borders Benjamin Lile, Nancy West, the dower, and Thomas Woods. Reg: 24 Oct 1844.

Page 370 - 12 May 1838. Benjamin McCuistion to John C. McCuistion. Deed, 17 acres. For love and affection Benjamin McCuistion has for his son John C. McCuistion, conveyed land in Bedford Co., TN, near and north west of Shelbyville, it being a part of a 62 acre tract granted to Benjamin McCuistion, Grant No. 2591. Borders John Mitchell. Wit: A. S. Lawrance and John McCuistion. Reg: 24 Oct 1844.

Page 371 - 12 Jun 1838. Matt S. Finch and wife to Julia A. to Laird B. Boyd. Relinquishment. Laird B. Boyd has paid in full for property, on obligation, on negroes. Wit: J. W. Ragsdale and John S. Davis. Reg: 29 Oct 1844.

Page 372 - 29 Oct 1844. James Lee to Catharine Lee. Deed. James Lee sold to Catharine Lee, all his interest in the estate of Peter Lee, deceased. Reg: 29 Oct 1844.

Page 375 - 26 Oct 1844. George Waite to Lydia M. Richardson. Deed, 75 acres. For love and affection George Waite has for Lydia M. Richardson, land in Bedford Co., TN, in District No. 22. Borders Templeton's Spring and Lydia M. Richardson, Evans & Norton's corner, and Fonville's line. Reg: 4 Nov 1844.

Page 376 - 7 Oct 1844. George Waite to Elizabeth P. Kingree. Deed, 80 acres. For love and affection George Waite has for Elizabeth P. Kingree, conveyed land in Bedford Co., TN, in District No. 22. Borders the Burgess' heirs, McKisick's old line, and McNatt's old corner. Reg: 4 Nov 1844.

Page 378 - 11 Nov 1844. Obadiah W. Knight to his children. Deed of Gift. For love and affection Obadiah W. Knight of Bedford Co., TN, has for his children, William Allen, John Wesley, Mary Jane, Elizabeth Bailey, and Gabriel Andrews Knight, as a portion with their mother Martha Ann, his late wife, and as he is expecting shortly again to marry and convey to the children, five negroes. Wit: William H. Wisener and Allen Knight. Reg: 12 Nov 1844.

Page 378 - 15 Nov 1844. Josiah Wheat and wife to John Ramsey. Deed in Trust. Josiah Wheat and Sarah Wheat his wife formerly Sarah Bryeans, of Bedford Co., TN, sold in trust to John Ramsey, land in Bedford Co., TN, to which the late John Bryeans had interest in at the time of his death and being on both sides of Big Sinking Creek, in District No. 18. Reg: 16 Nov 1844.

Page 385 - 15 Jan 1844. Fergus Hall to Harriett P. Thompson. Deed of Gift, negro girl Eliza. For love and affection for his daughter Harriett P. THompson, Fergus Hall conveys a negro girl Eliza to her. The slave is delivered unto William F. Thompson, husband of Harriett P. Thompson. Wit: James Thompson and L. W. Hall. Reg: 28 Nov 1844.

Page 399 - North Carolina to Robert Smith. No. 15. 5000 acres. Land on Duck River about 4 miles above the mouth of Sugar Creek. Borders lands of Amos Balch, William Galbreath, Jeremiah Chamberlain, dated 16 July 1788. Warrant No. 1883. Reg: 9 Dec 1844.

Page 401 - 28 Oct 1844. Elijah Bobo and Sarah Bobo to Samuel Bobo. Deed, Interest in estate. Elijah Bobo and Sarah Bobo his wife sold to Samuel Bobo, all of Bedford Co., TN, all the right, interest &c in estate, in William Pearson, deceased, being the daughter of William Pearson and entitled to one eighth share of the estate. Reg: 10 Dec 1844.

Page 402 - 9 Dec 1844. Manning G. Pearson to Samuel Bobo. Deed, interest in estate. Manning G. Pearson sold to Samuel Bobo, all his interest in the estate of William Pearson, deceased, he being a grandson of William Pearson, deceased, and his interest being one fifth of one eighth of said estate. Wit: G. W. Buchannan. Reg: 10 Dec 1844.

Page 406 - 6 Jun 1840. Jonathan Webster to Thomas Lipscomb. Relinquishment to negroes. Jonathan Webster conveyed unto Thomas Lipscomb all his right, title, claim &c to a family of negroes, now 11 in number, bequeathed to Jane Meadows during her life or widowhood by her husband Michael Meadows, deceased, which it being an undivided eleventh part of the remainder interest of said negroes after the death of Jane Meadows. Wit: J. W. Ragsdale and James McMichael. Reg: 12 Dec 1844.

Page 406 - 13 Dec 1844. Hiram Edde to Tarleton J. Reaves. Deed in Trust. Hiram Edde conveyed unto Tarleton J. Reaves, a deed in trust, for land whereon he now lives of about 200 acres, it being the same bequeathed to Hiram Holt by his father Joshua Holt. Reg: 14 Dec 1844.

Page 407 - 16 Dec 1844. William H. Craig to John S. Brown. Deed in Trust. William H. Craig conveyed unto John S. Brown, a deed in trust, 200 acres devised by John Dawdy to his two sons, John W. Dawdy and H. M. Dawdy. Land in Bedford Co., TN and adjoins lands of Edward John, W. R. Looney and others. Reg: 17 Dec 1844.

Page 411 - 20 Nov 1844. William S. Wisdom to Josiah Hastings and Sally Hastings. Power of Attorney. William S. Wisdom of McNairy Co., TN, appointed Josiah Hastings and his wife Sally Hastings his Attorney to sell and dispose of his interest that he purchased of them in the estate of Culberth Word. Reg: 18 Dec 1844.

Page 412 - 16 Dec 1844. Josiah Hastings and wife Sally to William Word. Deed, interest in estate. They conveyed unto William Word all the undivided interest in the estate owned by Josiah and Sally Hastings and now owned by William S. Wisdom, being one seventh part of said estate now remaining in the possession of widow of Culberth Word. Reg: 19 Dec 1844.

Page 414 - 23 Dec 1844. Samuel E. Dwyer to William Brown. Deed. Samuel E. Dwyer conveyed to William Brown, his interest in an undivided part of land which descended to him as one of the heirs of Daniel Dwyer, deceased, the same being the place where he resided at his death and being on north side of the Big Road leading from Shelbyville to Columbia, about two miles from Shelbyville. Reg: 24 Dec 1844.

Page 417 - 19 Aug 1844. Samuel C. Hooker and Sarah Hooker to Allen Wallace. Deed. Samuel C. Hooker and his wife Sarah Hooker of Marshall Co., Miss., sold Allen Wallace of Bedford Co., TN, on waters of the Wartrace Fork, belonging to the heirs of Robert Armstrong, Sr., deceased, the said Sarah being one of the heirs. The land contains 76 acres and bounded by lands of John Sutton, Sr., on which the late John B. Armstrong resided at the time of his death, the said Sarah being the relict and widow of the late John B. Armstrong, and she having since intermarried with Samuel C. Hooker. Reg: 1 Jan 1845.

Page 418 - 27 Dec 1844. Isreal Fonville and wife to William H. Burt. Deed. Isreal Fonville and his wife Julia Ann Fonville of Bedford Co., TN, sold to William H. Burt, land in Bedford Co., on waters of Powell Creek, in District No. 18, it being the land allotted to Julia Ann in the division of her father Jesse E. Williams, deceased, and known as Lot No. 1. Reg: 2 Jan 1845.

Page 419 - 30 Dec 1844. William B. M. Brame, Trustee &c to William H. Burt. Deed. Isreal Fonville by deed in trust to William B. M. Brame, dated 31 Mar 1842 and registered conveyed among other things all his right title and interest in land allotted to his wife Julia Ann in the division of the estate of her father Jesse E. Williams, deceased. Reg: 2 Jan 1845.

Page 421 - 8 May 1844. Elizabeth Reaves and others to T. J. Reaves. Bill of Sale. On 26 Dec 1842, Elizabeth Reaves conveyed a negro woman Eliza and her infant child to Tarlton J. Reaves, Alexander S. Reaves, Benjamin S. Reaves, Moses Reaves, and Pleasant H. Reaves. Tarlton gets two sixths, and the other four one sixth each reserving to herself in said slaves, a life estate. Wit: John Lacy and A. S. Reaves. Reg: 2 Jan 1845.

Page 424 - 20 Dec 1844. Martha Marshall to James H. Muse. Deed. Martha Marshall of Tipton Co., TN, conveyed to James H. Muse all her interest being one third in remainder of that portion of the land descended to the late Mary G. Muse formerly Mary G. Hartsfield on the death of her father the late Andrew Hartsfield and lately set apart by a division of the land in Bedford Co., TN on which A. Hartsfield lived at the time of his death. Mary G. being one fourth of the land, one third of which fourth descended to Martha Marshall on the death of Andrew W. Muse, subject to the life estate of James H. Muse. Andrew W. being a son of Mary G. and survived her some few months. Reg: 3 Jan 1845.
NOTE: A following instrument of John Hartsfield and James H. Muse, deed, on page 434 and 435. Reg: 3 Jan 1845.

Page 427 - 4 Jan 1845. Travis C. Nash, Jr. to Johanna Nash. Deed, interest in land. Travis C. Nash, Jr. of Bedford Co., TN conveyed unto Johanna Nash, all his interest as one of the heirs at law of Travis C. Nash, Sr., deceased, in the estate tract of land on which said Nash lived at the time of his death, on the waters of Fall Creek including the land he purchased from C. D. Steele, also the 10 acre Tennessee Grant, also land in Lincoln Co., TN, on headwaters of Mulberry Creek, his interest hereby conveyed is one fifteenth, to his mother Johanna Nash forever. Reg: 6 Jan 1845.

Page 427 - 4 Jan 1845. Travis C. Nash to Samuel A. Bell. Bill of Sale. Travis C. Nash on 27 Dec 1844 at the sale of the slaves belonging to the estate of his father Travis C. Nash, deceased, purchased a negro woman Matilda. He now sold unto Samuel A. Bell the said negro woman. Wit: Thomas C. Whiteside and J. M. Robinson. Reg: 6 Jan 1845.

Page 430 - 5 Oct 1844. James D. Clark and others to John M. Pressgrove. Power of Attorney. James D. Clark and Mary Clark, Hiram Maxfield and Judah Maxfield, all of Effingham Co., Illinois sold to John M. Pressgrove, land in Bedford Co., TN, it being known as the dower of the widow of John Sanders, deceased, late of Bedford Co., TN. Wit: E. W. Parkhurst and Tillman Clark. Reg: 7 Jan 1845.

Page 431 - 2 Dec 1844. John Morgan and others to John M. Pressgrove. Power of Attorney. John Morgan and Margaret Morgan and Rachel Pressgrove, all of Marshall Co., KY, owns lands in Bedford Co., TN and known as the dower tract of the widow of John Sanders, deceased, late of Bedford Co., appointed John M. Pressgrove as their Attorney to sell said land. Reg: 7 Jan 1845.

Page 432 - 29 Nov 1844. W. R. McFarlin and wife Elzira to W. R. Bresee. Deed. W. R. McFarlin and his wife Elzira McFarlin, sold to W. R. Bresee, their interest to the partition of Lot No. 14, in Shelbyville. Reg: 7 Jan 1845.

Page 433 - 7 Jan 1845. John Morgan and others by Jno. M. Pressgrove to Absalem Reaves. Deed, 43 acres. John Morgan and his wife Margaret Morgan, John M. Pressgrove and Rachel Pressgrove, of Marshall Co., KY, James D. Clark and Mary Clark his wife, Hiram Maxfield and his wife Judah Maxfield of Effingham Co., Illinois, sold to Absalem Reaves, land in Bedford Co., TN, on the North Fork. Reg: 8 Jan 1845.

Page 437 - 30 Nov 1844. Frederick Batte, Jr. to Thomas D. Tarpley. Deed, 55 acres. Frederick Batte, Jr. sold to Thomas D. Tarpley, it being his interest in land laid off as the dower of Rebecca Batte, widow of Henry Batte, deceased. Land in Bedford Co., TN, on waters of Weakley Creek and adjoining the lands of Jackson Lile, deceased, Edward Tarpley and the heirs of Henry Batte, deceased. Wit: Jennings Moore, D. A. Ozment, A. E. Atkinson and Minos F. Thompson. Reg: 9 Jan 1845.

DEED BOOK "OO" 1845 - 1846

Page 2 - 11 Jan 1845. William J. Peacock to Burrell Featherston. Deed. William J. Peacock conveys unto Burrell Featherston, all his right title and interest in the estate of his mother Anne Peacock, deceased. Reg: 11 Jan 1845.

DEED BOOK "OO"

Page 3 - 30 Dec 1844. Thomas Pettis and wife Sophia to John C. Coldwell. Deed, 76 acres. Thomas Pettis and his wife Sophia sold to John C. Coldwell, all their undivided interest, being one third, in tracts of land in Bedford Co., TN, on Duck River near Town of Shelbyville. Borders Wilson Coat's land. Another tract borders lands of the heirs of William Gilchrist, road leading from Shelbyville to McMinnville, James Deery. Reg: 13 Jan 1845.

Page 8 - 27 Nov 1844. Joshua White to William P. White. Deed, 140 acres. Joshua White of Marshall Co., TN, conveys to William P. White his son of Marshall Co., TN, for love and affection for his son, land in Bedford Co., TN. Borders lands of Bond's and Lyles' line. Reg: 17 Jan 1845.

Page 8 - 20 Nov 1844. Nancy Routon to James Deery. Deed in Trust. Nancy Routon conveyed to James Deery, her dower interest in the lands of my deceased husband A. B. Routon, in Bedford Co., TN, on waters of the Garrison Fork, for debt due to James Deery and due on 24 Sep 1845, the name of Hooper J. Routon, David Routon and Martha B. Routon signed as her surities. Wit: A. W. Majors and Ross D. Deery. Reg: 17 Jan 1845.

Page 11 - 10 Jan 1845. Thomas R. Talbot, A. Myers and others. Agreement &c. Thomas Talbot departed this life intestate in Bedford Co., TN, leaving Nancy Talbot his widow, and James R. Talbot, John H. Talbot, and Patsy Myers wife of Abram Myers, his only children. Thomas Talbot at the time of his death was the owner of slaves (4). James R. Talbot and John H. Talbot appointed administrators of the estate of Thomas Talbot, dec'd. The heirs have agreed to divide the slaves. Wit: J. Cleveland and Blan Maupin. Reg: 18 Jan 1845.

Page 21 - 13 May 1844. Shadrack S. Brown to Richard Warner. Deed. For love and affection Shadrack S. Brown has for his daughter Naomi Tilford wife of David Tilford of Bedford Co., TN, conveyed land in Bedford Co., about three miles north west of Shelbyville on the road leading to Columbia. Bounded by Joseph Green, lands of Joseph Robinson and Martin Phifer's heirs, common school land, and David Robinson. Reg: 27 Jan 1845.

Page 25 - 30 Dec 1844. J. M. Lorance to William Guy. Deed, 1/5th part of 192 acres. Joseph M. Lorance sold to William Guy, both of Bedford Co., TN, land in Bedford Co., in District No. 5, which descended from Margaret Lorance to her heirs, five in number. J. M. Lorance's interest being one fifth part. Bounded by lands of Capt. Z. B. Dozier, William Warren and William Guy. Wit: Preston Frazer and Lewis W. Shapard. Reg: 31 Jan 1845.

Page 26 - 23 Dec 1843. Thomas B. Carlton to James T. Byler and others, Trustees to Meeting House, 2 acres. Thomas B. Carlton of Bedford Co., TN, conveyed to James T. Byler of Williamson Co., TN and Thomas Cole of Williamson Co., TN, and Renwick A. Gault of Bedford Co., TN, Commissioners, for $5.00, land, the rail timber reserved for Carlton, in Bedford Co., on waters of Duck River. For the only use of a Liberty Meeting House. Wit: William C. Cook and Ivey Phillips. Reg: 1 Feb 1845.

Page 27 - 30 Jan 1845. Peter Miller to Nancy A. Porter and children. Deed of Gift. Peter Miller of Bedford Co., TN, for his daughter Nancy A. Porter and her nine (9) children, conveys negroes (3). Nancy A. Porter's children, to wit, Jane, Peter H., Mary N., Rachel G., Elizabeth M., Lucinda, Samuel H., James K., and Nancy Porter. Wit: D. D. Arnold and John M. Corbitt. Reg: 1 Feb 1845.

Page 31 - 22 Apr 1844. Moses Woodfin to W. H. Nailor. Deed, 33½ acres. Moses Woodfin sold to Wade Hampton Nailor a tract of land, being Lot No. 10, and the lot assigned to Moses Woodfin in the division of the tract of land on which his father Nicholas Woodfin lived. Borders lands of William Guy. and the Graveyard Lot. Wit: Thomas Haile, John Naler, J. D. Naler and Woodfin Naler. Reg: 4 Feb 1845.

Page 32 - 6 Feb 1845. Alexander B. Moon to Jennings Moore and James Ogilvie. Mortgage, 250 acres. Alexander B. Moon of Bedford Co., TN one part and Jennings Moore and James Ogilvie other part, conveyed land in Bedford Co., on Weakleys Creek. Borders lands of James H. Locke, Mrs. Farmer, Ann Wheeler a minor of Nathan Wheeler, and others. The land deeded to A. B. Moon by James T. McElvey of North Carolina, also a negro woman Fanny and her five children. Alexander B. Moon several years ago received from William Stokes of Lunenburg Co., VA, $2000.00 for which he executed to said Stokes his receipt or agreement in writing containing a stipulation that Moon should expend the same in the purchase of a tract of land for the use and benefit of Polly H. Jeffries, wife of Thomas B. Jeffries, during her life and at her death said land to be divided among her children. Reg: 6 Feb 1845.

Page 34 - 18 Jan 1845. Samuel B. McCuistion and others to John C. McCuistion. Deed. Samuel B. McCuistion, Piety A. McCuistion, and Elizabeth W. McCuistion, being heirs and distributees of Benjamin McCuistion, deceased, and all of lawful age, sold to John C. McCuistion, their undivided interest in lands in Bedford Co., TN, in District No. 6, on Hurricane Creek. Bounded by school land, Andrew Vannoy, and William Elliott. It being the dower tract allotted to their mother Sarah McCuistion during her lifetime, it being their 3/4th of same. Also, another tract of land bordering the school land, dower tract, Thomas Couch, Phillip's line, Hadley's old line, and William Elliott. Wit: Andrew Vannoy, James P. McCuistion, and Phillip Hodges. Reg: 7 Feb 1845.

Page 35 - 18 Jan 1845. Piety A. McCuistion to John C. McCuistion. Deed, 57¼ acres. Piety A. McCuistion sold unto John C. McCuistion, land in Bedford Co., TN, in District No. 6, on Hurricane Creek. Borders William Elliott, E. Payton, and William Watkins. Wit: Andrew Vannoy, James P. McCuistion, and Phillip Hodges. Reg: 7 Feb 1845.

Page 36 - 7 Feb 1845. Richardson Clardy and wife to Minos F. Thompson. Deed, 107 acres. Richardson Clardy and Adaline M. Clardy his wife, sold to Minos F. Thompson, land in Bedford Co., in District No. 11. Borders school land, a grant of William Lenoir, and John Thompson. Reg: 7 Feb 1845.

Page 38 - 13 Oct 1841. John Culver and D. W. Anglin and wife to Farwick Frazer. Deed. John Culver of Fentress Co., TN, David W. Anglin and Sally Anglin of Bedford Co., TN, sold to Farwick Frazer of Bedford Co., three twelfth part of an undivided tract of land in Bedford Co., TN, on the Bell Buckle Branch. They being the heirs of John Culver, Sr., deceased, to whom Martin Murphree had made a deed for 99½ acres. Borders Andrew Bailey and William Marsh, the Bell Buckle Branch, mouth of Sugar Camp Branch and include the spring, Dixon's line, Edward Cage and Coldwell's tract. Wit: Thomas Campbell and William P. Sample. Reg: 8 Feb 1845.

Page 42 - 1 Feb 1845. Ethern Jordan and others to Benjamin F. Greer. Deed, 50 acres. Eathern S. Jordan, Winston W. Jordan and Tabitha Jordan of Bedford Co., TN sold to Benjamin F. Greer of Bedford Co., land in Bedford Co., on waters of Sinking Creek and Powels Creek and on both sides of the road leading from Shelbyville to Columbia and Pulaski, being the one half of a 100 acre tract conveyed by Aaron Gambill to Zachariah Jordan and east half thereof. Bounded by Thomas Greer's lands. Wit: A. J. Greer and G. W. Greer. Reg: 11 Feb 1845.

Page 48 - 23 Mar 1844. John Phillips to James H. Curtis. Deed, 67 poles. John Phillips sold to James H. Curtis land in Bedford Co., TN, including the celebrated spring called Samaria, land near Richmond in Bedford Co. Borders land where James H. Curtis, Jr.'s dwelling house now stands. Wit: T. A. White and A. Freeman. Reg: 17 Feb 1845.

Page 65 - 4 Mar 1845. R. F. Arnold to Alexander J. Arnold. Deed of Gift. For love and affection has for his nephew Alexander J. Arnold, a brown filly. Alexander J. Arnold is the son of Absalom Arnold. Reg: 4 Mar 1845.

Page 69 - 4 Mar 1845. Thomas Davidson to Kimbro O. Chapman. Deed of Gift, in Trust. Thomas Davidson of Marshall Co., TN, for love and affection for his daughter Sophia Chapman, has delivered to Kimbro O. Chapman of Bedford Co., TN, negro slave Rose, for life. Reg: 8 Mar 1845.

Page 69 - 4 Mar 1845. Thomas Davidson to James Davis. Deed of Gift, in Trust. Thomas Davidson of Marshall Co., TN, for love and affection for his daughter Malinda P. Davis, conveyed unto her and delivered to James Davis, a negro slave Caroline, for life. Reg: 8 Mar 1845.

Page 78 - 26 Aug 1844. Margarett M. Arnold to James F. Arnold. Bill of Sale. Margarett M. Arnold sold to James F. Arnold a negro woman Ailsy and her child. Signed by the heirs of James Arnold, deceased. Marharett M. Arnold, Thomas M. Arnold, O. P. Arnold, THomas Cunningham, Martha Ann Arnold, Lemira M. Arnold, Sophronia Arnold, and Robert Petty. Wit: Charles F. Sutton and Joseph Galegy. Reg: 22 Mar 1845.

Page 86 - 2 Apr 1845. Joel Lorance and Mary Lorance to Mary Jane Kinney. Deed of Gift. For love and affection for Mary Jane Kinney, their niece, all of Bedford Co., TN, bequeathed a negro girl Selah Ann which is now in the possession of John Lorance in Noxubee Co., Mississippi. If Mary Jane Kinney dies without issue, the gift is to descend and equally divided amongst the children of Eliza Matilda Looney, the sister of Mary Jane Kinney. Wit: Andrew Vannoy and Thomas Lents. Reg: 10 Apr 1845.

Page 96 - 14 Apr 1845. Samuel J. Warner to Eunice Warner. Deed, interest in estate. Whereas by the Last Will and Testament of John Warner, Jr., deceased, Samuel Josiah Warner had interest in remainder to take effect and be united with possession after the death of his mother Eunice Warner, in two tracts of land in Bedford Co., TN, in District No. 21. One tract of 250 acres and the other whereon Eunice Warner now lives containing 250 acres and one Town Lot in Shelbyville and whereon Samuel Josiah Warner has an interest agreeable to the will of John Warner, deceased, in all the negroes and personal property belonging to the estate of John Warner, deceased, to take effect likewise at the death of Eunice Warner. Samuel J. Warner sold to Eunice Warner his interest in the estate. Wit: William Galbreath and Blount G. Green. Reg: 15 Apr 1845.

Page 98 - 7 Mar 1845. Poindexter Payne to Gabriel Maupin. Deed, 14 acres. Poindexter Payne sold to Gabriel Maupin, both of Bedford Co., TN, on the Barren Fork, it being No. 9 as laid off by the Commissioners in the division of the estate of Zebediah Payne, deceased. Bounded the river, and Lodwick Holt. Wit: John Turman, Robert H. Terry and Williamson Haggard. Reg: 23 Apr 1845.

Page 105 - 5 May 1845. James M. Elkins to Don C. Shriver. Deed, 75 acres. James M. Elkins sold unto Don C. Shriver, land in Bedford Co., TN, in District No. 3. Four of the 75 acres being which had been conveyed to the managers of the Horse Mountain Camp Ground for the use of the Methodist Church. Borders R. George and west of the top of the Horse Mountain. Reg: 5 May 1845.

Page 106 - 28 Apr 1845. Jemima H. Light to Samuel Carter and William B. M. Brame. Power of Attorney. Jemima H. Light of Bedford Co., TN, relying on the integrity of her friend Samuel Carter of Halifax Co., VA, appointed Samuel Carter for her Attorney to receive any money due her for rents &c of land, hire of negroes. Also, she has confidence in the integrity of her nephew William B. M. Brame of Bedford Co., TN, appointed him her Attorney to receive from Samuel Carter all monies due her. Wit: O. W. Knight and G. B. Knight. Reg: 6 May 1845.

Page 107 - 26 Dec 1844. William Jackson and others to David Potiller. Deed, 22 acres. William Jackson and Elizabeth J. Nelson now Elizabeth J. Jackson, his wife, and William Graham and Mary A. Nelson now Mary A. Graham, all of Bedford Co., TN, sold to David Potiller of Bedford CO., land in Bedford Co., on head waters of Wilson Creek in District No. 10. Bounded by Thomas Nunn, Thomas J. Nelson, James Garrett and David Potiller. Wit: William Elmore and William Taylor. Reg: 6 May 1845.

Page 109 - December Term 1844, Circuit Court Decree. Title to Joel Stallings. Circuit Court decrees that Joel Stallings was the purchaser of land that is in the interest of Benjamin Coffee and wife Nancy, Thomas Coffee and wife Priscilla, Lindsey Dobbs and wife Piety, Jacob Evans and Sally Evans, heirs at law of William Evans, deceased, their interest in two tracts, one of 75 acres in Bedford Co., on waters of East Fork of Rock Creek and headwaters of Bryeans Creek. Bounded by Peter Garren, Benjamin Coffey, Edward Bryeans, Joshua Musgrove, John T. Neil. Other tract of 38 acres, borders Jeremiah Forbes, Benjamin

Coffee's line. Reg: 14 May 1845.

Page 110 - 24 Feb 1845. Chancery Court Decree, Title to David Floyd. Michael Womack and wife Sally, Wiley B. Jones, Walton Watson and his wife Peggy, David D. Jones, George Davidson, Charles B. Jones, Charles W. Womack, Samuel Jones and Eliza Jane Jones by their guardian Rebecca Jones vs Joseph Watson and wife Tacy, Ellison Cox and wife Catharine, William Samuel Harrison, Charles W. Jones and Jonathan Samuel Jones. David Floyd purchased land mentioned in the pleadings, about 100 acres, sold by Robert P. Harrison. The Court ordered that all the interest &c of the widow and heirs at law of Charles Jones, deceased, be sold. Land on waters of Flat Creek. Bounded by William Boon and the dower lands of the widow of Charles Jones, Elijah and David Floyd, and Anthony Floyd and William Ray, and William Word. Reg: 17 May 1845.

Page 113 - 20 Jan 1845. George W. Hudlow and wife to Burrel Bobo. Interest in negroes. George W. Hudlow and Lucy Hudlow his wife, sold their interest in the proceeds from sale of negroes belonging to the estate of William Hurst, deceased, which were sold. Reg: 21 May 1845.

Page 114 - 20 May 1845. Thomas and Polly Pannell to Benjamin F. Pannell. Deed of Gift, on 200 acres of land. Thomas Pannell and Polly Pannell of Coffee Co., TN one part and Benjamin F. Pannell of Bedford Co., TN, for love and affection they have for their son Benjamin F. Pannell, conveys unto him land in Bedford Co., on the waters of the Garrison Fork. Borders lands of William Hooser and Francis King. Wit: John P. Steele and L. D. Pannell. Reg: 22 May 1845.

Page 120 - 2 May 1845. Thomas B. Mosely to Archelaus M. Hughes. Deed of Gift, slaves in Trust. Thomas B. Mosely of Bedford Co., TN, for love and affection for his two granddaughters Rebeckah Mosely Hughes and Sarah Mosely Hughes, conveys unto Archelaus M. Hughes to hold in trust, slaves, until either or both come of age or marry. Reg: 26 May 1845.

Page 124 - 19 Nov 1844. Neely Coble to Katharine and Larkin Jones. Deed of Gift. Neely Coble, for love and affection for his sister Katharine Jones and Larkin Jones and he being a fittified boy and is an idiot, convey unto them a lot of property that he bought at a sale on 12 Sep 1844, which property was sold by F. Shofner by a Deed of Gift by Samuel Jones to him, personal property. Wit: Daniel Hooser and Gabriel Shofner. Reg: 3 Jun 1845.

Page 124 - 9 Jul 1844. Reuben P. Sitliff to Gabriel Maupin. Deed, 17½ acres. Reuben P. Sitliff sold to Gabriel Maupin a tract of land in Bedford Co., TN, on waters of the Barren Fork near Rowsville, being a part of the tract of which Zebediah Payne died seized and possessed, being the portion allotted to Z. Payne, son of Zebediah Payne, deceased. Wit: G. W. Heard and F. Shofner. Reg: 3 Jun 1845.

Page 126 - 18 Feb 1845. Fergus Hall to John F. Hall. Deed of Gift, a negro girl Ardell. Fergus Hall of Bedford Co., TN, being of sound mind and disposing memory and for love and affection for his son John F. Hall of Bedford Co., TN, conveys unto him a negro girl Ardell. Wit: Francis F. Martin and Coleby C.

Brown. Reg: 6 Jun 1845.

Page 127 - Feb Term 1845, Chancery Court Decree. Title to James H. Locke. James H. Locke, administrator &c vs The creditors of Joseph Thompson, deceased. William S. Wade was purchaser of a three undivided fifth part of a twenty five acre tract which is near Thompson Ford, on north side of the river, it being the part of land of Joseph Thompson, deceased, which was allotted to William F. Thompson as one of the heirs of Joseph Thompson. deceased. Land borders lands of James H. Locke, Newton C. Thompson, school land, and Felix Turrentine. Another tract of 15 acres about one mile from Thompson Ford and bounded by John McMullin, John Thompson, William Lenoir's tract, Samuel Turrentine. James H. Locke has paid off all the purchase money and William S. Wade and Elizabeth Thompson relinquished their rights &c. Reg: 6 Jun 1845.

Page 129 - 7 Jun 1845. Elizabeth Ship, Sr. and others to Mary Kerby. Deed, 32 acres. Elizabeth Ship, Sr. and Valentine M. Kelly and Martha his wife, and Elizabeth Ship, Jr., and Sarah Ship, all of Bedford Co., TN, sold to Mary Kerby of Bedford Co., land in Bedford Co., on waters of Little Flat Creek. Wit: J. H. Miles and J. B. Reagor. Reg: 11 Jun 1845.

Page 132 - 19 Jun 1845. Flower Swift to Thomas Kimmons. Bill of Sale. Flower Swift of Bedford Co., TN, sold to Thomas Kimmons and his wife Polly, a negro girl Molly. Reg: 19 Jun 1845.

Page 135 - 25 Jun 1845. George Hudlow and wife, Allen Tribble and wife to Edmond Word. Deed, Interest in land, 150 acres. George Hudlow and Lucy Hudlow and Allen Trible and Sarah Trible his wife, conveyed unto Edmond Word, all the interest in two tracts of land in Bedford Co., TN, in District No. 22. Borders Hugh C. Hurst, Edmond Word and Polly Norman. Another tract bordering Thomas Dean and Reagor, Edmond Word and J. F. Norman. Reg: 1 Jul 1845.

Page 140 - 10 Feb 1834. Joseph Clark and William Moody to School Trustees for land. 1 acre. Joseph Clark and William Moody, both of Bedford Co., TN, conveyed to Moses Stone, James Kyser, and Hezekiah Brown, Trustees, for a school that is kept on said land and their successors forever for the good will that Clark and Moody has for a school to teach children, they do give the following land for that use. Land in Bedford Co., on headwaters of Big Flat Creek, it being a part of Clark's land and a part of Moody's land, and the school house is built on said lands. Borders lands of Clark and Moody and on the Big Flat Creek. Wit: Henry Dean and T. S. Brown. Reg: 10 Jul 1845.

Page 140 - 6 Jan 1845. James Robinson to Joseph Robinson. Deed, interest in land. James Robinson sold to Joseph Robinson, all his interest as one of the heirs at law of the late John Robinson, Sr., deceased, of Bedford Co., in the lands belonging to John Robinson at the time of his death in State of Kentucky and west of the Tennessee River and in different Counties. Wit: Alexanders Sanders. Reg: 10 Jul 1845.

Page 146 - 23 Jul 1845. Allen Kimbro and wife Mary to George Kimbro. Deed. Allen Kimbro and wife Mary Kimbro of Bedford

Co., TN, sold to George Kimbro of Bedford Co., their undivided interest, the same being one undivided twenty fifth part of a tract of land in Bedford Co., in District No. 25, on both sides of Thomas Creek, being the same land sold by John T. Neil by a decree of the Circuit Court to Robert Arnold, and Arnold sold to David Elkins, deceased. It adjoining the dower interest of Mary Coble out of the lands of her late husband Jacob Coble, deceased, of 149 acres. Reg: 25 Jul 1845.

Page 148 - 12 Jul 1845. Thomas Smith, Sr. to Elizabeth C. Kinnard. Deed of Gift, negroes. For love and affection Thomas Smith, Sr. has for his daughter Elizabeth C. Kinnard wife of William Kinnard, conveyed unto her and after her death to her children, negroes. Reg: 4 Aug 1845.

Page 151 - 16 Dec 1845. John S. Brown to William H. Wisener. Deed, 200 acres. Whereas William H. Craig executed a deed in trust to John S. Brown, one half of a tract of land, it being the same bequeathed by John Dawdy to his two sons John W. Dawdy and H. M. Dawdy, in Bedford Co., TN, on waters of Rock Creek. Craig failed to pay for tract of land. Ordered a public sale of land, William H. Wisener being the purchaser. Wit: H. M. Dawdy and A. J. Smith. Reg: 5 Aug 1845.

Page 152 - 8 Mar 1845. William P. Elkins and others to William Brown. Deed, 2 acres. William P. Elkins, Philip Elkins, James H. Cobb and Sarah his wife, and Mary Elkins, Allen Kimbro, H. H. Elkins, conveyed unto William Brown, land in Bedford Co., TN, in District No. 7, in the Town of Shelbyville. Bounded by Spring Street, old Corporation line and it being the place formerly owned by Joseph P. Stallard and bought by David Elkins, whose heirs they are, at Sheriff's Sale on 5 July 1841. Signed by William P. Elkins, James H. Cobb, Mary Elkins by her agent James H. Cobb, Allen Kimbro, John R. Hitt, D. D. Hitt, H. H. Elkins, and James Mullins. Wit: E. Cooper, J. Wortham, A. B. Coldwell, L. Shappard, and J. G. Barksdale. Reg: 5 Aug 1845.

Page 156 - 19 Aug 1845. Charlotte Head to James W. Head. Deed. For love and affection that Charlotte Head had for her son James W. Head, conveyed unto him two tracts of land in Bedford Co., TN, in District No. 8. Bounded by E. Wilson, and Claxton's fence. In all 52¼ acres. Second tract, being undivided interest in the tract of land in which was allotted to her daughter Mary Head in the division of the lands of her late husband Enoch Head, deceased, located in Bedford Co., on waters of Fall Creek. Bounded by Daniel Capps, Wilson Turrentine, James W. Head. About 80 acres. Her interest in the land is a one third part. Wit: Andrew Vannoy and David Burton. Reg: 16 Aug 1845.

Page 162 - 27 Aug 1845. Samuel Woodfin to Thomas Haile. Interest in negro. Samuel Woodfin, one of the heirs of the late Nicholas and Hannah Woodfin of Bedford Co., TN, deceased, sold unto Thomas Haile, all his interest in the family of negroes (3), belonging to the estate. Wit: J. H. Woodfin and Thomas Edwards. Reg: 30 Aug 1845.

Page 164 - 1 Sep 1845. William McKamie to James Dixon. Deed, 90 acres. Whereas by descent from John McKamie, Lucinda McCamie, Catharine McCamie, Ellen McCamie and himself William McCamie, has devised title to, and now hold equal interest in a tract of land in Bedford Co., TN, in District No. 21. Bounded by

DEED BOOK "OO"

Page 174 - 22 Aug 1845. Martha A. Stephens to Thomas Thompson. Relinquishment, 350 acre deed. Whereas by the Last Will and Testament of John Stephens, she is lawfully seized of a life estate in a tract of land in Bedford Co., TN, in District No. (blank). Bounded by lands of Robert and Leonard Temple, Richard H. Sims, Hubert Smith and the heirs of Coleman, and William Allen. It being the tract of land whereon Martha A. Stephens now lives, for love and affection she has for Thomas Thompson, sold to him her interest in her life estate. Wit: William G. Cowan and William Phillips. Reg: 20 Sep 1845.

Page 183 - 25 Sep 1845. William Eoff, Sr. to William Eoff, Jr. Deed of Gift, land of 414 acres. William Eoff, Sr. for love and affection for William Eoff, Jr., conveys land in Bedford Co., TN, in District No. 1, on the north waters of Puncheon Camp Creek, and a part of the tract formerly owned by Rody Boyd. Borders John Jakes. Wit: Edward A. Mosely and James Jakes. Reg: 4 Oct 1845.

Page 185 - 6 Oct 1845. G. M. Ray and Nancy J. Ray to Manuel Ray. Deed, 43 acres. G. M. Ray and his wife Nancy J. Ray sold to Manuel Ray, land in Bedford Co., TN, in District No. 24, on Thompsons Creek, being Lot No. 1 in the division of the lands belonging to the heirs of Thomas Bomar, deceased. Wit: Hezekiah Ray and J. D. Davis. Reg: 7 Oct 1845.

Page 185 - 6 Oct 1845. Wilson C. Arnold and wife to Robert Cannon. Deed, 50 acres. Wilson C. Arnold and his wife Margaret J. Arnold sold to Robert Cannon, land in Bedford Co., TN, about 1½ miles east of Shelbyville and on north side of Duck River. Borders lands of Robert Cannon, the heirs of Wilson Coats, and E. J. Frierson. It being Wilson C. Arnold and his wife Margaret J. place they now live on, and it being the whole tract conveyed by William S. Jett to Elizabeth Arnold formerly Elizabeth Sharp, by deed dated 10 July 1843. Reg: 7 Oct 1845.

Page 188 - 1 Sep 1845. Littleton Averett and wife to James W. Head. Deed. Littleton Averett and Sarah Averett his wife, conveyed to James W. Head, land in Bedford Co., TN, on waters of Fall Creek, in District No. 8. Borders lands of Daniel Capps, Wilson Turrentine, Hartwell Freeman and James W. and Charlotte Head. Land formerly owned by Enoch head, deceased. Reg: 9 Oct 1845.

Page 189 - 27 Aug 1845. Charlotte Head to James W. Head. Deed of Gift. For love and affection for her son James W. Head, conveyed unto him, her personal property &c, and that James W. Head is to support and maintain her during her natural life. Wit: Andrew Vannoy and David Burton. Reg: 11 Oct 1845. (Same page: James W. Head to Charlotte Head, Obligation)

Page 194 - 3 Mar 1845. Samuel and Evaline B. Simpson to John C. Coldwell. Deed, 1/3 of 76 acres. Samuel Simpson and Evaline B. Simpson formerly Eveline B. Coldwell of Gibson Co., Indiana, sold John C. Coldwell all their interest in two tracts of land in Bedford Co., TN, on waters of Duck River. Bounded by Wilson Coats' survey. Other tract borders road leading from Shelbyville to McMinnville. Reg: 18 Oct 1845.

Page 196 - 16 Oct 1845. Thomas C. Ryall and William P. Sims. Agreement or Bill of Sale. William P. Sims of Davidson Co., TN and Thomas C. Ryall of Bedford Co., TN, whereas by the will of Walter Sims which is on record in Davidson Co., TN, in item 35, states, "It is my will that at the death of my wife, all my slaves, with their increase, shall be equally divided between my daughter Elizabeth and my son William, except my slave boy Jefferson which is now the property of my son William" and whereas the Testators' daughter Elizabeth died bebore the Testator, there was a codicil made to his will, in which he devised to Elizabeth Scudder, daughter of his said Elizabeth, all that he had bequeathed to his daughter. Elizabeth Scudder has intermarried with Thomas C. Ryall and Mrs. Rebecca Sims wife of Walter Sims, deceased, is entitled to a life estate in the slaves. Reg: 23 Oct 1845.

Page 203 - 13 May 1843. Jacob Nichols and others to Robertson and Jacobs. Deed, 100 acres. Jacob Nichols, Susan Nichols, Sally Nichols and Katharine Nichols sold to Ezekiel M. Robinson and Alfred Jacobs, land in Bedford Co., TN, in District No. 1. Borders John G. Walker, heirs of A. B. Rowton, crosses Shelbyville to McMinnville road, and Mead Haile. Wit: Elzy Keeling, William Norton, and James Lambert. Reg: 8 Nov 1845.

Page 205 - 3 Nov 1845. William C. Freeman and wife to Samuel Doak. Deed, 80+ acres. William C. Freeman and Nancy R. Freeman his wife conveyed to Samuel Doak, land in Bedford Co., TN, on waters of Flat Creek. Borders Lewis Wilhoite's field, old Higginbotham tract, Elijah Lacy's corner, Hastings; tract, and school land and Jacob Albright, deceased, corner. Wit: John C. Hix. Reg: 11 Nov 1845.

Page 209 - 2 Aug 1842. Samuel and Suffiah Hawkins to Edward Martin. Interest in estate. Whereas by the Last Will and Testament of Cuthbert Word, deceased, who died in Bedford Co., TN, three negroes and other personal property was bequeathed to Jane Word widow of Cuthbert Word, deceased, during her natural life remaining to the seven children and heirs of Cothbert, among whom is Suffiah then married to William Bryant of Lincoln Co., TN, now married to Samuel Hawkins of Bedford Co., TN. Suffiah and Samuel Hawkins sold to Edward Martin all their right, title and interest in and to the one seventh part of the remainder interest in the three negroes and other personal property to be bequeathed to the seven children. Wit: William S. Carothers and Thomas Hastings. Reg: 15 Nov 1845.

Page 214 - 6 Oct 1845. Thomas Swann and Phebe Swann to Nicholas Swann. Power of Attorney. Thomas Swann and Phebe Swann his wife appointed Nicholas Swann of Noxubee Co., Mississippi, their Attorney to receive of and from the estate of Nicholas Woodfin, deceased, late of Bedford Co., TN, all property, effects or money that may be coming to them as legatees of the estate, to make settlement. Reg: 24 Nov 1845.

Page 220 - 26 Nov 1845. George Davidson & T. M. Coldwell to John Eakin and brothers. Deed, 552 acres. George Davidson and Thomas M. Coldwell conveyed to John Eakin, Thomas Eakin, and William Eakin, land in Bedford Co., TN, on waters of Wartrace Fork. Borders John Sutton, Sr. Wit: William B. M. Brame and William S. Jett. Reg: 2 Dec 1845.

Page 221 - 4 May 1844. Rebecca Woodfin to Woodfin Nalor. Deed, 34 acres. Rebecca Woodfin of Hickman Co., KY conveyed to

Woodfin Nalor of Bedford Co., TN, land in Bedford Co., being Lot No. 8 in the division of the land belonging to the estate of Nicholas Woodfin, deceased, it being the part she inherited as an heir of Nicholas Woodfin, deceased, and laid off bordering Lot No. 7. Reg: 4 Dec 1845.

Page 222 - 4 May 1844. John Woodfin to Woodfin Naylor. Deed, 19 acres. John Woodfin of Fayette Co., TN, conveyed to Woodfin Naylor of Bedford Co., TN, Lot No. 7 in the division of lands belonging to the estate of Nicholas Woodfin, deceased. Borders Lot No. 6. Reg: 4 Dec 1845.

Page 225 - 20 Nov 1845. Samuel Woodfin and others to Woodfin Naylor. Deed, 26 acres. Thomas Swann and Phebe Swann, daughter of Hannah Woodfin, deceased, Thomas Haile abd Hannah Hale, daughter of Hannah Woodfin, deceased, John Naylor and Sarah Naylor, daughter of Hannah Woodfin, deceased, Samuel Woodfin, W. H. Naylor sold to Woodfin Naylor, their undivided interest in the land allotted to Hannah Woodfin, deceased, being Lot No. 4 in the division of the land in the estate of Nicholas Woodfin, deceased, land in Bedford Co., TN, in District No. 5. Bounded by G. W. Campbell. Wit: John W. Naylor and John W. Edwards. Reg: 6 Dec 1845.

Page 232 - 18 Jun 1845. Martin Hoover to John P. Hoover. Deed of Gift, 250 acres. For love and affection for his son John P. Hoover, Martin Hoover conveyed unto him, land. Borders Henry Hoover and Frizzel's line. Wit: R. W. McKee and Jacob Hoover. Reg: 18 Dec 1845.

Page 234 - 4 Apr 1844. Michael F. and G. W. Parsons. Petition to sell slaves. George W. Parsons and Michael F. Parsons, administrators of George Parsons, deceased. Petition to sell slaves at public auction in Shelbyville. Margaret Parsons being the highest bidder of a negro woman Amy. Jacob Parsons her security. Reg: 22 Dec 1845.

Page 238 - 6 Jan 1845. John Oneal to the United Baptist Church. Deed, 1½ acres. For love and affection for the old United Baptist Chirch of Zion, convey unto them land in Bedford Co., TN, in District No. 18. Borders George Sharp near the Shelbyville road and Fayetteville road. Wit: Fielding Bell and William Stallings. Reg: 26 Dec 1845.

Page 241 - 4 Jul 1844. E. B. Hord and others to Lodwick Holt. Relinquishment to negro Patsy. Whereas Mary Hord sold to Lodwick Holt, a negro woman Patsy and on same day with C. F. Hord executed to L. Holt a bill for said negro woman and was registered. And whereas Mary Hord by the Last Will and Testament of her husband Edmund Hord, deceased, had only a life estate in the negro woman Patsy. Wit: Elijah Holt and William W. Holt. Signed by E. B. Hord, W. M. Hord, J. A. Hord, Susan S. Davidson, John Q. Davidson, Harriet C. Ferguson, H. C. Ferguson, and C. F. Hord. Reg: 3 Jan 1846.

Page 242 - 5 Feb 1841. John and Frederick Shofner, Executors to Austin Shofner. Deed, 283 acres. John and Frederick Shofner, Executors of the Last Will and Testament of Martin Shofner, deceased, of Bedford Co., TN, sold to Austin Shofner, land where Martin Shofner lived at the time of his death, on both sides of Thompson Creek, in District No. 25. Reserving two acres for the Upper Meeting House Tract which has been conveyed. Wit: N. K. Shofner and Allen Kimbro. Reg: 5 Jan 1846.

Page 250 - 20 Nov 1845. Mary Newsom to Tarlton J. Reaves. Deed, undivided interest in land, 130 acres. Mary Newsom formerly Mary Reaves, conveyed to Tarlton J. Reaves, all her interest as heir and devisee of Archibald Reaves and George Reaves in the tract of land on which Archibald Reaves lived at the time of his death. land in Bedford Co., TN, in District No. 22. Reg: 8 Jan 1846.

Page 250 - 19 Aug 1845. Edward B. M. Norville to Henry Brown. Deed, 23 acres. Edward B. M. Norville sold to Henry Brown, both of Bedford Co., TN, for the separate use and benefit of Emaline Norville wife of THomas Norville, William Henry Norville, Jane Norville, Benjamin L. Norville, Samuel Norville, Malinda Norville, and John Spencer Norville, children of Emaline Norville and such other children begotten of her body, land in Bedford Co., TN, in District No. 3. Borders Samuel Phillips, Abram Shriver and Thomas Norville. Reg: 8 Jan 1846.

Page 254 - 13 Jan 1846. Nancy Arnold to William D. Arnold. Deed of Gift. For love and affection for her grandson William D. Arnold, conveys a bay filly, not subject to debts of his father Absalom Arnold. Wit: Alsey Arnold and Asahel Cross. Reg: 13 Jan 1846.

Page 256 - 9 Jan 1846. Hiram Edde to Tarlton J. Reaves. Relinquishment Deed. Whereas the tract of land on which Hiram Edde now resides and which was devised to his wife by her father Joshua Holt, was sold by the Sheriff of Bedford Co., TN for an execution note against him. Felps being the purchaser. Reg: 14 Jan 1846.

Page 257 - 15 Jan 1846. Daniel R. Hime to William Hime. Deed, undivided interest &c, 82 acres. Whereas Daniel R. Hime has an interest in remainder after the death of Mary Ann Hime, who has a life time estate in the tract of land in Bedford Co., TN, in District No. 23. Bounded by Joseph Hastings. Also, he has interest in all perishable property that may be in the hands of Mary Ann Hime. Reg: 17 Jan 1846.

Page 259 - 17 Jan 1846. Lewis Hooker and Mary his wife to Archibald Prewitt. Deed, 36 acres. Lewis Hooker and Mary Hooker his wife conveys unto Archibald Prewitt, land in Bedford Co., TN, in District No. 3, it being Lot No. 1 in the division of the lands of Michael Holt, deceased, amongst his heirs. Lot is bounded by the dower tract of the widow of Michael Holt, deceased, and Nelson's line. Wit: Andrew Vannoy. Reg: 17 Jan 1846.

Page 266 - 24 Jan 1846. Malinda Dobbs and Margaret Spruce to James M. Neeley. Deed, 105 acres. Malinda Dobbs and Margaret Spruce of Bedford Co., TN, sold unto James M. Neeley of Bedford Co., land which descended to them from their father Jeremiah Dobbs, it being in Bedford Co., on Sinking Creek. Bounded by the west bank of Sinking Creek. Reg: 24 Jan 1846.

Page 267 - 23 Jan 1846. James T. and Katharine Arnold to Spencer Brown. Deed in Trust. James T. and Katharine Arnold sold in Trust to Spencer Brown, property. Wit: B. B. Morgan and T. W.

Terry. Reg: 27 Jan 1846.

Page 277 - 21 Nov 1845. Thomas Ramsey to Thomas Davidson and Obadiah Price. Deed, 1/10 of 252 acres. Thomas S. Ramsey sold to Thomas Davidson and Obadiah Price, all his undivided interest in and to two hundred and fifty two acres in Bedford Co., TN, in District No. 18, it being the interest that Thomas Ramsey bought of Radford Oneal and Diedama Oneal his wife, it being their interest in the tract of land on which John Bryant lived and died in Bedford Co., TN. Reg: 3 Feb 1846.

Page 282 - 5 Feb 1846. Absalom Arnold and wife Mary to William Jenkins. Deed, interest in dower. Absalom Arnold and Mary Arnold his wife formerly Mary Coble of Bedford Co., TN, conveyed to William Jenkins, all their right in and to one undivided tract of land of 134 acres, being the same as is now held by Mary Coble as dower, being the widow of Jacob Coble, deceased, and to which they are entitled at the death of Mary Coble as their portion as heirs at law of Jacob Coble, deceased. Reg: 5 Feb 1846.

Page 284 - 22 Dec 1845. Lemuel and Sally Snelling to John B. Snelling. Deed. Lemuel Snelling and Sally Snelling his wife conveyed to John B. Snelling, land in Bedford Co., TN, on waters of the Garrison Fork. Bordered by Brandon King and a spring branch. Reg: 6 Feb 1846.

Page 286 - 7 Jul 1845. Jesse S. M. Davis and wife to Elnathan Davis. Deed, undivided interest &c. Jesse S. M. Davis and Eliza Davis his wife of Attalia Co., Mississippi, sold to Elnathan Davis of Bedford Co., TN, all their interest in 100 acres, belonging to the heirs of Richard Ferrell, deceased, in Bedford Co., on Knob Creek. Eliza Davis being one of the heirs of the estate of Richard Ferrell, deceased. Signed by J. S. M. Davis and Louisa T. Davis. Reg: 11 Feb 1846.

Page 288 - 1 Oct 1842. Joseph K. Allen and others to Nathaniel White. Deed, 148½ acres. Joseph K. Allen of (blank) Co., Ill., Nancy Allen, Thomas Moore and Nancy C. his wife formerly Nancy C. Allen, George M. Ellis and Margaret B. his wife formerly Margaret B. Allen, Peterson J. Epps and Abigail his wife formerly Abigail Allen, Cyrus N. Allen, and James H. Allen of Bedford Co., TN, sold to Nathaniel White of Bedford Co., all their interest they have in and to three tracts of land which descended to them from their ancestor John Allen, deceased, on both sides of the Elk Ridge on headwaters of Sugar Creek and Cane Creek being the tract of land conveyed by Robert Morrison to John Allen. Borders William Clark, Bledsoe's line, Cunningham's line and Thomas Dryden. Reg: 13 Feb 1846.

Page 293 - 1 Feb 1845. William Thorn and Penny Thorn to John Oneal. Deed, 49 acres. William Thorn and Penny Thorn his wife sold to John Oneal, land in Bedford Co., TN, in District No. 18. Borders Ann Wilson now belonging to Fielding Bell, John Oneal purchase of John H. Anderson, John Stallings, and Rich Creek. The land being the land willed to Penny Thorn. Wit: James Stallings and William P. Oneal. Reg: 16 Feb 1846.

Page 294 - Tennessee Grant to Kimbrough Allison. No. 11228. 285 acres. 1¢ per acre, on 11 Feb 1827, land in Bedford Co., TN, on Wilson Creek. Bounded by William Stamper's corner,

Wilson Creek, John Atkinson and William Ogilvie. Reg: 16 Feb 1846.

Page 296 - 16 Feb 1846. THomas Holland to Green Holland. Deed, 17 acres. Thomas Holland sold to Green Holland land in Bedford Co., TN, in District No. 3. Borders Coats' line and James Holland. Reg: 18 Feb 1846.

Page 296 - 16 Feb 1846. Thomas Holland, Sr. to Green Holland. Bill of Sale. Thomas Holland, Sr. sold to Green Holland, in trust, for sole use and benefit of Thomas Holland's two granddaughters, Martha C. Holland and Mary C. Holland, daughters of Green Holland, conveyed a negro girl Mary Jane. Reg: 18 Feb 1846.

Page 297 - 16 Feb 1844. Solomon Bowers to Benjamin F. Bowers. Receipt &c. Received of Benjamin F. Bowers one of the heirs of John and Mary Bowers, deceased, in full of his share and interest left his mother by his father during her life, interest for the consideration above mentioned. Signed by Solomon Bowers. Reg: 18 Feb 1846.

Page 300 - 11 Sep 1845. Burrell Featherston to Mary S. Peacock. Deed, 162½ acres. Burrell Featherston conveyed for love and affection for his daughter Mary S. Peacock, land in Bedford Co., TN, on Bell Buckle Creek and it being also the tract of land on which Thomas J. Peacock now lives, and part of the land that Burrell Featherston bought of Felix G. Ake. Borders William P. Elkins, the Bell Buckle Creek, Oter Fork Creek, William J. Peacock, Mrs. Clardy, and Burrell Featherston. Wit: Robert A. Majors and John Douglas. Reg: 20 Feb 1846.

Page 303 - 23 Feb 1846. Solomon Ramsey to Solomon T. Ramsey. Deed of Gift, 101¼ acres. Solomon Ramsey for love and affection for his son Solomon T. Ramsey, land in Bedford Co., TN, and being the place whereon Solomon Ramsey now lives and on waters of Sinking Creek, in District No. 18. Bounded by Sinking Creek near John Bryant's Spring, David Dryden and William A. Gant. Wit: John D. Neill and Alexander J. Ramsey. Reg: 28 Feb 1846.

Page 304 - 31 Jan 1846. Peter Garron to William J. W. Wakefield. Deed, 65 acres. Peter Garron sold to William J. W. Wakefield, land in Marshall Co. and Bedford Co., TN. Bounded by John Woodward and Jane Wakefield now Jane Blackwell. Reg: 28 Feb 1846.

Pahe 307 - 6 Mar 1846. John Harrison and wife Nancy D. to James M. Neeley. Deed, undivided, 105 acres. John Harrison and Nancy Harrison his wife of Bedford Co., TN, sold to James M. Neeley of Bedford Co., all the right, title, claim and interest they have in and unto a tract of land which descended to them from Jeremiah Dobbs, the same being in Bedford Co., on Sinking Creek. Bounded by the west bank of Sinking Creek. Reg: 6 Mar 1846.

Page 308 - August Term 1845. Circuit Court Decree. Title to Joshua Woosley, for land. 100 acres. Widow and heirs at law of Asahel Cross. Bill for sale of land. John T. Neil appointed Commissioner to sell the lands mentioned, Jesse Rogers was the purchaser and has paid the purchase money except the share of Elijah Robinson and wife Spicy and is now due to them. The money was paid unto Elijah Robinson and the Court has decreed that all the right title &c which Willie Snell and Elizabeth his wife, Levina, Juliann, Robert, Caroline, Elizabeth, Sarah, James, Stephen, and Celia Rogers, Abijah Young and his wife Gincy, Curtis Jameson and wife Nancy, Elijah Robinson and wife Spicy, Amy, James, Cynthia Ann, and Willie Johnson, Eliza Jane, and William Cross, Cynthia Ann, James M. Cross, has in and to a tract of land in Bedford Co., TN, on waters of Beech Creek. Land being same tract of land purchased by Asahel Cross from Andrew Donalson to be devested out of them and vested in Joshua Woosley and the purchaser Jesse Rogers. Reg: 9 Mar 1846.

Page 309 - 2 Jan 1843. Green B. Carter and wife to Uriah Cross. Deed, undivided, 28 acres. Green B. Carter and Ann Carter his wife one of the heirs of George Crews, deceased, late of Bedford Co., TN, sold to Uriah Cross of Bedford Co., their interest in and to a tract of land that George Crews owned at the time of his death, on the north side of Duck River and on the north west side of Hambleton's (Hamilton) Creek and on the road leading from Shelbyville to Rowsville. Borders Robert Cannon's corner where an Old Still House formerly stood. Green B. Carter and Ann Carter his wife of Tippah Co., Mississippi. Reg: 9 Mar 1846.

Page 310 - 8 Apr 1841. Erasmus Walker and wife Ann P. to Mary Childress. Interest in land. Erasmus Walker and his wife Ann P. Walker of Marengo Co., Alabama, conveyed unto Mary Childress, land in Bedford Co., TN. Whereas Martin Phifer of North Carolina by his Last Will and Testament convey to John Phifer in trust for the use of said Mary Childress and her children by James Childress, land in Bedford Co., TN, and whereas Mary Childress, James L. Childress, John B. Read, and Erasmus Walker for a valuable consideration purchased of the said John Phifer, the land. The land being bequeathed by will of Martin Phifer to William D. Crawford and Elizabeth Doty, contains 1013 acres. Instrument written in Marengo Co., Alabama. Reg: 10 Mar 1846.

Page 311 - 5 Jan 1842. Mary Childress and James L. Childress to D. L. Barringer. Deed, 3/4 of 948 acres. Mary Childress of Marengo Co., Alabama and James L. Childress of Tuscaloosa, Alabama, conveyed to Daniel L. Barringer, their 3/4 part of a tract of land in Bedford Co., TN, on waters of Fall or Falling Creek and about four to five miles north of Shelbyville, it being a part of Lot No. 5 as by the return of William Houston, Caleb P. Houston and Price C. Steele, Commissioners selected to lay off said land to the children of William Crawford, of part of said Lot No. 5 with the exception of 400 acres to William and Elizabeth Crawford, children of William Crawford, was conveyed to the parties of the first part and to Ann Childress now Ann Walker and wife of Erasmus Walker, and to Susan Childress now Susan Read wife of John B. Read. Reg: 10 Mar 1846.

Page 312 - -- --- 1842. John B. Read and Susan W. Read to Daniel R. Barringer. Deed, 1/4 of 948 acres. John B. Read and his wife Susan Read of Marengo Co., Alabama, sold to Daniel L. Barringer of Bedford Co., TN, one undivided fourth part of a tract of land in Bedford Co., on waters of Fall Creek or Falling Creek and about four or five miles north of Shelbyville, it being part of division of Lot No. 5 and by the Commissioners selected to lay off and divide the 5000 acre granted by State of North Carolina to Martin Phifer, having laid off to William and Elizabeth Crawford, children of William Crawford of 400 acres conveyed to Mary Childress, James L. Childress, Ann Childress and Susan Childress now Susan Read wife of John B. Read, children of Mary by James Childress, deceased. Reg: 11 Mar 1846.

Page 317 - 11 Mar 1846. Elias Rambo and wife to William T. Thomason. Deed, 26¼ acres. Elias Rambo and Mary T. Rambo his wife, conveyed unto William T. Tomason, land in Bedford Co., TN, in District No. 10. Reg: 14 Mar 1846.

Page 318 - 11 Mar 1846. Elias Rambo and wife to John G. Hall. Deed, 86 acres. Elias Rambo and Mary T. Rambo his wife, conveyed unto John G. Hall, land in Bedford Co., TN, in District No. 10. Reg: 19 Mar 1846.

Page 323 - 29 Feb 1844. James L. Armstrong to Lydia Marshall. Deed of Gift. James L. Armstrong for love and affection for his daughter Lydia Marshall, conveyed unto her and at her death to her heirs, a negro girl Edy. Wit: H. J. H. Norville. Reg: 25 Mar 1846.

Page 328 - 31 Jul 1828. James Ray to Allen Perry and others. Deed to Camp Ground. James Ray conveyed unto Allen Perry, Richard Wright, James Ray, Robert Allison and Asa Stem, Trustees, land in Bedford Co., TN, on waters of Weakley Creek. Borders lands of Ray, for the purpose of a Camp Meeting Ground for the Methodist Church. Wit: Charles Wade, William Ogilvie and John P. Moon. Reg: 7 Apr 1846.

Page 330 - 16 Mar 1846. David J. Leathers to the heirs of Hugh Allen, deceased. Deed, 93½ acres. David J. Leathers of Rutherford Co., TN, conveyed unto the heirs of Hugh Allen, deceased, of Bedford Co., TN. The heirs, to wit, Joseph Allen, Benjamin Franklin Allen, Martha Jane Allen, James Thomas Allen, and Andrew Jackson Allen, which contract was made in the life time of Hugh Allen, deceased. Land in Bedford Co., on headwaters of Alexanders Creek. Bounded by Thomas P. Wells, John Woods, William G. Heights and Thomas Black. Wit: H. S. Misenheimer, R. T. D. Denniston, W. W. Dearing and James Alexander. Reg: 7 Apr 1846.

Page 331 - 20 Jan 1846. James A. Lentz to John F. Thompson. Deed, 14 acres. James A. Lentz sold to John F. Thompson, land in Bedford Co., TN, on south side of Duck River. Bounded by lands of John Lentz, Thomas Lentz's old tract, and Duck River. The land being the land willed to James A. by his father Jacob Lentz, deceased. Wit: Jacob Fisher and John Frazer. Reg: 7 Apr 1846.

Page 339 - 25 Aug 1845. Gwynn Foster to S. W. Bigham and others. Deed, 300 acres. Gwynn Foster of Bedford Co., TN, conveyed to S. W. Bigham, O. H. Bigham and Mrs. Bigham of Bedford Co., land in Bedford Co., on waters of the Wartrace Fork. Borders William Blakely and Foster, Reuben Curry, Robert Clarke, William Bigham, and Benjamin Webb. Wit: Robert Clark and Reuben Curry. Reg: 10 Apr 1846.

Page 343 - 20 Nov 1845. Thomas Haile and Hannah Haile to John Naylor. Deed, 17 acres. Thomas Haile and Hannah Haile sold to John Naylor, land in Bedford Co., TN, in District No. 5. Borders lands of landed estate of Nicholas Woodfin, deceased.

The land being Lot No. 6 in the division of the landed estate of Nicholas Woodfin, deceased, and allotted to Hannah Haile. Wit: Woodfin Naylor and W. H. Nailor. Reg: 13 Apr 1846.

Page 344 - 3 Apr 1846. Ransom White and Candis White to Jerome Albright. Deed, undivided interest, 225 acres. Ransom White and Candis White his wife sold to Jerome Albright, undivided share of land, subject to the widow's dower. Land in Bedford Co., TN, in District No. 22, on the headwaters of a western branch of Big Flat Creek. Bounded by school land, George Waite and Margaret Bennet, Lewis Wilhoite, and Tarlton Reaves. Being the lands Jacob Albright died seized and possessed of and place whereon he died, and during the land purchased by Jacob Albright, deceased, of Joseph Higginbotham, Edward Garrett and Isaac Bennett. Candis daughter of Jacob Albright, deceased. Wit: John Conwell and William M. Ellis. Reg: 13 Apr 1846.

Page 346 - 11 Apr 1846. James L. Scott to Elihu H. Bigham and Robert P. Bigham. Deed, 1/2 of 305 acres. James L. Scott of Marshall Co., Mississippi, sold to Elihu H. Bigham and Robert P. Bigham of Bedford Co., TN, one half of 305 acres in Bedford Co., TN, in headwaters of the North Fork and Falling Creek and east of the Turnpike, being part of a lot in the division of a tract of land granted by North Carolina to Matthew Locke, among the heirs and distributees of Matthew Locke and which lot fell to James Locke and that part assigned to James L. and Mary Scott in the division of land. Land borders lands belonging to the heirs of Joseph Loyd, deceased, and Joseph Kincaid. Wit: William D. Orr and N. Clark. Reg: 16 Apr 1846.

Page 347 - 11 Apr 1846. Joseph R. McKinley and James L. Scott to Elihu H. Bigham and Robert P. Bigham. Bond. Joseph R. McKinley of Bedford Co., TN and James L. Scott of Marshall Co., Mississippi, are bound unto Elihu H. Bigham and Robert P. Bigham for $1224.00. The condition of the obligation is such that whereas the above bound Joseph R. McKinley as agent and attorney in fact of John F.Woodfin and his wife Mary formerly Mary Scott, and James L. Scott for himself has sold unto Elihu H. and Robert P. Bigham, land in Bedford Co., on headwaters of the North Fork and Falling Creek, being part of a North Carolina grant to Matthew Locke and by descent vested in James L. Scott and Mary Scott now Mary Woodfin, she having intermarried with John F. Woodfin of Marshall Co., Mississippi. Wit: N. Clark and William D. Orr. Reg: 16 Apr 1846.

Page 349 - August Term 1845. Circuit Court Decree, Title, to George W. Heard. Acres. 69 acres, -4 acres. James M. Johnson, David Johnson, Powell Kimbro, Robert Patton and wife, Willis Johnson and others. Bill for sale of land and lots. Land of 69 acres, reserving 4 acres by Daniel Johnson in his life time to Charles Philpot, land in Bedford Co., TN, in District No. 25. Bounded by Isaac Barnett, Robert Puryear, the Shipman Creek, Heard & Lindley, and a street in Rowsville. Ordered by the Court all the right title &c of David Johnson, James M. Johnson, Powell Kimbro and Rebecca his wife, Robert Patton and Elizabeth his wife, Willis Johnson, William Johnson, John B. Johnson, Susanna Johnson, Eleanor Johnson, and Elizabeth Stewart, sold to George W. Heard. Reg: 22 Apr 1846.

Page 356 - 21 Mar 1846. Othneil Freeman and Sarah Freeman to Joel C. Russell. Interest in estate. Othneil Freeman and Sarah

M. Freeman of Bedford Co., TN, sold to Joel C. Russell of Bedford Co., their interest in and to the estate of William A. Russell, deceased. Wit: John Trice and S. T. Trice. Reg: 4 May 1846.

Page 358 - December Term 1845. Circuit Court Decree. Title to James H. Cobbs* and others. William P. Elkins, administrators &c vs Philip Elkins and others. Mary Elkins and Sarah Cobb formerly Sarah Elkins has been paid on 15 Dec 1845. Court satisfied that from the report that James H. Cobb and wife Sarah formerly Sarah Elkins and Mary Elkins has been paid in full for land mentioned. It is decreed that all claim &c which William P. Elkins, Philip Elkins, James Mullins, Dudley Hitt and wife Susan, John Hitt and wife Mariah, Harrison H. Elkins, James Elkins, Allen Kimbro and wife Mary, heirs at law of David Elkins, deceased. Land in Bedford Co., TN, in District No. 25. Borders F. Shofner, Webster's line and Esq. Coble's corner. Reg: 9 May 1846.
* Cobbs could be Coble.

Page 359 - 2 May 1846. Benjamin F. Bowers to Edmund Cooper. Deed in interest in estate. Benjamin F. Bowers sold to Edmund Cooper, all his interest &c which he has in the fund now in the hands of John T. Neil, Clerk of Circuit Court, arising from the sale of the lands of John Bowers, deceased, which came to Benjamin F. Bowers being a son of John Bowers, deceased, and by purchases made by him of the interests which Solomon Bowers, David Bowers, and Green Bowers had in said fund. Reg: 15 May 1846.

Page 360 - 24 Feb 1846. George and Anna Campbell to Samuel Anderson. Bill of Sale. George and Anna Campbell sold unto Samuel Anderson, a negro girl Lydia. Wit: Benjamin Gambill, Samuel Rone and Bradley Gambill. Reg: 15 May 1846.

Page 362 - 22 May 1846. James Deery to William B. M. Brame. Deed of Gift, 2¼ acres. For natural regard James Deery has for his son in law William B. M. Brame, conveyed unto him land in Bedford Co., TN, in District No. 7. Bounded by Alexander Eakin, E. J. Frierson, land belonging to the heirs of George Newton, deceased, and heirs of William Gilchrist. Reg: 22 May 1846.

Page 363 - 29 May 1846. John Mc. Nelson to Margaret M. and Elizabeth Jane Nelson. Deed of Gift, 4 acres. John Mc. Nelson for love and affection for his two children, Margaret Malvina Nelson and Elizabeth Jane Nelson, conveyed unto them land in Bedford Co., TN, in District No. 3. Wit: William S. Watkins and Thomas Thomas. Reg: 29 May 1846.

Page 364 - 26 Jan 1846. William H. Wisener to L. D. Stockdon. Deed, 100 acres. William H. Wisener of Bedford Co., TN, sold to Lorenzo D. Stockdon of Marshall Co., TN, land in Bedford Co., being a part of the land owned by John Dawdy in his life time and devised by him to his wife during her life, and then to his sons, Howel M. Dawdy and John W. Dawdy. Land bounded by the west bank of the Mill Dam and above the dam, Howel M. Dawdy and William H. Wisener, Albert Anderson and the Rock Creek. Reg: 29 May 1846.

Page 365 - April Term 1845. Circuit Court Decree. Title to Edmund Word. William Hastings, Mary Jane Hastings and Dennis Bryant and wife Elizabeth. Bill to sell land. Land in Bedford Co., TN, on waters of Flat Creek and bounded by William Hurst, Hugh C. Hurst, Josiah Hastings, and widow Hurst. Edmund Word being purchaser. Recorded: 8 May 1846.

Page 366 - 8 Oct 1845. Dennis Hemby to Washington Hartley. Deed of Gift, 100 acres. For love and affection Dennis Hemby has for Washington Hartley, conveyed unto him, land in Bedford Co., TN, in District No. 25. Bounded by Timothy Long and William Carr. Wit: Jesse Nutt and Daniel Hartley. Reg: 5 Jun 1846.

Page 367 - 1 Jun 1846. R. H. Richardson and others to George Waite. Power of Attorney. Josiah O. B. Richardson, Robert H. Richardson and Daniel C. King, all of Bedford Co., TN, appointed George Waite, Power of Attorney, to obtain possession of a negro woman Frances, who is now in the possession of Elijah Bomar and others. Wit: J. Wortham and Thomas Holland, Jr. Reg: 11 Jun 1846.

Page 368 - 9 Jun 1846. Washington P. Goodwin and Malinda Goodwin. Contract. Indenture made between Washington P. Goodwin one part and Benjamin Merret on behalf of his sister Malinda Goodwin other part, all of Bedford Co., TN. Washington P. Goodwin having lately intermarried, and by marriage Washington P. Goodwin became owner of all the personal property belonging to Malinda before her marriage, consisting of a negro woman Ailsey and other property. W. P. and Malinda has mutually agreed to live together and apart also agreed to share all property. Reg: 11 Jun 1846.

Page 372 - 22 Dec 1845. Lemuel and Sally Snelling to John B. Snelling. Deed. Lemuel Snelling and his wife Sally Snelling sold unto John B. Snelling a tract of land in Bedford Co., TN, on waters of the Garrison Fork. Bounded by the north bank of a Spring Branch and Brandon King's corner. Reg: 24 Jun 1846.

Page 375 - 22 Jun 1846. Zadock Wood of Coffee Co., TN, nominates and appointed his son Lewis Wood his Attorney to manage his business. Wit: Robert C. Walker and Joseph Helton. Reg: 25 Jun 1846.

Page 381 - 28 Sep 1840. William Gaston and wife to Samuel Morrow. Deed, 1/8 of 185 acres, undivided interest. William Gaston and his wife Elizabeth Gaston sold to Samuel Morrow an undivided interest in land in Bedford Co., TN, in District No. 1, on waters of Scotts Branch. Borders John Jakes, Harrison Gaston, Richard Gaither and Eli Eaton. The land being the dower interest and it also being descended to them by the late James Morrow, deceased. Wit: George D. Stephenson and Harrison Gaston. Reg: 24 Jul 1846.

Page 382 - 10 Aug 1841. John Sutton and wife Jane to Samuel Morrow. Deed, undivided interest. John Sutton and his wife Jane Sutton sold to Samuel Morrow, their undivided interest in land in Bedford Co., TN, in District No. 1, on waters of Scotts Branch. Bounded by John Jakes, Harrison Gaston, Richard Gaither and Eli Eaton. Their share is 1/8 of 185 acres. Wit: William Gaston and Harrison Gaston. Reg: 24 Jul 1846.

Page 390 - 11 Jul 1846. N. W. Springer and others to Hugh McCrory. Deed, undivided interest. Nathan W. Springer, William W. Rushing and Susan Rushing, conveyed to Hugh McCrory, all the undivided interest that they have in a tract of land in Bedford Co., TN, in District No. 9, of 115 acres. The tract being the same Sarah Springer died seized and possessed of, their interest being one ninth of said tract. Nathan W. Springer being one ninth and William W. Rushing and Susan Rushing being one ninth share. Land borders lands of Sarah Springer, James Hart, Mathis Price and Lydia Roane. Wit: James T. Springer and Jacob Hileman. Reg: 4 Aug 1846.

Page 392 - 27 Jan 1846. Lewis Roswell and wife to James M. Neeley. Deed, interest in land, 105 acres. Lewis Roswell and Sarah his wife of Benton Co., TN, sold to James M. Neeley of Bedford Co., TN, land that descended to them from Jeremiah Dobbs in Bedford Co., on east side of Sinking Creek. Bounded by Edward Stephenson, and on west bank of Sinking Creek. Wit: James Gordon. Reg: 4 Aug 1846.

Page 393 - 3 Aug 1846. Jane Doude to James M. Neeley. Deed, interest in land. Jane Doude of Ballard Co., KY, conveyed to James M. Neeley of Bedford Co., TN, all her interest in land that descended to her by her father Jeremiah Dobbs. The land in Bedford Co., TN, on east side of Sinking Creek. Borders Edward Stephenson, and on west bank of Sinking Creek. Reg: 4 Aug 1846.

Page 394 - 10 Jul 1841. William Leathers, Administrator to Thomas Johnson. Deed, 36 acres. William Leathers, an administrator of James Leathers, deceased, by powers vested in him in the life time of James Leathers, conveyed to Thomas Johnson, land in Bedford Co., TN and bounded by Caswell's tract. Land on Alexanders Creek. Wit: T. H. Leathers and Allen W. Leathers. Reg: 5 Aug 1846.

Page 397 - 10 Oct 1845. John Larue and Julia Adams and John H. Larue. Deed of Gift, 93¼ acres. For love and affection John Larue and Julia Adams has for John H. Larue, conveyed unto him land in Bedford Co., TN, in District No. 19. Bounded by Hart's corner, Gilchrist's line, and John Larue's line. Wit: Thomas Dryden and Isaac Larue. Reg: 6 Aug 1846.

Page 406 - 7 Aug 1846. P. C. Steele and others to Marinda Steele Deed, 179 acres. John P. Steele, Price C. Steele, Volney H. Steele, Carlos D. Steele, Jane Steele, James G. Neeley and Mary Neeley his wife formerly Mary Steele, and John Knott and Harriet Knott his wife formerly Harriett Steele, and Mintory Steele, the last two of whom are children of Wilson Steele, deceased, are children and heirs at law of Joseph Steele, deceased. This deed further states that Joseph Steele in his lifetime made division of his real estate between and amongst his children. And Wilson Steele who was also a heir and Marinda Steele his daughter. Land in Bedford CO., TN, on waters of Falling Creek and lands belonging to the widow and heirs of Thomas P. Burns, deceased, and lands belonging to the widow and heirs of Wilson Steele, deceased, lands of George Clanton, David Frizzell, and Price C. Steele. Reg: 11 Aug 1846.

Page 408 - 15 Aug 1842. Dennis Hemby to Timothy Long. Deed, 100 acres. For love and affection for Timothy Long, land in

Bedford Co., TN, in District No. 25. Borders lands of Dennis Hemby, Weaver's line, and Carr's line. Wit: Daniel Hemby and John Hemby. Reg: 11 Aug 1846.

Page 417 - 1 Jul 1846. William and Jane Dwyer to William G. Cowan. Deed, interest in land, 121 acres. William Dwyer and his wife Jane Dwyer of Jackson Co., Alabama, sold to William G. Cowan of Bedford Co., TN, land in Bedford Co., on waters of Little Flat Creek. Bounded by lands of the Widow Burrow, John Lacy, Widow Wilhoite, Pearce Wilhoite and others. The land being that which Willie Wilhoite, deceased, brother of Jane Dwyer, inhertied of the estate of his father Jacob Wilhoite. Reg: 21 Aug 1846.

Page 425 - 3 Sep 1846. Hiram Sutton and wife Nancy to William Hime. Deed, undivided interest, 82 acres. Hiram Sutton and Nancy his wife has interest in remainder, to take effect and be united with the possession after the death of Mary Ann Hime who had a lifetime estate in same, in land in Bedford Co., TN, in District No. 23. Land bounded by Joseph Hastings. Reg: 3 Sep 1846.

Page 425 - 1 Jul 1828. James Ray to Allen Perry and others, Trustees to Union Camp Ground. James Ray of Bedford Co., TN, conveyed unto Allen Perry, Richard Wright, James Ray, Robert Allison, and Asa Stem, Trustees, a tract of land in Bedford Co., on waters of Weakleys Creek. Bounded by James Ray's land. For the purpose of a Camp Meeting Ground for the reforming Methodist Church. Wit: Charles Wade, William Ogilvie and John P. Moon. On 6 Apr 1846, Willie Perry and John Thompson who being first duly sworn, is acquainted with said James Ray and the said James Ray had departed this life as they were informed. Reg: 7 Sep 1846.

Page 419 - 30 May 1846. William Hazlewood and wife to Daniel Looney. Deed, undivided interest. William Hazlewood and his wife Margaret formerly Margaret Ray, sold to Daniel Looney, the one eighth part of a tract of land undivided, late the property of William Ray, deceased, of which William Hazlewood and his wife Margaret are tenants in common with the other brothers and sisters and their representatives of William Ray, deceased. Wit: John Blackwell, Jr. and William Potter. Reg: 11 Sep 1846.

Page 430 - 10 Sep 1846. Mary Ann Hime to William Hime. Deed, 1 acre. Mary Ann Hime of Bedford Co., TN, conveyed unto William Hime, for and during her natural life, a tract of land in Bedford Co., in District No. 23, being a portion of her dower in lands of her late husband John Hime. Borders lands of Joseph Hastings, near the old Still House Spring. The one acre includes the old Still House Spring and Spring Branch. Reg: 11 Sep 1846.

Page 432 - 15 Sep 1846. Green M. Moore to James H. Bomar. Bill of Sale. Green M. Moore sold unto James H. Bomar, all his right &c to a negro boy Edmond, that was willed to him by John Moore, deceased, at the death of Eleanor Moore his wife. Reg: 16 Sep 1846.

Page 432 - 20 Jan 1840. William Conwell to Thomas Conwell. Received of Thomas Conwell his lawful guardian full and peaceable possession of a certain tract of land, on the head waters of

Big Flat Creek in Bedford Co., TN, willed to him by George King. Wit: John Conwell and Jerome Albright. Reg: 16 Sep 1846.

Page 433 - 17 Aug 1846. Richard Foreman to Rebeckah Foreman. Deed, part of Town Lot. Richard Foreman conveyed unto Rebeckah Foreman for and in consideration of her withholding her opposition to his getting a divorce and the Court having granted the same. A part of Lot No. 40 in Shelbyville, TN, it being a part of the lot on the north east corner of the Public Square. Borders the street running east from the Public Square, covering the front of the West Brick Room built by Richard Foreman. Reg: 18 Sep 1846.

Page 434 - 22 Sep 1845. George W. Record, Trustee to Blackman C. Dobson. Deed, 56 acres. Whereas Thomas C. Williams by deed dated 17 Jan 1843 conveyed to George W. Record of Marshall Co., TN, land in Bedford Co., TN, in District No. 18 and known as Lot No. 2 in the division of the lands of Jesse E. Williams amongst his heirs which plat is recorded in the Register's Office in Bedford Co., TN. G. B. Knight guardian of Elizabeth M. and other minor heirs of Jesse E. Williams, deceased. Trustee is to sell land and Blackman C. Dobson the purchaser. Reg: 22 Sep 1846.

Page 437 - 12 Sep 1846. William W. Hurst to John J. Hurst. Relinquishment &c. William W. Hurst sold to John J. Hurst, land in Bedford Co., TN, his interest as sold by decree of the Court upon the petition of Elizabeth Hurst, Hugh C. Hurst and others, widow and heirs at law of William Hurst, deceased. Land on waters of Big Flat Creek. Reg: 25 Sep 1846.

Page 437 - 23 Sep 1846. John T. Neil to Josiah T. Hughes, Jr. and John H. Hughes. Quit Claim, 50 acres. John T. Neil sold to Josiah T. Hughes and John H. Hughes, land in Bedford Co., TN, on waters of Little Sinking Creek. Borders lands of Josiah Hughes, deceased. Reg: 26 Sep 1846.

Page 438 - 10 Sep 1846. Josiah T. Hughes and others to William Gabbert. Deed, 61 acres. Agness Hughes, widow of Josiah Hughes, deceased, Charles Fisher and wife Nancy formerly Nancy Hughes, William S. Hughes, John H. Hughes, Benjamin Fugitt and wife Mary T. formerly Mary T. Hughes, Samuel W. Hughes, Josian T. Hughes, and Elizabeth Hughes, heirs of Josiah Hughes, dec'd, has sold to William Gabbert, land in Bedford Co., TN, in District No. 18. Borders lands of Moses Fugitt. Wit: William Galbreath. Reg: 26 Sep 1846.

Page 442 - 28 Sep 1846. Joseph S. Cates and wife Sophia to William Hime. Deed, interest in estate, 82 acres. Joseph S. Cates and Sophia Cates his wife has an interest in the remainder after the death of Mary Ann Hime, who has a lifetime estate in land in Bedford Co., TN, in District No. 23. Bounded by Joseph Hastings. Reg: 28 Sep 1846.

DEED BOOK "PP" 1846 - 1848

Page 1 - 30 Sep 1846. John S. Cates and wife to Joseph Hastings. Deed, 82 acres. Joseph S. Cates and Elizabeth Cates his wife has an interest in estate after the death of Mary Ann Hime who has a life time estate in land in Bedford Co., TN, in District

No. 23. Land borders Joseph Hastings, to convey said land to Joseph Hastings. Wit: Samuel Pratt and W. S. Wallace. Reg: 1 Oct 1846.

Page 3 - 31 Jul 1828. James Ray to Allen Perry and others. Deed to Union Camp Ground. James Ray of Bedford Co., TN, conveyed unto Allen Perry, Richard Wright, James Ray, Robert Allison, and Asa Stem, Trustees, land in Bedford Co., on waters of Weakleys Creek. Borders James Ray. The land is for the purpose of a Camp Meeting Ground for religious exercises for the reforming Methodist Church. Wit: Charles Wade, William Ogilvie and John P. Moon. Reg: 6 Oct 1846.

Page 7 - 5 Oct 1846. Nancy Young to William Young. Relinquishment Deed. Whereas by the Last Will and Testament of Nancy Young's deceased husband James Young, there was devised to her certain property, to have and to hold during her natural life and whereas she has disposed to give up a portion of the property, desires to convey and release to William Young, the Executor of her deceased husband, property. Wit: David Hunter and Horatio Clagitt. Reg: 10 Oct 1846.

Page 7 - 10 Oct 1846. Spencer and Partheny Brown to William Brown. Deed, 178½ acres. Spencer Brown and Partheny "Theny" Brown his wife sold to William Brown, land in Bedford Co., TN. Reg: 10 Oct 1846.

Page 9 - 20 Jun 1846. Thomas White and Airy A. White to William H. Burt. Deed, 41 acres. Thomas White and Airy A. White his wife formerly Airy A. Williams, sold to William H. Burt, land in Bedford Co., TN, in District No. 18, it being Lot No. 6 in the division of the lands of Jesse E. Williams, deceased, and was allotted to Airy A. White. The land adjoins the lands of John Dougle, school land, and Aaron Gambill. Reg: 13 Oct 1846.

Page 9 - 2 Oct 1846. Joseph Adams to William Mosely. Deed, 30 acres. Joseph Adams sold to William Mosely the southern half of a 60 acre tract given by Andrew Morrison to his son Andrew M. Morrison, in Bedford Co., TN, on waters of Sugar Creek. Wit: William H. Wisener and Samuel Doak. Reg: 15 Oct 1846.

Page 10 - 13 Oct 1846. George Davidson to George D. Allen. Deed of Gift, negro Catharine. George Davidson of Shelbyville, for love and affection for his grandson George Davidson Allen now an infant about 3 years old and residing with his father William A. Allen in Bedford Co., conveyed unto him a negro girl Catharine. Wit: William A. Allen and William B. M. Brame. Reg: 15 Oct 1846.

Page 10 - 17 Oct 1846. William Mosely to Isham Mosely. Power of Attorney. William Mosely of Bedford Co., TN, appointed his brother Isham Mosely of Bedford Co., his Attorney, to make a deed to William and John Blaine, for a tract of land on which he now lives. Reg: 17 Oct 1846.

Page 11 - 2 Oct 1846. William Mosely to Joseph Adams. Deed, 20 acres. William Mosely of Bedford Co., TN, sold to Joseph Adams, the northern half of a 60 acre tract of land given by Andrew Morrison to his son John Morrison. Land in Bedford Co., on waters of Sugar Creek. Borders land formerly owned by Milton Morrison and now owned by Joseph Adams. Wit: William H. Wisener and Samuel Doak. Reg: 20 Oct 1846.

Page 11 - 17 Oct 1846. Benjamin J. Ingram and wife to John V. Biddle. Deed, undivided interest. Whereas Theo. F. Bradford in his lifetime, to wit, on 15 Sep 1837, executed a Deed in Trust to Thomas Davis for the use and benefit of Eliza J. Howe and her two daughters Eliza Ann Howe and Cyntha B. Howe, which deed was made agreeable to the Last Will and Testament of John J. B. Welsh, which will bequeathed to his mother Eliza J. Howe, his whole estate during her natural life and after her death to descend to his two half sisters, viz, Eliza Ann Howe and Cyntha Briant Howe, and whereas Benjamin James Ingram has intermarried with Cyntha B. Howe and has interest in land in Bedford Co., TN, on Cribbs Branch, waters of the Barren Fork and whereon Eliza J. Howe now lives. All heirs sell land to John V. Biddle. Reg: 20 Oct 1846.

Page 12 - 17 Oct 1846. John V. Biddle to Eliza J. Howe. In Trust for the use and benefit of B. J. and C. B. Ingram, 136 acres. John V. Biddle conveyed unto Eliza J. Howe for the use and benefit of Benjamin J. Ingram and his wife Cyntha B. Ingram formerly Cyntha B. Howe, land in Bedford Co., TN, in District No. 2. Bounded by land Permelia Campbell deeded to John V. Biddle. Reg: 20 Oct 1846.

Page 12 - 29 Jun 1844. Spencer Brown and wife Partheny to the Cumberland Presbyterian Church. Deed, 1½ acres. Spencer Brown and his wife Partheny Brown formerly Partheny Pratt, deeded to the Cumberland Presbyterian Church, called New Hope, land in Bedford Co., TN, in District No. 23. Borders land of William Pratt. For the purpose for a church house and public burying ground. Wit: William Word and John Dunaway. Reg: 22 Oct 1846.

Page 19 - 28 Oct 1846. Circuit Court Decree, Title, to Martin Hancock. Sarah Burditt, Giles P. Burditt and Samuel S., Elizabeth, William M. Hampton, Kenneth L., and Sarah Burditt, who sue by their guardian Nathan Ivy and Polly Ann his wife, Thomas Gregory and James, and William Gregory, by their next friend Thomas Gregory. William Norton purchased mills &c and has paid part of the money and Court ordered half to be deeded to Martin Hancock of Coffee Co., TN and Hancock purchased other half from William Norton. The land and mills are on Noahs Fork in Bedford Co., TN. Reg: 2 Nov 1846.

Page 23 - 20 Jul 1846. Johanna Nash, Trustee to William Nash. Interest in land. Whereas Travis C. Nash, Jr. executed a Deed in Trust to his mother Johanna Nash on 4 Jan 1845, his interest in the landed estate of his father Travis C. Nash, deceased. His interest being one fifteenth part, conveys unto William Nash his interest. Reg: 9 Nov 1846.

Page 25 - August Term 1846. Circuit Court Decree, Title to Alexander Sanders and others. Alexander Sanders and Jane his wife, Joseph Robison and Jane Robison, the later being a minor who sues by her guardian Joseph Robison vs John Robison, Jr., William J. Robison and Frances Robison, widow, and Lewis, Richard, Jesse, Houston, Hannah and Robison, children of Alexander Robison, deceased. Decree for Title. Land in Bedford Co., TN, in District No. 7, about 2½ miles west of Shelbyville, several tracts. Reg: 13 Nov 1846.

Page 33 - August Term 1846. Circuit Court Decree, Title to James M. Robison. William Yates and his wife Mary Ann Yates, Edmund L. Hart and Nancy his wife, Philip G. Thompson and Caroline J. his wife, Elijah H. Moore, Harriett E. Moore, the latter of whom is a minor and sues by her guardian Leroy W. Barrett vs William McClure and Martha D. his wife, and Mary Moore. Court ordered that William Yates and others have an interest in land in Bedford Co., TN, on Sugar Creek, be devised of them and vested to James M. Robison. Reg: 26 Nov 1846.

Page 35 - 5 Sep 1846. C. D. Steele and others to Price C. Steele. Bill of Sale. The undersigned heirs and distributees of Joseph Steele, deceased, conveyed unto P. C. Steele all their undivided interest in a slave Daniel belonging to the estate of Joseph Steele, deceased. Signed by C. D. Steele, Marinda Steele, Jane B. Steele, Volney H. Steele, J. G. Neeley, M. P. Neeley, Mentoria Steele, John Knott, Harriett Knott, and John P. Steele. Wit: C. P. Houston and William T. Tune. Reg: 28 Nov 1846.

Page 36 - 26 Aug 1846. Richard Bandy to Richard T. Stone and others. Deed of Gift. Richard Bandy of Bedford Co., TN, for love and affection for his grand children, Richard Thomas Stone, Nancy Keziah Stone, and Sarah Philadelphia Stone, conveys a negro girl Lock. Wit: J. W. Swift and William S. Watkins. Reg: 1 Dec 1846.

Page 42 - 15 Aug 1846. Littleton Averett and wife to Isaac Rust. Deed, 102¼ acres. Littleton Averett and Sally his wife of Rutherford Co., TN, conveyed to Isaac Rust, land in Bedford Co., TN, on south side of Falling Creek. Bounded by Falling Creek, Jesse P. and Elizabeth Tucker's corner, Whitman's corner, Phifer's line and Withrow's old line. Reg: 8 Dec 1846.

Page 43 - 22 Dec 1845. C. M. Cobbs to George Davidson. Bill of Sale, interest in negroes. C. M. Cobbs sold to George Davidson, his interest in slaves belonging to the estate of the late Richard Daniel formerly of Halifax Co., VA. Wit: Wiley Daniel and Thomas M. Coldwell. Reg: 8 Dec 1846.

Page 45 - 19 Jun 1846. William Morgan and others to Elizabeth C. Morgan. Bill of Sale. Rutherford Co., TN. William Morgan, Simpson H. Morgan and John H. Morgan sold to Elizabeth C. Clark, alias Morgan, conveys a negro boy Elbert. Wit: Lewis Tucker and William C. Work. Reg: 9 Dec 1846.

Page 49 - 12 Nov 1846. John and Lina Mangrim to Addison Adams. Bill of Sale. John and Lina Mangrim conveyed to Addison Adams, a negro girl Ann. Wit: A. L. Adams and James Bigger. Reg: 10 Dec 1846.

Page 51 - 7 Dec 1846. L. D. Stockton to Howel M. Dawdy. Deed, 100 acres. L. D. Stockton of Marshall Co., TN, sold to Howel M. Dawdy of Bedford Co., TN, land in Bedford Co., being a part of a tract of land owned by John Dawdy in his lifetime and divided by him to his wife for her lifetime and then to his sons Howel M. Dawdy and John W. Dawdy. Wit: William H. Wisener and Thomas Coffey. Reg: 10 Dec 1846.

Page 51 - 7 Dec 1846. Lewis G. Ray to James Davis. Deed, 1/8 of 100 acres. Lewis G. Ray conveyed to James Davis, his undivided interest in the tract of land conveyed by John Ray to his son William R. Ray. Land in Bedford Co., TN, on waters of Sinking Creek, in District No. 19. Lewis G. Ray's interest descended to him on the death of William R. Ray as one of his heirs. Reg: 10 Dec 1846.

Page 54 - 30 Mar 1846. Clarissa Gilpin to James C. Snell. Deed, 30 acres. Whereas one W. H. Dyer on 19 May 1845 executed a deed to Nancy Brence wife of Alpheus Brence to the tract of land described during her natural life and remainder to Clarissa Gilpin might appoint to take the same, and in default of such appointment to the right heirs of Nancy Brence. Clarissa Gilpin in pursuance of Power of Appointment and for divers good causes me thereunto moving appoint James C. Snell to take the remainder of the tract of land after the death of Nancy. Land in Bedford Co., TN, on Sugar Creek. Bounded by Andrew Davidson's line formerly John Hall's line. Wit: John B. Neeley and Samuel Neeley. Reg: 11 Dec 1846.

Page 55 - 2 Mar 1846. Samuel B. McCuistion and others to Philip Hodge. Bill of Sale. Whereas the undersigned, all being lawful heirs and distributees of the late Sarah McCuistion of Bedford Co., TN, in and to a family of negroes belonging to Sarah McCuistion at the time of her death and now we the undersigned being willing that the said family of negroes not be separated and parted, conveyed unto Philip Hodge. Signed by S. B. McCuistion, John C. McCuistion, W. J. Chunn, W. W. Coldwell, P. A. Coldwell, Minos C. Hodges, E. W. Hodges, Thomas McCuistion, Nancy McCuistion. Wit: Thomas Lentz and Alfred Mallard. Reg: 11 Dec 1846.

Page 57 - 27 Nov 1846. Minos C. Dwyer to Samuel B. McCuistion. Deed, 103 acres. Minos C. Dwyer conveyed to Samuel B. McCuistion, all his undivided interest in land belonging to the heirs of Daniel Dwyer, deceased, in Bedford Co., TN, in District No. 6. Wit: William S. Watkins and Minos C. Hodge. Reg: 11 Dec 1846.

Page 58 - 9 Dec 1846. B. C. Dobson and wife to Abner Osborne. Deed, 56 acres. Blackman C. Dobson and Martha J. Dobson his wife formerly Martha J. Williams, conveyed to Abner Osborne, land in District No. 18. Reg: 12 Dec 1846.

Page 59 - 8 Feb 1845. Wilson Garrett and others to Samuel Coldwell. Deed, 46+ acres. Wilson Garrett, Nancy Martin, Sarah Martin, and Willson Garrett as Attorney for Joseph Garrett and Moses Garrett, sold to Samuel Garrett for $25.00 each to each of the legatees of the estate of Polly Garrett, deceased, viz, Wilson Garrett, Nancy Martin, Sarah Martin and Wilson Garrett as Attorney for Moses Garrett and Joseph Garrett, sold land in Bedford Co., TN, on waters of Big Flat Creek. Borders William Shook, Jas. C. Trible and Samuel Coldwell. Wit: Henry Dean and W. W. Coldwell. Signed by Wilson Garrett, Sarah Martin, Benhamin Martin, Nancy Martin, Asa Martin, and Wilson Garrett for Joseph and Moses Garrett. Reg: 12 Dec 1846.

Page 61 - 12 Dec 1846. John Streater to Nancy Streater. Relinquishment Deed. 194 acres. John Streater relinquished unto Nancy Streater, all his interest in lands lately occupied and held by his mother Mildred Streater now deceased. Land in Bedford Co., TN, on south side of Duck River, being part of a 1923 acre grant in the name of Dempsey Powell, which descended to Mildred Streater as one of the heirs of Dempsey Powell and known as Lot No. 1. Reg: 12 Dec 1846.

Page 63 - Tennessee Grant to John Thompson. 279 acres. No.14794. Land in Bedford Co., TN, survey date of 20 June 1836, on waters of the North Fork of Wilsons Creek. Reg: 14 Dec 1846.

Page 63 - Tennessee Grant to John Thompson. 200 acres. No. 15686. Land in Bedford Co., TN, survey date of 9 April 1838, west of North Fork and in District No. 11. Reg: 14 Dec 1846.

Page 68 - 20 Dec 1846. George Bussey to Jonathan Leggitt. Deed in Trust, 1 acre. George Bussey conveyed unto Jonathan Leggitt, both of Bedford Co., TN, for love and affection for said Leggitt, land whereon George Bussey now lives in Bedford Co., on both sides of Sinking Creek, in District No. 18, adjoining land of the heirs of John Bryeans and others, being the land he purchased of William A. Gaunt. Also, conveyed personal Property, reserving property for use and benefit for his use and his wife Lucy during their natural life and survivors of them. Reg: 23 Dec 1846.

Pahe 71 - 9 Dec 1846. John Dobbs to Tyree D. Dobbs. Deed. Fayette Co., Alabama. John Dobbs sold to Tyree D. Dobbs, all his interest in land lately owned by his father Jeremiah Dobbs, deceased, in Bedford Co., TN, on waters of Sinking Creek. Bounded by Jacob Moulder, Sinking Creek, and Edward Stevenson (Stephenson). Wit: Thomas Thornton and Orpha C. Thornton. Reg: 23 Dec 1846.

Page 71 - 18 Dec 1846. Tyree D. Dobbs and Rachel Dobbs to James M. Neeley. Deed. Tyree D. Dobbs of Fayette Co., Alabama and Rachel Dobbs of Bedford Co., TN, sold to James M. Neeley of Bedford Co., TN, their interest in land in Bedford Co., on east side of Sinking Creek. Borders Edward Stevenson (Stephenson). Wit: George Bussey and Jonathan Leggitt. Reg: 24 Dec 1846.

Page 73 - 22 Sep 1846. Anna Presgrove to James Presgrove and others. Deed, life estate, 260 acres. Whereas by the dower of Andrew Presgrove, deceased, Anna Presgrove is legally seized of a life estate in land in Bedford Co., TN, in District No. 8 and 9. Borders lands of John Rushing, Lander's land, Widow Allison's land, and heirs of Robert Allison, deceased. Being the same land that Andrew Presgrove her husband died seized and possessed of, conveys her life estate to the legal heirs of Presgrove, deceased, to wit, James Presgrove, Jno. H. and Nancy Featherston his wife, William Presgrove, Elizabeth Short, Harris S. and Ourcille(?) Wilson his wife, Nathaniel M. and Mary Wheeler his wife, and Jno. Presgrove. Wit: John Rushing and Alexander Landers. Reg: 25 Dec 1846.

Page 75 - 6 Dec 1846. Charles Pearson to Kindred Pearson. Deed, Interest in estate. Charles Pearson of Franklin Co., TN, conveyed to Kindred Pearson of Bedford Co., TN, all his interest in the proceeds of the sale of a tract of land in Bedford Co., and one Town Lot in Lynchburg, which property belonged to the estate of William Pearson, deceased, and sold in Nov 1845. Reg: 28 Dec 1846.

Page 76 - 22 Dec 1845. James T. Byler to Thomas Cole. Deed, 1/8 of 151 acres. James T. Byler sold to Thomas Cole, his interest in the estate of the late Abram Byler, deceased, his brother, both real and personal. His interest being one eighth of the property. Borders lands of Gault, Martha Gault, Johnson, and John Wray. Also a negro boy Frank. Reg: 28 Dec 1846.

Page 79 - 9 Jul 1838. Gabriel Low to Jason Winsett and others. Trustees of School House, Deed, 1 acre. Gabriel Low of Bedford Co., TN conveys unto Jason Winsett, Evan Wallace, Gabriel Low, Simeon Gilley and Ziza Moore, Trustees for Pleasant Hill School House of Bedford Co., for benefit of School House and goodwill for the neighborhood, he has given and conveyed to the Trustees of School House. The house may be used as a place of Public Worship, not to interfere with a school that may be taught in said house without the consent of the Trustees, a parcel of land on which said house is built. Wit: R. H. Parkerson and Hiram Maxfield. Reg: 31 Dec 1846.

Page 80 - 28 Nov 1846. Lemuel Snelling and others to John Snelling. Deed, 150 acres. Lemuel Snelling, Susannah Searcy, L. H. Arnold, James H. Arnold, all of Bedford Co., TN, sold to John Snelling of Bedford Co., land in Bedford Co., on waters of the Garrison Fork, adjoining lands with Sooter, James Chambers, Isaac West, Lemuel Snelling and George Thompson. Another tract borders Wason's land. Wit: James C. Searcy, James F. Snelling, and V. S. Searcy. Reg: 2 Jan 1847.

Page 86 - 28 Dec 1846. Joel and Matilda Shofner to Benjamin McFarlin. Deed, 104 acres. Joel and Matilda Shofner sold to Benjamin McFarlin, Sr., land in Bedford Co., TN, in District No. 23. It being the land that Robert McFarlin now lives on. Wit: William Woosley and Reuben Norman. Reg: 6 Jan 1847.

Page 87 - 14 Sep 1846. Needham and Sarah King to David King. Deed in Trust &c. Needham and Sarah King his wife sold to David King, their interest in the estate of William Pearson, deceased, the grandfather of Sarah. Deed in Trust. Reg: 6 Jan 1847.

Page 88 - 2 Jan 1847. Nancy Fugitt to Moses Cheves. Deed. Nancy Fugitt sold to Moses Cheves, both of Bedford Co., TN, her share or interest in two tracts of land in the name of Moses Fugitt, deceased, in Bedford Co., on waters of Little Sinking Creek. Borders lands of Richard Martin, lands of Moses Fugitt's Grant No. 11240, Josiah HUghes, Agness Hughes, Stephenson's line. Reg: 6 Jan 1847.

Page 92 - 28 Dec 1846. Sarag Aaron and others to James M.Neeley. Deed, 200 acres. Sarah Aaron, William H. Aaron, Samuel Blythe and Sarah his wife, the feme covert, Jackson Roberts and Nancy his wife, the feme covert, of Bedford Co., TN, sold to James M. Neeley of Bedford Co., land in Bedford Co., on west side of Sinking Creek. Bounded by Sinking Creek, Walter Bernard. Another tract borders Moses Aaron. Wit: John Pearson and James Pearson. Reg: 15 Jan 1847.

Page 97 - 7 Oct 1846. C. D. Westerman and wife to Nancy Fugitt. Deed, 95¼ and 115¼ acres. Clifford D. Westerman and his wife Fanny formerly Fanny Fugitt of Bedford Co., TN, sold to Nancy Fugitt all their interest in as heirs to land in Bedford Co., on waters of Little Sinking Creek, deeded by James Dickson to

Moses Fugitt in 1822. Wit: J. _. Brodie and Nicholas Dodd. Reg: 18 Jan 1847.

Page 101 - 16 Jan 1847. Richard Foreman to Thomas Foreman. Deed, 6¼ acres. Richard Foreman, for love and affection for his son Thomas Foreman, conveyed to him land in Bedford Co., TN, in District No. 7. Bounded by Old Nashville Road on Chockley's line, and Lipscomb's line. Wit: C. H. Wright and J. C. Wright. Reg: 23 Jan 1847.

Page 106 - 23 Aug 1845. Simon Battin to Sarah E. S. Smith. Deed of Gift. For love and affection Simon Battin has for Sarah E. S. Smith, infant daughter of his beloved wife Mary D. Batton, deceased. conveys 2/3 of the estate of Mary D. Batton his deceased wife. Wit: John Lane, D. M. Smith and Pinkney Smith. Reg: 1 Feb 1847.

Page 114 - 6 Feb 1847. James H. T. Lee and Elvira Bowles. Marriage Contract. Alvira Bowles and James H. T. Lee, both of Bedford Co., TN, that whereas a marriage is shortly intended to be had, and whereas Alvira Bowles is possessed of property and estate which she is desirous of securing to her sole and separate use during her lifetime. She has an undivided tenth part of land of which her father Claiborn Bowles died seized and possessed. Land in Bedford Co., in District No. 3, of about 50 acres, also slaves, also an interest in the estate of her late mother Mary Bowles who has Claiborn Bowles, Jr. as her Administrator of which the estate has not been settled. Wit: John Bowles and Claiborn Bowles. Reg: 8 Feb 1847.

Page 117 - 8 Feb 1847. Frederick Brown and Margaret his wife to G. W. Cunningham and others. Deed. Frederick Brown and Margaret M. Brown his wife formerly Margaret M. Cunningham, sold to George W. Cunningham, Jane E. Cunningham, J. W. C. Cunningham, and Josephus A. Cunningham, their interest in land in Bedford Co., TN, in District No. 20, on waters of Sinking Creek. The land being whereon Humphrey Cunningham lived at the time of his death. Bounded by George W. Cunningham, John Nance, Thomas Greer, Logan Henderson, William Potter. Their interest being one sixth part of 250 acres. Reg: 11 Feb 1847.

Page 118 - 18 Oct 1845. Margaret Cunningham to Josephus Cunningham. Deed. Margaret Cunningham of Bedford Co., TN, conveys to Josephus Cunningham, all her interest in a tract of land left at her disposal by Humphrey Cunningham, deceased, in Bedford Co., on waters of Big Sinking Creek. Borders G. W. Cunningham and William Potter, Nathaniel Porter, John Nance, and by Thomas Greer. Wit: Joseph Trice, Jr. and William Potter. Reg: 11 Feb 1847.

Page 120 - 13 Nov 1837. David Dryden and others to Thomas Dryden Power of Attorney. David Dryden, William Dryden, Samuel D. Walker and his wife Nancy, Andrew Grey and his wife Mary, and John G. Morrison and his wife Eliza N., all of Coles Co., Illinois, appointed Thomas Dryden of Bedford Co., as their Attorney, to sell the real estate belonging to them of the estate of Jonathan Dryden, deceased, late of Bedford Co. Reg: 13 Feb 1847.

Page 122 - 1 Feb 1847. Moses and Sarah Cheves to Nancy Fugitt. Deed, undivided interest in land. Moses Cheves and his wife

Sarah formerly Sarah Fugitt, sold to Nancy Fugitt, all their interest in land in Bedford Co., TN, in District No. 18, on waters of Sinking Creek. Bounded by George Doherty. Another tract bounded by William Martin, George Doherty. Reg: 15 Feb 1847.

Page 123 - 24 Nov 1845. Thomas and Phebe Swann (by Attorney) to Jacob Sivley. Bill of Sale. Thomas and Phebe Swann sold to Jacob Sivley, a negro woman Adaline and her three children now in possession of Thomas Haile, the property of Nicholas and Hannah Woodfin, deceased. Wit: William Tucker and Hiram J. Austin. Reg: 15 Feb 1847.

Page 123 - 10 Feb 1847. John Fugitt and Nancy Fugitt. Partition. Deed, 120 acres. Whereas by deed from Clifford Westerman and his wife Frances, Moses Cheves and wife Sarah, Benjamin Fugitt and Bedford Fugitt, we, Nancy Fugitt and John Fugitt have title to and hold undivided interest in a tract of land in Bedford Co., TN, on waters of Sinking Creek, in District No. 18. Borders R. H. Sims, Alexander Allen, and J. Dixon, now, the land has been partitioned. John conveys to Nancy Fugitt 60 acres of land. Bordered by R. H. Sims. Wit: John Stephenson and Moses Cheves. Reg: 15 Feb 1847.

Page 126 - 15 Feb 1847. Thomas Phillips to Adelia F. A. A. Nelson. Deed of Gift. Whereas John W. Nelson Deeded in Trust to Benjamin A. Nelson, dated 27 Feb 1846 and recorded in Bedford Co., TN. Land to be sold to highest bidder along with other personal items. Thomas Phillips has sold to Adeline Fitzgerald Allen Armore Nelson, daughter of John W. Nelson, for love and affection and good will, a brass clock made by Clark Gilbert & Co. at Winchester, Connecticut. Reg: 16 Feb 1847.

Page 129 - 13 Feb 1846. Martha Garrison and others to James C. Snell. Deed. Martha Garrison, Sr., Robert C. Garrison of Maury Co., TN, and Archibald M. Pickens and his wife Sarah W. Pickens of Giles Co., TN, all legal heirs of Samuel R. Garrison, dec'd., sold to Kames C. SNell of Bedford Co., TN, land in Bedford Co., being the western half of the tract of land formerly owned by Samuel R. Garrison, deceased, on waters of Sugar Creek, adjoining lands of Robert Riley and others. Bounded by land of the heirs of James Walker, deceased, Nathan Evans and James C. Snell. Reg: 22 Feb 1847.

Page 130 - 30 Oct 1841. George D. and Mary Stephenson to Samuel Morrow. Deed, 1/8 of 185 acres. George D. and Mary Stephenson sold their undivided interest in land in Bedford Co., TN, in District No. 1, on waters of Scotts Branch. Bounded by John Jakes, Harrison Gaston, Richard Gaither, and Eli Eaton. This land being their eighth part and it being the dower interest descended to them by the late James Morrow, deceased. Wit: William Gaston and Harrison Gaston. Reg: 22 Feb 1847.

Page 133 - 1 Sep 1845. John Woodfin to Thomas Haile. Bill of Sale. As an heir of the estate of Nicholas Woodfin, late of Bedford Co., TN, I am entitled to an undivided interest or childs part, of a negro woman Adeline and her daughter Sally. I have now sold same to Thomas Haile. Reg: 1 Mar 1847.

Page 136 - 17 Mar 1846. Worke land division to the Lorance heirs. (Plat on page 136). William Guy two shares by descent and purchase. Lewis W. Shuford, one share, in right of his wife Jane, and Edwin Deaton, one share, in right of his wife Mary. Wit: James Vannatta and William Weaver. Reg: 5 Mar 1847.

Page 140 - 16 Mar 1841. William D. Crawford to John Rendleman. Deed. William D. Crawford of Rowan Co., NC, sold to John Rendleman of Rowan Co., NC, an undivided half of four hundred acres in Bedford Co., TN, being part of a 5000 acre tract granted by State of North Carolina to the late Col. Martin Phifer and which 400 acres were willed by Col. Martin Phifer to his grandson William D. Crawford and his granddaughter (blank). The land lies about six miles from Shelbyville near the Turnpike Road leading to Nashville. Adjoining lands of Doc Houston and others. Wit: Charles Fisher. Reg: 15 Mar 1847.

Page 141 - 16 Mar 1841. John J. Shaver to John Rendleman. Deed. William D. Crawford of Rowan Co., NC deeded to John J. Shaver on 9 May 1840, all his estate for the benefit of John Rendleman, interest in undivided half of the land in Bedford Co., TN descended from Col. Martin Phifer. John J. Shaver sold same to John Rendleman. Wit: Charles Fisher. Reg: 15 Mar 1847.

Page 150 - 8 Feb 1847. Elizabeth Smalling and others to Susanna Lynch. Deed of Gift. Elizabeth B. Smalling, for good will and affection for her daughter Susanna Lynch, conveyed a negro boy Erie. Wit: John J. Shriver and Risdon Trott. Reg: 6 Apr 1847.

Page 154 - 10 Mar 1847. Elizabeth B. Smalling and others to B. F. Smalling. Bill of Sale. Elizabeth B. Smalling, for good will and affection for her son Benjamin F. Smalling, conveys a negro boy Isam. Wit: John J. Shriver and Risdon Knott. Reg: 8 Apr 1847.

Page 155 - 10 Mar 1847. James M. Smalling and others to Constantine W. Graham. Relinquishment. James M. Smalling and others, relinquished all their interest in a negro boy Brister. It being part of interest as the heir or legatees of Elizabeth B. Smalling. Signed by James M. Smalling, Susanna C. Linch, William Linch, and B. F. Smalling. Wit: John J. Shriver and Risdon Knott. Reg: 9 Apr 1847/

Page 156 - 26 Mar 1847. James M. Smalling and others to Constantine W. Graham. Relinquishment. James M. Smalling, William Linch, Susanna C. Linch and B. F. Smalling, relinquished all claim in interest of one fourth part of a negro woman Franky and a negro girl Harriett. They are heirs or legatees of Elizabeth B. Smalling who owns said negroes. Wit: John J. Shriver and Risdon Knott. Reg: 9 Apr 1847.

Page 157 - 13 Jan 1846. Andrew J. Tucker to James Wortham. Power of Attorney. Andrew J. Tucker appointed James Wortham his Attorney to deliver for him unto William Hammill, his interest in the lands upon which his father resided next before his death, of about 450 acres. Wit: Ed Wortham. Reg: 10 Apr 1847.

Page 157 - 26 Jul 1845. Thomas Shearin and others to William Hammill. Deed, 307+ acres in 4 tracts. John F. Thompson and Eritha Thompson his wife formerly Eritha Tucker, Thomas Shearin and wife Sarah Shearin formerly Sarah Tucker, William J. Pyland

and wife Elizabeth Pyland formerly Elizabeth Tucker, William E. Tucker of Bedford Co., TN, Andrew J. Tucker of Graves Co., KY, and John W. Tucker of Hickman Co., TN, and James F. Wortham and wife Nancy M. Wortham formerly Nancy M. Tucker of Haywood Co., TN, all being legal heirs of William Tucker, deceased, of one part, sold to William Hammill of Bedford Co., TN, land in Bedford Co., on south side of Duck River, in 4 tracts. One 100 acre tract borders John Rogers, Thomas Cook and the south bank of Duck River. Another 6+ acre tract borders Duck River originally William Tucker's corner. Another 21 acre tract that borders the bank of Duck River. Another 180 acre tract borders William E. Tucker, Josiah Davis, and Tucker and Roger's line, Owen Ballard, and Lane's line. Reg: 10 Apr 1847.

Page 160 - 18 Dec 1846. William Young and Nancy Martin to Eli Moss. Bill of Sale. William Young, Executor, and Nancy Martin, Executrix, of the Last Will and Testament of James Young, deceased, of Bedford Co., TN, sold to Eli Moss of Bedford Co., a negro woman Sóoky and a negro girl Mary Jane. Wit: John M. Stokes and William Mullins. Reg: 10 Apr 1847.

Page 160 - 25 Feb 1847. Thomas Coffey to Thomas W. Coffey. Deed of Gift, 105½ acres. Thomas Coffey conveyed unto Thomas W. Coffey, both of Bedford Co., TN. Thomas W. Coffey son of Thomas Coffey, land in Bedford Co., on East Fork of Rock Creek, in District No. 19. Land borders Archibald Adams, land Coffey bought of Thomas Allen, Shelbyville to Pulaski Road, W. Brown, center of road where Hannah Road crosses Shelbyville Road and near M. Smith and W. C. Swanson, and the lands belonging to the heirs of John Davis, deceased. Reg: 12 Apr 1847.

Page 161 - 31 Aug 1844. New Hope Baptist Church. Agreement. New Hope Baptist Church at New Hope Meeting House, Bedford Co., TN, having become divided forming two distinct parties or Churches, each claiming to be the original New Hope Church. We, the individuals composing said two parties enter into the following agreement and obligation relative to the occupancy, right of possession &c of the house, grounds &c belonging to New Hope Church, viz, We agree that each party being component parts of New Hope Church before the division is equally entitled to the grounds, house &c of said Church, for the purpose for which they were originally conveyed to Matt Martin, John B. Walker, Christopher Shaw, Vincent Smith, Jonathan Webster, James Slaton, and B. Martin, Commissioners of said Church by two deeds of conveyance, one from Andrew Erwin, the other from John Scott, and to prevent all future difficulties, and for the sake of convenience enter into the following further agreement, relative to the occupancy of said house and grounds by each party, viz, That part of the Church which do not oppose Missionary Societies and known as "The United Baptist Church" shall occupy the house and grounds of said Church from beginning on Friday before the second Sabbath in each month until ending on Thursday before the third Sabbath seven days; and beginning on Friday before the fourth Sabbath in each month seven days ending on Thursday following. That part of the Church which do oppose Missionary Societies and calling themselves "The Old United Baptist Church" shall occupy the house, grounds &c of said Church from, beginning on Friday before the third Sabbath in each month seven days ending on Thursday following; and from (beginning on) Friday before the first Sabbath in each month seven days ending on Thursday following. When a fifth Sabbath shall occur, it shall be occupied alternately. Signed by John Tillman, Clerk of the United Baptist Church at New Hope and F. H. Keller, Clerk of the Old United Baptist Church at New Hope. Wit: William P. Finch and Daniel Stephens. Reg: 12 Apr 1847.

Page 162 - 8 Jan 1847. Jane E. Springer to Hugh McCrory. Deed, undivided interest. Jane E. Springer sold to Hugh McCrory her undivided interest, her one ninth part of land in Bedford Co., TN, in District No. 9, of 115 acres, it being the tract that Sarah Springer died seized. Land borders Josiah Springer, James Hart, Mathis Price and Lydia Roane. Wit: W. W. Rushing and S. S. Whitworth. Reg: 12 Apr 1847.

Page 163 - 13 Apr 1847. Newton C. Thompson to James H. Lock. Deed, 1/5 of 25 acres. Newton C. Thompson sold to James H. Lock, both of Bedford Co., TN, land in Bedford Co., on north side of Duck River near Thompson's Ford, it being the part that fell to Newton C. Thompson at the death of William F. Thompson, deceased, one of the heirs of Joseph Thompson, deceased. Reg: 13 Apr 1847.

Page 164 - 20 Mar 1847. Henry Brown and Thomas Norville to Methodist E. Church. Deed, 1 acre. Thomas Norville and Henry Brown conveyed unto Abram Sriver (Shriver), J. A. Moore, Isaac West, R. J. King, G. M. Moore, J. J. Sriver (Shriver), B. B. Bomar, A. Sharp, and C. B. McGuyer, one acre of land in Bedford Co., TN, whereon Mount Moriah now stands and for many years as a Methodist Church. Thomas Norville and wife Emiline Norville and Henry Brown gave said one acre of land. Reg: 14 Apr 1847.

Page 168 - 3 Apr 1847. Hugh C. Hurst and others to Edmund Word. Deed of Release. By decree of Circuit Court of Bedford Co., TN, at August Term 1844, the lands belonging to the late William Hurst, deceased, were sold by the Clerk, on the petition of the heirs of said Hurst. Lands in Bedford Co., and Edmund Word was the purchaser. Said lands were sold subject to the widow's dower*. Wit: Samuel Doak and William Word. Reg: 19 Apr 1847.
*Signed by: Moses Neeley, Nancy Neeley, wife of Moses Neeley, America Hurst and H. C. Hurst.

Page 169 - 23 Nov 1846. William and Nancy Martin. Marriage Contract. William Martin and Nancy Martin his wife, and William Young, all of Bedford Co., TN. Whereas William Martin and Nancy Martin has lately intermarried, the said Nancy being the widow and relict of James Young, deceased, late of Bedford Co., and whereas James Young by his Last Will and Testament bequeathed to Nancy certain land, slaves and other property during her life or widowhood and further bequeathed that in the event of the marriage of his widow, she should receive out of his estate an equal part with his heirs and children, and whereas William Martin and Nancy his wife are willing and desirous that whatever property and money she has received, shall at their death, descend or go to the children of the said Nancy by her former husband James Young, deceased. Wit: J. W. Dickerson and Eliza Young. Reg: 21 Apr 1847.

Page 170 - 20 Apr 1847. George Davidson to William Young. Trustee, Bill of Sale. George Davidson sold to William Young as Trustee of William Martin and Nancy his wife, a negro girl Sindy. Reg: 23 Apr 1847.

Page 171 - 13 Mar 1847. Samuel Mason and wife to Alexander G. Ramsey and Jno. D. Neil. Deed, 1/5 of 101½ acres. Samuel Mason and his wife Margaret Mason sold to Alexander G. Ramsey and John D. Neill, the undivided interest in land in Bedford Co., TN, on Sinking Creek, in District No. 18. Bounded by lands of Michael Moore and David Dryden, Oneal's line, and John Bryean's heirs, and it being the land belonging to Solomon Ramsey on which he died. There are five heirs to the land. Wit: J. M. Harper and Thomas S. Ramsey. Reg: 23 Apr 1847.

Page 176 - 10 May 1847. Solomon G. Reeves and wife to A. B. Covington. Deed, 12¼ acres. Solomon G. Reeves and his wife Rachel Catharine sold to A. B. Covington, land in Bedford Co., TN, in District No. 11. Borders the dower tract and Lock's old line. Wit: A. Reeves and Levicy Covington. Reg: 11 May 1847.

Page 178 - 13 May 1847. Jeremiah Kimbro to Mary Franklin and her heirs. Deed of Gift. For love and affection Jeremiah Kimbro has for Mary Franklin, one half of his tract of land in Bedford Co., TN, in District No. 2, being and including the place whereon she now lives of about 50 acres. Borders Jeremiah Kimbro and his blacksmith shop and dwelling house. After the death of Mary Franklin, the land to be equally divided between Susan Franklin, Naomi Franklin and Ruth Franklin, daughters of Mary Franklin. Also, all the corn, wheat &c now on hand except a reasonable supply for Jeremiah Kimbro's wife Elizabeth Kimbro's support. Wit: A. M. Holt and D. P. T. House and Samuel Yates. Reg: 19 May 1847.

Page 181 - 22 May 1847. Powell Kimbro to Joseph Holt. Deed, interest in estate. Powell Kimbro sold to Joseph Holt all his interest in the estate of Jeremiah Kimbro which he lived at the time of his death. The land in Bedford Co., TN, in District No. 2. Also, sold his interest in the personal estate. Reg: 28 May 1847.

Page 185 - 21 May 1847. Absalom Reeves and wife Elizabeth to Jacob M. Parsons. Deed, 89 acres. Absalom Reeves and his wife Elizabeth sold to Jacob M. Parsons, land in Bedford Co., TN, in District No. 8. Borders John Allison, east bank of Alexanders Creek, Andrew Presgrove, B. Carr, mouth of Alexanders Creek. Wit: James M. Atkinson and Green M. Sikes. Reg: 31 May 1847.

Page 186 - 6 May 1847. Absalom Reeves and wife to John Allison. Deed, 69 acres. Absalom Reeves and Elizabeth Reeves his wife sold to John Allison a tract of land in Bedford Co., TN, in District No. 8. Borders west bank of the North Fork, Thomas Wheeler, Turrentine's line, John Sanders' Spring. Wit: James M. Atkinson and Green M. Sikes. Reg: 31 May 1847.

Page 187 - 11 Mar 1845. James F. Jameson and wife to Edwin Deaton. Deed, 1/5 of 192 acres. James F. Jameson and his wife Margaret Jameson of Rowan Co., NC sold to Edwin Deaton of Bedford Co., TN, land in District No. 5, his 1/5 interest in land, adjoining lands of William Guy, William Warren and Zachariah B. Dozier. Wit: James Smith and Robert W. Long. Reg: 3 Jun 1847.

Page 190 - 7 Jun 1847. David B. Johnson and wife and others to Joseph Holt. Deed, undivided interest. David B. Johnson and Eve Johnson his wife and John Lewis and Polly Lewis his wife sold to Joseph Holt their undivided interest in land in Bedford Co., TN, in District No. 2, on waters of the Barren Fork and it being the tract of land owned by Jeremiah Kimbro and on which he resided at the time of his death and it being the undivided share of Johnson and wife and Lewis and his wife as heirs of Jeremiah Kimbro, deceased. Wit: Minos Cannon. Reg: 8 Jun 1847.

Page 193 - 9 Jun 1847. John Hart to S. A. Bell and others. Trustees, Meeting House Deed. John Hart sold to Samuel A. Bell, John Overcast, Jonathan Cooper, Isaac B. Webb, A. J. Goodrum, and William K. Ransom, for respect he has for the Methodist Episcopal Denomination of Christians, conveys unto the Trustees of a Methodist Meeting House that is now being built on John Hart's land, known by the name of Harts Chapel. Borders lands of John Hart and on which he now lives, and John Knott. Reg: 12 Jun 1847.

Page 198 - 6 Jun 1847. William Boone to Milton N. Moore. Deed of Gift. William Boone of Bedford Co., TN, gives to his step son Milton N. Moore, all the property of Margarett Boone the wife of William Boone, brought into his house when he married her, and at the death of his mother Margarett Boone, all the property except the wearing cloths. Milton N. Moore is to take possession and if he should die without issue, the property goes to the daughters of David Owen, to wit, Elizabeth, Ruth, Lamiza Jane Abbott, Julian F. Owen, Margaret M. Owen, and Minerva E. Owen. Wit: B. Boone. Reg: 23 Jun 1847.

Page 199 - 28 Jun 1847. William M. Ayers and wife to Joseph Holt. Deed, undivided interest. William M. Ayers and Nelly Ayers his wife formerly Nelly Kimbro, sold to Joseph Holt, interest in tract of land in Bedford Co., TN, in District No. 2, on waters of the Barren Fork, being the tract of land on which Jeremiah Kimbro resided at the time of his death. Wit: William H. Wisener, Williamson Haggard and Eli Moss. Reg: 5 Jul 1847.

Page 201 - 3 Jul 1847. George W. Gambill to A. H. Gambill. Deed. George W. Gambill sold unto A. H. Gambill his distributive share and all his interest in the personal property of Benjamin Gambill, deceased, except his interest in the property of the widow of Benjamin Gambill, she has a life estate. Wit: Thomas C. Whiteside. Reg: 6 Jul 1847.

Page 201 - 12 Mar 1847. Solomon Brown and wife Eveline to Henry Brown. Deed, interest in 1/6 of 220 acres. Solomon Brown and his wife Eveline Brown sold to Henry Brown, all of Bedford Co., TN, land in Bedford Co., about one mile west of Shelbyville. Borders lands of Flower Swift, E. J. Frierson, Thomas Pettis, John T. Neil, and John McCuistion. Also the distributive share of Solomon Brown and Eveline Brown his wife in her right in the estate of Edward Kimmons, deceased. Wit: William Brown and Bartley Kimmons. Reg: 6 Jul 1847.

Page 204 - 26 Apr 1847. John F. Woodfin and wife Mary to Elihu H. Bigham and R. P. Bigham. 1/2 of 305 acres. John F. Woodfin and his wife Mary formerly Mary Scott of Marshall Co., Mississippi, sold to Elihu H. Bigham and Robert P. Bigham of Bedford Co., TN, land in Bedford Co., on headwaters of the North Fork and Falling Creeks and east of the Turnpike Road, being a part in the division of a 2500 acre tract granted by the State of

North Carolina to Matthew Locke, among the heirs and distributees of Matthew Locke and which fell to James Locke and part fell to James L. and Mary Scott. Reg: 17 Jul 1847.

Page 209 - 12 Apr 1846. James Mullins to Matilda Pannill. Deed of Gift. James Mullins for love and affection for his step sister Matilda Pannill, and for consideration of the undivided attention she has paid to him and his property for many years past and for her kindness and attention while he was on the bed of affliction, conveys unto her his negro girl Betsey. At the death of Matilda, to her heirs and if she should die without issue, the negro girl Betsey shall return to James Mullins or his lawful heirs. Reg: 23 Jul 1847.

Page 210 - 5 Jun 1847. Daniel Gober and wife Mary to Isaac Troxler. Bill of Sale. Daniel Gober and his wife Mary Gober sold to Isaac Troxler a woman slave Vinah. Wit: George Cortner, James Gober and Sullenger Holt. Reg: 31 Jul 1847.

Page 211 - 3 Jul 1847. James L. Payne to Isaac Troxler. Deed, 13 acres. James L. Payne sold to Isaac Troxler, land in Bedford Co., TN, in District No. 25, it being a part of Zebediah Payne's old tract and laid off to James L. Payne as his distributive share of his father. Bounded by the Barren Fork, Mary Ewell and Isaac Troxler. Wit: George Cortner and Eli Troxler. Reg: 2 Aug 1847.

Page 227 - 25 Aug 1827. John B. Newman and others to Hinckey Petway. Power of Attorney. Whereas James Lyle, late of Philadelphia, PA, Merchant, deceased, being in his life time seized in fee of land in the State of Tennessee, by his Last Will and Testament dated 24 July 1826, proven &c, did give and devise all and singular his estate real and personal unto John B. Newman, Hartwell Kuhn and Henry Beckett, all city Esquires, In Trust, for the use and behoof of Ellen Kuhn and Mary Beckett, the wives of Hartman Kuhn and Henry Beckett, respectively, they being his only children and heirs at law, they appointed Hinckey Petway of Nashville, TN as their Attorney to oversee all belongings held by James Lyle, deceased. Wit: William Whiteside and Fran. Hutchinson. Reg: 10 Aug 1847.

Page 234 - 24 Jul 1847. Archibald Prewit to Benjamin A. Nelson. Deed, 36 acres. Archibald Prewit sold to Benjamin A. Nelson, land in Bedford Co., TN, in District No. 3 and Lot No. 1 in the division of the lands of Michael Holt, deceased, amongst his heirs. Bounded by the dower of the widow of Michael Holt near Nelson's fence. Also conveyed to Nelson all his interest in the undivided interest which Lewis Hooker and his wife Mary Hooker will inherit of the dower of the widow of Michael Holt. Reg: 14 Aug 1847.

Page 235 - 14 Nov 1846. Matthew Shearin and wife to William O. Forbes. Bill of Sale. Matthew Shearin and his wife Elizabeth Shearin sold to William O. Forbes, a negro woman Abby. Wit: P. J. Epps and Ezekiel Roan. Reg: 21 Aug 1847.

Page 237 - 21 Aug 1847. Archibald Reaves to B. S. Reaves. Interest in estate. Archibald Reaves of Wilcox Co., Alabama sold to B. S. Reaves of same County and State, all his claim and interest in the estate of George Reaves, deceased, his brother, late of Bedford Co., TN. Wit: John J. Hurst and James C.

Norman. Reg: 21 Aug 1847.

Page 237 - 10 Aug 1847. James McMinn and wife to Samuel Woodfin. Deed, 26 acres. James McMinn and his wife Elizabeth of Hickman Co., TN, sold to Samuel Woodfin of Bedford Co., TN, land in Bedford Co., in District No. 5. Borders Thomas and Phebe Swann and Mathew's lot. Reg: 21 Aug 1847.

Page 239 - 16 Aug 1847. Benjamin Mosely and wife to Randolph Newsom. Deed, 116 acres. Benjamin Mosely and his wife Margaret Mosely sold to Randolph Newsom land in Bedford Co., TN, in District No. 20. Borders Newsom's line. Wit: W. P. Goodwin and L. W. Barrett. Reg: 28 Aug 1847.

Page 239 - 27 Aug 1847. William P. Elkins to Elizabeth Elkins. Deed of Gift. William P. Elkins for love and affection for his daughter Elizabeth Elkins wife of Harrison Elkins and the children of Elizabeth Elkins, a negro girl Matilda. Wit: William Galbreath and John T. Neal. Reg: 28 Aug 1847.

Page 240 - 3 Sep 1846. Granville H. Frazer to Preston Frazer. Deed. Granville H. Frazer. late of Texas, now in Bedford Co., TN, conveyed unto Preston Frazer of Bedford Co., all the lands and all real estate that may come to Granville H. Frazer by the Last Will and Testament of Mrs. Jane Frazer, being the mother of Granville H. Frazer. Reg: 28 Aug 1847.

Page 240 - 3 Sep 1846. Granville H. Frazer to Preston Frazer. Deed. Granville H. Frazer, late of Texas, now of Bedford Co., TN, sold to Preston Frazer of Bedford Co., all interest and claim in negro slaves that falls to Granville H. Frazer by the Last Will and Testament of Mrs. Jane Frazer, the mother of Granville H. Frazer. Reg: 28 Aug 1847.

Page 241 - 21 Aug 1847. Benjamin A. Nelson to John McGuire. Deed, 24 acres. Benjamin A. Nelson sold to John McGuire, land in Bedford Co., TN, in District No. 3, in Lot No. 1 in the division of lands of Michael Holt, deceased, amongst his heirs. Borders the dower's line, McGuire's line. Also, B. A. Nelson conveys to McGuire all his interest and claim that he holds in the undivided interest which Lewis Hooker and his wife Mary Hooker will inherit of the dower of the widow of Michael Holt, deceased, at her death, which was conveyed to Archibald Prewit, said Prewit to B. A. Nelson. Reg: 28 Aug 1847.

Page 243 - 13 Jul 1847. Moses Reaves to Benjamin S. Reaves. Power of Attorney. Moses Reaves of Wilson Co., Alabama, appointed Benjamin S. Reaves of same place, his Attorney to act in his place on any monies &c that may come to him from the estate of Archibald Reaves, Sr., late of Bedford Co., TN. Reg: 4 Sep 1847.

Page 245 - 4 May 1844. Morgan Smith and wife to John A. Moore. Bill of Sale. Morgan Smith and his wife Tabitha W. Smith, sold to John A. Moore, all their right and claim to a negro woman Sina. The negro woman Sina was willed to Sarah West, Frances Shriver and Tabitha Smith by John Moore, deceased. Wit: Redding George and Joseph W. George. Reg: 6 Sep 1847.

Page 248 - 30 Apr 1847. Thomas B. Mosely to Mary C. Davidson. Deed of Gift. Thomas B. Mosely, for his love and affection for his daughter Mary C. R. Davidson and having confidence in Samuel Davidson and John Q. Davidson, do nominate Samuel and John Q. Davidson as Trustees, conveys negroes (4). Wit: Mary Eddins and Rebecca Reddins. Reg: 6 Sep 1847.

Page 248 - 13 Jul 1847. John Larue to Hardin B. Larue. Deed of Gift, 100 acres. John Larue for love and affection for Hardin B. Larue, conveys land in Bedford Co., TN, in District No. 18. Borders John Larue, John T. Dabney, and east side of Rock Creek. Wit: John Oneal and John H. Oneal. Reg: 6 Sep 1847.

Page 251 - 30 May 1846. Jane Frazer to John S. Frazer. Deed, 110 acres. Jane Frazer for love and affection for John S. Frazer, conveys land in Bedford Co., TN, it being same Jane Frazer purchased of John S. Frazer and known as the Dalby place. Bounded by C. F. Sutton, Bradfords Creek, John Taylor, John S. Frazer, R. Chamber's line, and Sharp's line. Wit: G. H. Frazer and Newton C. Harris. Reg: 11 Sep 1847.

Page 251 - August Term 1847. Chancery Court Decree. Title to Alfred Campbell. 115 acres. Lemuel Broadaway, administrator of Daniel L. Mallard, deceased vs Minos Cannon and others. All the right claim and interest that Elizabeth A. Mallard, Nancy Mallard, Sarah Ann Mallard, and Alsey R. Mallard, heirs at law of Daniel L. Mallard, deceased, and Minos Cannon have in land in Bedford Co., TN, on waters of Big Flat Creek and bounded by James Reagor, Martin Friddle, Alfred Campbell, the Stage Road, and Anne Bromfield. Reg: 11 Sep 1847.

Page 252 - (no date). Chancery Court Decree. Title to Mary Dobson. Robert T. Cannon, administrator of Archibald Dobson, deceased vs The heirs and creditors of Archibald Dobson, deceased. The date set to sell two Lots, No. 33 and No. 34, on 10 May 1847, with all the improvements thereon (subject to the widow's dower). James Wortham was the purchaser for Mary Dobson was not accepted. The Court Decree was that all the right title and interest of Robert T. Cannon and Defendants Blackman C. Dobson, William D. Dobson and wife Martha, and Joseph Dobson, heirs at law of Archibald Dobson, deceased, or either of them in law or equity in and to said Lots No. 33 and No. 34 in the Town of Shelbyville. Reg: 11 Sep 1847.

Page 254 - 10 Jul 1846. David A. Ozment and wife to Frederick Batte. Deed. David A. Ozment and his wife Sarah Frances sold to Frederick Batte, all of Bedford Co., TN, land in Bedford Co., on waters of Weakley Creek, in District No. 9, it being an undivided interest in a tract of land belonging to the heirs of Henry Batte, deceased, it being the portion of land falling to Sarah Frances, daughter of Henry Batte. Reg: 18 Sep 1847.

Page 257 - 14 Jul 1847. Richard S. Williamson to Thomas G. Williamson. Quit Claim. On or about 11 Mar 1844, Richard S. Williamson recovered a judgement against Jordan C. Holt for $975.18 and the Court decreed that R. S. Williamson is to have the enjoyment of said sum money for his natural life and after his death descends to his three children, Thomas G. Williamson (other two names not named here). Whereas Thomas G. Williamson has, since the rendition of said judgement, married and R. S. Williamson desires that Thomas G. Williamson should now have his portion of monies. Now R. Williamson give and relinquish unto Thomas G., his son, all his right title, claim &c to one third or his part of said monies. Reg: 25 Sep 1847.

Page 261 - 30 Oct 1846. Thomas Greer, Sr. to George W. Greer. Deed, 381 acres. Thomas Greer, Sr. for love and affection for his son George W. Greer, conveyed unto him land in Bedford Co., TN, on east side of Sugar Creek, being a part of a 5000 acre granted by State of North Carolina to Alexander and Thomas Greer. Bounded by Robert J. Greer, Benjamin F. Greer, Byram's line, and the Sugar Creek. Wit: B. F. Greer and A. J. Greer. Reg: 28 Sep 1847.

Page 262 - 30 Oct 1846. Thomas Greer, Sr. to Benjamin F. Greer. Deed, 326 acres. Thomas Greer for love and affection for his son Benjamin F. Greer, land in Bedford Co., TN, on waters of Sugar Creek, being part of a 5000 acre tract granted by State of North Carolina to Alexander and Thomas Greer. Bounded by Robert J. Greer, John Harrison, Jonathan Mosely, and Bryam's line. Wit: G. W. Greer and A. J. Greer. Reg: 29 Sep 1847.

Page 265 - 20 May 1837. Samuel White to Nathaniel White. Quit Claim Deed. Samuel White of Cabarrus Co., NC sold to Nathaniel White of Bedford Co., TN, all his title claim and interest with all their profits and whatever to $4.00 paid by Nathaniel White, a tractof land of 40 acres in Bedford Co., on waters of Sugar Creek and being a part of the tract belonging to the heirs of Thomas White, deceased. Bounded by Davidson's land and N. White's land. Wit: George M. Ellis, William M. Pickens, O. W. Bradshaw, and A. H. Elliott. Reg: 2 Oct 1847.

Page 265 - 15 May 1847. Margaret H. White and others to Andrew S. Bayne. Deed, 40 acres. Margaret H. White and Joseph B. White of Cabarrus Co., NC and Margaret White, Samuel White and Nathaniel White of Bedford Co., TN, sold to Andrew J. Bayne of Bedford Co., land in Bedford Co., on headwaters of Sugar Creek, in District No. 20. Bounded by Bayne, Nathan Evans, James Ellis, and Margaret Stewart. Margaret H., Joseph, Margaret, Samuel, and Nathaniel White paid Margaret H., relict of John White, late of Cabarrus Co., NC $150.00. Wit: David B. McKinley, D. W. N. Faggert, A. H. Elliott, and O. W. Bradshaw. Reg: 2 Oct 1847.

Page 266 - 5 Jul 1847. Robert Preyer to J. H. Scott and others. Deed, 3/4 acre. Robert Preyer conveyed to J. H. Scott, R. L. Landers, A. L. Landis, Nicholas Lasater and Levi Turner, Trustees to superintend the building and management of a school house to be known as the Rowsville Schoolhouse. The house is to be kept forever for a school house, land in Bedford Co., TN, in District No. 25 near to Rowsville. Borders George Cortner and Reaves' line. Wit: G. W. Heard and S. B. Heard. Reg: 4 Oct 1847.

Page 270 - 28 Mar 1844. Alfred Burrow and others to Banks A. Burrow. Deed. Alfred Burrow, James Burrow, Jarrel J. Burrow and Frances Hill of Bedford Co., TN, sold to Banks A. Burrow, land in Bedford Co., on waters of Flat Creek, whereon their mother Mary Burrow now lives, said land being left to her during her natural life by their father William Burrow, deceased, said land being secured to him by four grants from State of Tennessee No. 19880 for 5 acres, No. 19881 for 10 acres, No. 19884 for 15 acres, No. 19885 for 60 acres, also one deed from Phillip

Burrow for 19+ acres and one from John Harrison for 19 acres, all the above land being in one tract and known as the property of William Burrow, deceased. Wit: Jarrel J. Burrow, Elender Austin, Pearce Wilhoite, Thomas Morris, M. M. Bedwell and William Bedwell. Reg: 9 Oct 1847.

Page 272 - 18 Aug 1846. William M. Harwell and wife to Levi C. Johnson. Deed, 70 acres. William M. Harwell and his wife Louiza Harwell formerly Louiza Nash, sold to Levi C. Johnson, land in Bedford Co., TN, in District No. 5. Bounded by Travis C. Nash, now deceased, Mrs. Hutton's land where she now lives, James Nash, a minor, and Lot No. 13 allotted to Benjamin F. Garrett and wife, and Lot No. 12 allotted to Harwell and wife by Commissioners who divided the estate of T. C. Nash, deceased. William M. Harwell and wife Louiza of Giles Co., TN. Reg: 16 Oct 1847.

Page 275 - 16 Oct 1847. James F. Arnold to Jos. H. M. McGrew. Deed, 50 acres and 9 acres. James F. Arnold has an interest in remainder to take effect and be united with the possession after the death of Margarett M. Arnold who has a lifetime estate in land in Bedford Co., TN, in District No. 4. Borders Charles Sutton, Jane Frazier, William McGrew, Sr. Reg: 16 Oct 1847.

Page 275 - April Term 1846. Circuit Court Decree to Henry Pickle. Title to land, 55 acres. Jane Buchanan and others. Exparte. Petition to sell land. Final decree. Court satisfied that at a former Term of Court, George Glascock, the original purchaser of the lands, came into court and asked to have his bid transferred to Major Pickle, which was done, and Major Pickle came into court and requested that all the right vested in him by the transfer from George Glascock be transferred to Henry Pickle and that the title of the heirs of John Buchanan to be vested in Henry Pickle. The Court ordered that all right, title, claim, and interest which Jane Buchanan, John W. Buchanan, William Sims and his wife Rebecca, Elijah Buchanan, Obadiah Buchanan, Eli Buchanan, Daniel Stephenson and Jemima his wife, Isaac Buchanan, Samuel B. Buchanan, Sarah S. Buchanan, Calvin E. Buchanan, Permelia J. Buchanan and George Glascock and Major Pickle, has in the land in Bedford Co., TN. Bounded by Edward Bryeans, Joseph Neil and Richard Martin. It being the land granted by State of Tennessee to Joseph Neil by Grant No. 7846 for 55 acres. Another tract bounded by Jesse Mize, Gaunt's line, Edward Bryeans, being 9 acres. It being granted by State of Tennessee to John Buchanan by Grant No. 15 and 128. This land vested into Henry Pickle and his heirs. Reg: 20 Oct 1847.

Page 278 - (no date). Alfred Balch to John C. Holt and others, Trustees &c, Deed. Alfred Balch sold to J. C. Holt, J. G. Barksdale, David Ruth, D. S. Evans, W. B. M. Brame, and T. C. Whiteside, Trustees of the "Baptist Church of Shelbyville" for $200.00, land or lot in Town of Shelbyville, Bedford Co., TN. Bounded by T. C. Ryall, and the McAdamized Street (graveled street), and J. A. Blakemore. It being Lot No. 3 in the Town. Reg: 22 Oct 1847.

Page 280 - 21 Oct 1847. James K. Norton and wife to John W. Norville. Deed, undivided interest, 270 acres. James K. Norton and his wife Mary Ann K. Norton sold to John W. Norville, all of Bedford Co., TN, their undivided one ninth part of a tract of land in Bedford Co., TN, in District No. 3. Bounded by Elijah Bomar, Daniel Gilchrist's land, and John W. Norville. It being that tract of land assigned to Elizabeth W. Norville for her dower interest in the lands of her deceased husband David Norville. Reg: 22 Oct 1847.

Page 283 - 3 Apr 1847. John Noblitt to Sarah Ann Noblitt. Deed, 5 acres. John Noblitt sold to Sarah Ann Noblitt, land in Bedford Co., TN, on the headwaters of Big Flat Creek. Bounded by a tract that Abraham Noblitt bought of Henry Dean. The land to belong to Sarah Ann Noblitt during her natural lifetime or widowhood and from the time of her death or marriage, to her children, to wit, Jasper, John, Marion, Harriett, Willie and Polly Ann Noblitt. Reg: 30 Oct 1847.

Page 289 - 4 Nov 1847. Phillip Burrow to Banks A. Burrow. Deed, undivided interest. Phillip Burrow sold to Banks M. Burrow, his interest in the land in Bedford Co., TN, on waters of Flat Creek whereon their mother Mary Burrow now lives. The land being left to Mary Burrow during her natural life by their father William Burrow, deceased. Wit: H. H. Holt and M. Holt. Reg: 6 Nov 1847.

Page 298 - 24 Nov 1847. James K. Norton and wife to Henry Stephens. Deed, 45+ acres. James K. Norton and his wife Mary Ann K. Norton and David J. Norville sold to Henry Stephens, land in Bedford Co., TN, on waters of Duck River. Bounded by widow Caruther's corner, Swinney tract, Younger's line, Lot No. 3 as allotted to the heirs of David Norville, deceased, and crossed the McMinnville Road. Reg: 26 Nov 1847.

Page 300 - 10 May 1847. Thomas Eakins and others to John W. Cowan. Deed. John Eakin, Alexander Eakin, Mary Jane Eakin, Nancy Nevins, William G. Cowan and his wife Sarah Cowan formerly Sarah Eakin of Bedford Co., TN, William Eakin and Thomas Eakin of Davidson Co., TN, and James J. McClelland and his wife Eliza formerly Eliza Eakin of Huntsville, Alabama, sold to John W. Cowan of Bedford Co., TN, all their interest as heirs at law and distributees of Jane Cowan, deceased, late of Bedford Co., land in Bedford Co., in Town of Shelbyville and known as Lot No. 28 and No. 29, the same being upon which Jane Eakin resided at the time of her death and on which John W. Cowan now resides. Wit: Thomas C. Whiteside and Thomas Lipscomb. Reg: 1 Dec 1847.

Page 302 - 10 May 1847. Thomas Eakin and others to Nancy Nevins. Bill of Sale. Thomas Eakin, William Eakin, Jno. Eakin, William G. Cowan, Alex. Eakin, Jane Cowan, Mary Jane Eakin, John W. Eakin, Sarah Eakin, Eliza McClelland, and J. J. McClelland sold to Nancy Nevins, a negro woman Lucinda. Wit: Thomas C. Whiteside and Thomas Lipscomb. Reg: 1 Dec 1847.

Page 303 - 18 Aug 1846. William M. Harwell and wife to Benjamin F. Garrett. Deed, 20¼ acres. William M. Harwell and his wife Louiza formerly Louiza Nash, sold to Benjamin F. Garrett, land in Bedford Co., TN, in District No. 5. Bounded by L. C. Johnson, Thomas Nash, William Nash, Garrett's line. Reg: 4 Dec 1847.

Page 307 - 27 Oct 1845. James Jackson and John C. Jackson to Nathan Jackson. Power of Attorney. James Jackson and John C. Jackson of Franklin Co., Alabama appointed Nathan Jackson of Bedford Co., TN as their Attorney to oversee their interest coming to them from the estate of Francis Jackson, deceased, their father, late of Rutherford Co., TN. Reg: 7 Dec 1847.

Page 308 - 12 Nov 1847. Joseph Hiles to Mary Ann Heard. Deed of Gift. For love and affection Joseph Hiles has for Mary Ann Heard, he conveys a negro girl Elender. Wit: Isaac Barnett and Lodwick Holt. Reg: 7 Dec 1847.

Page 308 - 3 Nov 1847. Benjamin F. Garrett and wife to Daniel Wadley. Deed, 56½ acres. Benjamin F. Garrett and his wife Emily formerly Emily Nash, conveyed unto Daniel Wadley, land in Bedford Co., TN, in District No. 5. Bounded by L. C. Johnson, Thomas Nash and William Nash. Wit: Thomas Nash and John P. Steele. Reg: 8 Dec 1847.

Page 310 - 12 Nov 1847. Joseph Hiles to Eliza Holt. Deed of Gift. Joseph Hiles for love and affection for Eliza Holt, conveys unto her a negro girl Julia. Wit: Samuel B. Heard and Isaac Barnett. Reg: 8 Dec 1847.

Page 318 - 6 Dec 1847. Neeley Kimbro to Daniel Hooser and others. Deed for Schoolhouse, 1 acre. Neeley Kimbro sold to Daniel Hooser, R. J. Williams and Martin Euless, Trustees, for $10.00, land in Bedford Co., TN, in District No. 25, on waters of Duck River. Bounded by Thomas Whiteside. It being part of a tract which Neeley Kimbro purchased of James H. Cobbs, deceased. Wit: James Mullins and J. T. Brittain. Reg: 10 Dec 1847.

Page 320 - 27 Jan 1844. William Hutson to Nancy Prince. Deed, 10 acres. This indenture made willed and bequeathed by William Hutson unto his daughter Nancy which is Jeremiah Prince's wife, conveyed unto her land in Bedford Co., TN, on Thompsons Creek. Bounded by John Powell and William Hutson. Wit: B. K. Daniel and John Massy. Reg: 11 Dec 1847.

Page 321 - 20 Nov 1845. Thomas Ramsey to Michael Moore. Deed. Thomas Ramsey sold to Michael Moore, land in Bedford Co., TN, it being the land that Ramsey bought from Elbert Bryeans dated 16 Sep 1844 and registered in Book NN, page 347, it being one undivided interest belonging to the heirs of John Briant, dec'd, it being one tenth part of the land, also, he holds one tenth interest of his wife, she being one of the heirs of John Briant, deceased. Reg: 14 Dec 1847.

Page 326 - 15 Nov 1847. Plat of Amos McAdams, deceased, lands in Bedford Co., TN. Whereas by the Last Will and Testament of Amos McAdams, deceased, late of Bedford Co. To Thomas McAdams 1/10 of value in land and known as Lot No. 4. To John McAdams 1/10 value in land and known as Lot No. 9. To William S. Hailey in right of his wife Malinda Hailey formerly Malinda Hailey (McAdams) 1/10 part known as Lot No. 7. To Nathaniel O. McAdams 1/10 part as Lot No. 3. To Daniel R. McAdams 1/10 part as Lot No. 5. To Robert P. McAdams 1/10 part as Lot No. 1. To Nancy McAdams 1/10 part as Lot No. 6. To Patience A. McAdams 1/10 part (now Patience Arnold) as Lot No. 2. To Andrew J. McAdams 1/5 part as Lot No. 8. Wit: Redding George, Morgan Smith, Henry Brown, Benjamin F. Whitworth, and John Hart. Executors of said will: John T. Neil and Nathaniel O. McAdams. Reg: 21 Dec 1847.

Page 332 - 21 Dec 1847. Alfred Kimery to Jacob Kizer. Deed, 104+ acres. Alfred Kimery of Hardin Co., TN sold to Jacob Kizer of Bedford Co., TN, land in Bedford Co., on Big Flat Creek. Bounded by Jesse Koonce, George Pratt and the Flat Creek. It excepting however and reserving such rights as Alfred Kimery has, conveyed to Turley Kimery, widow of Frederick Kimery, deceased, for her natural lifetime. Reg: 24 Dec 1847.

Page 333 - 21 Dec 1847. Elbowin Boules(Bowles) to Clabourn Boules (Bowles. Deed, 1/10 of 50 acres. Elbowin Boules sold to Clabourn Boules, all his right title, claim and interest which he has in the undivided tenth part of land which descended to jim jointly with others from Clabourn, deceased, in Bedford Co., TN. Bounded by Robert T. Cannon, Moriah Phillips, William Young, and THomas C. Whiteside. Also transfers unto Clabourn Bowles an undivided tenth part in negroe slaves, which descended to Elbowin Bowles from his brothers and sisters, from Joseph Olmer, late of Breckenham Co., VA, to wit, names negroes, Milly, Reuben, Edmund, William, Nancy, Jane and Albert and Isaac. Wit: Thomas H. Coldwell and Marion Miller. Reg: 24 Dec 1847.

Page 334 - 29 Nov 1847. Thomas E. Richardson and wife to Wynn D. Williams. Deed, 80 acres. Thomas E. Richardson and his wife Lydia M. Richardson of Coffee Co., TN, sold to Wynn D. Williams land in Bedford Co., TN, on headwaters of Sugar Creek. Bounded by Templeton's old corner, Morton & Evans' corner, and F. F. Fonville. Wit: Hiram S. Emerson and Robert J. Greer. Reg: 27 Dec 1847.

Page 335 - 25 Dec 1847. Thomas McGuire to Cornelius B. McGuire. Deed. Thomas McGuire for love and affection for his son Cornelious B. McGuire, land in Bedford Co., TN, all the lands he purchased from Nathaniel G. Brown, except that part sold and conveyed to B. B. Bomar in Bedford Co., on headwaters of Butlers Creek. Wit: Benjamin Ragsdale and Wiley Forster. Reg: 27 Dec 1847.

Page 344 - 6 Jan 1848. William Rucker to Thomas Black. Deed in Trust. Land and Personal Property. William Rucker conveyed to Thomas Black, in Trust Deed, land in Bedford Co., TN, in District No. 10. 120 acres. Bounded Willis D. Jenkins, Jordan Rucker, Keziah Rushing, John D. Cooper and Lewis Weatherford, it being the place whereon William Rucker now resides. Also one undivided interest in negroes, it being one tenth part of the negroes devised to William Rucker by the will of Elliott Rucker, deceased. Also personal property conveyed to Thomas Black. William Rucker is guardian of Margaret A. Stem formerly Margaret A. Kimmons and Violet A. Kimmons. Jackson Nichols and Enoch D. Rushing were his securities. Reg: 6 Jan 1848.

Page 355 - 31 Dec 1847. William S. Haley and wife to Thomas C. Whiteside. Deed, 46 acres. William S. Hailey and Malinda Hailey his wife formerly Malinda McAdams sold to Thomas A. Whiteside, land in Bedford Co., TN, on east side of Shelbyville, Murfreesboro and Nashville Turnpike, on the south fork of Falling Creek, being part of a 5000 acre tract granted to Caleb Phifer and part of a tract owned by Amos McAdams at the time of his death and devised by him to be divided between his children. Reg: 11 Jan 1848.

Page 360 - 8 Jan 1848. Elizabeth Jones to Michael F. Parsons. Deed, 4½ acres. Elizabeth Jones conveyed to Michael F. Parsons, land in Bedford Co., TN, on waters of Falling Creek, in District No. 8, it being Elizabeth Jones' distributive share of land formerly belonging to George W. Parsons, deceased. Bounded by the dower line. Wit: Jacob Fisher and Benjamin Parsons. Reg: 14 Jan 1848.

Page 361 - 13 Jan 1848. John H. Featherston and wife to James Presgrove. Deed, 40 acres. John H. Featherston and Nancy his wife sold to James Presgrove, land in Bedford Co., TN, in District No. 8. Bounded by North Fork and the Old Mill. Wit: William B. Wheeler and H. S. Wilson. Reg: 14 Jan 1848.

Page 362 - 19 Dec 1846. William Young, Executor to James W. Dickerson. Bill of Sale. William Young, Executor of the Last Will and Testament of James Young, deceased, sold to James W. Dickerson, a negro man Lewis. Reg: 14 Jan 1848.

Page 362 - 29 Dec 1847. William Young to James W. Dickerson. Deed, 241 acres. William Young, Executor of the Last Will and Testament of James Young, deceased, sold on 19 Dec 1846, land and it being the place whereon James Young resided at the time of his death. Bounded by Peter Miller's corner, H. Claggett's line, bank of Butler Creek, near the mouth of Cedar Branch, and Overton's & Whiteside's tract. Reg: 15 Jan 1848.

Page 364 - 14 Jan 1848. William H. Aaron and wife to Richard Warner. Deed, 200 acres. William H. Aaron and Delila his wife of Bedford Co., TN, sold to Richard Warner of Marshall Co., TN, land in Bedford Co., on south side of Duck River, it being the tract purchased by John Warner, Sr. from George Earnhart. Reg: 15 Jan 1848.

Page 366 - 13 Jan 1848. James E. Cunningham to George W. Cunningham. Deed, 250 acres. James E. Cunningham sold to George W. Cunningham all his interest &c that he as one of the heirs of Humphrey Cunningham, deceased, has in land in Bedford Co., TN, in District No. 20, on waters of Sinking Creek, it being the land whereon Humphrey Cunningham lived at the time of his death. Bounded by George W. Cunningham, John Nance, Thomas Greer, Logan Henderson and William Potter. Reg: 17 Jan 1848.

Page 367 - 5 Jul 1847. Reuben Smith to Jeremiah Cleveland. Power of Attorney. Greenville District, South Carolina. Reuben Smith of Greenville District, SC, appointed Jeremiah Cleveland of Bedford CO., TN, his Attorney to act for him as guardian appointed by Greenville District of SC, of his seven children, namely, John S., Amanda K., Ambrose R., Rosannah B., Nancy, Louisa B. and Reuben A. Smith, by my wife Nancy T., the daughter of William Pearson, Jr. who was the son of William Pearson, deceased. Jeremiah Cleveland is to ask, demand and receive from Kindred Pearson, administrator of the estate of William Pearson, deceased, the grandfather of his late wife Nancy Smith now deceased. Wit: William Choice. Reg: 18 Jan 1848.

Page 368 - 10 Sep 1847. Thomas Haile and wife to John Nailor. Deed, 17 acres. Thomas Haile and his wife Hannah Haile, conveyed to John Nailor dated 20 Nov 1845 and recorded. Hannah Haile formerly Hannah Woodfin. Land in Bedford Co., TN, in District

No. 5. Bounded by lands of Nicholas Woodfin, deceased. Wit: Woodfin Naylor and W. K. Ransom. Reg: 19 Jan 1848.

Page 369 - 1 Dec 1847. John and Woodfin Naylor to Ellis H. Haile. Deed, 114 acres. John and Woodfin Naylor of Bedford Co., TN sold to Ellis H. Haile of Rutherford Co., TN, land in Bedford Co., it being Lots No. 4, 5, 6, 7, and 8 in the division of Nicholas Woodfin, deceased. Bounded by Matthew Locke, W. H. Naylor, G. W. Campbell now W. Worke's land, Jane Statham, James Woods, and Samuel Woodfin. Wit: Isaac J. Miller and James D. Naylor. Reg: 19 Jan 1848.

Page 371 - 1 Jan 1848. Josephus A. Cunningham and wife to Dennis G. Smith. Deed, 54 acres. Josephus A. Cunningham and his wife Elizabeth sold to Dennis G. Smith, land in Bedford Co., TN. Bounded by B. C. Dobson and wife, and Alexander Allen. Reg: 20 Jan 1848.

Page 374 - 3 Dec 1847. John A. Hime to William Hime. Deed, undivided interest, 82 acres. John A. Hime has an interest in estate after the death of Mary Ann Hime who has a life time estate in the land in Bedford Co., TN, in District No. 23. Bounded by Joseph Hastings. Land and perishable property is conveyed to William Hime. Reg: 24 Jan 1848.

Page 376 - 20 Mar 1847. W. W. Coldwell and wife to Clement Cannon. Deed, 20 acres. William W. COldwell and wife P. A. Coldwell sold to Clement Cannon, land in Bedford Co., TN, on waters of Fall or Falling Creek, it being formerly owned by Ebenezer Wilson and sold to John Mason and by his heirs to Nathan H. Schooler and by Schooler to Benjamin F. McCuistion who died seized and possessed of the same. Said tract has been divided amongst the heirs of Benjamin F. McCuistion, deceased, into six lots. The Lot No. 5 conveyed. Bounded by Andrew Vannoy. Reg: 27 Jan 1848.

Page 377 - 28 Jan 1848. John Kimbro and others to John F. Hall. Deed, individed. John Kimbro, Ann Holt and William Holt, all of Bedford Co., TN, sold to John F. Hall, land in Bedford Co.,, in District No. 2, on waters of the Barren Fork, it being the tract on which Jeremiah Kimbro resided at the time of his death. Wit: Andrew Vannoy. Reg: 28 Jan 1848.

Page 378 - 15 Jan 1848. Shadrack S. Brown to Thomas J. Brown. Deed of Gift, 105 acres. Shadrack S. Brown for love and affection for his son Thomas J. Brown, conveyed unto him, land in Bedford Co., TN, in District No. 6, about two miles west of Shelbyville and on the north side of the Old Columbia Road, being the tract formerly owned by Daniel Dwyer, deceased. Wit: John T. Neil and James H. Neil. Reg: 25 Jan 1848.

Page 379 - -- Nov 1845. Isreal Harris and wife to James W. Head. Deed, 8 acres. Isreal Harris and his wife Martha Harris sold to James W. Head, land in Bedford Co., TN, in District No. 8. Bounded by Eben Wilson and James W. Head. Wit: E. Thomas and James O. Mohundro. Reg: 29 Jan 1848.

Page 380 - 12 Oct 1846. Sarah Lasater and Ireanny Green to Daniel Weaver. Deed. Sarah Lasater and Ireanny (Irena) Weaver conveyed all their right and interest in land which David Weaver, Sr., their father, deeded to them. Land on West Fork of Gages

Creek. Wit: M. W. Nutt and Lucretia Fielding Sherrill. Reg: 29 Jan 1848.

Page 389 - 20 Nov 1845. Thomas Ramsey and wife to Michael Moore. Deed, undivided interest. Thomas Ramsey and his wife Mary Ramsey sold to Michael Moore, land in Bedford Co., TN, on waters of Sinking Creek, it being one tenth part of a tract belonging to the heirs of John Bryant, deceased, which they hold by virtue of being heirs of John Bryant, deceased. Reg: 10 Feb 1848.

Page 391 - 10 Feb 1848. John Stephens*to Thomas Stephens* Deed, 252 acres. * Stevens in original book. John Stephens*for love and affection for his son Daniel Stephens and for consideration of $700.00 paid by the said Daniel Stephens for his brother Thomas Stephens, did transfer unto Daniel Stephens, two-thirds of a tract of land. One tract which John Stephens bought from the Executors of the Last Will and Testament of James Patton, deceased, of about 205 acres in Bedford Co., TN, on the Garrison Fork. Bounded by west side of the Garrison Fork, lands James Patton devised to his son James E. Patton, the road tract from Davis' Mill, Robert Hannah, and John Scott. Also, second tract of 30 acres on the Garrison Fork. Another tract. Bounded by John Stephens, G. G. Osborne, road leading from Davis' Mill to Shelbyville, William P. Finch's spring branch belonging to the Davidson tract or Armstrong line, of about 17 acres. Wit: F. H. Keller and C. Thomas. Reg: 10 Feb 1848.*Stephens in body of the instrument.

Page 394 - 18 Jan 1848. Jane H. Morrison to John W. Wiggins. Deed. Jane H. Morrison, late of Bedford Co., TN, now of Benton Co., Arkansas, did on 22 Sep 1838 together with her son John R. Morrison, executed a joint obligation to John W. Wiggins of Bedford Co., TN, for $1050.00. Conditioned that Robert A. and Leander B. Morrison, then minor children and heirs of Andrew Morrison, Jane's late husband, and formerly of Bedford Co., TN. When Robert A. and Leander B. comes of age of 21 years, are to make a good title to John W. Wiggins, to the land which was bequeathed to them by the Last Will and Testament of their father Andrew Morrison, deceased, late husband of Jane Morrison, it being the land whereon Andrew Morrison resided at the time of his death. Wit: Nathan Evans and Harrel Wiggins. Reg: 11 Feb 1848.

Page 396 - 19 Feb 1848. Thomas Webb and wife to Horatio Coop. Deed, 54 acres. Thomas Webb and Elizabeth Webb his wife formerly Elizabeth Loyd, conveyed to Horatio Coop, land in Bedford Co., TN, in District No. 5, being Lots No. 7, 8, and 9 in the division of the lands of Joseph Long, deceased. No. 7 had 18 acres, No. 8 & 9 had 36 acres. Borders Bingham's land. Reg: 12 Feb 1848.

Page 397 - 25 Dec 1847. John W. Cunningham to Josephus A. Cunningham. Deed, undivided interest. John W. C. Cunningham sold to Josephus A. Cunningham, land that he had belonging to the estate of Margaret Cunningham, deceased, being in Bedford Co., TN. Bounded by William Potter, G. W. Cunningham, John Nance and Richard Anderson. Wit: William Potter and Samuel F. Trice. Reg: 14 Feb 1848.

Page 399 - 28 Jan 1848. Alfred Poplin and others to William R. Baty. Deed, 45 acres. Martha Poplin and Alfred Poplin, Amyline

Deason and Keziah Taylor conveyed unto William R. Baty, land in Bedford Co., TN, in District No. 10. Bounded by Dougherty's line, Powell's line and Joel Rushing. Wit: William Taylor and Merryman Burns. Reg: 17 Feb 1848.

Page 405 - 26 Mar 1846. Robert N. Adams and wife to J. P. Mitchell. Deed. Robert N. Adams and Eliza A. Adams his wife conveyed to J. P. Mitchell, one fifth part of the land belonging to William Low at his death, which was and is the interest his wife Eliza Ann Lowe, one of the heirs of William Lowe, deceased, had in the land. Bounded by Archibald Adams, Thomas Davidson and Martin Smith. Land in Bedford Co., TN, in District No. 19. Wit: Thomas W. Coffey and Archibald Adams. Reg: 25 Feb 1848.

Page 407 - 21 Feb 1848. J. W. Brightwell to John Goodwin. Bill of Sale. J. W. Brightwell sold to John Goodwin, Harriett Ann, Eliza Jane and James Henry and George Washington Goodwin, a negro woman Jane. Reg: 25 Feb 1848.

Page 407 - 1 Mar 1848. John Wilson to A. L. Copeland. Deed, 50 acres. John Wilson on 29 Feb 1848 obtained a decree for title of land in Bedford Co., TN, to pay the administrators of T. J. Reaves, deceased, by the Clerk and Master and whereas A. L. Copeland agrees to pay same ($203.00). In the Bill of John Wilson against Mary Reaves and others. Reg: 2 Mar 1848.

Page 411 - 17 Feb 1848. Elizabeth and William A. M. Gilmore to Robert H. Majors. Deed, 112 acres. Elizabeth Gilmore and William A. M. Gilmore of Rutherford Co., TN, sold to Robert H. Majors of Bedford Co., TN, land in Bedford Co., on Wartrace Fork, in District No. 4. Bounded by Elnathan Davis and the lands Robert H. Majors bought of Theodocia H. Clardy and where he now lives. Wit: William J. Peacock and James R. Clardy. Reg: 7 Mar 1848.

Page 420 - 3 Mar 1848. John W. and Rhoda A. Foster to James G. Neeley. Deed, 60 acres. John W. Foster and Rhody A. Foster of Bedford Co., TN, sold to James G. Neeley, their undivided interest in land in Bedford Co., on waters of Fall Creek. Bounded by the widow and heirs of John Orr, deceased, and C. D. Steele, Samuel Doak, Daniel Wadley. It being the land on which Nancy A. Keele now lives. Reg: 16 Mar 1848.

Page 422 - 10 Sep 1847. David Weaver to Lucretia Fielder Sherrill. Deed, 20 acres. David Weaver for love and affection for Lucretia Fielder Sherrill, conveyed unto her land in Bedford Co., TN, in District No. 25. Bounded by west bank of the West Fork of Gages Creek, and Zachariah Weaver. Wit: Timothy Long, Lewis Holder, Thomas B. Kaar (Karr), and A. J. Green. Reg: 27 Mar 1848.

Page 423 - 25 Mar 1848. Rachel Culbertson and others to Valentine F. Lentz. Bill of Sale. Rachel Culbertson, John J. Lentz, Hiram Harris and John Harris, conveyed to Valentine F. Lentz, two slaves, Sam and Nance, which was bequeathed to them by Lawson Harris, deceased, by his Last Will and Testament which is one eighth. Wit: James Graham, Edward Graham, Joshua Crowell, William S. Jett, Hartwell Freeman, James Graham, James Graham and John Harris. Reg: 27 Mar 1848.

Page 423 - 25 Mar 1848. Ezekiel and Cynthia Cleck to Valentine F. Lentz. Bill of Sale. Ezekiel and Cynthia Cleck sold to Valentine F. Lentz, two slaves, Sam and Nance, left to them by Lawson Harris, deceased, by his Last Will and Testament. Reg: 27 Mar 1848.

Page 424 - 10 Sep 1847. David Weaver to Irena Green. Deed of Gift. 25 acres. David Weavers for love and affection for Irena Green, conveyed unto her land in Bedford Co., TN, in District No. 25. Bounded by John Kicks, mouth of Weavers Spring Branch where it empties into the West Fork of Gages Creek, and Mary Ewell. Wit: Timothy Long, Lewis Holder, Thomas B. Kaar and L. F. Sherrill. Reg: 27 Mar 1848.

Page 428 - 7 Jan 1848. Nancy G. and James A. Laird to James Mullins. Quit Claim. Nancy G. and James A. Laird released to James Mullins, land in Bedford Co., TN, in District No. 7, in Town of Shelbyville. Bounded by north of the Public Square and fronting on west side of Martin Street, it being the lot belonging to John H. Laird and whereon he resided at time of his death. Reg: 30 Mar 1848.

Page 429 - 16 Nov 1847. J. M. Doby and others to Thomas C. Whiteside. Deed, 379 acres. John M. Doby, Jos. Doby, M. P. Doby, William C. Doby, and James M. Doby of Lancaster District, South Carolina, the first being the husband and the four last named being the children of Elizabeth Doby, deceased, formerly Elizabeth Crawford, sold to Thomas C. Whiteside, land in Bedford Co., TN, on Falling Creek, about four or five miles from Shelbyville on the east side of the Turnpike leading from Shelbyville to Nashville. Land bounded by John C. Coldwell, land devised to Elizabeth Doby, deceased and her brother W. D. Crawford by their grandfather Martin Phifer and allotted to them by his will. Wit: A. A. Coffey and M. A. Tuttle. Reg: 1 Apr 1848.

Page 436 - 1 Nov 1847. A. Myers to Blan Maupin. Power of Attorney. A. Myers appointed Blan Maupin his Attorney to receive for him from James R. Talbert and John H. Talbert, a legacy, a distributive share which has descended to him from Thomas Talbert, deceased, late of Bedford Co., TN. Also, as above authorized with James Talbert as administrator of Nancy Talbert to recover any real or personal estate to come to him. Wit: Warner Wallace and A. D. L. Huffman. Reg: 4 Apr 1848.

Page 437 - 21 Mar 1848. James C. Nash to J. G. Neeley. Deed, undivided interest, 125 acres. James C. Nash sold to J. G. Neeley, his undivided interest in land in Bedford CO., TN and formerly owned by his father Travis C. Nash, deceased, on the waters of Falling Creek. Bounded by V. H. Steele, house of John Hutton, deceased, the house of T. C. Nash, deceased, and the heirs of Samuel A. Bell, deceased. Also, all his interest in two lots of land out of the estate of T. C. Nash, deceased, and owned by his father(brother) William Nash who died without issue. Wit: Kindred Pearson and John Newton. Reg: 5 Apr 1848.

Page 438 - 3 Jan 1848. James Ogilvie to B. Landers. Deed, 100 acres. James Ogilvie and his wife Jane G. Ogilvie sold to Bryant Landers of 11th District of Bedford Co., TN, land in Weakleys Creek. Bounded by J. Nichols, J. Wadley, Covington's heirs, D. W. Thompson, and the west bank of Weakleys Creek. Wit: William Collins and Gwynn Foster. Reg: 5 Apr 1848.

DEED BOOK "PP"

Page 443 - 25 Mar 1848. G. M. Ray to Baptist and Methodist Churches. Deed. G. M. Ray conveyed to Hezekiah Ray, Deacon of the Baptist Church and Solomon Ray, a class leader of the Methodist Episcopal Church and their successors forever, for the love and affection for his neighborhood, a tract of land for a Public Burying Ground, in Bedford Co., TN, in District No. 24, on the west side of Thompsons Creek. Reg: 7 Apr 1848.

DEED BOOK "QQ" 1848 - 1849

Page 4 - -- Aug 1845. Eliza J. Howe to J. J. Biddle and S. J. Ingram. Deed of Gift. Eliza J. Howe for love and affection for her two grandchildren, to wit, John James Biddle and Sarah Jane Ingram, the land where she now lives to be equally divided between them. Also, gives John James Biddle a negro boy, for him and his lawful heirs that is his brothers and sisters should hehave any and if not, for his mother to dispose of it as she may think proper. Also, gives to Sarah Jane Ingram a negro girl, to her and her lawful heirs if she should have any brothers and sisters, if not for her mother to dispose of it as she may think proper. Remainder to her two daughters their lifetime. Reg: 8 Apr 1848.

Page 9 - 24 Jun 1847. W. W. Hurst to Edmund Word. Deed, undivided interest. By Decree of the Circuit Court of Bedford Co., TN, at August Term 1844, the lands belonging to the late William Hurst, deceased, was sold on the petition of the heirs of William Hurst, deceased. The lands in Bedford Co., TN and Edmund Word was the purchaser. The lands was subject to the widow's dower. W. W. Hurst, one of the heirs of William Hurst, deceased. Wit: Amos Morrill and J. H. Reeves. William W. Hurst in Texas on 24 June 1847. Reg: (no date)

Page 10 - 3 Apr 1847. J. C. Hurst and others to E. Word. Deed. By Decree of the Circuit Court in Bedford Co., TN, August Term 1844, the lands belonging to the late William Hurst, deceased, was sold by the Clerk of the County and Edmund Word was the purchaser. The lands subject to the widow's dower. Signed by Moses Neeley, Nancy Neeley, America Hurst, H. C. Hurst, and John C. Hurst. Wit: Samuel Doak and William Word. Nancy Neeley wife of Moses Neeley. Reg: 12 Apr 1848.

Page 13 - 1 Jul 1846. Mary Barkley to John L. Barkley. Deed. Mary Barkley for love and affection for her son John L. Barkley, conveyed unto him, land in Bedford Co., TN, on north side of North Fork near the mouth of Weakleys Creek and known as the land given to Mary Barkley, Catharine Poole, William Lock, James Lock, and Mary Smith, by the Last Will and Testament of George Lock, deceased. Wit: Hardy W. Stricklin and A. C. Blair. Mary Barkley of Tippah Co., Mississippi. Reg: 12 Apr 1848.

Page 17 - 13 Apr 1848. John H. Barkley to James H. Lock. Deed, 424 acres. John H. Barkley of Wayne Co., TN sold to James H. Lock of Bedford Co., TN, land in Bedford Co., in District No. 11, on the waters of Weakleys Creek and the North Fork. Bounded by James H. Locke, William Locke's corner, George Lock, deceased, land, and land formerly of Mary Smith and now Alexander B. Moon. Wit: Joseph H. Brittain and H. C. Morgan. Reg: 13 Apr 1848.

Page 24 - 13 Apr 1848. Harrel Wiggins to Trustees. Deed, 3 acres. Harrel Wiggins sold to William Carlisle, Joseph Morton, and Miles Phillips, Trustees of the Big Spring School House and their successors in office, land in Bedford Co., TN, on waters of Sugar Creek. Bounded by Harrel Wiggins' original line, and to bank of the Dry Fork of Sugar Creek. If the land is not used for a school, the land is to return to Harrel Wiggins. Reg: 19 Apr 1848.

Page 25 - 6 --(Apr) 1848. Nathaniel O. McAdams and J. T. Neil, Executors &c to D. R. McAdams. Bill of Sale. Whereas by the Last Will and Testament of Amos McAdams, deceased, which was proven in Court, vested in the Executors to sell negro slaves, Daniel R. McAdams purchased same. The Executors has bargained and sold unto Daniel R. McAdams. Reg: 19 Apr 1848.

Page 26 - 18 Apr 1848. D. R. McAdams to John McAdams. Deed, 1/10 of 200 acres. Daniel R. McAdams sold to John McAdams, property, both real and personal, one tenth part of land in Bedford Co., TN, in District No. 6. It being that part of the real estate of Amos McAdams which he set apart in his Last Will and Testament to his wife Mariah McAdams for her during her natural life and at her death to his children. Land bounded by Andrew T. McAdams, Thomas C. Whiteside, John McAdams, Lydia Roan, John Eakin, and Payton H. Coats. Reg: 19 Apr 1848.

Page 28 - March Term 1848. Court Decree to Isham Oneal. 120 acres. Absolem B. Gaunt and Lewis Gaunt and others. John Aldridge and Martha his wife and others. John G. Mosely originally purchaser of land in Bedford Co., TN, the Court decreed that all the right title and interest which Absalem B. Gaunt, Lewis Gaunt, Jesse B. Gaunt, Elizabeth Gaunt, A. Gifford and Sarah Caroline his wife, John R., Lewis A., Bolin J., and Martha Jane Freeman, Mary Broughton, A. Bryan, L. G. Ray, John Cortner, Mary Bryan, James Gaunt, Samuel Harbour and wife Nancy, B. Bolin, Mary Caroline Bolin, Jesse G. Aldridge, Benjamin Broughton, Robert Gaunt, Elizabeth, John, William, and Eliza Jane Gaunt, Margaret Hazlewood, John R., Sarah and Nancy R. Ray, John Aldridge and Martha his wife, Riley Aldridge, Keziah Aldridge, Jinsey Barrett, Jacob Shaddy and wife Martha, and John G. Moseley, has in land in Bedford Co., TN, and bounded by David Dryden and Dr. A. B. Morton. About 50 acres. Land on Sinking Creek. Reg: 21 Apr 1848.

Page 34 - 22 Apr 1848. Rebecca Jones and others to J. J. Hurst. Deed, 103 acres. Rebecca Jones, Nancy Yates, Margaret Watson, Eliza Reese, C. B. Jones, Samuel Jones, S. W. Reese and Anthony Floyd, sold to John J. Hurst, land in Bedford Co., TN, it being the dower of Rebecca Jones, widow and relict of Charles Jones, deceased, in the tract of land of which Charles Jones, deceased, seized and possessed. The land in Bedford Co., on waters of Flat Creek in District No. 24. Bounded by William Boone, Anthony Floyd, David Floyd, Abram Reagor and Abram Shook, Nancy Yates daughter of Charles Jones and widow of Riley Yates, Margaret Watson widow of Walter Watson and daughter of Charles Jones, Charles B. Jones, Samuel Jones, Solomon W. Reese and Eliza A. Reese wife of Solomon W. and daughter of Charles Jones, being entitled as part of the heirs at law of Charles Jones, deceased, to five shares of the reminder interest in said land. And Anthony Floyd purchased from Wiley B. Jones, Michael Womack and Sarah his wife, and David D. Jones, heirs at law of Charles

Jones, land. Wit: H. L. Davidson, Ro. B. Davidson, Jno. Eakin and J. E. Pearson. Reg: (no date).

Page 39 - 11 Dec 1840. John Warran to William Warran. Deed of Gift, 75 acres. John Warran for love and affection for William Warran, conveyed land in Bedford Co., TN. Bounded by Nathan Chaffin and Milton Giles. Wit: William J. Frizzle and Samuel McKee. Reg: 2 May 1848.

Page 40 - 13 Feb 1847. Henry Clark to Ogilvie, Moon and Landers, Trustees of School. Henry Clark for love and affection for the morality and instruction of his neighborhood, the rising generation and the advancement of his own family, conveys unto James Ogilvie, A. B. Moon, and Briant Landers, good citizens of the neighborhood as Trustees for the use and continual benefit of a school and for a place of free worship for the same, land in Bedford Co., TN, in District No. 11, it being a part of his land that he now owns on west side of the road leading from Unionville to Crowell's Mill. Adjoining A. B. Covington. Wit: John L. Jackson, D. J. Wheeler and Jos. Anderson. Reg: 2 May 1848.

Page 40 - 20 Feb 1847. A. B. Covington to Moon, Landers and Ogilvie. Deed. A. B. Covington for love and affection for the neighborhood &c, conveys unto A. B. Moon, Briant Landers and James Ogilvie, land in Bedford Co., TN, in District No. 11 and being a part of his land on road from Unionville to Crowell Mills and adjoining Henry Clark. Wit: Henry Clark and Jacob Vincent. Reg: 2 May 1848.

Page 42 - 19 Nov 1847. W. F. Phifer and others to C. P. Houston. Power of Attorney. 540 acres. Mecklenburg Co., North Carolina and Lincoln Co., North Carolina. William F. Phifer, Martin L. Phifer, John F. Phifer, E. J. Erwin and Ann E. his wife, and Joseph H. Wilson and Mary L. his wife, all of North Carolina, appointed C. P. Houston of Bedford Co., TN, their Attorney, to sell land, it being a part of a 4766 acres which belonged to the late Col. Martin Phifer of Cabarrus Co., NC and devised by him in his Last Will and Testament, to the heirs of the late George Phifer, deceased. Land in Bedford Co., TN and known in the division as Lot No. 1, lying on the Dry Fork of Fall Creek. Borders North Fork of Fall Creek, Dry Fork of Fall Creek, and Murfreesboro Road. Mecklenburg Co., NC, the county of William F. Phifer, Martin L. Phifer, Joseph H. Wilson and Mary L. his wife. Lincoln Co., NC, the county of John F. Phifer, E. Jones Erwin and Ann E. his wife. Reg: 11 May 1848.

Page 45 - 26 Jul 1844. George Calhoon to George E. Calhoon. Deed, 181 acres. George Calhoon for love and affection for George E. Calhoon, conveys unto him land in Bedford Co., TN, in District No. 18. Bounded by Peter Garren. Wit: John Bell and R. Chapman. Reg: 12 May 1848.

Page 46 - 13 May 1848. William C. Swanson to Mrs. Massey and James Lester. Title Bond, 667 acres. William C. Swanson bound to Lemuel B. McConnico and James H. Lester. On 17 Sept 1847, William C. Swanson sold to Priscilla R. Massey and James H. Lester, land in Bedford Co., TN, on both sides of Sinking Creek. Bounded by Ray's dwelling house, land that John Ray sold to William M. and Charles S. Russell, Alexander Ray, Stephen Freeman, Comstock's line, Cortner's line, tract called the Mill

Tract, Sinking Creek, land George W. Ray conveyed to John Ray, Stephen Porter's old tract now Daniel Looney's tract, James Davis, and William R. Ray's corner. Reserving one half acre off for a grave yard which was not to be conveyed. Priscilla R. Massey has intermarried with Lemuel B. McConnico and he is to pay the purchase money for said land. Wit: G. B. Lester and M. A. Logan. Reg: 17 May 1848.

Page 48 - 17 Sep 1847. William C. Swanson to Mrs. Massey and James Lester. Deed, 666½ acres. William C. Swanson of Bedford Co., TN, sold to Mrs. Priscilla R. Massey of Lincoln Co., TN and James Lester, land in Bedford Co., TN, on waters of Sinking Creek in District No. 19 and 20. Bounded by Alexander Ray, Stephen Freeman, Thomas Mays, John Cortner, Daniel Looney, Washington Cunningham, James Davis, John Helton. Wit: John Woodward and Newton C. Gambill. Reg: 17 May 1848.

Page 50 - 23 May 1848. John J. Hurst to Eliza A. McCuistion. Deed, 103 acres. William W. Coldwell, Administrator of John C. McCuistion, deceased, paid John J. Hurst of Bedford Co., TN who sold to Eliza A. McCuistion widow of John C. McCuistion, deceased, for her and during her natural life time and the remainder interest to Mary Ann Amanda America McCuistion, land for and during the life of Rebecca Jones also eight undivided thirteenth of the tract of land, to take effect at the death of Rebecca Jones, to the said Eliza A. McCuistion for and during her natural life. Land bounded by William Boone, Anthony Floyd, David Floyd, A. Reagor and A. Shook. It being the tract assigned to Rebecca Jones for her dower by the Circuit Court, the lands of which her husband Charles Jones died seized and possessed. Reg: 23 May 1848.

Page 56 - 10 Dec 1847. L. W. Shuford and wife to Preston Frazier. Deed, 41 acres. Lewis W. Shuford and Jane A. W. Shuford his wife sold to Preston Frazier land in Bedford Co., TN, on waters of the North Fork. Bounded by lands of William Guy, deceased, Edward Deaton, lands of William Warren late deceased, and Lorance tract. The land Shuford lad by right of his wife Jane A. W. Shuford from estate of Alex (blank), deceased. Wit: William P. Temple and Granville H. Frazier. Reg: 30 May 1848.

Page 57 - 4 May 1835. M. McCorkle and others to William Guy. Deed, 31 acres. Matthew McCorkle, Charles Beaty, Gilbert Milligan and Rebecca Milligan his wife, George Little and Elizabeth S. Little his wife, and Alexander McCorkle, all of Lincoln Co., NC, sold to William Guy of Bedford Co., TN, all the land in Bedford Co., on waters of the North Fork. Bounded by William Guy whereon he lives and Brandon's and Locke's lines. It being the part of the division laid off to the heirs of Francis McCorkle and devises of Alexander Worke. Wit: James Crunkleton and Francis McCorkle. Reg: 31 May 1848.

Page 60 - 18 May 1848. William and Jane Kaar (Carr). Deed, 1/5 of 50 acres. William Kaar, Sr. and Jane his wife formerly Jane Brumfield, sold to James Cheshire, all of Bedford Co., TN, an undivided interest in land and being the one fifth part of a fifty acre tract in bedford Co., TN, on waters of Big Flat Creek. Bounded by lands of William M. Evans, Peter Tribble, widow Mallard now lives, lands of the late Alfred Campbell being the tract whereon Joseph Brumfield, deceased, resided at the time of his death and which one fifth part of said tract of fifty acres descended to William and Jane (Kaar), as heirs of Joseph Brumfield, deceased. Reg: 11 Jun 1848.

Page 62 - (no date). William Hudson to Mary Hudson. Deed, 10 acres. William Hudson for love and affection for his daughter Mary Hudson, conveyed unto her, land in Bedford Co., TN, on waters of Thompson Creek, it being the land on which the family of said Hudson now lives. Bounded by William Hudson and including the house and improvements. Wit: Staunton J. Green and William B. Holt. Reg: 5 Jun 1848.

Page 63 - 20 Sep 1834. Jonathan Mosley to Isham Mosley. Deed of Gift, 256 acres. Johnathan Moseley for love and affection for his son Isham Mosley, conveyed unto him, land in Bedford Co., TN, on both sides of Sugar Creek. Bounded by William Mosley's house where he formerly lived, Talbot's line, Joseph Gray, Thomas Greer, Randolph Newsom, and the banks of Sugar Creek. Wit: W. D. Orr and William Morton. Reg: 6 Jun 1848.

Page 66 - 24 Apr 1848. Elias Yates to Samuel Yates. Deed, 50 acres. Elias Yates for love and affection for Samuel Yates, conveyed unto him, land in Bedford Co., TN, on the waters of the Barren Fork. Bounded by Allen Knight, Nicholas Coble and Fergus Hall. Also another tract on the waters of Barren Fork and bounded by Jeremiah Kimbro and Fergus Hall. Wit: J. V. Biddle and William Meadows. Reg: 6 Jun 1848.

Page 68 - 18 Feb 1848. Louisiania Dwyer to Thomas J. Brown. Deed, undivided interest, 105 acres. Louisiania Dwyer sold to Thomas J. Brown, her interest in the land formerly owned by Daniel Dwyer, deceased, it being in Bedford Co., TN, in District No. 6, on the north side of the old Columbia Road. Bounded by lands of Shadrack S. Brown. Her interest being one eighth part of the land. Wit: B. F. Whitworth and Garrett Phillips. Reg: 7 Jun 1848.

Page 70 - 24 Jul 1826. Will of James Lyle, deceased.
James Lyle of Philadelphia, Merchant, do make this the Last Will and Testament.
1. Revoke all other wills made.
2. Appoint John B. Newman, Hartman Kuhn and Henry Beckett as Executors of his Last Will and Testament.
3. To John B. Newman gets all his lands, houses and lots, all his estate both real and personal to be divided into two equal parts. One equal part to his daughter Mary Beckett free of her husband, profits of her slave, and at her death goes to any children she may have. Other equal part to his daughter Ellen Kuhn and her children if she should have any.
4. If any of the Executors should die, the remaining Executors are to appoint another Executor.
5. In case Margaret Hamilton and Mary Hambleton should survive him and remain unmarried and from the unproductive character of their estate, they should make it convenient to have additional income and I direct the Executors to advance them any sum that is required by them to make up with their own income, a sum not to exceed $5000.00 per annum.
Wit: Dan C. Ellis and Charles Ingersall. Reg: 8 Jun 1848.

Page 75 - 13 Jun 1848. W. G. Cowan to A. L. Castleman. Deed, 6/7 of 121 acres. William G. Cowan sold to Arthur L. Castleman, land in Bedford Co., TN, on waters of Big Flat Creek, it being six sevenths part of a tract that Wiley Wilhoite inherited by the death of his father Jacob Wilhoite, deceased. Bounded by Polly Burrow, Eve Burrow, William Word, and Jacob Wilhoite's No. 1 survey for his heirs. Reg: 20 Jun 1848.

Page 76 - 6 Oct 1847. Pearce Wilhoite to A. L. Castleman. Deed, 1/7 of 121 acres. Pearce Wilhoite sold to Arthur L. Castleman his interest in land in Bedford Co., TN, on waters of Big Flat Creek, being the same tract allotted to Wiley Wilhoite out of the division of the land of Jacob Wilhoite, Sr., deceased, and known as Lot No. 3. Pearce Wilhoite's 1/7th part of 121 acres. Wit: William Campbell and John Wilson. Reg: 20 Jun 1848.

Page 79 - -- --- 1846. John and Nancy Streater. Division of slaves. Whereas at the decease of Mildred Streater, late of Bedford Co., TN, the undersigned as children and heirs of Mildred Streater, deceased, became joint owners of negro slaves. The children and heirs desirous of dividing slaves. To John Streater gets 16 valued at $4900.00. To Nancy Streater gets 14 valued at $4900.00. Wit: Asa Fonville and Richard H. Sims. Reg: 26 Jun 1848.

Page 84 - 26 Jun 1848. David King to Neadham King and wife. Quit Claim Deed. Whereas Neadham King and Sally(Sarah) King his wife, executed to David King three instruments of writing dated 14 Sep 1846 and recorded in Deed Book "PP", page 87 which deed conveyed to him all the right and title that Neadham King and Sarah King had in estate which descended to them by the death of William Pearson, deceased, the grandfather of Sarah King. Reg: 29 Jun 1848.

Page 85 - 8 Nov 1847. A. L. Erwin and wife to James Clardy. Deed, 196 acres. Adolphus L. Erwin and Mary G. Erwin his wife of McDowell Co., NC, sold to James Clardy, land in Bedford Co., TN. Bounded by lands of Martin Phifer, deceased. Wit: John L. Erwin and Jos. C. McDowell. Reg: 5 Jul 1848.

Page 93 - 8 Jul 1848. William Jenkins to James Carter. Deed, undivided interest, 34 acres. William Jenkins sold to James Carter, all his interest as assignee of Absalom and Mary Arnold one of the heirs at law of Jacob Coble, deceased, in one share of undivided tract of land laid off and known as the widow's dower, which at the death of the widow is to be divided among the heirs. Reg: 15 Jul 1848.

Page 95 - 9 Nov 1847. John M. Keller to Francis A. Keller and C. Thomas. Deed, undivided interest. John M. Keller sold to Francis A. Keller and Christopher Thomas, all his undivided interest in land of which his father Joseph Keller died and seized of about 250 acres. Land in Bedford Co., TN, on waters of the Garrison Fork. Wit: F. H. Keller and James Bramlett. Reg: 18 Jul 1848.

Page 107 - 1 Jun 1848. Robert and Amanda Wood to John Wood. Undivided interest. Robert H. Wood and wife Amanda Wood of Rutherford Co., TN, sold to John Wood of Bedford Co., TN, land in Bedford Co., on waters of Falling Creek. Bounded by near the mouth of Hurricane Creek. Containing in all the tract of Thomas Nash, deceased, 112 acres of which one seventh is a part of the undivided land granted by the State of North Carolina to Richard Trotter for 4000 acres deeded by Thomas J. Polk and Mary E. Polk to Dennis Springer and by Springer to the heirs of Thomas Nash, deceased. Wit: Jno. Woods. Reg: 8 Aug 1848.

Page 111 - 10 Mar 1847. William Linch and others to James M. Smalling. Bill of Sale. William Linch and Susannah C. Linch sold negroes to James M. Smalling. Wit: John J. Shriver and Risden Knott. Reg: 9 Aug 1848.

Page 112 - 10 Mar 1847. William Linch and others to James M. Smalling. Bill of Sale. Elizabeth B. Smalling for love and affection for her son James M. Smalling, conveys a negro boy Jack. Wit: John J. Shriver and Risden Knott. Reg: 9 Aug 1848.

Page 113 - 1 Jan 1848. W. F. Phifer and others to James Ogilvie. Deed, 273 acres. William F. Phifer, Martin L. Phifer of Cabarrus Co., NC and Joseph H. Wilson and M. L. Wilson his wife of Mecklenburg Co., NC, and John F. Phifer of Lincoln Co., NC, E. Jones Erwin and Ann E. Erwin his wife of Burk Co., NC, sold to James Ogilvie of Bedford Co., TN, land in Bedford Co., on waters of Fall Creek, the same being a part of a 4766 acre tract granted to Martin Phifer of North Carolina and divided by him to the heirs at law of the late George Phifer, deceased. Wit: R. P. Whiteside and M. R. Rushing. Reg: 10 Aug 1848.

Page 117 - 1 Jan 1848. W. R. Phifer and others to M. R. Rushing. Deed, 247 acres. William F. Phifer and Martin L. Phifer of Cabarrus Co., NC, Joseph H. Wilson and M. L. Wilson his wife of Mecklenburg Co., NC, John L. Phifer of Lincoln Co., NC, and E. Jones Erwin and Ann E. Erwin his wife of Burk Co., NC, sold to Milton R. Rushing of Bedford Co., TN, land in Bedford Co., on waters of Fall Creek, it being a part of a tract granted to Martin Phifer of NC and devised by him to the heirs at law of the estate of George Phifer, deceased. Wit: James Ogilvie. Reg: 12 Aug 1848.

Page 121 - 27 May 1848. John Burgess and others to William Kingree. Deed, 153 acres. John Burgess, Nancy Ann Burgess and Joseph L. Burgess sold to William Kingree, land in Bedford Co., TN. Bounded by George Waite, McKisick's old line, and Bennett's line. Wit: Jordan C. Holt and Edward Cooper. Reg: 14 Aug 1848.

Page 122 - 2 Aug 1848. William W. Daniel to John W. Cobbs. Bill of Sale. William W. Daniel sold to John W. Cobbs, all his interest in the estate of his deceased mother Frances Daniel, it being one sixth part of the estate, consisting in Henry, Royester, William, Minerva, and Ellen, and other property. Wit: Samuel T. Cannon and B. B. Morgan. Reg: 15 Aug 1848.

Page 126 - August Term 1843. Circuit Court Decree to James M. Johnson. Deed, 2 Lots. James M. Johnson, Daniel Johnson, Powell Kimbro and wife (blank), Robert Patton and wife (blank), and William Johnson and others. Exparte. Bill for the Sale of land. Lots sold in Rowesville, Bedford Co., TN, to James M. Johnson and paid all purchase money to the undersigned for the Lots. Complainants, Daniel Johnson, Powell Kimbro and Rebecca his wife, Robert Patton and Elizabeth his wife, Willis Johnson, William Johnson, John B. Johnson, Susannah Johnson, Ellenor Johnson and Elizabeth Stewart and Grayson H. Stewart her husband, had interest in Lots No. 16, 17, 18, and 19 and part of Lot

No. 14 and Lots No. 6 and 7, be devested out of them and vested in James M. Johnson. Reg: 17 Aug 1848.

Page 132 - 19 Aug 1848. Terril and Melissa Griggs to M. M. Holt. Deed, undivided interest, 50 acres. Terril Griggs and his wife Melissa formerly Melissa Holt, sold to Martin M. Holt, all their undivided interest, it being one sixth, in land in Bedford Co., TN, on road leading from Shelbyville to McMinnville and being about 2¼ miles from Shelbyville, it being the same allotted to the mother of Melissa as dower. The land which Benjamin Holt now resides. Reg: 19 Aug 1848.

Page 137 - 26 Feb 1848. Margaret Leathers and others to West C. Callen. Power of Attorney. Margaret Leathers, H. D. Callen and Elizabeth Callen his wife formerly Elizabeth Leathers of Carroll Co., Arkansas, appointed West C. Callen of Carroll Co., Arkansas, as their Attorney, to sell lands in Bedford Co., TN and Humphreys Co., TN, to which they are heirs to the estate of James Leathers, deceased. Wit: John R. Lipps and Jacob H. Meek. Reg: 24 Aug 1848.

Page 139 - 15 Jun 1848. W. C. Callen and wife to Frederick Batte. Deed, undivided interest. W. C. Callen and Martha B. Callen his wife of Carroll Co., Arkansas, sold to Frederick Batte of Bedford Co., TN, all their interest and right in 40 acres by heirship in land in Bedford Co., on waters of Weakleys Creek and Alexander Creek, it being known as the estate of James Leather, deceased. Wit: William M. Berry and T. Denton. Reg: 24 Aug 1848.

Page 140 - 20 Apr 1848. John V. Leathers and others to Frederick Batte. Deed, undivided interest. John V. Leathers, H. D. Callen and Elizabeth Callen his wife, all of Carroll Co., Arkansas, and Elija Smotherman and his wife Nancy Smotherman of Rutherford Co., TN, sold to Frederick Batte of Bedford Co., TN, all their undivided interest in 40 acres of land in Bedford Co., received by heirship, land in the estate of James Leathers, deceased. Land on Weakley and Alexander Creeks. Bounded by William Allison. Wit: Elbert A. Smotherman and James Holden. Reg: 24 Aug 1848.

Page 145 - 20 Apr 1848. Elija Smotherman and others to Elija Dunn. Deed, 65 acres. Elija Smotherman and Nancy his wife formerly Nancy Leathers of Rutherford Co., TN, also H. D. Callen and Elizabeth his wife formerly Elizabeth Leathers, also John V. Leathers, residents of Carroll Co., Arkansas, sold to Elija Dun of Bedford Co., TN, land they inherited as heirship of the estate of James Leathers, deceased, it being on waters of Weakleys Creek and Alexanders Creek. Bounded by Samuel Smotherman. Wit: Frederick Batte, Elbert A. Smotherman and James Holden. Reg: 26 Aug 1848.

Page 146 - 15 Jun 1848. W. C. Callen and wife to Elija Dunn. Deed, undivided interest. W. C. Callen and Martha B. Callen his wife of Carroll Co., Arkansas, sold to Elija Don of Bedford Co., TN, all their interest amounting to 6½ acres by heirship in the estate of James Leathers, deceased. Wit: William M. Berry and T. Denton. Reg: 26 Aug 1848.

Page 150 - 25 Jul 1848. Caleb Phifer and others to Benjamin Whitworth. Deed, 941 acres. Caleb Phifer, John F. Phifer,

George L. Phifer, E. R. Gibson and wife Elizabeth, Robert W. Allison and wife Sarah Ann, Mary B. Phifer and Martin Phifer of Cabarrus Co., NC, sold to Benjamin F. Whitworth of Bedford Co., TN, land in Bedford Co., on the Dry Fork of Fall Creek, in District No. 2, in the partition of lands of Martin Phifer between his children and the Lot assigned to John Phifer. Reg: 26 Aug 1848.

Page 154 - 12 Jul 1847. John C. McCuistion's Will.
John C. McCuistion of Lamar Co., Texas, being sick and weak in body, make his Last Will and Testament.
1. Commends himself to the Almighty God.
2. To his beloved wife Eliza Ann McCuistion, one half of his estate, both real and personal.
Daughter, Mary Ann Amanda America McCuistion to receive the remainder. John C. McCuistion owns land in Cherokee Co., Texas, said land to return to Frost Thom. Anthony McCuistion of Lamar Co., Texas, was appointed Executor of the Last Will and Testament. Wit: William H. Newland and G. G. Bonner. Probated in Sept Term 1847.

Page 171 - 2 Sep 1848. George W. Brown to William H. Brown. Deed or Transfer. Whereas by the Last Will and Testament of Shadrack Brown, deceased, George W. Brown holds equally with nine other heirs at law, in estate of Shadrack Brown, deceased, sell his interest in Town Lots No. 60 and 68 in Shelbyville to one half of the two lots, to William H. Brown. Wit: Edw. Cooper. Reg: 4 Sep 1848.

Page 178 - 24 Mar 1848. Circuit Court Decree to G. B. Sharpe. Deed, 99 acres. John Snelling and wife Phereby, John S. Arnold and his wife Sarah, and others, petition for sale of land &c. Grimes B. Sharpe purchased the lands. Land in Bedford Co., TN, on waters of Duck river. The land being the land allotted and set apart to Mary McGuire in the division of lands of William Ditto, deceased, known as Lot No. 3 with the exception of about 22 acres heretofore allotted to Archibald Pruett and wife and Andrew E. Mullins and wife. Reg: 6 Sep 1848.

Page 184 - 18 Apr 1848. Kindred Pearson to John Newton and others. Deed, for School House of 6 acres. Kindred Pearson conveyed unto John Newton, William C. Nix and James F. Farrar, in Trust for the use of schools and for no other purpose, land in Bedford Co., TN, in District No. 24, on headwaters of Big Flat Creek. Bounded by James F. Farrar and Elija Bobo. Wit: Watson Floyd and William B. Pearson. Reg: 8 Sep 1848.

Page 187 - 31 Jul 1848. Peyton Still and wife to Parthena E. Rushing and others. Deed, 52 acres. Peyton Still and his wife Sarah Jane Still of Bedford Co., TN, sold to Parthena Elizabeth Rushing, Sarah Ann Rushing, Telitha Jane Rushing, Mary Palestine Rushing, minor children of the late Asa Rushing, deceased. John Rushing is guardian of the minor children. Land in Bedford Co., being the land of which Asa Rushing died seized and possessed, their interest in the tract being the dower interest of Sarah Jane Rushing who was the widow of Asa Rushing. Wit: Hartwell Freeman and Nicholas Harris. Reg: 14 Sep 1848.

Page 188 - 15 Sep 1848. William W. Ramsey and others to Thomas A. Neill. Deed. William W. Ramsey, Alexander G. Ramsey, and John D. Neill and his wife Sarah Elizabeth, sold to Thomas A.

Neill, land, except the dower interest of Nancy Ramsey, in Bedford Co., TN, in District No. 18. Bounded by the west bank of Sinking Creek, David Dryden and William A. Gaunt. Wit: Michael Moore and William N. Moore. Reg: 18 Sep 1848.

Page 189 - 20 May 1846. Jane Frazer to G. H. Frazer. Deed of Gift. Jane Frazer for love and affection for her son Granville H. Frazer, all the land whereon she now lives, being in Bedford Co., TN, on Bradfords Creek and bought of Edward Cage and the lands bought of widow Green, also the land bought of John Taylor, also the lands bought of Col. James Arnold, deceased, all of Bedford Co. She also conveys slaves. Wit: Robert Dennington and Giles R. Bowers. Reg: 19 Sep 1848.

Page 194 - 21 Sep 1848. H. A. Barnett and wife to J. M. H. Coleman. Deed, undivided interest. Hugh A. Barnett and Lucy B. Barnett his wife formerly Lucy B. Coleman, sold all their interest in a tract of land in Bedford Co., TN, in District No. 21, being the one half of the tract of land devised in the will of Jesse Coleman, after the death of their mother Frances Coleman. Reg: 21 Sep 1848.

Page 199 - 3 Mar 1843. C. D. Steele and wife to Samuel Doak. Bill of Sale. C. D. Steele and his wife Katharine Steele, sold to Samuel Doak, 9 slaves, bequeathed to Katherine, in the Last Will and Testament of James Cooper, deceased. She being one of his legal heirs and being one eighth part. Reg: 27 Sep 1848.

Page 200 - 15 Nov 1845. Preston and John Frazer to G. H. Frazer. Deed. G. H. Frazer of Bedford Co., TN of one part and John S. Frazer of Bedford Co. G. H. Frazer for $600.00 paid and sold to John S. Frazier, one land warrant on the Republic of Texas, unlocated Colony for 1280 acres of land, it being for the service of Smith Newton in the Texan Army, dated 12 Apr 1838. Wit: N. C. Harris and James Denniston. This instrument made 18 Nov 1846 by Preston Frazer one part and Granville H. Frazer other part. Preston sold to Granville H. Frazer, all lands and slaves which may fall to Granville H. Frazer at Mrs. Jane Frazer's death, being the same which was transferred to Preston Frazer dated 3 Sep 1846 by Granville H. Frazer. Reg: 28 Sep 1848.

Page 202 - 28 Sep 1848. John M. Haggard to Williamson Haggard. Interest in estate. John M. Haggard of Perry Co., Illinois, sold to Williamson Haggard of Bedford Co., TN, all his interest in both real and personal of their father Samuel Haggard, deceased. It being one fifth of the estate. Wit: George W. Buchanan, J. M. Jackson and W. B. M. Brame. Reg: 29 Sep 1848.

Page 203 - 4 Mar 1844. William Houston to E. H. McKre. Deed, 60 acres. In the year 1834, there was a Trust Reposed in William Houston to purchase land for a house for his late sister Sarah M. L. McKre, which Trust was executed, and now she having departed this life, conveys the land to her youngest son E. Hamilton McKre, subject to a life estate in behalf of his father William E. McKre. The land was purchased from James C. McKre. Land in Bedford Co., TN, on west side of Fall Creek, in District No. 5. Bounded by Caleb Phifer, William Houston's land purchased of Margaret E. McKre. Wit: Caleb P. Houston and Will Houston, Jr. Reg: 2 Oct 1848.

DEED BOOK "QQ"

Page 217 - 27 May 1848. Vilsey and John Baker to William Kingre. John Baker and Vilsey Baker his wife sold and conveyed to William Kingre, lands in Bedford Co., TN, they being the lands William Burgess died seized and possessed and their interest being the dower interest of Vilsey Baker in three tracts. One tract being the place where Baker now lives. Reg: 6 Oct 1848.

Page 232 - 20 Oct 1848. William Murphree to Christian Churches. Deed, 1 acre. William Murphree of Bedford Co., TN, for love and affection and good will for the churches, he conveyed one acre of land including Cross Road Meeting House in his tract of land on the headwaters of Falling Creek. Bounded by the road leading to Salem Camp Ground. Reg: 20 Oct 1848.

Page 236 - 25 Oct 1848. James Purvis and wife to Franklin McElwrath. Undivided Interest. James Purvis and Margaret M. Purvis his wife formerly Margaret M. McElwrath, sold to Franklin McElwrath, , their undivided interest in the land belonging to the heirs of Joseph McElwrath, deceased. Land in Bedford Co., TN, in District No. 6, on Parch Corn Creek. Their interest being one sixth of 313 acres. Wit: Andrew Vannoy. Reg: 26 Oct 1848.

Page 241 - 25 Oct 1848. William Martin to Wilson Garrott and Patsy Martin. Deed of Gift, 130 acres. William Martin for love and affection for his son in law Wilson Garrott and William Martin's daughter Patsy Martin, conveyed land in Bedford Co., TN, in District No. 24. Bounded by William Martin, Keeble Terry, and Bobo's line. Wit: John P. Steele and George W. Buchanan. Reg: 28 Oct 1848.

Page 244 - 21 Nov 1848. W. B. Norville to Mary Ann Norton. Bill of Sale. Whereas Mary Ann Norton formerly Mary Ann Norville in consideration of an agreement and promise of her husband James K. Norton that he would purchase for her a negro woman, conveyed her lands. Reg: 30 Oct 1848.

Page 250 - 16 Sep 1848. Uriah Call and others to J. A. Cox. Undivided interest. Uriah Call and Sarah Call late Sarah Cox, John Hill and Nancy Hill late Nancy Cox, heirs at law to the estate of Caleb Cox, deceased, all of Carroll Co., Arkansas, sold to Jackson A. Cox of Carroll Co., Arkansas, their interest in the estate of Caleb Cox, deceased, of Bedford Co. Wit: John W. Peel and T. Denton. Reg: 6 Nov 1848.

Page 252 - 18 Sep 1848. J. J. Pennington and wife to J. A. Cox. Undivided interest. J. J. Pennington and Artelisa Pennington his wife late Artelisa Cox, an heir to the estate of Cabel Cox, deceased. J. J. and Artelisa Pennington of Carroll Co., Arkansas, conveyed their interest in the estate of Caleb Cox, deceased, to J. A. Cox of Bedford Co., TN. Wit: B. H. Berry and Robert Searcy. Reg: 6 Nov 1848.

Page 253 - 5 Oct 1848. Benjamin Lile to Elizabeth Knott. Deed to interest in money. Benjamin Lile of Bedford Co., TN, conveyed to Elizabeth Knott, money, it being the money willed to him by Jackson Lile, deceased, his father, which money was to remain in his mother's hands, Elizabeth lile, until her death, then to be handed over to Benjamin Lile by Jackson Lile, Jr., who is Executor of Jackson Lile, deceased, at the death of Elizabeth Lile. Jackson Lile, Sr. made a will. Wit: William Taylor and

J. R. Stem. Reg: 8 Nov 1848.

Page 255 - 2 Nov 1848. Harris Owen to Mary E. Owen. Relinquishment. Harris Owen for love and affection for his wife Mary E. Owen and his children born now, and which may be born during their marriage, the legacy left to her by the Last Will and Testament of her deceased brother James H. Cobb, with John W. Cobb the Administrator with the will annexed, who refuses to pay over her legacy until it is secured to Mary E. Owen and her children. Harris Owen therefore conveyed to Mary E. Owen during her natural life and at her death to her children of their marriage, all estate left by James H. Cobb, deceased. Wit: A. C. Wood and Samuel T. Cannon. Reg: 8 Nov 1848.

Page 255 - 3 Nov 1848. Milly Whitesell to Jeremiah Whitesell. Deed of Gift, 50 acres. Milly Whitesell for love and affection for Jeremiah Whitesell, conveyed to him her land in Bedford Co., TN, in District No. 20. Bounded by Coat's tract, Thomas Kimmons, D. L. Barringer and Fanny Barrett. It being the tract left Milly Whitesell by her father Jacob Wilhoite. Jeremiah Whitesell being son of Milly Whitesell. Wit: John T. Neil and James H. Neil. Reg: (no date).

Page 256 - 26 Oct 1848. Joseph Alexander and wife to Alfred Campbell. Deed, 38 acres. Joseph Alexander of Missouri and wife Betsey Ann Alexander, sold to Alfred Campbell of Bedford Co., TN, the interest &c in which Betsey Ann Alexander did have in her former state of widowhood to dower out of the lands of Daniel L. Mallard, deceased, it being one third part of the land on Big Flat Creek, including a saw mill and grist mill and whereon Betsey Ann now lives the only tract Daniel L. Mallard owned at the time of his death. reg: 9 Nov 1848.

Page 257 - 6 Nov 1848. Harrison Smith and wife to James H. Harrison. Undivided interest, 188½ acres. Whereas by descent from Jonathan Harrison, deceased, William T. Harrison, Cleveland L. Harrison, Thomas F. Harrison, James H. Harrison, George W. Smith and his wife Margaret, Susanah E. Harrison and himself Harrison Smith and his wife Polly Ann, received title to an equal and undivided interest in a tract of land in Bedford Co., TN, on waters of Rock and Sinking Creeks. Bounded by James Dillard and T. W. Harper, William Williams, James H. Harrison, Nathaniel Porter, John Blackwell and J. M. Gibson. The land bought from Lewis Medlin and Owen Medlin deeded same to Mary Harrison the Executrix of Jonathan Harrison, deceased. Mary Ann same as Polly Ann Harrison. Reg: 9 Nov 1848.

Page 260 - 2 Nov 1848. Nathan Evans to A. H. Evans. Deed, 146½ acres. Nathan Evans for love and affection for his son A. H. Evans, conveyed unto him his tract of land in Bedford Co., TN, in District No. 22. Bounded by James McKisick's survey and George Waite. Reg: 9 Nov 1848.

Page 261 - 27 Oct 1846. William Burrow to Banks A. Burrow. Undivided interest. William Burrow sold to Banks A. Burrow, interest in land in Bedford Co., TN, on waters of Flat Creek and whereon Mary Burrow now lives and which tract was left to Mary Burrow during her natural life by William Burrow, deceased, and was granted to William Burrow by the State of Tennessee. Wit: John T. Neil and Joel R. Deason. Reg: 9 Nov 1848.

Page 262 - 17 Feb 1847. Robert S. Johnson and wife to Banks A. Burrow. Undivided interest. Robert S. Johnson and Martha Johnson his wife formerly Martha Burrow of Walker Co., Alabama, conveyed unto Banks A. Burrow of Bedford Co., TN, land in Bedford Co., on waters of Flat Creek, it being the land whereon Mary Burrow now lives and which was willed to Mary Burrow during her life by William Burrow, deceased. Wit: John Irvin. Reg: 9 Nov 1848.

Page 269 - 2 Jul 1841. Little Rock, Washington Co., Arkansas. Will of Col. Archibald Yell. After the death of Archibald Yell, to descend to his beloved children. To his daughter Mary S. Yell, all the servants, three in Arkansas, which he received by her mother Mary Scott. Also one negro which he is entitled from the estate of Miss Meadows of Bedford Co., TN, 4. Also to all his children his servants (8) to be sold. To his son Clinton, his gold watch and to Jane her mother's gold watch. To Clinton gets the mill farm whereon Archibald Yell's brother resides now. To Elizabeth, lands in Jefferson Co., Arkansas, 400 acres. To Artemisia his Eutaw Farm of Fayetteville, Arkansas of 400 acres. Each child to receive their portion of his estate as they marry or arrive at the age of twenty one years. He appointed James McKisick and Gen. William Moore, his Executors. Wit: R. W. Johnson and Richard C. Hawkins. Proven: 26 Oct 1847.

Page 270 - 17 Nov 1848. C. D. Cooper and wife to Thomas P. Cooper. Undivided interest, 120 acres. C. D. Cooper and Elizabeth Cooper his wife, sold to Thomas P. Cooper, for the consideration of the support of Nancy Rogers, Bedford Rogers and Martha A. Rogers during their natural life or so long as they may be willing to live with him the said Thomas P. Cooper as one of his family or during their single life, an undivided interest in land that John Rogers died seized and possessed of in Bedford Co., TN, in District No. 11. Bounded by James Rogers, Isom Stammers, J. R. Haskins, and Littleton Clark. Wit: Addison Adams and James R. Haskins. Reg: 18 Nov 1848.

Page 271 - 16 Nov 1848. J. W. McGimsey and wife to James G. Neeley. Deed, 12+ acres. John W. McGimsey and his wife Mary McGimsey sold to James G. Neeley, land in Bedford Co., TN, on the waters of Fall Creek. Bounded by the heirs of Samuel A. Bell, deceased, Benjamin F. Garrett and Lot No. 5 in the division of T. C. Nash, deceased. Mary McGimsey formerly Mary Nash. Reg: 18 Nov 1848.

Page 281 - 18 Sep 1843. L. B. McConnico to R. A. Hill. Deed for negroes. Lemuel B. McConnico sold to Robert A. Hill, both of Williamson Co., TN, negroes he owned, whereas he is desirous of securing to his daughter Angelina B. Claud wife of Edwin J. Claud. For love and affection L. B. McConnico has for his daughter Angelina B. Claud, conveyed slaves unto R. A. Hill. Wit: John W. Miller and Lemuel Farmer. Reg: 2 Dec 1848.

Page 297 - 17 Dec 1839. John Cunningham to Patsey Cunningham. Deed of Gift. John Cunningham of Warren Co., TN, for love and affection for his daughter in law, the wife of his son Richard Cunningham, conveyed unto her and her heirs namely, Patsey now Patsey Haggard, Margaret now Margaret Sheppard, Jane Cunningham, Mary Ann now Mary Ann Bowers, and Angelina Cunningham, 4 negroes. Wit: William Kinnard. Reg: 8 Dec 1848.

Page 303 - 13 Dec 1848. Thomas Holland, Sr. to Martha A. Jones. Deed of Gift. THomas Holland, Sr. for love and affection for Martha Ann Jones, daughter of Robert N. and Elizabeth Jones, conveyed unto her a negro girl Delila. Reg: 12 Dec 1848.

Page 303 - 6 Dec 1848. Joseph McKamie and wife to Thomas C. Whiteside. Deed, 42 acres. Joseph McKamie and Nancy McKamie his wife, lately Nancy McAdams, sold to Thomas C. Whiteside, all of Bedford Co., TN, land in Bedford Co., on the Nashville, Murfreesboro and Shelbyville Turnpike Road on the south fork of Falling Creek. The land known in the division of the lands of Amos McAdams, deceased, made by Reding George, B. F. Whitworth, and others, as Lot No. 6, being the lot assigned to Nancy McAdams. Reg: 15 Dec 1848.

Page 308 - 18 Dec 1848. Seborn Bartlett and wife to Horatio Coop. Deed, 20 acres. Seborn Bartlett and Jane Bartlett his wife formerly Jane Loyd, sold to Horatio Coop, land in Bedford Co., TN, in District No. 5, and being Lot No. 3, in the division of lands of Joseph Loyd, deceased, amongst the distributees of his estate. Bounded by William Murphree and the dower's tract. Wit: Andrew Vannoy and John H. Oneal. Reg: 19 Dec 1848.

Page 312 - 4 Mar 1848. Elijah Rushing and wife to A. Burrow. Undivided interest. Elijah Rushing and Evaline Rushing his wife, sold to A. Burrow, their undivided interest in land in Bedford Co., TN, on waters of Flat Creek where Mary Burrow now lives, which tract of land was left to Mary Burrow during her life by William Burrow, deceased, and was granted to William Burrow by the State of Tennessee. Elijah Rushing and Evaline Rushing of Walker Co., Alabama. Reg: 21 Dec 1848.

Page 313 - 21 Aug 1848. Tucker & Minter, Executors of Nancy Manor, deceased, to Samuel G. Thompson. Deed, 187 acres. Whereas Nancy Manor, deceased, late of Rutherford Co., Tn, at the time of her death was vested with title to a tract of land in Bedford Co., TN, in District No. 9. Bounded by James Clark, Jane Harris, Ann Guy, John Key, Richard Landers, lands of the late William Guy, deceased, and the land Nancy Manor held as security for a debt of John Wilson. Nancy Manor made and published her Last Will and Testament and recorded in Rutherford Co., TN. Wit: Alexander G. Key and John W. Key. Reg: 21 Dec 1848.

Page 320 - 28 Dec 1848. Thomas J. Bingham to W. W. Gill. Undivided interest, 1/7 of 166 acres. Thomas J. Bingham and wife Sarah Bingham, has an interest in the remainder to take effect and be united with the possession after the death of Margarett Bennett who has a life estate in same in the one seventh part of a tract of land in Bedford Co., TN, in District No. 22. Bounded by Sarah Albright widow of Jacob Albright, Jacob Castleman, Winston W. Gill and William Kingree. It being the place whereon Margarett Bennett now resides. Wit: Andrew Vannoy and John S. Frazer. Reg: 2 Jan 1849.

Page 326 - 2 Jan 1849. L. C. Johnson to Johanna Nash. Undivided interest. Levi C. Johnson sold to Johanna Nash, all interest &c he and his wife Elizabeth Johnson has in the estate, as one of the heirs at law of William Nash, deceased, it being the personal estate. Wit: G. W. Buchanan and Henry Cannon. Reg: 3 Jan 1849.

Page 332 - 11 Mar 1848. William Falk and others to William Hoover. Deed, 34 acres. William Falk, Jr. and Rebecca Falk, Ann Freeman, Sally Gibbs, all of Bedford Co., TN, sold to William Hoover's line, E. Gibbs and James Smalling. It being on headwaters of Fall Creek. Wit: William Murphree and Joseph H. Freeman. Reg: 6 Jan 1849.

Page 334 - 1 Jan 1849. W. B. Fonville to W. B. M. Brame. Deed, Undivided interest of 100 acres. Washington B. Fonville sold to William B. M. Brame, his interest in land belonging to and laid off to himself, sisters, Virginia and Ann O. and brother, William B. Fonville, being a portion of the tract that belonged to his grandfather Melchisedec Brame, deceased. One fourth of which is hereby conveyed. Land in Bedford Co., TN, on waters of Powell Creek. Bounded by R. H. Sims, Asa Fonville, William Collins and the Brame land. Wit: William S. Jett and J. W. Thompson. Reg: 8 Jan 1849.

Page 337 - 9 Jan 1849. William and Nancy Martin. Agreement. Whereas William and Nancy Martin was on the 7th Nov 1846 lawfully married. Nancy Martin formerly Nancy Young, the widow of the late James Young, deceased, made a marriage contract and registered in the Register's Office in Bedford Co., TN, and dated 23 Nov 1846. They revoke and make null and void all claims that each on either may have to personal property of each on either by marriage contract. Wit: Drury D. Martin and Wilson Garrett. Reg: 9 Jan 1849.

Page 350 - 4 May 1846. Warren and Bingham to Common School Commissioners. 261 poles. John Warren and Samuel M. Bingham conveyed unto William Linch, Samuel M. Bingham and William W. Miller, District School Commissioners in District No. 4, for the use of schools and also preaching by the Methodist, Presbyterians and Baptist, land in Bedford Co., TN, on waters of the Wartrace Fork. Bounded by Samuel M. Bingham, John Warren. Wit: Thomas Warren and N. L. Majors. Reg: 18 Jan 1849.

Page 353 - 20 Jan 1849. James H. Ellis to William Ellis. Deed in Trust. James H. Ellis' wife Irena Ellis is entitled by the Last Will and Testament of her late grandfather James Ellis, late of Lincoln Co., TN, of two negroes, also other estate such as stock, money and other effects which is yet to be divided and set apart to her. James H. Ellis is willing to make suitable settlement on his wife out of the property for the support &c of her and her children. Also for consideration of $1.00 to him paid by William Ellis, the brother of his wife, of Lincoln Co., TN, James H. Ellis conveyed unto William Ellis all rights to negroes and other property of his wife. Reg: 22 Jan 1849.

Page 356 - 12 Dec 1848. Court Decree to Robert T. Cannon. Deed, 137 acres. John McGuire, Administrator, Catharine Lee and others. Robert T. Cannon the purchaser of land. Court ordered that the monies be paid over to the parties entitled to the same, their portion arising from the sale of the lands, but before he pays the shares belonging to the married woman over their husbands, he shall examine them apart from their husbands. Catharine Lee as guardian of Mary Lee and Peter Lee, minors. It was ordered that all the interests &c which Claiborne Bowles and wife Melinda, Calaway Walker and wife Elizabeth, William M. Lee, James H. Lee, John S. Lee, Green D. Lee, Lucy King, Mary Lee, and Peter Lee as the heirs at law of Peter Lee, deceased, has in land which Peter Lee died seized and possessed and which was not included in the dower allotted to Catharine Lee as widow of Peter Lee, and which part adjoins the lands of Kinchen Stokes, Mrs. Robinson and others, in District No. 3 of Bedford Co., TN. Reg: 24 Jan 1849.

Page 362 - 10 Nov 1848. James R. Terry and others to Odd Fellows. Deed, 1 Lot. James R. Terry, William Brown, Benjamin F. Whitworth and Joseph Thompson, a committee appointed by Chosen Friends Lodge No. 11 of The Independent Order of Odd Fellows of Tennessee. It being a subordinate of the Grand Lodge of the Independent Order of Odd Fellows of the State of Tenn= essee, to purchase a building and as Trustees purchased a parcel of land, it being of Lot No. 54 in the Town of Shelbyville, of John Eakin, William Eakin and Thomas Eakin. Bounded by the Old Bank House. Wit: George W. Buchanan and James L. Scudder. Reg: 26 Jan 1849.

Page 367 - 5 Apr 1847. Court Decree to John N. Helton. Deed, 97 acres. Lewis G. Ray and Others, Petition to sell land. Petition for the sale of land, it being in Bedford Co., TN, on waters of Sinking Creek, in District No. 19. Bounded by lands sold by John Ray, Sr. to Alexander Ray, Jane Ray's dower corner and James Davis' corner. Reg: 29 Jan 1849.

Page 368 - 24 Jan 1849. Dickerson Weaver and wife to Enoch Deason. Deed, Undivided interest, 100 acres. Dickerson Weaver and wife Elenor Weaver sold to Enoch Deason, land in Bedford Co., TN, in District No. 5, all of their undivided interest in land of John Deason, deceased. Interest in dower accepted. Reg: 29 Jan 1849.

Page 373 - 10 Jan 1849. H. P. Kimsey to Austin Shofner. Deed of Conveyance. Whereas Adam Euless departed this life some few years ago having previously made and published his Last Will and Testament of the provisions of which after the death of his wife, certain property both real and personal and money go to his wife Margaret Kimsey, a daughter of Adam Euless. Humphrey P. Kimsey has conveyed to Austin Shofner all effects that may come to his wife Margaret Kimsey. Wit: William McFar- land and J. L. Short. Reg: 31 Jan 1849.

Page 378 - 29 Jan 1849. Clement Cannon to Thomas B. Cannon. Deed, 10 acres. Clement Cannon for love and affection for Thomas B. Cannon, conveyed unto him, land in Bedford Co., TN, adjoining the Town of Shelbyville. Bounded by Robert Moffatt, Martin Street, George Davidson, Brittain's corner, and the east bank of Duck River. Reg: 5 Feb 1849.

Page 379 - 23 Dec 1848. Elizabeth Daniel and others to E. J. Frierson. Deed, 50 acres. Elizabeth Daniel, Catharine N. Daniel, and Wiley F. Daniel, sold to E. J. Frierson, land in Bedford Co., TN, about four miles south east of Shelbyville. Bounded by the Executors of James Lile, deceased, James Deery, and John Hastings. Wit: A. C. Wood and John W. Cobbs. Reg: 5 Feb 1849.

Page 383 - 18 Jan 1847. E. G. Cook as Attorney to H. S. Shofner. Deed, 65 acres. Edmund G. Cook, Henry Harman, Mary Harman, Catharine J. Cook, nearest heirs of Henry Cook, deceased, of Cooper Co., Missouri, sold to Hezekiah S. Shofner of Bedford

Co., TN, all their right, title, interest &c in land granted to Henry Cook assignee of Peter Shofner by the State of Tennessee. The land in Bedford Co., on waters of Thompsons Creek. Bounded by Jesse Rogers and where he now lives. Wit: H. P. Kimsey and P. L. Shofner. Reg: 6 Feb 1849.
Page 384 - Another instrument selling land, it joins above tract. Reg: 6 Feb 1849.

Page 393 - 22 Jan 1849. Thomas Holland, Sr. to Nathan Ivy and William Galbreath. Deed in Trust. Thomas Holland, Sr. of Bedford Co., TN, for love and affection for his beloved wife Sarah Holland, conveyed unto his friends, William Galbreath and Nathan Ivey, land in Bedford Co., TN. Adjoining lands of James G. Barksdale and others, except for 40 acres which has been conveyed to Nathan Ivey. Thomas Holland, Sr.'s sons are Thomas and Green Holland. Wit: John A. Moore and J. McGuyre. Reg: 10 Feb 1849.

Page 401 - 17 Feb 1849. Decree of Court to Benjamin H. Berry & Co. Town Lot. Kindred Pearson, John Eakin and wife Lucretia and others vs Kindred G. Pearson and others, heirs of William Pearson, deceased, sold a Town Lot in Lynchburg, Lincoln Co., TN, to Benjamin H. Berry & Co. Reg: 17 Feb 1849.

Page 403 - -- --- 1848. J. Cleveland and others to Rail Road Company. "The undersigned owners of real estate situated in the State of Tennessee do hereby bind ourselves, our heirs and assigns. In consideration of the benefits to accure to us from the construction of the Nashville and Chattanooga Railroad Company, such titles as we may now have or may hereafter acquire to the amount of land required by the Charter of said Company to build the said Railroad upon, as soon as the road shall have be permanently located upon any of our lands within said State. In witness whereof we have hereunto set our hands and seal, this year of our Lord, one thousand eight hundred and forth eight. Witnesses present: William D. Stone, N. F. Carr. Signatures of land owners: H. B. Coffey, Jeremiah Cleveland, R. T. Cannon, William Young, Trigg & Davidson, J. B. Bates, Matthew Mullins, O. H. Bigham & Co., Robert Clark, Theodocia H. Clardy, William J. Peacock, Burrell Featherston, George Cortner, John Norvell, C. L. Cannon, Curry McGuire, N. C. Harris, Sarah Troxler, Rice Coffey, A. Erwin, William Thomas & Brothers, Joshua P. Miller, Nathan Chaffin, and R. D. Rankin. Reg: 20 Feb 1849.

Page 406 - 21 Feb 1849. Samuel K. Bates and wife to Stephen V. Butts(could be Bates). Deed, 57 acres. Samuel K. Bates and Jane S. Bates his wife formerly Jane Thompson, sold to Stephen Butts(Bates), land in Bedford Co., TN, in District No. 5. Bounded by lands of William Guy. Reg: 22 Feb 1849.

Page 407 - 22 Feb 1849. Williamson Haggard to R. B. Parks and others. Deed in Trust. For $300.00 paid by Louisa Elizabeth Shaw wife of William R. Shaw, R. B. Parkes, Annis Marilda Parkes and Frances Ann Haggard his wife(of Williamson Haggard), paid to Williamson Haggard and he paid to Rufus B. Parks, Deed in Trust, as trustee of Frances Parks mother of the aforesaid children, including Rufus B. Parks. Wit: George W. Buchanan and John P. Steele. Reg: 23 Feb 1849.

Page 411 - 8 Jun 1848. William Thorn and others to Theophalus Williams. Deed, 115 acres. William Thorn, James Thorn, Patsy Thorn, Prestly Thorn and Emeline Thorn, all of Bedford Co., TN, sold to Theophilus Williams of Bedford Co., TN, their undivided interest shares of land in Bedford Co., on west waters of Bryans Creek. Another tract bordering Henry Pickle and Benjamin Dorman. Wit: Lewis Gaunt, Prestly Thorn and James M. Leggett. Reg: 27 Feb 1849.

Page 420 - 2 Mar 1849. Jeremiah Prince and Others to H. Bennett. Deed, 10 acres. Whereas William Hudson executed a Deed of Gift dated 27 Jan 1844 to his daughter Nancy Prince, wife of Jeremiah Prince, for land in Bedford Co., TN, on Thompsons Creek and recorded in Book "PP", page 320, sold same to Hezekiah Bennett. Bounded by John Powell. Reg: 3 Mar 1849.

Page 424 - 6 Mar 1849. Harpers Invincible Straw Cutter. Lawrence A. Harper of Russellville, Logan Co., KY, did obtain Letters Patent of the U. S. for a certain Straw Cutter, or Corn Choppers, which Letters Patent bear date 15 Aug 1848 and on record in Patent Office of the U. S. Harper sold said Patent to William M. Word and John H. Oneal. Wit: T. K. Browr and David Kirkpatrick. Reg: 7 Mar 1849.

Page 438 - 7 Jun 1847. James Christian and wife to William Hime. Deed, 28 acres, Lot No. 5. James Christian, Sophronia Christian his wife formerly Sophronia Hime, sold to William Hime, land in Bedford Co., TN, being the tract allotted to Sophronia in the division of the lands of John Hime, deceased, out of a 100 acre tract. Bounded by Pratt's line. Wit: S. B. Hart. Reg: 10 Mar 1849.

Page 439 - 24 Jan 1849. James Christian and wife to William Hime. Deed, undivided interest, 82 acres. James Christian and Sophronia his wife has interest in remainder to take effect and be united with the possession after the death of Mary Ann Hime who has a lifetime estate in the same, in land in Bedford Co., TN, in District No. 23. Bounded by Joseph Hastings' land. Wit: S. B. Hart. Reg: 10 Mar 1849.

Page 458 - 5 Dec 1848. Decree to Isaac Shook. Deed, 194 acres. It appearing to the Court that the lands of William Shook, deceased, be sold for partition amongst the distributees entitled to the same. Isaac Shook became purchaser. All heirs of William Shook are of age of twenty one years and are anxious to receive their share which is in the hands of their guardians. Abram Shook, Executor of the Last Will and Testament of William Shook, deceased. The Trustee of Anna W. Floyd will execute Bond. The Trustee of the children of Elenor Morgan and of Jacob Shook and of William Shook and of James Shook to execute Bond. It is also ordered by the Court that all right, title claim and interest which Abram Shook, John Shook, Jonathan Shook, Levi Shook, Montgomery C. Shook, John B. Shook, Marion M. E. Shook, Minerva Shook, Angaline Shook, Tebitha Shook, Marion Shook, Levi C. Shook, Leroy C. Shook, James C. Shook, Elenor W. Shook, Mary J. Robinson, John H., William B., and George R. Shook, Enoch Floyd and wife Anna W. FLoyd, and Elvira W., Eliza A., Harris P., Isaac S., Robert G., and Sally B. Morgan, and Albert W. Shook have in and to the land in Bedford Co., TN. Bounded by William W. Coldwell, Thomas McFarland, Martin S. Holt, Thomas Dean, William Word, and James Tribble. Reg: 24 Mar 1849.

DEED BOOK "QQ"

Page 460 - 27 Feb 1849. Court Decree to Jeremiah Jacobs. Decree, 100 acres. Court decreed that all the right, title, claim and interest which William Wood, Mary L., Ann, James M., Martha, Tabitha, John W., Frances and Mary A. Robinson and Jacob, Susan, Sarah and Catharine Nichols and Alfred Jacobs and William have in the following, land in Bedford Co., TN, in District No. 1. Bounded by John G. Walker, A. B. Rowton, Mead Hale's line. Said land to be vested to Jeremiah Jacobs. Reg: 3 Apr 1849.

Page 461 - 30 Mar 1849. E. H. Popejoy and E. Popejoy to W. W. Miller. Deed in Trust. Edward H. Popejoy and Elizabeth Popejoy conveyed to William W. Miller, land in Bedford Co., TN, in District No. 2. Bounded by John Scott, John S. Davis and I. J. Miller. Wit: John S. Davis and Daniel Stephens. Reg: 3 Apr 1849.

Page 473 - 23 Mar 1849. P. Frazer, G. H. Frazer and John S. Frazer. Agreement. A suit is now pending in the Chancery Court of Bedford Co., TN wherein Granville H. Frazer is complainant and Preston and John S. Frazer are the Defendants, in which suit said Granville seeks to set up a certain Deed of Gift or a writing purporting to be a Deed of Gift from his mother Jane Frazer and dated 20 May 1846, purporting to convey to Granville H. Frazer certain property. Jane Frazer in the month of June or July 1847 made and published her Last Will and Testament which has since been proven and recorded. The Will bequeathed part of said land to John S. Frazer and Preston Frazer. Wit: James R. Terry and Thomas P. Powell. Reg: 9 Apr 1849.

Page 477 - 14 Dec 1848. John and <u>Levi</u> Harris to James Lawrence. Power of Attorney. John and <u>Lewis</u> Harris appointed James Lawrence as their Attorney to sell and convey in a deed in a tract of land descending to them by their father John T. Harris, deceased, late of Bedford Co., TN, it being the tract of land on which he lived at the time he died. Wit: Frederick Batte and Edwin Batte. Reg: 10 Aug 1849.

Page 478 - 22 Jan 1849. Zebidee Harris to James Lawrence. Power of Attorney. Zebidee Harris appointed James Lawrence his Attorney to sell and convey land, his undivided interest as an heir at law, in lands of John T. Harris, deceased, in Bedford Co., TN, in District No. 10. Bounded by F. S. Brown, L. B. Knott, Mary Ann Little, William Brown, and John Jackson. Wit: William Taylor and Thomas Black. Reg: 10 Apr 1849.

Page 480 - 23 Apr 1846. Absalom L. Landis to John Landis. Absalom L. Landis sold to John Landis land in Bedford Co., TN, on waters of Thompson Creek, in District No. 25 and known in the division of the lands of Christopher Landis, deceased, as Lot No. 8 and falling to Robert L. Landis. Bounded by east bank of Thompson Creek. Wit: William Jenkins and Martin Eulis. Reg: 11 Apr 1849.

Page 483 - 26 Feb 1849. Frances Wilson and Others to Richard O. Robinson. Power of Attorney. Frances Wilson, William L. Robinson, Jesse L. Robinson and Elizabeth H. Malone, all of San Augustine Co., Texas, appointed Richard O. Robinson as their attorney, to receive the money now in the hands of the Clerk of the Circuit Court of Bedford Co., TN, arising from the sales of the lands of the late John Robinson, deceased of Bedford Co.,

Tennessee, which may be coming to her as the widow of Alexander Robinson, deceased, being one third of his share during her natural life. Reg: 12 Apr 1849.

Page 487 - 16 Apr 1849. W. J. Peacock and his wife to Thomas J. Peacock. Deed, 160 acres. William J. Peacock and Catharine T. Peacock his wife sold to Thomas J. Peacock, all interest in a tract of land on which Thomas J. Peacock now resides. Land in Bedford Co., TN. Bounded by William P. Elkins, bank of the Bell Buckle Creek, the west bank of Otter Creek, William J. Peacock, Mrs. Clardy, Burrell Featherston's land he purchased of Feliz G. Ake, and James Thomas. Reg: 16 Apr 1849.

Page 494 - 26 Apr 1849. William Galbreath, Nathan Ivy and Others to R. Matthews. Deed, 7 acres. Whereas Thomas Holland, Sr. by Deed dated -- day of 1849, conveyed unto us in Trust for the benefit of himself and his wife Sarah T. Holland, all of his property both real and personal. The property was still liable for payment of Thomas Holland, Sr. contracted previously. Now it is necessary to sell portion of the land to pay debts. Land bordered Nathan Ivey, James Wortham, Rufus Holland, and Thomas Holland. Reg: 27 Apr 1849.

Page 502 - 26 Feb 1849. David Floyd to Mary Craig and others. Deed, 107½ acres. David Floyd sold and conveyed to Mary A. Craig and her four children, Mary Ann Craig, Henry C. Craig, Robert McNeill Craig and Rebecca N. Craig, land in Bedford Co., TN, in District No. 24. Bounded by David A. Floyd, Thomas W. Frost, William C. Hix, Lemuel Broadaway, and Thomas Dean. Wit: W. W. Coldwell and George W. Buchanan. Reg: 2 May 1849.

Page 509 - 5 Apr 1849. Thomas Holland to Nathan Ivy. Bill of Sale. Thomas Holland conveyed to her a negro girl Tempe, in Trust, for her during his natural life. Wit: Thomas Thomas and B. A. Nelson. Reg: 16 May 1849.

Page 516 - 17 Apr 1849. James H. Kincaid and wife to John T. and J. H. Neil. Deed, 2 Lots. James H. Kincaid and wife Caroline C. Kincaid formerly Caroline C. McGimpsey of Platt Co., Missouri, sold to John T. and James H. Neil of Bedford Co., TN, land in Bedford Co., in Shelbyville, being part of Lots No. 80 and 81. Bounded by Public Square and Spring Street. The land sold belonging to James H. Kincaid and his wife Caroline C. Kincaid and Joseph Kincaid and wife (blank) E. Kincaid, and John W. McGimpsey. Wit: Fielden Lankford and John B. Stone. Reg: 23 May 1849.

DEED BOOK "RR" 1849 - 1850

Page 1 - 25 May 1849. Shrewsberry B. Blackwell to John Blackwell. Deed, 172 acres. Whereas Shrewsberry B. Blackwell of Bedford Co., TN inherited from his father John Blackwell and had devised to him by the will of John Blackwell and had given to him by Deed of Gift from Blackwell. The one seventh part of all the real and personal property of which John Blackwell died seized and possessed. One tract being in Marshall Co., TN and bounded by B. Smiley, George Woodward, Glenn heirs, and Josiah Blackwell. It being the place whereon John Blackwell resided at the time of his death, and other property. Reg: 25 May 1849.

Page 4 - 30 May 1849. R. J. Williams to Samuel D. Coble. Deed in Trust &c. Richard J. Williams sold to Samuel D. Coble, Deed in Trust, of land in Bedford Co., TN, in District No. 25. Bounded by Mary Coble, Martin Eulis and Thomas C. Whiteside. It being the dower interest which was allotted to his wife Mary Williams out of the lands of her former husband Jacob Coble, and upon which he now resides. Also, all the interest he had, one tenth part, of 70 acre tract adjoining the dower tract, it being during the joint lives of Mary and R. J. Williams. Also, negro slaves and other property. R. J. Williams is indebted to Samuel D. Coble. Reg: 30 May 1849.

Page 5 - 29 May 1849. William M. Wilhoite and Eliza J. Coble. Marriage Contract. Articles of Agreement between William M. Wilhoite and Eliza J. Coble, both of Bedford Co., TN, that whereas a marriage is shortly to be had and that Eliza J. Coble being seized and possessed in her own right of some estate, both real and personal, which they are desirous to secure. Eliza J. Coble has interest in lands of which her father Jacob Coble died seized and possessed and not being sold, being her undivided interest in about 60 acres assigned to Mary Coble the widow of Jacob Coble, deceased, as her dower and on which she now resides. Two tracts on both sides of Thompson Creek and Duck River. Wit: Richard J. Williams and James Carter. Reg: 30 May 1849.

Page 15 - 4 Jun 1849. William Haithcoat to C. Bowls. Bill of Sale. William Haithcoat sold to C. Bowls, his interest &c which he has as one of the heirs, in the Last Will and Testament of his grandfather Joseph Palmore of Buckingham Co., Virginia, and he (William Haithcoat) being one of the children of Poley Bowls, deceased, conveyed negro slaves. Wit: J. W. Allen and James H. T. Lee. Reg: 5 Jun 1849.

Page 16 - 4 Jun 1849. Robert Cannon from Chancery Court Decree for land. George W. Haywood, Administrator of William Gilchrist vs Malcom Gilchrist, Catharine Mary Gilchrist, Adelaid Gilchrist and Sarah Gilchrist, and the creditors of said Gilchrist. Court ordered all interest &c to be sold and Robert Cannon being the purchaser. Land in bedford Co., TN, in Shelbyville. Reg: 6 Jun 1849.

Page 17 - 8 Sep 1848. John Wood Decree of Court for land. James Foster, Administrator of Hugh Allen, deceased, vs Martha Allen and Others. On 11 Sep 1847, offered the lands not included in the widow's dower in two Lots or tracts. Hugh McBride having highest biddes was purchaser. Another tract purchased by Thomas Davis. Reg: 7 Jun 1849.

Page 20 - 1 Jun 1844. Nancy Wilson and A. B. Moon to Anderson and Others. Trustees. Deed, 3 acres. Nancy Wilson and A. B. Moon donated and conveyed to John Thompson, Joseph Anderson, John C. Wilson, William M. Shaw, and Alexander B. Moon, Trustees of the Episcopal and Protestant Methodist Denominations, as a place of worship but not as a Camp Ground. The land in Bedford Co., TN, in District No. 11. Wit: James Ogilvie, A. Wilson and William Wortham. Reg: 11 Jan 1849.

Page 22 - 7 Jun 1849. William Brown to Trustees of Cumberland Presbuterian Church. Newcum Thompson, L. D. Pannell, C. B. Wood, and W. W. Hendrix, all of Bedford Co., TN, Trustees for the Cumberland Presbyterian Church in Shelbyville, bought of William Brown, land in Shelbyville, Lot No. 22. William Brown is to remove all the buildings on said lot. Reg: 15 Jun 1849.

Page 24 - 16 Jun 1849. John McAdams to Daniel R. McAdams. Deed, 1/10th of 200 acres. John McAdams sold to Daniel R. McAdams, property, both real and personal, to wit, the one tenth part of a tract in bedford Co., TN, in District No. 6, it being a part of the real estate of Amos McAdams, which he set apart in his will to his wife Mariah McAdams during her natural lifetime and at her death to his children. Bounded by Andrew J. McAdams, Thomas C. Whiteside, John McAdams, Lydia Roan, John Eakin and Peyton H. Coats. John McAdams is a son of Amos and Mariah McAdams. Reg: 16 Jun 1849.

Page 33 - -- Jun 1849. Shrewsberry Blackwell to Robert Blackwell. Deed of Gift. Shrewsberry Blackwell for love and affection for his son Robert Blackwell, conveyed unto him land on which Shrewsberry Blackwell now live and in Bedford Co., TN, on east fork of Rock Creek on the Marshall County line. Bounded by R. Stephenson, T. W. Coffee, J. Price, Colson G. Woodward, and Mrs. Rodes. Wit: James C. Russell and Green Lovett. Reg: 29 Jun 1849.

Page 36 - 4 Jan 1848. Abel Rushing and Others to Alfred Mustain. Deed, 116 acres. Abel Rushing of Rutherford Co., TN, Milton R. Rushing and John Rushing of Bedford Co., TN, sold to Alfred Mustain, land in Bedford Co., on both sides of Alexander Creek. Bounded by the mouth of Alexander Creek, George Alexander, George Wadley, widow Short, the North Fork of Duck River. Wit: Abraham Winsett and N. M. Wheeler. Reg: 30 Jun 1849.

Page 40 - 2 Jul 1849. Mary Fonville with Ewing, Hardison & Fonville. Agreement. Mary Fonville widow of Asa Fonville and Samuel Ewing, James Y. Hardison and James Fonville. Whereas Asa Fonville by his Last Will and Testament bequeathed to Mary property by Asa Fonville before his intermarriage with Mary. The will is now being contested by the heirs at law of Asa and Mary is not liable for the debts of Asa. Mary Relinquished all right and claim to all that part of the estate of Asa. Reg: 2 Jul 1849.

Page 53 - 26 Jul 1849. Mary L. Nowlin to J. W. Nowlin. Deed of Gift. Mary L. Nowlin for love and affection for her son J. W. Nowlin, conveyed a negro girl Charlotte. Reg: 27 Jul 1849.

Page 33 - 27 Jun 1849. J. F. Bowls to Claiborn Bowls. Deed, undivided interest. J. F. W. Bowles sold to Claiborn Bowles, his one ninth part of a tract of land which descended to him, jointly with others from Claiborn Bowles, deceased, it being in Bedford Co., TN, in District No. 3. Bounded by Robert Cannon, Mariah Phillips, William Young and Thomas Whiteside. Also conveys negroes. Reg: 29 Jun 1849.

Page 56 - 27 July 1849. Isreal Harris and wife to John M. Warner. Deed, 23 acres. Isreal Harris and wife Martha Harris formerly Martha Head, sold to John M. Warner, land in Bedford Co., TN, in District No. 8. Reg: 31 Jul 1849.

Page 71 - 7 Sep 1842. Ewel heirs to David Weaver. Deed, 6 acres.

Martha and William P. Chamlin. Ann and Asa Elkins, Lucy and Wilson Hall, John Ewel, Catharine and George W. Heard, Thomas Ewel, Virginia and J. H. Scott, P. K. Ewel, Sharah and Alexander Kimbro, and Joseph Ewel, heirs of John Ewel, deceased, conveyed to David Weaver, land in Bedford Co., TN, in District No. 25. Wit: A. L. Landis and G. W. Harris. Reg: 9 Aug 1849.

Page 74 - 10 Aug 1849. John H. Wood and wife to Robert H. Wood. Deed, 74 acres. John H. Wood and his wife Nancy Wood, sold to Robert H. Wood, land in Bedford Co., TN, in District No. 9, on the headwaters of Weakleys Creek. Bounded by John McGowen and Jasper Daisey. Wit: John A. Reed and Barram Lamb. Reg: 10 Aug 1849.

Page 79 - 1 Aug 1849. Joseph Hasty and wife to John Kizer. Deed, 74 acres. Joseph Hasty and wife Mary Ann Jane Hasty, sold to John Kizer, all of Bedford Co., TN, land in Bedford Co., on Big Flat Creek. Bounded by Hiram Eddy, tract on which Britain Daws now lives, Jacob Kizer and Kimery tract. Also, another tract on Big Flat Creek. Bounded by land formerly owned by Hiram Holt now belonging to Hiram Eddy and Sally Hix. Reg: 13 Aug 1849.

Page 81 - 26 Jan 1846. Nicholas Harris and wife to Michael F. Parsons. Deed, 6 acres. Nicholas Harris and wife Mary Ann Harris formerly Mary Ann Parsons, sold to Michael F. Parsons, land, it being their distributive share of land formerly belonging to George W. Parsons, deceased. Land in Bedford Co., TN, on waters of Falling Creek, in District No. 8. Bounded by J. Harris, Parson's tract, and Mrs. Parsons. Wit: George W. Parsons and John W. Parsons. Reg: 13 Aug 1849.

Page 82 - 15 Dec 1848. James P. Allison to J. P. and Mary King's heirs. Deed, 70 acres. James P. Allison for love and affection for the children of James P. King and Mary King, conveys unto them land in Bedford Co., TN, in District No. 11. Bounded by Jane Snell, A. Wilson and K. Allison. Wit: M. Blanton and W. W. Jenkins. Reg: 14 Aug 1849.

Page 94 - 19 Jul 1849. John Sutton to Mary B. and Narcissa Sutton. Deed of Gift. John Sutton for love and affection for his two daughters, Mary B. Sutton and Narcissa W. Sutton, both minors, conveyed to them for their natural life, a negro woman Sarah Ellen and her children, also a negro boy Harry to Mary B. To Narcissa W. conveys a negro woman Mary and her children, also a negro boy Harrison. Wit: Thomas C. Whiteside. Reg: 22 Aug 1849.

Page 97 - 13 Feb 1846. Robert C. Garrison and others to Nathan Evans. Deed, undivided interest. Robert C. Garrison and Martha Garrison (Sen.) of Maury Co., TN, Archibald M. Pickens and his wife Sarah W. Pickens of Giles Co., TN, all legal heirs of Samuel R. Garrison, deceased, sold to Nathan Evans of Bedford Co., TN, land being in the eastern half of the tract of land formerly owned by Samuel R. Garrison, deceased. Land in Bedford Co., TN, on waters of Sugar Creek and adjoining lands of Nathan Evans. Bounded by heirs of James Walker, deceased, Nathan Evans, and James C. Snell. Reg: 24 Aug 1849.

Page 101 - 27 Aug 1849. Francis Bush and others to T. P. Green. Deed, undivided interest. Elisha Brown and Mary Ann Brown formerly Mary Martin, Francis Bush and Elizabeth Bush formerly Elizabeth Martin, sold to Townson P. Green, land in Lincoln and Bedford Counties, TN, on headwaters of East Mulberry, their part being two tenths of the tract belonging to the estate of John Martin, Sr., deceased. Bounded by Martin M. Holt, James Ivey, William Hix, and Lorenzo Buchanan. Reg: 27 Aug 1849.

Page 103 - 16 Aug 1849. Shrewsberry Blackwell and others to James W. Coffee. Deed, 50 acres. Shrewsberry B., Zeno C., Robert B., Sumner and Elizabeth Blackwell, sold to James W. Coffee, land. Bounded by Richard Stephenson and James W. Coffey's line. Wit: William Wood and Thomas Coffey. Reg: 28 Aug 1849.

Page 104 - 16 Aug 1849. S. B. Blackwell and others to Jerman Woodward. Deed, 50 acres. Shrewsberry S., Zeno C., Robert B., Sumner and Elizabeth Blackwell, sold to Jerman Woodward, land. Bounded by James Price, Robert J. Alison, Jerman Woodward, Allen Rhodes, and James W. Coffey. Wit: William Wood and Thomas Coffey. Reg: 28 Aug 1849.

Page 110 - 1 Sep 1849. W. G. Rives and wife to William B. M. Brame. Deed, undivided interest, 1/4 of 100 acres. Willis G. Rives and wife Virginia sold to William B. M. Brame, land in Bedford Co., TN, in District No. 21, it being the fourth of their undivided interest and which descended to Virginia as one of the heirs of Melchesidec Brame, deceased. Wit: W. S. Jett and J. H. Thompson. Reg: 1 Sep 1849.

Page 113 - 1 Sep 1849. E. P. Winn and others to John Wadley. Bill of Sale. E. P. Winn, S. Winn, P. Primrose, J. G. Primrose, James Winn, M. Winn, T. J. Primrose, B. C. Primrose, J. R. Lane and M. L. Lane, sold to John Wadley, a negro man Jo. Wit: Thomas J. Wadley and Charles F. Haskins. Reg: 4 Sep 1849.

Page 114 - 3 Sep 1849. E. and J. W. Rucker to Frederick Batte. Deed, 60 acres. Elliotte Rucker and John W. Rucker sold to Frederick Batte, land in Bedford Co., TN, on waters of Weakleys Creek. It being the south east corner of a tract of land willed to them by their father Elliott Rucker, deceased. Wit: Anderson Landers and William H. Low. Reg: 4 Sep 1849.

Page 122 - 7 Sep 1849. James E. Wray to John M. Wray. Deed, undivided interest in estate. James E. Wray sold to John M. Wray all his interest in both real and personal and mixed estate of his father John Wray, deceased, which consists of one tract of land lying in Bedford Co., TN, in District No. 10 of 340 acres and negroes. Wit: William Neal and Hannibal M. Owen. Reg: 10 Sep 1849.

Page 124 - 7 Jul 1849. S. R. Harris to James Lawrence. Deed, 30 acres. S. R. Harris has interest remainder to take effect and be united with the possession after the death of Esther Harris who has a life estate in the same, in a tract of land in Bedford Co., TN, in District No. 10. Bounded by John Jackson. Wit: G. W. Bandy and Richard Bandy. Reg: 11 Sep 1849.

Page 129 - 25 May 1849. Plat of Peter Crowell. Land on Sinking Creek of Bedford Co., TN. 451 acres.

Page 130 - 11 Jun 1849. Heirs of Peter Crowel, deceased. Division of land. Samuel Crowel, Charles Crowel, David R. Keel and wife Cloey, John Crowel and wife Sophia, and J. B. Jones, the heirs and distributees of Peter Crowel, deceased, late of Bedford Co., TN, agreeable to the Last Will and Testament of said Peter Crowel, deceased, to divide said estate among the heirs. Samuel Crowel has Lot No. 1, Charles Crowel has Lot No. 2, David R. Keel and wife Cloey has Lot No. 3, John Crowel and wife Sophia has Lot No. 4, James B. Jones who represents Henry Crowel has Lot No. 5. The widow's dower is not included. Land in Bedford Co., on Sinking Creek, in District No. 18. Wit: Jos. Anderson and John C. Anderson. Reg: 14 Sep 1849.

Page 133 - 15 Sep 1849. John Blackwell to Robert Matthews. Deed to interest in an estate. John Blackwell sold to Robert Matthews all the interest that he has in the interest of Shrewsberry B. Blackwell which John Blackwell purchased from Shrewsberry in John's father John Blackwell, deceased, estate. John Blackwell conveyed to Robert Matthews the interest. Reg: 15 Sep 1849.

Page 139 - 19 Sep 1849. John Tillman to Barkley M. Tillman. Deed in Trust, 220 acres. John Tillman for love and affection for his daughter Rachael M. Tipton wife of Edmund W. Tipton, and for love and affection for Edmund W. Tipton, sold unto Barkley M. Tillman, all his interest in land in Bedford Co., TN. Bounded by Anthony Thomas, John Tillman's line and Edward A. Moseley. Also conveyed negroes. Reg: 20 Sep 1849.

Page 140 - 20 Sep 1849. George Presgrove and wife to Samuel Clark. Deed, 43 acres. George Presgrove and wife Susanah Presgrove sold to Samuel Clark, land in Bedford Co., TN, on waters of Alexanders Creek. Bounded by James Harris formerly lands of Joseph P. Morris and William Allison. Wit: John P. Steele, William S. Puckett and John Fisher. Reg: 20 Sep 1849.

Page 143 - 18 Sep 1849. Thomas Holland and wife to James G. Barksdale. Deed, 30 acres. THomas Holland and wife Sarah T. Holland, William Galbreath and Nathan Ivey, sold to James G. Barksdale, land in Bedford Co., TN, in District No. 3. Bounded by Barksdale's line and Holland's house. Reg: 21 Sep 1849.

Page 145 - 18 Sep 1849. Thomas Holland and wife to Nathan Ivey. Deed, 1½ acres. Thomas Holland and wife Sarah T. Holland and William Galbreath, sold to Nathan Ivey, interest in land in Bedford Co., TN, in District No. 3. Bounded by Barksdale's line and Gilchrist's line. Reg: 21 Sep 1849.

Page 148 - 22 Sep 1849. William A. Young to Mary J. Evans. Deed of Gift. William A. Young for love and affection for his daughter Mary Jane Evans, wife of A. J. Evans, conveyed unto her land in Bedford Co., TN, in Shelbyville, Lot No. 99. Wit: James R. Scudder and J. W. Buchanan. Reg: 25 Sep 1849.

Page 148 - 24 Sep 1849. Green B. Newsom to Eliza Newsom. Deed of Gift, 194 acres. Green B. Newsom husband of Eliza Newsom of Bedford Co., TN, conveyed unto her, land in Bedford Co., in District No. 20. Bounded by Gaunt's line and George Davis. Wit: J. H. M McGrew and Terry D. Thompson. Reg: 25 Sep 1849.

Page 153 - 21 Sep 1849. John T. Davis and wife to T. G. W. Wright. Deed, undivided interest. John T. Davis and wife Elizabeth Caroline Davis formerly Elizabeth Caroline Ferrill of Attalia Co., Mississippi, sold to T. G. W. Wright their undivided interest in land in Bedford Co., TN, in District No. 2, and it being the land whereon Richard Ferrill, deceased, resided at the time of his death. Reg: 29 Sep 1849.

Page 155 - 3 Oct 1849. Lewis Obryan and others to F. A. Martin. Deed, undivided interest. Lewis Obryan and Rebecca Obryan and Thomas J. Martin, heirs of John Martin, deceased, sold to Franklin A. Martin, all their undivided interest in land in Bedford Co., TN, it being the lands of which John Martin, Sr. died seized and possessed. Wit: M. M. Holt and Francis Bush. Reg: 2 Oct 1849.

Page 156 - 23 Jul 1849. David Anderson to David Anderson, Jr. Bill of Sale. David Anderson sold to his son David Anderson, Jr. of Hickman Co., TN, a negro girl Mary Ann and a negro boy Anderson. Wit: Jos. Anderson and William Crowell. Reg: 2 Oct 1849.

Page 158 - 17 Feb 1849. Charles L. Hoover to Thomas Warren. Bond for Title. Charles L. Hoover sold to Thomas Warren, land in Bedford Co., TN, in District No. 4, it being one half of the tract of land John Warren bought by Andrew Erwin. Wit: William T. Tune and H. B. Warren. Reg: 3 Oct 1849.

Page 159 - 8 Nov 1845. William Casteele and wife to G. P. Burditt. Deed, undivided interest. William Casteele and his wife Elizabeth G. Casteele, sold to Giles P. Burditt, land in Bedford Co., TN, it being their undivided interest willed to William Burditt's widow Sarah Burditt the wife of William Burditt, Jr., deceased, by William Burditt, Sr., deceased, and after the death of Sarah Burditt, to the heirs of William Burditt, Jr., deceased. Land on waters of Noah's Fork and it being the land whereon the wife of William Burditt, Sr. now resides. Wit: Giles B. Raney and Nathan Ivy. Reg: 4 Oct 1849.

Page 160 - 2 Oct 1849. Nathan Ivy and wife to Giles P. Burditt. Deed, undivided interest. Nathan Ivy and Polly Ann his wife, sold to Giles P. Burditt, land in Bedford Co., TN, it being willed to William Burditt's widow Sarah Burditt wife of William Burditt, Jr., deceased, by William Burditt, Sr., deceased. Reg: 4 Oct 1849.

Page 161 - -- Oct 1849. Francis M. Miller and wife to William B. Cooper. Deed, interest in land &c. Francis M. Miller and Amandy M. Miller his wife, sold to William B. Cooper, land in Bedford Co., TN, on waters of Battes Creek, adjoining lands of Mariah Phillips, William Young, Thomas C. Whiteside, Robert Cannon, and land formerly owned by Claiborne Bowles, deceased. Also conveyed negroes. Reg: 5 Oct 1849.

Page 166 - 5 Oct 1849. Court Decree to Edmund Word. 97+ acres. Pascal Brown, Jesse W. Brown, Joel Whorley and wife Cynthia, Elizabeth Brown, John Brown, Robert A. Brown, Daniel Brown, William Brown, and Henry Brown. Exparte. Bill for Sale of Land. Clement Cannon, Sr. was purchaser of land. The land in Bedford Co., TN, on waters of Sugar Creek. Reg: 9 Oct 1849.

Page 169 - 29 Feb 1848. Samuel Crowell to James B. Jones. Deed, undivided interest. Henry Crowell sold to James B. Jones, undivided interest as the heir of Peter Crowell, lands, being one fifth part. One tract on both sides of Big Sinking Creek, of 4½ acres. Another tract on Sinking Creek. Another tract on Big Sinking Creek. Also, another tract on Sinking Creek. Another tract on south side of Duck River. And other tracts. Wit: James M. Baxter and William H. Aaron. Reg: 10 Oct 1849.

Page 172 - 10 Jan 1840. Francis Garrett and others to James S. Holt. Deed, 4/10 of 77 acres. Francis Garrett, William Garrett, Allen and Louisa M. Gilliam, Wilburn and Sarah H. Holt, sold to James S. Holt, land in Bedford Co., TN. Wit: Willis Green and A. M. Garrett. Reg: 11 Oct 1849.

Page 174 - 23 Sep 1848. Marinda Steele and others (to James G. Neeley). Deed, 43¼ acres. Marinda Steele, Jane Knott wife of Thomas Knott, Thomas Knott, P. C. Steele, John Knott and his wife Harriett Knott, Mintoria Steele, and E. N. Steele, sold to James G. Neeley, land in Bedford Co., TN, on waters of Falling Creek. Bounded by Fall Creek. The land descended to them by the decease of Joseph Steele, they being heirs and distributees at law. Signed by Marinda Steele, Thomas Knott, Jane Knott, Volney H. Steele, P. C. Steele, C. D. Steele, John P. Steele, John Knott, Harriett Knott, Mintoria Steele, and Ellen Steele. Reg: 11 Oct 1849.

Page 181 - 4 Oct 1849. Thomas McAdams to Peter S. Deckard, Executor. Deed, 43 acres. Thomas McAdams sold to Peter S. Deckard, Executor of John W. Holder, deceased, of Franklin Co., TN, the lands being a part of Virginia Hart's share of her father John W. Holden, deceased. The land on Falling Creek and on east side of Nashville, Murfreesboro and Shelbyville Turnpike Road and it being part of tract owned by Amos McAdams, deceased, at the time of his death and directed by him to be divided between his children. Lot No. 4 allotted to Thomas McAdams. Wit: Thomas C. Whiteside and John T. Neil. Reg: 15 Oct 1849.

Page 182 - 28 Mar 1849. Mahala and Matilda Elkins to John Q. Davidson. Agreement. Mahala and Matilda Elkins of Bedford Co., TN, of one aprt and John Q. Davidson of second part. Mahala and Matilda Elkins being old and infirm and unable to provide for themselves, conveyed unto John Q. Davidson, a negro and her children in exchange for his support for them in the life time. Wit: William Norton and Jonas Myers. Reg: 15 Oct 1849.

Page 185 - 18 Oct 1849. Robert Mathews to Gabriel Blackwell. Deed, undivided interest. Robert Mathews sold to Gabriel Blackwell of Marshall Co., TN, all the remainder interest in the estate of John Blackwell, deceased, that Robert Mathews purchased from John Blackwell, dated 15 Sep 1849, in his father's estate that he purchased from S. B. Blackwell. Reg: 22 Oct 1849.

Page 189 - 20 Oct 1849. L. B. McConnico to M. P. Gentry. Deed, 628½ acres. Lemuel B. McConnico of Williamson Co., TN, sold to Meredith P. Gentry of Williamson Co., TN, land in Bedford Co., TN, on both sides of Sinking Creek, except the parcel thereof known as the graveyard, containing one half of one acre. Land bounded by Ray's dwelling house, Alexander Ray, land of John Ray conveyed to W. M. and C. S. Russell, Stephen Freeman,

Cortner's line, Stephen Porter's old tract now Daniel Looney's corner, James Davis, and William R. Ray. Also personal property. Wit: John Marshall and M. H. Nicholson. Reg: 24 Oct 1849.

Page 195 - 20 Oct 1849. Flower Swift to Harriett E. Swift. Deed of Gift. Flower Swift for love and affection for his daughter in law Harriett E. Swift wife of Jacob W. Swift, and her children, conveyed unto her a negro girl Margaret. Wit: J. R. Terry and William H. Wisener. Reg: 1 Nov 1849.

Page 195 - 27 Oct 1849. Henry Crowell to William Brown. Bill of Sale to undivided interest. Henry Crowell has an undivided interest in remainder to be united with the possession and take effect after the death of his mother Eve Crowell, sold to William Brown, the remainder interest in three negroes belonging to the estate of Peter Crowell, deceased. The negroes was by the Last Will and Testament of Peter Crowell, deceased, bequeathed to Henry's mother Eve Crowell during her natural life and after her death to be divided between Henry's two brothers, Samuel and Charles and his two sisters, Chloea and Sophia and himself (Henry). Reg: 1 Nov 1849.

Page 201 - 2 Jun 1847. Hiram Harris to James A. Lentz. Deed, 67½ acres. Hiram Harris sold to James A. Lentz, land in Bedford Co., TN, in District No. 18. Bounded by John Lentz, Adam Culps, John M. Warner, and the bluff of Duck River. The exception of the interest of Mary Lentz the widow of Jacob Lentz, deceased, in fifty two acres with the building &c. Reg: 2 Nov 1849.

Page 205 - -- Jan 1848. Harriett and W. F. Thompson to Jonas Myers. Quit Claim to negroes. Harriett Thompson and William F. Thompson sold to Jonas Myers, three negroes. Wit: John F. Hall and A. D. THompson. Reg: 6 Nov 1849.

Page 205 - 5 Nov 1849. J. M. Elkins to H. H. Elkins. Bond for Title. J. M. Elkins sold to Harrison H. Elkins, land being part of the tract on which William P. Elkins, deceased, resided at the time of his death. Reg: 6 Nov 1849.

Page 208 - 5 Nov 1849. John Butler to James W. Proby. Power of Attorney. John Butler appointed James W. Proby his Attorney to receive for him monies due his wife or to him in right of his wife, as one of the distributees and heirs of Peter R. Proby, deceased, in the hands of Clerk of Circuit Court of Bedford Co., TN. Reg: 7 Nov 1849.

Page 211 - 15 Sep 1849. Harrel Wiggins to William O. Forbes and wife. Bill of Sale. Harrel Wiggins for love and affection for his son in law William O. Forbes and his wife Nancy the daughter of Harrel Wiggins, conveyed unto them a negro boy Samuel. Reg: 8 Nov 1849.

Page 219 - 10 Nov 1849. William B. M. Brame to Edmund Cooper. Trustee Deed. William B. M. Brame for natural love and affection for his wife and children, sold to Edmund Cooper, three lots in Twown of Shelbyville, Lots No. 25, 26, and 27, including the dwelling house in which W. B. M. Brame now lives, also a negro boy Fed, a negro woman Pollie and others, to hold said land and negroes for benefit of his wife Mary Ann Brame during her natural life and for her separate use, and at her death to his children by Mary Ann Brame or any children that might be born. Reg: 12 Nov 1849.

Page 224 - 16 Nov 1849. James Deery to J. H. and R. D. Deery. Deed of Gift to Town Lot. James Deery for love and affection for his two sons James H. Deery and Ross D. Deery, conveyed unto them a Lot of ground in Bedford Co., Shelbyville, TN, on the north side of the Public Square, on which the Brick House in which Amzi Bradshaw now lives adjoining the Shelbyville Inn and the east half of the framed house adjoining the Brick House. Wit: William H. Wisener and James L. Scudder. Reg: 19 Nov 1849.

Page 237 - 29 Sep 1849. Andrew H. Elliott and wife to Matt Martin. Deed, 1/5 of 300 acres. Andrew H. Elliott and wife Sarah E. Elliott, sold to Matt Martin, land in Bedford Co., TN, on the Garrison Fork and Noahs Fork. Bounded by Matt Martin, Thomas Mason and McMichael. The same being two tracts of land adjoining, owned by Abram Rowten, the Executor of Sarah E. Elliott. Wit: L. P. Fields and Joseph Tillman. Reg: 30 Nov 1849.

Page 247 - 31 Aug 1849. Mathew T. and Elizabeth Cunningham to S. B. Gordon. Deed, 100 acres. Mathew T. and Elizabeth Cunningham sold to Samuel B. Gordon, land in Bedford Co., TN, in District No. 23, on headwaters of Big Flat Creek. Wit: Newton B. Cunningham and W. C. Gordon. Reg: 5 Dec 1849.

Page 248 - 31 Aug 1849. Mathew and Elizabeth Cunningham to W. C. Gordon. Deed, 48 acers. Mathew T. Cunningham and Elizabeth Cunningham, sold to William C. Gordon, land in Bedford Co., TN, in District No. 23. Wit: Newton B. Cunningham and Samuel B. Gordon. Reg: 5 Dec 1849.

Page 264 - 18 Dec 1849. F. A. Martin and others to William Dillingham. Deed, 7/10 of 100 acres. F. A. Martin, John Martin, Jr., Thomas J. Martin and Nancy W. Martin, Elizabeth Bush, Mary Ann Brown and Rebecca O. Bryant, sold to William Dillingham, land in Bedford Co., TN and in Lincoln Co., TN. it being the land of which John Martin died seized and possessed. Signed by F. A. Martin, John Martin, Nancy W. Martin and T. P. Martin. Reg: 31 Dec 1849.

Page 269 - 21 Dec 1849. A. L. Nash to James G. Neeley. Deed, undivided interest. Augustus L. Nash sold to James G. Neeley all his undivided interest in land in Bedford Co., TN, on waters of Fall Creek. Bounded by lands of the heirs of John Hutton, deceased, V. H. Steele, heirs of Samuel A. Bell, deceased, heirs of T. C. Nash, deceased. Being the dower tract on which Mrs. Joanna Nash lives, being one fifteenth part of said tract also one fourteenth of a fifteenth of the tract and all that A. L. Nash may have by descent in the tract at the termination of the dower. Recorded 2 Jan 1849(1850).

Page 274 - 2 Jan 1850. Nathaniel O. McAdams to W. W. Arnold. Deed, 40 acres. Nathaniel O. McAdams sold to W. W. Arnold, land in Bedford Co., TN, it being Lot No. 3 in the division of the lands of Amos McAdams, deceased, which was set apart to Nathaniel O. McAdams. Bounded by Fall Creek and the Turnpike. Reg: 4 Jan 1850.

Page 285 - 10 Jan 1850. John Keck to Sarah Holt. Deed of Gift. John Keck for love and affection for his daughter Sarah Holt wife of Jesse Holt, conveyed unto her land or part of his land in Bedford Co., TN, in District No. 25, of 49½ acres. Bounded by George Cortner. Wit: J. H. Scott and D. P. T. House. Reg: 11 Jan 1850.

Page 285 - 10 Jan 1850. John Keck to Delila E. Newton. Deed of Gift. John Keck for love and affection for his daughter Delila Elizabeth Newton wife of John E. Newton, conveyed unto her, land or part of his tract in Bedford Co., TN, in District No. 25. Bounded by George Cortner. Wit: J. H. Scott and D. P. T. House. Reg: 11 Jan 1850.

Page 286 - 11 Jan 1850. John Keck to Lucy E. Holder. Deed of Gift. John Keck for love and affection for his daughter Lucy E. Holder wife of Joseph Holder, conveyed unto her part of his land in Bedford Co., TN, in District No. 25. Wit: J. H. Scott and D. P. T. House. Reg: 11 Jan 1850.

Page 286 - 11 Jan 1850. John Keck to John M. Keck. Deed of Gift, Lot No. 4. John Keck for love and affection for his grandson John M. Keck, son of George Keck, conveyed unto him part of his land in Bedford Co., TN, in District No. 25. Wit: J. H. Scott and D. P. T. House. Reg: 11 Jan 1850.

Page 287 - 11 Jan 1850. John Keck to Mary Ann Farris. Deed of Gift, Lot No. 5. John Keck for love and affection for his daughter Mary Ann Farris wife of James Farris, conveyed unto her part of his land in Bedford Co., TN, in District No. 25. Wit: J. H. Scott and D. P. T. House. Reg: 11 Jan 1850.

Page 288 - 11 Jan 1850. John Keck to Jesse Holt. Deed of Gift. John Keck for love and affection for Jesse Holt, conveyed unto him a negro boy Thadius and other personal property. Wit: J. H. Scott and D. P. T. House. Reg: 11 Jan 1850.

Page 289 - 11 Jan 1850. George F. M. Davis and his wife Cyntha to John Wallace. Deed, 65 acres. George F. M. Davis and his wife Cyntha sold to John Wallace, land in Bedford CO., TN, in District No. 23. Bounded by lands of John Hime, deceased, and the dower tract. Including what is called the Rocky Springs. Reg: 12 Jan 1850.

Page 290 - 9 Jan 1850. Priscilla Primrose and others to William Allison. Deed, 197½ acres. The heirs of Thomas Primrose, deceased, to wit, widow Priscilla Primrose, T. J. Primrose, Sophia Winn, Mary Winn, James Winn, Elvy F. Williams, E. P. Winn, Robert Williams, John G. Primrose, J. R. Lane, Martha J. Lane and Benjamin C. Primrose of John G. Primrose, sold to William Allison, land in Bedford Co., TN, on west side of Alexander Creek. It being the place where the widow Primrose now lives. Bounded by Alexander Creek, Brandon family tract, Henry Dean, Tarpley's line, Harris' line, Ebenezer Alexander, Lander's line, and others. Wit: Robert Williams and E. P. Winn. Reg: 12 Jan 1850.

Page 294 - 26 Dec 1849. Agreement between William P. Sims and Thomas C. Ryall and E. J. Ryall. William P. Sims of Wilson Co., TN and Thomas C. Ryall and his wife Elizabeth Ryall of Bedford Co., TN, on 16 Oct 1845 executed an agreement in reference to the slaves therein mentioned. Whereas by the will of Walter Sims which is on record in Davidson Co., TN, Item No. 35, it is the will that at the death of his wife, all the slaves, shall be divided between his daughter Elizabeth and his son William R. The slave boy Jefferson which is now in the possession of his son William. Daughter Elizabeth died before the Testator, she had a daughter Elizabeth Scudder to inherit her mothers share. The said Elizabeth Scudder intermarried with Thomas C. Ryall. Mrs. Rebecca Sims wife of the Testator Walter Sims, deceased, is entitled to a life estate in the slaves. Mrs. Rebecca Sims has departed this life since the death of the agreement. Signed by William P. Sims, Thomas C. Ryall and Elizabeth L. Ryall. Reg: 15 Jan 1850.

Page 298 - 11 Jan 1850. G. F. M. Davis and wife to William Hime. Undivided interest in land. George F. M. Davis and Cyntha Davis his wife has inherited in remainder to take effect and be united with the possession after the death of Mary Ann Hime who has a life time estate in the same, in a tract of land in Bedford Co., TN, in District No. 23. Bounded by Joseph Hasting. Reg: 16 Jan 1850.

Page 303 - 30 Oct 1849. Jno. L. Neill and his wife Sally to Sarah Searcy and others. John L. Neill and Sally Neill his wife sold to their children Sarah C. Searcy, Mary C. Smith, Matty B. Hughs, Rachel E. Neill, John L. Neill, Jo., James F. Neill, Arabella R. Neill, Archer Neill, also their grandson Thomas V. Parish infant son of Thomas H. Parish and Virginia Parish and for love and affection for their children and their grandchild, conveyed to them the land conveyed to them or family of Mrs. Rachel Martin by deed devised in the will of Mrs. Rachel Martin, deceased, late of Bedford Co., TN. Wit: Willis Cannon and Daniel Stephens. Reg: 18 Jan 1850.

Page 309 - 24 Dec 1849. William Stewart to Alfred Campbell. Deed, undivided interest. William Stewart of Lawrence Co., Missouri, transferred and conveyed unto Alfred Campbell of Bedford Co., TN, all his interest in 50 acres in Bedford Co., on the waters of Big Flat Creek, it being the land purchased of Peter F. Brumfield, deceased, in 1841. Wit: James L. Cook and H. Haley. Reg: 24 Jan 1850.

Page 310 - 22 Aug 1842. Elizabeth P. Lavender and Acton Young to J. G. Henderson &c. Elizabeth P. Lavender of Williamson Co., TN and Acton Young of Bedford Co., TN sold to James G. Henderson, property also property that her father may have given her during his lifetime. Her father was Nelson Lavender. And whereas, a marriage is shortly intended to be had between Elizabeth P. Lavender and Acton Young, they conveyed to secure her property &c. Wit: Benjamin W. Morris and William Y. Bennett. Reg: 25 Jan 1850.

Page 315 - 29 Jan 1850. Smith Arnold to George W. Cunningham. Bill of Sale. Whereas previous to the intermarriage between Smith Arnold and my wife Elizabeth Arnold formerly Elizabeth Sharp, it is agreed that Smith Arnold would settle upon her and her children, a negro woman Mariah and her daughter, which belonged to Elizabeth at the time of their marriage, now sell slaves to George W. Cunningham. Wit: John T. Neil and Arey E. Kincaid. Reg: 5 Feb 1850.

Page 319 - 7 Feb 1850. John and Polly Lane to Thomas C. Whiteside and John Hart. Deed & Trust. John Lane and Polly Lane his wife sold to Thomas C. Whiteside and John Hart, all interest in land in Bedford Co., TN, on the Nashville, Murfreesboro and Shelbyville Turnlike Road, adjoining Whiteside & Hart and known in the lands of Amos McAdams, deceased, as Lot No. 5. Bounded by lands of John and Polly Lane in her right as a sister, heir and distributee of Daniel R. McAdams, deceased, in his estate. Reg: 11 Feb 1850.

Page 336 - 21 Feb 1850. John Little to J. M. Townsend. Deed, 137 acres. John Little sold to J. M. Townsend, land in Bedford Co., TN, in District No. 3. Bounded by Kinchen Stokes, Mrs. Robertson and others. The same being the tract purchased by R. T. Cannon at public sale, which Claiborn Bowles and wife, Malinda Calaway, Walker and wife Elizabeth, William M. Lee, James H. Lee, Green D. Lee, Lucy King, Mary Lee and Peter Lee, as the heirs at law of Peter Lee, deceased, property. The dower, allotted to Catharine Lee as widow of Peter Lee. Reg: 22 Feb 1850.

Page 339 - 25 Feb 1850. Jacob Whitesell to Joshua Hall. Deed. Jacob Whitesell sold Joshua Hall, land in Bedford Co., TN, in District No. 20. Bounded by Joshua Hall, Mary D. Whitesell, the same being a dower interest, Jeremiah Whitesell, James Coats, it being the same land which John Whitesell, Sr., died seized and possessed of and which is now by his widow Milly Whitesell, she having dower in land, and in which Jacob Whitesell and other heirs possess a remainder interest, subject to the dower of Milly Whitesell. Wit: James L. Scudder. Reg: 25 Feb 1850.

Page 340 - 12 Feb 1850. Nathan Evans to Sarah J. Goggins. Deed of Gift, 105 acres. Nathan Evans for love and affection for his daughter Sarah Jane Goggin, bequeathed to her a tract of land in bedford Co., TN, on waters of Flat Creek. Bounded by John Robinson, Winston Gill and the road leading from Shelbyville to Fayetteville. Reg: 26 Feb 1850.

Page 344 - 4 Feb 1850. Catharine R. Greer and A. J. Greer to James Stallings. 50 acres. Catharine R. Greer, Executrix, and A. Jackson Greer, Executor of the Last Will and Testament of Thomas Greer, Sr., late of Bedford Co., TN, sold to James Stalling, land in Bedford Co. (Will dated 25 Nov 1847) Will appointed Catharine R. Greer and A. Jackson Greer, Sr. The land sold located on headwaters of Powells Creek. Bounded by land deeded by Aaron Gambill to Malinda H. Doty and Preston L. Doty. Wit: James C. Gambill and B. Gambill. Reg: 6 Mar 1850.

Page 361 - 1 Dec 1849. L. and J. Harris to James Lawrance. Deed, undivided interest, 30 acres. Whereas Levi and John Harris has a fee simple interest remainder to take effect and be united with the possession after the death of Easther Harris who has a life estate in the same, sold to James Lawrance, land in Bedford Co., TN, in District No. 10. Bounded by John Jackson. Wit: William Taylor and William S. Knott. Reg: 15 Mar 1850.

Page 367 - 25 Dec 1845. Mary Bryant to Goodrum Davis. Deed, 38 acres. Mary Bryant sold to Goodrum Davis land in Bedford Co., TN, in District No. 9. Bounded by William Jones and Joseph Rushing. Signed by Hezekiah Bryant and Mary Bryant. Wit: John Jackson and Thomas W. Hill. Reg: 20 Mar 1850.

Page 371 - 25 Aug 1849. Francis Miller and others to Mariah E. Phillips. Deed, 50 acres. Francis Miller of Georgia, Jerry Arnold Miller and Candas Miller, Nancy A. Porter, Robert Lacy and his wife Amia Lacy of Bedford Co., TN, sold to Mariah E. Phillips of Bedford Co., land in Bedford Co., on north side of Duck River, on one of the branches of Butlers Creek. Borders the land of Mariah E. Phillips, John Overton and Whiteside, land William Hooser purchased of Peter Miller, deceased and now owned by Mariah E. Phillips. Signed by Jeremiah A. Miller, Francis Miller, Candas Miller, Nancy A. Porter, Robert Lacy, and Amia Lacy. Wit: William Young, Eliza C. Young and James Mullins. Reg: 21 Mar 1850.

Page 383 - 25 Feb 1850. George W. McQuiddy and others to John W. Williams. Deed. George W. McQuiddy and wife Emily M. formerly Emily M. Davis, William T. Edmundson and wife Sarah formerly Sarah A. Davis, W(iley). F. Stone and wife Mary R. Stone formerly Mary R. Davis, William H. Burt and wife Virginia P. formerly Virginia P. Davis, Nathan A. Yeargan and wife Charlotte S. formerly Charlotte S. Davis, for and consideration of the fact that Henry Davis in his lifetime sold a tract of land designated in the plan of the Town of Fairfield in Bedford Co., TN and known as Lot No. 4, sold to John W. Williams. Wit: T. H. Patterson and Hollen Collins. Emily M. McQuiddy appeared in Davidson County, TN to be examined. Charlotte S. Yeargan was examined in Rutherford Co., TN. Mary R. Stone appeared in Marshall Co., TN to be examined. T. H. Patterson and Hollen Collins appeared in Marshall Co., TN. William T. Edmundson appeared in Bedford Co., TN. Reg: 2 Apr 1850.

Page 392 - 11 Nov 1848. Garrett Phillips and others to Joshua White. Deed, 140 acres. Garrett Phillips of Bedford Co., TN, America White, Benjamin F. White and John H. White of Marshall Co., TN, sold to Joshua White of Marshall Co., TN, land in Bedford Co., on Dry Branch of Duck River. Bounded by lands of Lyles. Wit: L. Bullock, Martin Cleveland and Richard Hester. Reg: 4 Apr 1850.

Page 408 - 16 Apr 1850. Rebecca Loyd to William Loyd. Deed. Rebecca Loyd sold to William Loyd formerly owned by Joseph Loyd, deceased, consisting of a dower for life in the tract, for which William Loyd has paid for said land. Wit: Lewis Fowler and James P. Loyd. Reg: 8 Apr 1850.

Page 434 - 26 Apr 1850. Court Decree to John G. Walker. Deed, 53 acres. The Circuit Court in 1850, John Manning, Joseph Manning, Cloah Jane Manning, and Martha Ann Parthenia Manning, minors by their guardian John E. Sharber. Exparte. John G. Walker became purchaser of lands. Land bounded by the north side of Noahs Fork of Duck River, Dr. Norton's corner and Samuel Bird. Reg: 26 Apr 1850.

Page 438 - 30 Mar 1850. Minos C. Hodges and wife to Robert Cannon. Deed, 18 acres. Minos C. Hodges and his wife Elizabeth W. Hodges formerly Elizabeth W. McCuistion, sold to Robert Cannon, land in Bedford Co., TN, in District No. 6, on the south side of the south fork of Fall or Falling Creek. It being part of a tract of land formerly owned by Ebenezer Wilson ans sold by him to John Mason and by Mason's heirs to Nathan H. Schooler and by Schooler to Benjamin F. McCuistion who died seized and possessed and which said tract has been allotted and divided to the legatees of Benjamin F. McCuistion, deceased, into 6 lots, the number of distributees. Bounded by Fall Creek, near the old Nashville Road and Clement Cannon. Reg: 29 Apr 1850.

Page 440 - 25 Apr 1848. Nathaniel White and Robert E. Bradshaw to THomas Dryden and others. Deed, 3 acres, Trustees. Nathaniel White and Robert E. Bradshaw conveyed unto Thomas Dryden, Andrew Bain and William A. Morrison, Trustees of New Providence Church, for love and good will for the people of the New Providence Church and other Christian Denominations, for $1.00, a tract of land in Bedford Co., TN, in District No. 20, on headwaters of Sugar Creek, it being part of several tracts belonging to White and Bradshaw where they now live. Bounded by R. E. Bradshaw, Bluford Davidson, deceased line, and Nathaniel White. For the purpose of building a house for the use of the New Providence Church which is in connection with Shilo Presbyterian but to be free for the use of any other branch of the Presbyterian Church or any other Orthodox Denomination of Christians in good standing. When not occupied by said church, but should New Providence Church change its connection, it is still to have control of the said House of Worship. Wit: Samuel Hill and James C. Dryden. Reg: 30 Apr 1850.

Page 441 - 1 Sep 1849. David R. Adams and wife to George W. Woodward(Woodard). Deed, 73 acres. David R. Adams and Lisa (Elisa) Adams his wife formerly Lisa Woodard both of Wayne Co., TN, sold to George W. Woodward, their claim and interest in a tract of land in Bedford Co., TN, on waters of Flat Creek. It being in the name of Solomon Woodard, their interest being one tenth part, which descended to them as heirs at law of Solomon Woodard, deceased. Bounded by John Woodard, Hugh McCall, William Holston, John Casteele, and George W. Woodard. Wit: John McGee and Brad C. Lancaster. Reg: 30 Apr 1850.

DEED BOOK "SS" 1850 - 1851

Page 1 - 3 May 1850. W. W. Whitesell to J. Hall. Deed, undivided interest. William W. Whitesell sold to Joshua Hall, land in Bedford Co., TN, in District No. 20. Bounded by Joshua Hall, Mary D. Whitesell's dower tract, Jeremiah Whitesell, and James Coats. It being the same land which John Whitesell, Sr. died seized and possessed of and which is now held by his widow Emily Whitesell, she having dower and in which William W. Whitesell and other heirs possess a remainder interest subject to the dower of Milly Whitesell. Reg: 3 May 1850.

Page 15 - 12 Sep 1849. John Sutton and Rebecca J. Harris. Agreement. John Sutton and Rebecca J. Harris, agreed to let Rebecca Harris have a mulatto girl slave for six years from 12th March 1849 until 12 Mar 1854. Rebecca Harris is to feed and cloth her and have her to do necessary housework and not to remove her from Bedford Co., TN. Should Rebecca Harris should die before her time is out, she is to be returned to John Sutton of his daughter Narcissa Sutton. Wit: N. C. Harris and William Taylor. Reg: 14 May 1850.

Page 23 - 22 Dec 1849. Robert W. Locke and wife to George W. Brown. Deed, interest in estate. Robert W. Worke and wife Tabitha formerly Tabitha Brown sold to George W. Brown, all their interest in the estate of Shadrack Brown, deceased, being one tenth of the estate. Wit: J. W. Tilford and H. L. Brown. Reg: 24 May 1850.

Page 28 - 4 Apr 1850. Court Decree to Griffin Randol and others. Deed, 110+ acres. Jackson Wallis and others vs George W. Brown and others. Final Decree. It appears to the court that all the purchase money for the land has long been paid and is now ordered that all rights, title &c of the heirs of Thomas Brown, deceased, named in the pleadings in and to the land purchased of Griffin Randol be vested unto him. The said lot is located in District No. 19 of Bedford Co., TN. Bounded by Thomas Brown's improvements, Joseph Hall, John Woodward, top of a ridge, and James M. Brown and others. Reg: 29 May 1850.

Page 35 - 27 Apr 1850. Nancy Kelley to Peterson Grammer. Power of Attorney. Nancy Kelley formerly Nancy Noblett of Benton Co., Arkansas, appointed Peterson Grammer of Bedford Co., TN, her Attorney to demand, receive of and from the guardian of the estate belonging to John Jackson Noblett, deceased, all her estate both real and personal which he may have as guardian. Wit: John R. Davis and A. Whinery. Reg: 6 Jun 1850.

Page 38 - 7 Jun 1850. John Fisher and wife to John F. Thompson. Deed, 23 acres. John Fisher, Jr. and Christina Fisher his wife conveyed to John F. Thompson, land in Bedford Co., TN. Bounded by land of Thompson Thompson, deceased. Reg: 8 Jun 1850.

Pahe 41 - 5 Jun 1850. Martin Sims and wife to Joel Darnal. Deed, 138 acres. Martin Sims and Charlotte Sims his wife formerly Charlotte Bryans sold to Joel Darnal, land in Bedford Co., TN, in District No. 18. Bounded by John Baker now owned by Harry M. Oneal, Edward Bryans, near a grave yard, and Musgraves' line. Reg: 11 Jun 1850.

Page 51 - 16 Feb 1850. Isham Stammers to J. R. Haskins. Deed, 100 acres. Isham Stammers has interest in remainder to take effect after and be united with the possession after the death of Elizabeth Haskins who has a life estate in the same, in a tract of land in Bedford Co., TN, and District No. 11. Bounded by A. L. Adams, Daniel Collins, Susan Stammers, William Collins, and Jackson Nichols. Reg: 21 Jun 1850.

Page 53 - 6 Nov 1849. Samuel P. Balch and wife to Jordan C. Holt. Deed, undivided interest. Samuel P. Balch and wife Hannah Balch of Marshall Co., Mississippi, sold to Jordan C. Holt of Bedford Co., TN, all rights, title &c they have in and to the estate of Joshua Yates, deceased, late of Bedford Co., TN. Wit: William Chunn and Mathew Hearn. Reg: 23 Jun 1850.

Page 54 - 27 May 1850. Jones and others to Mariah Phillips. Deed, 40 acres. William B. Jones, Harrison Jones, John McLean, Martha E. formerly Martha E. Jones, and Robert Jones of Fayette Co., Georgia, being grandchildren and heirs of the estate of Peter Miller of Bedford Co., TN, sold to Mariah Phillips of Bedford Co., their entire interest in land formerly owned by Peter Miller, it being the land Peter Miller lived at the time of his death in bedford Co., TN, in District No. 3. Bounded by Mariah E. Phillips's land, William Hooser purchased of Peter Miller and now owned by Mariah E. Phillips, and the land Daniel Johnson sold to Mariah E. Phillips. Wit: Jared Irwin Whitaker and Jesse L. Blalock, Jr. Reg: 22 Jun 1850.

Page 56 - 8 Apr 1850. Thomas Thompson and others to John F. Thompson. Deed, 45 acres. Thomas Thompson, Michael B. Thompson, John M. Warner and wife Harriett R. formerly Harriett R. Thompson, sold to John F. Thompson, land in Bedford Co., TN, in District No. 8, being several lots. Bounded by tract laid off for dower to Christiana Thompson, land laid off and sold as the share of Jacob Thompson, deceased, and John Fisher. Another tract bounded by Jones Mill tract, on John Fisher's line and Phifer's line. Reg: 22 Jun 1850.

Page 57 - 21 Jun 1850. T. L. and J. D. Logan to David S. Logan. Deed, undivided interest, 46 acres. Tarlton L. Logan and John D. Logan sold to David S. Logan, their interest in an undivided tract of land belonging to the heirs of Benjamin Logan, deceased, in Bedford Co., TN, in District No. 19, on waters of Rock Creek. Bounded by William Farrar and Isom Oneal. Wit: Robert C. Dysart and William M. Alford. Reg: 24 Jun 1850.

Page 60 - 10 Dec 1849. Court Decree to James Harris for 48 acres. Jacob M. Parsons, Administrator of M. F. Parsons, deceased, and Zilphia Parsons. Exparte. Petition for dower. On 3 Sep 1849 offered for sale, negro woman. Zilphia Parsons' bid being highest, was purchaser. Land was offered for sale by Jacob M. Parsons, Administrator of Michael F. Parsons and Zilphia Parsons widow of Michael F. Parsons. Exparte. Land in the 8th District, bordering lands of George W. Parsons, widow of Zilphia Parsons' dower, Jacob M. Thompson, lands belonging to the estate of Thompson Thompson, deceased, Margaret Parsons' dower, N. Thompson, Zilphia Parson, and Martha and Margaret C., Jacob T., George W., John W., and Sarah Parsons, the children of Michael F. Parsons, deceased. James Harris being the highest bidder. Reg: 26 Jun 1850.

Page 63 - 15 Jun 1850. John B. Johnson to Trustees of Ebenezer Church. Deed. John B. Johnson conveyed unto Trustees of Ebenezer Meeting House, being a place of Public Worship of a portion of the Methodist Episcopal Church, South, land in Bedford Co., TN, it being a part of the tract of land John B. Johnson now lives. Borders lands of Mrs. Letitia Cannon or her children. Trustees Nimrod Burrow, D. R. Jackson, William B. Snell, Herrod F. Holt, and Robert D. Miller. Reg: 29 Jun 1850.

Page 64 - 14 Dec 1849. Harbert Thorne to A. B. Gaunt. Power of Attorney. Harbert Thorne of Wayne Co., TN, appointed Absalom B. Gaunt of Wayne Co., TN, his Power of Attorney, to sell land in Bedford Co., TN, on Sinking Creek, it being the tract of land on which Harbert Thorne's father William Thorne lived up to the time of his death. Reg: 1 Jul 1850.

Page 71 - -- --- 1848. John Nelson and others to Rail Road Company. Right of Way. The undersigned owners of real estate situated in State of Tennessee, do hereby bind ourselves, our heirs and assignees, in consideration of the benefits to accord to us from the construction of the Nashville and Chattanooga Railroad over our lands, to execute to the said Nashville and Chattanooga Railroad Company. Such titles as we may now have, or may hereafter acquire to the amount of land required by the Charter of said Company to build the said Railroad upon, as soon as the road shall have been permanently located upon any of our lands within said State. In witness whereof we have hereunto set our hands and seal this year of our Lord, 1848.

DEED BOOK "SS"

Signature of land owners: John Nelson, N. Sugg, Cintha Anne MtGomery(Montgomery), F. Shofner, Gabriel Shofner, Robert Puryear, Isaac Troxler, N. Lasater, L. Holt, D. Hickerson, John Keck, John Jamerson, Isaac Barnett, Zephaniah Weaver, Moses Ayres, Amos Ladd, John J. Kelton, Landerville Montgomery, Susan Montgomery and Esther Montgomery. Wit: William J. Osborne and Blan Maupin. Reg: 9 Jul 1850.

Page 72 - 5 Jul 1850. Jacob Fisher to Zelphia Parsons. Bill of Sale. For love and affection for his niece Zelphia Parsons and her children, Martha Ann Parsons, Margaret Christine Parsons, Jacob F. Parsons, George W. Parsons, John T. Parsons and Sarah Elizabeth Parsons, conveyed unto them a negro woman Nicey. Reg: 9 Jul 1850.

Page 76 - 13 Jul 1850. William Eoff, Sr. to William Eoff, Jr. Deed of Gift. For love and affection for his son William Eoff, Jr., William Eoff, Sr. conveyed unto him negroes. Reg: 13 Jul 1850.

Page 79 - 9 Jul 1850. I. N. and E. Rone and wives to Nicholas Burns. Deed. Isaac N. and his wife Eliza Jane Rone and Ezekial Rone and his wife Lucinda Rone, sold to Nicholas Burns, land in Bedford Co., TN, on head waters of Sugar Creek, a tract contains about 40 acres and was conveyed to William Stagg by Daniel Saling by deed, dated 12 Oct 1819, the interest half conveyed is two sixths of all the lands of which said William Stagg died seized and possessed in Bedford Co., TN, being the share of the said Eliza Jane and Lucinda in said land which descended from their father William Stagg. Land sold to Nicholas Burns. Reg: 22 Aug 1850.

Page 80 - 12 Nov 1849. Allison Cox and wife to Thomas Cox. Power of Attorney. State of Mississippi, County of Tippah. Allison Cox and Catharine Cox his wife appointed Thomas Cox of Bedford Co., TN, their Attorney, to sell their interest in the dower lands of Rebecca Jones of Bedford Co., TN, being part of the lands that belonged to Charles Jones, now deceased. Reg: 24 Jul 1850.

Page 82 - 24 May 1850. Thomas Musgraves to the heirs of Richard Musgraves. Deed, 9½ acres. Thomas Musgraves for love and affection for the heirs of Richard Musgraves, viz, William Everet Musgraves, James Raford Musgraves, and Nancy Richard Musgraves, conveyed unto them his tract of land in Bedford Co., TN, in District No. 18, it being a part of the sixth lot of school land lying on the waters of Sinking Creek. Wit: Jacob B. Anderson and Allen S. Musgraves. Reg: 24 Jul 1850.

Page 87 - -- Jan 1850. Joseph Watson and wife to Eliza A. Coleman. Deed, undivided interest, 103 acres. Joseph Watson and wife Tacy Watson of Pike Co., Arkansas, sold to Eliza A. Coleman formerly Eliza A. McCuistion, widow of John C. McCuistion, deceased, and remainder interest to Mary Ann Amanda America McCuistion, part of the dower of Rebecca Jones widow of Charles Jones, deceased, in the tract which Charles Jones died seized and possessed of, land in Bedford Co., TN, on waters of Flat Creek, in District No. 24. Bounded by William Boone, Anthony Floyd, David Floyd, Abram Reagor and Abram Shook. Wit: John Bassey and THomas Fawcette. Reg: 30 Jul 1850.

Page 89 - 3 Aug 1850. Robert G. Morgan to Mitchell E. W. Dunaway. Deed, 104 acres. Robert G. Morgan has a fee simple interest to take effect and united with his possession after the death of Rebeka L. Morgan who has a life estate in the same, in a tract of land in Bedford Co., TN, in District No. 23. Land borders lands of Robert Morgan and Mrs. L. Cannon's tract. Reg: 3 Aug 1850.

Page 91 - (no date). William Dryden and others to William Gammill. Deed, 233 acres. The heirs of Jonathan Dryden, deceased, late of Bedford Co., TN, to wit, William Dryden, David Dryden, Samuel Dryden, Jonathan B. Dryden, Samuel Walker and his wife Nancy formerly Nancy Dryden, Andrew Gray and his wife Màry formerly Maru Dryden of County of (blank), State of Illinois, and John G. Morrison and his wife Eliza N. formerly Eliza N. Dryden of Coles Co., Illinois, and Joseph Dickson in right of his wife Rebecca formerly Rebecca Dryden, and Thomas Dryden and James E. Bradshaw and his wife Barbara A. formerly Barbara A. Dryden of Bedford Co., TN, it being the land held by Jonathan Dryden at the time of his death, containing several grants. Reg: 6 Aug 1850.

Page 97 - 3 Aug 1850. Rebecca Morgan to M. E. W. Dunaway. Deed, 104 acres. Whereas by the will of Robert Morgan, Rebecca Morgan is lawful seized of a life estate in a tract of land in Bedford Co., TN, in District No. 23. Bordered by the original tract of Robert Morgan, sold to M. E. W. Dunaway said land. Reg: 8 Aug 1850.

Page 101 - 7 Mar 1850. Jas. Ogilvie and others to Jennings Moore. Deed, 60 acres. We, James Ogilvie and Richard C. Ogilvie, Kimbrough Allison and his wife Sarah Allison, Leonard Bullock and his wife Ann Bullock, Augustine Wilson and his wife Nancy Wilson, Briant Landis and his wife Margaret Landis, Milton R. Rushing and his wife Tabitha Rushing, sold to Jennings Moore, land in Bedford Co., TN, in District No. 11. Bounded by widow Covington and Thomas Allison. Signed by James Ogilvie, R. C. Ogilvie, Milton R. Rushing, Tabitha Rushing, K. Allison, Sarah Allison, A. Wilson, Nancy Wilson, L. Bullock, Ann Bullock, Briant Landis and Margaret Landis. Wit: E. A. Wilson, W. E. Jeffries and J. R. Stem. Reg: 9 Aug 1850.

Page 102 - 7 Mar 1850. James Ogilvie and others to Briant Landis. Deed, 195 acres. We, James Ogilvie and Richard C. Ogilvie, Kimbrough Allison and his wife Sarah Allison, Leonard Bullock and his wife Ann Bullock, Augustine Wilson and his wife Nancy Wilson, Milton R. Rushing and his wife Tabitha Rushing, sold unto Briant Landis, land in Bedford Co., TN, in District No. 11. Bounded by widow Ogilvie's dower, the bank of Clems Creek, Wilson's corner, William A. Shaw, A. B. Moon, Thomas Jeffries, Henry Clark and widow Covington's dower. Wit: J. R. Stem and William E. Jeffries. Reg: 9 Aug 1850.

Page 103 - 7 Mar 1850. James Ogilvie and others to Richard C. Ogilvie. Deed, 190 acres. We, James Ogilvie, Kimbrough Allison and his wife Sarah Allison, Leonard Bullock and his wife Ann Bullock, Augustine Wilson and his wife Nancy Wilson, Briant Landis and his wife Margaret Landis, Milton R. Rushing and his wife Tabitha Rushing, sold unto Richard C. Ogilvie, land in Bedford Co., TN. Borders lands of Widow Covington, Jennings Moore, A. Wilson and Bryant Landis, the land being the land on which Richard C. Ogilvie now lives. Reg: 9 Aug 1850.

Page 112 - 12 Aug 1850. G. B. Sharp to A. E. Mullins. Deed, 99 acres. G. B. Sharp sold to A. E. Mullins, land in Bedford Co., TN, on Duck River, it being the tract or lot of land allotted and set apart to Mary McGuire in the division of lands of William Ditto, deceased, known as Lot No. 3, with the exception of about 22 acres heretofore allotted to Archibald Prewitt and wife and A. E. Mullins and his wife. Reg: 16 Aug 1850.

Page 112 - 15 Dec 1845. William C. Hix to J. R. Hix. Deed, 103 acres. William C. Hix sold to Joshua R. Hix, all his interest in land in Bedford Co., TN, on waters of Big Flat Creek. It being the tract on which William C. and Joshua R. and Sally Hix now lives, being the lands bequeathed to William C. and Joshua R. at the death or marriage of their mother Sally Hix by their father William Hix, deceased. Wit: J. N. Hix and K. M. Pybas. Reg: 16 Aug 1850.

Page 113 - 27 Jul 1849. Jefferson Wilson and others to Jno. C. Wilson. Bill of Sale. We, Jefferson Wilson, William Wilson, William M. Shaw in rite of his wife Mahala, and Joseph Anderson in rite of his wife Lucinda, Augustine Wilson, sold to Jno. C. Wilson, two negroes, Milley and her son Sid. The slave descended to Jefferson and others by the Last Will and Testament of John Wilson, deceased, of Orange Co., NC. Wit: Alex. B. Moon and John H. Shaw. Reg: 16 Aug 1850.

Page 121 - 15 Aug 1850. John M. Wray to Jones Floyd. Deed, 77 acres. John M. Wray sold to Jones Floyd, land in Bedford Co., TN, in District No. 10, it being the part or portion of land that descended to John M. Wray from his father John Wray, deceased. Bounded by James Smith, Samuel Wray, Thomas Martin and wife, H. Pope, and James Wray. Wit: Daniel D. Russell and Chesley Williams. Reg: 27 Aug 1850.

Page 123 - 21 Aug 1850. Bazeel Green and wife to Daniel Stephens. Deed. Bazeel Green and Mary C. Green his wife formerly Mary C. Adcock, sold Daniel Stephens, land in Bedford Co., TN, in District No. 2, on the ridge dividing the waters of Straight Creek and Knobb Creek. Bounded by lands of heirs of Ephraim B. Galegles, and passes through the farm of Jos. Keller. The land is same that Thomas Drake purchased of Isaac Holmes in 1827, and which agreeable to the Last Will and Testament of Thomas Drake is devised to them and Martha Taylor formerly Martha Drake, and in which said land Catharine Drake, widow of Thomas Drake, has a dower of 40 acres, during her lifetime. Reg: 27 Aug 1850.

Page 133 - 9 Sep 1850. Warren Landers and wife to R. T. Landers. Deed, undivided interest. We, Rilday Landers formerly Rilda Deason, and Warren Landers, sold to R. T. Landers their eleventh part of the lands of John Deason, deceased, except their interest in the part of land as may be assigned to Sarah Deason for her dower. The land in Bedford Co., TN, in District No. 5. Reg: 17 Sep 1850.

Page 134 - 19 Sep 1850. James A. Lentz to Benjamin Earnhart. Deed, 70 acres. James A. Lentz sold to Benjamin Earnhart, the 52 acres of land, subject to the life estate of James A. Lentz's mother, Mrs. Mary Lentz, which was willed to James A. Lentz by his father, at the death of James's mother, the land in Bedford Co., TN, in District No. 18 and on which Mary Lentz now lives. Also, another tract of land, adjoining the above tract and containing about 18 acres and formerly owned by Alsey Freeman, also, a small island, containing 2 or 3 acres in the river below the tract of land, which he entered and which he has a grant. Reg: 20 Sep 1850.

Page 140 - -- Aug 1850. Court Decree to Thurza Sheppard and others. John T. Neil, Administrator of Lewis Sheppard, deceased vs the widow and heirs of Lewis Sheppard, deceased, bill for the sale of land and dower. Thurza Sheppard became the purchaser of Lot No. 53 out of which the widow's dower had been assigned her. The Lot is in Shelbyville. Reg: 26 Sep 1850.

Page 140 (First page numbered 140) - 18 Jul 1850. Newton B. Cummings to Trustees of Flat Creek Academy. Deed. Newton B. Cummings sold for $50.00 to the Trustees, Thomas Dean, Elisha Bobo, W. J. Gordon, W. W. Coldwell, and Isaac Shook, of Flat Creek Academy, land in Bedford Co., TN, on waters of Big Flat Creek. Bounded by Barrett Stephens, N. B. Cummings, and Isaac Shook. Includes free use of N. B. Cumming's spout spring for the benefit of the Academy. Wit: Robert H. Terry and Nimrod Burrow. Reg: 26 Sep 1850.

Page 140 (Second page numbered 140) - 22 Mar 1848. Freeman Burrow and Elenor Austin to Jerrel Burrow. Deed, undivided interest. We, Nelly Austin of Lincoln Co., TN, Freeman Burrow of Fayette Co., TN, sold to Jerrel Burrow, land in Bedford Co., TN, on waters of Flat Creek, where our mother Mary Burrow now lives, it being left to her, during her natural life by our father William Burrow, deceased. Wit: William Word and Pearce Wilhoite, Thomas Ramsey and M. C. Jones. Signed by Freeman Burrow and Elenor Austin. Reg: 26 Sep 1850.

Page 147 - 7 Aug 1847. Abel F. Price to Abel R. Jackson. Power of Attorney. Abel F. Price of Memphis, TN sold to Abel R. Jackson of Howard Co., Missouri, appointed Abel R. Jackson, his Attorney, to sell and collect from his lands in Bedford Co., TN. The land owned by the late James Staton at the time of his death, lying on Straight Creek. James Staton, deceased, who was the grandfather of Abel F. Price. Reg: 3 Oct 1850.

Page 148 - 30 Nov 1849. Abel R. Jackson, Attorney to Prior M. Jackson. Deed. Abel F. Price of Memphis, TN by his Attorney Abel R. Jackson of Howard Co., Missouri, sold to Prior M. Jackson of Howard Co., Missouri, the land in the estate of James Staton, deceased, who died in Bedford Co., TN. James Staton was the grandfather of Abel F. Price. Land on Straight Creek. Reg: 3 Oct 1850.

Page 148 - 27 Sep 1850. Prior M. Jackson and wife to Jas. C. Word and others. Deed. Prior M. Jackson and wife Martha E. of Howard Co., Missouri, sold to James C. Word, James P. Finch and Elnathan Stephens, land in Bedford Co., TN. Bounded by Hannah, Crittendon's Spring, James P. Finch, Mrs. Staton, and John S. Woods. Martha Jackson is granddaughter of James Staton and Martha Staton. Abel F. Price also being a grandson of James and Martha Staton*(*could be Slaton). Abel F. Price's mother is dead but left three children of which Abel F. Price is one. Reg: 4 Oct 1850.

DEED BOOK "SS"

Page 154 - -- Sep 1850. Simpson Misenheimer and wife Tempy to J. A. Blakemore. Deed. Simpson Misenheimer and wife Tempy formerly Tempy Keele, sold to J. A. Blakemore, land in Bedford Co., TN, on waters of Falling Creek. Adjoining lands of Samuel Doak, Daniel Wadley and James G. Neeley, lands of the heirs of John Orr, deceased, heirs of Thomas P. Burns. The land being on which the widow Nancy A. Keele now lives, their interest being one sixth part. Reg: 7 Oct 1850.

Page 154 - 20 Oct 1848. Elizabeth Hufman to George and Alfred Hufman. Deed, personal property. Elizabeth Hufman for love and affection for her two sons George and Alfred Hufman, personal property. Elizabeth Hufman of Coffee Co., TN and George and Alfred Hufman of Bedford Co., TN. She conveyed unto her two sons personal property. Wit: Isaac Barnett and S. D. Bates. Reg: 7 Oct 1850.

Page 156 - 7 Oct 1850. John E. Scruggs to Elizabeth Sharp. Deed of Gift. John E. Scruggs conveyed to Elizabeth Sharp wife of William H. Sharp, for love and affection, for her beloved daughter Elizabeth who has heretofore intermarried with William H. Sharp, a negro girl Corry. Wit: Mede G. Haile and Orville Muse. Reg: 7 Oct 1850.

Page 156 - 26 Sep 1850. W. J. Culverhouse and wife to James G. Neeley. Deed, undivided interest. William J. Culverhouse and Frances his wife, sold to James G. Neeley their undivided interest in land in Bedford Co., TN, on the waters of Falling Creek. Bounded by lands of the widow and heirs of John Orr, deceased, C. D. Steele, or Samuel Doak, Daniel Wadley and said Neeley. The land being a part of a tract of land on which Nancy Keele now lives, of 60 acres. Reg: 7 Oct 1850.

Page 168 - 14 Oct 1850. James A. Loyd and wife to Jonathan J. Cooper. Deed, 85 acres. James A. Loyd and Mary M. Loyd his wife sold to Jonathan J. Cooper, their interest in a tract of land that John Kent, deceased, owned, being in Bedford Co., TN, in District No. 5. Bounded by Issah Webbs. Reg: 18 Oct 1850.

Page 169 - 10 Oct 1850. Plat of Yell land. E. Bomar had surveyed and marked the two tracts of land on which his sons, William and John, live. Land in bedford Co., TN. Borders lands of Isaac West, Yell's land, E. M. B. Norville, Thomas Norville, Sam Phillips and the Shelbyville and McMinnville Road. Reg: 23 Oct 1850.

Page 171 - 15 Oct 1850. James W. Golerthun to Mrs. Sarah Golerthun. Deed, 20 acres and 7 acres. James W. Golerthun sold to Mrs. Sarah Golerthun, his claim and interest in land set apart to the heirs of John W. Golerthun, deceased, in Bedford Co., TN, in District No. 3. Bounded by John S. Arnold, D. H. Williams, A. Pruitt. Also, a 7 acre tract granted to John W. Golerthun, deceased, by the State of Tennessee, in Bedford Co., in District No. 3. Borders A. Sharp, J. S. Arnold, and A. Pruitt. Wit: A. Pruitt and W. W. Payne. Reg: 25 Oct 1850.

Page 172 - 28 Oct 1850. Synthia Haggard to Williamson Haggard. Deed. Cynthia Haggard sold to Williamson Haggard, all her claim and interest in the estate, both real and personal set forth in the Last Will and Testament of Samuel Haggard, deceased, it being one seventh part of the interest of one full share or heir of the estate. Wit: Robert Mathews and Samuel W. Haggard. Reg: 29 Oct 1850.

Page 173 - 30 Sep 1850. Catharine R. and A. J. Greer to Isom Oneal. Deed, 100 acres. Catharine R. Greer and A. Jackson Greer, Executors of the Last Will and Testament of Thomas Greer, Sr., late of Bedford Co., TN, sold to Isom Oneal of Marshall Co., TN, the land in Bedford Co. Will dated 25 Nov 1847. Land borders lands of James Null, Sr., Gaunt's heirs, David Dryden, Henderson's line, dividing the spring now used by Andrew Neill. Reg: 29 Oct 1850.

Page 178 - 4 Nov 1850. William Gabbert to Nancy and Elizabeth Gabbert. Deed, 145 acres. William Gabbert for love and affection for his two daughters, Nancy and Elizabeth Gabbert, conveyed unto them his tract of land in Bedford Co., TN, in District No. 20. Bounded by Sugar Creek. Wit: James H. Neil and R. J. Greer. Reg: 5 Nov 1850.

Page 182 - April Term 1850. Circuit Court. William O. Pepper and wife Sophia A. and Barkley M. Tillman and wife Elizabeth F. Exparte. The land being in Haywood Co., TN, 318½ acres, and Town Lot and parts of Town Lots in Shelbyville, Bedford Co., TN. Reg: 14 Nov 1850.

Page 184 - 9 Nov 1850. James Carlile to George Brown and wife. Deed, 112 acres. James Carlile sold to George Brown and Nancy Brown his wife, land in Bedford Co., TN, on waters of Sugar Creek, in District No. 20. Bounded by William Gammil, Thomas and Alexander Greer, Joshua Holt. Wit: R. J. Greer. Reg: 15 Nov 1850.

Page 185 - 9 Nov 1850. George Brown and wife to James Carlile. Deed, 82 acres. George Brown and Nancy Brown his wife, sold to James Carlile, land in bedford Co., TN, on Sugar Creek, in District No. 20. Bounded by Sugar Creek. Reg: 15 Nov 1850.

Page 187 - 15 Nov 1850. George W. Smith and wife to James H. Harrison. Deed, undivided interest. Whereas by descent from Jonathan Harrison, deceased, William T. Harrison, Cleveland L. Harrison, Thomas F. Harrison, James H. Harrison, Harrison Smith and his wife Polly Ann Smith, Susanah E. Harrison, and George W. Smith and his wife Margaret P. Smith, received title to an undivided interest in land in Bedford Co., TN, on waters of Rock and Sinking Creeks, sold to James H. Harrison, said land. Bounded by Thomas W. Harper, James Dillard, Nathaniel Porter, and James W. Wallace. The land being the land purchased of Lewis Medlin of Jonathan Harrison, deceased. Reg: 16 Nov 1850.

Page 188 - 24 Jun 1850. T. B. Mosley, Sr. to T. B. Mosley, Jr. Deed, 52½ acres. THomas B. Mosley, Sr. for love and affection for his son THomas B. Mosley, Jr., conveyed unto him, land in Bedford Co., TN, in District No. 4. Bounded by Orville Muse, the Wartrace Fork of Duck River, Thomas B. Mosley, Jr. Wit: William F. Bradford and Rebecca M. Sercia(Searcy). Reg: 21 Nov 1850.

Page 196 - 26 Nov 1850. C. R. and A. J. Greer to Richard Anderson. Deed, 104 acres. Catharine R. Greer, Executrix, and

A. Jackson Greer, Executor of the Last Will and Testament, dated 25 Nov 1847, of Thomas Greer, Sr., late of Bedford Co., TN, sold to Richard Anderson, land in Bedford Co., on waters of Little Sinking Creek. Bounded by Samuel and Richard Anderson, including the place whereon Elijah Anderson formerly lived. Reg: 26 Nov 1850.

Page 197 - 29 Dec 1842. John Byler and others to Noah Putnam. Deed, 43 acres. John Byler, William L. Byler, Jacob Byler, James T. Byler, John M. Maxwell guardian to the minor heirs, Elvira his wife, Isaac D. Maxwell guardian to the minor heirs of his wife Nancy, THomas Byler the right of his wife Mary T. and James P. Smith the right of his wife Orpha D., sold unto Noah Putnam, land in Bedford Co., TN, in District No. 10. Bounded by John Byler, the Murfreesboro Road, William Taylor, Thomas P. Carlton, and the Nashville Road. Wit: E. D. Rushing and W. B. Marchant. Reg: 26 Nov 1850.

Page 198 - 19 Nov 1850. A. S. Riggs to James Dixon. Deed, 85½ acres. Whereas by descent from David Riggs, Adam S. Riggs obtained land in Bedford Co., TN, in District No. 21 and sold to James Dixon. Land bounded by James Dixon, Newton Cummings, Rev. William J. Garrett, Henry Cannon, and Richard Phillips. Wit: R. Dixon and C. C. Dixon. Reg: 26 Nov 1850.

Page 200 - 2 Nov 1850. Thomas Allison to Kimbrough T. Allison. Deed, 82 acres. Thomas Allison bequeathed to his son Kimbrough T. Allison as part of his legacy in his estate in Bedford Co., TN, in District No. 11, on Clems Creek. Bounded by David Ozment. Wit: R. M. Fain, John D. Cooper and Lemuel Call. Reg: 29 Nov 1850.

Page 218 - 2 Dec 1850. Jarrel J. Burrow to Banks A. Burrow. Deed, undivided interest. Jarrel J. Burrow sold unto Banks A. Burrow, land in Bedford Co., TN, on waters of Flat Creek, whereon their mother Mary Burrow now lives. Said land being left to her during her natural life by their father William Burrow, deceased. The land being secured by four grants from State of Tennessee, No. 19880 for 5 acres, No. 19881 for 10 acres, No. 19884 for 15 acres, and No. 19885 for 60 acres, also one deed from Phillip Burrow for 19+ acres. All the above land known as property of William Burrow, deceased. Reg: 4 Dec 1850.

Page 223 - 25 May 1850. E. B. and R. P. Throgmorton to E. Stephens. Deed. Edward and Robert P. Throgmorton by Attorney Daniel Stephens, Executors of Robert P. Throgmorton, late of Bedford Co., TN, deceased, sold to Elnathan Stephens, that whereas the late R. Throgmorton died seized and possessed of land in Bedford Co., lying adjoining each other, which land, by his Last Will and Testament directed his Executors to sell for the benefits of his heirs. James L. Armstrong the purchaser. Armstrong on 11 Nov 1849, sold to Elnathan Stephens, land in Bedford Co., on waters of Straight Creek. Wit: John T. Davis and H. J. H. Norville. Reg: 10 Dec 1850.

Page 226 - 4 Dec 1850. Andrew Erwin to William J. Webster. Deed, 250 acres. Andrew Erwin sold to William J. Webster, as Trustee for Mary J. Erwin formerly Mary J. Camp by virtue of a marriage contract entered into between Andrew Erwin and Mary J. Camp on 24th Nov 1847. Recorded in Register's Office of Madison Co., Alabama, land in Bedford Co., TN, between the

Garrison and Barren Forks of Duck River, about two to three miles above the junction of said stream, being part of the tract commonly known as the brick house tract. Bounded by John Q. Davidson, T. G. W. Wright, Warner Wallace, Archibald Murphey, Anne Hitchcock and William Pepper. Wit: Jno. R. Eakin and William T. Myers. Reg: 10 Dec 1850.

Page 242 - 16 Dec 1850. William Young to Elizabeth P. Young. Deed of Gift. William Young for love and affection for Elizabeth Young wife of my brother Acton Young, and her children, he gives to James G. Henderson of Williamson Co., TN, the property purchased from Acton Young on 2 March last. Wit: J. W. Dickerson, J. P. Steele and Edmund Cooper. Reg: 17 Dec 1850.

Page 245 - 30 Nov 1850. Robert Temple and others to Forbes, Wiggins &c. Deed, 150 acres. Robert H. Temple, W. Preston Temple, R. H. Powel and his wife Jane T. Powel formerly Jane T. Temple, and William J. Stegall and his wife H. Malvina Stegall formerly Malvina Temple, sold to Riley H. Forbes, Harbert Wiggins and John H. Oneal, land in Bedford Co., TN, in District No. 18, it being land of Dempsey P. Temple. Wit: Volney H. Steele, E. J. Graham and Sam H. Whitthorn. Reg: 2 Dec 1850.

Page 253 - 25 Dec 1850. James T. Cunningham to William Brown. Deed, 103 acres. James T. Cunning has a fee simple interest in remainder to take effect and be united with the possession of the death of Martha Cunningham who has a life estate in the same, in a tract of land in Bedford Co., TN, in District No. 4. Bounded by the mouth of Anderson Creek, William Waite, the road leading from Davis Mill to Shelbyville, Norville's line, and Wartrace Fork. Wit: James L. Scudder and W. H. Wisener. Reg: 25 Dec 1850.

Page 258 - 17 Dec 1850. G. R. Bowers and wife to William Brown. Deed. Giles R. Bowers and Mary Ann Bowers formerly Mary Ann Cunningham, sold to William Brown, all their interest in land, it being the tract on which Richard Cunningham resided at the time of his death, in Bedford Co., TN. Bounded by the mouth of Alexanders Creek, William Waite, lands of Richard Cunningham, the road leading from Davis Mill to Shelbyville, Norville's line and Wartrace Fork. Their interest in the land being a lien upon the same for $100.00, in trade or cash, by James T. Cunningham after the death of the widow of said Richard Cunningham, deceased. Reg: 2 Jan 1851.

Page 261 - 25 Feb 1850. Joel A. Wallis to Hiram C. Kinnard. Deed, undivided interest. Joel A. Wallis sold to Hiram C. Kinnard land known as the dowry formerly Cynthia Cathy now Cynthia Wallis, which dowry was transferred by her husband Alfred Y. Wallis, his interest in her dowry to Allen Wallis in a Deed of Trust in 1842 and by Public Sale to Joel A. Wallis. The land in Bedford Co., TN. Bounded by heirs of William Sharp and A. Mullins, and Mrs. Eakin. Wit: Samuel Phillips and David Blessing. Reg: 4 Jan 1851.

Page 268 - 2 Jan 1851. Jesse W. Brown and wife to Kenneth Pybas. Deed, 210 acres. Jesse W. Brown and Martha Brown his wife formerly Martha Yeats, daughter of Joshua Yeats, deceased, sold to Kenneth M. Pybas, land in Bedford Co., TN, in District No. 21. Bounded by Jacob Greer, Michael Holt, Jordan C. Holt, W. P. Goodwin. The land being the tract of land that Joshua Yeats died possessed and on which he resided at the time of his death and by his Last Will and Testament he devised in part to his wife during her lifetime or widowhood and to her children, it being the interest of Martha Brown as one of his children. Reg: 7 Jan 1851.

Page 270 - 6 Jan 1851. Jordan C. Holt, Sr. to Jordan C. Holt, Jr. Deed, 97 acres. Jordan C. Holt for love and affection for Jordan C. Holt, Jr., conveyed land in Bedford Co., TN, in District No. 22. Bounded by a ridge between Flat Creek and Sugar Creek, McKisick's and McCamey's lines, Joshua Holt, Nathan Evans, and the Fayetteville Highway. Reg: 7 Jan 1851.

Page 271 - 26 Dec 1850. Elizabeth Rogers and others to James R. Haskins. Deed, 58 acres. Elizabeth Rogers, David Rogers and Samuel C. Rogers sold to James R. Haskins, land in Bedford Co., TN and in Marshall Co., TN, in District No. 11 in Bedford Co., and in District No. 8 in Marshall Co., TN. Bounded by George Tillman and graves old north border line. Wit: Jas. Anderson and Isham Stammer. Reg: 7 Jan 1851.

Page 272 - 7 Jan 1851. G. W. Thompson to Sarah E. Thompson. Deed of Gift. George W. Thompson for love and affection for his niece Sarah Emma Thompson, daughter of Michael F. Thompson and Martha Thompson, conveyed unto her personal property. Wit: John T. Neil and James Davis. Reg: 7 Jan 1851.

Page 283 - 30 Dec 1850. Thomas Jackson and others to Abner C. Potts. Deed, 102 acres. We, Thomas Jackson, Nathan Jackson, John C. Jackson and by N. Jackson agent for Francis Johnson, sold to Abner C. Potts, land in Bedford Co., TN, in District No. 11. Bounded by the bank of North Fork, Wheeler's line, Old school land, Reeves' line and Williams' line. Wit: F. H. Jackson and James E. Arnold. Reg: 9 Jan 1851.

Page 288 - 11 Jan 1851. Joseph Hastings to Joharriet and William Woosley. Deed of Gift, 54½ acres. Joseph Hastings for love and affection for his daughter Joharriet Woosley and her husband William Woosley and for their support, give and donate to them, land in bedford Co., TN, in District No. 23. Bounded by Robert McFarlin, F. A. Ross and Baker's Spring. Reg: 13 Jan 1851.

Page 292 - 16 Jan 1851. Andrew N. Harper to James W. Wallace. Deed in Trust. Andrew N. Harper sold unto James W. Wallace, both real and personal interest in Andrew N. Harper's father's estate, Samuel Harper, deceased. Wit: THomas J. Bartley and B. B. Harper. Reg: 16 Jan 1851.

Page 293 - 2 Dec 1850. Thomas Nash to Joannah Nash. Power of Attorney. Thomas Nash of Washington Co., texas, appointed Joannah Nash of Bedford Co., TN, his Attorney to sell his lands in Bedford Co., TN. Wit: Patrick Gorman and John C. Tucker. Reg: (no date).

Page 295 - 16 Jan 1851. Thomas and Sarah Holland to William Gosling. Deed, 5½ acres. Thomas Holland, Sr. did on 22 Jan 1849, conveyed unto William Galbreath and Nathan Ivy as Trustees, both real and personal property. The Trustees for Thomas Holland and wife during their lives, sold to William Gosling, land in Bedford Co., TN. Bounded by William Gosling, Henry

Davis, and R. Mathews. Wit: B. A. Nelson and James M. (blank). Reg: 18 Jan 1851.

Page 298 - 20 Jan 1851. James Davis and others to Nelson Gabbart. Deed, 320 acres. We, James Davis, Daniel Davis, Newsom THompson, 3rd and wife Catharine Thompson formerly Catharine Davis, and John Davis, sold to Nelson Gabbart, land in Bedford Co., TN, in District No. 19. Bounded by A. Helton. Another tract. Another tract bounded by Francis Smith and J. H. Smith sold to James Davis and Zachariah Davis. Reg: 21 Jan 1851.

Page 299 - 20 Jan 1851. James Davis and others to Newcum Thompson, 3rd. Deed, 100 acres. James Davis, Daniel Davis and John Davis, sold Newcum Thompson, 3rd, their undivided interest in land in bedford Co., TN, in District No. 19. Borders Lewis Medlin and W. Brown. Reg: 23 Jan 1851.

Page 300 - 10 Nov 1849. W. P. Bobo and others to Samuel Bobo. Deed, 108½ acres. Thomas E. Simpson and Salina his wife, Nathan A. Hodges and Elizabeth his wife, Lucretia J. Bobo, Burrell Bobo and Washington P. Bobo, sold to Samuel Bobo, all of Bedford and Lincoln Counties, TN, all their interest in land in Bedford Co., in District No. 24, on Big Flat Creek. The land being the same upon which Elijah Bobo formerly lived and which descended to them from Sarah Pearson and also to the said Samuel Bobo. Wit: Kindred Pearson and Rufus Smith. Reg: 23 Jan 1851.

Page 302 - 21 Jan 1851. W. W. Arnold and wife to Joseph H. McCamy. Deed, 52 acres. W. W. Arnold and Patience A. Arnold formerly Patience A. McAdams sold to Joseph H. McCamy, land in Bedford Co., TN, in District No. 6, it being Lot No. 2 in the division of land of Amos McAdams, deceased, amongst his heirs, allotted to Patience A. McAdams. Bounded by Knott's line and Caleb and Martin Phifer's survey. Reg: 27 Jan 1851.

Page 306 - 22 Jan 1851. Rector Haggard and wife to William Brown. Deed. Rector Haggard and Martha Haggard his wife formerly Martha Cunningham, sold to William Brown, land in Bedford Co., TN, it being the tract of land on which Richard Cunningham resided at the time of his death. Bounded by the mouth of Andersons Creek, lands formerly owned by William Waite, lands owned by Richard Cunningham and on the road leading from Davis Mill to Shelbyville, Norville's line, Wartrace Fork. Their interest in land being a lien upon the same for the payment of $100.00 in trade a cash price by James T. Cunningham after the death of the widow of Richard Cunningham, deceased. Wit: A. Vannoy and J. W. Crutcher. Reg: 28 Jan 1851.

Page 309 - 6 Jan 1851. Mary Dobson to Mrs. Elliott and others. Bill of Sale. Mary Dobson for love and affection for her children, Justina E. S. Elliott, Mary T. Drumgoole and Clement C. Ashburne, give unto them her interest to slaves. Wit: Robert H. Majors and William T. Wells. Reg: 30 Jan 1851.

Page 316 - 10 Nov 1849. William Yeats to K. L. Pybas. Deed. William Yeats of Marshall Co., Mississippi sold to Kenneth L. Pybas of Lincoln Co., TN, undivided interest in a tract of land in Bedford Co., TN, as described in the Last Will and Testament of Joshua Yeats the above named William Yeats as a legatee.

Wit: Joseph Morton and J. D. Clift. Reg: 5 Feb 1851.

Page 317 - 20 Sep 1848. A. P. Brents and wife Nancy to James C. Snell. Deed, 30 acres. Alphus P. Brents and wife Nancy, sold to James C. Snell, land in Bedford Co., TN, on waters of Sugar Creek. Bounded by land formerly Andrew Davidson, and Robert Riley. Alphus P. Brents and Nancy C. Brents of Marshall Co., Mississippi. Reg: (no date).

Page 332 - 27 Nov 1848. J. P. Mitchell to Senior Low. Deed, undivided interest. Jefferson P. Mitchell sold and conveyed to Senior Low, land in bedford Co., TN, in District No. 19, it being the one fifth part of a tract of land that belonged to the heirs of William Low, deceased, and which J. P. Mitchell purchased of R. N. Adams and Eliza A. Adams, which is undivided. Land borders Archibald Adams, Thomas Davidson and Martin Smith. Wit: William P. Oneal and James M. Forbes. Reg: 12 Feb 1851.

Page 336 - 13 Feb 1851. William Loyd to A. S. Lawrance. Deed, Dower interest. Whereas Rebeca Loyd being lawfully seized and possessed of a life estate by the statue of dower in a tract of land, deed bearing date 16 Apr 1850, conveyed to her life estate therein to William Loyd, sold to Andrew S. Lawrance. Land bounded by Robert Clinkenbeard and Joseph Loyd's Old Tract. Reg: 13 Feb 1851.

Page 337 - 13 Feb 1851. John J. Dickey and wife to A. S. Lawrance. Deed, 23+ acres. John J. Dickey and Martha Ann Dickey formerly Martha Ann Loyd, sold to Horatio Coop, land in Bedford Co., TN, in District No. 5, it being Lot No. 4, in the division of the lands of Joseph Loyd, deceased. Bounded by William Murphey's line. Reg: 13 Feb 1851.

Page 338 - 13 Feb 1851. J. J. Dickey and wife to A. S. Lawrance. Deed. John J. Dickey and Martha Ann Dickey formerly Martha Ann Loyd has an interest in remainder to take effect at the death of Rebecca Loyd, in a tract of land, sold to A. S. Lawrance, it being the dower to Rebecca Loyd, widow of Joseph Loyd, deceased. Reg: 13 Feb 1851.

Page 340 - 14 Feb 1851. Margaret C. Key to A. G. Key. Bill of Sale. Margaret C. Key for love and affection for her son Alexander G. Key and his wife Ann E. Key and their present children, Susan Margaret Key, Delia Ann Key, William Alexander Key, and Martha Frances Key and such children as may be hereafter born unto Alexander G. and Ann E. Key, conveyed unto them a negro girl Winney Margaret. Wit: John W. Key and John S. Sch<u>luter</u>(?). Reg: 14 Feb 1851.

Page 343 - 17 Nov 1847. Francis V. Story to Joseph Robinson's heirs. Deed. Francis V. Story executed to Joseph Robinson, his written Obligatory Bond to real estate. Joseph Robinson has died. The Administrator of Joseph Robinson paid said Story full amount of note. Story conveyed unto Robert J. Robinson, Rufus A. Robinson, Margaret F. Robinson, and THomas D. Robinson, minor children and heirs at law of Joseph Robinson, deceased. The land being in Shelbyville, Lot No. 55. Bounded by Lot on which the "Shelbyville Inn" is now located. Also another Lot adjoining the above lot. Recorded: 24 Feb 1851.

Page 344 - Abner Freeman to Meeting House. Deed, 1 acre. Abner Freeman of Lincoln Co., TN, conveyed unto Isaac Bennet, Peterson Grammer and Henry Dean and successors of Bedford Co., TN, for $50.00, land in Bedford Co., on headwaters of Big Flat Creek. Bounded by a road leading from John Noblets to William Bartletts, in and around the Meeting House Mount Hermon. Wit: William C. Freeman and James A. Simmons, Thomas Morris and Saffield N. Morris. Reg: 24 Feb 1851.

Page 349 - 3 Feb 1851. Harrel Wiggins to Church. Deed, 3 acres. For the purpose of encouraging the worship of the Almighty God, and good will, Harrel Wiggins has for the preaching of the Gospel, he gives and conveyed to James Nelson and Jordan Epperson, Deacons in the Missionary Baptist Church on Sugar Creek, known as Big Spring Church, land, being a part of the tract of land on which Harrel Wiggins now lives. Bounded by the 3 acres of land belonging to the Big Spring School House. Reg: 1 Mar 1851.

Page 364 - 18 Mar 1851. James Carter to Samuel D. Coble. Deed, undivided interest. James Carter sold to Samuel D. Coble, land in Bedford Co., TN, in District No. 25, on Thompsons Creek, it being laid off to Mary Coble now Mary Williams, wife and relict of Jacob Coble, deceased, and it being one undivided child's part which was conveyed by Absalom Arnold and wife to William Jenkins and from William Jenkins to James Carter. Reg: 18 Mar 1851.

Page 367 - 27 Feb 1851. Thomas Eakin and others vs John M. Bass and others. Deed, 5 acres. Alcy Dunston, colored, in the year 1845 or 1846 purchased from John Eakin & Co., the tract of land which was paid in full but has never received a conveyance of the title of said land from Thomas Eakin, William S. Eakin, John R. Eakin, Argyle P. Eakin, Julia A. Eakin, Sarah J. Eakin, Alexander E. Eakin, Thomas L. Eakin, Jas. H. Eakin, George W. Eakin, Albert Eakin, Charles Eakin, and Lucretia Eakin and defendants Felicia Jane W. and Anne Eakin, in and to said tract of land. Bounded by Town of Shelbyville, John T. Neill, lands of Gen. Robert Cannon, land formerly owned by Mrs. Morgan. Reg: 22 Mar 1851.

Page 371 - 21 Jan 1851. W. W. Arnold and wife to Joseph H. McCamy. Deed. W. W. Arnold and Patience A. Arnold his wife conveyed unto Joseph H. McCamy, land in bedford Co., TN, in District No. 6, it being Lot No. 2 in the division of the land of Amos McAdams, deceased, among his heirs, allotted to Patience A. Arnold in the division. Patience A. Arnold being at the time under the age of 21 years, and now having arrived to the age of 21 years. Reg: 26 Mar 1851.

Page 373 - 1 Apr 1851. Joseph White and Ruthy Lewellen. Marriage Contract. They contemplate entering into Holy Matrimony, but before doing so, being convinced it being to each's advantage, as to the disposition of the property of which Ruthy Lewellen is the owner and to insure its safety to her and her children, such as she may be the mother of at the time of her death. Her land in Bedford Co., TN, on waters of Sugar Creek. Bounded by lands of Susan Davidson, Nicholas Burns and Mathew Shearin. The land being same land on which Mrs. Lewellen now resides. Also personal property. Wit: W. W. Evans and Nathaniel White. Reg: 2 Apr 1851.

Page 388 - 5 Apr 1851. William O. Pepper and wife to Stephen Hoit. Bond for Title. William O. Pepper and wife Sophia A. Pepper bound unto Stephen Hoit. They conveyed unto Stephen Hoit, land in Bedford Co., TN, on north side of Duck river and two miles below the Town of Shelbyville, being all the tract of land given by John Sutton, Sr. to his sons William B. Sutton and Charles F. Sutton, except 50 acres heretofore sold to Newcom Thompson. Wit: William H. Wisener and Sam H. Whitthorne. Reg: 8 Apr 1851.

Page 394 - 4 Mar 1851. David G. Weaver to John T. Weaver. Deed, 70 acres and 26 acres. David G. Weaver sold to John T. Weaver, land in Bedford Co., TN, in District No. 25, near Normans Creek, a branch of the Baren (Barren) Fork where the widow Sarah Weaver now lives. Bounded by Ephraim Weaver, Normans Creek, G. Hofmand's line, G. H. Hofmans' corner, and Hollins' line. Also, a tract bounded by J. Speers, Moss' line and Calahan's line. Wit: Nicholas Lasater and George Hufman. Reg: 7 Apr 1851.

Page 396 - 5 Apr 1851. P. H. Reaves to A. S. Reaves. Deed, 131 acres. P. H. Reaves sold to A. S. Reaves, his interest in a tract of land in Bedford Co., TN, on waters of Big Flat Creek, now in the possession of Elizabeth Reaves. Bounded by Lacy's land, Eve Burrow, lands of Wilhoite & Campbell, Freeman's tract. It being the tract of land which descended to the heirs of Archibald Reaves, deceased. It being P. H. Reaves' interest in the same being the one eighth part thereof. Reg: 9 Apr 1851.

Page 398 - 6 Apr 1851. Isam Oneal to John P. Oneal. Deed. Isam Oneal sold to John P. Oneal, in Trust, for his five children now born, and such others as may hereafter be born by his present wife, should she die or by any future marriage, land in Bedford Co., TN. Bounded by James Neill, Sr., deceased, lands of Guants' heirs, David Dryden, Henderson's line, Andrew Neil's spring and Gilchrist's line. It being the same tract of land purchased by Isam Oneal of Catharine and Archibald J. Greer, Executors &C of Thomas Greer. Wit: G. W. Cunningham and George W. Buchanan. Reg: 12 Apr 1851.

Page 402 - 12 Apr 1851. Jacob Kizer to J. J. Kimery. Deed of Gift, 105 acres. Jacob Kizer for love and affection for his grandchildren, the children of my daughter Elizabeth Kimmery, deceased, to wit, John J. Kimmery, Margaret R. and William E. Kimmery, conveyed unto his heirs, real estate and personal property, to wit, land in Bedford Co., TN, on east side of Big Flat Creek. Bounded by John and Robert Reed, John Koonce, A. Reed and J. Reed. Edwin Kimmery the father of the above minor children is raising and providing for the minor children. Reg: 12 Apr 1851.

Page 403 - 12 Apr 1851. Jacob Kizer to John Kizer. Bill of Sale. Jacob Kizer for love and affection for his son John Kizer, give to him a negro woman Eliza. Reg: 12 Apr 1851.

Page 406 - 25 Mar 1851. Pherby L. Cathey to H. C. Kinnard. Deed, 22 acres. Pherby L. Cathey of Christian Co., KY sold to H. C. Kinnard of Bedford Co., TN, her interest in the tract of land conveyed to James S. Cathey by William Lee, laid off and set apart, it being about 22 acres. Also the interest in her mother's dower. Wit: Anderson Sharp, A. E. Mullins and Allen Wallis. Reg: 22 Apr 1851.

Page 412 - 2 Jan 1851. Martin Hoover to Daniel D. Hoover. Deed of Gift, 200 acres. Martin Hoover for love and affection for his son Daniel D. Hoover, give my Deed of Gift, land in Bedford Co., TN. Bounded by James M. Hoover, Henry Pruett, John W. Rawlings, John P. Hoover, and John Frizzell. Wit: John McKee and James M. Hoover. Reg: 28 Apr 1851.

Page 413 - 2 Jan 1851. Martin Hoover to James M. Hoover. Deed of Gift. Martin Hoover for love and affection for his son James M. Hoover, land. Bounded by Frizzell's line, Puiett's line, and John Pruett. Wit: D. D. Hoover and John McKee. Reg: 28 Apr 1851.

Page 415 - 9 Jun 1848. John Capley and wife to Richard Warner. Deed, 200 acres. John Capley and his wife Rebecca of Bedford Co., TN, sold to Richard Warner of Marshall Co., TN, their interest in a tract of land in Bedford Co., on south side of Duck River, it being the tract of land purchased by John Warner, Sr. from George Earnhart. John Capley and Rebecca his wife had two shares in the above land as heirs at law of said John Warner, Sr., deceased, conveyed unto Richard Warner. Wit: Green L. Neeley and William H. Aaron. Reg: 9 May 1851.

Page 419 - 26 Apr 1851. Richard C. Ogilvie to Jennings Moore and others. Deed, 1 acre. Richard C. Ogilvie conveyed unto A. B. Moore, Jennings Moore, G. L. Poplin, R. W. Fain, Joseph Brown, B. Landers and A. Wilson, for $20.00, land in Bedford Co., TN, for subscription to the Unionville Female Academy, a tract of land bounded by Jennings Moore and Widow Covington. This land is sold for the purpose of building a Female Academy. Wit: D. A. Ozment, C. C. Covington, and Thomas B. Allison. Reg: 10 May 1851.

Page 422 - 17 Apr 1851. Claiborne W. Coats to William Gosling. Deed, 160 acres. Claiborne W. Coats has an interest in land on which his mother Celia Coats now lives, the same being the dower allotted to her on the death of his father Wilson Coats which land will come into his possession after the death of his mother Selia. Land in Bedford Co., TN, in District No. 3 and No. 7. He sold to William Gosling. The lands bounded by lands of Wilson Coats, deceased. Reg: 13 May 1851.

Page 426 - 15 May 1851. Friar Trail to Eliza Jane Frazer. Marriage Contract. Friar Trail and Eliza Jane Frazer is contemplating entering in the Holy Bonds of Wedlock and desire to secure the welfare of each to make the following agreement. Friar Trail agrees that Eliza Jane Frazer shall have and hold all the property both real and personal that may come unto her possession and at her death to descend to her children. Wit: E. D. Fonville, William T. Wells and Robert H. Majors. Reg: 16 May 1851.

Page 427 - 25 jul 1850. L. W. Hall to W. and L. Hickerson. Deed. Wilson Hall sold to William and L. Hickerson, land in Bedford Co., TN, in District No. 2, on waters of Barren Fork of Duck River, it being the tract of land on which Fergus Hall resided at the time of his death. Wit: J. G. Wilson and C. F. Hord. Reg: 16 May 1851.

Page 429 - 25 Mar 1851. Joel A. Wallis to P. L. Cathey. Bill of Sale. Joel A. Wallis sold to Pheriba L. Cathey of Hopkins-ville, Christian Co., KY, a negro man Moses. Wit: James M. Porter and Samuel M. Gentry. Reg: 17 May 1851.

Page 430 - 29 Jan 1851. Anne Hitchcock to William J. Webster. Deed, 250 acres. Anne Hitchcock sold to William J. Webster, Trustee for Mary J. Erwin, (by virtue of a marriage contract entered into between herself and her husband Andrew Erwin, which contract was afterwards reformed by a decree of Chancery Court at Huntsville, Alabama), a tract of land in Bedford Co., TN between the waters of the Garrison Fork and Barren Fork of Duck River, being the land conveyed to Anne Hitchcock by Andrew Erwin. Bounded by the Garrison Fork, Kinchen Stokes' land now occupied by John M. Stokes, Old Brick House tract, Archibald Murphy, tract of William J. Webster, Trustee for Mary J. Erwin. Wit: Henry Hitchcock and Jno. R. Eakin. Reg: 19 May 1851.

Page 431 - 25 Apr 1851. James H. Deery and R. D. Deery to James A. Deery and brothers. Deed. James H. Deery and Ross D. Deery of Bedford Co., TN, sold to James A. Deery, William B. Deery and Robert E. Deery of Allisonia, Franklin Co., TN, the amount due and owing by James Deery, to the estate of his brother William Deery, deceased, dated 19 Jan 1846 and payable one day after to James A. and William B. Deery as Administrators of the estate of the deceased, conveyed land in Bedford Co., in Town of Shelbyville, on north side of the Public Square, on which the Brick House, west of the Shelbyville Inn is situated. Reg: 19 May 1851.

DEED BOOK "TT" 1851 - 1852

Page 1 - 25 Mar 1851. James C. Wallace and Wilie B. Wallace of DeKalb Co., Missouri, appointed John P. Steele of Bedford Co., TN, his Attorney, to convey and dispose of all their interest in an undivided tract of land in Bedford Co., TN, on Wartrace Fork, it being the land recovered by James C. Wallace and Wilie B. Wallace in a suit in Circuit Court of Bedford Co., TN, with Thomas Mosley. Reg: 24 May 1851.

Page 3 - Same as above instrument. Reg: 26 May 1851.

Page 5 - 25 Jan 1848. John Stallings to William Stallings. Deed of Gift, 30 acres. John Stallings for love and affection for his son William Stallings, land in Bedford Co., TN, in District No. 18. Bounded by John Oneal. It being near where William Thorn now lives. Wit: John Oneal and H. B. Branwell. Reg: 26 May 1851.

Page 6 - 26 May 1851. A. H. Gambill to Jos. Trice. Interest in land, 135 acres. A. H. Gambill has interest to take effect and be united with the possession after the death of Rachel Gambill who has a life estate in same in the one eighth part of land in Bedford Co., TN, in District No. 20, sold to Joseph Trice. Land bounded by Joseph Trice, Robert Logan, J. H. Price, P. Nance, it being the land formerly owned by Benjamin Gambill, deceased and was executed to A. H. Gambille as one of the heirs of Benjamin Gambille, and also to the one eighth of personal property now in possession of Rachel Gambille devised to her during her natural life by Benjamin Gambille and at her death to descend to his heirs of which A. H. Gambille is one. Reg: 27 May 1851.

Page 17 - 4 Mar 1851. James Bell to George N. Arrington. Power of Attorney. James Bell and Eliza Bell his wife of Marion Co., KY, appointed George N. Arrington of Coffee Co., TN, their Attorney to sell and dispose of their interest in descended to them from the estate of George Newton, deceased, and from his wife Ellen (Helen) Newton. Reg: 7 Jun 1851.

Page 19 - 28 May 1851. James Deery to William B. M. Brame. Deed. James Deery for natural regard for his son in law William B. M. Brame, conveyed unto him a piece of ground. Bounded by Barksdale and Tillman, property (formerly Gilchrist's). Reg: 9 Jun 1851.

Page 19 - 28 May 1851. James Deery to Gideon P. Baskette. Deed. James Deery for natural regard for his son in law Gideon P. Baskette, conveyed unto him a piece of ground. Bounded by the Barksdale and Tillman's property and Brame's property. Reg: -- Jun 1851.

Page 21 - 30 May 1851. L. C. Johnson and wife to James G. Neeley. Deed. Levi C. Johnson and Elizabeth J. Johnson sold to James G. Neeley, their interest in land in Bedford Co., TN, on waters of Falling Creek. Bounded by Volney H. Steele, land of Samuel A. Bell, deceased, land belonging to the heirs of Travis C. Nash, and John Hutton, deceased, it being where Joannah Nash now lives. Reg: 10 Jun 1851.

Page 22 - 30 May 1851. Alex Eakin to Lucretia Eakin. Deed, 8 acres. Alexander Eakin sold to Lucretia Eakin, land in Bedford Co., TN, in District No. 6. Bounded by Nashville, Murfreesboro and Shelbyville Turnpike Road, heirs of John Eakin, deceased, and Benjamin Brown. Reg: 10 Jun 1851.

Page 27 - 9 Dec 1850. James Gilliam, Mary Ann Gilliam and William H. Gilliam, Elizabeth Caroline Gilliam and Catharine G. Garrett sold to Elijah Holt, their shares of 77 acres of land in Bedford Co., TN. Their share being three tenths. Wit: M----- Gilliam and Sullinger Holt and James W. Culley. Reg: 16 Jun 1851.

Page 28 - 18 May 1840. Eliza J. Howe and Eliza A. Howe to James S. Holt. Deed, 15 acres. Eliza J. Howe and Eliza A. Howe and Cynthia B. Holt sold to James S. Holt, land in Bedford Co., TN, in District No. 2. It being two shares in Hosea Garrett tract, now owned by James S. Holt. Wit: James W. Culley and Sullinger Holt. Reg: (no date).

Page 32 - 12 Jun 1851. William Woods and wife to Phillip Hodges. Deed, 50 acres. William Woods and Mary S. his wife formerly Mary S. Watkins sold to Phillip Hodges, land in Bedford Co., TN, on the Hurricane Fork, in District No. 6. Bounded by John and William Payton. The land being the tract of land purchased by Thomas G. Watkins, deceased, from Henry Skidmore and deeded to him on 7 Feb 1827. Reg: 18 Jun 1851.

Page 34 - 14 Jun 1851. Littleberry Still to Greenberry Still and others. Deed, 50 acres. Whereas John Thompson executed to the undersigned on 25 Oct 1849, land in Bedford Co., TN, in District No. 8. The land was a fund bequeathed to Littleberry Still in trust for the use of his children, four sons, Greenberry Still, Thomas, William and James by his sister

Rebecca Still, late of Williamson Co., TN. In consideration that the Last Will and Testament of his sister Rebecca Still, deceased, may be more fully carried out. Littleberry relinquished all claim and rights of his four sons (above named). Bounded by John Wilson, Claxton's line and Turrentine's line. Reg: 19 Jun 1851.

Page 35 - 24 Jun 1851. Jesse Muse to Susannah Muse. Whereas Aaron Gambill departed this life a few days ago, leaving among other heirs at law who are entitled to his real and personal estate of which Aaron Gambill died seized and possessed, my wife Susannah Muse, she being entitled as a child of Aaron Gambill to the 1/11th part of the estate of which he died, including one tract of land in Bedford Co., TN and two negroes. Reg: 24 Jun 1851.

Page 36 - 23 May 1851. Joseph Greer to John A. and Lewis V. Greer. Joseph Greer of Harrison Co., Texas sold to John A. and Lewis V. Greer of San Augustine Co., Texas, his interest in 4 negroes and increases. Whereas Thomas Greer, Sr., deceased, by his Last Will and Testament bequeathed the said negroes to Catharine R. Greer, his wife during her life, remainder to her and his children of whom I, Joseph am one. Reg: 25 Jun 1851.

Page 38 - 12 Jun 1851. F. M. Miller and wife to Edmund Cooper. Deed. F. M. Miller and his wife Amanda B. Miller sold to Edmund Cooper, 9 slaves, they being our ninth part. Reg: 26 Jun 1851.

Page 44 - 28 Jun 1851. G. W. King and wife to Nicholas P. Burns. Deed. George W. King and Lovina King his wife formerly Lovina Staggs, sold to Nicholas P. Burns, all their interest in land in Bedford Co., TN, on the headwaters of Sugar Creek, it being the land owned and possessed by William Staggs at the time of his death. Reg: 8 Jul 1851.

Page 49 - 8 Jul 1851. Henry Davis to Mary Siddon. Deed of Gift. Henry Davis for love and affection for his daughter Mary Siddon, wife of Abraham Siddon, conveyed unto her for life, a negro slave Betsey. He loan to my daughter Polly the negro girl and at his death and use it as part of his estate. Wit: Edmond Cooper and Henry Cooper. Reg: 12 Jul 1851.

Page 53 - 15 Jul 1851. Jordan C. Holt to Elenor C. Pybas. Deed, 205 acres. Jordan C. Holt, Sr. for love and affection for his daughter Elenor C. Pybas, conveyed unto her, land in Bedford Co., TN, on waters of Big Flat Creek, in District No. 21. Borders lands of Jordan C. Holt, Michael Holt, Jacob Greer and W. P. Goodwin. The land being the interest of S. P. Balch and wife Hannah Balch, conveyed to Jordan C. Holt by them, in the lands of which Joshua Yeats, deceased, died seized and possessed, it being one eighth part of the tract. Reg: 18 Jul 1851.

Page 56 - -- Jan 1851. Jordan C. Holt to Francis F. Holt. Deed, 35+ acres. Jordan C. Holt sold to Francis F. Holt wife of Isaac B. Holt, land in Bedford Co., TN, on Flat Creek, in District No. 21, including the grist and saw mill on said land. Bounded by lands Michael Holt conveyed to John H. Reaves in 1841, land on which Isaac B. Holt now resides. Reg: 15 Jul 1851.

DEED BOOK "TT"

Page 59 - 1 Jul 1851. Gabriel Barns to John Barns. Gabriel Barns of Shelby Co., Alabama, sold to John Barns, one undivided tenth part of the estate of his mother Susan Barns, also conveyed Log Mill to Susan by her father Swepson Sims, for her life and heirs, of which Gabriel Burns is an heir. Land in Bedford Co., TN, being the plantation on which Susan Barns lived at the time of her death, also slaves and other property. Wit: Hiram Sumner and P. D. Marony. Reg: 28 Jul 1851.

Page 60 - 5 Apr 1847. John R. Proby and others. Petition to sell land. 30-40 acres. Sale of land on 27 Mar 1847, the land which the heirs at law of Peter R. Proby, deceased, had interest in, on which a saw and grist mill on Duck River in Bedford Co., TN formerly known as Troxler's Mills and more recently known as Clark's Mills. John Huffman became purchaser. Reg: 28 Jul 1851.

Page 61 - 28 Jul 1851. William Primrose and wife Elizabeth Primrose to Jeremiah Culberhouse. Deed. William Primrose and his wife Elizabeth, sold to Jeremiah Culberhouse, their interest in land in Bedford Co., TN, in District No. 9. Bounded by Moses Culberhouse and H. W. Jones. The land being one undivided eighth part and being the land assigned to Nancy Culberhouse for her dower. Reg: 29 Jul 1851.

Page 63 - 1 Jul 1851. James A. Deery, William B. Deery to Robert E. Deery to William S. Eakin. James A. Deery, William B. Deery and Robert E. Deery of Franklin Co., TN, sold to William S. Eakin of Davidson Co., TN, land in Bedford Co., TN, in Shelbyville, on the north side of the Public Square, one of the lots. Bounded by the Shelbyville Inn, Public Square, The Brick House erected by James Deery. The lot being the lot conveyed to James A., William B., and Robert E. Deery by James H. and Ross D. Deery in 1851, also other lots. One lot executed by them jointly with Elizabeth Deery as security, dated 1851. Wit: R. D. Deery and Thomas C. Whiteside. Reg: 29 Jul 1851.

Page 64 - 27 May 1851. Thomas Haskins and wife to Edward Tarpley. Power of Attorney. Sumter Co., Alabama. Thomas Haskins and Jane Haskins his wife, daughter of Thomas Culberhouse, deceased, of Sumter Co., Alabama, sold to Edward Tarpley of Bedford Co., TN, all their interest in to or out of the estate of Thomas Culberhouse, deceased, Bedford Co., TN, property in hands of John L. Cooper, Administrator of the estate or in hands of John T. Neil. Land in Bedford Co., on Alexanders Creek, in District No. 9. Bounded by Thomas Primrose, Henry Jones, C. G. McLane, the heirs of John Taylor, deceased. Wit: C. Frost and William S. ---man(?). Reg: 30 Jul 1851.

Page 66 - 30 Jul 1851. William Pratt to Catharine Pratt. Deed of Gift, 366½ acres. William Pratt for natural love and affection for his wife Catharine Pratt, all his interest he may have in property both real and personal conveyed by Willis Cannon and wife Letitia Cannon, dated 13 Feb 1833. To their children, Catharine Cannon, Samuel T. Cannon, Martha Cannon, Jason H. Cannon, and Letsy Cannon, land on south side of Duck River, in District No. 23 in Bedford Co., TN. Bounded by John Johnson, M. E. W. Dunaway, John Read, and James Wortham. Also, conveyed slaves. Reg: 30 Jul 1851.

Page 67(?) - 10 Jun 1851. Barrum Lamb and Lucy Lamb to (Edward) Tarpley. Deed. Barrum Lamb and wife Lucy Lamb, daughter of Thomas Culberhouse, deceased, sold their interest in estate of Thomas Culberhouse, being held jointly by his heirs, except dower set apart. The land in Bedford Co., TN, on Alexander Creek, in District No. 9. Bounded by John E. Haskins, Henry M. Jones, C. G. McLane and Jeremiah and Moses Culberhouse. Wit: H. W. Jones and J. A. Tarpley. Reg: 30 Jul 1851.

Page 68 - 7 Jul 1851. James Deery to James H. and Ross D. Deery. Deed of Gift. James Deery for love and affection for his two sons James H. and Ross D. Deery, conveyed unto them, land in Bedford Co., TN, in and or near Shelbyville, being all the land on which he now lives, except what may be north of Union Street, a new Street recently opened, and except the land conveyed to William B. M. Brame and G. P. Baskette. The sons are not to take possession until the death of James Deery and their mother Elizabeth Deery. Reg: 31 Jul 1851.

Page 69 - 7 Jul 1851. James Deery to Gideon P. Baskette. James Deery for natural regard for his son in law Gideon P. Baskette, give and conveyed unto him, land in or near Shelbyville, lying north of a piece of ground recently conveyed to Baskette by James Deery. Bounded by J. H. Graham, Hugh Wardlow, W. B. M. Brame. Baskette is not to take possession until after the death of James and Elizabeth Deery. Reg: 31 Jul 1851.

Page 73 - 14 Jan 1839. Nathan Evans and others to Joseph G. Dyer. Deed. Whereas by descend from Alexander Greer, deceased, our father, we, Mary McKisick, Andrew Greer, Nathan Evans, Jane McKisick, Frances Greer, Alexander Greer, and James E. Whitney have derived title to and now hold equal and undivided interest in two tracts of land in Lincoln Co., TN, on the headwaters of Mulberry, a north branch of Elk River and in District No. __. First tract of 150 acres and adjoining the lands of Daniel Warren and others. Second tract of 100 acres bounded by school land and adjoining lands of Joseph Brim and others. Nathan Evans and others sold to Joseph G. Dyer the above land. Wit: C. C. Taliaferro and William McClure. Reg: 6 Aug 1851.

Page 78 - 9 Jan 1851. Robert B. Maupin to Sarah L. Caruthers. Deed, 11 acres. Robert B. Maupin for love and affection for Sarah L. Caruthers, conveyed to her land in Bedford Co., TN, in District No. 2. Bounded by road leading to Trigg's Mill. Wit: James L. Maupin and Blan T. Maupin. Reg: 7 Aug 1851.

Page 90 - 5 Aug 1851. J. J. McGowen to I. W. McGowen. Deed. John James McGowen sold to I. W. McGowen, his divided part of a legacy left by their grandfather William Holmes, in negroes, to his daughter Sarah Ann McGowen who was their mother. Wit: William G. Hight and J. M. Barber. Reg: 13 Aug 1851.

Page 97 - 9 Jun 1851. John M. Keller to Francis A. Keller and Christopher Thomas. Deed, 250 acres. Whereas John M. Keller had an interest in remainder, to take effect and be united with the possession after the death of Mrs. Ann Keller who has a life estate in the same for her lifetime or widowhood in land in Bedford Co., TN, on the waters of the Garrison Fork of Duck River, it being the land of which his father Joseph Keller died seized and possessed and whereas John M. Keller by deed bearing date 9 Nov 1847, conveyed unto Francis A. Keller and Christopher

Thomas, his undivided interest in land. Wit: Robert C. T. Keller and Benjamin H. Keller. Reg: 15 Aug 1851.

Oage 98 - 16 Aug 1851. L. A. Smith and wife to Michael Shofner. Deed, 17 acres and 101 acres. L. A. Smith and wife Virginia formerly Virginia Franklin, sold to Michael Shofner their undivided interest, it being one half, in two pieces of land in Bedford Co., TN, in District No. 3, on Duck River. First tract bounded by north bank of Duck River and Shofner's line. Second tract bounded by north bank of Duck River and the first tract. Reg: 19 Aug 1851.

Page ?? - 29 Sep 1847. Rachel Franklin to Michael Shofner. Deed, 118 acres. Rachel Franklin relinquishes and quit claim in one undivided interest in land on which Peter Franklin lived at the time of his death. Land on Duck River in Bedford Co., TN. Wit: L. Shofner and J. C. Tune. Reg: 19 Aug 1851.

Page 104 - 8 Aug 1851. Edward Tarpley to Jeremiah Culberhouse. Deed. Edward Tarpley sold to Jeremiah Culberhouse, his interest in estate or land in the estate of Thomas Culberhouse, deceased, as conveyed to him by Thomas Haskins and Jane Haskins his wife and wife and daughter of Thomas Culberhouse, deceased, land in Bedford Co., TN, except the dower set apart for widow of Thomas Culberhouse, deceased. Land transferred to Tarpley by Barum Lamb and his wife Lucy Lamb. Land in District No. 9. Wit: William Taylor and H. W. Jones. Reg: 27 Aug 1851.

Page 109 - 1 Sep 1851. Eliza Davidson to Thomas H. Davidson. Deed of Gift. Eliza Davidson for love and affection for her son Thomas H. Davidson, give and transfer to him at her death, her negro boy Benjamin. Wit: William F. Davidson and John H. Davidson. Reg: 4 Sep 1851.

Page 110 - 28 Aug 1851. T. W. Bigham and others to O. H. Bigham. Deed, 631 acres. S. W. Bigham, M. S. Bigham, E. H. Bigham, Jr., R. P. Bigham, Wilson Bates and Ursula G. Bates his wife, and W. N. Bigham, conveyed to O. H. Bigham, their undivided interest in a certain tract of land which was deeded to the heirs of Robert Bigham, deceased, by M. and D. Gilchrist. Wit: John I. Allen and Reuben Curry. Signed by T.(S)W. Bigham, M. S. Bigham, E. W. Bigham, R. P. Bigham, Wilson Bates and Ursula G. Bates and W. N. Bigham. Reg: 4 Sep 1851.

Page 121 - 15 Sep 1851. L. C. Elliott to Ruthy White. Deed, 12 acres. Lorenzo C. Elliott sold to Ruthy White wife of Joseph White, land in bedford Co., TN, on waters of Sugar Creek. Bounded by lands of Benjamin Delk, Allen Newsom and Mrs. Staggs. Reg: 11 Sep 1851.

Page 123 - 10 Sep 1851. Thomas Walker and Susan Walker to W. K. Ransom. Deed. Thomas H. Walker and Susan Walker his wife, sold to W. K. Ransom, their interest in the lands of John Deason, deceased, in Bedford Co., TN, in District No. 5. Reg: 16 Sep 1851.

Page 123 - 15 Sep 1851. James Morris and wife to O. H. Bigham. Deed, 630 acres. James Morris and Mary A. L. Morris his wife, sold to O(liver). H. Bigham, their interest in a tract of land Robert Bigham, deceased, bought of M. and D. Gilchrist. Wit: Solomon Claxton and M. L. Bigham. Reg: 16 Sep 1851.

DEED BOOK "TT"

Page 127 - 15 Sep 1851. William B. Phillips and wife to William F. Cooper. Deed, 174 acres. William B. Phillips and wife Malinda formerly Malinda A. Cooper, sold to William F. Cooper, their undivided interest being our eighth thereof, of a tract of land, being the same land willed by Charles Cooper to his wife Sarah Cooper during her life and on which she now resides in Bedford Co., TN. Also their undivided interest in slaves. Reg: 17 Sep 1851.

Page 128 - 2 Aug 1851. Thomas Smith to Benjamin Moseley. Deed, 507 acres. Thomas Smith, Sr. and Mary (Polly) Smith his wife, sold to Benjamin Moseley, land in Bedford Co., TN, in District No. 19. Bounded by Nathan McAdams. Wit: David Yancy and William Kinnard. Reg: 19 Sep 1851.

Page 129 - 16 Sep 1851. William H. Gill to A. and M. Hudlow. Deed, 75 acres. William H. Gill sold to Andrew and Margarett Hudlow, land in Bedford Co., TN, on waters of Big Flat Creek. Bounded to John White, Samuel Wilson, Reeses and Phillips' corner. Including the cabins and plantations owned by William H. Gill. Wit: John D. Whitaker and William M. Goggin. Reg: 19 Sep 1851.

Page 130 - 17 Sep 1851. Thomas Smith and wife to Thomas Allison and others. Deed in Trust. Thomas Smith and Polly (Mary) Smith sold to Sarah Allison formerly Sarah Smith, Davidson M. Smith, Elizabeth Kinnard formerly Elizabeth Smith, Thomas Smith, John M. Smith, Martha Durrett formerly Martha Smith, Mary M. McAdams formerly Mary M. Smith, and Ann C. King formerly Ann C. Smith, and Lucinda McDonnold formerly Lucinda Smith, for love and affection for the above named, conveyed all their interest in and to the estate of Abram Medearis, deceased, late of the county of (blank) State of North Carolina. Reg: 20 Sep 1851.

Page 135 - 22 Sep 1851. Wiley T. Tune to John McAdams. Deed, undivided interest. Wiley T. Tune sold to John McAdams, his interest in the estate of Lurany Tune, his mother, it being the remainder that he would receive after the death of his mother Lurany Tune, it being 1/12th part of the estate. Reg: 25 Sep 1851

Page 136 - 23 Sep 1851. George W. Greer and wife to Leroy W. Barratt. Deed, 108 acres. George W. Greer and wife Adria J. Greer sold to Leroy W. Barratt, land in bedford Co., TN, in District No. 20. Bounded by land formerly owned by John Barratt, Henry Turpin and Alexander Greer. Reg: 25 Sep 1851.

Page 137 - 22 Apr 1851. Peter Waite and others to Orville Muse. Deed, 177 acres and 70 acres and 50 acres. Peter Waite, G. W. Waite and Francis P. Waite. Bill for sale of land. The above named sold to Orville Muse, land in Bedford Co., TN, on Wartrace Fork of Duck River. Bounded by Orville Muse, Benjamin Merrett, H. Moseley, lands of Isaac Muse, deceased, the lands of Richard Cunningham, deceased, William M. McGrew and William Waite, and is composed of a tract of land conveyed to William Waite, deceased, by John Slade in 1820. Also, a tract conveyed by John Cartnell to William Waite in 1828. Peter Waite, George W. Waite and Charlotte Waite, children and heirs of William Waite, deceased. Reg: 26 Sep 1851.

Page 138 - 26 Sep 1851. S. H. Bigham and others to John P. King. Deed, 171 acres. Samuel B. Bingham, Oliver H. Bingham, and Moses S. Bingham, sold to John P. King of Augusta, Georgia, land in Bedford Co., TN, and in Rutherford Co., TN, on both sides of the Nashville and Chattanooga Railroad. Bounded by A. M. Webb, Hiram Pearson, Daniel Gilchrist, Robert Clark, John D. Bigham, and Benjamin Webb. Wit: James H. Neil and John T. Neil. Reg: 29 Sep 1851.

Page 142 - 8 Sep 1851. Bigham and others to A. M. Webb. Deed, 128 acres. S. W. Bigham, O. H. Bigham and M. S. Bigham, sold to Anderson M. Webb, land in Bedford Co., TN. Bounded by Benjamin Webb's tract where he now lives, Pearson's tract, R. Curry, and M. S. Bigham. Wit: William H. Duncan and Benjamin Webb. Reg: 30 Sep 1851.

Page 145 - 3 Feb 1851. James Fulton to Helen M. Newton. Bill of Sale. James Fulton sold to Helen M. Newton, his interest in a negro boy Alfred, being now in the possession of Helen M. Newton. The slave was sold by order of court as property of Helen M. Newton's late husband George Newton. Reg: 2 Oct 1851.

Page 154 - 12 Sep 1851. Thomas J. Bartley and wife to J. W. Wallace. Deed, undivided interest. Thomas J. Bartley and his wife Elizabeth Bartley formerly Elizabeth Harper, sold to James W. Wallace of Bedford Co., TN, all his interest both real and personal in the estate of Samuel Harper, deceased. Reg: 3 Oct 1851.

Page 156 - 29 Aug 1851. Kizziah Hays and others to Thomas Hatchett. Deed, 130 acres. Kizziah Hays, Cooper Hays, Nelly Hays, Mary Hays, and William Haggard and his wife Mahala Haggard formerly Mahala Hays, sold to Thomas Hatchett, land in Bedford Co., TN, on waters of Wartrace Fork, in District No. 4. Borders Boze(Boaz) land, McMahan's land, A. Moseley's corner James Frizzell, and James Hail's corner. Wit: Jas. Haile and Nathan Frizzell. Reg: 7 Oct 1851.

Page 166 - 13 Oct 1851. B. S. Warren and others to J. H. M. McGrew. Deed, 159 acres. B. S. Warren and his wife Mary, George R. Moseley and wife Lucy E., Penny Ann Allbright and Sarah K. Allbright, heirs at law of Jacob Allbright, deceased, sold to J. H. M. McGrew, their undivided interest in land not assigned for dower for the widow of Jacob Allbright, deceased, of which he died seized and possessed in Bedford Co., TN, in District No. 23, on waters of Flat Creek. Reg: 14 Oct 1851.

Page 168 - 13 Oct 1851. J. H. M. McGrew to Spencer Brown. Deed. J. H. M. McGrew sold to Spencer Brown, one half of the interest this day conveyed to him by Benjamin S. Warren and his wife Mary, George B. Moseley and wife Lucy E., Penny Ann Allbright and Sarah Catharine Allbright, heirs at law of Jacob Allbright, deceased. Reg: 14 Oct 1851.

Page 168 - 28 Jun 1851. Pleasant M. Yell to Samuel Phillips. Power of Attorney. 90 acres. Pleasant M. Yell of Limestone Co., Texas, appointed Samuel Phillips of Bedford Co., TN, to sell and convey land in Bedford Co., TN, it being the land conveyed to him by Piercy Yell, his father. Bounded by Joseph Kennedy. Wit: J. E. Collett and A. E. Haynes. Reg: 14 Oct 1851.

Page 177 - 13 Oct 1851. H. W. Landers and Rilda Landers to W. K. Ransom. Deed. H. W. Landers and wife Rilda Landers sold to W. K. Ransom, their undivided interest in the dower land of Sarah Deason, widow of John Deason, deceased. Reg: 21 Oct 1851.

Page 178 - 13 Oct 1851. Enoch Deason to William K. Deason. Deed. Enoch Deason sold to W. K. Ransom, land in Bedford Co., TN, in District No. 5, being the land owned and possessed by the late John Deason, deceased, and at the time of his death. His interest being one undivided child's part. Wit: A. Vannoy. Reg: 21 Oct 1851.

Page 179 - 4 Oct 1851. Jefferson M. Stone and Ann O. Stone to William B. M. Brame. Deed, 25 acres. Jefferson M. Stone and Ann O. Stone of Lincoln Co., TN, sold to William B. M. Brame, land in Bedford Co., TN, in District No. 21, on waters of Powell Creek, being the fourth part, their undivided interest in and to 100 acres which descended to Ann O. Stone as one of the heirs of Melchesdic Brame, deceased. Reg: 21 Oct 1851.

Page 181 - -- Oct Term 1851. James W. Pennington. Petition to sell land, 60 acres. Charles H. Pennington, Eliza Pennington, Hawkins Hendon and others. Land in Bedford Co., TN, on the Little Sinking Creek and adjoining the lands of Andrew Neill and others. Bounded by road leading from Shelbyville to Pulaski, Andrew Neill and Little Sinking Creek and Thomas Moore. James W. Pennington purchaser. Reg: 21 Oct 1851.

Page 183 - 8 Aug 1851. Martha Ann McCrory. Decree from Circuit Court, 115 acres. Price C. Steele, Amdinistrator of Hugh McCrory, deceased, Martha Ann McCrory, widow. Exparte. To sell land to pay debts. Petition for dower and to sell land. Land in Bedford Co., TN. Martha Ann McCrory being the purchaser. All the interest that Price C. Steele, Administrator of Hugh McCrory, deceased, and Rebecca Ann Mc<u>Rory</u> and Sarah Jane Mc<u>Rory</u>, minors and only heirs at law of Hugh Mc<u>Rory</u>, deceased. Land bounded by Price C. Steele, James Hart, Joseph Springer and Washington Cooper and Lydia Roane. Reg: 22 Oct 1851.

Page 187 - 18 Oct 1851. Augustine Rowland to John W. Watkins. Augustine Rowland sold to John W. Watkins, Trustee of Elizabeth Rowland who signs and becomes a third party to this instrument, witnesses that whereas on -- day March 1851, Augustine Rowland and Elizabeth intermarried with each other and Elizabeth determined to separate herself from her husband, John W. Watkins became Trustee of property. Reg: 28 Oct 1851.

Page 192 - 21 Oct 1851. Benjamin H. Keller to Joseph W. C. Keller. Deed, 250 acres. Whereas Benjamin H. Keller has interest in the remainder to take effect and be united with the possession after the death of Mrs. Ann Keller who has a life estate during her life time or widowhood in a tract of land in bedford Co., TN, on waters of the Garrison Fork, it being the same land of which her father Joseph Keller died seized and possessed and whereas Benjamin H. Keller by deed transferred unto Joseph W. C. Keller, his undivided interest. Wit: F. A. Keller and J. M. Keller. Reg: 3 Nov 1851.

Page 194 - 4 Nov 1851. Elizabeth Patton to Kenneth M. Pybas. Deed, 210 acres. Elizabeth Patton of Marshall Co., Mississippi, sold to Kenneth M. Pybas, land in Bedford Co., TN, in District No. 21. Elizabeth Patton formerly Elizabeth Yeats and daughter of Joshua Yeats, deceased. Land bordered by lands of Jacob Greer, Michael Holt, Jordan C. Holt, and W. P. Goodwin. The land being the land Joshua Yeats died seized and possessed and on which he resided at the time of his death and by his Last Will and Testament, he divided in part to his wife during her life or widowhood and to his children, of which Elizabeth Patton as one of his children. Reg: 5 Nov 1851.

Page 196 - 11 Oct 1851. Mary Elizabeth Pursell and Margret Ann Norvell of Dyer Co., TN, appointed George R. Norvell their Attorney to sell and convey land in Bedford Co., TN, it being their interest in the estate of David Norvell, deceased. Wit: S. D. Norvell and H. F. Norvell. Reg: 5 Nov 1851.

Page 197 - 10 Oct 1851. Charles W. Lewis and Louisa Lewis to Don C. Moore. Power of Attorney. Charles W. Lewis and Louisa Lewis his wife of Randolph Co., Arkansas, appointed Don C. Moore of Randolph Co., Arkansas, their Attorney to sell and convey their interest in Tennessee, in estate of Tabitha Green, dec'd, late of Bedford Co., TN, who died seized and possessed in Lots in Shelbyville leaving Louisa Lewis as one of her lawful heirs. The Lot on which David Green now resides. Wit: L. C. Moore. Reg: 6 Nov 1851.

Page 198 - 5 Nov 1851. Charles W. Lewis and Louisa Lewis to Don C. Moore. Power of Attorney. Charles W. Lewis and Louisa Lewis appointed Don C. Moore, all of Randolph Co., Arkansas, their Attorney to convey unto Isaac Green, all interest in Town Lots of which Tabitha Green died seized and possessed and being the place wherein David Green and family now live, also adjoining Lot. Reg: 6 Nov 1851.

Page 203 - 3 Nov 1851. Robert Norvell and others to Jno. W. Norvell. Deed, undivided interest, 270 acres. Robert Norvell and George R. Norvell in their own right and Mary Elizabeth Pursell and Margaret Ann Norvell by their Attorney George R. Norvell, sold to John W. Norvell their undivided interest ninth part of a tract of land in Bedford Co., TN, in District No. 3, it being the place whereon John W. Norvell now resides and formerly owned by David Norvell, deceased. Bounded by Elijah Bomar, Gilchrist and Daniel Gilchrist. Reg: 7 Nov 1851.

Page 210 - 3 Nov 1851. Tabitha Brown to S. S. Brown. Rellinquishment. Whereas Shadrack S. Brown, husband of Tabitha Brown, by his Last Will and Testament, devised to her during her natural life, slaves and at her death the slaves to be divided amongst his children. She releases unto her children the right to divide said slaves. For her love and affection for T. J. Brown, G. W. Brown, William Brown, Weakley Locke and wife Tabitha, Samuel Suddarth and wife Keziah, Naomi Tilford, Elizabeth Robinson, Mary Sanders, and William and Martha Brown, children of Sterling Brown, deceased, and Richard Warner and wife Lucy. Wit: Thomas J. Brown, Richard Warner, James C. Burnett, G. W. Brown and H. L. Brown. Reg: 16 Nov 1851.

Page 211 - 14 Oct 1851. Randolph Newsom and others to Eliza J. Newsom and children. Deed of Gift. The Executors of the Last Will and Testament of William McGrew, deceased, and by said will vested money to Eliza J. Newsom and children from proceeds of the sale of the property belonging to the estate of William McGrew, deceased. Signed by Randolph Newsom, G. W. McGrew, and J. H. M. McGrew. Reg: 17 Nov 1851.

Page 213 - 29 Oct 1851. Letitia Cannon, Relinquishment to her heirs. Deed, 200 acres. Whereas Willis Cannon on 26 Jan 1826 by deed executed seceral tracts of land in Bedford Co., TN, to John McNary THompson for the benefit of Letitia Cannon who was then the wife of Willis Cannon. And whereas Willis and Letitia on 13 Feb 1833 by deed, executed to their children for love and affection, to wit, Catharine, Samuel T., Martha, Jason T., and Letsy Cannon, Jr., conveyed unto them two tracts of land also other property. And whereas Catharine jointly with her husband William Pratt filed their Bill in Chancery Court 15 Aug 1851 against Samuel T. Cannon, Jason T. Cannon, and Martha jointly with her husband George W. Thompson, and Letsy, Jr. and her husband Joseph H. M. McGrew, desiring to divide said land. Reg: 17 Nov 1851.

Page 217 - 28 Aug 1851. John W. Harrison and wife to J. Culberhouse. Deed, undivided interest. John W. Harrison and his wife Lucy Harrison and daughter of Thomas Culberhouse, deceased, both of Fayette Co., TN, sold to Jeremiah Culberhouse of Bedford Co., TN, their interest in the estate of Thomas Culberhouse, deceased, with John L. Cooper as Administrator of estate. The land in Bedford Co., TN, on Alexanders Creek in District No. 9. Bounded by John Haskins, Henry Jones, C. G. McLane and Moses and Jeremiah Culberhouse. Reg: 18 Nov 1851.

Page 218 - 22 Aug 1851. Thomas Culberhouse to Jeremiah Culberhouse. Deed, undivided interest. Thomas Culberhouse, son of Thomas Culberhouse, deceased, of Henry Co., TN, sold to Jeremiah Culberhouse of Bedford Co., TN, his interest in estate of Thomas Culberhouse, deceased, land in Bedford Co., TN, in District No. 9. Bounded by John Haskins, Henry Jones, C. G. McLane, Moses and Jeremiah Culberhouse. Reg: 18 Nov 1851.

Page 221 - 20 Nov 1851. J. A. Phillips to William Phillips. Deed, to negroes in trust for his son. Jesse A. Phillips for Natural love and affection for his sons Amzi A. Phillips and Trenton C. Phillips, conveyed unto William Phillips, all his interest in slaves, in trust for his sons who are now minors, Amzi being 12 years old and Trenton C. being 10 years of age. When the youngest arrives at the age of 21 years, they are to receive said slaves. Wit: Williamson Haggard and Alex. Eakin. Reg: 20 Nov 1851.

Page 225 - 12 Nov 1851. Samuel Suddrath and wife to Nepoleon B. Suddrath and others. Deed. Samuel Suddrath and wife Kisiah Suddrath, late Brown, deceased, daughter of Shadrack Brown, deceased, sold to Nepoleon B. Suddrath and John B. Suddrath, all of Simpson Co., KY, the entire interest of Kisiah and Samuel, both jointly in the estate of Shadrack Brown, deceased, in Bedford Co., TN, of both real and personal property. Reg: 22 Nov 1851.

Page 229 - 14 Nov 1851. William J. Webster, Trustee to John R. Eakin. Deed, 67 acres. We, Mary J. Erwin wife of Andrew Erwin, Andrew Erwin and William J. Webster, Trustee for the said M. J. Erwin, by virtue of a marriage contract, entered unto the said M. J. Erwin, then M. J. Camp, and the said A. Erwin at Huntsville, Alabama on the 24th Nov 1847, sold unto John R. Eakin, land in Bedford Co., TN, near the Garrison Fork of Duck River. Bounded by John Q. Davidson, T. G. Wright, William J. Webster, Wallace's line, near Maupin Spring and near the graveyard field, and A. Murphy's line near the graveyard, and W. Pepper's line. William J. Webster of Maury Co., TN. Mary J. Erwin of Davidson Co., TN. Reg: 22 Nov 1851.

Page 233 - 24 Nov 1851. Madison L. Burrow to William Campbell. Deed, 250 acres. Madison L. Burrow sold to William Campbell, land in Bedford Co., TN, in District No. 22, it being the land devised by Ephraim Burrow in his Last Will and Testament to his wife Eve Burrow during her natural life and at her death to be divided between his two children, Madison L. Burrow and Lethe Burrow who has intermarried with William Campbell. Borders John C. Hix, Elijah Lacy and William Barrett, John Wilson, Joseph Parker, Polly Burrow, William Campbell and Elizabeth R---(?) and upon which land William Campbell, Madison L. Burrow and Mrs. Eve Burrow now reside. Reg: 28 Nov 1851.

Page 237 - 1 Dec 1851. James Edde to Edmond Cooper. Deed, undivided interest, 130 acres. James Edde sold all interest in land devised to his mother Candace J. Edde during her life by her father Joshua Holt and at her death to descend to her children. Land in Bedford Co., TN. Bounded by Herrod F. Holt, Edmund Cooper and others. Reg: 1 Dec 1851.

Page 239 - 2 Oct 1850. Zebedee Harris to James Lawrance. Deed, undivided interest, 30 acres. Zebedee Harris has interest remainder to take effect and be united with the possession after the death of Esther Harris who has a life estate in same, in land in Bedford Co., TN, in District No. 10. Bounded by John Jackson. Wit: D. G. Denson and J. H. Locke. Reg: 2 Dec 1851.

Page 242 - 18 Nov 1851. Mary Shaw. Relinquishment to heirs. Whereas by the Last Will and Testament of the late C. Shaw, deceased, Mary Shaw has a life estate in several negroes, conveyed unto her heirs, T. C. D. W. Shaw, C. G. W. B. Shaw and R. E. C. P. Shaw. Wit: A. R. Wood, L. P. Fields and Willis Cannon. Reg: 3 Dec 1851.

Page 243 - 18 Nov 1851. Mary Shaw to T. L. D. W. Shaw and others. Relinquishment. Mary Shaw for love and affection for her three sons, T. L. D. W. Shaw, C. G. W. B. Shaw and R. C. C. P. Shaw, negroes. Wit: A. R. Wood, L. P. Fields and Willis Cannon. Reg: 3 Dec 1851.

Page 244 - 1 Dec 1851. William O. Forbs and John W. Wiggins, Executors. Deed, 307 acres. William O. Forbs and John W. Wiggins, Executors of Harrel Wiggins, deceased, sold to Harbert Wiggins, land in Bedford Co., TN, in District No. 20, on waters of Sugar Creek of which there is one Church House Lot, one School House Lot and Graveyard, in all three lots. Bounded by George W. Fogleman, John W. Wiggins, Hugh Hurst, Moses Neeley, Samuel Neeley, William Gabbard, and Noah Scales. Wit: A. Vannoy and D. H. Williams. Reg: 3 Dec 1851. NOTE: On page 246, some part of land above was sold by Harbert Wiggins to William O. Forbs.

Page 247 - 18 Nov 1851. Mary Shaw to T. L. D. W. Shaw and others. Relinquishment. Mary Shaw gave T. L. D. W. Shaw,

C. G. W. B. Shaw and R. C. C. P. Shaw, a lot of negroes and have mutually agreed to divide slaves. Wit: A. R. Wood, L. P. Fields and Willis Cannon. Reg: 4 Dec 1851.

Page 250 - 5 Dec 1851. George J. Black and wife to James Woods. Deed, undivided interest. George J. Black and Francis Black his wife, sold unto James Woods, all their interest in the personal estate of Eve Burrow, deceased. Francis Black being a child of Eve Burrow. Wit: George W. Buchanan. Reg: 5 Dec 1851.

Page 251 - 29 Nov 1851. C. C. Covington to Louisa Covington. Bill of Sale. Christopher C. Covington sold to Louisa Covington, his interest in four negroes which was his distributive share by right of inheritance as one of the heirs of Jesse Covington, deceased. Reg: 5 Dev 1851.

Page 256 - -- Dec 1851. Newcom Thompson, Sr. to J. T. Brittain and wife. Deed, 231 acres. Newcomb Thompson, Sr. for love and affection he has for Jason T. Brittain and wife Mary Ann Brittain, conveyed unto them, land in Bedford Co., TN, in District No. 8. At the death of either or both, Jason T. and Mary Ann Brittain, land to go to their heirs. The land bounded by the bank of Duck River. Newcomb THompson, Sr. now lives on part of said land. Reg: 8 Dec 1851.

Page 260 - 17 Oct 1851. Milton Moss to John T. Neil and Thomas C. Whiteside. Deed, 102 acres. Milton Moss of Pickens Co., Alabama, sold unto John T. Neil and Thomas C. Whiteside, all his undivided interest as one of the heirs of Mathew Moss, deceased, in land in Bedford Co., TN, in District No. 25. Borders lands of Middleton Holland and the heirs of Franklin Holland, John (blank), Richard F. Callagohan, and John S. Hight. It being the land of which Milton Moss' father Matthew Moss died seized and possessed in Bedford Co., TN, and on which he resided at the time of his death, his interest being one undivided tenth part. Wit: Eli Moss and James Stallings. Reg: 8 Dec 1851.

Page 267 - 1 Dec 1851. George W. Bell to Benjamin Whitworth, Caleb P. Houston and James Ogilvie. Trustees, 1 acre. George W. Bell conveyed to Benjamin Whitworth, Caleb P. Houston, and James Ogilvie as Trustees for a branch of three Cumberland Presbyterian Church called Bell Mount, land in Bedford Co., TN, in District No. 5. Bounded on road of Nashville, Murfreesboro and Shelbyville Turnpike where the Davis' Mill Road crosses the Turnpike. The land on which Cumberland Presbyterian Church called Bell Mount stands. Reg: 11 Dec 1851.

Page 274 - -- --- 1847. B. J. Rowland to Trustees of Bethlehem Church. Deed. Benjamin J. Rowland sold to Trustees of the Bethlehem Church, to wit, Augustine Rowland, Phillip Hodges, Alfred Mallard and S. A. Bell, land in Bedford Co., TN, in District No. 6 and adjoining one acre of land deeded by John Burns for the use of the Methodist Episcopal Church, of 12 poles. Bounded by James Clardy. Reg: 13 Dec 1851.

Page 276 - 1 Dec 1851. R. T. Landers and wife to W. K. Ransom. Deed, undivided interest. R. T. Landers and Terry Landers sold to W. K. Ransom, their interest in the land of John Deason, deceased, being in Bedford Co., TN, in District No. 5. Reg:

Reg: 13 Dec 1851.

Page 290 - 5 Apr 1851. William O. Pepper and wife to Stephen Hart. Title Bond. William O. Pepper and wife Sophia A. Pepper conveyed unto Stephen Hart, land in Bedford Co., TN, on north side of Duck River about two miles below Town of Shelbyville, being all the land given to John Sutton, Sr. to his sons, William B. and Charles F. Sutton, except 50 acres sold to Newcom Thompson, Sr. Wit: W. H. Wisener and Samuel H. Whitthorne. Reg: 29 Dec 1851.

Page 292 - 20 Dec 1851. B. M. and E. F. Tillman to William O. Pepper. Deed, 350 acres. Barkley M. Tillman and Elizabeth F. Tillman his wife, sold to William O. Pepper, land in Bedford Co., TN, in District No. 7, deeded to the heirs of William B. Sutton, deceased, by John Sutton, Sr. Bounded by Wilhoite's line, Samuel Patton, the Duck River, and Samuel Thompson. Reg: 29 Dec 1851.

Page 295 - 7 Jul 1851. Newton C. Gambill and others to James C. and T. J. Gambill. Power of Attorney. 183 acres. Newton C. Gambill, J. H. Gambill, B. Gambill, Aaron Gambill, Jesse Muse, Susanah Muse, James Ellis, Ellena Ellis and William Gambill, appointed James C. Gambill and Thomas J. Gambill their Attorney to convey and sell their tract of land lately owned by Aaron Gambill, deceased, it being in Bedford Co., TN, on the road leading from Shelbyville to Farmington. By their Attorney Thomas J. Gambill, Attorney in fact. Reg: 30 Dec 1851.

Page 312 - 19 Sep 1851. Tempy Bledsoe and others to Ransom Stephens. Title Bond. Tempy Bledsoe, William Bledsoe, and Annis Bledsoe, obligation to Ransom Stephens, sold unto them, land in Bedford Co., TN, on waters of Little Sinking Creek. Bounded by Hugh Hurst, Henderson's line. Which land the said Stephens has this day paid for said land, all the land that Jacob D. Bledsoe, John C. Bledsoe and Louiza F. Bledsoe has in three fifths of the above land, as heirs of Henry Bledsoe, deceased. Wit: John B. Smith and John W. Bledsoe. Reg: 9 Jan 1852.

Page 315 - 19 Sep 1851. Tempy Bledsoe and others to Ransom Stephens. Deed, 62 years. Tempy Bledsoe, William P. Bledsoe and Annis Bledsoe, sold to Ransom Stephens, their interest in the lands of the heirs of Henry Bledsoe, deceased. Tempy Bledsoe widow of Henry Bledsoe and William P. and Annie, as heirs, land in Bedford Co., TN, on waters of Little Sinking Creek. Bounded by Hurst's line and Henderson's line. Wit: John B. Smith and John W. Bledsoe. Reg: 9 Jan 1852.

Page 320 - 29 Dec 1851. B. M. D. Burrow to Alfred Burrow. Deed, undivided interest &c. B. M. D. Burrow sold unto Alfred Burrow, all interest that he has in an undivided interest in the estate of his deceased father Ephraim Burrow, 10 negroes, some at the place where his mother Eve Burrow died and other property of his deceased father. Reg: 10 Jan 1852.

Page 332 - 22 Jan 1852. Jesse Chockley and wife to Nicholas Burns. Deed. Jesse Chockley and Charlotte Chockley his wife formerly Charlotte Staggs, sold to Nicholas Burns, their interest in land in Bedford Co., TN, on headwaters of Sugar Creek, it being the land owned by William Staggs at the time of his death.

Reg: 23 Jan 1852.

Page 333 - 17 Jan 1852. Robert W. Locke to THomas B. Jeffress. Deed, 111 acres. Robert W. Locke sold to Thomas B. Jeffress, his undivided interest that he now holds in land set apart and willed to his mother during her natural life, Martha Locke, but now Martha Mayfield by William Locke, deceased, land in Bedford Co., TN, on Weakley Creek and now in possession of Martha Mayfield. Bounded by Jeffress, Jackson Nichols, Henry Clark and others. Wit: Joseph Anderson and J. M. Johnson. Reg: 23 Jan 1852.

Page 335 - 3 Jan 1852. William J. Chunn to Phillip Hodges, Alfred Mallard and others. Deed, 1/2 acre. William J. Chunn conveyed unto Phillip Hodges, Alfred Mallard and others, Trustees for the Methodist Episcopal Church, South, land adjoining the Meeting House deed and known as Burns Meeting House on Fall Creek, Bedford Co., TN, in District No. 6. Bounded by the Meeting House acre of land deeded by John Burns to said Church. Reg: 26 Jan 1852.

Page 336 - 24 Jan 1852. John Williams to Martha Ruby. Deed of Gift. John Williams for love and affection for his daughter Martha Ruby the wife of John B. Ruby, conveyed unto her during her life free from the control of her husband and at her death descends to her children, a negro woman Phillis. Reg: 24 Jan 1852.

Page 337 - -- --- 1852. Edmund Cooper, Trustee to Thomas Kimmons. Deed. Whereas Joshua Hall by deed 13 Dec 1850, conveyed to him in Trust, land in Bedford Co., TN, in District No. 20, it being two undivided seventh part of the land now in the possession of Milley Whitesell and which belonged to her during life and at her death goes to the children of John Whitesell. The share of Jacob Whitsell and William Whitsell. Reg: 29 Jan 1852.

Page 338 - 30 Jan 1852. Ellis Huddleston to Rebecca Mullins. Bill of Sale. Ellis Huddleston in right of his wife Mary Ann formerly Mary Ann Mullins, derived a title to one seventh part interest in a negro woman Jane. Wit: Andrew Vannoy and James Anderton. Reg: 30 Jan 1852.

Page 340 - 30 Jan 1852. Joshua Phillips to James Smith. Deed, 222½ acres. Whereas Joshua Holt, Sr. by his Last Will and Testament, devised to his daughter Jane Phillips, conveyed a tract of land in Bedford Co., TN, in District No. 22. Bounded by Hosea F. Holt, Robert S. Dwiggins, Herod G. Holt, James Smith, part of the school land bought by Benjamin Phillips, and Joshua Holt, to be enjoyed by Jane Phillips and at her death to be equally divided between all the children of Jane Phillips of which Joshua Phillips is entitled to one share. Reg: 3 Feb 1852.

Page 341 - 30 Jan 1852. Martin Cougill to James M. Neeley. Deed, 492½ acres, in three tracts. Martin Cougill and Luanna Cougill his wife, sold to James M. Neeley, granted and a quit claim, on land in Bedford Co., TN, on the waters of Sinking Creek, which was granted to William Hartsfield by the State of Tennessee. Bounded by Lewis Tillman and William Hartsfield and Edward Stephenson, James M. Neeley, Jacob McLour, James B.

Jones and others. Reg: 3 Feb 1852.

Page 371 - 17 Feb 1852. Richard Foreman, Sr. to Lewis F. Sears. Deed, 1 acre. Richard Foreman, Sr. sold to Lewis F. Sears, for love and affection for him, land in Bedford Co., TN, in District No. 7. Bounded by Edmund Green and the west side of the old Nashville Road. Reg: 17 Feb 1852.

Page 374 - 24 Jan 1852. William F. Phifer and J. H, Wilson and wife. Power of Attorney. Mecklenburg Co., NC. William F. Phifer and Joseph H. Wilson and Mary L. his wife, appointed Caleb P. Houston of Bedford Co., TN as their Attorney to receive from him any money &c, that belonging to the undersigned, arising from sale of property in vicinity of Shelbyville which belonged to Col. Martin Phifer and at his death descended to his heirs at law. Reg: 23 Feb 1852.

Page 386 - 24 Feb 1852. Silas Pratt and wife to Hiram Edde. Title Bond. Silas Pratt and wife Patience sold to Hiram Edde, land devised to her from her mother during her life and at her death descended to her children by Joshua Holt. Land in Bedford Co., TN, in District No. 22 and No. 23. Wit: William H. Wisener. Reg: 3 Mar 1852.

Page 386 - 9 Feb 1852. Nathaniel White and wife to William A. Morrison. Deed, 144½ acres. Nathaniel White and Mary S. White his wife, formerly Mary S. Allen, sold to William A. Morrison, land conveyed to them by the heirs of John Allen, deceased. Land on both sides of the Elk Ridge on the headwaters of Sugar and Cane Creeks, it being the land conveyed by Robert Morrison to John Allen. Reg: 3 Mar 1852.

Page 388 - 20 Feb 1852. Jacob Greer to Nancy C. Kimery. Deed of Gift. Jacob Greer for love and affection for his daughter Nancy C. Kimery, conveyed unto her a negro woman Minerva and child and other personal property, and at her death descends to her children. Wit: W. P. Goodwin and J. M. Greer. Reg: 3 Mar 1852.

Page 392 - 11 Nov 1851. John W. McGimsey and wife to James G. Neeley. Deed, 125 acres. J. W. McGimsey and wife Mary McGimsey, sold to James G. Neeley, land in Bedford Co., TN, on waters of Falling Creek. Bounded by Volney H. Steele, heirs of Samuel A. Bell, deceased, the heirs of Travis C. Nash, deceased, and heirs of John Hutton, deceased. It being land that Johannah Nash now lives on. Reg: 9 Mar 1852.

Page 393 - 4 Mar 1852. John P. Steele and J. H. Neil to Mary Whiteside. Bill of Sale. John P. Steele and J. H. Neil executed to Mary Whiteside wife of Russell P. Whiteside of Marshall Co., TN, a negro man Jackson. Reg: 9 Mar 1852.

Page 397 - 26 Jan 1852. George B. Sumner and wife to Margaret Muse. George B. Sumner and Nancy C. Sumner his wife, sold to Margaret Muse, their interest in all debts due the estate of Richard Muse, deceased, or now known, in land whereon Margaret Muse now lives. Wit: P. W. Davis, William H. Finch and Lewis Haggard. Reg: 10 Mar 1852.

Page 398 - Margaret Muse to Preston W. Davis of Marshall Co., TN. Trust Deed of above land and property.

Page 400 - 8 Mar 1852. William J. Chunn to Peter E. Clardy and others. Trustees, School House, 1/2 acre. William J. Chunn conveyed unto Michael Dixon and Peter E. Clardy also William J. Chunn as Trustees, land in Bedford Co., TN, on waters of Fall Creek near to Burns Meeting House. Bounded by the Meeting House, Clardy's line. The land set apart for the purpose of building a good and comfortable School House. Reg: 16 Mar 1852.

Page 400 - 19 Feb 1851. Martha Allen to Thomas W. Davis. Deed, 33 acres. Whereas by the statues of dower of Hugh Allen, Martha Allen is seized of a life estate in land in Bedford Co., TN, in District No. 9, sold to Thomas W. Davis. Bounded by A. P. Mohumdro and Davis' corner. Wit: James Foster and William E. Davis. Reg: 23 Mar 1852.

Page 402 - 8 Mar 1852. W. W. Reese to L. Leftwich and others. Deed, 115 acres. W. W. Reese sold to L. Leftwich and A. G. Gill, Trustees for Charity Church, James D. Cole and A. D. Summerford, Trustees for Concord Church, D. A. Gilbert and William Armstrong, Trustees for Hannah's Gap Church and their successors in office, land in the Counties of Lincoln and Bedford, TN. Bounded by the County Line, B. Phillips, J. Polk and W. Bagley. Wit: W. W. Gill and John Wagster. Reg: 24 Mar 1852.

Page 403 - -- Mar 1852. A. J. Evans and wife to Claiborn McQuistion. Town Lot Deed. A. J. Evans and Mary Jane Evans sold to Claiborn McQuistion, land in Bedford Co., TN, in Town of Shelbyville, Lot No. 99. Reg: 24 Mar 1852.

Page 407 - 25 Feb 1845. Solomon Hornaday and others to John Anthony. Deed. Solomon Hornaday, David Low, John Low, Barbery Anthony and Elizabeth Brinkley, the nearest heirs of Samuel Low, deceased, and P. L. Shofner, purchaser of her share of Barbery Anthony, sold to John Anthony, land in Bedford Co., on waters of Thompsons Creek. Bounded by an entry of John Low, Adam Anthony, Epps and Allen Parker. Wit: H. Kimsey and J. L. Span. Reg: 29 Mar 1852.

Page 409 - 2 Jan 1852. William O. Pepper and wife to Newcum Thompson. Deed, 99¼ acres. William O. Pepper and Sophia A. Pepper formerly Sophia A. Sutton, sold to Newcum Thompson, Sr., land in Bedford Co., TN, in District No. 7, on north side of Duck River and about 1½ miles west of Shelbyville. Bounded by William B. Sutton. Reg: 31 Mar 1852.

Page 411 - April Term 1850. Circuit Court Decree. John F. Norman and wife and William Woosley, guardian and others. Petition to sell land and slaves. Charles T. Philpot was purchaser of the land belonging to the heirs of Nathaniel and Sally Hubbard, deceased, all the interest which Robert McElvany and his wife Nancy, John F. Norman and wife Milley, William Heaslett and wife Malvina, John W. Davis and wife Sally, Nathaniel Hubbard, William Hubbard, and Elizabeth Hubbard, have in the land in Bedford Co., TN, of 68 acres, on waters of Big Flat Creek and being the lands assigned to Sarah Hubbard, widow of Nathaniel Hubbard, deceased. Reg: 31 Mar 1852.

Page 412 - 1 Jun 1842. Stephen Porter and others to Nathaniel Porter. Deed, 200 acres. Stephen Porter, Samuel Porter, John Porter and George W. Cummings and Sarah his wife formerly Sarah

H. Porter, and Stephen A. Porter of Marshall Co., TN, and William W. Porter of the Territory of Iowa, sold to Nathaniel Porter of Bedford Co., TN, land in Bedford Co., on Sinking Creek. Bounded by Dougherty survey, Sinking Creek and known as Stephen Porter's old corner, Mathew Brooks, Lewis G. Ray, Daniel Looney and Cunningham's line. Wit: William W. Porter and J. W. C. Cunningham. Reg: 3 Apr 1852.

Page 416 - 24 Jun 1851. John Eakin Executors to John Hart. Deed. Alexander Eakin, John W. Cowan, William G. Cowan and John R. Eakin, sold land in Bedford Co., TN, in District No. 6, land on Shelbyville to Murfreesboro Turnpike Road. Bounded by Enoch William, B. F. Whitworth now Whiteside. Reg: 5 Apr 1852.

Page 418 - 1 Jan 1852. William G. Cowan to J. R. Eakin and J. W. Cowan. Deed, Town Lot. William G. Cowan sold to John W. Cowan and John R. Eakin, Trustees, of Julia A. and Sarah J. Eakin, the heirs, a certain house and lot on the Public Square in Shelbyville, it being the brick two story now occupied by said Cowan. Eakin and Cowan was appointed by the Last Will and Testament of John Eakin, deceased, and trustees for the daughters Julia A. and Sarah J. Eakin. Wit: Robert Cowan and Samuel Cowan. Reg: 4 Apr 1852.

Page 427 - -- Feb 1852. Mary C. Foster to Randolph Newsom. Deed. Whereas in the Last Will and Testament of Mary C. Foster's grandfather William McGrew, deceased, proven and recorded in Bedford Co., TN. In one of the clauses of the Will is the following that his daughter Frances having married the second husband, the share given to her is not to be paid to her present husband but to be settled on her as one of his daughters Eliza J. and Charlotte unless he will enter into an obligation to his Executors to give to her daughter, Mary C. Foster, at his death. Randolph Newsom who is the husband of Mary C. Foster's mother Frances has executed his bond. Wit: L. W. Barrett and H. C. Hurst. Reg: 7 Apr 1852.

Page429 - 3 Apr 1852. T. B. Jeffress to J. J. Long and wife. Thomas B. Jeffress gave to his son in law J. J. Long and wife Nancy C. Long, land in Bedford Co., TN that he sold to Samuel G. McGowan. Land in District No. 11. Wit: Ed Wortham and Samuel G. McGowan. Reg: 8 Apr 1852.

Page 436 - 10 Jan 1851. Thomas E. Martin and wife to Thomas Martin. Power of Attorney. Thomas E. Martin and wife Mary C. Martin appointed Thomas Martin as their Attorney to sell land in Bedford Co., TN, in District No. 10. Bounded by Hardy Pope, Thomas Carlton, J--- FLoyd and John King. Thomas E. Martin and wife Mary C. Martin of Izard Co., Arkansas. Reg: 10 Apr 1852.

Page 437 - 10 Jan 1852. Thomas E. Martin and wife Mary C. to Woddy S. Taylor. Deed, 39 acres. Thomas E. Martin and Mary C. his wife of Izard Co., Arkansas by their Attorney Thomas Martin of Williamson Co., TN, sold to Woddy S. Taylor, land in Bedford Co., TN, in District No. 10. Wit: William Little and James Mankin. Reg: 10 Apr 1852.

Page 439 - 17 Feb 1852. John W. Simpson to William Little and Robert Allison. Deed, 1/2 acre. John W. Simpson has interest in remainder to take effect and be united with the possession after the death of Emily Weaver who has a life estate in the same, in land in Bedford Co., TN, in District No. 10. Bounded by John Little and William Little. Wit: E. D. Winsett and R. S. Gantt and W. S. Taylor. Reg: 12 Apr 1852.

Page 449 - 9 Oct 1851. R. J. A. Allison to Hiram H. Holt. Deed, 158 acres. Robert J. A. Allison sold to Hiram H. Holt, land in Bedford Co., TN and in Marshall Co., TN, in Districts No. 19 and No. 5, on headwaters of the East Fork of Rock Creek. Bounded by Thomas SMith. Out of which tract there is exception, one fourth acre where James Sheppard's daughter was buried which is not hereby conveyed. Wit: Joseph Trice, Jr. and Benjamin Mosley. Reg: 15 Apr 1852.

Page 453 - 25 Mar 1852. Aly(female) Dunston to William V. Beasley and others. Trustees of B. Church. Aly Dunston sold and conveyed unto William V. Beasley, William B. M. Brame, James G. Barksdale, Williamson Haggard, John C. Holt and Thomas C. Whiteside, Trusteesof the Baptist Church at Shelbyville, land in Town of Shelbyville, Bedford Co., TN. Bounded by Aly Dunston, William Galbreath. Wit: B. M. Tillman and John Armstrong. Reg: 16 Apr 1852.

Page 457 - -- Feb 1851. Minos Cannon, Jr. to James Wortham. Deed, 45 acres and 136 acres. Minos Cannon, Jr. sold to James Wortham, his interest in land in Bedford Co., TN. Bounded by a tract of land it being the land allotted to Minos Cannon of the land of his father Minos Cannon, deceased, and it being Lot No. 1 on west and north side of Duck River and bounded by the dower of his mother, and the banks of Duck River. Also, his remainder interest in the original tract of land allotted to his mother and bounded by Clement Cannon, Duck River, Big Flat Creek and Galbert's old line. Also, undivided interest in Lots No. 3 and No. 4, it being allotted to James Wortham and wife Catharine and his brother John M. Cannon, who is now dead. Also other lands. Reg: 21 Apr 1852.

Page 463 - 13 Apr 1852. Benjamin T. Hollins to Eliza J. Wallis. Deed of Gift, 4 acres. Benjamin T. Hollis for love and affection for his daughter Eliza J. Wallace, conveyed unto her, land in Bedford Co., TN, near Shelbyville. Bounded by land formerly owned by S. C. Roberts and others and which John P. Steele has resided for several years, William F. McRee and the Railroad. Wit: Robert Mathews and George W. Buchanan. Reg: 23 Apr 1852.

Page 468 - -- Apr 1852. David Blessing and wife Polly Blessing to Celia Caroline and Manervy E. Blessing. David Blessing and his wife Polly Blessing formerly Polly Coats for love and affection for their daughters Celia Caroline Blessing and Manervy Emeline Blessing, conveyed unto them their interest in a negro slaves belonging to the estate of Wilson Coats, deceased, also their interest in the estate of Bailey Washington Coats, deceased, John Bedford Coats and Henry C. Coats, deceased, children of Wilson Coats, deceased. Reg: 3 May 1852.

Page 474 - -- Apr 1851. Circuit Court Decree to William M. Russell and others. Deed, 50 acres. Joshua Hall, Administrator of George W. Whitesell, deceased, vs Mary D. Whitesell and others, heirs of George W. Whitesell, deceased. Petition to sell land. William M. Russell being the purchaser and resold to Thomas J. Mays and others. The above decree was unexcepted to court. Reg: 10 May 1852.

Page 478 - 3 May 1852. Daniel McCaughlin and wife to William Kingry. Deed, 153 acres. Daniel McCaughlin and wife Nancy A. McCaughlin formerly Nancy A. Burgess, sold to land in Bedford Co., TN, it being land belonging to William Burgess at the time of his death and descended to his heirs of which Nancy A. being one of them. Bounded by George Waite, McKisick's line and Bennett's line. Wit: George W. Buchanan. Reg: 3 May 1852.

Page 479 - 15 May 1852. J. W. Allison to Thomas C. Allison. Trust Deed. John W. Allison sold to Thomas C. Allison, property of slaves and all his interest in the estate of his mother Elizabeth after deduction for a debt which he owed her estate. J. W. Allison is indebted to Jane Robinson as her guardian also to Lewis Gant also indebted to his brother James Allison. Reg: 17 May 1852.

Page 481 - 15 May 1852. Silas Woodbury to Mary E. and Silas Woodbury. Deed of Gift. Silas Woodbury for love and affection for his children, Mary E. Woodbury and Silas Henry Woodbury, conveyed unto them, land in Shelbyville, Bedford Co., TN. Silas Woodbury is to keep control of said land as long as he and his wife lives. Wit: H. L. Davidson and Robert B. Davidson. Reg: 17 May 1852.

Page 485 - 20 Aug 1849. Richard Warner to Eunice Warner. Deed, undivided interest. Whereas by the Last Will and Testament of John Warner, Jr., deceased, William Dixon Warner had an interest in remainder to take effect and be united with the possession after the death of his mother Eunice Warner, in 2 tracts of land in Bedford Co., TN, in District No. 21. One tract whereon Eunice Warner now lives, also one Town Lot in Shelbyville also slaves, all belonging to John Warner, deceased. Wit: G. W. Brown and Hiram Harris. Reg: 19 May 1852.

Page 486 - 12 May 1852. Eunice Warner to John W. Rutledge. Deed, undivided interest. Whereas the Last Will and Testament of John Warner, deceased, William Dixon Warner had an interest in remainder to take effect and united with the possession after the death of his mother Eunice Warner, in 2 tracts of land in Bedford Co., TN, one whereon Eunice Warner now lives. Conveyed to John W. Rutledge the said land. Wit: Samuel J. Warner and Hiram Harris. Reg: 19 May 1852.

Page 487 - (Same as above instrument) Reg: 20 May 1852.

Page 492 - 23 Apr 1851. John P. Bryan* Elizabeth Carlton and Mary Bryan to Milton A. Haynes. John P. Bryan and Elizabeth Carlton of Marshall Co., TN, and Mary Bryan, only surviving children and heirs at law of Hezekiah Bryan, deceased, conveyed unto Milton A. Haynes, land in Bedford Co., TN, it being the land granted to Ira Williard for Military Services in the War of 1812, in the Military Bounty Tracts in the State of Illinois. Said land being the same conveyed by said Williard to Fanning Jones and by Fanning Jones to Hezekiah Bryan. Wit: Benjamin H. Bryant and John W. Bryant.*<u>Bryan</u> possibly <u>Bryant</u>. Reg: 26 May 1852.

Page 501 - 1 Apr 1852. Chancery Court Decree to Martin Euliss. Deed, 69 acres. James C. Carter and Frances his wife and others vs Benjamin Coble and others. Bill for Sale of land. John W. Cobb the purchaser of the lands and he sold his interest to Martin Euliss. Reg: 1 Jun 1852.

Page 503 - 29 Apr 1852. Nancy Parker to Commissioners of School House. Nancy Parker agree that the School House and sufficient portion of land around the house in order to give room for school privileges, she gives land on east side of land adjoining Thomas Roberts' tract on Thompsons Creek. Wit: B. K. Daniel and H. Bennett. Reg: 3 Jun 1852.

Page 503 - 8 Jan 1852. Robert Mathews to the School Commissioners. Robert Mathews will permit and authorize the School Commissioners to hold and keep a Public School lease for 10 yeras on his land, it purchased of Joab Short, in the house where the school is now kept. Wit: George W. Buchanan and John Bennett. Reg: 3 Jun 1852.

Page 514 - 7 Jun 1852. M. B. Thompson to John F. Thompson. Quit Claim, 80 acres. M. B. Thompson conveyed Quit Claim unto John F. Thompson, the interest he has in dower tract of his mother Christina Thompson, in the lands of her husband Thompson Thompson, deceased. Land in Bedford Co., TN, in District No. 8. Reg: 10 Jun 1852.

Page 514 - 7 May 1852. Willis W. Dearing to C. P. Houston and others, School Commissioners, 128 poles. Willis W. Dearing conveyed unto C. P. Houston, G. W. Bell, William K. Ransom, James Ogilvie and B. F. Whitworth, as Trustees for the use of building a School House on to be known as Dearing Academy, in Bedford Co., TN, in District No. 5. Bounded by west side of Nashville, Murfreesboro and Shelbyville Turnpike, it being C. P. Houston's corner, to build a School House. Reg: 10 Jun 1852.

Page 515 - 14 Jun 1852. James R. and Mary Ann Farriss to George Cortner. Deed, 41 acres. James R. and Mary Ann Farriss sold to George Cortner, land in Bedford Co., TN, in District No. 25. Bounded by Jesse Hart, corner of Sarah Troxler's tract, Lucy Holden, the Barren Fork of Duck River, Huffman's Mill and the Shelbyville Road. Wit: W. L(?). Troxler and Alexander Cortner. Reg: 14 Jun 1852.

Page 517 - 18 Dec 1851. Newcome Thompson to Newcome Thompson, Jr. Deed, 200 acres. Newsome Thompson, Sr. sold to his nephew Newcome Thompson, 2nd, land in Bedford Co., TN, in District No. 7. Bounded by the north bank of Duck River and land belonging to the heirs of William B. Sutton, deceased. Wit: William B. M. Brame and William S. Jett. Reg: 14 Jun 1852.

Page 519 - 18 May 1852. John Scott to E. A. Mosley and others. Trustees, 4 acres. John Scott, for $15.00, the amount of his subscription formerly subscribed for the building of Duck River Male Academy, sold and conveyed to E. A. Mosley, Matt S. Finch, A. H. Coffee, J. Cleveland, J. G. Barksdale, Robert Buchanan, S. B. Heard, H. C. Ferguson, Alfred Ransom, David Wagster, A. G. Gill, H. C. Hurst, R. M. Whitman, John Fitzpatrick, N. R. Martin, G. G. Osborne, W. W. Miller, E. Stokes, Lewis Tillman, and John McQuiddy, Trustees of Duck River Male Academy, land in Bedford Co., TN and in the vicinity of Fairfield. Bounded by land Scott deeded to New Hope Baptist Church at Fairfield. Wit: John S. Davis, William D. Clark and R. W. Beachboard. Reg: 14 Jun 1852.

Page 525 - 16 Aug 1851. John W. Cobb and others to Euliss & Jenkins. Deed, 150 acres. John W. Cobb and Sarah Cobb, widow &c. Petition for dower for Sarah Cobb, of James H. Cobb, deceased. Land in Bedford Co., TN, in District No. 25. The land whereon Martin Euliss and William Jenkins bid for said land and they being best bidder. Reg: 23 Jun 1852.

Page 535 - -- --- 1852. Dabney Ewell and others. Petition to sell land. Land belonging to estate of John Ewell, deceased. Dabney one of the heirs. Reg: 14 Jul 1852.

Page 540 - 21 Nov 1851. G. W. Brown, N. B. Suddrath and J. B. Suddrath to G. W. Brown. George W. Brown of Bedford Co., TN, and N. B. Suddrath and J. B. Suddrath of Kentucky, sold to George W. Brown, both real and personal estate of Shadrack Brown, deceased, whether in the hands of Administrtors in remainder after the termination of the life estate of Tabitha Brown, except their share of proceeds of sale of the slaves. Wit: Edmund Cooper and Henry Cooper. Reg: 19 Jul 1852.

Page 541 - 7 Jul 1852. William G. Cowan and others to Mayor and Alderman of Shelbyville. William G. Cowan, Alexander Eakin and John W. Cowan conveyed to George W. Ruth, Newcum Thompson, George W. Fogleman, Samuel Morton, William Word, L. D. Pannel, and James J. Barksdale as Mayor and Alderman of Shelbyville, a part of Lot No. 1 and No. 2, in Shelbyville, known as the graveyard. Bounded by the graveyard. Recorded 21 July 1852. Also on page 542, Graveyard adjoins Baptist Church. George W. Ruth, Mayor of Shelbyville.

Page 544 - 26 Jul 1852. John Williams to Thomas Williams. John Williams, growing old and unable to manage and control his farm and slaves, wants his debts paid and property sold to benefit his wife and children, conveyed all properties over to Thomas Williams, both real and personal. The land on which John Williams now lives, it being land he purchased of Benjamin F. Greer. Bounded by D. L. Barringer, James Gant, Green Newsom, Killingsworth's tract and others. Reg: 27 Jul 1852.

Page 548 - 7 May 1852. David A. and Sarah F. Ozment to Thomas D. Tarpley. Deed, undivided interest, 7½ acres. David A. Ozment and Sarah Frances Ozment his wife sold to Thomas D. Tarpley, their undivided interest in the dower of Rebecca Batte, widow of Henry Batte, deceased, land in Bedford Co., TN, in District No. 9. Bounded by lands of Henry Batte, deceased and the dower tract of 84 acres. Wit: Richard Ozment and E. G. Carter. Reg: 28 Jul 1852.

Page 551 - 5 Jul 1852. John W. Ash and Susanna M. Ash to Daniel W. Dollar. Power of Attorney. John W. Ash and Susanna Margaret Ash of Lacleda Co., Missouri, formerly Susanna Margaret Dollar, appointed Daniel W. Dollar, their Attorney, to receive any money, good effects of John H. Dollar and Ceily Dollar, the daughter of Michael Holt, the heirs of said Michael Holt, deceased, Susanna Margaret Dollar who is now known in law by Susanna M. Ash, by her late marriage with John W. Ash, of John H. Dollar and Ceily Dollar, one of the heirs of said John H. Dollar and Ceily Dollar his wife. Reg: 6 Jul 1852.

Page 554 - 26 Jul 1852. James Story to Julia A. McEwen. Deed of Gift. James Story of Bedford Co., TN, conveyed unto his daughter Julia A. McEwen of Davidson Co., TN, for love and affection for his daughter, a negro girl Eliza. Reg: 5 Aug 1852.

Page 559 - Joseph Holder and wife to George Cortner. Deed, 43 acres. Joseph and Lucy E. Holder sold to George Cortner, land in Bedford Co., TN, in District No. 25. Wit: Jesse Holt and Alexander Cortner. Reg: 9 Aug 1852.

Page 560 - -- Aug 1852. Samuel J. Warner and wife to John F. Thompson. Deed, undivided interest. Samuel J. Warner and Margaret Warner formerly Margaret Thompson, sold unto John F. Thompson, their interest in land in Bedford Co., TN, in District No. 8, being the same set apart to Margaret Thompson in the division of the lands of Thompson Thompson, deceased. Reg: 9 Aug 1852.

Page 563 - 16 Apr 1852. Joshua White to John White. Deed, 140 acres. Joshua White of Marshall Co., TN, for love and affection for his son John H. White, conveyed land lying in Bedford Co., TN. Bounded by Robert Mathews, Charles Batts, and Robert Mathis. Wit: Leonard Bullock and Garrett Phillips. Reg: 10 Aug 1852.

Page 574 - 5 Dec 1851. Thomas Webb to A. S. Lorance. Thomas Webb sold to A. S. Lorance, his undivided interest which Jordan Loyd had in and to the remaining interest in the dower estate of Rebecca Loyd widow of Joseph Loyd, deceased. Wit: W. W. Webb and Isaiah Webb. Reg: 16 Aug 1852.

Page 574 - 14 Aug 1852. James F. Shearin and wife to J. M. Ledbetter. Deed, 320 acres. James F. Shearin and his wife Elizabeth formerly Elizabeth Hamble of Marshall Co., TN, sold to J. M. Ledbetter of Bedford Co., TN, land in Bedford Co., in District No. 11. Bounded by John Rogers' land he sold to J. M. Ledbetter, Duck River, Marman (Mariman) Burns, and Richard Warner and others. Reg: 16 Aug 1852.

Page 577 - 19 Jul 1849. H. M. Dawdy to Edward Johnson. Deed, 11 acres. Howel M. Dawdy sold to Edward Johnson, with the exception of Mary Dawdy his mother, having it subject to her control during her life time, land in Bedford Co., TN, on the waters of the East Fork of Rock Creek. Bounded by Albert Anderson. Wit: Albert Anderson and E. A. Craige. Reg: 17 Aug 1852.

Page 581 - 11 Feb 1839. William, Ezekiel and Joseph Click to James Click. Deed, 199 acres. William Click, Ezekiel Click and Joseph Click, grandchildren of Ezekiel Reynolds, sold to James Click, land bounded by land on south bank of Duck River, and Reynolds' line. Wit: Hiram Harris and Henry Hay. Reg: 18 Aug 1852.

Page 582 - 30 Jan 1851. John K. Knight to William G. Knight. Power of Attorney. John K. Knight appointed William G. Knight his Attorney to receive from Leroy W. Barrett or any other person having possession of a legacy bequeathed to him by Allen Knight, now deceased, late of Bedford Co., TN. Wit: S. M. Holt and George M. Holt. Reg: 18 Aug 1852.

Page 586 - 14 Apr 1852. Circuit Court Decree. 1591 acres. John Phifer, Caleb Phifer, Martin Phifer, George Phifer, E. R. Gibson and wife, and others*, heirs of Martin Phifer, deceased. Bill for the sale of land. William G. Cowan became the purchaser of the land. Tract bounded by Hurricane Creek, Columbia Road, James Clardy, Deason's line, and Mrs. Stewart's line. *Others, E. R. Gibson's wife Elizabeth formerly Elizabeth Phifer, Robert W. Allson and wife Sarah Ann formerly Sarah Ann Phifer, Mary B. Phifer, John P. Young, William Phifer, Martin L. Phifer, John F. Phifer, E. Jones Erwin and wife Ann E. Erwin formerly Ann E. Phifer, S. H. Willson and wife Mary L. formerly Mary L. Phifer, James Erwin and wife Margarett formerly Margarett Phifer, Ann Crawford and Mary Childress and their heirs of said Martin Phifer, deceased. Reg: 2 Jun 1852.

Page 590 - 21 Aug 1852. Samuel J. Warner and wife to John F. Thompson. Deed, undivided interest. Samuel J. Warner and wife Margaret A. Warner formerly Margaret Thompson, sold to John F. Thompson, his interest in and to the dower interest of Christina Thompson in the lands of her husband Thompson Thompson, deceased. Land in Bedford Co., TN, in District No. 8. Reg: 25 Aug 1852.

Page 591 - 3 Oct 1851. William Pratt and others to Henry McGrew. Deed, 200 acres. William Pratt, Catharine Pratt, G. W. Thompson, Martha M. Thompson, Samuel T. Cannon, Willis Cannon and Jason T. Cannon, sold for the benefit of the children of Willis and Letitia Cannon, by note of Henry McGrew in the hands of William J. Whitthorne, land in Bedford Co., TN, being part of land formerly belonging to the estate of Walter Simms, deceased. Bounded by Minos Cannon, Edmund Green and John G. Sims. Reg: 25 Aug 1852.

Page 593 - 3 Oct 1851. William Pratt and others to H. L. Davidson. Deed, 165 acres. William Pratt and others (same as above) sold land to H. L. Davidson, land in Bedford Co., TN, on south side of Duck River. Bounded by Nathaniel Johnson now John B. Johnson, old Winchester Road, Chandler's Mills, and Robert Morgan. With the exception of the ten acres sold by Willis Cannon to John B. Johnson which is not here conveyed. Also other land. Reg: 2 Aug 1852.

Page 597 - -- Apr 1852. G. P. Burditt and others to L. P. Fields. Deed, 135 acres. Giles P. Burditt, William M. Burditt, A. H. Burditt and K. L. Burditt sold to L. P. Fields, all their interest in land in Bedford Co., TN, on Noah Fork of Duck River. Bounded by John L. Davis, Matt Finch and Thomas B. Moseley, being the land on which Patience Burditt, deceased, resided at the time of her death. Wit: Thomas C. Whiteside and Robert B. Davidson. Reg: 31 Aug 1852.

Page 598 - 4 Aug 1852. Rancolph Newsom and Terry D. Thompson, Executors to R. L. Singleton. Deed, 47 acres. Whereas Sterling Newsom departed this life lately in Bedford Co., TN, of which he was a citizen, previously made and published his Last Will and Testament, was proven and registered and in which Randolph Newsom was appointed Executor. The Will stated the estate to be sold and was purchased by Robert L. Singleton. Bounded by road of Skull Camp Ford, Cowan's Mills, The Graveyard. Wit: James W. Johnson and R. N. Jones. Reg: 31 Aug 1852.

Page 602 - 3 Jun 1852. John A. Bradshaw and wife to C. P. Houston. Power of Attorney. Davidson Co., NC. John A. Bradshaw and Mary Burton his wife, appointed Caleb P. Houston of Bedford Co., TN, their Attorney, to handle their affairs in the estate of John Phifer, deceased, late of (blank) Co., NC, Mary Burton Bradshaw being one of the heirs. Reg: 7 Sep 1852.

INDEX

INDEX

D

E

I

J

K

L

Mc

Q

R

S